THE ETERNAL PEOPLE

*God in Relation to Israel:
Post-New Testament Israel*

WILLEM J. OUWENEEL

AN EVANGELICAL INTRODUCTION TO
REFORMATIONAL THEOLOGY
VOL IV/1B

PART IV: CONSUMMATION:
THE LIVED SHAPE OF THEOLOGY

AN EVANGELICAL INTRODUCTION TO REFORMATIONAL THEOLOGY

Part I: Scripture: The Revealed Source For Theology
   I/1 *The Eternal Word:* God Speaking To Us
   I/2 *The Eternal Torah:* Living Under God

Part II: God: The Personal Source Behind Theology
   II/1 *The Eternal God:* God Revealing Himself To Us
   II/2 *The Eternal Christ:* God With Us
   II/3 *The Eternal Spirit:* God Living In Us

Part III: Redemption: The Christ-Centered Heart of Theology
   III/1 *The Eternal Purpose:* Living In Christ
   III/2 *Eternal Righteousness:* Living Before God
   III/3 *Eternal Salvation:* Christ Dying For Us
   III/4 *Eternal Life:* Christ Living In Us

Part IV: Consummation: The Lived Shape of Theology
   IV/1a *The Eternal People:* God in Relation To Israel: Israel in the Tanakh and the New Testament
   IV/1b *The Eternal People:* God in Relation To Israel: Post-New Testament Israel
   IV/2 *The Eternal Covenant:* Living With God
   IV/3 *The Eternal Kingdom:* Living Under Christ

Part V: Method: The Comprehensive Foundation of Theology
   V/1 *Eternal Truth:* The Prolegomena of Theology

THE ETERNAL PEOPLE

*God in Relation to Israel:
Post-New Testament Israel*

WILLEM J. OUWENEEL

PAIDEIA
PRESS

Eternal People: God in Relation to Israel: Post-New Testament Israel

This English edition is a publication of Paideia Press (P.O. Box 1000, Jordan Station, Ontario, Canada L0R 1S0). Copyright © 2020 by Paideia Press. All rights reserved. Except for brief quotations in critical publications or reviews, no part of this book may be reproduced in any manner without prior written permission from Paideia Press at the address above.

Unless otherwise indicated, Scripture quotations are from the ESV® Bible (The Holy Bible, English Standard Version®). Copyright © 2001 by Crossway, a publishing ministry of Good News Publishers. Used by permission. All rights reserved.

Scripture quotations or references marked as NKJV are taken from the New King James Version®. Copyright © 1982 by Thomas Nelson, Inc. Used by permission. All rights reserved.

Scripture quotations or references marked as NIV are taken from the Holy Bible, New International Version®, NIV®. Copyright © 1973, 1978, 1984, 2011 by Biblica, Inc.™ Used by permission of Zondervan. All rights reserved worldwide. www.zondervan.com. The "NIV" and "New International Version" are trademarks registered in the United States Patent and Trademark Office by Biblica, Inc.™

Book Design by: Steven R. Martins and Paul Aurich

ISBN 978-0-88815-329-6

Printed in the United States of America

Table of Contents

Series Preface		i
Author's Preface		v
Abbreviations		vii
Chapter 1	Judaism and Christianity	1
Chapter 2	Bible and Tradition	51
Chapter 3	Historical Supersessionism and Historical Judaism	101
Chapter 4	Theological Supersessionism	153
Chapter 5	The Sufferings of Israel	201
Chapter 6	The Rejection and Preservation of Israel	247
Chapter 7	Earlier Jewish-Christian Relationships	293
Chapter 8	Later Jewish-Christian Relationships	343
Chapter 9	Israel and the Palestinians	389
Chapter 10	Zionism and Islam	443
Chapter 11	Supersessionism and Millennialism	495
Chapter 12	God's Dwelling Place	543
Chapter 13	The Messianic Kingdom of Israel	587
Chapter 14	*Tiqqun:* The Restoration of People, City, and Temple	633
Bibliography		677
Scripture Index		703
Subject Index		721

Table of Contents Expanded

Series Preface		i
Author's Preface		v
Abbreviations		vii
1 Judaism and Christianity		1
1.1	Israel in Hebrews	2
1.1.1	Hebrews 4:9	2
1.1.2	Hebrews 8	5
1.2	The "City"	7
1.2.1	Heavenly Capital of the Kingdom?	7
1.2.2	The Intermediate State?	8
1.2.3	Heavenly and Earthly Sides	10
1.3	Hebrews 12:22–24	12
1.3.1	Four Aspects	12
1.3.2	Four More Aspects	13
1.4	Paul: Exposition and Application	16
1.4.1	*Remez* and *D'rash*	16
1.4.2	*G'zerah shavah*	18
1.4.3	The Supersessionist Error	20
1.5	Post-Acts 15 Christendom	22
1.5.1	"Christians" Growing Away from Jews	22
1.5.2	The Apostolic Council in Jeruslem	23

		1.5.3 Jews Do Not Become Gentiles, and Vice Versa	26
	1.6	Identity and Animosity	29
		1.6.1 Seven Similarities	29
		1.6.2 Animosity	31
	1.7	Torah or No Torah?	34
		1.7.1 Three Viewpoints	34
		1.7.2 Under the Torah of Christ	37
	1.8	Legalism	39
		1.8.1 What Is It?	39
		1.8.2 Four More Aspects	42
	1.9	The Non-Legalistic Life under the Law	44
		1.9.1 The *Telos* of the Law	44
		1.9.2 God-Given Religion	46
		1.9.3 Similarities and Differences	47
2	Bible and Tradition		51
	2.1	Sabbath versus Sunday	51
		2.1.1 Four Views	51
		2.1.2 Personal View	53
		2.1.3 The "First Day of the Week"	55
	2.2	Evaluation	57
		2.2.1 Significance of the Sabbath	57
		2.2.2 No New Testament Sabbath Commandment	58
		2.2.3 The Sabbath and the Other Feasts	61
	2.3	Scripture and Tradition	64
		2.3.1 Orthodox-Jewish and Roman Catholic View	64
		2.3.2 Unbiased Reading	68
		2.3.3 Protestant Traditionalism	71

2.4		Truth Elements in Tradition	75
	2.4.1	The Oral Word of God	75
	2.4.2	The Proper Balance	77
2.5		Rabbinic Judaism	79
	2.5.1	The "Traditions of the Forefathers"	79
	2.5.2	From Oral to Written Tradition	82
2.6		The Mishnah	84
	2.6.1	*Zugot* and *Tannaim*	84
	2.6.2	The Babylonian Yeshivas	87
2.7		The Talmud	89
	2.7.1	More on the Gemarah	89
	2.7.2	The Status of the Talmud	91
2.8		The Talmud on Jesus and the Chritians	93
	2.8.1	Rumors and Lies on Both Sides	93
	2.8.2	"Brothers" and "Life Forevermore"	96
	2.8.3	"Brothers" in Genesis	97

3 Historical Supersessionism and Historical Judaism   101

3.1		Historical Background	102
	3.1.1	The Chasm Opens	102
	3.1.2	Initial Tolerance	103
	3.1.3	Rising Anti-Semitism	105
	3.1.4	The "Guilt" of Israel	107
3.2		The Scapegoat	110
	3.2.1	Substitution	110
	3.2.2	Money Business	112
	3.2.3	Israel and Job	113

	3.3	The Crucifixion of Christ	115
		3.3.1 Projection	115
		3.3.2 Sacrificial Chicken or Roast Chicken?	116
		3.3.3 Recent Times	118
		3.3.4 Israel and Edom	120
	3.4	"Jesus Cannot Be the Messiah"	122
		3.4.1 First Reason: Necessity of Repentance	122
		3.4.2 Second Reason: Jews and Gen-tiles Equal?	125
		3.4.3 Third Reason: Jesus Did Not Bring the Kingdom	126
		3.4.4 Fourth Reason: "Deification" of Jesus	128
		3.4.5 Fifth Reason: More on the Divinity of Christ	132
		3.4.6 Sixth Reason: The Hidden Messiah	135
	3.5	Attempts to Get Rid of Israel	137
		3.5.1 No Place for Israel	137
		3.5.2 Recent Insights	140
	3.6	The Three Options	143
		3.6.1 Expulsion	143
		3.6.2 Extermination or Conversion	145
		3.6.3 Assimilation	147
4	Theological Supersessionism		153
	4.1	Back to the Torah	153
		4.1.1 The Eternal Torah	153
		4.1.2 A Remnant "Seeing"	156
	4.2	Again, Jesus and the Torah	159

	4.2.1	"But I Say to You . . ."	159
	4.2.2	Jesus' Four Comments	160
	4.2.3	In Summary	162
4.3	Damage Caused by Supersessionism	163
	4.3.1	Historical Roots of Supersessionism	163
	4.3.2	Theological Roots of Supersesionism	166
	4.3.3	Theological Decline of Supersessionism	168
4.4	Church and Heaven Cut the Line	171
	4.4.1	The Underlying Logic	171
	4.4.2	The Five Replacements	173
4.5	Christian Expectation	177
	4.5.1	The Kingdom of Heaven or Heaven?	177
	4.5.2	Dante Alighieri and Thomas à Kempis	180
	4.5.3	John Bunyan	182
	4.5.4	Summary	184
4.6	Again, the Anti-Semitic Breeding Ground	185
	4.6.1	Church Fathers	185
	4.6.2	Martin Luther	188
	4.6.3	Calvinism	190
4.7	Who Are the Jews?	193
	4.7.1	Nazis and Palestinians	193
	4.7.2	Other Theories	195
	4.7.3	Conclusion	198
5	The Suffering of Israel	201
	5.1. The Innocent	202

	5.1.1. Two Apples of the Eye	202
	5.1.2 Stealing the Honey	203
	5.1.3 Direct and Indirect Government	205
5.2	The Holocaust	206
	5.2.1 Terminology	206
	5.2.2 Israel's First Mass Destruction	207
	5.2.3 Not Keeping *From* But Keeping *Through*	209
5.3	Vicarious Suffering	210
	5.3.1 What Is It?	210
	5.3.2 The *Shoah* in Isaiah 53?	212
	5.3.3 Counterarguments	214
	5.3.4 Derivative, Figurative	215
5.4	More on Job and Israel	218
	5.4.1 Representation	218
	5.4.2 The *Tamidim*	220
	5.4.3 Job and Joseph K.	223
5.5	Various Types in the Tanakh	224
	5.5.1 Prophets and Psalms	224
	5.5.2 Esther and Mordecai	226
	5.5.3 Jonah and the Sea	228
5.6	Scapegoat and Exile	230
	5.6.1 *Shoah* and Sacrifice	230
	5.6.2 The *Galut* As Atonement	232
	5.6.3 Two Observations	234
5.7	More on the *Galut*	236
	5.7.1 Penance in Patience	236
	5.7.2 The Solitude of the *Galut*	238
5.8	The *Lamed-Waws*	240
	5.8.1 The Thirty-Six *Tzaddiqim*	240

	5.8.2	The Last *Lamed-Waw*	243
6	The Rejection and Preservation of Israel		247
	6.1	Jesus and Israel—Who Killed Whom?	247
		6.1.1 The Cruel Friends	247
		6.1.2 The Torah-Less	250
		6.1.3 Only the Crowd in Pilate's Court	251
	6.2	"His Blood Be On Us"	252
		6.2.1 A Double Blunder	252
		6.2.2 The Effect of the Blood	254
		6.2.3 Under the Blood	256
	6.3	Rejection and Preservation	257
		6.3.1 The Bundle of the Living	257
		6.3.2 Similar Metaphors	260
	6.4	Why the "Rejection"?	261
		6.4.1 God's Punishment?	261
		6.4.2 Ignorance and Unintentionality	263
		6.4.3 False Witnesses	265
	6.5	Ignorance Versus Responsibility	267
		6.5.1 Tension	267
		6.5.2 The "Veil"	268
	6.6	"What If . . . ?"	270
		6.6.1 "What If Israel Had Accepted Its Messiah?"	270
		6.6.2 Stop Being a Jew?	272
		6.6.3 The "Veil" Over the Gentile's Heart	274
	6.7	Israel's "Conversion"	276
		6.7.1 What Is Conversion?	276
		6.7.2 Various Cases	277

	6.8	Two Israels	279
		6.8.1 Christ *or* the Torah?	279
		6.8.2 Christ *and* the Torah	281
		6.8.3 The Godly Jew	283
	6.9	What Is Anti-Semitism?	286
		6.9.1 No Hatred of Jews in the New Testament	286
		6.9.2 Hatred of Jews in the Church	289
		6.9.3 The Jewish Identity	290
7		Earlier Jewish-Christian Relationships	293
	7.1	Some Church Fathers	294
		7.1.1 Chrysostom and the Jews	294
		7.1.2 Jerome and the Jews	295
		7.1.3 Augustine and the Jews	297
	7.2	Anti-Jewish Church Decisions	300
		7.2.1 The Visigoths	300
		7.2.2 Other Powers	301
	7.3	The Popes	303
		7.3.1 Pope and Emperor	303
		7.3.2 Examples	306
	7.4	Modern Amillennialism	308
		7.4.1 Amillennialism and Two Millennialisms	308
		7.4.2 The Power Interests of Amillennialism	310
	7.5	What Does Amillennialism Involve?	
		7.5.1 The Millennium	313
		7.5.2 Who Has World Dominion Today?	314
		7.5.3 Why Is Amillennialism Attractive?	316
	7.6	The Iberian Jews	320

	7.6.1	What Are *Marranos*?	320
	7.6.2	The Inquisition	322
	7.6.3	Marranos in the Netherlands	324
	7.6.4	Famous Marranos	326
7.7	The Disaster Year 1492		328
	7.7.1	Columbus	328
	7.7.2	The Last Iberian Muslim Kingdom	330
	7.7.3	Jews and Protestants	332
7.8	Jewish-Christian Disputes and Processes		333
	7.8.1	"Jesus Cannot Be the Messiah"	333
	7.8.2	Three Disputes	336
	7.8.3	The Accusation of Ritual Murder	338
8	Later Jewish-Christian Relationships		343
8.1	The Reformed and the Jews		343
	8.1.1	The Second Reformation	343
	8.1.2	Anti-Semitism	346
	8.1.3	Abraham Kuyper	348
8.2	The Jewish Influx into the Netherlands		351
	8.2.1	Sephardic Jews	351
	8.2.2	"Dutch Jerusalem"	352
	8.2.3	Ashkenazi Jews	354
8.3	The State of Israel		355
	8.3.1	Three Miracles	355
	8.3.2	Two More Miracles	357
8.4	"Messianic Jews"		360
	8.4.1	A New Movement	360

		8.4.2	The Jewishness of Messianic Jews	361
		8.4.3	Judeophilia	364
	8.5	Jewish Cultural Blessing	366
		8.5.1	Jewish Pioneers and Founders	366
		8.5.2	Jewish Medical and Natural Scientists	368
		8.5.3	Jewish Philosophers	369
		8.5.4	Jewish Composers and Writers	370
	8.6	Christian Misunderstandings About Jews	372
		8.6.1	Five Misunderstandings	372
		8.6.2	Three More Misunderstandings	374
	8.7	Jewish Misunderstandings About Christians	376
		8.7.1	Three Misunderstandings	376
		8.7.2	The Fourth Misunderstanding	377
		8.7.3	The Fifth Misunderstanding	379
		8.7.4	The Sixth Misunderstanding	380
		8.7.5	The Seventh Misunderstanding	382
		8.7.6	The Eighth Misunderstanding	383
	8.8	Peace and Its Bringer	386
		8.8.1	Varieties of Peace	386
		8.8.2	The Bringer of Peace	386
9	Israel and the Palestinians	389
	9.1	Introduction	389
		9.1.1	Black and White	389

	9.1.2	Irreparable?	392
	9.1.3	A Middle Course	394
9.2	Critics of Israel		396
	9.2.1	Jewish and Christian Critics	396
	9.2.2	Dutch Kairos-Sabeel Critics	399
	9.2.3	An Arab Critic	401
9.3	Historical Aspects		404
	9.3.1	The Palestinians	404
	9.3.2	No Peace Possible	407
	9.3.3	A Preliminary Theological Question	411
9.4	Political Aspects		413
	9.4.1	The Attitude of Israeli Politics	413
	9.4.2	The Attitude of Palestinian Politics	415
	9.4.3	The Living Conditions of the Palestinians	417
9.5	Deeper Backgrounds		419
	9.5.1	Racism? Fascism?	419
	9.5.2	Palestinian "Sojourners"	421
	9.5.3	Criticizing Israel	423
9.6	Religious Aspects		425
	9.6.1	The Temple Mount	425
	9.6.2	The Two-Ways Doctrine	428
	9.6.3	Recognizing the State of Israel?	430
9.7	On Rights and Promises		432
	9.7.1	Who Has the "Oldest Rights"?	432
	9.7.2	Who Has the Solution?	434
9.8	Claiming the Holy Land		436
	9.8.1	Whose Is It Anyway?	436

		9.8.2 Repentance and Confession	437
		9.8.3 Restoration of the Land and of the Hearts	438
	9.9	Taking and Giving	440
		9.9.1 Do Not Steal Your Presents	440
		9.9.2 Biblical Evidence	441
10	Zionism and Islam		443
	10.1	Zionism and Religion	444
		10.1.1 Dividing Up God's Land	444
		10.1.2 "Occupied" Territories?	446
		10.1.3 The PLO Charter	449
	10.2	Terrorists or Liberators?	450
		10.2.1 Who Are the Terrorists?	450
		10.2.2 What Is the Opinion of the Muslim Majority?	452
	10.3	A Political or a Terrorist Solution?	453
		10.3.1 A Hopeless Political Situation	453
		10.3.2 Palestinian As Well As Jewish Terrorism	455
	10.4	Israel and Islam	457
		10.4.1 Jerusalem and the Quran	457
		10.4.2 Islamic Eschatology	460
		10.4.3 What Is "Extreme"?	461
	10.5	The Goals of Islam	463
		10.5.1 Islam and Peace	463
		10.5.2 Islam and Patience	465
		10.5.3 "Where Was God/Allah?"	467
	10.6	Moses, Jesus, Muhammad	469
		10.6.1 Similarities Between Judaism and Islam	469
		10.6.2 Jesus Versus Muhammad	471

10.7	Jews and Muslims	473
	10.7.1 Islam and Judaism	473
	10.7.2 Kill the Jews, or Tolerate Them?	475
	10.7.3 Foes or Friends?	477
10.8	Return to God and to the Land	479
	10.8.1 The Essence of Believing	479
	10.8.2 The Paradox	481
	10.8.3 Infidelity and Repentance	482
10.9	Ishmael and the Palestinians	485
	10.9.1 Promises for Ishmael	485
	10.9.2 Isaac and Ishmael	488
	10.9.3 Summary	490
10.10	Arabs in the Messianic Kingdom	491
	10.10.1 *Ha'Aretz*	491
	10.10.2 From Egypt to Assyria	492
11 Supersessionism and Millennialism		495
11.1	Modern A- and Post-Millennialism	496
	11.1.1 Reformed Amillennialism	496
	11.1.2 Abraham Kuyper	497
	11.1.3 H. Berkhof	500
11.2	Other Reformed Theologians	501
	11.2.1 G. C. Berkouwer	501
	11.2.2 J. A. Heyns	503
	11.2.3 J. van Genderen	504
11.3	Modern Post-Millennialism	506
	11.3.1 Classical and Dominionist Post-Millennialism	506
	11.3.2 Re-Introduction of the Mosaic Torah	508
	11.3.3 Amillennial Differences of Opinion	510

11.4	Modern Pre-Millennialism	511
	11.4.1 Its Rise	511
	11.4.2 Its Spreading	514
	11.4.3 Millennial Dispensationalism	517
11.5	Evaluation	520
	11.5.1 Comparison	520
	11.5.2 Integration	522
11.6	Objections Against Amillennialism	524
	11.6.1 Satan Bound	524
	11.6.2 First and Second Resurrection	525
	11.6.3 Three Court Hearings	528
11.7	The Messianic Kingdom	530
	11.7.1 The Kingdom in Glory	530
	11.7.2 Acts and Revelation	531
	11.7.3 The Jewish Kingdom	533
11.8	The Torah Is Still Functioning!	536
	11.8.1 The Restored Sacrificial Ministry	536
	11.8.2 Attempts to Rebuild the Temple	538
	11.8.3 Other Mosaic Elements	540
12 God's Dwelling Place		543
12.1	Jerusalem: Dwelling Place of God	544
	12.1.1 Earthly Versus Spiritual	544
	12.1.2 Why Not "Primitive"?	546
	12.1.3 Symbolic Dwelling	548
12.2	Concrete Reality	550
	12.2.1 Concrete Dwelling	550
	12.2.2 Life-Threatening Sanctity	551

	12.2.3 God's Most "Concrete" Dwelling	552
12.3	Dwelling Places of God	554
	12.3.1 Introduction	554
	12.3.2 God's Heavenly Abode	555
	12.3.3 The Tabernacle	557
	12.3.4 Tabernacle and Torah	559
12.4	From the Tabernacle to the Temple	562
	12.4.1 The Tabernacle in the Holy Land	562
	12.4.2 The Ark in the Holy Land	564
	12.4.3 The Third Tent	566
12.5	The Two Temples	568
	12.5.1 Seeking the Place	568
	12.5.2 The *Shekhinah* in the Temple of Solomon	571
	12.5.3 The Temple of Zerubbabel and Herod	573
12.6	Christ and the Ecclesia	575
	12.6.1 Jesus Christ	575
	12.6.2 The Ecclesia	577
	12.6.3 The Individual Believer	579
12.7	The Remaining Dwelling Places of God	580
	12.7.1 The Millennial Temple	580
	12.7.2 The Immovable "Tent" Jerusalem	581
	12.7.3 The "Booth" of David	582
12.8	Finally	583
	12.8.1 The Eternal State	583
	12.8.2 Summary	584

13 The Messianic Kingdom of Israel — 587

- 13.1 The Beginning of the Messianic Kingdom — 588
  - 13.1.1 A Jewish Kingdom — 588
  - 13.1.2 A Cup and a Stone — 590
- 13.2 Foreshadows — 592
  - 13.2.1 David and Solomon — 592
  - 13.2.2 David and the Ark — 595
  - 13.2.3 Christ on Mount Zion — 597
- 13.3 The Place of Zion — 598
  - 13.3.1 The Holy Mountain — 598
  - 13.3.2 The *Shekhinah* in Exile — 600
  - 13.3.3 Four Exiles — 602
  - 13.3.4 Three Replacements — 604
- 13.4 Zion Restored — 605
  - 13.4.1 God's Dwelling Place Forever — 605
  - 13.4.2 *Sh'ar Yashub* — 607
- 13.5 Blessing on Zion — 608
  - 13.5.1 Three Groups of Jews — 608
  - 13.5.2 Return of the Dispersed to Zion — 609
  - 13.5.3 A Special Relationship — 611
  - 13.5.4 From Where Do the Dispersed Come? — 612
- 13.6 The Restoration of Israel — 615
  - 13.6.1 Once More: Jacob and Esau — 615
  - 13.6.2 Judgment and Peace for Edom — 617
- 13.7 The King and His Bride — 619
  - 13.7.1 A Heavenly and an Earthly Bride — 619
  - 13.7.2 The Wedding — 620

	13.7.3 The Divorce	622
	13.7.4 Re-Accepted	624
13.8	The Dominion of Christ	626
	13.8.1 The King	626
	13.8.2 Four Aspects	628
	13.8.3 The Basis: Christ's Redemptive Work	630

14 *Tiqqun*: The Restoration of People, City, and Temple — 633

14.1	Restoration of City and Temple	634
	14.1.1 Rebuilding	634
	14.1.2 Descent of the *Shekhinah*	636
14.2	The Grand City	638
	14.2.1 The New Names of the City	638
	14.2.2 Living in the City	640
14.3	Israel During the Messianic Kingdom(1)	642
	14.3.1 Israel's Seven "Seasons": Introduction	642
	14.3.2 The Seven "Seasons": Survey	644
14.4	The Twelve Tribes	646
	14.4.1 The *Tzaddiqim*	646
	14.4.2 Physical Restoration	647
14.5	Israel During the Messianic Kingdom (2)	648
	14.5.1 God Dwelling In the Midst	648
	14.5.2 Heavenly and Earthly Saints	650
	14.5.3 Navel of the Earth	650
14.6	The Blessings for the Nations	653
	14.6.1 Feast	653
	14.6.2 An Illustrious Trio	657

	14.6.3 Questions	659
14.7	The New Heavens and the New Earth	661
	14.7.1 One People	661
	14.7.2 New Questions	663
	14.7.3 The "Tabernacle" On the New Earth	664
	14.7.4 Fourteen Mountains	665
14.8	The *Go'el*	667
	14.8.1 The Four Tasks of the *Go'el*	667
	14.8.2 Prophetic Realization	669
	14.8.3 Final Remarks	673
Bibliography		677
Scripture Index		703
Subject Index		721

Series Preface

BY MEANS OF THIS PREFACE, the editor and publisher of this series wish to help the reader both understand and process the content of these volumes.

The capacities and erudition of Dr. Willem Ouweneel need no demonstration or defense from us. His voluminous work and prodigious writing stand as a testimony to his love for the Lord Jesus Christ, God's Word, and God's people.

But these volumes present ideas that will surprise some, anger others, and possibly confuse still others. Both the editor and publisher disagree with some of Dr. Ouweneel's assertions and conclusions, but this is not the place for offering our counterarguments. That requires an altogether different venue. Nevertheless, discerning readers will legitimately wonder why this editor and publisher invested effort and resources in putting these volumes into print.

At least three reasons justify that investment. Each of them is very sensitive.

The first reason is: *self-examination*. Some of our readers may conclude that, in presenting his exegetical, doctrinal, and historical case, Dr. Ouweneel is "coloring outside the lines" of what they have come to believe. He challenges deeply and firmly held convictions and beliefs, like those associated with Israel, with the law of God, with election and reprobation, with infant baptism, with covenant theology, and with justification. At each point, his challenges call us readers to self-examination, regarding our love for Scripture, for the God of Scripture, and for the Truth revealed and incarnated personally in Jesus Christ. One of Ouweneel's challenges is for us believers in Jesus Christ who are Reformed and Presbyterian church members to recognize that there are millions, even billions, of Jesus-believers who disagree with us *and are nevertheless genuine Christians.* And they ought to be acknowledged as such.

The second reason is: *repentance.* Coming, as they do, from one who lives and teaches outside the orbit of many of our readers, Dr. Ouweneel's observations about the state of our (numerous) churches and of our (interminable) doctrinal squabbles ought to embarrass us Reformed and Presbyterian church members. Our incessant polemicizing, our cantankerous stridency, and our offenses against the unity of Christ's church seriously compromise the gospel's witness to the watching world. Brothers and sisters, we must repent of these, for the sake of the gospel, for the sake of the church's witness, and for the sake of our children.

The third reason is: *ecumenicity.* This reason may indeed strike you as strange, but one of the salutary outcomes of reading Dr. Ouweneel's arguments can be this: *not* that you surrender your commitments and convictions that are being challenged, but instead that you come to *respect* and *love* those Jesus-believers who don't share them with you. These Christians are those whose spiritual pilgrimage and gospel-guided history have not brought them to the same place on the road, but who nonetheless are walking the same road as we.

You may well be asking: How, then, is this different from advocating doctrinal relativism? If these distinctive features of Reformed confession and theology are biblical, then why is Dr. Ouweneel being given a microphone for proclaiming his criticisms and rejections of these distinctive emphases of Reformed teaching? The short answer is this: So that from this brother in Christ, this close cousin in the faith, this fellow pilgrim-soldier, we may learn how to lock arms with other Jesus-believers as we face unbelief in our day, even if we can't hold hands. So that we may learn what it means to be Jesus-believers *first*, Reformed or Presbyterian confessors *second*, and only then, *thirdly, theological advocates.*

So we leave you with this challenge: Why do you believe what you believe? What is your biblical warrant? Dr. Ouweneel presents fairly the various positions prevalent within Christianity. The reader will learn why others believe what they believe, and why they don't emphasize certain teachings in the same way that we do.

These books, then, are *not* for the faint of faith. But they *are* for those wanting to grow up and mature into the unity of faith in our Lord Jesus Christ (John 17: 20-23; Eph. 4:13).

Nelson D. Kloosterman, editor
John Hultink, publisher

Author's Preface

For an introduction to the present two-volume work on Israelology, see the Author's Preface in the first volume (vol. IV/1a). This first volume focused on biblical Israel, the Israel we find throughout both the Tanakh and the New Testament. This second volume focuses on the Israel in post-biblical times until today, as well as on its prophetic future.

As a Bible translation I am using the ESV (English Standard Version), unless otherwise indicated.

I wish to warmly thank my editor, Dr. Nelson D. Kloosterman, and my publisher, Mr. John Hultink, for their constant support and encouragement.

Loerik (Houten, Netherlands), Summer 2021
Willem J. Ouweneel

P.S. The national anthem of the modern state of Israel is called *HaTikvah* ("The Hope"). It is marvelous, but religious Jews have rightly objected that God and the Torah are not mentioned in it. Therefore, Rabbi Abraham Isaac Kook (1865–1935), the first Ashkenazi chief rabbi of British Mandatory Palestine in the land of Israel, wrote an alternative anthem titled *HaEmunah* ("The Faith"). It goes like this:[1]

Leʻad chayyah bilbabēn   Forever lives in our hearts

---

1. For transliteration and pronunciation, see vol. IV/1a, chapter 1, note 1.

THE ETERNAL PEOPLE: GOD IN RELATION TO ISRAEL

ha'emunah hane'emanah	the faithful faith
lashub el eretz k'doshēn	to return to our holy land,
ir bah David chanah.	to the city where David settled.
Shamah na'amod l'goralēnu	There we shall stand in view of our destination,
ab hamon qanah	which the father of a multitude[2] acquired,
shamah nichyē chayyēnu	there we shall live our life,
chayyé 'adat mi manah.	the life of the innumerable congregation.
Shamah na'abod Elohēnu	There we shall serve our God
b'chedvah b'gilah ubirnanah	with joy, bliss and song,
shamah na'alēh l'raglēnu	there we shall pilgrimage
shalosh pa'amim b'shanah.	three times a year.
Torat chayyim chemdatēnu	The Torah of life[3] is our desire,
mipi elyon nitnah	given from the mouth of the Most High,
netzach hi nachalatēnu	forever it is our heritage,
mimidbar matanah.	from the wilderness it was given.

---

2. I.e., Abraham (see Gen. 17:5 and footnote).
3. Cf. Lev. 18:5, "You shall therefore keep my statutes and my rules; if a person does them, he shall live by them." Deut. 32:47, "[The Torah] is your very life."

Abbreviations

AMP	Amplified Bible
AMPC	Amplified Bible, Classic Edition
ASV	American Standard Version
BRG	BRG Bible
CEB	Common English Bible
CEV	Contemporary English Version
CJB	Complete Jewish Bible
DARBY	Darby Translation
DLNT	Disciples' Literal New Translation
DRA	Douay-Rheims 1899 American Edition
ERV	Easy-to-Read Version
ESV	English Standard Version
EXB	Expanded Bible
GNT	Good News Translation
GNV	1599 Geneva Bible
GW	God's Word Translation
HCSB	Holman Christian Standard Bible
ICB	International Children's Bible
ISV	International Standard Version

JUB	Jubilee Bible 2000
KJ21	21st Century King James Version
KJV	King James Version
LEB	Lexham English Bible
MEV	Modern English Version
MOUNCE	Mounce Reverse-Interlinear New Testament
MSG	The Message
NASB	New American Standard Bible
NIRV	New International Reader's Version
NMB	New Matthew Bible
NCV	New Century Version
NET	New English Translation
NIV	New International Version
NLV	New Life Version
NKJV	New King James Version
NOG	Names of God Bible
OJB	Orthodox Jewish Bible
PHILLIPS	J. B. Phillips
RSV	Revised Standard Version
TLB	Living Bible
TLV	Tree of Life Version
TPT	The Passion Translation
VOICE	The Voice
WE	Worldwide English (New Testament)
WEB	World English Bible
YLT	Young's Literal Translation

Other Sources:

BT	Kelly, W., ed. 1856–1920. *Bible Treasury: A Monthly Review of Prophetic and Practical Subjects*. Available at https://bibletruthpublishers.com/bible-treasury/lpvl22465.
COT	Commentaar op het Oude Testament
CNT	Commentaar op het Nieuwe Testament
CR	*Corpus Reformatorum*. 1st series and 2nd series. Vols. 1–87. Brunswick: Schwetschke, 1834–1900.
CW	Darby, J. N. n.d.-a *The Collected Writings of J. N. Darby*. Kingston-on-Thames: Stow Hill Bible and Tract Depot.
DJG	Green, J. B. and S. McKnight, eds. 1992. *Dictionary of Jesus and the Gospels*. Downers Grove, IL: InterVarsity Press.
EBC	The Expositor's Bible Commentary
EDR	Evangelische Dogmatische Reeks
EGT	Expositor's Greek Testament
EJ	Skolnik. F. 2007. *Encyclopedia Judaica*. 2nd ed. 14 vols. Farmington Hills, MI: Keter Publishing House Ltd.
KDC	Keil, C. F. and F. Delitzsch. 1976–1977. *Commentary on the Old Testament*. 10 vols. Grand Rapids, MI: Eerdmans.
KV	Korte Verklaring der Heilige Schrift
NICNT	New International Commentary on the New Testament
NICOT	New International Commentary on the Old Testament
NIGTC	New International Greek Testament Commentary

RC	Dennison, J. T., Jr., ed. 2008–2014. *Reformed Confessions of the 16th and 17th Centuries in English Translation*. 4 vols. Grand Rapids, MI: Reformation Heritage Books.
RD	Bavinck, H. 2002–2008. *Reformed Dogmatics*. Edited by J. Bolt. Translated by J. Vriend. 4 vols. Grand Rapids, MI: Baker Academic.
SBB	Soncino Press Books of the Bible
ST	Chafer, L. S. 1983. *Systematic Theology*. 15th ed. 8 vols. Dallas, TX: Dallas Seminary Press.
SYN	Darby, J.N. n.d.-b. *Synopsis of the Books of the Bible*. 5 vols. London: G. Morrish.
TDNT	Kittel, G. et al., eds. 1964–1976. *Theological Dictionary of the New Testament*. Translated by G. W. Bromiley. 10 vols. Grand Rapids, MI: Eerdmans.
TNTC	Tyndale New Testament Commentaries

Chapter 1
Judaism and Christianity

In [the] office of firstborn, the Jew is in a certain sense untouchable. His humanity exists so to say immediate, by the grace of God, whereas the Greek must create himself the beautiful and good of his humanity. Therefore, the Jew to a certain extent is also taboo; it is forbidden, and also dangerous, to touch him. Consequently, around the Jews that mysterious tension arose, which everyone knows from history and, even more so, from the youngest experience [i.e., the Shoah]. In the force field in which this tension occurs the world is least of all in balance. It is constantly sparking there, as if humanity were still originating.

Oepke Noordmans (emphasis added)[1]

---

1. Noordmans (1956, 312–13); Oepke Noordmans was one of the most influential Dutch Reformed theologians of the twentieth century.

1.1 Israel in Hebrews
1.1.1 Hebrews 4:9

THE NEW TESTAMENT EPISTLE to the Hebrews was written by an unknown Christian author from the circle of the apostles, and addressed to Jesus-believers of Jewish descent who were living in the Holy Land during a time when the temple ministry still existed.[2] For our purpose—designing a Christian Israel theology—this letter is extremely significant because its origin lies, as it were, at a crossroads of Judaism and Christianity (cf. §1.5 for these terms). The letter is thoroughly Jewish, as is evident from the innumerable references, both direct and indirect, to the Tanakh (the Old Testament); not only to persons in the Tanakh persons but especially to the tabernacle ministry (interestingly not at all to the temple ministry, indicating that the letter went back to the basics of Jewish history). The letter is also thoroughly Christian by placing at the center Jesus Christ as the Messiah (anointed King) of Israel, as the Son of God and the Son of Man, as both high priest and atoning sacrifice.

It is difficult to find in the letter some direct and decisive evidence for the notion of a future national restoration of Israel, but it contains enough material that is compatible with such a notion and is less doubtful than other interpretations.[3] Let me give some examples.

The writer observed, "So then, there remains a Sabbath rest [one Gk. word: *sabbatismos*] for the people of God" (Heb.4:9). There have been many suggestions as to the meaning of this expression. The following ones must be rejected because they have nothing to do with the notion of the Sabbath as such: (a) the *sabbatismos* is *not* the rest for the believer's conscience (see on this point 9:9, 14; 10:22). (b) It is *not* the celebration of the Sabbath by Messianic Jews.[4] (c) It is *not* a reference to the intermediate state of the believer (the stage between physical death and physical resurrection).[5] (d) And

---

2. See the introduction in Ouweneel (1982b).
3. See more extensively, Ouweneel (1982b, ad loc., plus references).
4. *Contra* Stern (1999, 673).
5. See Ouweneel (2012a, §§3.1–3.2; and 2022).

it is *not* a reference to the new heavens and the new earth.[6] Only one interpretation remains: the *sabbatismos* is a reference to the Messianic age and kingdom. It is entirely compatible with similar expressions in the same letter: "the world to come" (2:5), the "age to come" (6:5)—the time when everything will be "in subjection" to Christ" (2:8-9), the "city to come" (13:14), and especially this statement: "Therefore let us be grateful for receiving a *kingdom that cannot be shaken*" (12:28).

The term *sabbatismos* reminds us of Psalm 92, called "A Song for the Sabbath." It says,

> For behold, your enemies, O Lord,
>> for behold, your enemies shall perish;
>> all evildoers shall be scattered.
> But you have exalted my horn like that of the wild ox;
>> you have poured over me fresh oil.
> My eyes have seen the downfall of my enemies;
>> my ears have heard the doom of my evil assailants.
> The righteous flourish like the palm tree
>> and grow like a cedar in Lebanon.
> They are planted in the house of the Lord;
>> they flourish in the courts of our God (Ps. 92:10-13).

According to Rashi,[7] this psalm was referring to the world to come, which will be an "endless Sabbath." Thus, in my view, the Sabbath rest could not be referring to anything but the peace and rest of the Messianic kingdom, established by and belonging to the Son of Man. We read of the latter that he is "Lord of the Sabbath" (Luke 6:5), which (also) means, Lord of the future Sabbatical world. The Ruler, set over the "world to come," will be the Lord of the great Sabbath, that is, the world of the seventh "day" of God's redemptive history.[8] It is the "day" in which all previous eras, times and epochs

---

6. Cf. the Marginal Notes of the Dutch States' Translation (1637): ". . . the spiritual and eternal rest."
7. Cohen (1985, 304); Rashi is the acronym of the great Jewish French Bible expositor, Rabbi Shlomo Yitzchaki.
8. See extensively, Ouweneel (2011, chapter 14).

will culminate, called in Ephesians 1:10 the "fullness of the [consecutive] times [ages, epochs]" (Gk. *plērōma tōn kairōn*).⁹ As Paul says, God has made "known to us the mystery of his will, according to his purpose, which he set forth in Christ as a plan for the fullness of *times*, to unite all things in him, things in heaven and things on earth" (Eph. 1:9-10).

If we were to think of six time periods of world history, the Sabbath is the seventh "day" (era, epoch), the completion and culmination of all God's ways with the world throughout history. The new heavens and the new earth will be an "eighth day,"¹⁰ which is the beginning of a new "week."¹¹

The Bible speaks of various "days" in connection with God:

(a) There is the "day of God" (Gk. *hē theou hēmera*, 2 Pet. 3:12, which in my view is identical with the "day of eternity," *hēmera aiōnos*, in v. 18);

(b) there is also the "day of the Lord" (Gk. *hēmera kuriou*, 1 Thess. 5:2; cf. 2 Pet. 3:10; cf. also the Tanakh expression "day of the LORD," *yom YHWH*, from Isa. 13:6 to Mal. 4:5). As I see it, this day is the day of the coming of the Messiah and the age of his kingdom, whereas the "day of God" is the day of the new heavens and the new earth.

(c) In a similar vein, the present era could be called the "day of Man" (or "Man's day," cf. 1 Cor. 4:3, Gk. *anthrōpinē hēmera*, although here, the expression has the meaning of a tribunal). In summary, in God's redemptive dealings with the world, the sixth "day" (the day on which humanity was created) is the day of Man, the seventh "day" is the day of the Lord (the Messiah), and the eighth "day" is the day of (the Triune) God.

---

9. *Not* "fullness of time" (sing., ESV, RSV)—a confusion with Gal. 4:4, *plērōma tou chronou*, a time coming to its fulfillment.
10. *Contra* Booth (1999), who referred the "sixth day (of creation)" to the Messianic kingdom, and the "seventh day" to the new heavens and earth.
11. Cf. Exod. 22:30; Lev. 12:3; 14:10, 23; 15:14, 29; see also Luke 9:28; John 20:26.

1.1.2 Hebrews 8

When in Hebrews 8 the writer extensively quoted Jeremiah 31:31–34 and introduced the theme of the new covenant, we must constantly keep in mind that he is writing to Jesus-believing Jews:

> For if that first covenant had been faultless, there would have been no occasion to look for a second. For he finds fault with them when he says:
>
> "Behold, the days are coming, declares the LORD,
>   when I will establish a new covenant with the house of
> Israel
> and with the house of Judah,
>   not like the covenant that I made with their fathers
>   on the day when I took them by the hand to bring
>   them out of the land of Egypt.
> For they did not continue in my covenant,
>   and so I showed no concern for them, declares the
>   Lord. . ." (Heb. 8:7–9).

First and foremost, the covenant was intended for "the house of Israel and the house of Judah." We cannot read the letter with the assumption that although it was primarily addressed to Jesus-believing Jews, it makes no distinction between Jesus-believing Jews and Jesus-believing Gentiles. Notice phrases such as "God spoke to the fathers" (1:1) and "the people of God" (4:9), which referred primarily to (the remnant of) the people of Israel. To be sure, we have seen that Gentile Jesus-believers have been admitted under the "roof" of this new covenant's blessings (cf. Matt. 26:28; 2 Cor. 3:6), but nowhere in the Bible were they referred to as the Lord's actual covenant partner in the covenant mentioned in Jeremiah 31 (see vol. IV/1a, chapter 5).[12]

The new covenant is formally established with "Israel," which referred to the ten tribes, and with "Judah," which

---

12. See extensively, Ouweneel (2011, chapters 1–4).

referred to the two tribes (Judah and Benjamin),[13] and this event will occur at the beginning of the Messianic kingdom. The latter claim is clear from Jeremiah 31 and its entire context. Nevertheless, the readers of the letter to the Hebrews were also involved with this, for they constituted the remnant from Israel, chosen by grace in the present time, as we saw in Romans 11:5. In this way, they received the pre-fulfillment of the promises that one day will be true for all (converted) Israel (Rom. 11:26).

If the writer of Hebrews applied the covenant-making of Jeremiah 31:31–34 to his readers in this way, it seems clear that the entire eschatological context of Jeremiah 31 is implied and included in his argument. Let me mention seven aspects of this context.[14]

(1) The fulfillment was placed in the "latter days" (Jer. 30:24, Heb. *be'acharit hayyamim*, more precisely, "at the end of the days," DARBY, JUB, YLT). This is a typically eschatological expression, referring to the end times and the arrival of the Messianic kingdom[15] (but cf. Heb. 1:2; 1 Cor. 10:11; 1 John 2:18, where the present era is seen to presage that coming time).

(2) The restoration is Israel is preceded by what is called the Great Tribulation (Jer. 30:7; cf. Dan. 12:1; Matt. 24:21; Rev. 3:10; 7:14).

(3) The unbelieving majority of the people is judged (Jer. 30:11; 31:30).

(4) All nations, in particular those that have lifted themselves up against Israel, are judged by, and subjugated to, the Messiah (Jer. 30:8, 11, 16-17).

(5) The Messiah, who is the Son of David, is the One bringing about the restoration of Israel, and is the focal point of the Messianic kingdom that will follow that judgment (Jer. 30:9, 21).

---

13. Cf. 2 Sam. 2:10; 20:2; 1 Kings 12:16–17, 20–23; 2 Chron. 11:3, 12, 23; 14:8; 15:2, 8–9.
14. Ouweneel (1982b, 1:109–110).
15. Num. 24:14; Deut. 4:30; Isa. 2:2; Jer. 23:20; 48:47; 49:39; Dan. 2:28; 10:14; Hos. 3:5; Micah 4:1; see vol. IV/1a, chapter 5, note 11.

(6) The future restoration of Israel involves both the ten tribes and the two tribes, which will return to the Promised Land *from* all the nations of the earth (Jer. 30:3-4; 31:9, 15, 27, 31).

(7) Righteousness, joy, and peace will rule in Israel, without ever again being disrupted by any power (Jer. 30:18-20; 31:4-7, 24-25, 38-40).

It is fascinating to discover how differently Hebrews 8 is interpreted when one wears different paradigmatic spectacles. Hebrews 8 makes clear, in the spirit of Jeremiah 31, that the New Covenant is not (to be) made with the Ecclesia as such, but with the literal two and ten tribes of Israel. One interpreter has seen the exact opposite in Hebrews 8, namely, proof that the author of Hebrews "sees in the Church of Jesus Christ the fulfillment of the prophecy concerning the new covenant as described in Jeremiah 31."[16] He overlooked the fact that the letter was addressed to Hebrews, that is, Jesus-believing Jews—not to the Ecclesia (of Jews and Gentiles) as such (although the writer knew, of course, about the Ecclesia: ". . . the assembly (or, church) of the firstborn [Gk. *ekklesia prōtotokōn*] who are enrolled in heaven," Heb. 12:23).

1.2 The "City"
1.2.1 Heavenly Capital of the Kingdom?

Several times, the letter to the Hebrews speaks of a mysterious "city." Abraham "was looking forward to the city that has foundations, whose designer and builder is God. . . . [the patriarchs] desire a better country, that is, a heavenly one. Therefore God is not ashamed to be called their God, for he has prepared for them a city" (11:10, 16). Later, "[Y]ou have come to Mount Zion and to the city of the living God, the heavenly Jerusalem" (12:22). And finally: "[H]ere we have no lasting city, but we seek the city that is to come" (13:14).

This "city" is not simply "heaven," whether in the intermediate state (between death and resurrection) or in eternity (the new heavens and the new earth). Rather, in the context of this letter it must be the city that can perhaps be best de-

---

16. Maljaars (2015, 125).

scribed as the heavenly capital of the "world to come" (2:5) in the "age to come" (6:5), that is, of the Messianic kingdom, the "kingdom that cannot be shaken" (12:28).[17] We may compare this with the "new Jerusalem" mentioned in Revelation 21:2 and 21:9–22:5, which has been viewed as well as the heavenly capital of the Messianic kingdom. We are dealing here, so to speak, with the heavenly side (sphere, realm) of the Messianic kingdom. During the time when Israel will be again as the stars of the sky and the sand on the seashore, and will inherit its earthly country, the risen saints—including the patriarchs, but also the Jesus-believing first readers of the letter to the Hebrews—will inherit the heavenly country (11:14–16).

The patriarchs had looked forward to the time when their offspring would possess the Promised Land, that is, Canaan, later called the "land of Israel" (from 1 Sam. 13:19 to Matt. 2:21). The Jesus-believing first readers of the letter to the Hebrews were already living in the "land of Israel," though under the occupying Romans. They looked forward to a different Promised Land. What was this? First in the Roman Catholic, and later in the Protestant tradition, Christians began increasingly to understand this Promised Land to be "heaven," the place where believers supposedly go when they die.[18]

1.2.2 The Intermediate State?

In fact, this expectation of going to heaven immediately upon death, which pushed the significance of the resurrection and of the second coming of Christ to the background of theological thinking, is a distinct aspect of supersessionism. That is to say, just as ethnic Israel with its earthly promises was replaced by the church with its spiritualized promises, just as circumcision was replaced by infant baptism, and just as the Sabbath (Saturday) was replaced by—or was supposed to have switched to—Sunday (matters to which we will return), similarly the expectation of the Messianic kingdom (at the second coming of Christ) was replaced by the expectation of heaven (after death). Because of this, the Messianic kingdom was no

---

17. Ouweneel (1982b, 2:57, 59).
18. But see extensively, Ouweneel (2020b; 2022).

longer of interest to Christians. Since it was only heaven that counted, *the* central and climactic question of gospel preaching and of many very orthodox sermons became: "Where will you go when you die?" instead of, for instance: "Christ is coming soon—are you ready?"

Even today, when millions of Christians have learned to look forward again to the second coming of Christ and the establishment of his kingdom, and have again learned to interpret the Tanakh prophecies concerning Israel literally, this expectation of heaven after death is still very strong. Many who have come to surrender their supersessionism still do not see all the aspects and consequences of this misleading teaching; they may have rejected its main components, but they often do not recognize the harmful implications of supersessionism, and thus continue to embrace them. Supersessionism is embedded in Christian thinking to such an extent that it takes the greatest spiritual energy to rid oneself of all its implications.

This is all the more serious because, in the New Testament, ever since the ascension of Christ the notion of "expecting" (waiting for, looking forward to) *always* referred to the second coming and the Messianic kingdom (and ultimate eternity), and *never* to "heaven" (as the supposed destination reached immediately upon death). Here are a few New Testament examples, first from Hebrews itself.

> Christ, having been offered once to bear the sins of many, will appear a second time, not to deal with sin but to save those who are eagerly *waiting* for him (Heb. 9:28).
>
> [O]ur citizenship is in heaven, and from it we *await* a Savior, the Lord Jesus Christ (Phil. 3:20)
>
> ... how you turned to God from idols to serve the living and true God, and to *wait* for his Son from heaven (1 Thess. 1:9-10)
>
> ... *waiting* for our blessed hope, the appearing of the glory of our great God and Savior Jesus Christ (Titus 2:12-13)
>
> ... *waiting* for and hastening the coming of the day of God,

because of which the heavens will be set on fire and dissolved, and the heavenly bodies will melt as they burn! But according to his promise we are *waiting* for new heavens and a new earth in which righteousness dwells (2 Pet. 3:12-14).[19]

Only when we understand the real nature of genuine Christian "waiting" will we understand Hebrews 11:10, about Abraham "looking forward to the city that has foundations." Entirely in line with an age-old tradition, older expositors in particular thought here of the heavenly bliss, or at best of the new heaven and earth.[20] However, in the context of the letter we must insist that the patriarchs—as far as the Holy Spirit enabled them to discern this—looked forward to the blessed rule of the Son of Promise (2 Cor. 1:20-21), the true "Seed" (Offspring) of Abraham (Gal. 3:16), the great Shiloh (Gen. 49:10 KJV), the Son of Man (Dan. 7:13-14; Heb. 2:6-9). One day, they, or their offspring, would under him receive their heritage in the land that had been promised to them since Genesis 12. In Jesus' own words (John 8:56): "Your father Abraham rejoiced that he would see *my day*. He saw it and was glad." At that point, Abraham was not looking forward to his death or to heaven, but to the *day* of the great Messiah, who will be manifested here on earth in all his glory, power, and majesty; or he was looking forward to "the *days* of the Son of Man" (Luke 22:17, 26).

1.2.3 Heavenly and Earthly Sides

On the day when the people of Israel will inherit the earthy land, namely, in the Messianic kingdom, the patriarchs will not miss out on the fulfillment of the promises. They will inherit the "land," too, namely, "from above," from the heavenly side of it, so to speak. This will also involve their reigning with Christ from heaven *over the earth* (cf. Rev. 20:4, 6). They will not receive the earthly land with the earthly Jerusalem, but rather—in their resurrection bodies—a heavenly country, which will contain the new, heavenly Jerusalem, the "Jerusa-

---

19. See also Luke 12:36; 23:51; Rom. 8:19, 23–25; 1 Cor. 1:7–8; Gal. 5:5; Jude 21.
20. http://biblehub.com/hebrews/11-10.htm.

lem above" (Gal. 4:25-26), though in view of the kingdom of God, which will be established *on earth*.²¹ However, this does not at all diminish the reality that many Israelites *in their mortal bodies* will inherit the *earthly* land with the *earthly* Jerusalem and the *earthly* temple.

During the Messianic kingdom, the earthly and the heavenly sides will be closely connected. How would heavenly believers be able to reign over the earth if they, when necessary, could not appear to the earthly inhabitants, presumably similar to the way angels appeared to humans throughout redemptive history? I have no direct biblical evidence for this, but such a situation seems plausible to me. I imagine that it will be like the ladder in Jacob's dream, "set up on the earth, and the top of it reached to heaven. And behold, the angels of God were ascending and descending on it" (Gen. 28:12). As Jesus said, "[Y]ou will see heaven opened, and the angels of God ascending and descending on the Son of Man" (John 1:51).

It will be a unanimous community of heavenly and earthly saints, the former in their resurrection bodies, the latter still in their mortal bodies (apparently, they will be transformed only at the end of the Messianic kingdom). As Jesus said, "I tell you, many will come from east and west and recline at table with Abraham, Isaac, and Jacob in the kingdom of heaven [i.e., the heavenly kingdom on *earth*]" (Matt. 8:11). In hell, "there will be weeping and gnashing of teeth, when you see Abraham and Isaac and Jacob and all the prophets in the kingdom of God but you yourselves cast out. And people will come from east and west, and from north and south, and recline at table in the kingdom of God" (Luke 13:28-29).

This Messianic kingdom is the "day of the Lord," to which the patriarchs were looking forward. This was the time to which the saints in Jerusalem at the time of Messiah's birth were looking forward as well: ". . . waiting for the consolation of Israel" (Luke 2:25), "waiting for the redemption of Jerusalem" (v. 38). The "heavenly country" of Hebrews 11:16 is the country of that "day of the Son of Man," just as the "world to

---

21. See vol. IV/1a, §14.9 on the various spiritual meanings of "Jerusalem."

come" (2:5) and the "city to come" (13:14) are the world and the city of the "age to come" (6:5).

1.3 Hebrews 12:22-24
1.3.1 Four Aspects

In Hebrews 12:22-24, the various aspects of the Messianic kingdom according to its heavenly side are enumerated. Zion, according to its spiritual sense, is the comprehensive term for this new order of things—which does not mean in the least that there will not be the earthly Zion with its own significance, about which the Tanakh prophecies speak extensively.[22] This is the enumeration in Hebrews 12:22-24:

"[Y]ou have come to
- [a] Mount *Zion* and to
- [b] the *city* of the living God, the heavenly Jerusalem, and to
- [c] innumerable *angels* in festal gathering, and to
- [d] the *assembly* (Gk. *ekklesia*) of the firstborn who are enrolled in heaven, and to
- [e] *God*, the judge of all, and to
- [f] the spirits of the *righteous* made perfect, and to
- [g] *Jesus*, the mediator of a new covenant, and to
- [h] the sprinkled *blood* that speaks a better word than the blood of Abel."

Let us briefly look at the first four of these eight aspects:

(a) The spiritual Zion is implied, for instance, in Galatians 4:21-31, where it represents the new covenant in contrast to Mount Sinai, which represents the system of Judaism; see especially the reference in verse 27 to Isaiah 54:1.

(b) The "city of the living God, the heavenly Jerusalem" is, as argued above, the heavenly capital of the Messianic kingdom, which is explicitly a kingdom *on earth*; the heavenly Jerusalem and the earthly Jerusalem will be counterparts, so to speak.

(c) We now come to the inhabitants of the heavenly city, viewed, as it were, from the "outside" to the "inside," that

---

22. See Isa. 2:3; 30:19; 31:4; 33:20; 35:10; 37:32; 51:3, 11, 16; 59:20; 62:11; Jer. 31:12; Joel 2:32; 3:16–17, 21; Obad. 17, 21; Micah 4:2, 8, 13; Zeph. 3:14, 16.

is, first the angels are mentioned, that is, the servants in the kingdom (cf. Heb. 1:14; Ps. 103:21).

(d) Then, there is the "church of the firstborn," which is a community in which every member will possess the spiritual birthright of a firstborn. The parallel with Israel is obvious here: initially the firstborn of the people were dedicated to the Lord (Exod. 13:2, 11-16; 22:29; 34:20). Later, the firstborn were replaced by the tribe of Levi (Exod. 28-29; Num. 3:5-13). In other words, Israel's priests originally came from the firstborn (cf. Exod. 20:20-25; 24:5), but later they came from the Levites. It is highly interestingly—and not often noticed—that the Ecclesia was called both: it is the company of the firstborn, as our verse says, but also a company of priests.[23] During the Messianic kingdom, there will be mortal priests serving in the earthly temple (see extensively in Ezek. 40-48), and there will be heavenly priests (glorified saints), the "firstborn," serving in the heavenly temple (Rev. 1:6; 5:10; 7:15; 11:19; 20:6). Both heaven and earth will be reverberating with the praise and worship of God's priests.

1.3.2 Four More Aspects

If [a] "Zion" represents the entire new order of things involved in God's New Covenant, we then have [b] the "city of God," and then the inhabitants: [c] the outer circle of the angels and [d] the inner circle of the glorified saints belonging to the Ecclesia.

(e) Then, at the center is God, who as the Judge will eventually judge all people, and is also the Supreme Ruler. He is the "Judge of all the earth";[24] as the apostle Paul says, "[W]e will all stand before the judgment seat of God" (Rom. 14:10). To this, we may add that, according to Jesus' own words: "the Father judges no one, but has given all judgment to the Son, ... he has given him authority to execute judgment, because he is the Son of Man" (John 5:22, 27). Therefore, Paul can also speak of "Christ Jesus, who is to judge the living and the dead" (2 Tim. 4:1). Or hear what Paul had to say on the Areop-

---

23. 1 Pet. 2:5, 9; Rev. 1:6; 5:10; 20:6; cf. Heb. 3:6; 7:25; 10:19–22; 13:15.
24. Gen. 18:25; Ps. 7:11; 50:6; 58:11; 82:8; Eccl. 3:17; Acts 10:42; Rom. 2:16.

agus (Acts 17:31): God "has fixed a day on which he will judge the world in righteousness by a man whom he has appointed; and of this he has given assurance to all by raising him from the dead."

(f) From the heavenly company we move to those who lived on this earth before Messiah's coming. Those—Jews and Gentiles—who were acknowledged by the Judge as *his* people before the Ecclesia was revealed are the righteous ones in the Tanakh: the *tzaddiqim*. They are described here as "made perfect." This is not so much a moral, but rather an eschatological characterization: having been brought to the state of perfection, namely, the perfection of resurrection, or of the resurrection body[25] (cf. AMP, ". . . bringing them to the final glory"; CJB, ". . . who have been brought to the goal"). Compare here Hebrews 11:39-40, "And all these [believers mentioned in the Tanakh], though commended through their faith, did not receive what was promised, since God had provided something better for us, that apart from us they should not be made perfect." I understand this to teach that Tanakh and New Testament saints will reach perfection at the same moment, that is, their resurrection at the beginning of the Messianic kingdom. All the deceased Tanakh and New Testament saints are waiting in their graves, and will experience the rising of their bodies ("perfection") at the same time.

(g) Then follows another focal point in this summing up: Jesus, who is the mediator between the two parties involved in the New Covenant (cf. 1 Tim. 2:5; Heb. 9:15). The one party is God, who takes the initiative in establishing the covenant, the other party consists of the ten and the two tribes of Israel. Thanks to this New Covenant, made with Israel, there will again be a blessed people of God on earth during the Messianic kingdom. Jesus will be the mediator for this earthly company, just as he is the mediator for the deceased saints of the Tanakh who, in the resurrection, will receive "the promised eternal inheritance" (Heb. 9:15).

---

25. This is something very different from having been "taken up in heaven," as Bavinck (*RD* 4:281) suggests. Here again, the heavenly bliss, not the Messianic kingdom, is mistakenly being viewed as the ultimate goal of redemption.

(h) There is no covenant of God that is not founded on sacrificial blood (cf. Gen. 8:20; 15:9; Exod. 24:8). But all this blood of the thousands of animal sacrifices possessed its value only because it anticipated the blood of Jesus. It is the latter, and only the latter, that constitutes the foundation for all earthly as well as heavenly blessings of God. As the writer said, Jesus

> entered once for all into the holy places, not by means of the blood of goats and calves but by means of his own blood, thus securing an eternal redemption. For if the blood of goats and bulls, and the sprinkling of defiled persons with the ashes of a heifer, sanctify for the purification of the flesh, how much more will the blood of Christ, who through the eternal Spirit offered himself without blemish to God, purify our conscience from dead works to serve the living God (Heb. 9:12-14).

Under the ancient, Sinaitic order of things, God's voice "shook the earth." But under the new, Messianic order of things, God's voice one day "will shake not only the earth but also the heavens." This will involve "the removal of things that are shaken—that is, things that have been made—in order that the things that cannot be shaken may remain" (Heb. 12:26-29). The "unshakable kingdom" (v. 28 NABRE) will be realized in the "world to come" (2:5) during the "age to come" (6:5), when the Son of Man will establish his kingdom on earth in glory. He receives this kingdom from God's hands (Dan. 7:13-14), and the believers receive it from *his* hands (cf. Luke 12:32; 22:29). When, soon, the redeemed Israelites will be subjects of the King on earth, the heavenly saints (resurrected Tanakh and New Testament believers) will be co-rulers with the Messiah, that is, *from* heaven and *over* the earth. In summary:

(a) *Mortal* believers (i.e., on earth) are never co-rulers of Christ, but always subjects in his kingdom, whether this involves Israel or the Ecclesia.

(b) *Glorified* believers (i.e., in heaven) are co-rulers with Christ (Rev. 20:4-6)—but, of course, in a certain sense they too remain subjects of the King (22:3). They will be kings, but he is the King of kings (19:16).

1.4 Paul: Exposition and Application
1.4.1 Remez and D'rash

No doubt, Paul's references to the Tanakh sometimes employ the literal meaning of the passages involved, whereas at other times he made only a practical application. In such cases, the passages were not cited according to their original meaning, as established by the principles of ordinary grammatical-historical biblical exegesis. Entirely in line with rabbinic tradition,[26] Paul often made free applications of the Tanakh. The rabbis as well as Paul were interested not only in the *P'shat* (the text's direct, clear meaning), but also in the deeper *Remez* (allegorical or typological meanings), the still deeper *D'rash* (the midrashic meaning or homiletical application), and the deepest *Sod* (the text's esoteric or mystical meaning).[27] One of the mistakes of supersessionism's exegetical method is not distinguishing between these four layers of exposition, and as a consequence, using certain *applications* that Paul made as a key for interpretating the Tanakh prophecies.

Some helpful examples of *Remez* or *D'rash* are the following.

In Romans 10, Paul wished to illustrate in what way and to what extent the "voice" of the gospel has gone out to both Jews and Gentiles, and to this end he quoted from Psalm 19 (verse 4): "Their voice has gone out to all the earth, / and their words to the ends of the world" (Rom. 10:18). Of course, Paul was well aware of the literal meaning of Psalm 19:4, since this statement described the "language" going out from the celestial bodies. But apparently Paul was not afraid that his readers would point out to him that he was mistreating the text by not sticking to its *P'shat* interpretation. On the contrary, he assumes that his readers would understand that such

---

26. Of course, extant rabbinic writings appeared much later than Paul's writings; but it is obvious that the Mishnah scholars and Paul—Rabbi Sha'ul, pupil of Gamaliel I the Elder (Acts 22:3)! – go back to the same rabbinic tradition; cf. Flusser (1981).
27. Cf. https://en.wikipedia.org/wiki/Pardes_(Jewish_exegesis). The first letters of these words form the acronym *PaRDeS*, which is the Hebrew word for "paradise."

passages can also be understood in the sense of *Remez* and *D'rash*. Moreover, the application that the apostle made here is not as arbitrary as it may seem: there *is* a close coherence between the general revelation as it comes to us through nature and the special revelation as it comes to us through the apostles.[28]

Another example: God told Abraham that, in his "seed" (offspring), all the families or nations of the earth would be blessed.[29] Here, the word "seed" referred either to Abraham's son Isaac or to Abraham's entire progeny, that is, Israel in particular. Paul referred to this as follows: "Now the promises were made to Abraham and to his offspring. It does not say, 'And to offsprings,' referring to many, but referring to one, 'And to your offspring,' who is Christ" (Gal. 3:16). Of course, Paul knew very well that "seed" (Heb. *zera'*, Gk. *sperma*) can have a collective meaning (cf., e.g., "I will surely multiply your offspring [Heb. *zera'*] as the stars of heaven and as the sand that is on the seashore," Gen. 22:17). However, in a midrashic way, he emphasized the singular of *zera'/sperma*, and freely applied this to that one Israelite who has been appropriately referred to as the personification of Israel: Jesus Christ. In a similar way, Hosea 11:1 ("out of Egypt I called my son"), which was clearly referring to the "son" Israel,[30] can be applied to Christ in person, as indeed occurred in Matthew 2:15. Here again, the underlying thought is that Christ is the true Israel, or the true personification of Israel.

One final example: we read in Jeremiah 31:15, "A voice is heard in Ramah, / lamentation and bitter weeping. / Rachel is weeping for her children; / she refuses to be comforted for her children, / because they are no more." From the context, the clear *P'shat* interpretation is that Rachel was weeping over her (grand)children, Ephraim and Manasseh, who, together with the other northern tribes, had been deported to Assyria. In Matthew 2:17-18, this verse was applied to Herod's cruel infanticide in Bethlehem, shortly after the birth of Jesus. The

---

28. See Ouweneel (2012b, chapters 1–4).
29. Gen. 12:3; 18:18; 22:18; cf. 26:4; 28:14.
30. Exod. 4:22; Deut. 1:31; 8:5; cf. the plural in 14:1; Hos. 1:10.

link between the two passages is the fact that Rachel's tomb lay in the neighborhood of Bethlehem (Gen. 35:19). From the high place of her tomb, this "mother in Israel"[31] observed as it were this horrendous event in Bethlehem and wept over the little boys who perished there. Again, this was a typically midrashic application of the original passage. Viewed from our grammatical-historical tradition of biblical exegesis, these examples may strike us as strange—but from the standpoint of rabbinic tradition they are perfectly normal.

1.4.2 *G'zerah shavah*

Another example of a midrashic approach is found in one of the seven exegetical rules of Rabbi Hillel (d. AD 10),[32] called *g'zerah shavah*, freely rendered as the hermeneutic of parallelism. It means that an analogy between two passages is assumed when in both passages an identical root, word, or phrase occurs.

This hermeneutic is found in Peter's sermon on the Day of Pentecost. In Acts 2:25-28 we read that he quoted Psalm 16:8-11, of which he provided a Messianic application in terms of the resurrection of Christ. The pivotal line here is this: "[B]ecause [the Lord] is at my right hand, I shall not be shaken" (Ps. 16:8b). Peter subsequently (Acts 2:35) linked the expression "my right hand" with Psalm 110:1, "The Lord says to my Lord: / 'Sit at my right hand, / until I make your enemies your footstool.'" Here, the Messianic context is even clearer: because *he* was at *my* right hand when I was on this earth, *I* will be at *his* right hand when I am in heaven. In those days, it was quite common to link such passages containing similar words and phrases, and then look for a deeper coherence.[33]

We read in Hebrews 3:7-11 that the writer quoted Psalm 95:7-11, and in 4:4-5, he linked this with Genesis 2:2, apparently because of the similar words "day," "works," and "rest." Through these parallel terms, the writer assumed a deeper

---

31. Cf. this expression in Judg. 5:7 (Deborah) and 2 Sam. 20:19 (the town Abel of Beth-maacah).
32. Regarding him, see Ouweneel (2014, 93–96).
33. See, e.g., Stern (1999, ad loc.); Shulam (2010, 52–53).

coherence between Genesis 2 and Psalm 95. The influence of Rabbi Hillel would have been one of the causes for Jewish interpreters easily assuming such connections.

Our purpose with all these examples is to demonstrate the serious error of supposing that when they dealt with the Tanakh, New Testament writers always followed our own modern grammatical-historical approach.

Other examples may further elucidate this point. A typical case of a midrashic interpretation was the application of Israel passages to converted Gentiles. See, for instance, Isaiah 49:8, "In a time of favor I have answered you; / in a day of salvation I have helped you." This statement as quoted in 2 Corinthians 6:2 and applied to the gospel work among the nations. What Isaiah told *Israel* was repeated by Paul, but then applied to (believing) *Gentiles*, without at all suggesting that believing Gentiles have now become Jews. This is clear from the fact that Isaiah 49:8-26 is God's reply to "Zion," which had gone through miserable circumstances but is ultimately restored.

Another example is Hosea 1:10, "[T]he number of the children of Israel shall be like the sand of the sea, which cannot be measured or numbered. And in the place where it was said to them, 'You are not my people [Heb. *Lo-'Ammi*],' it shall be said to them, 'Children of the living God.'"

This statement was quoted in Romans 9:26 and 1 Peter 2:10 in such a way that *Lo-'Ammi* was referring not to the people of Israel temporarily set aside—which, according to the grammatical-historical method would be the *only valid* interpretation—but to the Gentile world, from which some people come to faith in Jesus Christ, and thus become "people of God."

Consider Hosea 2:23 as well: "[A]nd I will sow her for myself in the land. / And I will have mercy on No Mercy [Heb. *Lo-Ruchamah*], / and I will say to Not My People [Heb. *Lo-'Ammi*], 'You are my people [Heb. *'Ammi*]'; / and he shall say, 'You are my God.'" This is quoted in Romans 9:25 and applied to the Gentile world. To believe that Paul was simply providing an *exegesis* of Hosea 2:23 is just as mistaken as believing that

Matthew 2:17-18 is *simply* providing an *exegesis* of Jeremiah 31:5, or that Romans 10:18 is *simply* providing an *exegesis* of Psalm 19:4. In all three instances, the writers were providing a free, creative application, about which we might raise our modern scholarly eyebrows, but which in New Testament and rabbinic times was quite common.

1.4.3 The Supersessionist Error

Of course, supersessionists have used these quotations to defend their thesis that the church is the true, spiritual Israel. Our first volume on Israelology (vol. IV/1a in this series) offers an extensive refutation of this error. This error consists simply in confusing *P'shat* with *Remez/D'rash*, that is, confusing the grammatical-historical interpretation with the midrashic application of the text. No fair grammatical-historical exposition of Hosea 1-2 could understand *Lo-'Ammi* there as a reference to the yet unconverted Gentile world. In Hosea, *Lo-'Ammi* was not referring to those who, until now, are *not yet* God's people (the Gentiles), but rather to those who once *were* God's people, but now, because of their sins, temporarily bear the stamp of Not-My-People. By origin, the Gentiles are not God's people because they have never been called to this special position; Israel was *temporarily* (and *formally*) not God's people because it *had* been called to be God's people but had desecrated this calling through their sins.[34] These two things are entirely different. Of course, the apostle Paul knows this very well, too; today, he would perhaps reply: But please note, I am not doing *P'shat* but *D'rash*!

The citation in the New Testament of the Tanakh passages mentioned must necessarily create problems for all those to whom—since the Renaissance and the Enlightenment—grammatical-historical exegesis is the only acceptable approach. Orthodox Jews view every word of the Tanakh as divinely inspired, whereas one Jewish tradition neverthe-

---

34. *Originally,* Israel was of course a nation like all others; cf. this interesting comparison: "'Are you not like the Cushites to me, O people of Israel?' declares the LORD. 'Did I not bring up Israel from the land of Egypt, and the Philistines from Caphtor and the Syrians from Kir?'" (Amos 9:7).

less speaks of "seventy meanings" in each verse.³⁵ This was explained in the book *Ayin Panim baTorah* ("Seventy Faces [= Meanings] in the Torah"), written by Abraham ben Samuel Cohen of Lask (1797). The *P'shat* (the literal and most obvious meaning of the text) comes first, followed by many other interpretations or applications of the text, given as *Remez*, *D'rash*, and *Sod*. In other words, we must not believe that this Jewish tradition suggests that there are seventy different *grammatical-historical* interpretations of each verse. This would be simply absurd and would in fact destroy all serious exegesis. Why do we have serious exegetical commentaries on the Tanakh by Jewish commentators like Rashi (Shlomo Yitzchaki), Rambam (Moses ben Maimon, or, Maimonides), Ramban (Moshe ben Nachman, or, Nachmanides), Abraham Ibn Ezra, Jacob Sforno, and David Kimchi, if for each interpretation that they provide we could respond: Where are the other sixty-nine interpretations?

Apparently, the method of dealing with the sacred text being described here is also the—truly Jewish—method the apostles used in dealing with the Tanakh, without this approach at all detracting from (their respect for) the verbal text and its primary meaning. On the contrary, the apostles had an eye for a text's deeper expository layers than just what lay on the grammatical-historical surface. The same Paul who quotes the Tanakh so freely—which means that, in addition to *P'shat*, he also appreciated *Remez*, *D'rash*, and *Sod*—also implicitly emphasized that the Bible writers used *words* of the Holy Spirit (1 Cor. 2:13); each word, every tittle, each jot, and every nuance is God-breathed, and thus important. But the same is true for *every* method of expounding the text— no matter how much difficulty modern Western expositors may have with this. Just think of the severe difficulty that Reformed theology has always had with typology, whereas the New Testament itself gives us so many examples of this.³⁶

---

35. Talmud: Shabbat 88b (to be read in the light of Sanhedrin 34a; see the quotation at the beginning of this chapter); see further Num. Rabbah 13–15.
36. See especially Rom. 5; 1 Cor. 10 and 15; Gal. 4; Heb. 3–4; Heb. 11.

1.5 Post-Acts 15 Christendom
1.5.1 "Christians" Growing Away from Jews

For a proper understanding of our subject, a clear and accurate view of the relationship between Christianity and Judaism, and thus of the distinct future of the Ecclesia and Israel, is of the utmost importance. The word "distinct" does *not* mean here a kind of "two-ways doctrine" for Jews and Gentiles: both the Ecclesia and Israel will ultimately reach their destination solely in and through Jesus Christ, on the basis of his work of redemption accomplished on the cross.

It might be viewed as an argument for supersessionism—and as a difficulty for classical dispensationalists—that the separation between Judaism and what we now call Christianity occurred at a relatively late stage. No doubt, none of the apostles would have described Christianity as a new religion, clearly distinct from Judaism. On the contrary, the time of the Gospels and the book of Acts featured the growing movement of the Jesus-confessing Jews, just as there were the Pharisaic, Sadducean, Herodian, Essene, and other movements. There were even social and ethnic distinctions: Acts 6:9 speaks of "those who belonged to the synagogue of the Freedmen (as it was called), and[37] of the Cyrenians, and of the Alexandrians, and of those from Cilicia and Asia."

In Acts, Jesus-confessing persons are referred to as the "sect [i.e., religious party] of the Nazarenes," or "Nazoreans," that is, followers of Jesus of Nazareth, or of Jesus the Nazarene (Matt. 2:23) (Acts 2:22; 3:6; 4:10; 6:14; 22:8; 26:9). In those days, the term "Christians" (Gk. *christianoi*, i.e., followers of Christ; Acts 11:26; 26:28; cf. 1 Pet. 4:16) was simply a synonym of "Nazarenes." Interestingly, their faith community was described as "the Way," which is the way to life, to salvation, to the kingdom of God, Jesus himself being the Way.[38] In a sense, since the word "Christ" means "Messiah" (Anointed One), the term *christianoi* could preferably be translated as something like "Messianists" or "Messiah-confessors," so that

---

37. Some translate this word "and" as "composed of" or "including."
38. Acts 9:2; 19:9, 23; 24:14, 22; cf. 16:17; 18:25, 26; perhaps a reference to passages such as Matt. 3:3 (Isa. 40:3); 7:13–14; John 14:6.

readers avoid the mistake of viewing Christianity as a new, separate religion. Nowhere in Acts, or in the New Testament, for that matter, is Christianity presented as a distinctly new religion.

However, in post-New Testament times, as faith in Jesus increasingly became especially a matter of Gentiles (not obliged to keep the Mosaic Torah), it became increasingly inevitable that, generally speaking, the word "Jews" came to mean more and more the vast majority of *Jesus-rejecting* Jews, whereas the term "Christians" increasingly came to refer to the great mass of *Jesus-confessing* Gentiles. Strictly speaking, however, this contrast is inaccurate; more concretely, we should never speak of "Jews and Christians." This is because, since the first century of the present era, there have *always* been both Jesus-confessing and Jesus-rejecting Jews, and *always* Jesus-confessing and Jesus-rejecting Gentiles, or, there have *always* been Jewish Christians and Gentile Christians. The categories "Jews" and "Christians" overlap: this overlapping part is roughly formed by two segments:

(a) Traditional Jesus-believing Jews, today sometimes called "Hebrew Christians"; they do not maintain the Mosaic Torah and usually belong to traditional Christian denominations. Throughout church history, there have always been such "Hebrew Christians" in churches, sometimes maintaining at least something of their Jewish origins, but in many cases totally assimilating to "other" Christians.

(b) Those who today are often referred to as "Messianic Jews"; they do maintain the Mosaic Torah (just as orthodox Jews, but often more as liberal Jews) and usually form their own "Messianic" (read, Jesus/Yeshuah-believing) communities.

1.5.2 The Apostolic Council in Jerusalem

The basis for the unintended, but actual separation between non-Jesus-believing Jews and Jesus-believing Gentiles—say, for the sake of convenience, "Jews" and "Christians"—was laid at the Apostolic Council of Acts 15. Before this decisive moment, Gentiles who learned to love and serve the God of Israel, had two options: either they fully joined Judaism ("proselytes";[39] Matt. 23:15; Acts 2:10; 6:5; 13:43), or they assumed a more or less Jewish manner of life without undergoing proselyte baptism, and without the males being circumcised. In Greek, they were called *sebomenoi*, "devout," "worshiping," "God-fearing." A well-known example is the Roman centurion Cornelius (Acts 10:7); Acts 13:50 spoke of the "devout women of high standing" in Pisidian Antioch, and Acts 17:4 he mentioned in one breath the "devout Greeks and not a few of the leading women" (also see v. 17).

The rabbis distinguished between the *gēr tzedeq*, that is, the Gentile who had fully become a Jew, and the *gēr toshav*, the "gate proselyte" or half-proselyte, who served the God of Israel but had not submitted to the entire Mosaic Torah. The latter expression (lit., "resident sojourner") was derived from the expression "the sojourner within your gates" (Exod. 20:10; Deut. 5:14). As the term indicates, the situation presupposed here was that of the Promised Land rather than that of the Diaspora.

The Apostolic Council made the historic decision *not* to place Jesus-believing Gentiles under the Mosaic Torah, which also implied that the males were not obligated to be circumcised. This was a universal decision in the sense that no element or component part of the Sinaitic Torah was exempted from it. Speaking purely formally, not even a small part of the Mosaic Torah, like the Ten Commandments, actually applies to Jesus-believing Gentiles. To be sure, Christians are not allowed to curse, to steal, to murder, to lie, to commit adultery, and so on—*not* because these are prohibited by the Ten Commandments as part of the Mosaic Torah, but rather because such behaviors conflict with the law of Christ (Gal. 6:2) (which in its kernel, is, of course, no other Torah than the eternal Torah to which Moses had already referred[40]).

The decision of the Apostolic Council had far-reaching consequences, but was made explicitly under the guidance of

---

39. The term comes from the Gk. term *prosēlutos*, "newcomer," and hence "convert"; in the Septuagint, it is a word for "stranger" (e.g., Exod. 12:49).
40. See extensively, Ouweneel (2001a; 2020a).

the Holy Spirit (Acts 15:28). The Gentiles who came to believe in Jesus became, so to speak, *gērim toshavim*, which entailed three realities: (1) Jesus-believing Gentiles did not join Judaism, (2) Jesus-believing Gentiles were not viewed as "Jews" in any sense, yet (3) in some sense Jesus-believing Gentiles were united with Jesus-believing Jews. This unity consisted in this: the God of Israel had become *their* God, the Messiah of Israel had become *their* Savior and Lord, and the book of Israel had become *their* book.

Please notice, by the way, that the important decision *not* to require Jesus-believing Gentiles to observe the 613 commandments and prohibitions of the Torah was not primarily an idea of Paul, the "apostle of the nations (or, the Gentiles)."[41] Not he but James, Jesus' half-brother (Gal. 1:19), and Peter, the "minister to the circumcised" (Gal. 2:8), played the decisive role in the deliberations. In the end, everyone did agree that Gentile Jesus-believers es should not be turned into "Jews." *Jesus-believing Gentiles are not "Jews" (in any sense whatsoever); they never were, and never will be.* This is a huge challenge to supersessionism. But perhaps the correlative challenge is far more devasting to supersessionism: *Jesus-believing Jews were "zealous for the Torah," and they remained so* (Acts 21:20). Read this conclusion one more time: Jesus-believing Gentiles never became "Jews," and Jesus-believing Jews never ceased being Jews faithful to the Mosaic Torah (as is still the case among many "Messianic" Jews today).

In the New Testament era, Jesus-believing Jews never formally or emotionally abandoned their religion in order to adopt another religion. On the contrary, they kept living, as faithfully as possible, according to the Sinaitic Torah and the "customs of the fathers" (Acts 28:17). They would have abhorred of the idea of having joined another religion—instead, they believed that Jesus was the *fulfillment* of their Tanakh religion. This was not some kind of weakness on their part, which disappeared with and after the fall of Jerusalem (AD 70), as some have suggested; no, they ceased living as Jews

---

41. Rom. 1:5; 11:13; 15:16, 18; Gal. 1:16; 2:2, 8–9; Eph. 3:1–8; 1 Tim. 2:7; 2 Tim. 1:11; 4:17.

only when the Gentile Church began increasingly to compel them to abandon their Jewish customs, as we shall see.

1.5.3 Jews Do Not Become Gentiles, and Vice Versa

The entire notion of the existence of a "spiritual Israel" is wrongheaded from the very beginning: believing Gentiles never became Jews, and believing Jews never stopped being Jews. They did share in the same salvation in Christ, they belonged to the same body of Christ, and they were living stones in the same spiritual temple of God. Yet, they remained different. To be sure, "in Christ" there is neither Jew nor "Greek" (read: Gentile) but "in Christ" there is no male and female either (Gal. 3:28). Just as the differences between males and females remain very important in practice—why else would Christians marry?—the same is true for Jews and Gentiles. The Jesus-believing Jew is under both the Mosaic Torah and the Torah of Christ (which are one in their essence), whereas the Jesus-believing Gentile is under only the Torah of Christ (Gal. 6:2).

Understanding precisely what occurred in Acts 15 is inexpressibly and essentially important for our grasp of the gospel. If supersessionism were right, Gentile Jesus-believers would simply have become proselytes of Israel, and thus in fact "Jews." Then the males would have been obliged to be circumcised, and all these believers would have had to observe all 613 commandments of the Mosaic Torah. In this respect, supersessionism is very inconsistent. Of course, we know the reply to this problem: it claims that in Christ, the Mosaic Torah has come to an end (despite Matt. 5:17 and against the spirit of Rom. 10:4). But if this claim were true, *why did Jesus-believing Jews continue by faith to observe the Mosaic Torah, intentionally and without any apostolic criticism?* Even the apostle Paul continued by faith to observe the Mosaic Torah throughout all his life, as he said explicitly at the end of Acts to the Jewish leaders in Rome: "I had done nothing against our people or the customs of our fathers."[42] (28:17). Paul had no difficulty circumcising Timothy because the young man

---

42. See Stern (1999, ad loc.) for this and other Bible passages quoted in the text.

had a Jewish mother (Acts 16:3).[43] At a certain moment, he even took the vow of the Nazirite (18:18), entirely according to the Law of Moses.

Paul continued telling people, "I *am* [not, I *was*] a Pharisee" (Acts 23:6). This was not hypocritical because he still had all the characteristics of the primordial Pharisee:

(a) He was an orthodox Jew, faithful to the Mosaic Torah and to all rabbinic interpretations of the Torah insofar as they were in harmony with the Torah.

(b) He accepted the entire Tanakh as inspired by God, and therefore also believed in angels and in the resurrection of the dead (Acts 23:6-9).

In Acts 3:1 we read that the apostles "Peter and John were going up to the temple at the hour of prayer, the ninth hour," apparently to take part in the evening sacrifice and the gathering linked with it. Of the apostle Paul we even read more clearly that he brought sacrifices in the temple. He told Governor Felix about his journey to Jerusalem: "After an absence of several years, I came to Yerushalayim to bring a charitable gift to my nation and to offer sacrifices. It was in connection with the latter that they found me in the Temple. I had been ceremonially purified, . . ." (Acts 24:17-18 CJB). Several translations prefer "offerings" to "sacrifices," or they eliminate from the text altogether the idea of animal sacrifices (ERV). But it is impossible to interpret the Greek term *prosphora* here in any other sense than animal sacrifices; what else would he have been doing in the temple? In other words, he was not *persuaded* to offer sacrifices after he had arrived in Jerusalem; rather, he had intended to do so all along.

After having arrived in the city, the Jesus-believing Jews told Paul:

> "[T]hey have been told about you that you teach all the Jews who are among the Gentiles to forsake Moses, telling them not to circumcise their children or walk according to our customs. What then is to be done? They will certainly hear that you have come. Do therefore what we tell you. We have four men who are under

---

43. Titus was *not* circumcised because he was a full Gentile (Gal. 2:3).

a vow; take these men and purify yourself along with them and pay their expenses, so that they may shave their heads. Thus all will know that there is nothing in what they have been told about you, but that you yourself also live in observance of the law. But as for the Gentiles who have believed, we have sent a letter with our judgment that they should abstain from what has been sacrificed to idols, and from blood, and from what has been strangled, and from sexual immorality." Then Paul took the men, and the next day he purified himself along with them and went into the temple, giving notice when the days of purification would be fulfilled and the offering presented for each one of them (Acts 21:21-26).

Let us carefully consider what is happening here. The Jesus-believing Jewish leaders agreed entirely with Paul about not requiring Jesus-believing Gentiles to observe the Torah of Moses, but requiring them only to abstain from idolatry, from eating blood or strangled animals (which still contained the blood), and from sexual immorality.[44] In other words, they accepted that these believers were not placed under the Mosaic Torah. However, with the Jesus-believing Jews it was a different story. The (false) rumor was circulating that during his journeys, Paul was not only telling believing Gentiles, *but also believing Jews*, that they were no longer obligated to observe the Sinaitic Torah. *This is exactly what supersessionism teaches, too.* But Paul was not. The leaders gave Paul the opportunity to refute this rumor, and Paul did so gladly. In his group were four men who had taken the Nazirite vow (Num. 6), and now had reached the end of their vow's period. Paul was advised to pay for the rituals involved in the vow's conclusion, and even to finance the related sacrifices in the temple. Without any problem, Paul accepted the request, *to prove that Jesus-believing Jews are still under the Mosaic Torah.*[45]

---

44. For the meaning of this, see Ouweneel (2020a, ad loc.).

45. Out of embarrassment, supersessionists have viewed this as weak indulgence; so, e.g., Matthew Henry (http://biblehub.com/acts/21–21.htm). However, Acts 24:17 tells us that one of Paul's explicit goals for going to Jerusalem was to offer sacrifices in the temple.

Just as surely as Gentiles were not placed under the Mosaic Torah, so surely were Jesus-believing Jews not exempted from it. That is, there was no question of Jesus-believing *Jews* having become *gērim toshavim* as well. In the entire book of Acts, Jesus-believing Jews were, and always remained, faithful observers of the Mosaic Torah. It would be a fatal mistake to enforce the entire Mosaic Torah with respect to Jesus-believing Gentiles. But it is an equally fatal mistake to compel Jesus-believing Jews to renounce the Mosaic Torah—something that has occurred frequently throughout church history: among the Eastern Orthodox, among the Roman Catholics, and later among many Protestant churches (and among some Jesus-believing Jewish leaders today).

1.6 Identity and Animosity
1.6.1 Seven Similarities

It is challenging to obtain an accurate picture of those early decades when there were still fewer Jesus-believing, non-Torah-observing Gentiles ("Christians") than non-Jesus-believing, Torah-observing Jews. But this gradually changed. When "Christians" became an increasing majority, especially throughout the Middle East, the situation of two distinct religions emerged, not necessarily theologically, but phenomenologically. Moreover, the animosity of Christians toward Jews increased because Christians saw them as stubbornly refusing to admit the obvious, namely, that Jesus was the Messiah of Israel. It is important, however, to remember the seven essential elements that the two groups shared and continue(d) to share.[46]

(1) Christians and Jews could not deny that they basically served the same God: the God of the patriarchs, the God of Israel, the God of the Bible. Of course, during the coming centuries the nuances in their picture of this God gradually grew: the image of the God who supposedly manifested himself in Jesus Christ and the image of the God who supposedly rejected Jesus Christ became increasingly different.

---

46. Cf. vol. IV/1a, animosity toward the Jews grew §8.2, for a similar enumeration, which is elaborated here more extensively.

THE ETERNAL PEOPLE: GOD IN RELATION TO ISRAEL

(2) Both originate with the patriarchs, Abraham in particular: all Jews are physical descendants of Abraham, all pious Jews are both physical and spiritual descendants of Abraham (Rom. 4:11), and all Jesus-believing Gentiles are spiritual descendants of Abraham (v. 12). It is "in" (through, because of) Abraham, Isaac, and Jacob that all families and nations—Jews and Gentiles—of the world are blessed (Gen. 12:3; 18:18; 22:18; 26:4; 28:14) (on the condition of repentance and faith).

(3) Their love and reverence for, and study of, the Tanakh, including the Mosaic Torah, which forms the foundation for all biblical writings. The Tanakh is the sacred book of both Jews and Christians (see, e.g., Rom. 1:2; 3:2). When Jesus in the Gospels and the apostolic writers in their letters spoke of "the Scripture(s)" (more than fifty times from Matt. 21:42 to 2 Pet. 3:16), they were referring to the Tanakh, the entire Tanakh, and nothing but the Tanakh.

(4) Their faith in divine forgiveness and atonement exclusively on the basis of a vicarious sin offering: "It is the blood that makes atonement for the soul" (Lev. 17:11 NKJV), on the condition of the sinner's repentance and faith. "Without the shedding of blood there is no forgiveness of sins" (Heb. 9:22). During times when no temple was available, Jews believed, and believe, that certain prayers could make up for the lack of bloody sacrifices, but deep in their hearts they must know that this is not biblical.[47]

(5) Their expectation of the coming of Messiah on the clouds of heaven, and the establishment of the Messianic kingdom of peace and justice:

> I saw in the night visions,
> and behold, with the clouds of heaven
> > there came one like a son of man,
> and he came to the Ancient of Days
> > and was presented before him.

---

47. We cannot appeal here to passages in which morality is ranked above sacrifices (e.g., Isa. 1:11; Hos. 6:6; Micah 6:6–8) because the contrast here is not with the (God-given!) the sacrificial ministry as such but with a *sinful* sacrificial ministry (cf. Mal. 1:8, 14).

> And to him was given dominion
>> and glory and a kingdom,
> that all peoples, nations, and languages
>> should serve him;
> his dominion is an everlasting dominion,
>> which shall not pass away,
> and his kingdom one
>> that shall not be destroyed (Dan. 7:13-14; cf. Matt. 24:30).

(6) Both (orthodox) Jews and Christians believe that the only life that pleases God is a life lived according to his Torah, which in the broadest sense is the entire Word of God as we have it in the Holy Scriptures: "How can a young man keep his way pure? / By guarding it according to your word" (Ps. 119:9). Jewish Zechariah and Elizabeth were the great example of this: "[T]hey were both righteous before God, walking blamelessly in all the commandments and statutes of the Lord" (Luke 1:6).

(7) In addition to the central notion of obedience is the central notion of confidence (faith, trust) in God; obedience without faith *and* faith without obedience do not make someone a *tzaddiq* (a "righteous" person): "[T]he righteous shall live by his faith [i.e., confidence in God]."[48] In the New Testament, this means *in concreto* faith in God's Son and Sent One, Jesus Christ, and following in his footsteps. But this does not alter the fundamental similarity between believing Jews and Christians: confidence in God, for the present and for the future (trusting his promises).

1.6.2 Animosity

The seven shared features just mentioned closely connect (genuine) Judaism and (genuine) Christianity, and they are standing together against *all* other religions.[49] Recall the

---

48. Hab. 2:4; cf. Gen. 15:6; Rom. 1:17; Gal. 3:11; Heb. 10:38.
49. At best, Islam can claim, rightly or wrongly, to tie in with point (1), and it also has a certain respect for the Tanakh (point 2), called by them the *Tawrat* or *Taurat*, derived from Torah; see Surah 5:44; 7:157; 48:29; in the hadith: Abu Dawood nr. 4431.

shared bridge between the two groups: the "Messianic" (Jesus-believing) Jews. But apart from this relatively small group, there is a deep divide between the *physical* (almost entirely non-Jesus-believing) progeny of Abraham (which also includes the Arab desert tribes; see Gen. 25) and the *spiritual* progeny of Abraham, those who do not necessarily descend from him physically but who do walk in the same footsteps of faith as he did.[50] This faith is, above all, the confidence that God will fulfill his unbreakable promises in none other than the Son of Promise (cf. Gen. 15:4-6; 2 Cor. 1:19-20).

Unfortunately, it was inevitable, human speaking, that animosity would grow between these two groups. We read in the book of Acts that especially the non-Jesus-believing Jews persecuted Jesus-believers (frequently out of jealousy; see 5:17; 13:45; 17:5-8). But since especially the fourth century, Jesus-believing Gentiles ("Christians") have persecuted non-Jesus-believing Jews. Jews have blamed Christians in particular for three things:

(1) The Christians declared the Mosaic Torah to have been annulled and to have become obsolete (whereas Jesus himself had said that he had not come to "abolish" the Law and the Prophets; Matt. 5:17).

(2) The Christians called a certain person "Messiah" despite the fact that, as the prophets had foretold of the true Messiah (see, e.g., Isa. 9:6-7), this person had not brought universal peace and justice to the world (notice that Jesus himself had said, "Do you think that I have come to give peace on earth? No, I tell you, but rather division," Luke 12:51).

(3) The Christians paid homage appropriate to God alone to a person who may have been special, but in the end was nothing but an ordinary human being.

Christians in turn blamed Jews for three things in particular:

(1) Although Jesus of Nazareth had given a multitude of proofs that he was the Messiah, especially by fulfilling a mul-

---

50. Rom. 4:9–12; Gal. 3:7–9, 27–29; cf. Matt. 3:9; John 8:33, 37, 39–41, 56.

titude of prophecies, the great majority of Jews refused to accept him as such.

(2) Moreover, the Jews in Jerusalem had delivered Jesus into the hands of the Roman authorities in order that he be executed, so they bore full responsibility for his death.[51]

(3) In the Roman Empire, the Jews sided several times with the authorities *against the Christians.*

Jesus' tone regarding Jerusalem was sad (Luke 13:34): "O Jerusalem, Jerusalem, the city that kills the prophets and stones those who are sent to it! How often would I have gathered your children together as a hen gathers her brood under her wings, and you were not willing!" Later he said (Luke 19:42), "Would that you, even you, had known on this day the things that make for peace! But now they are hidden from your eyes." The apostle Paul's tone was sharp (1 Thess. 2:14–16): ". . . the Jews, who killed both the Lord Jesus and the prophets, and drove us out, and displease God and oppose all mankind by hindering us from speaking to the Gentiles that they might be saved [cf. Acts 13:45; 14:2; 17:5]—so as always to fill up the measure of their sins. But wrath has come upon them at last!"[52]

Please notice that, as the context makes clear, Paul was speaking about the Jews in Judea, *not* about all the Jews of his time, nor about all Jews of all times—an absurd claim made later by millions of Christians. This same limitation applies to Matthew 27:25 ("His blood be on us and on our children!"), which is not a self-cursing involving all Jews of all times and all places. Paul accused the Jews in *Jerusalem, not* the Jews in the entire land of Israel, for the death of Jesus; read Acts 13:27–29, where he explicitly made this distinction in a sermon in Pisidian Antioch. Only those Jews were co-responsible for the death of Jesus who had delivered him on false

---

51. Acts 2:23; 3:14–15; 4:11; 5:30; 7:51–52; 10:39; 13:28; cf. Matt. 17:20; 20:18–19.
52. It goes far too far when Jansen (1981, 27, 30–31, 64, 145) speaks here of anti-Semitism within the New Testament, because Paul was not speaking of "the" Jews' generally, but only of the guilty ones, especially the leaders (see ESV note). Regarding anti-Semitism in church history, see Jansen (1999).

charges to the Roman authorities and had demanded that he be executed.[53]

Despite these reproaches against Israel, we must keep in mind that both Jesus and Paul foretold the *restoration* of Israel (the *tiqqun*, as the rabbis called it). Jesus told the Jewish leaders (not in a threatening, but in a predictive manner: "See, your house [i.e., the temple] is left to you desolate. For I tell you, you will not see me again, until you say, 'Blessed is he who comes in the name of the Lord' [Ps. 118:26]" (Matt. 23:38-39). This will occur only at the re-appearance of the Messiah; only then will the destruction and desolation of the temple come to an end though its reconstruction. The apostle Paul wrote:

> Now if their trespass means riches for the world, and if their failure means riches for the Gentiles, how much more will *their full inclusion* mean! ... For if their rejection means the reconciliation of the world, *what will their acceptance mean but life from the dead?* ... I do not want you to be unaware of this mystery, brothers: a partial hardening has come upon Israel [so that they do not recognize their Messiah], until the fullness of the Gentiles has come in. *And in this way all Israel will be saved* (Rom. 11:12, 15, 25-26).

For in those days, they finally *will* recognize their Messiah.

1.7 Torah or No Torah?
1.7.1 Three Viewpoints

The Apostolic Council mentioned in Acts 15 had many theological and practical consequences, including many misunderstandings. Nowadays, we can encounter at least three very different views concerning this Council.

---

53. Matt. 27:22-26; John 19:6-16; cf. the sharp language of Acts 2:23; 3:15; 5:30; 7:52.

(1) Philosemitic[54] Christians claim that the Apostolic Council has been misunderstood. They refer to James' remark (v. 21), "For from ancient generations Moses has had in every city those who proclaim him, for he is read every Sabbath in the synagogues." They believe that Jesus-believing Gentiles must definitely be circumcised, must attend synagogue services in order to become familiar with the Mosaic Torah, and, as far as possible, must observe the 613 commandments of the Mosaic Torah.[55] At various places one can find congregations and communities where Jesus-believing Gentile men are, kindly or severely, pressured toward circumcision, despite these Pauline warnings: "Was anyone at the time of his call uncircumcised? Let him not seek circumcision. For neither circumcision counts for anything nor uncircumcision, but keeping the commandments of God" (1 Cor. 7:18b–19). "I, Paul, tell you that if you let yourselves be circumcised, Christ will be of no value to you at all" (Gal. 5:2 NKJV).

Of course, philosemites are very facile at arguing away such warnings. As I heard one Messianic rabbi argue: We must observe the commandments of Yeshuah—his commandments cannot be different from those of Moses—one of the Mosaic commandments requires circumcision—so Gentile Yeshuah-believers must be circumcised. Period.

(2) By way of contrast, many Christians cannot understand that, after the Day of Pentecost or after the Apostolic Council (Acts 15), Jesus-believing Jews simply continued observing the Mosaic Torah because, in their view, the Mosaic Torah was abolished and was made obsolete through the cross.

Indeed, today thousands of Messianic (Jesus-believing) Jews do the same: they have their little boys circumcised (they do not believe that circumcision has been replaced by infant baptism), and have their children baptized when

---

54. The term "philosemitism" means (an exaggerated) love for Jews; its opposite is "anti-Semitism": an aversion toward Jews. Aalders (1985, 15) used the term "judaeofilie" (judeophilia).

55. See, e.g., http://www.unlearnthelies.com/understanding-acts-15.html.

these have come to personal faith. They maintain the Sabbath and the biblical festivals (Lev. 23; Deut. 16), as well as the food laws (Lev. 11; Deut. 14), to mention some important matters. Some opponents of modern Messianic Jews argue that the Bible's Jesus-believing Jews continued to observe the Torah only for a short time. With the fall of the temple and the sacrificial ministry, this phenomenon ceased, *precisely as God intended*. Thus, modern Messianic Jews who continue to observe the Mosaic Torah are mistaken.[56] I view this as a clear circular argument: because these opponents believe that the Messianic Judaism was a temporary matter, they "conclude" that Messianic Judaism was a temporary matter.

This claim that the Mosaic Torah became obsolete with Jesus Christ appeals to Ephesians 2:14–15, which many translations render in a way that is thoroughly misleading and therefore regrettable. According to the ESV, Paul wrote that Christ "has broken down in his flesh the dividing wall of hostility by abolishing the law of commandments expressed in ordinances [Gk. *to mesotoichon tou phragmou lysas, tēn echthran en tē sarki autou, ton nomon tōn entolōn en dogmasin katargēsas*], ..." I strongly prefer the CJB: Christ "has broken down the *m'chitzah* which divided us by destroying in his own body the enmity occasioned by the *Torah*, with its commands set forth in the form of ordinances." *What Jesus abolished was not the Torah but the enmity between Jews and Gentiles* that had been occasioned by the Torah.

(3) The viewpoint that I defend is squarely opposed to the two previous ones: after the Apostolic Council, Jesus-believing Jews remain Torah-observers, whereas Jesus-believing Gentiles are not required to become Torah-observers. *And this disparity remains the same today*, despite the fact that the two groups are fundamentally one in Christ. It is a grievous error to *require* Jesus-believing Gentiles to be circumcised

---

56. One argument is that they are clinging to the "shadows" (Col. 2:17) instead of clinging to Christ alone. But in that text, Paul's point was: Do not make the shadows more important than the substance (Christ); his point was *not*: the "shadows" have become obsolete; on the contrary, *he himself still observed the "shadows."*

and to observe the Mosaic Torah. Conversely, it is also a grievous error to *require* Jesus-believing Jews to cease observing (insofar as this is possible) all the 613 commandments of the Mosaic Torah. The latter Torah remains in force for Israel as long as this earth exists (see, e.g., Lev. 16:34; 1 Chron. 16:17), just as the Sinaitic Covenant was and is everlasting; it is not replaced by the New Covenant, but the latter is a renewal and extension of the Old Covenant. In the Messianic kingdom, the Jews—who will all believe in Jesus by then—will still celebrate the Sabbath and the Jewish festivals (Isa. 56:2–6; Ezek. 45–46; Zech. 14:16–19), uncircumcised Jewish males will have no place among them (Isa. 52:1; Ezek. 44:7, 9), and eating pork will still be condemned (Isa. 65:4; 66:3, 17). There is an uninterrupted continuity between Tanakh orthodox Jews, Yeshuah-believing Jews, and Jews during the Messianic kingdom.

1.7.2 Under the Torah of Christ

In their essence, the ways of life of Jewish Jesus-believers and of Gentile Jesus-believers are not all that far apart. On the one hand, there was Rabbi Simlai (third century) who, as far as we know, was the first to state that the Mosaic Torah contains exactly 613 commandments;[57] these have been enumerated and explained by the great Jewish scholar Maimonides (Moses ben Maimon, d. 1204). By contrast, it may appear that Christians possess only one commandment; as Jesus said, "A new commandment I give to you, that you love one another: just as I have loved you, you also are to love one another" (John 13:34; cf. 1 John 3:23; 4:21). The new element in this commandment is that Jesus did not make *self-love* the model for brotherly love, unlike the Mosaic Torah ("you shall love your neighbor *as you love yourself*," Lev. 19:18 GW), but Jesus made *his own love* to be the model for brotherly love: love one another "just as *I* have loved you." At the same time, this commandment was an old commandment (cf. 1 John 2:7–8), for it was Jesus himself who was summarizing the Mosaic Torah as follows:

---

57. Talmud: Makkot 23b.

THE ETERNAL PEOPLE: GOD IN RELATION TO ISRAEL

> [O]ne of them, a lawyer, asked him a question to test him. "Teacher, which is the great commandment in the Law?" And he said to him, "'You shall love the Lord your God with all your heart and with all your soul and with all your mind" [Deut. 6:5; 10:12; 30:6]. This is the great and first commandment. And a second is like it: "You shall love your neighbor as yourself" [Lev. 19:18]. On these two commandments depend all the Law and the Prophets" (Matt. 22:35-40).

That is, these two commandments constitute the core, the essence, of the entire Tanakh (i.e., the Torah, the Prophets, and the Writings; cf. Luke 24:44). Jesus quoted both core commandments directly from the Torah. According to Jesus, the double commandment of love is the heart of the Torah, even of the entire Tanakh, and many Jews would agree with Jesus on this point. Take, for instance, the concise way Hillel the Elder summarized the Torah,[58] which amounts to the same thing: "What is hateful to you, do not do to your fellow: this is the whole Torah; the rest is the explanation; go and learn."[59]

The Apostle Paul gave us the same basic rule:

> Owe no one anything, except to love each other, for the one who loves another has fulfilled the law. For the commandments, "You shall not commit adultery, You shall not murder, You shall not steal, You shall not covet [Exod. 20:13-17], and any other commandment, are summed up in this word: "You shall love your neighbor as yourself" [Lev. 19:18]. Love does no wrong to a neighbor; therefore love is the fulfilling of the law (Rom. 13:8-10).

Notice that Paul was referring here to no other law than the Torah of Moses. The eternal Torah, no matter what external form it may have throughout history, always has this core rule: "We love (or, Let us love)" (1 John 4:19); in Greek this is

---

58. Talmud: Shabbat 31a.
59. Jesus gave the same rule, but stated positively: "So whatever you wish that others would do to you, do also to them, for this is the Law and the Prophets" (Matt. 7:12).

just one word: *agapōmen*. If I were to summarize the Law of Christ in one word it would be this *agapōmen*: "Love [God and each other]!" Indeed, the Love Commandment is one (double) commandment—but functions as the focal point of an entire array of commandments. The New Testament speaks of Jesus' "commandments" in the plural,[60] and in his Great Commission he said, "Go . . . and make disciples of all nations, baptizing them in the name of the Father and of the Son and of the Holy Spirit, teaching them to observe *all that I have commanded*[61] *you*. And behold, I am with you always, to the end of the age" (Matt. 28:19-20).

The New Testament also spoke about the "Law of Christ" (Gk. *nomos tou Christou*, cf. *ennomos Christou*, "under the law of Christ," 1 Cor. 9:21), and about the "law of the Spirit of life in Christ Jesus" (Rom. 8:2),[62] but we have already seen that in its essence this law does not differ from the law of Moses. The difference is only this: the New Testament "law" in its moral *essence* is the law of Moses *plus* two necessary *keys* to this law (cf. Luke 11:52, "the key of knowledge"): first, Christ, and second, the Holy Spirit (the "Spirit of life"). Why is this? Because first, Christ is the One *imposing* this Law on his followers; second, Christ is the *norm* (measure, criterium) of this Law; and third, Christ is the *example* to follow in observing his commandments. And the Holy Spirit is the *power* believers need for observing of the Law of Christ.[63]

1.8 Legalism

1.8.1 What Is It?

Living according to a law is not legalism—legalism is living according to a law in a wrong way. It is a fundamental error

---

60. John 14:15, 21; 15:10; 1John 2:3–4; 3:22, 24; 4:2; 5:3; 2 John 1:6; Matt. 5:19; 1 Cor. 7:19; Rev. 12:17; 14:12); but cf. also "the commandment [sing.] of the Lord and Savior" (2 Pet. 3:2).
61. The Gk. noun for "commandment" is *entolē*, and the related Gk. verb for "to command," is *entellomai*.
62. Assuming that the Gk. *nomos* here means "Torah," and not "principle"; cf. what immediately precedes these words: Rom. 7:21–25, where *nomos* in some cases has this meaning.
63. See extensively, Ouweneel (2001a, 2020a).

to assert that Jews are legalistic simply because good Jews try to observe the Torah. If this were so, Christians are legalistic, too, because they are bound to the Law of Christ (Gal. 6:2), the commandments of Jesus. In this respect, there is no difference between Jews and Christians at all. No person serving God is without God's commandments, because such serving is defined by, and bound to, God's commandments. Even in the eternal state, God's "slaves" (Gk. *douloi*) will "serve" him (verb *latreuō*, Rev. 22:3 DLNT, HCSB, JUB, LEB), that is, in the quality of "slaves," as people forever submitted to God, to his orders and ordinances.

In genuine legalism and among real legalists, at least seven aspects are present.

(1) Legalists observe the law with the expectation of being able to please God—or to inherit the Messianic kingdom—*in one's own power*, that is, apart from God's grace and from the guidance of his Holy Spirit.

Comment. As a matter of principle, the true *chassid* ("godly" person, whether Jew or Christian) lives by the mercy of God. Under the Old Covenant, the sacrificial ministry formed the counterpart of the Torah: on the one hand, there was the commandment, on the other hand, there was the atoning sacrifice in case someone had unintentionally[64] transgressed the commandment and was truly humbled about this (cf., e.g., Prov. 28:13). The Ten Commandments were not given to a nation that had to enter fellowship with God through keeping his commandments, but rather they were given to people whom he had redeemed: "I am the LORD your God, who brought you out of the land of Egypt, out of the house of slavery" (Exod. 20:2; Deut. 5:6).[65] First came the grace of redemption, then came the Torah as the gracious rule of life for the already redeemed people, and then the grace of forgiveness if and when the Torah was broken. This sequence characterized the Old Covenant, and in principle it characterizes the

---

64. Cf. Lev. 4:2, 13, 22, 27; 5:15; Num. 15:28; Ezek. 45:20; see also "ignorant/-ce" in Acts 3:17; 1 Tim. 1:13.

65. In the Jewish enumeration, this is the first of the *Ashēret haDibrot* ("Ten Words"; Exod. 34:28; Deut. 4:13; 10:4).

New Covenant as well. Both Judaism and Christianity share a divine order in which law and grace are harmoniously interwoven (which interwovenness must be correctly understood).

(2) Legalism is focused on the *form* of the law, not its *content*—on the outward, not the inner, aspect of the law. This is what Jesus meant when he spoke about legalistic people who in a scrupulous manner keep the smallest details of the law but lose sight of its core intention. In Jesus' words, some people "tithe mint and dill and cumin, and have neglected the weightier matters of the law: justice and mercy and faithfulness" (Matt. 23:23; see the entire passage: vv. 23–28). These are the people "straining out a gnat [a small unclean animal] and swallowing a camel [a big unclean animal]," focusing upon details, overlooking the things that really matter.[66]

Comment. The true *tzaddiq*, faithful to God's commandments, is not a nitpicker, but is always focused on the actual core of the Torah; in Jesus' words, "justice and mercy and faithfulness," and, "justice and the love of God" (Luke 11:42). What matters is the "spirit" of the Torah (of Moses, or of Christ), not the details isolated from that spirit. "[W]hat does the LORD require of you / but to do justice, and to love kindness, / and to walk humbly with your God?" (Micah 6:8).

(3) Legalists look down on the ignorant: ". . . this crowd that does not know the law is accursed" (John 7:49), that is, those who do not (sufficiently) know the law, or who do know it, but (according to the nitpickers) inadequately put it into practice. These are the people who are described in the Talmud as the *'am ha'aretz* (lit., "people of the land"[67]), the uneducated Jews, who because of their ignorance are sloppy in observing the Torah, or have hardly studied it.[68]

---

66. Jewish psychiatrist Immanuel Velikovsky tells the story of the biologist who was on his honeymoon in the Amazon, and was told by a terrified servant that a crocodile had eaten his bride. The nitpicker replied: "That's not possible, for there are no crocodiles here; it must have been a caiman." The essence of the message escaped him.
67. Cf. the meaning in, e.g., Lev. 4:27; 20:4; 2 Kings 15:5; 16:15.
68. E.g., Pesachim 49a,b.

Comment. The true *tzaddiq*, faithful to God's law, realizing his/her own shortcomings, will not despise the ignorant, but rather wishes to be "an instructor of the ignorant, a teacher of the immature" (Rom. 2:20 HCSB). They also realize that their own responsibility—as one who knows the commandment—is all the greater: it is better to know no law (but to keep it unconsciously) than to know it without doing it (vv. 12-16). "[H]e who increases knowledge increases sorrow" (Eccl. 1:18). Or as Paul wrote, "Now concerning food offered to idols: we know that 'all of us possess knowledge.' This 'knowledge' puffs up, but love builds up. If anyone imagines that he knows something, he does not yet know as he ought to know. But if anyone loves God, he is known by God" (1 Cor. 8:1-3).

Paul was a learned man (Acts 22:3; Gal. 1:14; Phil. 3:5-6). But amazingly, the first followers whom Jesus chose were "uneducated, common men" (Acts 4:13), such as fishermen. They could read and write, but possessed no rabbinic training. People asked about Jesus himself, "How is it that this man has learning, when he has never studied?" (John 7:15).

1.8.2 Four More Aspects

(4) Legalists observe the Torah, at least outwardly, in order to gain the esteem of others; as Jesus said, "Beware of practicing your righteousness before other people in order to be seen by them, for then you will have no reward from your Father who is in heaven" (Matt. 6:1; read vv. 1-8; cf. also 23:5).

Comment. The person who properly observes the law (whether Jew or Christian) acts exclusively out of love for God and love for their neighbors, and guards against seeking honor from others (cf. John 12:43)—although we must admit that even the greatest *tzaddiq*, apart from Jesus, still works from the flesh. We are reminded of what the Roman poet Terence said: "Nothing human is alien to me" (Lat. *nihil humanum a me alienum puto*).

(5) The legalist tries to acquire a higher degree of piety than others, *or* a higher degree of power over others, by supplementing the law of God with many human-made com-

mandments and prohibitions; as Jesus said of the Jewish spiritual leaders, "They tie up heavy burdens, hard to bear, and lay them on people's shoulders, but they themselves are not willing to move them with their finger" (Matt. 23:4).

Comment. The person who properly observes the law is the very opposite: strict toward oneself, mild toward others. A person who is strict toward oneself must never be called a legalist. Real legalists love to be strict toward others; they are arrogant and judgmental. This is one of the most powerful tools in the hands of cult leaders: imposing heavy rules upon their followers.

(6) Legalists allow themselves great liberty with regard to things *not* mentioned in the law. Thus, a person can be a "pious" Jew or Christian—and even be recognized as such—and at the same time be a chain smoker, an excessive drinker, or addicted to gambling, since the law does not explicitly refer to these and many other bad things. Additionally, in strict legalistic Christian circles people forbid ladies wearing trousers or television sets (all with an appeal to "appropriate" Bible verses), but permit expensive cigars and big fancy cars (because no Bible verses forbid these).

Comment. The person who properly observes the law observant acts not only according to the letter ("if it is not forbidden in the Torah, it is allowed") but also according to the spirit of the law.[69] When we discern the Torah's profoundest intentions, we know what God expects of us, also in areas of life that are not explicitly mentioned in the law. The true sons of God are those who are being led by the Spirit of God (Rom. 8:14).

(7) Legalists try to do their best in the eyes of others, while simultaneously trying to escape the reach of the law by softening certain commandments, or by declaring them to be inapplicable to them. As Jesus said, "For God commanded, 'Honor your father and your mother,' and, 'Whoever reviles father or mother must surely die.' But you say, 'If anyone tells his father or his mother, "What you would have gained from me is given to God," he need not honor his father.' Thus you

---

69. Cf. Rom. 2:29; 7:6; 2 Cor. 3:6 ("the letter kills, but the Spirit gives life").

have made the commandment of God of no effect by your tradition" (Matt. 15:4-6).

Comment. For one who properly observes the law, the law is a love letter from God; their attitude is this: "Your wish is my command." True love never tries to escape the law, but rather proclaims, "Oh, how I love your law" (Ps. 119:97), which necessarily includes the exclamation, "Oh, how I love *doing* your law," and I love doing it because I love the One who gave the law, knowing that he gave a law that demonstrates his own love for *me*.

1.9 The Non-Legalistic Life under the Law
1.9.1 The Telos of the Law

The true *tzaddiqim* in Israel have *never* been legalists; therefore, it is pure nonsense to say that Judaism is by nature a legalistic religion.[70] Those who can truly say, "I find my delight in your commandments, which I love" (Ps. 119:47; cf. vv. 48, 97, 113, 127, 159, 163, 165) cannot possibly be legalistic. Those who can genuinely say, "The law of the LORD is perfect, / reviving the soul; ... / the precepts of the LORD are right, / rejoicing the heart" (Ps. 19:7-8) cannot be legalistic. Regarding two godly Jews, Zechariah and Elizabeth, we are told: "They were both righteous before God, walking blamelessly in all the commandments and statutes of the Lord" (Luke 1:6). Not only is there not a grain of legalism here, but this description ought to be equally true of Christians: the true, godly Christian is "righteous before God, walking blamelessly in all the commandments and statutes of Christ."

Therefore, I cannot repeat enough that *neither* Jesus *nor* his apostles "abolished" the Torah of Moses, certainly not in terms of its (eternal) core and intention.[71] On the contrary,

---

70. In his writings, rabbi and New Testament scholar Pinchas Lapide has often argued that Judaism is a religion of pure grace; see, e.g., Lapide (2004; 2011). Wilson (1989, 21) quoted Lapide saying that the rabbis never viewed the Torah as the path of redemption to God, that Jews consider salvation to be God's exclusive prerogative, and that therefore they advocated pure grace. All masters of the Talmud taught that salvation can be attained "only through God's gracious love."
71. Regarding this matter see extensively, Ouweneel (2001a, 2020a).

Jesus did not "abolish" the "Law and the Prophets" but "fulfilled" them (Matt. 5:17). This seems to imply at least three things.

(1) In Jesus, the prophetic predictions have been fulfilled in principle; compare the next verse: ". . . until heaven and earth pass away, not an iota, not a dot, will pass from the Law until all is accomplished."

(2) In Jesus, the Torah has been brought to its perfection; compare Matthew 5:48: the true keeper of the Torah will be perfect as his heavenly Father is perfect.

(3) Jesus is the *telos* of the Torah, as Paul said in Romans 10:4, "Christ is the *telos* of the law for righteousness to everyone who believes." The Greek word *telos* does not mean that in Christ the law has come to an "end," but rather that he is the "aim, goal, sense, meaning, deepest content" of the Torah. If Christ is the "end," he is not the end of the Torah as such—how else could Paul speak of the Torah of Christ (1 Cor. 9:21; Gal. 6:2)?—but the end of a human-made order of things in which people think they can acquire righteousness by their personal faithfulness to the Torah (accomplished in their own strength). Time and again, such a view has turned out to be a failure. People will "fulfill" the Torah only if they begin entrusting themselves to Christ. Jesus Christ is the goal for everyone who believes in him.

This is the only way we also understand that other statement by Paul: "[Y]ou are not under law but under grace" (Rom. 6:14). Romans 8:4 and 13:8-10 make clear that this does *not* mean that believers have nothing to do with any form of "law" anymore. Rather, it means that believers are not under an order of things in which salvation depends on their own works of law, but under one in which the grace of God triumphs over all their sins and shortcomings with respect to God's law. Of course, this does not acquit them from the duty of trying in every situation to "discern what is the good and acceptable and perfect will of God,"[72] if only they realize that this can be accomplished in the power of the Holy Spirit alone.

---

72. Rom. 12:2; cf. Heb. 13:20, 21; 1 Pet. 2:15; 1 John 2:17.

1.9.2 God-Given Religion

The apostle Paul never opposed Judaism as such, for the Jewish religion is an order of things that has been given at Mount Sinai to Israel by God himself, *and given forever*. Therefore, the apostle said, "[T]he law [of Moses] is holy, and [each] commandment [of it] is holy and righteous and good" (Rom. 7:12). It is inconceivable that God would have given his people a legalistic system, or a system that could have been called inferior in any other respect. Legalism never comes from God, but is always a work of sinful human flesh, whether we encounter it with Jews or Christians, or any other religion. Both Judaism and Christianity are rooted in the grace of God (Exod. 34:6-7):

> The LORD, the LORD, a God merciful and gracious, slow to anger, and abounding in steadfast love and faithfulness, keeping steadfast love for thousands [or, to the thousandth generation], forgiving iniquity and transgression and sin, but who will by no means clear the guilty, visiting the iniquity of the fathers on the children and the children's children, to the third and the fourth generation [i.e., of those who hate me; Exod. 20:5; Deut. 5:7[73]].

If things go well, people move from legalism to grace; and people always move from grace to the law, not vice versa. Those who have learned to live by the mercy of God learn also to love God's law, or the law of Christ. Gentiles undergoing the *mikveh* in the sense of proselyte baptism (plus circumcision), thus joining Judaism, begin to learn all the riches of the Torah of Moses. Jews or Gentiles undergoing the *mikveh* in the sense of Christian baptism, thus joining Christianity, begin to learn all the riches of the Torah of Christ (cf. Matt. 28:19, which basically says, "Baptize them, then teach them my commandments"). First conversion, then baptism, then Torah teaching, according to the sequence Israel experienced: first the deliverance from Egypt, then "baptism" in the Red

---

73. This essential addition, which in some passages is present only implicitly, is highly important for avoiding any thought that innocent children are punished for their ancestors' sins (cf. Ezek. 18:14–20).

Sea (cf. 1 Cor. 10:1–2), then the Torah-giving on Mount Sinai. In both cases, the *tzaddiq* arrives at the Messianic kingdom of peace and justice. The parallelism is valid even in its details.

Notice the verb "to teach" (Gk. *didaskō)* in Matthew 28:20. The word *torah* comes from the Hebrew root *y-r-h*, which has the same meaning: "to teach." In Isaiah 2:3 and Micah 4:2 we find this root as well:

> "Come, let us go up to the mountain of the LORD,
> to the house [i.e., temple] of the God of Jacob,
> that he may teach [*y-r-h*] us his ways
> and that we may walk in his paths."
>
> For out of Zion shall go forth the law [or, teaching, *torah*] and the word of the LORD from Jerusalem.

A related key word in Matthew 28:19 is "to make disciples" (Gk. *mathēteuō*), in which we find the Greek noun *mathētēs*, "disciple." The Hebrew equivalent is *talmid* (1 Chron. 25:8), from the root *l-m-d*, "to teach" (from which also the word *Talmud* was derived). We find this verb many times in Psalm 119: "Teach me your statutes" (vv. 12, 26, 64, 68, 124, 135; cf. 33, 171). The disciple is the pupil learning from their m/Master the commandments of God. This is not harsh, severe teaching, but always sweet, just as a father or mother teaches his/her child; compare Proverbs 1:8; 3:1; 4:2; 6:20; 7:2, which speak of the *torah* ("law," but here better: "teaching, instruction") by a father or a mother for his or her children.

1.9.3 Similarities and Differences

We find at least seven *similarities* between the Mosaic order of law and the New Testament order of law.

(1) Both *begin* with the redeeming God who redeems, who *then* gives his people the rules for the fellowship with him, rules encompassing all of life, individually and collectively.

(2) In both cases, the Torah, according to its profoundest essence, is more far-reaching than, at first sight, the Ten Commandments might lead us to think. On the one hand the rabbis, and on the other hand Jesus and the apostles, have

uncovered much of these riches.

(3) In both cases, there is a remedy for transgressing God's commandments, namely, through the atoning sacrifice, provided by God himself, and necessary for blotting out the sin committed.

(4) Both orders begin with an excellent teacher: Moses and Jesus, respectively.

(5) Both orders contain a law: the Mosaic Torah and the Messianic Torah, respectively, but in their eternal essence this is the same law: the eternal Torah.

(6) Both orders are, according to their actual nature, primarily an order of divine love and mercy, as a counterpart of the law.

(7) Both orders fundamentally condemn legalism, and presuppose love in the hearts of those who endeavor to observe God's law; that is, the law is not a yoke weighing down on the shoulders (cf. Acts 15:10) but a law written in the hearts of the *tzaddiqim*.[74]

The three main *differences* between the Mosaic order of law and the New Testament order of law are equally important.

(1) The former stipulates animal sacrifices (which by themselves can never bring about true atonement [Heb. 10:4], and since the destruction of the temple, are no longer possible). The latter stipulates the sacrifice of Christ, which is sufficient once and for all (see especially Heb. 9–10).

(2) Moses was a sinful servant of God, Jesus was the sinless Servant as well as Son of God (cf. Heb. 3:1–6). As a consequence, Moses was not a perfect example for keeping the law that he preached—which is why he was not allowed to enter the Promised Land—but Jesus was; as he said for instance: "[L]earn from me, for I am gentle and lowly in heart, and you will find rest for your souls" (Matt. 11:29).

(3) Moses could present the law to Israel, but he was unable to provide the strength to effectively observe that law.

---

74. Deut. 6:6; Jer. 31:33; cf. Ps. 40:8; 119:11, 34, 36, 69, 80, 111–112, 161; 2 Cor. 3:3.

Jesus *is* able: he granted his people the Holy Spirit, by which God's love has been poured out into the hearts of believers (Rom. 5:5). As a consequence, believers *are* able to love by the strength of that Spirit, and thus are able to fulfill all other commandments as well. (The fact that, in practice, they do not always do so, is because they still have the sinful nature[75] within them.)

If genuine Christians serve God by the Spirit of God (Phil. 3:3), this does not mean that genuine Israelites, who endeavor to observe God's law out of the inner love toward God, would *not* do so by the Holy Spirit. Long before the coming of Jesus, Zechariah and Elizabeth were godly Jews who fulfilled the law and knew the power of the Holy Spirit in their lives, even though they might not have been able to identify it (Luke 1:6, 41, 67).

---

75. In Jewish parlance: *yetzer hara* ("evil inclination"), standing over against the *yetzer hatov* ("good inclination"); cf. Mishnah: Aboth III.18.

Chapter 2
Bible and Tradition

"Is not my word like fire," declares the LORD, *"and like a hammer that breaks the rock in pieces?"*
                                    Jeremiah 23:29

In R[abbi] Ishmael's School it was taught: **And like a hammer that breaks the rock in pieces:** *i.e., just as [the rock] is split into many splinters, so also may one Biblical verse many [elsewhere: seventy] teachings.*
    Talmud: Sanhedrin 34a (emphasis added)

2.1 Sabbath versus Sunday
2.1.1 Four Views

THE ISSUE OF THE SABBATH (Heb. *shabbat*) is a beautiful example of (a) the power of tradition, (b) the similarities and differences between Judaism and Christianity, and (c) certain errors of supersessionism.[1] It is valuable to review various views that theologians have chosen regarding Sunday.[2]

---

1. These same features characterize the issue circumcision versus infant baptism; regarding this, see Ouweneel (2011, §6.2).
2. See extensively, Ouweneel (2001a, Appendix III).

(a) The first view is represented by Seventh Day Adventist, Messianic Jewish, and other theologians who wish to *retain Saturday* as the day of rest for God's people in the present Christian era. This view entails the claim that the New Testament Ecclesia remains formally obligated by the Mosaic Torah, or at least the Ten Commandments, and therefore also by the Fourth Commandment: "Remember/Observe the Sabbath day, to keep it holy" (Exod. 20:8; Deut. 5:12). This view interprets the commandment literally; therefore, Saturday is the sacred day of the week, both for Jews and for Jesus-believing Gentiles.

(b) Second, many Roman Catholics and many Reformational Christians (Lutheran, Calvinist, Anglican) wish to *observe Sunday* as the sacred day of the week, the obligatory day of rest of the new era. This view also entails the claim that the New Testament Ecclesia remains formally obligated by the Fourth Commandment. However, these Christians believe that in the present Christian era, God has replaced the seventh day with the first day of the week. Therefore, according to this view, Sunday (often called Lord's Day) is now the God-given "Sabbath," both for Jews and for Jesus-believing Gentiles. Jews who observe Saturday are considered to be mistaken: they should come to faith in Jesus the Messiah, and begin celebrating the first day as the sacred day of the week. This is the most widespread view among established churches.

(c) Some "free church" Evangelical believers wish to *observe Sunday* as a sacred day. But these Christians believe that the New Testament Ecclesia is no longer obligated by the Mosaic Torah, and therefore is not bound to the Fourth Commandment. Yet, they wish to maintain that God gave Christians Sunday as a special day, the sacred day of the week. However, they reject the idea that Sunday has replaced Saturday as a day of rest; Sunday is not a new Sabbath. These Christians believe in an independent historical origin of the Sunday as the sacred day, and thus also reject the idea of Sunday as a day of mandatory rest.

(d) Some "free church" Evangelical believers wish *not to recognize any day of mandatory rest*.[3] These Christians, too, believe that the New Testament Ecclesia is no longer obligated by the Mosaic Torah, and therefore is not bound to the Fourth Commandment. Moreover, they believe that in the New Testament era, God has not set apart any day of the week as sacred. These Christians do not necessarily object to regularly assembling on Sunday, as long as Sunday is not viewed as intrinsically more sacred than other days, and as long as Sunday is not made a day of compulsory rest. To this end, they might quote passages like these:

> One person esteems one day as better than another, while another esteems all days alike. Each one should be fully convinced in his own mind. The one who observes the day, observes it in honor of the Lord. The one who eats, eats in honor of the Lord, since he gives thanks to God, while the one who abstains, abstains in honor of the Lord and gives thanks to God (Rom. 14:5–6).

> Therefore let no one pass judgment on you in questions of food and drink, or with regard to a festival or a new moon or a Sabbath (Col. 2:16).

2.1.2 Personal View

In my view, Gentile Christians are *neither formally nor morally* obligated by the Fourth Commandment (*contra* [a] and [b] above). This is because only the ethnic people of Israel was obligated by the Mosaic Torah, the cornerstone of which is the Sabbath.[4] Therefore, the claim that in the New Testament era God has not set apart any sacred day of the week (view [d]) cannot be refuted by arguing that an explicit New Testament Sabbath Commandment was unnecessary because the Fourth Commandment had already been given to Israel. We cannot assert that Germany does not need certain laws because France already has them; this is a *non sequitur*.

---

3. This is the view of "Messianic" Jew Arnold Fruchtenbaum (1994).
4. Exod. 20:8–11; 31:13–15; 35:2, 3; Lv 19:3, 30; 23:3; 26:2; Num. 15:32–36; Deut. 5:12–15; cf. Ezek. 20:12–24; 22:8, 26; 44:24.

The argument must be turned around: those who adhere to view (b) must supply clear evidence from the New Testament that the Sabbath, or the sacred day of the week, has been moved from Saturday to Sunday. Many who have carefully examined the matter have concluded that the New Testament offers not the slightest evidence for this claim.[5] From the New Testament one might conclude that during the early period of church history, Sunday was viewed as a special day. But this conclusion is quite different from the claim that Sunday has become the new Sabbath.

Let us look a little more closely at the supersessionist logic on this point. The claim that Sunday has replaced Saturday as the weekly day of rest rests on the following two theses:

(1) All Christians are obligated by the Fourth Commandment.
(2) The New Testament identifies Sunday as the new day on which God's people come together.

Conclusion: Sunday must be observed as the new "Sabbath."

This is my reply:

(1) Jesus-believing Gentiles are not obligated by the Fourth Commandment at all.

(2) Even if they were obligated by the Fourth Commandment, a special day of *assembling together* is not the same as a special day of *compulsory rest,* which was and is the primary purpose of the Sabbath.[6] The Sabbath is a feast day, but also an day of obligatory rest; Sunday is a day for assembling together and worshiping God. There is no New Testament evidence that Gentile Christians were obligated to observe the

---

5. In recent times, some Reformed theologians also have reached this conclusion; see, e.g., J. Douma's helpful discussion of the Fourth Commandment (1996, 138–42).

6. The Heb. noun *shabbat* comes from the verb *sh-b-t*, "to stop (working)," hence, "to rest"; see Gen. 2:2, "And on the seventh day God finished his work that he had done, and he rested [Heb. *sh-b-t*] on the seventh day from all his work that he had done."

"Sabbath" on Sunday, nor that they were obligated to observe Sunday as a day of mandatory rest. Even in Israel, every Sabbath was a feast day, but not every feast day (such as the weekdays during *Pesach* and *Sukkoth*) was a Sabbath.

(3) Actually, even if the two theses mentioned above were correct, the conclusion does not necessarily follow from them. Supersessionists might just as legitimately have concluded that in the New Testament era God left the Fourth Commandment intact—the weekly Sabbath always occurs on Saturday—but added to this a new obligatory feast day: the first day of the week.

2.1.3 The "First Day of the Week"

Of course, no Christian would deny that the New Testament attaches special value to the "first day of the week." Let us consider this expression a little more closely.

The Greek uses the expression *prōtē* sabbatou (Mark 16:9) or *mia sabbatou* (1 Cor. 16:2), both of which contain the word *sabbaton*. This word is clearly related to the Hebrew word *shabbat*. Christian Sabbath observers have used this as an argument that Sunday had become the new Sabbath, *or* that the passages mentioned do not speak of Sunday at all but of Saturday.[7] However, the New Testament expression was "the first [day] of the *sabbaton*," which is something quite different from "the (first) Sabbath." The straightforward explanation is that both the Greek *sabbaton* and the plural *sabbata* do not at all mean "Sabbath" here—what would "first of the Sabbath" mean?—but these words rather mean "week," period of seven days, of which the Sabbath is the culmination. A nice demonstration that this is the proper interpretation is the Greek phrase *dis tou sabbatou* (Luke 18:12): "twice a week." This example is decisive for the conclusion that, in certain cases, the Greek word *sabbaton* means not "Sabbath" but "week."

Clearly, the New Testament does emphasize the "first day of the week." Jesus rose from the tomb "after the Sabbath,

---

7. See, e.g., https://bible-menorah.jimdofree.com/english/resurrection-on-sabbath/mk-16–9/.

toward the dawn of the first day of the week" (Matt. 28:1: Gk. *Opse de sabbatōn, . . . eis mian sabbatōn*). Notice that we find the word *sabbaton* here in its two meanings; and notice, too, that Jesus did not rise from the dead *on* the Sabbath, but *after* the Sabbath, that is, on Sunday. On this day, Jesus gathered with his disciples, and did so again exactly a week later, that is, the following Sunday.[8]

Seven weeks later, on the Day of Pentecost—again on the first day of the week[9]—Jesus poured out the Holy Spirit (Acts 2; cf. Lev. 23:15-16). The Jesus-believers in Troas also gathered on the first day of the week. The sentence, "On the first day of the week, when we were gathered together to break bread, . . ." (Acts 20:7), suggests that this was their custom. It seems that the apostle Paul, who apparently had arrived on a Monday, waited in Troas "for seven days" (vv. 5–6) until the first day of the week, because he knew that believers gathered on Sundays.

On the first day of the week the Corinthian believers, at Paul's command, put aside money for Paul's collection (1 Cor. 16:2), which suggests that they had the custom of gathering on that day. The evidence is scarce, but it does suggest that the first day of the week played a special role in the life of the early Christians.

However, what it does *not* suggest, let alone prove, is that in the new era, the first day of the week had been formally appointed to be a special, new, sacred feast day, or that it was to be the new "Sabbath" in the sense of a day of compulsory rest.[10]

---

8. Mark 16:2, 6; Luke 24:36–49; John 20:19–29.
9. See Ouweneel (2001b, ad loc.).
10. The Gk. phrase *hē kuriakē hēmera*, "the Lord's Day," in Rev. 1:10 should not be confused with the Gk. phrase *hēmera [tou] kyriou*, "day of the Lord," in Acts 2:20; 1 Cor. 5:5; 1 Thess. 5:1–2; 2 Pet. 3:1, 10. More importantly, the phrase in Rev. 1:10 cannot really function decisively in this discussion because it can be interpreted in several ways.

2.2 Evaluation
2.2.1 Significance of the Sabbath

In summary, on the one hand the apostles never explicitly or implicitly applied the Sabbath commandment to Gentile Christians. On his missionary journeys, as part of his strategy the apostle Paul did go to synagogues on Sabbaths, but this clearly was to meet the Jews there for the purpose of evangelizing them.[11] On the other hand, the apostles never instituted the Sunday as an obligatory feast day, nor as a day of mandatory rest. So what conclusion must we draw? At a minimum, we may observe the following somewhat contradictory features.

On the one hand (cf. next section), even though Gentile Christians are not obligated by the Mosaic Torah, in a more elevated form nine of the Ten Commandments are certainly part of the Messianic Torah; so why not the one remaining commandment, the Sabbath commandment? Moreover, this commandment is not only part of the Ten Words, but has a much wider impact by going back to the week of creation: "[O]n the seventh day God finished his work that he had done, and he rested on the seventh day from all his work that he had done. So God blessed the seventh day and made it holy, because on it God rested from all his work that he had done in creation" (Gen. 2:2-3). What else could the Israelite hearers of the Torah have concluded from this than that this day was intended as a day of blessing and hallowing *for all humanity?*

To be sure, we never read that the patriarchs observed the Sabbath. However, even before Sinai, the Sabbath appeared to be known to Israel. In Exodus 16:23-29, that is to say, *before* the Torah-giving at Mount Sinai, we read of the Sabbath four or five times; Moses said, "This is what the Lord has commanded: 'Tomorrow is a day of solemn rest [Heb. *shabbaton*], a holy Sabbath to the Lord'. . . . today is a Sabbath to the Lord. . . . on the seventh day, which is a Sabbath. . . . The Lord has given you the Sabbath."

---

11. Acts 13:14, 42, 44; 16:13; 17:2; 18:4.

This clearly indicates that the significance of the Sabbath was far broader than the framework of the Mosaic Torah. The Sabbath was instituted not only for the Jews, but "for humans" (Mark 2:27 CEB), "for the good of human beings" (GNT), for the physical and spiritual well-being of all humanity. It was instituted not only for the Jew but also for "the sojourner who is within your gates" (Exod. 20:10; Deut. 5:14). Think of the many Gentiles who were blessed on Sabbath days (Acts 13:43–44; 18:4). Hence, it is understandable that, during the Messianic kingdom, the Gentiles too will observe the Sabbath:

> Blessed is the man who . . . keeps the Sabbath, not profaning it, ... [T]he eunuchs who keep my Sabbaths, / who choose the things that please me / and hold fast my covenant, ... [T]he foreigners who join themselves to the LORD, / to minister to him, to love the name of the LORD, and to be his servants, / everyone who keeps the Sabbath and does not profane it, / and holds fast my covenant—these I will bring to my holy mountain, / and make them joyful in my house of prayer; / their burnt offerings and their sacrifices / will be accepted on my altar; / for my house shall be called a house of prayer / for all peoples (Isa. 56:2–7).

2.2.2 No New Testament Sabbath Commandment

On the other hand, the New Testament provides no clue whatsoever that Gentile Christians observed the Sabbath formally or informally, whereas we do have indications, scarce though they be, that they met on the first day of the week.[12] So why would Christians not accept Sunday as an appropriate day for corporate worship, without that day being a day of compulsory rest? If Gentile Christians observe the first day of the week as a sacred day of worship, is it not sensible to combine this day with that regular day of rest that every human being needs?

---

12. Mark 16:2, 6; Luke 24:36–49; John 20:19, 26; Acts 2:1; 20:7; cf. 1 Cor. 16:3. See above for a refutation of the absurd idea that these passages were referring to the Sabbath. Mark 16:1–2 explicitly tells us that this day came immediately *after* the Sabbath.

The advantage of the Sabbath-on-Saturday view is that it upholds the continuing validity of the entire *corpus* of Ten Commandments within the Torah of Christ and does justice to the fact that the Sabbath Commandment has a wider (creational) significance than the other Nine Commandments. The advantage of the Sabbath-on-Sunday view is that the New Testament does supply indications of *Gentile* Christians celebrating the first day of the week, but no indications of *Gentile* Christians celebrating the seventh day of the week. This is not so amazing: the first day of the week was the day of the resurrection of Christ as well as of the outpouring of the Holy Spirit. No day has greater Messianic significance than the first day of the week.

By now, several conclusions have emerged.

(a) No one can deny to Jesus-believing Jews the right, if not the duty, to observe the Sabbath (and do so on Saturday, not Sunday).

(b) We may deny that Jesus-believing Gentiles have the duty to observe the Sabbath, but we cannot deny their *right* to do so.

(c) We may deny that Jesus-believing Gentiles have the duty to observe Sunday as a day of corporate worship and of rest, but we cannot deny their *right* to do so. We simply do not have direct clues, either way, regarding the duty of Gentile Christians in this respect. We must therefore leave room for view (d) (see §2.1.1), and say that in the New Testament era, God has not identified any day of the week as especially sacred.

(d) At any rate, *God has not abolished the Sabbath*, just as he has not abolished the smallest part of all the Mosaic Torah. The Sabbath—i.e., Saturday—will be observed during the Messianic kingdom, not only by Israel but also by believing Gentiles.[13] From the beginning of creation, there has never been a time during which the Sabbath disappeared; it was there at least in Genesis 2 and in Exodus 16, and from the Sinai until now, and it will be there as long as the earth endures in its present form.

---

13. Isa. 56:1–7; 66:23; Ezek. 44:24; 45:17; 46:1, 3, 4, 12.

As argued earlier, the Messianic kingdom as such will be the great Sabbath of world history; God travels along his pathway through redemptive history until this ultimate "Sabbath rest" (Gk. *sabbatismos*, Heb. 4:9; see §1.1.1) is realized. We find this view not only in rabbinic sources, but also in the writings of the church fathers and the Reformers.[14] Thus, though many excellent Gentile Christians observed Sunday, they have always acknowledged that in a certain sense God himself still observes the Sabbath, as he did at the creation and toward which he continues to move in redemptive history.[15] Today we are living during the "sixth day," so to speak, and God is moving toward the great "seventh day" of redemptive history, as foreshadowed by the seven days of the creation week. Whatever day Gentile Christians may observe as their usual day for corporate worship, the Sabbath is a spiritual reality that we must take into account, and it will be such as long as the earth endures.

Let me add this historical note: it is *not* true that Sunday observance was instituted for the first time by Emperor Constantine in his Sunday Law of AD 321 (or that he adopted this from the pagans: Sunday, day of the sun god),[16] or by the Council of Laodicea in AD 364. Therefore, the celebration of the Lord's resurrection cannot be rejected by means of such a simple argument, even though significant and undeniable supersessionist anti-Semitism clearly lay behind this fourth-century practice. In reality, the celebration of Sunday as the day for corporate worship was generally practiced outside the land of Israel as early as the beginning of the second century. Later church councils merely confirmed an already well-established institution; their underlying supersessionism was bad enough, but does not diminish the long pedigree of the tradition of Sunday observance.

However, what the councils did under the influence of rising supersessionism was definitely wrong. They changed Sunday, an established feast day and a day of corporate wor-

---

14. Ouweneel (2001a, §2.3.1).
15. Gen. 2:2–3; Exod. 20:8–11; 31:13–17; 35:2–3.
16. So, e.g., https://sabbathsentinel.org/2016/10/13/constantine-march-321-ad/.

ship, into a day that was also a *day of mandatory rest*, to which they applied an entire bevy of Tanakh Sabbath regulations. This was an egregious error, from both a theological and a practical point of view. There is nothing against the *voluntary* celebration of the first day of the week as a special day of *worship*. But there is everything against the *involuntary* observation of it as a *day of compulsory rest*. No one would deny that a weekly day of rest may be beneficial for hard working people. But this is quite different from claiming that Sunday is the "Christian Sabbath," and that therefore, according to the Tanakh Sabbath ordinances, work is *forbidden* (except for priests and pastors, and other traditionally exempted works of necessity and mercy).

2.2.3 The Sabbath and the Other Feasts

In Leviticus 23:3, the description of the weekly Sabbath appears immediately before that of the seven annual feasts (Heb. *mo'adim*[17]) (Lev. 23:4-44), and apparently was viewed in close connection with them.[18]

(1) *Pesach* (v. 5): the Feast of Passover, in remembrance of the exodus from Egypt, on the 14th of the month of Abib (later called Nisan).[19]

(2) *Matzot* (vv. 6-8): the Feast of the Unleavened Loaves, in coherence with *Pesach*, during the week following upon *Pesach*.[20]

(3) *Yom habBikkurim* (vv. 9-14): the Day of Firstfruits (the first sheaf of the barley harvest) (cf. 1 Cor. 15:20), on the first day after the Sabbath[21] during the week of *Matzot*.

---

17. The literal meaning of this Heb. word is "appointed [times]" (from the root '-y-d, "to appoint").
18. See extensively, e.g., Ouweneel (2001b); Cohen Stuart (2003); Van der Poll (2008); I am leaving out of consideration here the feasts that originated much later: *Purim* and *Chanukkah*.
19. Cf. these New Testament passages: Matt. 26:2, 17–19; Luke 2:41; John 2:13, 23; 6:4; 11:55; 12:1; 13:1; 18:28, 39; 19:14; Acts 12:4; 1 Cor. 5:7; Heb. 11:28.
20. Cf. these New Testament passages: Matt. 26:17; Mark 14:1, 12; Luke 22:1, 7; Acts 20:6; 1 Cor. 5:8.
21. Tradition differs on the meaning of this "Sabbath": is it the regular Sabbath

(4) *Shavu'ot* (vv. 15-22): the Feast of Weeks or Pentecost[22] (originally feast of the wheat harvest, later that of the Torah-giving), seven weeks after the "Sabbath" in *Matzot* (see note 21 below) (Acts 2:1; 20:16; 1 Cor. 16:8).

(5) *Yom t'ru'ah* (vv. 23-25): the Feast of the Blast (viz., of the shofar; in the Jewish civil year this is *Rosh haShanah*, "beginning of the year," i.e., the Jewish New Year) (cf. Matt. 24:31), on the first day of the seventh month (in the religious year, i.e., the first month in the civil year).

(6) *Yom hakKippurim* (vv. 26-32): in short, *Yom Kippur*, Day of the Atonements, in short, Day of Atonement (see especially Heb. 9), on the 10th of the seventh month.

(7) *Sukkot* (vv. 33-43): the Feast of Booths, the final harvest feast, but also the memorial of the wilderness journey (John 7:2), from the 15th to the 22nd of the seventh month.

The Christian church has historically displayed an ambivalent attitude toward these biblical festivals. Most of them have fallen into disuse, but two of them were adopted and given a Christian content. These were, first, *Pesach*, because Christ had risen from the dead at the Passover feast, and second, *Shavu'ot*, because at this feast the Holy Spirit had been poured out (Acts 2). But these new, Christian feast days have little to do with their original meanings.

(a) In the Christian celebration of Easter, nothing remains of the Passover night of Exodus 12, and in the Christian celebration of Pentecost, nothing remains of the wheat harvest or of the Torah-giving, which are characteristic of the Feast of Weeks.

(b) In many countries, not even the names were retained: *Pesach* became Easter (in German: *Ostern*, derived from the Germanic goddess Ostara), and *Shavu'ot* became Whitsun(-

---

during this week (as the Sadducees and modern Messianic Jews believe; in this case, both *Yom habBikkurim* and *Shavu'ot* are always on Sunday), or is it the first day of Matzot (the 15th of Abib) (as the Pharisees and modern orthodox Jews believe)? In the latter case, *Shavu'ot* is always on a fixed date: the 6th of the month Sivan.

22. The name "Pentecost" comes from Gk. *pentēkostē*, "fiftieth [day]," because this feast is celebrated on the fiftieth day after *Yom habBikkurim*.

day) in many English speaking countries (probably after the white garments of those to be baptized at this feast). (In the name "Pentecost," at least some of the original meaning was retained, but now it became the fiftieth day after Easter, no longer the fiftieth day after *Yom habBikkurim*).

(c) Anti-Semitic feelings prompted Emperor Constantine the Great to disconnect these feasts as much as possible from Judaism by changing their dates (AD 325). In fact, it was for the same reason that the "Sabbath" was moved from Saturday to Sunday: the remembrance of the Jewish source was retained, but at the same time, an intentional cleft was created between Judaism and Christianity, between Jews and Christians.

In practice, the "Christian" feast days were instead filled with non-Jewish (pagan) elements. This may be seen especially in the example of Christmas, which goes back to, among other things, the ancient pagan feast celebrating the winter solstice (Dec. 25). In certain European regions, even the pagan name was retained: *Yule* in Scandinavian countries, *Joelfeest* in Dutch regions, *Julfest* in German regions. Because Christmas had no Jewish prototype, its pagan elements have been retained here more clearly than in other cases. But even *Easter* and *Ostern*, though going back to biblical *Pesach*, remind us more of ancient Germanic pagan origins (including the Easter bunny and Easter eggs) than of Jewish elements. Strictly speaking, it is simply incorrect to claim that *Pesach* was "fulfilled" in Christian Easter: first, *Pesach* never was a resurrection feast, and second, Easter is the "resurrection story" wrapped—not in a Jewish but—in a pagan garment.

But please notice, this does not change the fact that the biblical *mo'adim* do have a spiritual meaning that is highly important, also for Gentile Jesus-believers. This is why Jewish Jesus-believers have the *duty*, but Gentile Jesus-believers have the *right* and *privilege*—not the duty—to take part, at the invitation of Jews, in celebrating the biblical *mo'adim*. The *mo'adim* are not "Jewish" feast times but *biblical* feast times, and as such are inherently and perpetually significant. Moreover, Gentile Jesus-believers are, or at least should be, highly interested in the redemptive-historical and prophetic meaning of these festivals.

(1, 2) *Pesach* and *Matzot*: the sacrifice of Christ as the true Passover lamb, and the Christian celebration that is based upon it.[23]

(3) *Yom habBikkurim:* the day of the resurrection of Jesus Christ, who is the "firstfruits [Gk. *aparchē*] of those who have fallen asleep" (1 Cor. 15:20).

(4) *Shavu'ot*: God's Sinaitic covenant with Israel; in its renewed form (after the Day of Pentecost in Acts 2), Gentile believers are also welcomed to its celebration.

(5) *Yom t'ru'ah*: the re-appearance of the Messiah with the blast of the trumpet.[24]

(6) *Yom Kippur*: the high priest returns from the sanctuary after having sprinkled the blood, and presents himself to his people (Lev. 16): the day of atonement for Israel at the second coming of Christ.

(7) *Sukkot*: the Feast of Booths, the presaging *par excellence* of the Messianic kingdom.

2.3 Scripture and Tradition
2.3.1 Orthodox Jewish and Roman Catholic View

Observing regular religious feast days is a matter of both Jewish and Christian tradition. Traditions are fixed ways of acting that Jews and Christians (and many others, of course) have continued to follow for centuries. The word "tradition" comes from Latin *tradere*, "to hand down"; traditions are long-established customs and beliefs handed down from one generation to the next. In a sense, there is nothing wrong with a good "custom": when Jesus was twelve years old, he went with his parents to Jerusalem for the Feast of *Pesach* "according to custom" (Luke 2:42). When his ministry began, "as was his custom, he went to the synagogue on the Sabbath day" (4:16; cf. Acts 17:1-2, where we read the same about the apostle Paul). And during the last night of his life on earth,

---

23. 1 Cor. 5:7–8; cf. John 1:29, 36; 1 Pet. 1:19; Rev. 5–7 and 13–21.
24. Cf. Matt. 24:31; 1 Cor. 15:52; 1 Thess. 4:16; Rev. 8:2.

Jesus "went, as was his custom, to the Mount of Olives" (Luke 22:39) in order to pray there. There is nothing wrong with keeping the feast, going to believers' gatherings, and praying regularly.

However, there is more to tradition than this. In order to understand modern Judaism, as well as important aspects of traditional Christianity (Roman Catholic, Eastern Orthodox, Protestant, Evangelical), it is useful to pay some attention to this role of tradition in religious life.

There is a remarkable similarity between Jews and Roman Catholics—regarding a point in which they both differ from Protestants—when it comes to reading the Bible.

Let us consider first the great rabbinic expositors, for instance, the difference between the Bible commentaries by Rashi (Rabbi Shlomo Yitzchaqi) and those by Abraham Ibn Ezra. Ibn Ezra chose to omit the midrashic (say, homiletical and typological) traditions from his Bible commentaries; these commentaries thus resemble the grammatical-historical commentaries that we in the Western Christian world have been used to for centuries: what does the text say, and what does it not say? With Rashi, however, we often experience a feeling of alienation: how can Rashi possibly derive this or that from the text? This is precisely the point: strictly speaking, he does not "derive" it from the text. Rather, he argues this: This was how sages of former ages dealt with the text, and I take that seriously.

In this way, a problem is created that may be likened to problems that Protestant expositors often experience with Roman Catholic dogmas or interpretations.[25] Take, for instance, the matter of praying for and to, and the intercession by, deceased saints. Rome appeals to various deuterocanonical texts (2 Maccabees 12:38-45; 15:11-16). Protestants find such an appeal rather strange. How can one derive from such passages a complete Christian dogma—one that plays such an enormous role in the practice of faith? Or take the appeal to 1 Corinthians 3:13-15 in the defense of the doctrine of purgatory:

---

25. Cf. Ouweneel and De Korte (2010, chapter 3).

> [T]he quality of each person's work will be seen when the Day of Christ exposes it. For on that Day fire will reveal everyone's work; the fire will test it and show its real quality. If what was built on the foundation survives the fire, the builder will receive a reward. But if your work is burnt up, then you will lose it; but you yourself will be saved, as if you had escaped through the fire.

Protestants argue that they find nothing in this passage about a place or a state through which believers must first pass in order to be purified before they may enter heaven. These Protestants do not understand that in the Roman Catholic Church, such an appeal to the Bible has a very different function than in Protestant theology. Roman Catholics do not believe in praying to the deceased *on the basis of* 2 Maccabees 12, nor do they believe in purgatory *on the basis of* 1 Corinthians 3. Rather, they accept these doctrines as true because they have arisen early, sometimes very early, within the church, have become part of church tradition, have been endowed with the moral authority of great Christian thinkers, and have been sanctioned by the church—the latter is decisive. The *church* has accepted and preached these doctrines for centuries, and the church cannot err, for Jesus himself promised that he would guide her: "When the Spirit of truth comes, he will guide you into all the truth, for he will not speak on his own authority, but whatever he hears he will speak, and he will declare to you the things that are to come" (John 16:13).

These Roman Catholic appeals to Scripture function only *a posteriori*, whereas in Protestant thought they function *a priori*. Protestants wish to *prove* their doctrines from the Bible, for this is their only source of knowledge of spiritual truth (though Protestantism contains its own traditionalism; see §2.3.3). Roman Catholics, by contrast, do not need such proofs from Scripture because they *already know* that the doctrines involved must be true because these teachings have been endowed with the authority of the *church*. And the church knows that this or that doctrine is true because, from early days, it has been taught by (some of) its great sages. And why should we claim to understand things better than these sages of long ago, who stood so much closer to the time of the apostles? It comes in handy if after making our argument we can find certain biblical indications of a certain doctrine, but strictly speaking this is not necessary.[26]

In fact, it works precisely the same way within orthodox Judaism, although here the *formal* authority of some institution, such as the church, is lacking. This formal authority of the church goes back to the *moral* authority of the church's sages (church fathers, council fathers, popes). Jews appeal to this *moral* authority of their sages alone, whether the *Zugot* (sages from ca. 170 to 30 BC), the *Tannaim* (sages from ca. 10 to 220 of the present era, mentioned in the Mishnah; see below), the *Amoraim* (sages from about 200 to 500, mentioned in, and composers of, the Gemarah; see below), and so on. The wisdom of these sages as written down in the Talmud (i.e., Mishnah and Gemarah) functions similarly to that of the Roman Catholic Church. The truly orthodox Jew can never deviate from what he recognizes as the general teaching of the Talmud, and the truly orthodox Roman Catholic can never deviate from the church's doctrines as laid down in Council decisions, Creeds, and Papal Dogmas. The orthodox Jew reads the Tanakh through the glasses of the Talmud; the orthodox Roman Catholic reads the Bible (Tanakh and New Testament) through the glasses of the church's written creeds and dogmas.

It is amazing to see how little understanding some Protestant theologians had, or have, for this state of affairs. In his commentary on Leviticus, the Reformed theologian A. Noordtzij repeatedly "corrected" Rashi and other Jewish exposi-

---

26. If we still wonder where tradition gets its wisdom from, one helpful rule is this (and it works in Judaism, in Roman Catholicism, as well as in Protestantism): a certain doctrine must at least reflect the "spirit" of Scripture. A striking Roman Catholic example is this: if God *can* do a thing, and (for logically compelling reasons) *must* have done it, then it reflects the spirit of Scripture to assume that he *has* done it. Thus, there *must* be a purgatory in order to render the believing souls fit for heaven. Mary *must* have been born by immaculate conception in order to guarantee the sinlessness of her Son. There *must* be a central leadership in the church in order to guarantee its unity and continuity. And so on.

tors because he could not find in the text what these Jews had found in it. Those who read the text with an open mind, in a supposedly unbiased way, may often conclude that Noordtzij was right. But this is precisely the point: the rabbis Rashi and Ibn Ezra did not *wish* to read the text with an open mind, in a supposedly unbiased way. Noordtzij interpreted the text like a modern individualist who believed he could read the text as it addressed him personally (as a trained theologian). Rashi and Ibn Ezra knew themselves to be part of a community, not only a contemporaneous one but one that extended back many centuries. To them, tradition was sacred. They would be filled with indignation if they had witnessed Noordtzij's approach, who really seemed to believe that in his exegesis he could begin anew. Conservative Roman Catholics would never think this way, nor would Ibn Ezra, and Rashi least of all.

2.3.2 Unbiased Reading

Imagine some highly intelligent Indian or Chinese who has never heard of the Bible. Give them an English version of the book of Leviticus, or perhaps a Hebrew version; to make it easier, let them begin in Genesis. In this case, what would an open-minded, unbiased reading of the Bible look like? Are there differences between such a brilliant outsider and a brilliant theologian like Noordtzij. Would we still call Noordtzij's approach "open-minded, unbiased," in a way similar to the "open-minded, unbiased" way our Asian friend is reading the Bible? Of course not. Noordtzij brought to his interpretation all *his* knowledge of theology, *his* Western way of thinking, as a theologian steeped in Reformed schooling, and more broadly, in a Protestant stream of thought, dating back several centuries, marked either by medieval scholasticism, or by Enlightenment rationalism, or by Protestant mysticism, or by Protestant rationalism, or some mixture of all these elements.

Noordtzij and our imaginary Asian reader have each been socialized in entirely different ways of thinking. We understand this infinitely better since philosopher of science

Thomas S. Kuhn introduced us to the notion of paradigms,[27] and since the application of his notion to theological thinking.[28] *There is no such thing as an open-minded, unbiased reading of the Bible,* neither by Noordtzij nor by my Asian, neither by Jewish expositors, nor by Roman Catholic theologians, neither by the most conservative, nor by the most modernist theologians. Believers may count upon the guidance of the Holy Spirit, but they must also realize that they read the Bible through the glasses of a certain paradigm (framework of thought) in which they have been trained. If it were different, we would never understand how so many readers have relied on the guidance of the Holy Spirit and yet have reached such divergent exegetical conclusions. Even the orthodox Jewish or Roman Catholic scholar who feels strongly bound to the traditions of his ancestors is a different person than his predecessors of, say, three centuries ago because he or she lives in a different age, culture, and paradigm.

In practice, all Bible reading occurs somewhere between the extremes of "my open mind (my conscience, my intellect) only" and "my tradition (my church, my sages) only." The former extreme is mistaken because there *is* no such thing as a completely open mind; all our Bible study is driven by our paradigm. But the latter extreme is also mistaken, because what are the sages of long ago other than brilliant men who approached the text with *their* supposed "open minds," or within *their* paradigms? Why would the past have produced more such sages than the present? Jesus *criticized* those who thought that the "old wine" was automatically better than the "new wine" (Luke 5:39). And we must similarly criticize those who think that the "new wine" is automatically better (for instance, more "scientific") than the "old wine." Protestants, including Noordtzij (and so many others), have their own traditions, which sometimes are any less powerful than Jewish or Roman Catholic traditions (see next section). And conversely, Jews and Roman Catholics are just as much

---

27. Kuhn (1996).
28. See, e.g., Spykman (1992); see my more recent introductions: Ouweneel (2014b; 2014c).

bound to the rules of grammatical-historic interpretation as is *all* ancient and modern literature. They cannot avoid "reading what they are reading," no matter how strong their dogmatic biases may be.

Here is the middle path: on the one hand, we must all be aware of our paradigm glasses, no matter how objective and unbiased we try to be. On the other hand, a person can never deny that they are reading what they are reading, in whatever frame of thought they may have been socialized. Formulated a little differently: on the one hand, we are not the first people who read the Bible, and so we must not pretend that we can begin from ground zero; we stand on the shoulders of the giants of the past (without denying that there may be such giants in our own time, too). On the other hand, there may be moments when we say, as Luther did at the Diet of Worms (in my words): If all the councils and all the popes have said such and such, but I read in the Bible to say so and so, the I will believe the Bible.[29]

The only real difference is this. When reading the Bible, (orthodox) Jews and (orthodox) Roman Catholics begin with submission to a specific authority; for Jews this is the Talmud (plus the great medieval interpreters of the Talmud, and the great medieval Tanakh expositors); for Roman Catholics this is the creeds and the dogmas of their church. Officially speaking, (orthodox) Protestants do not possess such an authority telling him how they should read the Bible; for them it is *sola Scriptura* ("Scripture alone") (in how far this is really the case will be discussed in the next section). All three orthodox groups just mentioned believe in the guidance of the Holy Spirit. But Jews see this especially in the way the Spirit has led the *Zugot*, the *Tannaim*, the *Amoraim*, and so on (see previous section). Roman Catholics see this especially in the way the Spirit has led the church fathers and the council fathers, whereas orthodox Protestants see the guidance of the Spirit

---

29. Stated more formally, "Unless I am convinced by the testimony of the Scriptures or by clear reason (for I do not trust either in the pope or in councils alone, since it is well known that they have often erred and contradicted themselves), I am bound by the Scriptures I have quoted and my conscience is captive to the Word of God"; see Brecht (1985–1993), 1:460.

especially in the way *they themselves* trust in the leading of the Spirit.

We must not exaggerate these differences, though. On the one hand, it might seem that for Jews or Roman Catholics the Bible text as such is not very important, and of course this is not the case. Or it might seem that the modern sages are not very important, and this is not the case either. On the other hand, Protestants are usually well aware of the tremendous significance and influence of twenty centuries of Christian thinking, which strongly shapes their own thinking. Even the word "formal" (as in the phrase "formal authority") must be relativized: in practice, every Christian denomination develops its own traditions, including traditional doctrines, which are binding on its members to such an extent that the distinctions between "formal authority" and "moral authority" become blurred.

2.3.3 Protestant Traditionalism

All those who know the history of Protestant theology realize that, when it comes to the influence of tradition, the differences with orthodox Judaism, orthodox Roman Catholicism, and orthodox Protestantism (Lutheran, Calvinistic, Anglican, Evangelical) are only relative. *Every* Protestant movement that has experienced some decades or centuries of development contains its own specific doctrines. These might not go back directly to Scripture—why else would *other* movements not have discovered these same truths?—but the Bible teachers involved are convinced that they are "according to the spirit of Scripture." Those who criticize Jews or Roman Catholics for adhering to doctrines that might not conflict with Scripture but cannot be directly derived from Scripture must first clean up their own backyards. Consider these few examples.[30]

(a) As far as I know, orthodox Jews are the *only* ones who believe that God demands that they maintain two separate

---

30. The author welcomes correction through further insight into these examples, whose description may be tainted by oral tradition rather than drawn from written sources.

kitchens, one for dairy products and one for meat (such with a quaint appeal to Exod. 23:19; 34:26; Deut. 14:21).

(b) As far as I know, Roman Catholics are the *only* Christians who believe that Matthew 16:18 teaches the institution of the central (read: papal) leadership of the church (Peter supposedly being the "rock" on which the church is built, and Peter being the first pope, representing all the later popes).

(c) As far as I know, Lutherans are the *only* (or at the least the *mainline*) Christians who believe that, after his ascension and glorification, and Jesus Christ is omnipresent not only according to his divine nature, but also corporally (i.e., according to his human nature) (which is the basis for the doctrine of consubstantiation).

(d) As far as I know, consistent Reformed Christians are the *only* ones who believe that the relationship between God and humans is always of a covenantal nature, and that there is not only an election from eternity but also a reprobation from eternity.

(e) As far as I know, Baptists are the *only* (or at the least the *mainline*) Christians who believe that a person becomes a member of the body of Christ on the basis of believers' baptism (by misinterpreting 1 Cor. 12:12–13).

(f) As far as I know, Pentecostals are the *only* (or at the least the *mainline*) Christians who believe in (the necessity) of a "second blessing," that is, receiving the indwelling Holy Spirit through the laying on of hands (some time) *after* a person has come to faith in Jesus Christ.

(g) Latter-day saints ("Mormons") are the *only* religious group that believes 1 Corinthians 15:29 to mean that a person can be baptized for deceased persons (especially ancestors) who in this way are saved.

We could supply more examples. Every religious movement has such traditions, or doctrines clothed in tradition, that receive an increasingly immutable status.

Often, traditions are far more sacred than people realize—or wish to realize—simply because they consider it the most normal thing in the world to believe or do this or that.

In a certain sense, traditions within Protestantism are even more dangerous than traditions in Judaism or Roman Catholicism, because they often go unnoticed and are thereby unconsciously placed above God's Word. As Jesus told the Pharisees, "You leave the commandment of God and hold to the tradition of men. . . . You have a fine way of rejecting the commandment of God in order to establish your tradition!" (Mark 7:8-9). And the apostle Paul told the Colossian believers, "Watch out, so that no one will take you captive by means of philosophy and empty deceit, following human tradition which accords with the elemental spirits of the world but does not accord with the Messiah" (Col. 2:8 CJB).

Within Protestantism, traditionalism is clothed in various garments, particularly in the form of the ancient confessions, in particular the Apostle's Creed, the Nicene-Constantinopolitan Creed, among Reformed Christians the three Forms of Unity (the Belgic Confession, the Heidelberg Catechism, and the Canons of Dordt), among Presbyterians the Westminster Standards (the Confession, and the Shorter and Larger Catechisms), further the Lutheran confessional documents (Augsburg Confession and Luther's Catechism), and so on. Many times, the incantation of "Scripture and Confession"[31] has played a decisive role in both theological and practical questions of church and faith. In such cases, the confession did not formally function on the same level as Scripture, but actually and virtually it did.

This is similar to the Jewish doublet of Tanakh and Talmud, in which the Talmud functions perhaps not formally but actually and practically on the same level as the Tanakh.[32] To get an idea of this process, just ask how much time an (ultra-)orthodox Jew spends studying the Tanakh, and how much time he spends studying the Talmud.

Traditionalism also comes to light in the veneration people have for the advanced age of a certain tradition. Here

---

31. Even occurring in book titles: see Van Sliedregt (1994).
32. If the Mishnah is considered to be (the record of) the so-called Oral Torah, given to Moses on Mount Sinai, there would be no *a priori* reason why the Mishnah would have less divine authority than the Tanakh.

again, supersessionism is an excellent example because it is encountered already among preeminent church fathers of the fourth and fifth century, first and foremost with Augustine. Considering the intimate loyalty to Augustine expressed by both the Augustinian (!) monk Martin Luther and the humanist John Calvin, what traditional Protestant would dare to contradict (the three of) them?[33] People *think* they are objectively interpreting Scripture as they (unconsciously?) *do* so along the lines of Augustine, Martin Luther, Philip Melanchthon, John Calvin, Theodore Beza, and their successors. Indeed, if Luther and Calvin—and Melanchthon and Beza[34]—thoroughly agreed on certain matters, such as supersessionism, infant baptism, Sunday observance, amillennialism, and so on, and if even the great majority of the theologians of the Dutch Second Reformation, British Puritanism, and German Pietism endorsed these views, what traditional Protestant would dare to preach a different view?

The same phenomenon appears within orthodox Judaism. If Rashi, Ibn Ezra, Nachmanides, Gersonides, Maimonides, Jacob Sforno, and David Kimchi explain a Tanakh passage in such and such a way, what modern Jewish author calling himself orthodox would dare to deviate from this? Or if the Talmud, as well as the *Yad haChazaqah* by Maimonides and the *Shulchan Aruch* by Joseph Qaro, say that in a given situation a Jew must act this or that way, how many Jews would call themselves orthodox while daring to interpret the Torah differently?

Dutch Reformed supersessionists might appeal to the rhymed Psalms of 1773, where we find, for instance, the famous expression *in Isrel ingelijfd* ("incorporated into Israel," Psalm 87, stanza 4). The Annotations tell us:

> As if he [i.e., the Psalm writer] said: The time shall come, that it shall be said of the Philistines, Tyrians and Moores [Ethiopi-

---

33. Although how many Protestants would still defend Augustine's support for the Roman Catholic Church over against the Donatists?
34. And, in the Netherlands, the highly revered Annotations to the States Translation of 1637, even if these do not have the formal authority of the Forms of Unity.

ans], that they are born at Jerusalem (which is the mother of us all), Gal. 4.26, that is in the Church of God: *i.e.* that they do belong to the Church of God, and to the heavenly Jerusalem.[35]

What opposition can the modern Protestant mount against the overwhelming power of such a magnificent tradition"? Nevertheless, millions of Christians nowadays are fully convinced that supersessionism, no matter how strongly supported by tradition, has no biblical basis. This should tell us something. These Christians may say, as a variant upon Luther's words (see note 29): Unless I am convinced by the testimony of the Scriptures or by clear reason (for I do not trust creeds or confessions or catechisms alone, since it is well known that they have often erred and contradicted themselves), I am bound by the Scriptures I have quoted and my conscience is captive to the Word of God. None of this reduces the responsibility of either Luther or the anti-supersessionists to thoroughly defend their own assertions from Scripture. And this is precisely what I am seeking to do in these volumes on Israelology.

2.4 Truth Elements in Tradition
2.4.1 The Oral Word of God

One important, positive element in all tradition(alism) is this: it is quite possible and conceivable that ancient traditions have retained certain truths that are not explicitly revealed in the Bible, but that were common knowledge among, for instance, post-exilic Jews and early church fathers, respectively. We know this through apocryphal Jewish and early rabbinic writings, and through early Christian writings like those of the Apostolic Fathers. Protestants may be reluctant to adopt such elements, and understandably so; yet, they must exhibit a certain benevolence with regard to the possibility of such extra-biblical, yet divine truths.

Both the Jews and the Roman Catholics have constructed an entire doctrine around their respective sacred traditions. Take the Jewish notion of the "Oral Torah" that God, through Moses, supposedly gave to Israel at Mount Sinai, the written

---
35. Haak (1918, ad loc.).

THE ETERNAL PEOPLE: GOD IN RELATION TO ISRAEL

record of which we would find in the Mishnah. The idea that God gave Israel certain instructions that are not recorded in the written Torah, regarding, for instance, how exactly the tabernacle had to be constructed, is quite conceivable. It is equally conceivable that God gave oral elaborations about putting into practice many of his commandments and prohibitions. But for liberal Jews and for Christians, the claim that everything in the Mishnah goes back to such oral instructions by God, given already at Mount Sinai, goes too far.

Protestants have similar objections regarding the Roman Catholic doctrine implying that although the church consists of fallible believers, *as church* she is in fact infallible, because she is guided and protected by the Holy Spirit (John 16:13).[36] Protestants cannot accept this because they view many Roman Catholic dogmas as unbiblical. That is, if the Bible says A, and tradition says B, or even non-A, then the Bible is right, not tradition. Here is a small sampling.[37]

103. Mary was conceived without any stain of "original sin" (the inherited sinful nature).
108. Mary, when she passed away, was assumed body and soul into heaven.
134. The grace by which we are justified may be lost, and is indeed lost through every grievous [mortal, serious] sin.
147. The pope is infallible when he speaks *ex cathedra*.
176. Baptism confers the grace of justification.
189. The body and the blood of Christ together with his human soul and his divine nature, and thus the whole Christ, are truly present in the Eucharist.

But, let us not lose sight of the many *dozens* of vital Roman Catholic dogmas with which orthodox Protestants can

---

36. In 1870, this doctrine was set forth in the dogma of papal infallibility: when the pope speaks *ex cathedra*, he speaks free of error.
37. The numbering comes from http://www.traditionalcatholicpriest.com/wp-content/uploads/2017/12/A-List-Of-The-Dogmas-Of-The-Catholic-Church.pdf.

wholeheartedly agree! And let us always be open to ancient Jewish or Christian insights, even if they cannot be explicitly found in Scripture. There is great wisdom in this statement by the apostle Paul: "So then, brothers, stand firm and hold to the traditions that you were taught by us, either by our spoken word or by our letter" (2 Thess. 2:15). That is, the Thessalonian believers may have learned "traditions" (doctrines and practices handed down) from the apostle that were contained in his spoken word but in none of his letters. In this sense, I would venture to say that, strictly speaking, the well-known motto of *sola Scriptura* as such is illogical.[38] Paul had preached the word of *God* to the Thessalonians (cf. 1 Thess. 2:13), which had reached them, and the Vulgate puts it, *sive per sermonem, sive per epistolam nostrum* (2 Thess. 2:2). The *preached* word of Paul was just as much Word of God as the *written* word of Paul. It is in principle possible that some of this *preached* word of God was retained in early Christian writings, though not in the *written* New Testament.

This claim is not be asserted in order to fling open the door for all kinds of new doctrines derived from, for instance, the Apostolic Fathers. But this claim ought to create more respect for tradition than is customarily acknowledged among many Christians. For if we do not have such respect, we will never understand and appreciate Jewish tradition, and thus we will never understand and appreciate the true nature of orthodox (rabbinic, Talmudic) Judaism.

2.4.2 The Proper Balance

The Protestant believer may personally choose to appeal to the Bible alone; but the Protestant theologian of academic quality will gladly take seriously early Christian writings as well as rabbinic writings when studying the things of God. Consider this simple distinction: at a Bible school or a confessionally bound theological academy, the students learn

---

38. As a hermeneutical principle, *sola Scripture* cannot be found in Scripture. Strictly speaking, it may come as a surprise that this motto is self-contradictory—that is to say: "Scripture alone" is not Scriptural!

what "the Bible says" (therefore, all denominations must have their own Bible schools, for at all these schools the Bible is thought to say different things). But at a non-confessionally bound theological academy (but one that moves within Nicene boundaries), the students learn what twenty-five centuries of Jewish and Christian scholars have taught about the Bible. The former type of school may produce pastors; the latter type of school may produce scholars. This latter type does not necessarily teach relativism, as if all theologies are equally good or bad. But it does contain something of the wisdom of Rabbi Simeon ben Zoma, who said, "Who is wise? He who learns from everyone. As is stated: 'From all my teachers I have grown wise' [Ps. 119:99]."[39]

Notice the distinction between "everyone" and "all my teachers." Of course, we do not learn as much from some people as we do from other people around us. But some—or many—of them may become true teachers for us, if we are just prepared to listen to them, even if they proceed from very different paradigms.

This is the balance one must seek to find: the balance between listening to all and knowing where one stands themselves. On the one hand, we can learn from all orthodox[40] Bible scholars, Jewish, Roman Catholic, or Protestant, and perhaps even from all liberal Bible scholars, Jewish, Roman Catholic, or Protestant. On the other hand, there are moments when we speak as Luther did: *It is written*,[41] no matter what all the rabbis, all the popes, all the councils, and all our cherished Protestant theologians may have said. If we do the former too much—listening to everyone—we get confused and distracted, we become relativists, we become "children, tossed to and fro by the waves and carried about by every wind of doctrine, by human cunning, by craftiness in deceitful schemes" (Eph. 4:14).

---

39. Aboth IV.1.

40. Here the term "orthodox" means believing that the Tanakh, or the Tanakh and the New Testament, respectively, are the inspired and divinely authoritative Word of God.

41. As Jesus did so often: Matt. 4:4–10; Mark 7:6; 11:17; Luke 4:4–10; 10:26; 19:46; 22:37; 24:46; John 8:17.

But if we do the latter too much—appealing to the Bible in our own way—we become individualists, arrogant, know-it-alls, people who think they have a monopoly on biblical wisdom. We must seek the balance between "Learn to always listen to what others may have to say" and "Learn to testify to your own deepest convictions." It is the balance between "always learning and never able to arrive at a knowledge of the truth" (2 Tim. 3:7) and daring to say, "I know whom I have believed" (2 Tim. 1:12).

Finally, let me emphasize again that there is not necessarily anything wrong with customs and traditions as such (see §2.3.1). Traditions become problematic only in two situations: first, when they clearly conflict with (the spirit of) Scripture (see, e.g., Matt. 15:1-6), and second, when they degenerate into tradition*alism*, that is, when they receive an unassailable status, which in the end may even surpass that of Scripture (cf. Mark 7:8-9, 13; Col. 2:8). As one theologian has put it, in Evangelical Protestantism, traditionalism is even more dangerous than traditionalism in Judaism, Roman Catholicism, or Eastern Orthodoxy because it often goes unnoticed and unrecognized; yet, it is invariably present, and thus can be unconsciously confused with the Word of God and can annul the latter.[42] This is perfectly correct—the problem is only that no Christian would likely admit to being a traditionalist, or a confessionalist, or a legalist for that matter. "-Isms" can be eliminated only if they are acknowledged and confessed, and this usually occurs only if the Holy Spirit is allowed to enlighten the hearts (cf. Eph. 1:17-18).

2.5 Rabbinic Judaism

2.5.1 The "Traditions of the Forefathers"

We have seen that Judaism cannot be simply evaluated on the basis of the Tanakh, just as Roman Catholicism cannot be evaluated solely on the basis of the New Testament. Each must be evaluated on the basis of their concomitant *tradition*. To put it simply: Judaism is Torah plus rabbinic tradi-

---

42. Koivisto (1993, 147); he used the word "tradition," whereas "traditionalism" would have been more accurate.

tion, and Roman Catholicism is New Testament plus church tradition. We could also put it this way: Christians view the Tanakh through the glasses of the New Testament, whereas Jews view the Tanakh through the glasses of rabbinic tradition, that is primarily, the Talmud. Therefore, no one can begin to understand modern Israel or Judaism without some basic knowledge of this rabbinic tradition.

Many supersessionists are far too negative about this rabbinic Judaism. It is true, many philosemites express excessive admiration for this Judaism ("Judaeophilia"), as if the rabbis possess *the* true key to understanding the Tanakh.[43] They do not, for this key is Christ—whom they reject. But this does not render everything in Judaism worthless. Above, I have quoted Simeon ben Zoma (first half second century), who identified as wise those who are prepared to learn from everyone, which is perfectly correct. Here is a simple—somewhat exaggerated—example: those who interpret the Israel prophecies literally can often learn more from supersessionists than from thinkers sympathetic to them, because the former present with new viewpoints and new challenges. (Of course, the opposite is equally true: supersessionists could learn much from those who interpret the Israel prophecies literally.) Therefore, it is incorrect that Christians could learn nothing from the rabbis.[44] Jesus said of them, "The scribes and the Pharisees sit on Moses' seat, *so do and observe whatever they tell you*"—although Jesus added, ". . . but not the works they do" (Matt. 23:2–3).

---

43. Cf. Paas (2014, 222–24, including the reference to M. Boertien, 260–65).
44. For dozens of years, the many volumes of the Talmud and of the Soncino Bible commentaries have found a home on my bookshelves, and are consulted regularly.

According to tradition (!), rabbinic tradition began with the "scribe"[45] Ezra (see Ezra 7:6, 11-12, 21).[46] Here, the term "scribe" means as much as Torah scholar. His task was not primarily that of doing grammatical-historical exegesis, which would be developed in later Judaism and Christianity, but rather a practice-oriented interpretation of the Torah. Notice the brief description of Ezra:

> Ezra had set his heart
> [a] to *study* the Law of the LORD, and
> [b] to *do* it and
> [c] to *teach* his statutes and rules in Israel (Ezra 7:10).

The goal of this practical teaching of the "statutes and rules" of the LORD was to standardize the faith practice of the Jews, both in the Holy Land and scattered to remote countries. This initiative led to schools (*yeshivas*), in combination with the first synagogues that had developed already during the Babylonian exile.[47] The *yeshiva* (lit., "sitting [together]") is the place for the learned debate among the Torah scholars concerning the proper understanding of the Torah, as well as for teaching younger Jewish men. Until AD 70, the most important *yeshiva* was in Jerusalem, and after the destruction of city and temple it moved to Jamnia (or Javne)—at the instigation of Jochanan ben Zakkai—and still later also to places like Lud and Tiberias.

All these studies focused on the question: How exactly does Adonai want us to put the 613 commandments of the Torah into practice? For instance, how exactly must the Sabbath be observed (what is commanded, what is allowed, what is prohibited)? How exactly must we observe the food laws,

---

45. Heb. *sophēr* (from the root *s-ph-r*, "to write"); in the pre-exilic books of the Tanakh, this term had more the meaning of "secretary" (e.g., 1 Chron. 24:6; 27:32), whereas in the case of Ezra and the New Testament "scribes" the term had more the meaning of "Bible scholar" (cf. German *Schreiber* and *Schriftgelehrter*, respectively; Dutch: *schrijver* en *schriftgeleerde*).
46. Regarding him, see Ouweneel (2014a, 79–82).
47. In Yiddish, the "synagogue" is still called *Schul*, from German *Schule*, i.e., "school," underscoring the teaching function of the synagogue.

the marriage laws, the moral laws? How do we properly practice civil and criminal justice? What exactly is "clean" and "unclean" in the cultic sense (cf. Lev. 11 and Deut. 14)? All these studies and debates led to an extensive casuistry. From Ezra until the early centuries of the modern era—a total of five or six centuries—this casuistry was handed down in a purely oral way. In such cases, the question always arises how *accurate* such an oral tradition can possibly be. The answer is, probably (much) more accurate than we modern people can imagine, because the art of memorizing today is a mere shadow of what it was in those days.

2.5.2 From Oral to Written Tradition

The criterion for all such studies was primarily what Jesus called the "traditions of our ancestors" (Matt. 15:2 GW, NOG). The Gospel writer Mark explains to his Gentile readers:

> [T]he Pharisees and all the Jews do not eat unless they wash their hands properly, holding to the tradition of the elders [or, ancestors], and when they come from the marketplace, they do not eat unless they wash. And there are many other traditions that they observe, such as the washing of cups and pots and copper vessels and dining couches. And the Pharisees and the scribes asked him [i.e., Jesus], "Why do your disciples not walk according to the tradition of the elders, but eat with defiled hands?" (Mark 7:3-5)

Similarly, the apostle Paul spoke of the "traditions of our fathers" (Acts 28:17 CJB) and the "traditions handed down by my forefathers" (Gal. 1:14 CJB). Thus, the Torah scholar always first listens to what the "(fore)fathers" have taught concerning a certain question, and this he knows through oral tradition, which was later written down in the Mishnah. His own insight begins to play a role only during the interpretation and elaboration of this tradition. The idea behind this is the conviction that the fathers know better than we do because they were closer to the source. This source is the Oral Torah, which—as the scholars told us—was given by God to Moses at Mount Sinai, in addition to the Written Torah (the five books of Moses). This Oral Torah contains the authentic interpretation of the Written Torah; tradition tells us that Moses passed it on to Joshua, Joshua to the elders of Israel, and so on.

Orthodox Jews believe that this "traditioning" (passing on) of the Oral Torah was done so accurately that the Mishnah (see next section) is entirely or largely the written record of this oral teaching. Liberal[48] Jews greatly respect Jewish tradition, but view the Mishnah as only one possible, though from a historical perspective, certainly a very important interpretation of the Torah. In this case, the liberal view is more appealing than to orthodox view. On the one hand, some Jewish traditions go all the way back to their Sinaitic beginnings; on the other hand, in the Mishnah we find various differences of rabbinic opinion, about which more authorities have struggled throughout the centuries to determine who of the fathers was closer to the truth.

For centuries it had been strictly forbidden to record the Oral Torah in writing; it had to be handed down in orally. The reason for this was simple: if the LORD had given the Oral Torah in an oral form, in addition to the Written Torah, how could the later Torah scholars imagine themselves to be wiser than God, and put this tradition in written form? Had this been God's intention, he himself would have given it in written form. However, after the AD 70 (the fall of Jerusalem), and especially after AD 135 (the crushing of the uprising under Bar Kochba), the situation changed drastically.

First, the material to be handed down had become so vast that it could no longer be memorized and supervised by individuals.

Second, the Jews were more and more dispersed over large distances; the danger existed that quite different "Jewish traditions" would develop, say, in the West and in the East.

---

48. "Liberal" must not be confused with "liberal" Christianity, which has removed itself much farther away from biblical teaching. In a sense, when it comes to one's attitude toward "tradition," liberal Judaism is related to orthodox Judaism more or less as orthodox Protestant thought is related to orthodox Roman Catholic thought.

Third, the events around the years 70 and 135 had shown how vulnerable the Jewish people were; only a few pupils of Rabbi Aqiva[49] who had survived the massacre would have been able to pass on the Oral Torah. Imagine what the situation would have been if they had been massacred, too! No, in the end it became inescapable that the Oral Torah was recorded in a written form. What for more than thousand years had not been necessary now became inevitable. Scholars were convinced that Adonai would understand and accept this. The result was the *Mishnah*, a word derived from the root *sh-n-h*, "to study by repetition."[50]

2.6 The Mishnah
2.6.1 *Zugot* and *Tannaim*

The *Mishnah* is the first major written documentation of the Jewish oral traditions, and thus also the first major work of rabbinic literature. It records about seven centuries of oral tradition: from about 500 BC until about AD 200. Early compendia were the Mishnah of Rabbi Aqiva and the Mishnah of his pupil, Rabbi Meir. It was only around 200 that the (provisionally) definitive Mishnah, composed by Rabbi Yehudah haNasi ("Judah the Prince"), was produced, which was eventually called *the* Mishnah.

From the beginning, there have been debates about the relationship between the divine and the human in the Mishnah. Is this book really a reflection of some Oral Torah that God gave to Moses at Mount Sinai? Or does the book contain human, and thus fallible interpretations of the written Torah? Rabbi Yeshuah (Jesus) clearly belonged to the critics of the oral traditions. In his day, he warned against the "traditions of our (fore)fathers."[51] This was *not* because he had anything against traditions as such (cf. Matt. 23:3a; Acts 28:17; Gal. 2:19); recall how his followers spoke of the traditions *they* had handed down to *their* followers (1 Cor. 11:2; 2 Thess.

---

49. Regarding this important figure, see Ouweneel (2014a, 159–62).
50. Cf. the related word *shanah* (known from *Rosh haShanah*), which means "year," literally something that repeats (renews, duplicates) itself.
51. See especially Matt. 5:17–48; 15:1–20; 23:1–33; Mark 7:1–13.

3:6). No, Jesus was warning against *wrong* traditions, namely, those that violate the spirit of Torah, either by diluting it or by constraining it (always to the advantage of those who acted this way). Jesus also saw the danger of legalism, ritualism, and hypocrisy in the way certain traditions were absolutized. Interestingly, part of his criticism is also found in the Talmud, for instance, where the Talmud describes seven types of Pharisees: the five hypocritical kinds, and the two sincere ones.[52]

The Mishnah contains especially these two methods of rabbinic investigation (derivation from the Torah):

(a) The *casuistic-juridical* method, starting from legal-ethical questions, not from Bible passages (cf. [b]). This approach is called *halakhah*, a word derived from the Hebrew root *h-l-kh*, "to go, to walk." The term refers to the "way" along which a person is walking, their "way of life."[53] Halakhic teaching refers to the way the Mosaic laws must be interpreted, that is, must be put into practice. Halakhah is the answer to the continual Jewish question, "What must I do in this particular situation, and in what way does Adonai wish me to do it?"

(b) The *homiletic* method, identified by a Hebrew word referred to as *aggadah* or *haggadah*, usually derived from the root *n-g-d*, "to declare, make known, expound." Later, this was better known as *midrash*, a term largely overlapping with *(h) aggadah*, and partly with *halakhah*. Midrash is derived from the root *d-r-sh*, "to seek, examine, inquire." This category contains stories, legends, fables, and parables with an educational meaning.[54] The word *midrash* is found in the Tanakh in 2 Chronicles 13:22; 24:27, and rendered, for instance, as "com-

---

52. Talmud: Sotah 22b; hypocritical Pharisees, e.g., those who have bloody heads because they walk with their heads down in order not to watch women—and consequently bump into walls. Sincere Pharisees are those who act out of love to God, or out of fear toward God.
53. As we saw, the movement of the Jesus-believing Jews was described as "the Way" (Acts 9:2; 18:25–26; 19:9, 23; 24:14, 22)—a similar idea. What matters is not the knowledge in your head, but the way along which you walk.
54. Cf. the fables in the Tanakh: Judg. 9:7–15; 2 Sam. 12:1–6; 2 Kings 14:9 (2 Chron. 25:18), but also the many parables of Jesus in the New Testament Gospels.

mentary," "treatise," or "story" of a certain prophet or book. In *(h)aggadah* and *midrash,* the Tanakh is not interpreted in a grammatical-historical manner, but applied, more or less as this occurs in Christian allegories and typology, but also in sermons (homiletics is [the scholarly study of] the art of preaching). In both cases, such application sometimes occurs in a very free and fanciful manner (cf. §1.4.1).

The Mishnah contains references to, and quotations from, dozens of sages (i.e., Torah scholars). The oldest mentioned are, as said before, the *Zugot* (lit., "pairs," like Rabbi Hillel and Rabbi Shammai). Then there are the so-called *tannaim* ("teachers"), like Rabbi Gamaliel I (the teacher of Rabbi Shaul, the later apostle Paul, Acts 22:3), Rabbi Jochanan ben Zakkai (the man who arranged with the Romans to continue the Pharisaic school after the fall of Jerusalem), the severe Rabbi Gamaliel II (grandson of Gamaliel I), who was the *nasi* ("prince," here: chairman of the Sanhedrin or Jewish Council) at Jamnia. Under him, we find the famous Rabbi Aqiva, and Rabbi Shimon (son of Gamaliel II), *nasi* at Usha (near Akko). Under him, we find Rabbi Meir, Rabbi Shimon bar Jochai, and Rabbi Yehudah haNasi (Judah the Prince).[55]

The Mishnah contains six parts, which contain a total of sixty-three so-called "tracts" (treatises, chapters); these are:

(1) *Zeraim* ("seeds"): regulations concerning prayers, blessings, and tithes, and many agricultural laws;

(2) *Mo'ēd* ("appointed [time]"): regulations concerning the Sabbath and the Jewish festival times;

(3) *Nashim* ("women"): regulations concerning marriage and divorce;

(4) *N'ziqin* ("damages, offenses"): regulations concerning civil and criminal justice;

(5) *Kod'shim* ("holy things, sacred matters"): regulations concerning sacrifices and worship ministry;[56]

---

55. All these rabbis are discussed in Ouweneel (2014a: see the Index of Persons).
56. After AD 70, most of these cannot be practiced because there is no temple, yet formally every Jew is still "under" them, "bound" to them.

(6) *Toharot* ("purities, clean matters"): regulations concerning cultic cleanness and uncleanness.

2.6.2 The Babylonian Yeshivas

One pupil of Rabbi Judah the Prince was the well-known Rabbi Abba Arikha, called Rav for short; he became the founder of the yeshiva in the Babylonian city of Sura. Almost as authoritative was another pupil of Rabbi Judah the Prince: Samuel (Sh'mu'el) of Nehardea, known as Mar Samuel ("Mar" is a title comparable to that of Rav or Rabbi[57]). He was not only a Torah scholar and a judge, but also a physician and an astronomer. Rav was a transitional figure between the *Tannaim* (along with the *Zugot*, these were the oldest rabbis quoted in the Mishnah) and the *Amoraim* (the earliest rabbis after the composition of the Mishnah). Mar Samuel was the main figure among the actual *Amoraim* (lit., the "speaking ones," those speaking on the teachings of the Mishnah).

Mar Samuel was born in Babylonian Nehardia and made the yeshiva there prosper and flourish. Promising young Torah students in Babylon no longer needed to go to the Holy Land for their studies. On the contrary, the yeshivas in Sura and Nehardia (today this is Falluja in Iraq), and later the ones in Pumbedita (not far from Nehardia) and Machuza, eventually became far more famous than the Palestinian[58] ones. This explains why the Babylonian *Gemarah*,[59] the ancient rabbinic commentary on the Mishnah, is much more prestigious than the Palestinian or Jerusalem *Gemarah*. Mishnah and Gemarah together constitute what today is called the *Talmud*.[60] In other words, the so-called Babylonian Talmud has much more authority than the so-called Palestinian or Jerusalem Talmud. When Jews speak of "the" Talmud, they

---

57. Cf. *Maran* (= "our Lord") in *Maranatha*, i.e., "Our Lord is coming," *or* "Our Lord, come!" (1 Cor. 16:22).
58. The term "Palestinian" is the Roman name for everything about the Holy Land; even the Jews who had returned to the Holy Land in the beginning of the twentieth century were called "Palestinians." The appellation has nothing to do with those Arabs who call themselves "Palestinians" today.
59. The term comes from the root *g-m-r*, "to finish, complete."
60. The term comes from the root *l-m-d*, "to learn" or "to study."

invariably mean the Babylonian Talmud (Heb. *Talmud Bavli*).

After the death of Rav, Nehardea became the most important yeshiva, and Mar Samuel the most influential Torah scholar. Even the most important Palestinian Torah sage of that moment, Rabbi Jochanan bar Nappachah (or, Naphchah) (i.e., "son of the smith"), also a (very young) pupil of the then old Judah the Prince, acknowledged Mar Samuel as his superior. Conversely, after Mar Samuel had passed away, this Rabbi Jochanan was considered to be the greatest Torah scholar of his time, also by the Babylonian Jews. He was the founder of the important yeshiva in the Palestinian city of Tiberias, at the Sea of Galilee. Just as Rav and Mar Samuel laid the foundation for the Babylonian Gemarah, so Rabbi Jochanan laid the foundation of the Palestinian Gemarah.

Among the Babylonian *Amoraim*, the rabbis who have contributed to the Babylonian Gemarah, eight generations of scholars are distinguished. Abba Arikha and Mar Samuel belonged to the first, and Rabbi Ravina II to the eighth generation. His actual name was Rav Avina bar Rav Huna (Rabbi Avina son of Rabbi Huna). He was also called Ravina ha'Acharon ("the last one").[61] This name hints at his peculiar role in Judaism: according to tradition, he was the rabbi who put the last touches to the Babylonian Gemarah, and thus to the Babylonian Talmud.

Ravina was a pupil of his uncle, Ravina I and of Rav Ashi, who had restored the yeshiva in Sura. Together, Ravina I and Rav Ashi had begun composing the Babylonian Gemarah. Ravina II, one of the successors of Rav Ashi as leader of the yeshivah in Sura, finished this work. He did so under difficult circumstances because fanatic Gentiles tried to violently force the Jews to work on a Sabbath or a feast day, and thus to desecrate this day.

The role of Ravina II did not imply that he finished the *written* edition of the Talmud. The so-called *Savoraim* ("reasoners"),[62] the scholars working after the (provisional) com-

---

61. Not to be confused with the *acharonim*; see the Vernacular in Ouweneel (2014a).
62. Ouweneel (2014a, Excursus 21).

pletion of the Gemarah, still did editorial work on it for centuries. Thus, there has been much discussion about the question how large the contribution of Rav Ashi and Ravina II might have been exactly.

Rav Jose (also called Rabba Jose, Rava Jossi, or Rav Joseph, not to be confused with Rabbi Jose ben Halafta of the second century) is considered to have been the first of the *Savoraim*. He was the head of the yeshivah in Pumbedita of 476. He too must have played an important role in establishing the final version of the Babylonian Gemarah.

2.7 The Talmud

2.7.1 More on the Gemarah

The Jewish community in Babylonia was headed by an *exilarch* or *Resh Galuta*, the Greek and Hebrew terms for "head of the exiles." This person descended from the ancient dynasty of King David, and in the eleventh century was still honored as a kind of viceroy, also by the Persian rulers. A remarkable fact! Ezekiel tells us about a "prince" or "ruler" (Heb. *nasi*)[63] who, during the Messianic kingdom, will rule in Israel.[64] Those who take the Israel prophecies literally generally assume that this will be an earthly, Davidic prince who, as a mortal man, will be the earthly representative of the glorified Messiah in heaven.[65] In view of this future reality, it is of interest that in the Middle Ages people identified such a royal lineage from the house of David. And thus, presumably also today.[66]

During those centuries, Babylonia—modern Iraq—has ex-

---

63. He will not be called *melekh*, "king," for this title is reserved for the Messiah himself.
64. Ezek. 44:3; 45:7–9, 16–17, 22; 46:2, 4, 8, 10, 12, 16–18, 21–22.
65. See, e.g., Grant (1931, ad loc.); Gaebelein (1972, ad loc.).
66. The great Rabbi Isaac Abravanel (or Abarbanel) claimed to be a descendant of King David, and had many descendants until the present time (e.g., the Russian writer Boris Pasternak, d. 1960), who thus are David's descendants as well; see https://en.wikipedia.org/wiki/Abravanel. The great Rashi also had thousands of descendants, extending to today, being himself a descendant of Rabbi Hillel the Elder, whose mother was a descendant of Shephatiah, one of David's sons (2 Sam. 3:4), a half-brother of King Solomon.

perienced a richly flourishing Jewish life, especially in Sura, located east of the Euphrates, not far from the modern city of Kufah. For centuries in the Jewish communities in Sura, Pumbedita, and Nehardea, rabbinic debates occurred concerning the interpretation and bearing of the Mishnah. As we saw, the Gemarah was the written documentation of these debates. While the Mishnah was the practical commentary on the Torah, the Gemarah was the practical commentary on the Mishnah; after the completion of the Gemarah, throughout many subsequent centuries practical commentaries on the Gemarah were produced, some of them in a written form. And after this, written commentaries appeared in which these commentaries were debated. This development of sources resembles an onion with layer after layer. On the one hand, veneration for the Talmud is enormous. On the other hand, infinitely *debating* the Talmud, in an oral or a written form, will continue until the Messiah comes.

As we have seen, the Babylonian-Jewish and the Palestinian-Jewish communities each produced their own Gemarah, of which the former was to gain far more respect than the latter. What is decisive is not the *country*—although the Holy Land is infinitely more elevated than pagan Babylonia—but the prestige and the authority of the rabbis involved.

(a) The *Talmud Bavli* ("Babylonian Talmud") is the one and only Mishnah plus the Babylonian Gemarah; it was completed around the year 500. This work, containing many volumes, was written in a Syriac-related Aramaic and rabbinic Hebrew. It offers the reader comments on thirty-seven of the sixty-three Mishnah tracts.

(b) The *Talmud Yerushalmi* ("Jerusalem Talmud," also called "Palestinian Talmud") is the one and only Mishnah plus the Palestinian Gemarah. It was written in the Palestinian variant of Aramaic, and was completed around the year 425. It offers the reader comments on thirty-nine of the sixty-three Mishnah tracts.

Amazingly, the composition of the Gemarah took so many centuries but only a few more than half of the Mishnah tracts were dealt with. One of the most famous Mishnah tracts on which there is no Gemarah is the tract (Pirkē) Aboth ("Fathers," that is, "Chapters of the Jewish Fathers").

2.7.2 The Status of the Talmud

In the Talmud, the discussions of the rabbis have often been noted down in great detail, which of course is of great historical importance in order to understand the development of Talmudic thinking. These extensive reports help us understand that "the opinion of the Talmud" rarely exists, because we often find an entire array of opinions side by side. It is necessary to study Mishnah and Gemarah in their entirety, to become steeped in the Talmud, in order to establish the main lines and the consensus, of Talmudic teaching. This explains why the study of the Talmud demands an enormous amount of time and patience. Unfortunately, many Christians have shown little understanding of this basic fact. Some of them have quoted one single rabbinic opinion as a way to ridicule the entire Talmud. Such a foolish attitude testifies to shallow insight into the matter, and little respect for such a monument of wisdom as the Talmud. Many villainous attacks of the Talmud from so-called "Christians" have found their origins in this misunderstanding.[67]

Clearly, the status of the Talmud is enormous. No one can pretend to understand post-New Testament Judaism without some knowledge of the Talmud and the process that led to its origins.[68] To judge medieval and modern Judaism by what we know—or think we know—from the New Testament is unfair. The study of the Talmud and the practice of its rules of life form the foundation of all (orthodox) Jewish life to this very day.

The Talmud is important for Christian theology and Christian ecumenism as well, because this multi-volume work sheds light on many different aspects of the Tanakh,

---

67. Sometimes Christians are as bad at listening as Jews; Talmud tract Aboth V.15 distinguishes four types of hearers: the sponge (absorbing everything, good and bad), the funnel (letting everything pass through, good and bad), the strainer (letting out the wine, retaining the dregs), and the fan (letting out the chaff, retaining the fine flour).
68. A well-known annotated edition in the English language is Epstein (1978).

as well as on the developmental history of Judaism since the completion of the canon of the Tanakh,[69] and on the study of relationships between Jews and Christians throughout the ages.

(Ultra-)orthodox Jews declare the Talmud to be sacred, and they attempt to erase from it all (apparent) contradictions and to canonize all its judicial opinions. Less orthodox Jews believe that the Talmud is there to be *investigated*, not to be accepted and followed in every detail. In this view, the Talmud offers an ancient, prestigious, and morally authoritative interpretation of the Torah, which is nevertheless not formally binding in all respects for all Jews of all times. To put it in Christian terms, the Talmud was not inspired in the sense of 2 Timothy 3:16-17, as the Tanakh is: "All Scripture is breathed out by God and profitable for teaching, for reproof, for correction, and for training in righteousness, that the man of God may be complete, equipped for every good work."

As Christians we might compare the Talmud with the writings of the Apostolic Fathers (Clement of Rome, Ignatius of Antioch, Polycarp, Papias of Hierapolis) and of early church fathers (Greek: Justin Martyr, Irenaeus, Athanasius; Latin: Tertullian). These writings are highly revered and are extensively studied—but they are not Scripture. In our modest opinion, they may even deviate from Scripture here and there. Just as in the case of the Talmud, they must be *investigated*, but they must not be believingly accepted and followed in every detail. To be sure, both the orthodox Jew and the orthodox Christian must have very good reasons to deviate from what their respective "fathers" have taught—but ultimately only Scripture and our faithful understanding of it is divinely authoritative. There is no Judaism without the Talmud, just as there is no serious Christian theology without a thorough knowledge of the early church fathers.

According to our modern Western sensitivities, there are

---

69. Good introductions are Neusner (2003) and Steinsaltz (2009); from a Christian perspective, Strack (1945) is still authoritative; cf. also Strack and Billerbeck (1922–1928).

too many tasteless sophisticated exaggerations in the rabbinic debates, but these were already criticized by Jews themselves in those days. Heavy *halakhic* (judicial) discussions alternate in the Talmud with *(h)aggada* (stories, fables, parables, etc.). The result is a seemingly chaotic encyclopedia or treasury, the precipitate of seven centuries of Judaism in one multi-volume work. In these volumes, more than one thousand rabbis express their views, debating among themselves issues that are religious, judicial, scientific, medical, astronomical, and educational in nature. Thereby the *entire* public and private lives of the Jews are discussed and debated from an orthodox religious viewpoint. The Talmud is a cultural monument, and for that reason alone educated Christians find that it possesses great historical importance.

Naturally, the completion of the Gemarah did not mean an end for rabbinic discussions. Just as the *Amoraim* commented upon the views of the *Tannaim*, new generations arose that subsequently discussed the views of the *Amoraim*. The early generations of rabbis that arose after the completion of the Gemarah are called *Savoraim*. These scholars lived between 500 and 700 and added material that ultimately became part of the Talmud we have today. Thus, if the rabbinic tradition began with Ezra, the entire history of the Talmud's development encompasses no less than about twelve hundred years.[70] This time span exceeds the nearly one thousand years[71] between Moses and Malachi, the period in which the Tanakh must have originated. (Compare the origin of the New Testament, which probably occurred within half a century, and according to some, within a few decades.)

2.8 The Talmud on Jesus and the Christians
2.8.1 Rumors and Lies on Both Sides

The debate between Jews and Christians is governed by the vital issue of what the two Talmudim say about Jesus, about

---

70. The process of the actual writing took "only" three hundred years, between about 200 and about 500, and five hundred years between 200 and 700.
71. This number accords with traditional chronology; modern chronology stipulates about eight hundred years.

his mother Mary, and about the Christians. Three matters complicate this issue.

(1) In the past, Christian authorities have occasionally forced the Jews to produce censured editions of the Talmud, in which true or alleged statements about Jesus and Mary were omitted. Later, it was often difficult to establish the original text of the Talmud, and thus which statements about Jesus and Mary were authentic.

(2) Another difficulty involves determining which statements in the Talmud really deal with Jesus and Mary, or have been misunderstood in this respect. The minimalists claim that there are very few statements about Jesus and Mary, whereas the maximalists say there are many. Since the thirteenth century, and especially since the seventeenth century, many publications have appeared, often written by Christianized Jews, discussing the allegedly negative statements in the Talmud about Jesus and Mary. In the twentieth century for the first time, more objective scientific studies on this matter appeared.[72]

(3) It is unclear whether the passages alleged to be about Jesus are speaking about the historical Jesus, or are simply reflecting on Christian testimony about him, or are merely presenting rumors that the rabbis had heard about him. We should not forget that during the first centuries of the present era the Babylonian Jews lived far away from the Holy Land; any stories they might have heard about the ministry and the death of Rabbi Yeshuah (Jesus) and the "Nazarenes" (the early Jesus-believing Jews) were at best distorted.

In rabbinic literature, Jesus is referred to as Yeshu—as modern Israelis do—but it is quite certain that many persons identified by the name Yeshu do not refer to the New Testament Jesus. An important example is Yeshu ben Pandera or Panthera, someone named Yeshu who was the son of a Roman soldier of this name. Some have suggested that this Pandera had an illegitimate relationship with Mary, the mother of Jesus. However, others have argued that this man is de-

---

72. Krauss (1902); Schäfer (2007).

scribed as having spoken with Rabbi Aqiva shortly before the latter's martyrdom (AD 135). This is about hundred years after Jesus' death. We have the same problem with expressions such as *oto ish* ("that man"),[73] or *peloni* ("So-and-so"),[74] or *naggar bar naggar* (the "carpenter son of a carpenter"), or *ben charsh etaim* ("son of a/the wood worker"), or *talui* (the "hanged one"). In many cases, it is doubtful whether these expressions refer to Jesus. He is described as a Torah teacher with five disciples, as a healer, as a wizard (because of the miracles he did), as having been hung during *Pesach*, and as burning in hell.[75] With regard to his supposed magic, Jesus' question to the Pharisees is of interest: "[I]f I cast out demons by Beelzebul, by whom do your sons cast them out? Therefore they will be your judges" (Matt. 12:27).

All the alleged evidence taken together is very meager. In fact, it is an ancient misunderstanding, even an outright false accusation, that Jesus and Christianity are fiercely attacked in the Talmud. The meager anecdotal material, if it refers to Jesus and the Christians, could be simply understood to arise from Jewish rejection of Jesus as their Messiah. But there is hardly any direct confrontation with Christianity, since the Babylonian Jews knew far too little about it.

We do hear, though, of disputes in rabbinic literature that especially Rabbi Gamaliel II would have had with the *minim* ("heretics," lit., "kinds," as *min* in Gen. 1), or "philosophers."[76] Some believe that these designations refer especially to the Christians, others that they refer to the Sadducees, or the Gnostics, or the Karaites (Jews who rejected the Oral Torah), or other heretical Jewish movements. Again, there is far too little basis for the claim that these disputes are evidence of the hatred of the Jews toward the Christians.

---

73. E.g., Aboda Zarah 6a.
74. E.g., Chagigah 4a.
75. In boiling hot feces: Gittin 56b–57a (uncensored version); see further especially Sanhedrin 43a, 43b, 67a, 103a, 107b, Aboda Zarah 6a, 17a, 27b, Chagigah 4b, Shabbat 104b; Tosefta: Chullin II.22–24.
76. Yebamoth 102b; Midrash Psalms on Ps. 10; Exod. Rabbah 30.

In their criticism of Jesus and the Christians, the rabbis were never harsher and more unreasonable than the Christians were in their criticism concerning the Jews and the Talmud—but often no less harsh or unreasonable, either. What is more absurd: the assertion that Jesus (the Righteous One, as even his enemies had to admit![77]) was sent to hell to lie there eternally in boiling feces, or the insinuation that Jews, who are not allowed to eat any form of blood,[78] for the preparation of *matzes* (*matzot*, unleavened loaves) would use the blood of ritually murdered Christian boys (see §7.3.1)? This ridiculous myth is still being spread today by Muslim propagandists, but the lie was invented long ago by "Christians." What a shame, all those lies, all those fairy tales that Jews and Christians have told about each other throughout the centuries.

2.8.2 "Brothers" and "Life Forevermore"

For a long time, the relationships between Jews and Christians seemed to share this destiny: Jews would continue to live with absurd ideas about Jesus and Christianity, and Christians with absurd ideas about Jews, Judaism, and the Talmud. The Jew and the Christian are like two brothers in a family, who sometimes have violent arguments with each other, yet always remain brothers. Alas, since Cain and Abel, fratricide—one brother murdering the other—belongs to the primordial sins of humanity. Both parties, Jews and Christians, have made themselves guilty of this, though Christians far more than Jews, if only because of their enormous advantage in number.

In this context, Psalm 133 is quite remarkable. It is a pilgrimage song (Heb. *shir hama'aloth*, lit., "song of ascents," viz., song sung when going up to Jerusalem), one of the fifteen (and possibly more) such songs (Ps. 120–134) that the Israelites sang as they went up to the temple in Jerusalem for the three pilgrimage feasts (Heb. *shalosh r'galim*). All these

---

77. Cf. some modern testimonies: Boteach (2012); Moffic (2016).
78. Gen. 9:4; Lev. 3:17; 7:26–27; 17:10, 14; 19:26; Deut. 12:16, 23; 15:23; cf. 1 Sam. 14:33; Ezek. 33:25.

psalms also have a profound prophetic meaning referring to Israel's return to Jerusalem in the end times, and the Messianic kingdom. Psalm 133 reads as follows:

> Behold, how good and pleasant it is
>   when brothers dwell in unity!
> It is like the precious oil on the head,
>   running down on the beard,
> on the beard of Aaron,
>   running down on the collar of his robes!
>
> It is like the dew of Hermon,
>   which falls on the mountains of Zion!
> For there the Lord has commanded the blessing,
>   life forevermore.

The latter expression, "life forevermore" or "everlasting life" (Heb. *chayyim 'ad ha-'olam*) underscores the prophetic significance of the psalm: this is the "everlasting" life that the orthodox Jew longs to receive, or to enter, one day; as Jesus said,

> [T]here is no one who has left house or brothers or sisters or mother or father or children or lands, for my sake and for the gospel, who will not receive a hundredfold now in this time, houses and brothers and sisters and mothers and children and lands, with persecutions, and *in the age to come eternal life*.[79]

This life of the "age to come" is the life of the Messianic kingdom, as Jesus said, "'Come, you who are blessed by my Father, inherit the *kingdom* prepared for you from the foundation of the world'. . . . And these [i.e., the wicked] will go away into eternal punishment, but the righteous into *eternal life*" (Matt. 25:34, 46).

2.8.3 "Brothers" in Genesis

In the Bible, the book of Genesis is *the* book about the relationships between brothers: between Cain and Abel (Gen. 4),

---

79. Mark 10:29–30; cf. v. 17; Matt. 19:16, 29; 25:46; Luke 10:25; 18:18, 30; Dan. 12:2.

between the sons of Noah (Gen. 9), between the sons of Terah (Gen. 11), between Abraham and Lot,[80] between Isaac and Ishmael, between Jacob and Esau, and between Joseph and his brothers. Some of these brotherly relationships are very sad—but three of them are restored in the Messianic kingdom, namely, the last three just mentioned.

(a) *Isaac and Ishmael.* According to the view of Muslims, "Ishmael" represents the Arab desert tribes (cf. Gen. 21:20-21; 25:12-18), and thus the world of the Islam (see more extensively chapter 10). Although Muslims have often treated the Jews better than Christians did—think of medieval Spain!—the tension between Jews and Muslims today is extremely threatening. However, in the Messianic kingdom, these brothers will "dwell together in harmony"; this was illustrated in the harmonious way in which Isaac and Ishmael together buried their father Abraham (Gen. 25:9-10). The only condition will be that both these Jews and these Muslims will bow together before the God of Israel, the Messiah of Israel, and submit to the book of Israel.

Philosemitic Christians, who see a future only for the Jews in the Promised land, but not for Palestinians, need to be reminded of Ezekiel 47:21-23:

> "So you shall divide this land among you according to the tribes of Israel. You shall allot it as an inheritance for yourselves *and for the sojourners who reside among you* and have had children among you. They shall be to you as native-born children of Israel. With you *they shall be allotted an inheritance* among the tribes of Israel. In whatever tribe the sojourner resides, there you shall assign him his inheritance," declares the Lord God.

There is a future for the Palestinians in the land of Israel—but a future very different from what many Israelis, Palestinians (also Christian Palestinians[81]), and global politicians seem to be able to imagine.

---

80. These are in fact uncle and nephew, yet they are called "brothers": Abram said to Lot, "There should be no arguing between you and me, or between your herdsmen and mine, because we are brothers" (Gen. 13:8 NCV).
81. Cf. Kant (2015).

(b) *Jacob and Esau*. As we explained in the first volume of our Israelology, in the rabbinic tradition, Esau—that is, Edom—represents the Roman Empire, which since the fourth century was the Christian Roman Empire, or, in the broader sense, Christianity.[82] The tensions between Jacob and Esau began when they were very young boys, just as the tensions between Jews and Christians began early after the beginning of the first century. For a long time, Esau constituted a threat for Jacob, but fortunately there was reconciliation (Gen. 33). Yet, they kept going their separate ways, as Jacob put it: "Let my lord [i.e., Esau] pass on ahead of his servant [i.e., Jacob], and I will lead on slowly, at the pace of the livestock that are ahead of me and at the pace of the children, until I come to my lord in Seir" (Gen. 33:14). Rashi said of this that Jacob and Esau will meet each other in Seir only when Obadiah's prophecy is fulfilled: "Saviors shall go up to Mount Zion / to rule Mount Esau [or, mount of Esau, i.e., Seir], / and the kingdom shall be the LORD's" (21; see §3.3.4).

This will become true in the Messianic kingdom. Then, Jews and Christians will meet each other in the one God, and in the one Messiah, and in the one book. *Both* will have to be purified to this end: Jacob (cf. Zech. 13:8-9) and Esau (cf. Isa. 34 and 63). At that time, the blind spot of "Jacob" will be healed, viz., Jesus. And then, the blind spot of "Esau" will be healed, viz., Israel.

(c) *Joseph and his brothers*. Jacob's sons brought a lot of evil upon their brother Joseph, just as the Israelites brought a lot of evil upon their brother Jesus. Both delivered their brother over to the pagans (cf. Matt. 20:19; Acts 2:23). Without the brothers being aware of this, Joseph became the viceroy of Egypt, and without the Jews being aware of this, Jesus was glorified at God's right hand, and to him was given all power in heaven and on earth (Matt. 28:18). However, in the end, Joseph made himself known to his brothers (Gen. 45), and in the end, Jesus will make himself known to his brothers, namely, at his second coming: "I will pour out on the house of David and the inhabitants of Jerusalem a spirit of grace

---

82. See extensively, Ouweneel (2003, §4.2).

and pleas for mercy, so that, when they look on me, on him whom they have pierced, they shall mourn for him, as one mourns for an only child, and weep bitterly over him, as one weeps over a firstborn" (Zech. 12:10; cf. Rev. 1:7).

However, just as in the case of Joseph and his brothers, this lamentation will become a song of joy, when the brothers humble themselves before their Messiah, and when it becomes manifest that Jesus will forgive them. Then, Jesus will express the truth that Joseph expressed earlier to his brothers: "[D]o not be distressed or angry with yourselves because you sold me here, for God sent me before you to preserve life. . . . God sent me before you to preserve for you a remnant on earth, and to keep alive for you many survivors" (Gen. 45:5, 7). "Do not fear, for am I in the place of God? As for you, you meant evil against me, but God meant it for good, to bring it about that many people should be kept alive, as they are today" (50:19–20). These are statements with a profound Christological as well as redemptive-historical as well as prophetic significance.

Chapter 3
Historical Supersessionism and Historical Judaism

See, LORD, and raise up for them their king, the son of David, to rule over Israel, your servant, in the time which you chose, o God, undergird him with the strength to destroy the unrighteous rulers, to cleanse Jerusalem from gentiles who trample her to destruction. . . . He will distribute them [i.e., the Israelites] in their tribes upon the land. . . . And he will have gentile nations serving him under his yoke and he will glorify the LORD in [a place] visible [from] the whole earth. And he will cleanse Jerusalem to [reach] a sanctification as [she has] from the beginning so that nations will come from the ends of the earth to see his glory, bringing as gifts her children who had become quite weak, and to see the glory of the LORD with which God has glorified her. . . . This is the beauty of the king of Israel whom God knew, to raise him over the house of Israel to discipline it. . . . Blessed are those born in those days to see the good things for Israel which God will cause to happen in the assembly of the tribes. May God hurry up his mercy over Israel; may he deliver us from the impurity of

> *unhallowed enemies. The* LORD *himself is our king forever hereafter.*
>
> Psalms of Solomon
17:21–22, 28, 30–31, 42, 44-46

3.1 Historical Background

3.1.1 The Chasm Opens

IF SUPERSESSIONISM LACKS A firm biblical basis, how could it have come to development during church history? The answer must not be sought in the exegesis of the Tanakh and the New Testament, nor in systematic theology. It seems clear that no unbiased Bible exegesis—if such a thing exists at all—would ever have produced any form of replacement theology. This means that the answer to our question must lie exclusively in church history.

It is my thesis that supersessionism finds its roots first in anti-Judaism, and later in anti-Semitism, which we find rising already during the first centuries of church history. Anti-Judaism is a rejection of the Jewish religion as it developed in the post-New Testament era, and anti-Semitism is a rejection of "the" Jew as such. Before continuing, I declare emphatically that I am *not* asserting that every modern supersessionist is an anti-Semite. But I am claiming that the roots of supersessionism lie in early Christian anti-Judaism and anti-Semitism, even if many modern supersessionists are perhaps unaware of this. Let us therefore begin by looking at some historical facts.

In the first century of the present era, Judaism unfortunately split into a faction that followed Jesus of Nazareth as its Messiah, Savior, and Lord, and a faction that believed following Jesus would betray the core and essence of Judaism, namely, keeping the Torah.[1] *They thought it was either Jesus or the Torah.* This was, and is, a serious and deeply tragic misunderstanding, existing still today, which the early Christians strongly helped to foster: if you wish to follow Jesus, which

---

1. Cf. Rubenstein and Roth (1987, 31–45).

means, join "our" church, you must surrender "your" Mosaic Torah. In earlier chapters we have seen what a gross error this was, on the part of both Jews and Christians. Jesus Christ is the very *telos* (sense, meaning, goal, fulfillment) of the Torah (Rom. 10:4). The "shadows" of the Torah have found their fulfillment in him who is its "substance": Jesus Christ (Col. 4:17). Just as Jesus is the true personification of Israel, so too he is the true embodiment of the Torah. Speaking of "shadows": "[S]ince the law has but a shadow of the good things to come instead of the true form of these realities, it can never, by the same sacrifices that are continually offered every year, make perfect those who draw near" (Heb. 10:1). The sacrificial laws are not obsolete, but rather are *fulfilled*, namely, in the one and only sacrifice of Jesus Christ (cf. vv. 5–10).

Those Jews who have accepted Christ have not done away with the Torah, but they do possess the Torah now in a sense much fuller and richer than those who have only the shadows. The Torah has been fulfilled—brought to its true fullness—by Christ, as he himself explained (Matt. 5:17). The *moral* dimension of the Torah has been elaborated in the "law of Christ" (Gal. 6:2; cf. 1 Cor. 9:21), and the *ceremonial* element—insofar as such a distinction can be made at all—is like a prophetic word that in Christ has become reality. Therefore, Jews need not and must not choose between Jesus and the Torah. Rather, they must *observe* the Torah—but they must choose between an unfulfilled Torah and a fulfilled Torah, between the "shadows" and the "substance." They must choose between a Torah with Jesus or a Torah without Jesus. But the idea of having to choose between the Torah and Jesus is, in my view, virtually a demonic falsehood, spread by Jews themselves, but especially by Christians. And perhaps, if Christians had never spread it, Jews might not ever have believed this false idea.

3.1.2 Initial Tolerance

After some argument within their constituency, the apostles of Jesus decided not to impose the Mosaic Torah on Gentile Jesus-believers (Acts 15; see §1.5). They did so specifically under the guidance of the Holy Spirit (Acts 15:28). But the Jews who had come to faith in Jesus, including the apostles, unashamedly continued to participate in the temple ministry and observe the ceremonial laws. Even Paul, the apostle to the Gentiles,[2] continued to observe the Mosaic Torah as best as he could.[3] After the fall of Jerusalem (AD 70), when the temple ministry ended, eventually not much remained of this Jewish type of Christianity. This process was enhanced by the growing pressure of Gentile Christians on Jewish converts to abandon the Mosaic Torah. In this way, the chasm was widened between "the Jews" (read: the 98% non-Jesus-believing Jews) and "the Christians" (read: the 99% non-Jewish Christians). This process was enhanced by the growing animosity between the two (see §1.6).

At first, the relationship between Judaism and Christianity was not necessarily strained; but it was ambivalent.[4] For instance, it is certainly remarkable to see how, during the period of the book of Acts, Jewish Jesus-believers in Palestine could confess and live their faith without being disturbed or criticized by both non-Jesus-believing Jews and Jesus-believing Gentiles. We find the ambivalence particularly among the Pharisees. We must remember that the apostle Paul had grown up as a Pharisee, and shared with the Pharisees their love for the entire Tanakh and their belief in the resurrection, as well as their loyalty to the ancestral traditions: "Brothers, I *am* [present tense!] a Pharisee, a son of Pharisees. It is with respect to the hope and the resurrection of the dead that I am on trial" (Acts 23:6).[5] The Pharisee Gamaliel I, Paul's own teacher, adopted a moderate attitude toward Jesus-confessing Jews (Acts 5:34-40; cf. 22:3). When Paul was interrogated by the Jewish Council, the Pharisees publicly sided with their former ally, and even considered the possibility that an angel spoke through him (Acts 23:6-9). Conversely, it was precisely the Jesus-confessing Pharisees who wished to force the

---

2. Rom. 1:5; 11:13; Gal. 2:7-8; 1 Tim. 2:7.
3. Acts 3:1; 9:20; 13:5, 14, 43; 14:1; 17:1, 10, 17; 18:4, 18-19, 26; 19:8; 20:16; 21:21-26; 24:27; 28:17; 1 Cor. 16:8.
4. See Ouweneel (2000a, §6.3.2).
5. Acts 23:6; cf. 22:3; 24:21; 26:5; 28:17; Gal. 1:14; Phil. 3:5-6.

Jesus-confessing Gentiles to become full-fledged proselytes (Acts 15:5).

Gradually, this—not all too generous—form of peaceful coexistence changed. With the rise of Christianity, the Jews could not see anything else than a threat of Israel's unique election, and they gradually assumed a more hostile attitude (cf. Acts 13:45-51; 14:1-15, 19). In spite of his great love for them (Rom. 9:2-3), the apostle Paul sometimes reproached the Jews quite sharply for this (1 Thess. 2:14-16). Conversely, in this matter (Gentile) Christians were not innocent either: it did not take long for many of them to develop a nasty anti-Semitism. This happened, first, because of their disappointment that the Jews had not accepted their Messiah. Second, many Christians developed the false idea that, at Calvary *all* the people of Israel had become guilty of the death of the Messiah. Third, Christians also developed the false idea that they themselves were the real "Jews," the true "Israel." Thereafter, the history of the relationship between Judaism and Christianity has mainly been one of continual misunderstanding, and often of hatred and envy. Even today, where things have changed so much for the better, it is shocking to find so many misconceptions on both sides.

3.1.3 Rising Anti-Semitism

Let us carefully realize what happened here. First, Israel was no longer allowed to exist in a *theological* sense, for the church claimed the title "Israel" entirely for herself. If the church is indeed the true "Israel," irritation about some other Israel claiming to be "Israel" could only increase. Throughout the centuries, this necessarily led to a steadily growing hatred toward Israel. If initially Israel was no longer allowed to exist in a *theological* sense, it was ultimately no longer allowed to exist in a *physical* sense, either. Let me give a shocking example: Adolf Hitler's anti-Semitism is historically inconceivable apart from the anti-Semitism of Martin Luther—especially in his two publications of 1543⁶—which would fester for centuries in the German mind.

However, Luther's anti-Semitism is historically inconceivable without the much older supersessionism of the (Roman Catholic) Middle Ages, and even before them. After the fourth century, this doctrine had conquered the Christian church, in particular through the great church father Augustine. Since its beginning, supersessionism was linked with anti-Semitism, to some extent in the case of Augustine himself, and much more strongly in the case of church fathers such as Chrysostom and Jerome (see the quotations above chapter 7).

It seems that only after the horrendous *Shoah* (or Holocaust)⁷ an essential change took place in this relationship. On the one hand, many Christians developed a much greater understanding of the essence of Judaism, of the disasters of Jewish history, and of the Jewish roots of Christianity. On the other hand, many Jews developed more interest in and understanding of the person of (the Jew) Jesus of Nazareth. In the French novel *The Last of the Just*, by A. Schwarz-Bart, Ernie Levy said this to his fiancée Golda about Christians:

> . . . I've been in their churches and I've read their gospel. Do you know who the Christ was? A simple Jew like your father. A kind of Hasid." . . . [H]e was really a good Jew, you know, sort of like the Baal Shem Tov⁸—a merciful man, and gentle. The Christians say they love him, but I think they hate him without knowing it. So they take the cross by the other end and make a sword out of it and strike us with it! . . .
>
> . . . Poor Jesus, if he came back to earth and saw that the pagans had made a sword out of him and used it against his sisters and brothers, he'd be sad, he'd grieve forever. . . . [H]e was a little

---

6. On the Jews and their Lies and Of the Unknowable Name and the Generations of Christ; see Falk (1992).
7. *Shoah* is a Heb. term meaning "ruin" (e.g., Isa. 10:3; 47:11); *holocaust*, a Gk. term meaning "burnt offering" ("that which is burned up entirely"; cf. *holokautōma* in Lev. 1, LXX); see §5.2.
8. Father of Hassidism, d. 1760; regarding him, see Ouweneel (2014a, 440–43).

old-fashioned Jew, a real Just Man, ...[9] [H]e and your father would have got along together. I can see them so well together, you know. "Now," your father would say, "now my good rabbi, doesn't it break your heart to see all that?" And the other would tug at his beard and say, "But you know very well, my good Samuel, that the Jewish heart must break a thousand times for the greater good of all peoples. That is why we were chosen, didn't you know?" And your father would say, "Oi, oi, didn't I know? Didn't I know? Oh, excellent rabbi, that's all I do know, alas. . . ."[10]

3.1.4 The "Guilt" of Israel

It is no easy task to acquire proper insight into the deepest roots of the hatred that, throughout the centuries, so many Christians, or rather, alleged Christians, harbored against the Jews. Was it the latter's strangeness, their being so different, so elusive? Was it what the grand vizier Haman told the Persian King Ahasuerus? "There is a certain people scattered abroad and dispersed among the peoples in all the provinces of your kingdom. Their laws are different from those of every other people, and they do not keep the king's laws, so that it is not to the king's profit to tolerate them" (Est. 3:8).

Is this essentially the same phenomenon as the three men who visited Job in his misery, and were called his "friends" (Job 2:11), yet who accused him so fiercely? Was this only because of their ideas about God ("if you suffer, you are apparently being punished, so you must have sinned"), or was there more to it? How is it possible that we sometimes even perceive undertones of real hatred toward Job, especially in chapters likes Job 20 and 22? When the "friends" are "theorizing" about him and his misery, they are searching for the causes of Job's sufferings. But what seems to lead them to hatred and disgust is that, in doing so, they *encounter Job's innocence.*

---

9. Cf. Matt. 27:19, 24; Acts 3:14; 7:52; 22:14; James 5:6 [?]; 1 Pet. 3:18; 1 John 2:1.
10. Schwarz-Bart (1985, 324); regarding this novel, see more in chapter 5 below.

This is the hatred that is born—not from the other's (non-existing) guilt but—from jealousy, as in the case of the hatred of Joseph's brothers: *the hatred of the guilty ones toward the innocent one.*

This is what the godless Jewish psychoanalyst Sigmund Freud has called "projection": projecting one's own negative features on an innocent victim. The attitude of "Christians" toward Jews throughout the centuries is perhaps explained in no better way than through this term "projection." In Jesus' day Jews projected their own guilt on Jesus, and throughout the centuries Gentiles have been projecting their own guilt on the Jews.

In her magnificent book on Job, the Jewish German writer Margarete Susman wrote that all hostility toward Israel is connected to the Jewish acceptance of the Torah.[11] The Jewish people are "mercilessly persecuted by the nations" both because, on the one hand, the Torah is perfect and because, on the other hand, Israel has failed with regard to the Torah. However, when we ask *why* the latter is so—since *no other* nation would have performed any better under the Torah—"we encounter the real root of the hatred toward Jews of all times." Israel is persecuted because it "stands over against the general guilt in a different way than all [other] nations," namely, "the way Job stands over against it." All other nations have "confirmed" (read: continued) their own guilt (of violent disobedience) time and again, always in the same ways. As distinct states, that is, as structures of power, they have "done their share in attack, self-defense, defending their borders against those of others," and in this way, "each in their own manner have given expression to the general guilt, which debouches in the hostility of all against all."

However, with Israel it is very different. It has remained faithful "to its origin in view of the goal of humanity that is not to be lost," Susman wrote. Therefore, although Israel was equally guilty with regard to the Torah, it has not "con-

---

11. Susman (1948, 90). Cf. Joseph (1929, 153): "By taking upon himself the yoke of the Law, Israel has been self-doomed to a life of trial." Israel at Mount Sinai promised three times that it would fulfill the Torah (Exod. 19:8; 24:3, 7).

firmed" (continued) this guilt through on-going violence: "Just as Job, it has rejected this guilt, and, in the formation of its reality, as a people it has directly submitted itself to the command of the Absolute, which from the beginning had been entrusted to this people."

Before the Babylonian exile, when Israel was not only a nation but also a nation state—in any pre-modern sense of the term—it behaved in many respects just like the other nations, and has been terribly punished for this. According to the spirit of the Torah, from the beginning Israel *in principle* declined all wars and all violence. But it was only during the Babylonian exile that this became concrete reality, for in this period Israel was not *able* to fight aggressive wars or defensive wars. It was *sinful* like other nations; but it did not make itself *guilty*, as did nations that possess a nation state structure.

There is tremendous tension here, because in later periods Israel resorted to the weapons many times: the Maccabees did so in their fight against the Syrian rulers (167–164 BC), and the Jewish rebels did so in their fight against the Roman rulers, with such low points as the Jewish War (66–70) and the resurgence of Bar Kochba (132–135) in the present era. And as far as the modern state of Israel is concerned, in some respects it is just as guilty as many other states (see extensively chapters 9–10 below).

However, during the Babylonian exile, and especially during the time after AD 70 (if we ignore Bar Kochba for a moment), Israel was *not* as guilty as the other nations, *and therefore, due to the projection mentioned, receives all the blame for everything that went wrong*. It does not practice violence, but itself must endure all the violence of the nations. Generally speaking, it endures this with passive patience, during the pogroms, all the way to the destruction camps of the Holocaust: Auschwitz, Sobibór, Majdanek. Why was this?

3.2 The Scapegoat
3.2.1 Substitution

Here we will encounter the mystery of substitution: the sacrifice vicariously dying for others.[12] The innocent one is hated by the guilty ones, but he is also the very one who bears the guilt of the guilty ones. This is true for the servant of the LORD in the book of Isaiah:

> Surely he has borne our griefs
> and carried our sorrows;
> yet we esteemed him stricken,
>   smitten by God, and afflicted.
> But he was pierced for our transgressions;
>   he was crushed for our iniquities; . . .
> like a lamb that is led to the slaughter,
>   and like a sheep that before its shearers is silent, . . .
> (Isa. 53:4-5, 7)

Here we find the picture of a lamb; in Leviticus 16:21-22 we find a description of the so-called "scapegoat":

> Aaron shall lay both his hands on the head of the live goat, and confess over it all the iniquities of the people of Israel, and all their transgressions, all their sins. And he shall put them on the head of the goat and send it away into the wilderness by the hand of a man who is in readiness. The goat shall bear all their iniquities on itself to a remote area, and he shall let the goat go free in the wilderness.

Both the servant-lamb and the goat are types of Christ as the true personification of Israel, but in a derivative sense they are also types of true Israel.[13] Of course, Israel does not and cannot *atone* for the sins of the nations, that is, blot them

---

12. See more extensively in chapter 5 below.
13. Rubenstein (1968, 110; cf. 121) argues that, at the heart of *Yom Kippur* lies the concept of the vicarious ritual atonement. But although this dogma touches the core of both the Day of Atonement and Christianity, it satisfies very few Jews. All too often, says Rubenstein, the Jewish community itself has been the vicarious victim, used by incited and mentally disturbed people as a magical sacrifice for their own guilt and mischief.

out before a holy and righteous God. Yet, Israel is a substitute in the sense that the term "scapegoat" has acquired in ordinary life: an innocent victim bearing the consequences of the wrongdoing of others. This scapegoat was the only innocent one among the people, yet all the guilt of the people was placed upon it (Lev. 16:21). During its *galut* (exile), Israel has been the great scapegoat of all the nations, in particular the "Christian" ones, as the innocent one charged with the terrible guilt of these nations. The servant—whether Israel or its Messiah—is both lamb and goat,[14] and thus has been the great burnt offering and sin offering for the world. In this sin offering, as Susman says, "the two forms of salvation in history breaking apart"—she means Christianity and Judaism—"are so intimately one"—namely, through the unity of Christ and Israel—"that they still seem to be enclosed by the same core."[15]

Only Christ is the true sin offering, which *blots out* the sins of those to whom the sacrifice applies. But in a derivative sense, both Israel and Christ are the lamb that is led to the slaughter, as well as the innocent scapegoat, which bears the sins of others, as if not these others but the goat itself had committed them. In the *galut*, Israel is lamb and goat, "without power, without a state, without weapons, without form or beauty, without an actually visible existence, weak, worthless: the human being [in its essence]."[16] Here, the *Ecce Homo*, "Behold, the man," or rather, "Behold, this is what the human being is" (John 19:5),[17] is projected upon the entire nation of Israel, of which Jesus is the true personification. Or, even stronger than "human being": "I am a worm and not a man, / scorned by mankind and despised by the people" (Ps. 22:6). This is the Messiah, but it is also Israel, "you worm Jacob, you maggot [MSG: fragile insect] Israel" (Isa. 41:14 NABRE). For

---

14. More precisely, the "lamb" is the male young (often: one year old) sheep, sometimes goat (Exod. 12:5); the goat is the male adult goat (Lev. 16:6)
15. Susman (1948, 113).
16. Susman (1948, 127).
17. Gk. *Idou, ho anthrōpos*, not "Behold, the man (Gk. *anēr*)," but *anthrōpos*, i.e., "human being," a member of the human race.

those who have seen the movie *Schindler's List* made by the Jewish film maker Steven Spielberg, I quote these words by Susman concerning the insignificance and defenselessness of this nation: "The only liberation battle, which it fought in Warsaw, dying, without any hope, as a tiny bunch surrounded by mountains of power and destructive rage, only for its own soul, impresses us as the most shocking confirmation of the radical solitude and desolation of the people."[18]

3.2.2 Money Business

When explaining the hatred of "Christian" nations toward Israel, we found one important cause: projection of their own guilt upon innocent Israel, just as the friends did toward Job. This was closely linked with a second cause for this hatred, namely, the financial power that Israel acquired in Europe, especially during the Middle Ages. Few Christians realize the cause of this power.[19] Everywhere, the Jews were driven out of every honest profession, until only the financial business remained for them. In the entire medieval world, taking interest was prohibited, a rule that, remarkably enough, had been adopted from the Torah: "If you lend money to any of my people with you who is poor, you shall not be like a moneylender to him, and you shall not exact interest from him" (Exod. 22:25; Lev. 25:36-37; Deut. 23:19-20). However, when successful people needed great sums of money, this Jewish prohibition was lifted precisely for the Jews—and just as easily re-instituted for them as well. The consequence was that the Jews learned to live from the interest, and—human that they were—in doing so easily learned to develop a desire for money. Everywhere in literature we encounter this *Geldjud* ("money Jew"), and always in an anti-Semitic context, whether this be Shylock in William Shakespeare's *The Merchant of Venice* (1598), Nathan the Wise in Gotthold E. Lessing's play of this name (1779), Isaac of York in Walter Scott's novel *Ivanhoe* (1819), or the Jew Joseph Süss Oppenheimer in Lion Feucht-

---

18. Susman (1948, 124).
19. Ibid., 101.

wanger's novel *Jew Suss* (1921-1922).[20] This Jewish financial history either produced the great Jewish capitalists, such as the Rothschilds (beginning with Mayer Amschel Rothschild, d. 1812), or the very opposite: the greatest Jewish communist revolutionaries,[21] such as Karl Marx, Leon Trotzky, Rosa Luxemburg, Isaac Deutscher, György Lukács, and the South African communist leader Joe Slovo.[22]

In 1850, the great composer but fierce anti-Semite, Richard Wagner, wrote:

> The Jew ... rules, and will rule as long as money remains the power over against which all our doing and acting loses its strength.... What the serf, in the form of misery and need, has paid as interest to the lords of the Roman and medieval world, is converted into money by the modern Jew: who notices that the blood of numerous generations sticks to the innocently looking piece of paper [against which one has borrowed money]?[23]

3.2.3 Israel and Job

This historical link between the Jews and money reminds us of a remarkable passage in the Talmud,[24] where Rabbi Samuel ben Isaac says, "What is meant by the verse, *Thou has blessed the work of his hands?* [Job 1:10] Whoever took a farthing from Job was blessed; even to buy from and to sell to him

---

20. A corrupted movie version of this book (*Jud Süss*) was shown by the Nazis everywhere in occupied Europe; as a student, I saw this horrendous movie in a closed performance (ca. 1965).
21. Vladimir Ilyich Lenin was probably at least one-fourth Jewish: his mother's father, Israel Blank, was a Jewish Russian, as was his mother's mother, Anna Grosschopf, according to some sources. If the latter is correct, Lenin would be considered a Jew in the Talmudic sense. During the Soviet era, Lenin's Jewish roots were systematically covered up.
22. See also chapter 5 note 55. Several decades ago, my wife and I lodged a colleague of mine for three months; she was Jewish as well as a communist as well as American—a remarkable combination. We have seldom known a more sensitive and idealistic person, one who showed no hostility at all to the gospel. At present, she is a well-known scholar in the United States.
23. Wagner (n.d., 68). We must add here, though, that Wagner had a number of genuine friendships with Jews; see extensively, Brener (2006).
24. Talmud: Pesahim 112a (see also Baba Bathra 15b).

is advisable." What a painful contrast between this and the false accusation in Job 22:6-9 made by one of his "friends" (who, as we remember, represented the Gentile nations):

> [Y]ou have exacted pledges of your brothers for nothing [or, without reason]
>   and stripped the naked of their clothing.
> You have given no water to the weary to drink,
>   and you have withheld bread from the hungry. . . .
> You have sent widows away empty,
>   and the arms of the fatherless were crushed.

Job himself, representing Israel, said of this:

> . . . I delivered the poor who cried for help,
>   and the fatherless who had none to help him.
> The blessing of him who was about to perish came upon me,
>   and I caused the widow's heart to sing for joy.
> I put on righteousness, and it clothed me;
>   my justice was like a robe and a turban.
> I was eyes to the blind
>   and feet to the lame.
> I was a father to the needy,
>   and I searched out the cause of him whom I did not know.
> I broke the fangs of the unrighteous
>   and made him drop his prey from his teeth (Job 29:12-17).

Which of the two pictures of Job, that is, Israel, that are presented here is closer to the truth? Is it the picture that Job/Israel gives of himself/itself, or the picture that the "friends," that is, the nations, give of Job/Israel? The answer is given by the LORD himself at the end of the book in saying to Eliphaz and the other "friends": "My anger burns against you and against your two friends, for you have not spoken of me what is right, as my servant Job has" (Job 42:7). Please notice that the LORD does not say, "you have not spoken of *Job* what is right" (although that would have been perfectly true, too), but "of *me*." The great truth expressed here is this: anyone who does not speak right of Israel does not speak right of the God of Israel.

3.3 The Crucifixion of Christ

3.3.1 Projection

As we saw, the first complaint against Israel was pure projection: placing one's own guilt on the innocent other. The second complaint involved an alleged guilt into which the Christian nations themselves had forced the Jews: the financial superiority that the Jews acquired in Europe.

The third and most serious complaint involved turning things upside down in a similar way: the people who, for the salvation of the world, had *given birth* to the "Savior of the world" (John 4:42; 1 John 4:14), became the people who supposedly *crucified* the "Savior of the world." They did indeed participate in this crucifixion (Acts 2:23, 36; 4:10), but the main responsibility was borne by "the Gentiles" (Matt. 20:19), specifically Pontius Pilate, representative of the emperor of the nations (Matt. 27:26).[25] However, the "Christian" Romans of later centuries reversed this responsibility and placed all the blame on the Jews. Jesus had said, "[S]alvation is from the Jews" (John 4:22), but soon "Christians," in a devilish way, reversed this: "All mischief is from the Jews."[26] Israel brought the Savior to the world, and in the name of this Savior, the "Christian" world brought the greatest misery upon Israel.[27]

Rabbi Richard Rubenstein argued that in Christian thought, the Jews play a double role: they deliver both the incarnated God and the latter's murderers.[28] Of interest here is the link between Jesus' birth and his death.

Although national socialism had sunk to the deepest level of pure paganism, it still had the audacity to assert, in the line of Luther and those following his anti-Semitic ideas, as one of its most serious complaints against Israel, that it had "murdered Jesus Christ." The greatest murderer of Jews of all

---

25. In Luke 2:1 and Acts 17:6, and perhaps in other, similar places, the term *oikoumenē* ("world") is a clear reference to the Roman Empire.
26. The word play works better in German and Dutch: "salvation–mischief" is *Heil–Unheil*, or *heil–onheil*, respectively.
27. Susman (1948, 123).
28. Rubenstein (1968, 21–22).

times, Adolf Hitler, had the temerity to write about the Jew:

> His life is only of this world, and his mentality is as foreign to the true spirit of Christianity as his character was to the great Founder of this new creed, 2,000 years ago. The Founder made no secret of his estimation of the Jewish people. When necessary, he drove those enemies of the human race out of the temple of God; then, as always, they used religion as a means of advancing their commercial interests. In return, Christ was nailed to the cross.[29]

That a mad fanatic could publish such things is bad enough; that he could exterminate almost six million Jews is breathtakingly worse. That throughout the centuries, thousands of "Christians" have endorsed the opinion just quoted is an equally egregious fault—for who can count the number of Jews who, during the centuries before the *Shoah*, have perished as a consequence of such "Christian" arguments?

After the triumph of official Christianity in the fourth century, Christians had three courses of action: force the Jews to be "converted," or chase them out of their respective countries, or destroy them (see below). If a Jew refused the first option, the second one awaited them, and if they refused the second option, the third one awaited them. The "Christians" told the Jews: *We* are now the true Jews. You have no right to live as Jews among us—so convert and be baptized. The worldly rulers said, You have no right to live as Jews among us—so get out. The Nazis said, You have no right to live—so die.[30]

3.3.2 Sacrificial Chicken or Roast Chicken?

In the gripping novel by the Jewish French author André Schwarz-Bart, *The Last of the Just*, young Ernie Levy asks his grandfather:

> ... "Is it [God] then who asks the Germans to *persecute* us? Oh,

---

29. Hitler (2018, 308); notice that Hitler wrote about Jesus as if the latter were not a Jew himself.
30. Hilberg (1985, 8–9).

Historical Supersessionism and Historical Judaism

Grandfather, then we aren't like other men! We must have done something to him, to God, otherwise he wouldn't be angry at us that way, at just us, the Jews. Right?" .... "Oh, Grandfather, tell me the truth! We aren't like other men, are we?" "Are we men?" Mordecai said.[31]

The Nazis said that the Jews were not human beings, but dogs, lice, vermin that must be eradicated—which indeed they did with an *insecticide*: the gas Cyclon B. However, the Nazis could never have said such things if "Christians" had not asserted for centuries that, as Ernie says, the Jews "did something to God." And this "something" is a matter regarding which *they*, these "Christians," thought they needed and were permitted to be the instruments of torture. Therefore, with some justification Rubenstein calls national socialism "a Jewish-Christian heresy," and not paganism. It presupposes, says he, both the Jewish-Christian "myth" (he means, story of God) and the Jewish-Christian ethos, although both were rejected by national socialism.

Later is the novel mentioned above, the character Mordecai Levy wonders about the purpose of the "useless" persecutions of the Jews; but then he corrects himself and says, "But after all, are we Jews not the sacrificial tribute, the tribute of suffering that man—um—offers to God? Praised be his name ... O Blessed ...." Here again we encounter the profound thought of substitution, of the innocent vicariously paying for the guilty. However, his son Benjamin (Ernie's father) replies:

> "Ah, my dear father!" Benjamin said then, brokenhearted, "if all that were God's will, who would not rejoice? But I think we are the prey of the wicked—simply a prey. And tell me, my venerable little father, does the chicken rejoice that it serves to glorify God? No, and you know it very well, the chicken is altogether sorry—and *reasonably* so—to have been born as a chicken, slaughtered as a chicken and eaten as a chicken. There is my opinion on the Jewish question."[32]

---

31. Schwarz-Bart (1985, 174–75).
32. Ibid., 267.

Here we have "the Jewish question" formulated in all its sharpness and bitterness. Are the Jews a sacrificial chicken for the honor of God—or only a roast chicken to be eaten by the "bad" people? Or do they have in themselves something of both? In Benjamin's view, the "bad" people are, of course, "the Christians"; during the *Shoah* it was very hard to distinguish the Nazis from (the majority of) the "Christians," who had been slaughtering Jews for so many centuries already. Consider this pungent example: on May 6, 1939, a number of theologians of the *Deutsche Christen* ("German Christians," that is, Nazi-minded Protestants) met in Eisenach in order to establish a church institute with the goal of removing from the Lutheran church all that was Jewish. Until 1945, this institute was very active in publishing anti-Jewish books, and even published a Bible freed of all its Jewish elements.[33]

The great majority of the Germans in those days confessed the Roman Catholic or the Protestant faith—just as the great majority of the Germans wholeheartedly supported Adolf Hitler. They did so despite the fact that, since the publication of *Mein Kampf* ("My Struggle," 1924), they could all have known what Hitler thought of the Jews. It is just naïvete to claim that only the "pagan" Nazis supported Hitler's plans with the Jews. "Christians" did so as well, not only inside but also outside Germany and Austria. These "Christians" may have been ignorant and stupid, and no doubt many were—but theirs was a *culpable* ignorance and stupidity.

3.3.3 Recent Times

Are things much better after the *Shoah*? Are there not many Christians, still today, who have great trouble seeing and acknowledging the place that "the Jew," or the people of Israel, or the state of Israel, are allowed to have in our present world? They can hardly understand and accept that ethnic Israel still exists, and *if* it still exists, why it does not accept Jesus, who "so obviously" is the Messiah of Israel. They overwhelm the Jews with their well-intended, but unwise and a-historical urge to convert them. They fail to realize or understand that

---

33. See extensively, Kant (2015, especially chapter 4).

after 1,700 years of persecution of the Jews "in the name of Jesus," we Christians can speak with Israel about Jesus only with the greatest modesty and reluctance. We do so not in an intrusive way, but only in a testifying way, only where the God-given opportunity arises. We do so not to persuade the Jew, but only to testify about what Jesus the *Jew* means for *us*, Gentile believers. And the rest we leave to the Holy Spirit.

Today, Christian nations find themselves in the position of the friends of Job:

> After the Lord had spoken these words to Job, the Lord said to Eliphaz the Temanite: "My anger burns against you and against your two friends, for you have not spoken of me what is right, as my servant Job has. Now therefore take seven bulls and seven rams and go to my servant Job and offer up a burnt offering for yourselves. And my servant Job shall pray for you, for I will accept his prayer not to deal with you according to your folly. For you have not spoken of me what is right, as my servant Job has." So Eliphaz the Temanite and Bildad the Shuhite and Zophar the Naamathite went and did what the Lord had told them, and the Lord accepted Job's prayer (Job 42:7-9).

On the one hand, these Christian nations still exhibit the same obtuseness with regard to Israel as did the friends with regard to Job. Job's friends did not understand Job, and it seems they did not *wish* to understand him either. He did not fit into their theological views, just as Israel has never fit into the theological views of many Christians. And if we do think that the Jew fits into our ideas and our mindsets, this might very well be because we have always endeavored to press the Jew into them, so that they would be someone in *our* image and after *our* likeness. That is, the Jew had to surrender their Jewish identity, join some Christian denomination, and become a "Gentile among the Gentiles."

On the other hand, Job's friends were totally dependent on the sacrifice that Job offered with and for his friends, as the text said. This means that the starting point is recognizing that the true God is, first and foremost, the God *of Israel*, that our Redeemer is, first and foremost, the Messiah *of Isra-*

el, that salvation is *from the Jews*, and that God's sacred book originally is a book *of the Jews*. Without this recognition, how could there be any salvation for the Gentiles? To what extent are Gentiles prepared to acknowledge that they can stand before God only through the sacrifice that is "from the Jews"? In other words, Jews and Gentiles are saved only through a sacrifice *brought* by a Jew, and brought according to the sacrificial regulations of the Jewish Torah. There is no other way. A sacrifice separated from its Jewish rules and context *is* no sacrifice acceptable to God.

Many Jews do not know Jesus as the *Messiah* of Israel, and this is saddening. They know only of *animal* sacrifices, and not of the fulfillment of these sacrifices in their Messiah. In their turn, however, many Christians do not know Jesus as the Messiah of *Israel*, and this is saddening, too. Jews sever the sacrifice from Jesus, and Gentiles sever Jesus from Israel. Thus, the chasm remains, with both parties sadly erring. For the majority of both groups, this will last until Jesus himself, at his coming, brings the two together *in* himself—or will we be allowed to experience some of this reconciliation already before that time?

3.3.4 Israel and Edom

Since the beginning of the third exile (AD 70), we find non-Jesus-confessing Jews and Christians (i.e., Jesus-confessing Jews and Gentiles), each group going its own way. Jacob (Israel) and Esau (Edom, "Rome"[34]) have parted, and one might easily think, for good. Jacob told Esau:

> My lord knows that the children are frail, and that the nursing flocks and herds are a care to me. If they are driven hard for one day, all the flocks will die. Let my lord pass on ahead of his servant, and I will lead on slowly, at the pace of the livestock that
>
> are ahead of me and at the pace of the children, until I come to my lord in Seir (Gen. 33:13–14).

---

34. With the ancient rabbis, "Edom" was a current designation for the (pagan, later Christian) Roman Empire; see extensively, Ouweneel (2003, chapter 4).

Four hundred warriors (Gen. 32:6) cannot move together with masses of children, herds, and flocks.[35] These groups form two totally different worlds. The "Christian" nations with their magnificent cathedrals, as well as their mighty armies and weapons, cannot move together with poor, unarmed Jewish families stuck away in their ghettos with their poor little synagogues. However, the two did not part forever; on the contrary, they go different ways that, in the end, lead to the same goal, Interestingly (see §2.8.3), it is not that Christians will ultimately join Israel in some way or another, but rather the opposite: as Jacob says, *he*, Jacob, will come to Seir, the mountains of Edom; that is, he will come to his brother Esau. When the two parties ultimately meet—in the Messianic kingdom—it is not just Esau coming to Jacob, but Jacob coming to Esau. It is equally true to say that in the end, Edom will come to Zion (cf. Isa. 2:2) as it is to say that in the end, Israel will come to Seir. They will be reconciled in Christ, who will be just as much in Zion as in Seir (figuratively speaking).

When the two finally meet, what will be the greatest miracle: that the heart of "Jacob" (Israel) will be turned to that of "Esau" (the nations), or that the heart of "Esau" will be turned to that of "Jacob"? The latter, I think, just as it was in Genesis 33, where Jacob was afraid of Esau, not the other way around. In the age-old fight for the birthright—which Jacob stole twice from Esau (Gen. 25:29-34; 27:1-40)—Esau, with his embrace, will finally *acknowledge* Jacob's birthright. But to arrive at this point, each and every form of supersessionism must vanish. Esau did not "become" Jacob, just as the church never "became" Israel in any sense. There are about 2.3 billion (nominal) Christians, which is about 150 times more than the 16 million Jews. Yet, even today, it is first Jacob, then Esau. First the Jew, then the Greek.[36] In Genesis, every older brother—Cain, Japheth,[37] Haran, Ismael, Esau, Reu-

---

35. See Ouweneel (2003, §4.2).
36. Acts 13:46; Rom. 1:16; 2:9–10.
37. At least, this is the rendering of the Septuagint, Symmachus, Onkelos, Rashi, Ibn Ezra, and Luther read Gen. 10:21 ("Shem . . . Japheth the great [= greater, elder]"); others (incl. modern translations) read the text such that Shem was the elder one, but I think the former view is the correct one.

ben—must give way to the, or a, younger brother.[38] This may be used as an argument against supersessionism because, in the supersessionist representation of things, the "church existing from Adam" is older than Israel.

3.4 "Jesus Cannot Be the Messiah"

Israel has chosen to reject Jesus as the Messiah, and it knows exactly *why* it has done so. In line with 2 Corinthians 3:14–15, *we* speak of a veil that lies over Israel's heart. But such a veil does not necessarily imply that Israel's ideas about Jesus are blurred. On the contrary, Israel has very clear ideas about why it *cannot* accept Jesus of Nazareth as the Messiah of Israel. In this and the following sections, I mention six of Israel's reasons.[39]

3.4.1 First Reason: Necessity of Repentance

The first reason is this. Like John the Baptist, Jesus denied that merely because one belonged to the chosen people, one would therefore have access to the kingdom of God. Jesus preached emphatically that the Jew could enter only on the condition of humbling themselves, confessing their sins, repentance, and "new birth":[40]

> "Truly, truly, I say to you, unless one is born again he cannot see the kingdom of God." Nicodemus said to him, "How can a man be born when he is old? Can he enter a second time into his mother's womb and be born?" Jesus answered, "Truly, truly, I say to you, unless one is born of water and the Spirit, he cannot enter the kingdom of God." (John 3:3–5).

Jesus straightforwardly told Israel that he had come *not*

---

38. Examples outside Genesis: Moses was the youngest in the family (Exod. 7:7), Gideon was the youngest in *his* family (Judg. 6:15), and David was younger than all his brothers (1 Sam. 16:11; 1 Chron. 2:15).
39. For the first two, see more extensively, Ouweneel (2000a, §6.2.3).
40. See also Matt. 5:3, 10, 19–20; 6:33; 7:21–23; 13:19–23; 18:3–4; 19:14; 21:31. The phrase "new birth" is what Ezek. 36:26 calls receiving a "new heart" and a "new spirit."

for those Jews who imagined that they did not need repentance and conversion (Luke 5:32; 15:7), but rather for the "lost sheep of the house of Israel" (Matt. 10:6; 15:24). As he explained in a parable, which referred to Israel as represented by the self-righteous Pharisees and scribes who stood before him:

> What man of you, having a hundred sheep, if he has lost one of them, does not leave the ninety-nine in the open country, and go after the one that is lost, until he finds it? And when he has found it, he lays it on his shoulders, rejoicing. And when he comes home, he calls together his friends and his neighbors, saying to them, "Rejoice with me, for I have found my sheep that was lost." Just so, I tell you, there will be more joy in heaven over one sinner who repents than over ninety-nine righteous persons who need no repentance (Luke 15:4–7).

For the self-confident Jew this was a hard pill to swallow, and remains so today. The Jewish German thinker Franz Rosenzweig had almost become a Christian, but he was impeded by one obstacle. This was the statement of Jesus: "I am the way, and the truth, and the life. *No one comes to the Father except through me*" (John 14:6). Rosenzweig thought: This may be true for the *goyyim*, but not for God's chosen people, because these *are* already with the Father.[41] He forgot that Jews was speaking here to Jews, not to Gentiles. Nevertheless, the great Jewish historian of religion, Hans Joachim Schoeps, expressed his approval of Rosenzweig on this point.[42] As to the positive aspect of Rosenzweig's view, Abraham Joshua Heschel wrote that a Jew must acknowledge the eminent role and place of Christianity in God's plan for the redemption of humanity.[43] The Gentiles must indeed be redeemed, but Israel has already received (the guarantee of) redemption. The Messianic Jew Jakob Jocz wrote that it was Rosenzweig's greatest mistake that he gave to "Israel" a purely ethnic in-

---

41. Quoted by Heering in Heering et al. (1987, 10).
42. See his article in Kac (1986, 57).
43. Quoted by L. R. Dewitz in ibid., 80.

terpretation by making blood relationship the guarantee of Israel's election.[44]

What a tragic error on the part of Rosenzweig, Schoeps, and others, an error exposed by the very Jesus who was rejected by the majority of Jews for this very point. Did they not remember the tenth plague of Egypt, which killed all the firstborn sons of Egypt, but which would have also killed the firstborn of Israel, if they had not found refuge behind the blood of the *Pesach* lamb? They were saved not because of their descent or election, but because of the lamb's blood. And this is a perpetual truth. No Israelite has ever received, or will ever receive, eternal redemption apart for the blood of the Lamb. And there can be no doubt as to who or what this Lamb is: "Cleanse out the old leaven that you may be a new lump, as you really are unleavened. For Christ, our Passover lamb, has been sacrificed. Let us therefore celebrate the festival, not with the old leaven, the leaven of malice and evil, but with the unleavened bread of sincerity and truth" (1 Cor. 5:7-8). The apostle Peter wrote (mainly) to Jewish believers, "[Y]ou were ransomed from the futile ways inherited from your forefathers, not with perishable things such as silver or gold, but with the precious blood of Christ, like that of a lamb without blemish or spot" (1 Pet. 1:18-19).

Why did the call to repentance and conversion irritate so many Jews? Was this not the pride and trouble of Job himself, a type of Israel, who, though guiltless (but not sinless), in the end could not do else than come to God, saying, ". . . therefore I despise myself, / and repent in dust and ashes" (Job 42:6)? And humanly speaking, did not God have expend significant effort in bringing Job that far? To come back to Rosenzweig once more, Messianic Jew David Stern asked the speculative question, whether, if Messianic Judaism had existed in his day, Rosenzweig might have become a Messianic Jew.[45]

---

44. See his article included in ibid., 92.
45. Stern (1997, 21); but see chapter 8.

3.4.2 Second Reason: Jews and Gentiles Equal?

In the eyes of the Jews of his day, and many Jews thereafter, it was challenging enough that, according to Jesus, the access to the kingdom of God—including the future Messianic kingdom—depended, and depends, on repentance and new birth. But what was more challenging was that, according to Jesus, because of these conditions access to the kingdom of God was open equally to Jew and Gentile. Jesus added—which was still more unacceptable—that, if the Jews continued to reject the true way to the kingdom, the kingdom would ultimately be given to others:

> Jesus said to them, "Have you never read in the Scriptures: 'The stone that the builders rejected has become the cornerstone; this was the Lord's doing, and it is marvelous in our eyes' [Ps. 118:22-23]? Therefore I tell you, the kingdom of God will be taken away from you and given to a people producing its fruits. And the one who falls on this stone will be broken to pieces; and when it falls on anyone, it will crush him [cf. Isa. 8:14-15]. (Matt. 21:42-44).[46]

Notice the response of the spiritual leaders as Luke describes it: "'What then will the owner of the vineyard do to them? He will come and destroy those tenants and give the vineyard to others.' When they heard this, they said, 'Surely not!'" (Luke 20:15-16). This is the "Surely not!" that we hear from Jews to this day.

To be sure, Jesus always acknowledged the divine election of Israel (Matt. 10:5-6; 15:21-28). But when it comes to eternal salvation, he taught that there is no basic difference between Israel and the nations. The majority of the Jews considered this to be a serious threat for the unique identity of, and thus for the continued existence of, ethnic Israel.

Humanly speaking, there was an element of truth in this view. If Israel had been assimilated into Christian nations, ethnic Israel would have ceased to exist. In that case, the Israel prophecies in the Tanakh could never have been fulfilled. (Here is a good question for supersessionists: For what

---

46. Cf. Matt. 8:10–12; 12:38–42; 13:37–38; Luke 11:29–32; 13:28–30.

purpose did God providentially ensure that ethnic Israel retained its identity to this very day?)

I may add here that Rabbi Sha'ul (the apostle Paul) taught the very same thing as Rabbi Yeshuah (Jesus): "I am not ashamed of the gospel, for it is the power of God for salvation to everyone who believes, to the Jew first and also to the Greek" (Rom. 1:16). "What then? Are we Jews any better off? No, not at all. For we have already charged that all, both Jews and Greeks, are under sin. . . . For there is no distinction: for all have sinned and fall short of the glory of God, and are justified by his grace as a gift, through the redemption that is in Christ Jesus, whom God put forward as a propitiation by his blood, to be received by faith" (Rom. 3:9, 22–25).

3.4.3 Third Reason: Jesus Did Not Bring the Kingdom

One of the most tragic misunderstandings existing between Jews and Christians is an argument heard repeatedly from Jews. It is this: the Tanakhic prophecies have linked the coming of the Messiah with certain effects that did not occur during the time of Jesus, or shortly after. If P necessarily leads to Q, and X does not lead to Q, then X cannot be P. Thus, Jesus cannot possibly be the Messiah.

An example of this reasoning is encountered with the great Jewish Spanish expositor Rabbi Nachmanides. During the (in)famous dispute of Barcelona (1263)—where Nachmanides finally had to flee because he was threatened with death—he argued as follows: Did the prophet not say that the Messiah would reign from sea to sea, and from the River (Euphrates) to the ends of the earth (Ps. 72:8; Zech. 9:10)? But Jesus did not become a world ruler, but during his life was persecuted by his enemies, hid himself from them, in the end fell into their hands, and was unable to save himself. So how could he have saved all Israel?[47] Even after his death, he

---

47. Quoted in Lapide (1984, 77–78). He also mentions (92) a similar argument supplied by the last great Jewish thinker of the Middle Ages: Don Isaac Abravanel (or Abarbanel). Such an argument also occurs in the mentioned novel by Schwarz-Bart (1985, 7). Cf. the argument of the Jews at the cross: "He saved others; he cannot save himself. He is the King of Israel; let him come down now from the cross, and we will believe in him. He trusts in God; let God

did not rule, for the power of Rome was not *his* power; on the contrary, already before people began believing in him, Rome exercised dominion over the largest part of the world. After the Romans accepted belief in Jesus on the part of their citizens, many kingdoms perished, and now those who venerate Muhammad possess an empire that is larger than the Roman one has ever been.

Nachmanides also argued that the Tanakh prophet had announced that, in the time of the Messiah, no one would teach the art of war to others (Isa. 2:4; Micah 4:3), and the world would be full of the knowledge of the Lord, as the waters cover the sea (Isa. 11:9). However, from Jesus' day until today, the world has been filled with murders, robberies, and lootings—and Christians have waged more wars and spilled more blood than any other religious people in history.

The tragedy of this argument of Nachmanides is first, that we encounter a series of misunderstandings regarding the gospel. Nachmanides did not know of the resurrection of Jesus, he did not know his last words on earth ("All authority in heaven and on earth has been given to me," Matt. 28:18), he did not know of the Jews Stephen (Acts 7:55-56) and Paul (Acts 22:14, 18; 1 Cor. 9:1) who both saw Jesus glorified in heaven.[48] But second, what is more tragic is that all prophesied effects of the coming of the Messiah have not (yet) been fulfilled *precisely because Israel has not (yet) accepted him.* The Messianic kingdom did not arrive because Israel rejected him—but Israel uses this very argument of the kingdom not having arrived to continue rejecting him. This appears to be unintentional; rather, it is a tragic misunderstanding. In one of his sermons to the Jews in Jerusalem, the apostle Peter appealed to the nation: if you accept your Messiah now, the kingdom will come immediately:

> Repent therefore, and turn back, that your sins may be blotted out, that times of refreshing may come from the presence of the

---

deliver him now, if he desires him" (Matt. 27:42–43).
48. Cf. Acts 2:33–34; 5:31; Rom. 8:34; Eph. 1:20; Col. 3:1; Heb. 1:3, 13; 8:1; 10:12; 12:2.

Lord, and that he may send the Christ [i.e., Messiah] appointed for you, Jesus, whom heaven must receive until the time for restoring all the things about which God spoke by the mouth of his holy prophets long ago (Acts 3:19-21).

Humanly speaking, Israel did not seize this opportunity. On the contrary, a short while later, the Jewish crowd stoned Stephen (Acts 7). This opened the door to a new work of the Holy Spirit: the dispersion of the Jesus-believing Jews, the conversion of Rabbi Sha'ul (the later apostle Paul), and the beginning of a global work among the Gentiles. These events only widened the chasm between Israel and the early Christians (Jewish and Gentile).

Nevertheless, there was one point where Nachmanides hit the nail on the head. To be sure, it was because the Jews rejected their Messiah that the Messianic kingdom was postponed in the first place. However, it was *the alleged "followers" of Jesus who themselves have deepened the absence of peace, the disharmony, the injustice.* It was "Christians" who gave the very worst conceivable testimony of Jesus. If today a Jew has negative feelings when hearing the name "Jesus," this is not so much because of the portrait of Jesus in the New Testament. This result is far more because of seventeen centuries of abominations that "Christians" have inflicted upon Jews in the name of this Jesus.

3.4.4 Fourth Reason: "Deification" of Jesus

There is a profoundly Jewish truth that seemed to be violated in Christianity (even though this, too, was a sad Jewish misunderstanding). What component in the Jewish doctrine of God is more important than this, that God does not have a form; as Moses had said, "Then the LORD spoke to you out of the midst of the fire. You heard the sound of words, but saw no form [Heb. *t'munah*]; there was only a voice" (Deut. 4:12; cf. v. 15). Therefore, Israel was not allowed to make any form of God: "You shall not make for yourself a carved image, or any likeness of anything [Heb. *t'munah*] that is in heaven above, or that is on the earth beneath, or that is in the water under the earth" (Deut. 5:8; cf. Exod. 20:4).

To be sure, it is said of Moses that he beheld "the form [Heb. *t'munah*] of the LORD" (Num. 12:8; see next section). But this cannot have meant anything more than a glory, a shining, not a shaped image. However, the New Testament presents Jesus as someone who was "in the form [Gk. *morphē*] of God" (Phil. 2:6), as the "image of the invisible God" (Col. 1:15; cf. 2 Cor. 4:4), the "radiance of the glory of God and the exact imprint of his nature" (Heb. 1:3). Margarete Susman wrote of this: ". . . the decision was made on the *form*. The Son is form; where Israel remained pure Israel, Israel did not understand or grasp him; because of the formless One, because of the invisible, only audible appeal, it has remained outside the heavenly and earthly community of humanity: outside the church and history."[49]

Indeed, Judaism has always taken offense at what it has called the "deification" of Jesus. Jesus "was even calling God his own Father, making himself equal with God" (John 5:18). "[Y]ou, being a man, make yourself God" (10:33). "[H]e has made himself the Son of God" (19:7). Jews often viewed this as a form of idolatry. According to Christians, God does have a form, an image, as presented in Jesus, and this is worshiped as God. This constitutes the worship of an image, and thus transgresses what Christians call the Second Commandment. We hear this complaint from the great medieval rabbis such as Rashi and Rabbi Joseph Kimchi.[50] Even in the twentieth century, Franz Rosenzweig, said, "We have crucified Christ and believe me, we would do it again. We alone in the entire world . . . if we would stand again over against a frenzy craving for idolatry, over against a crowd demanding the deification of a man."[51] That is, this Jewish nation would do what King Hezekiah did: "[H]e broke in pieces the bronze serpent that Moses had made, for until those days the people of Israel had made offerings to it" (2 Kings 18:4). But we ask Rosenzweig: Where was this frenzy crowd craving for idolatry, this crowd demanding the deification of a man? The only crowd

---

49. Susman (1948, 155; italics added).
50. See Lapide (1984, 81–83).
51. Rosenzweig (1935, 670–71).

we know of is the one demanding that Pontius Pilate would send Jesus to the cross for the very reason that "he has made himself the Son of God" (see above). Rosenzweig viewed this killing Jesus as a noble act, which only Israel could carry out because, thanks to the Torah, no nation was so strongly against any veneration of images.

Of course, the truth was that Jesus was not deified at all by Christians. The word "deification" suggests that, before this, he was not God, and that he was *made* God by his admirers. But this is not New Testament teaching at all; quite the opposite. It was not a Man who was "deified" (made God), but God was "humanified" (made a Man):

> In the beginning was the Word,
> > and the Word was with God,
> and the Word was God.
> > He was in the beginning with God....
> And the Word became flesh and dwelt among us,
> > and we have seen his glory,
> glory as of the only Son from the Father,
> > full of grace and truth (John 1:1-2, 14).

One does not have to agree with this, but at least this is New Testament teaching, which ought not to be dismissed or distorted for the sake of the argument.

Susman refers to the example of the great Dutch painter Vincent Van Gogh, whom she calls "one of the profoundest, truest Christians of our time, and certainly of all times, and one of the greatest artists of our world."[52] The former claim is rather exaggerated—but a fact not known to many is that in his younger period Van Gogh worked for some years (1876-1880) as a teacher of religion and as an evangelist in England and Wallonia (the French-speaking part of Belgium).[53] However, it is equally clear how he later came into a conflict with God, and lost a good deal of his beliefs.[54]

---

52. Susman (1948, 157).
53. Hulsker (1989, 7; cf. his letters: 18, 21–30, 59).
54. Ibid., 66–68, 100, 147–48, 159, 165, 197, 202, 236, 252, 280, 335–37, 371, 382, 416, 445, 503, 514, 516.

According to Susman, Van Gogh wrestled for years with how he could depict Christ, discovering at the end of his (short) life that Christ cannot be depicted. Every time Christ's presence inspired him, he painted him as the sun, which is like a halo around an invisible head. Here is a remarkable example: the painting *The Resurrection of Lazarus* (Van Gogh Museum, Amsterdam) shows the dead Lazarus and his two sisters (John 11), but not Jesus; we do see, though, a sun brightly shining over everything. What Susman wished to say is that the Gentile Christian Vincent Van Gogh apparently had understood this profoundly Jewish thought better than many other Christians, viz., if Jesus Christ cannot be depicted, then the purely divine even less.[55]

Another remarkable example is that of the Jewish composer Arnold Schoenberg.[56] The main topic of his opera *Moses and Aaron* (1932) is the depiction of two ideas of God, which we encounter with Moses and Aaron, respectively, but also within Schoenberg himself. His Moses is dominated by the almost compulsive idea that God cannot, and must not, be depicted in any possible way.[57] Aaron, however, wonders if Israel is indeed capable of loving and worshiping a God whose image it may not depict. When Moses gives to the people, who are still in Egypt, a very lofty description of the God who cannot be imagined, Aaron explains this to the nation in words that aim at appealing to the people. After the miracles that Aaron accomplishes the people seem to be convinced about this new God. But when they have arrived at Mount Sinai, and Moses had been on the mountain forty days, Aaron made the golden calf (see Exod. 32).

This was a painful moment in the opera. Aaron excused himself to the returning Moses, and testified of his love for the people as well as for the God who cannot be depicted.

---

55. This reminds me of the *Ben Hur* movie of 1959, in which Christ is shown only from behind; we never see his face.
56. Ouweneel (2000a, Intermezzo I.3).
57. Schoenberg, too, sticks to this principle: when God spoke to Moses from the burning bush, he did not hear the voice of a bass, but a spoken chorus plus six singing voices from the orchestra pit.

But he emphasized that this God can be explained to the people only in a mediating fashion. Moses maintained his doctrine concerning the emptiness of all idolatrous images, and destroyed the tablets of stone, after Aaron had called these "also just an image." Moses even called the pillar of cloud and fire "idolatrous images," but Aaron interpreted them as signs that do not depict God himself but the path to him. Moses finally becomes desperate because of his incapacity to express the idea of God in an undistorted way.

3.4.5 Fifth Reason: More on the Divinity of Christ

Another Jewish misunderstanding involves the following. Susman argued that Judaism and Christianity separated "when answering the question whether Christ is God, whether he is the Lord of the world, whether he is its Creator."[58] But, according to Susman, it is more important that the two separated not in *answering*, but in *asking* the question:

> The Jewish person cannot at all ask this question as a question concerning an objective, expressible reality of God. He can only allow himself to be grasped directly by this reality. Job's question is never and nowhere: Who are you?[59] What is your essence, your form? His only cry is: What do you want from me? How am I supposed to bow to your will?[60]

Here we encounter an important distinction between Judaism and Christianity. Almost from the beginning, Gentile Christian thinkers were Greeks and Romans, and thus were influenced by Greek and Roman thinking. As a consequence, throughout the centuries Christians have continually asked questions about essences (ontological, metaphysical questions), also concerning God.[61] Job did not ask a question

---

58. This is a false assumption; Jesus was not the Creator of the world but the Triune God was: the work of creation went forth *from* the Father, was *performed* through the Son (John 1:3; Col. 1:16; Heb. 1:2), in the power of the Holy Spirit.
59. Notice the difference with Acts 9:5: Saul of Tarsus does not ask about the *being* of his Interlocuter, but about his identity: "Who are you, Lord?"
60. Susman (1948, 159).
61. This is *not* true of the New Testament as such; Gen. 1:1 immediately presents

about essence, but a question of faith. The latter presupposed the essence of God, for those who ask, "What do you want?" no longer need to ask, "Who are you?"[62] Susman says that it is not correct that Job "believes" in God: "Job does not believe[63] in God; he has experienced him; God has crashed into him; how then could he ask about his being?"

Many Christians have personally experienced God precisely as Job did. Some of them are philosophers (or theologians), whose philosophical-theological questions by nature create a distance between the thinker and the God who is being investigated. But if they are good Christians, such matters do not interfere with their personal, existential relationship with God.

To be sure, it might seem that, here and there, the Tanakh, too, seems to delve in what we would call philosophical matters, such as when the LORD says of Moses, "With him I speak mouth to mouth, clearly, and not in riddles, and *he beholds the form of the LORD*" (Num. 12:8). But this hardly means anything more than "he beholds the LORD *himself*," or than what we read in Exodus 24:10-11: ". . . they saw the God of Israel. There was under his feet as it were a pavement of sapphire stone, like the very heaven for clearness. . . . [T]he chief men of the people of Israel . . . beheld God" (Exod. 24:10-11). That is, they saw a glow, a shining; they could not see who and what God is in his essence:

> Moses said, "Please show me your glory." And he said, "I will make all my goodness pass before you and will proclaim before you my name 'The LORD.' And I will be gracious to whom I will be gracious, and will show mercy on whom I will show mercy. But," he said, "you cannot see my face, for man shall not see me and live" (Exod. 33:18-20).

---

us with God without first asking philosophical questions about him (see next section)—and John 1, Col. 1, and Heb. 1 do the same.

62. See previous note: after the question, "Who are you, Lord?", Saul asks, "What shall I [i.e., What do you want me to] do, Lord?" (Acts 22:10).

63. Here the term "believing" apparently means intellectually accepting God as an idea, without any existential encounter with him; but this is not necessarily the biblical idea of "believing" (cf. John 14:1).

What Moses asked here was not whether he was allowed to see the essence, the being of God. What he wanted to behold was the mystery of the tension between God's holiness—which cannot tolerate sin—and his mercy toward sinners, as God had just been showing to his people. It is only in Jesus and his work on the cross that this mystery becomes fully visible.

When Ezekiel beheld the Lord, he saw only this: ". . . above the expanse over their heads there was the likeness of a throne, in appearance like sapphire; and seated above the likeness of a throne was a *likeness with a human appearance*" (Ezek. 1:26). Daniel seemed to see more of the form of the Lord (Dan. 7:9), but when we compare verses 13 and 22, this form seems to merge with that of the Son of Man. This important datum is entirely confirmed in Revelation 1:13-16, where the same description is applied to Jesus; in the picture given, Jesus has the features both of the Ancient of Days (God) and of the Son of Man in Daniel 7. And when Isaiah sees the glory of the Lord (Isa. 6:1), John 12:41 reveals to us that it was the glory of Jesus that he actually saw.

Here, we can formulate the profoundly tragic Jewish misunderstanding in a sharp way, as we did above. Jesus is not the Man who was later deified by Christians, but Jesus is the Lord, God—God the Son—the eternal Logos, who was with God, and who was God (John 1:1), who became Man (v. 14); he was the "only God"—that is, God the Son—who from eternity was in the bosom of the Father (v. 18). Perhaps nowhere does the Tanakh testify of this in a deeper and more touching—yet still hidden—way than in the word that the Lord himself has spoken: "'I will pour out on the house of David and on those living in Yerushalayim a spirit of grace and prayer; and they will look *to me, whom* they pierced.' They will mourn for him as one mourns for an only son; they will be in bitterness on his behalf like the bitterness for a firstborn son" (Zech. 12:10 CJB).

We encounter a similar misunderstanding among some Christians, who seem to think that, first there was God, and then he turns out to have a divine Son and a divine Spirit, as if from nowhere Christians have smuggled in these two divine persons, so that God suddenly turns out to be three persons. No wonder that Jews believe that Christians are polytheists: they have three gods, the Father, the Son, and the Holy Spirit. But no, together with Israel, Christians can—as I myself have done many times—whole-heartedly confess the *Sh'ma*: "Hear, O Israel: The LORD our God, the LORD is one" (Deut. 6:4).[64] According to Christians, God is not God plus something later added to him; they did not deify Jesus (nor the Holy Spirit). Christians confess *one God*, but they believe that this God has been, *from eternity*, and will be *in eternity*, Father, Son, and Holy Spirit. The great majority of Jews does not agree with this—but this does not entitle them to accuse Christians of some form of tritheism.[65]

3.4.6 Sixth Reason: The Hidden Messiah

This brings us to the sixth and final reason why Jews rejected Jesus as the Messiah of Israel. Under the influence of Hellenism, Christian theology repeatedly inquired about the being (essence) of God, and endlessly speculated about this. In the Jewish view, God's being is an *a priori* about which one does not ask questions, but which one takes as a starting point, in order to inquire about what really matters in practical life: the *will* of God for us humans. The Tanakh begins not by speculating about God's being, but by simply positing that he is there, and by telling us how he imposes his will on his creation: "In the beginning, God created the heavens and the earth. . . . And God said, 'Let there be light,' and there was light. . . . And God said to [the first humans], 'Be fruitful and multiply and fill the earth and subdue it,'" etc. (Gen. 1:1-3, 28).

In general, Judaism did not reject the facts of Jesus' life and death—and sometimes even those of his resurrection[66]— but only the question concerning his supposed being. As we

---

64. ESV note: "Or, 'The LORD our God is one LORD; or, 'The LORD is our God, the LORD is one'; or, 'The LORD is our God, the LORD alone.'"
65. This is not to deny that, at times, a certain (inclination to) tritheism has been expressed by Christians, such as with Roscelin of Compiègne.
66. See orthodox Jewish scholar Pinchas Lapide (1983).

heard from Susman, it rejected not only the answer to this question but also the question as such. Jewish philosopher Martin Buber called Jesus the greatest, purest, and most legitimate among the prophets of Israel—but added that Israel cannot call him "Messiah" because of the very self-manifestation of his Messiahship, "because in Israel, within history, the Messiah must remain concealed."[67]

In my view, this is a more correct and profound thought than it might seem at first glance, even if it might not be interpreted according to Buber's intention. As I see it, his thesis—with which I do not agree—means that, *if* Jesus were the Messiah, no Jew has the right to pronounce this now, before the appointed time. *If* he were the Messiah, this must remain a mystery until the actual arrival of the Messiah on the clouds of heaven (Dan. 7:13). I am under the strong impression that Jews like Margarete Susman, but also Franz Rosenzweig, Martin Buber, and many other serious Jews would rejoice—openly or secretly—if the coming Messiah exhibited the physical features of Jesus of Nazareth.[68] However, presumably they would all agree that, before the time has come, this secret must not be broadcast; I suppose that, in some cases, they would not even dare to declare this secret *to themselves*.

In order to illustrate this, let me give two quotations from orthodox Jewish authors. The first one is from the Jewish historian of religion, Hans Joachim Schoeps:

> The church of Jesus Christ has not preserved a portrait of its lord and savior. If Jesus would come back tomorrow, no Christian would know his face. However, it is quite well possible that he who will come at the end of the days, he who is expected by the synagogue as well as by the church, will be one, with one and the same face.[69]

---

67 Quoted by Susman (1948, 159–60).

68. As I heard an Israeli rabbi say, "I do not believe that Jesus is the Messiah—but *when* the Messiah comes, I hope it is Jesus." And I heard a Dutch rabbi say that when the Messiah comes, it is "quite possible" that he will have the features of Jesus.

69. H. J. Schoeps, quoted in Kac (1986, 58).

The second quotation comes from orthodox Jewish New Testament scholar Pinchas Lapide:

> To me, it is a fact beyond any doubt that in God's redemptive plan, actually unknown to me, a central role was attributed to Jesus, because it was in his name that the Western world has been brought to the faith in the one God. If Paul turns out to be right . . . and if Jesus turns out to be the coming Redeemer, then all Israel will definitely welcome him as the Anointed [i.e., Messiah] of the Lord.[70]

Similar thoughts had already been expressed by great orthodox Jewish scholars such as Rabbi Moshe ben Maimon (Rambam, or Maimonides) in his *Laws of Kings and Wars*,[71] and Rabbi Jacob Emden in his work *Seder 'Olam*, a commentary on the Mishnah.[72] According to Emden, it was Jesus' (and Paul's) intention to convert the Gentile world to the (alleged) seven Laws of Noah: "Do not deny God [by idolatry], do not murder, do not steal, do not commit sexual immorality, do not blaspheme, do not eat of a living animal, establish courts and legal systems to ensure obedience to these laws." Jesus, not as a heretic, but as a mighty instrument of God—this is some kind of a confession!

3.5 Attempts to Get Rid of Israel

3.5.1 No Place for Israel

Thus, Israel continues to reject its own Messiah, Jesus of Nazareth, as it continues to blame Christians for not seeing and accepting the convincing arguments why Jesus cannot be the Messiah of Israel. Throughout the centuries, the great majority of these Christians were supersessionists, that is, people claiming that *they* were the true "Israelites," that God continued his redemptive history with *them*, and that the only hope and future for the Jews lay in accepting Jesus and Christianity. Thus, tension necessarily and inevitably arose between

---

70. In: Lapide and Rahner (1984, 79).
71. *Melakhim uMilchamot*; English translation: https://www.chabad.org/library/article_cdo/aid/1188343/jewish/Melachim-uMilchamot.htm.
72. Hamburg 1752, p. 32b–34b (see *Jewish Encyclopedia*, "Gentile").

the two groups, for both claimed to be the true people of the God of the Bible. This was certainly not only a theological tension—too often it was also a historical, social, and political tension. A nation was rejecting the New Testament and the superiority of the church, continuing to claim for itself the name "Israel," and through its defenseless vulnerability it constituted a perpetual complaint against Christians, continually provoking the latter's hatred and aggression.

As Margarete Susman put it, "in the Christian world, the reality 'Israel' has become church, congregation"; this is the essence of supersessionism. It was all the more irritating for "Christians" that ethnic Israel continued to survive alongside them.[73] This Israel was never entirely destroyed, nor did it ever fully merge with Christians. It has existed and continues to exist to this very day—a pain in the neck for every consistent supersessionist. The German theologian and church leader, Ludwig Lemme of Heidelberg, said in 1913, in quite an outright way: "Judaism is an anachronism—for a long time it ought not have existed any longer."[74] This is harsh, but from a supersessionist viewpoint, utterly consistent. There can be no separate place for Judaism alongside Christianity.

Jewish author Richard L. Rubenstein accurately reflected the Christian—read: supersessionist—view by observing that the Jews still being alive was itself an offense to the claims of the church.[75] This eminently exposes the anti-Judaistic tendencies in supersessionism: after Christianity arrived there can no longer be any place for Judaism; now that the "spiritual Israel" exists in the world, ethnic Israel need no longer exist. And, as we have seen so often in world history, such anti-Judaism very easily becomes anti-Semitism, and comes to oppress and persecute ethnic Israelites.

Christians are Israel's natural friends because these (claim to) serve—not just any God but—the God *of Israel* and to venerate—not just any religious book but—the book *of Isra-*

---

73. Susman (1948, 50; cf. 78, 92–94).
74. Quoted by Jocz (1981, 50).
75. Rubenstein (1968, 19).

el. However, it is these "friends" who have repeatedly poured out their disgust and disapproval upon Israel, just as Job's "friends" did to *him.* For almost two thousand years, Job/Israel has been saying, even screaming in the face of these "friends" something that no "friend" can ever take away from him/it:

> For I know that my Redeemer lives,
> and at the last he will stand upon the earth.
> And after my skin has been thus destroyed,
> yet in my flesh I shall see God (Job 19:25-26).

The Hebrew word for "my Redeemer" *Go'ali,* that is, "my *Go'ēl.*" Job knew that the *Go'ēl* is on his side; no "friend" can take that away from him. This *Go'ēl* will also be the Redeemer of Israel in the end times.[76] Job also knew, just as Israel does, that one day, he whom we call the Messiah will "stand upon the earth [lit., dust]." Through all his misery, Job/Israel will arrive at the day of resurrection and redemption, and behold the glory of God:

> Arise, shine, for your light has come,
> and the glory of the Lord has risen upon you. . . .
> . . . and you shall know that I, the Lord, am your Savior
> and your Redeemer [Heb. *Go'ēl*], the Mighty One of Jacob
> (Isa. 60:1, 16).

Job knew "my personal Redeemer lives," but *go'ēl haddam* (see especially Num. 35) means "redeemer of blood," that is, the "avenger of [innocent] blood [poured out]": "my avenger lives"—the One who will avenge me over against my "friends," who really are my enemies. God will redeem *me,* but he will also execute vengeance on *you,* my so-called "friends." Vengeance may involve punishment, but Job/Israel would already be quite happy if he/it is justified, vindicated, rehabilitated in the eyes of the "friends." Indeed, we already found in Job 42:7-8 that God's anger burned against Job's friends because of the way they had treated him; in do-

---

76. See especially Isa. 41:14; 43:14; 44:6, 24; 47:4; 48:17; 49:7, 26; 54:5, 8; 59:20; 60:16; 63:16; see further in §14.8.

ing so, they had not spoken rightly about *God*. Those who do not speak rightly about the apple of God's eye (Deut. 32:10), do not speak rightly about God himself: ". . . he who touches you [i.e., Israel] touches the apple of his eye" (Zech. 2:8). This is a sin that can be blotted out only through a sacrifice (Job 42:8).

This Israel, this pain in the neck of supersessionist Christians, which ought not to exist anymore, still exists and is in a better condition than it has been for centuries. Christians, including apostate Christians like the Nazis, have repeatedly tried to apply three well-known methods against the Jews: forced conversion, expulsion, and extermination. Both Roman Catholics and Protestants—Lutherans and Calvinists, though the latter least of all (see §4.6.3)—have been guilty of this. As Richard L. Rubenstein and John A. Roth put it, the Holocaust has shown how much more difficult it is to convert baptized Christians into genuine Christians than it is to change them into anti-Semite murderers, accomplices of murder, and indifferent bystanders. So-called Christians have not only killed their brother, as Cain did to Abel, but also had the audacity of asking: "[A]m I my brother's keeper?" (Gen. 4:9), that is, am I responsible for the vicissitudes of Israel? Cain's natural way (cf. Jude 11) is crowded with travelers. The rough Avenue of the Righteous[77] is not. Unless Christians join those who took the latter road, they betray him whom they claim to follow, and crucify those whom they should embrace, according to Rubenstein and Roth—sharply but appropriately.[78]

3.5.2 Recent Insights

A very different attitude emerged for the first time among some Reformed theologians during the Second Reformation in the Netherlands, among British Puritans,[79] and later

---

77. The "Avenue of the Righteous" (viz., of Gentiles who took care of the Jews in their miserable circumstances) is an avenue of trees near the *Yad Vashem* monument in Jerusalem. Cf. Jesus' words about the "narrow" and the "wide gate" (Matt. 7:13–14).
78. Rubenstein and Roth (1987, 228).
79. One remarkable example was the Anglican preacher of York, Edmund Bunny,

among a larger group of Evangelical theologians. This was the consequence of the rediscovered view that they cherished with regard to the future position of Israel mentioned in the prophecies in the Tanakh.

We should not idealize these recent views, though. Now and then, Evangelical Christians, like many others, demonstrated a susceptibility to various conspiracy theories. One theory accuses various groups, not least the Jews—the Jewish bankers!— of trying to seize global power.[80] Numerous publications and websites tell us that the Jewish bankers were responsible for the Armenian genocide and many other disasters, including World War II, to say nothing of more recent developments in the United States.

Another very common belief among nineteenth-century Evangelicals was that the Jews had caused their own sufferings throughout so many centuries because they had called down the blood of Christ upon themselves (Matt. 27:25).[81] (When the pendulum swung back, liberal expositors accused Matthew and other New Testament writers that they themselves had anti-Jewish sentiments.[82]) But on the whole we can say that, where the renewed understanding of the prophecies in the Tanakh, and thus of the future of Israel, began to prevail, the attitude toward the Jews began to change. Israel was no longer just a nation suffering under the chastising hand of God, but a nation that was being prepared by God for a future that he had announced to them many centuries ago.

Israel was indeed a nation in a "fiery furnace" like the one in which Daniel's three friends had been cast. But what the Jews did not know was that *the Son of God was with them in the fire* (Dan. 3:25 NKJV). God had never promised his people that he would keep them from all disaster and misery, but he

---

who wrote *The Scepter of Judah* (1584) and *The Coronation of David* (1588), in which he interpreted the Israel prophecies literally; cf. http://1024project.com/2014/01/14/the-puritans-and-israel/ for many other examples.

80. For an excellent refutation, see Cohn (1967).
81. So, e.g., Grant (1897, 260).
82. Cf. Jansen (1981, 27, 30–31, 64, 145); see the refutation by France (1989, 238–41).

did promise that he would be *with them* in the midst of every disaster:

> When you pass through the waters, I will be with you;
>   and through the rivers, they shall not overwhelm you;
> when you walk through fire you shall not be burned,
>   and the flame shall not consume you (Isa. 43:2).

More movingly still, "In all their affliction *he was afflicted*" (Isa. 63:9). This thought was poignantly expressed by Dutch resistance fighter Floris Bakels, who, during World War II, spent three years in Nazi concentration camps.[83] When he was asked, "Where was God in Auschwitz?," his reply was, "In Auschwitz." The God who—silently—was with Daniel's friends in the fiery furnace, was—silently—with his people even in the gas chambers, though this confession may leave us with thousand questions.

To be sure, *millions* of Israelites have been overwhelmed by the rivers and consumed by the flames—and by the gas. But not Israel as a whole. The nation has survived all the "breakers and waves" that have gone over it (cf. Ps. 42:7), and all the fires that have threatened to consume it, including those of the ovens in the Nazi destruction camps. It survived, and for the first time in history, millions of Christians rejoiced, and looked forward to the great things that God was going to do with and among this nation.

This entailed not only a *theological* reformation but also a *metahistorical* and *existential* reformation. For the first time in history, a multitude of Christians rose to stand at the side of Israel, inspired by the rediscovered, deep roots of their faith. In this way, this Evangelical movement, which included Lutherans, Calvinists, and Anglicans, has become a *positive sign of the end times*, and a flaming testimony over against the traditional spiritualistic supersessionism, developed especially by and since Augustine. Again, of course there is no *direct* causal connection between anti-Semitism and supersessionism, but in practice such a connection has arisen all too often. Where do conspiracy theories come from in which

---

83. Cf. Bakels (2016).

Jews play a central—and always negative—role? From Christians who have rediscovered the prophecies in the Tanakh? *Or* from supersessionists?

3.6 The Three Options
3.6.1 Expulsion

If the church was indeed the true "(spiritual) Israel," there were only three options available to "impenitent" Jews—the "murderers of Christ"—namely, the three options mentioned earlier (apart from the very rare *voluntary* conversion): (1) expulsion, (2) extermination, (3) forced conversion and assimilation. These are the three gross sins committed against Israel by numerous "Christians" throughout the centuries: the Jew had to leave—or had to become a Christian, even if it were only outwardly and nominally. Let us briefly look at these options.

In the first place, many "Christian" nations were culpable for Israel's *expulsion*. In 1290, the Jews were expelled from England. In 1306, they were expelled from France, and in 1492 the massive expulsion of the Jews from Spain occurred. Then there were the many expulsions, throughout the centuries, from German-speaking and Eastern European countries.

Often, such expulsion occurred for economic reasons. For instance, in fifteenth-century Poland, Jewish life acquired a remarkable autonomy, prestige, and influence. However, a century later, when the country was looted by Cossacks, Russians, and Swedes, the Jews had to pay back double. They were decimated by Poland's enemies, and subsequently persecuted by the Polish people on the basis of the accusation that the Jews had supported the enemy.[84]

One reason for expulsion was that the Jews were repeatedly and systematically blamed for every disaster that fell upon a country. An infamous example is that in various European countries during the Middle Ages, the Jews were accused of causing the black plague (pestilence). (It was a fact that Jews got less sick from this plague, not because they had

---

84. Rubenstein and Roth (1987, 51).

caused the plague, but because they did not drink from polluted wells, and practiced much better hygiene and medical care.)[85]

The counterpart of expulsion (driving them out) is the refusal to admit Jews (letting them in), which actually amounts to the same thing: there was no place for them in the "inn" of Western society and culture (cf. Luke 2:7). Between 1920 and 1939, the Americans had a policy in which the flight of European Jews to the United States was actively impeded. Switzerland did the same with respect to German and Austrian Jews. From 1939, the British managed to close Palestine almost entirely to the Jews.[86] If the Nazis killed almost six million Jews, this high number could be reached because countries such as the United States, Great Britain, Switzerland and others had refused to admit Jews who wished to flee from rising and threatening Nazism. In this way, such countries unconsciously cooperated in the Holocaust. With a variant upon a famous Jewish saying: *whoever fails to save a life, it is considered as if he failed to save an entire nation.*[87]

As far as the Netherlands is concerned: the fact that, especially in the seventeenth century, many Jews found this country to be a safe haven was due far more to the liberal rulers in the cities than to the Reformed preachers. And the fact that, of the approximately 140,000 Jews who lived in the Netherlands before World War II, about 101,800 succumbed (approximately 84%), was due not only to the German occupation but also to the laxity of many Dutch people.[88]

---

85. As far as I know, the Jews have not yet been accused of causing the Covid-19 pandemic.
86. Rubenstein and Roth (1987, 101–102).
87. Jerusalem Talmud, Sanhedrin 4:1 (22a): "Whoever destroys a soul, it is considered as if he destroyed an entire world. And whoever saves a life, it is considered as if he saved an entire world." The saying became world famous through the movie *Schindler's List*.
88. Cf. Belgium: ca. 40%; France: ca. 25%; Luxemburg: ca. 20% (https://nl.wikipedia.org/wiki/Holocaust_in_Nederland).

3.6.2 Extermination or Conversion

Second, *all* "Christian" nations have been guilty of Israel's *destruction*. The war of 1939–1945 was a *world* war, that is, involving all the nations of the world. They either fought on the side of Germany (Italy, Hungary, Bulgaria, Yugoslavia, Japan, etc.), and thus, to some extent, took part in the crime of the *Endlösung* (a Nazi term, meaning "final and definitive solution" of the Jewish question, namely, extermination). Or they fought against Germany and its allies, thus doing everything possible in order to defeat Hitler. However, these nations did little or nothing to disturb him in implementing the *Endlösung*. They were definitely aware of what was going on; since 1942, the Allied forces had known what was happening in Auschwitz and other concentration camps. However, preventing their own defeat was an infinitely higher priority than saving the Jews.[89] For instance, the Allied powers could have bombed the railways leading to the concentration camps, but they did not care. As the Bible says, "[W]hoever knows the right thing to do and fails to do it, for him it is sin" (James 4:17; cf. Luke 12:47). Of course, the Germans and their allies were to be blamed first for the massive destruction of the Jews—but all the allied nations were guilty, too, because they did so little to prevent the destruction. Many occupied countries did shockingly little to impede the deportation of the Jews living among them. Even today, more than three-quarters of a century after the Holocaust, the "Christian"nations are still in the debt of the Jews—think, for instance, of the bank deposits of the *Shoah* victims—and seem to care little about it. Or think of the art objects that the Nazis stole from the Jews, some of which can still be found in various museums that seem rather reluctant to return them to the families involved.

According to the deeper sense of the Torah, the commandment "You shall not kill" means not only that people should not take other people's lives, but also that people should ensure that other people will not lose their lives. "You shall not kill" also means: Protect your neighbor's life. The New Tes-

---

89. Rubenstein and Roth (1987, 183–86).

tament expresses the same thought: "This is how we know what love is: Jesus Christ laid down his life for us. And we ought to lay down our lives for our brothers and sisters" (1 John 3:16).

Here we find the deepest meaning of the sixth commandment: You shall love your brother so much that you are prepared to put your life at risk for him in order to save *his* life.

If we understand this, we can understand why the Jews in Jerusalem could be called "murderers" of Jesus (Acts 7:52). This is because they may not have touched him—the leaders did physical beat him (Matt. 26:67-68)—but they had done nothing to save his life; on the contrary, they begged Pilate for the death penalty (John 18:28-40). In precisely the same way, the Christian world has become "murderers" of the Jews, throughout the centuries, but surely during the Holocaust. Around the year 30, hundreds of Jerusalem Jews killed "our" Lord;[90] this is horrible. But hundreds of millions of "Christians" have killed six million Jews—is this less horrible? There can be no shared future for Jews and Christians under the one God of Israel unless each group confesses its guilt—acknowledging that "Christian" guilt is unspeakably much larger than Jewish guilt.[91]

Daniel had no part at all in the sins of his forefathers; yet he said (speaking for the entire nation), "To us, O LORD, belongs open shame, to our kings, to our princes, and to our fathers, because *we* have sinned against you. To the Lord [*Adonai*] our God belong mercy and forgiveness, for *we* have rebelled against him" (Dan. 9:8-9; cf. vv. 5-6, 11, 14-15).

Let me put it this way, as a paraphrase of Zechariah 12:10: God will pour out on all Christians and the entire church the Spirit of grace and supplication. They will look on the one they have pierced, Israel, and they will mourn for him as one mourns for an only child, and grieve bitterly for him as one

---

90. Philosemitic Christians sometimes deny this, and claim that it was not the Jews but the Romans who killed Jesus; but this goes against the explicit and emphatic testimony of the apostles and Stephen in Acts 2:23; 3:15; 7:52; 10:39; 13:28.
91. See Ouweneel (2000a, 232–36).

grieves for a firstborn son. For this is what Israel is according to the LORD himself: "Israel is my firstborn son" (Exod. 4:22). Jews killed God's Firstborn Son, and they will have to confess this when they stand before the judgment seat of Christ (2 Cor. 5:10). Christians killed God's firstborn son, and they will have to confess this when they stand before the judgment seat of Christ (2 Cor. 5:10). This will be *the* condition for entering into the Messianic kingdom.

3.6.3 Assimilation

Perhaps the last of the three options mentioned, *forced conversion*, was after all the most effective method to eliminate the Jews. Apart from the Holocaust, the continued existence of Israel was threatened at least as much by this much older danger: *assimilation*. We distinguish between, on the one hand, forced conversion as it was practiced in Spain during the late Middle Ages: conversion or death (or, at best, expulsion), and, on the other hand, forced conversion implying that if the Jew did not convert they were tolerated but not allowed to participate in social, cultural, and economic life. Since the Enlightenment, the temptation of this option for the Jewish intelligentsia was enormous, especially in the Western European countries: the Jew only needed to be sprinkled with water in the name of the Triune God—Roman Catholic or Protestant, depending on the country or region—and the entire Western culture and society opened up to them.

As evidence, consider the Western, and sometimes purely Christian, first names of famous (and sometimes infamous) Jews like Alfred Adler, George L. Beer, Leonard Bernstein, Jerome Blum, Niels Bohr, Ambrósio Brandão, Sydney Brenner, René Cassin, Gerald Edelman, Paul Ehrlich, Albert Einstein, Andrew Fire, Viktor Frankl, Sigmund Freud, Jerome I. Friedman, Gregor Gysi, Theodor Herzl, François Jacob, Franz Kafka, Paul Levy, Max Liebermann, Gustav Mahler, Pierre Mendès France, Felix Nussbaum, Marc L. Polansky, Arnold Schoenberg, Dominique Strauss-Kahn, Martin Rodbell, Steven Weinberg. And so on.

Let me choose here two examples of famous composers around the beginning of the twentieth century: Gustav Mahler (1860-1911) and Arnold Schoenberg (1874-1951). Both were of Jewish descent, and both were baptized in order to gain access to all the opportunities and open doors in the Western cultural world without truly accepting any form of Christian beliefs. Mahler was baptized a Roman Catholic, but was a pantheist and mystic in some general deistic sense. Schoenberg was baptized a Lutheran, but thirty-five years later he returned to his original Jewish beliefs. Two examples, in a sense tragic, of Jewish geniuses who felt obliged to join the "Christian" world—but, in their heart of hearts, never did. They could not deny themselves. They were a bit like the many Jews who had been forced to converted, and thus to assimilate, but who then fled from Spain and Portugal. They were welcomed in Amsterdam (sixteenth and seventeenth centuries), where they could be what they had always been, dress as they had always dressed, celebrate the festivals as they had always done: *as Jews*, clearly distinct from Christians.

There was also another, very different way of assimilation: forced conversion to (atheistic) *communism*. In the Soviet Russia, which was just as anti-Semitic as former Russia, there was hardly any place for Jews practicing their Jewish religion. Many of them assimilated by burning their Jewish family papers, throwing away all the other aspects of their Jewish identity, trying to behave as staunch Russians, assuming Russian names and even joining the communist party. They still had a Jewish heart, but their (grand)children had forgotten all about their Jewish past. And if I may be a bit cynical: what was the practical difference between joining a Christian denomination *or* a communist party, if the hearts were far away from what they joined? The effect was the same: their (grand)children were fully assimilated.

In modern times, to a great extent the Holocaust was a powerful means to put an end to this assimilation. No one in his right mind would care to speculate about the "usefulness" or the "advantage" of the *Shoah*—the *Shoah* was way too horrible for this. And yet, humanly speaking, nothing has furthered the revival of Jewish self-awareness and identity more than the *Shoah* did.

Of course, we should not forget Zionism here, which had arisen near the end of the nineteenth century. Amazingly, this began as a thoroughly secular movement, related to socialism and communism, with hardly any Messianic awareness, only with the ardent desire of a homeland for the Jews. At first, the Jewish Austrian journalist Theodor Herzl had not even necessarily thought of Palestine—the Holy Land of the past. However, precisely this intense longing for a Jewish state in the ancient land of Israel—humanly speaking, would this have been conceivable without the Holocaust? Nearly a thousand days after the end of the *Shoah*, which occurred on August 14, 1945, on May 14, 1948, the state of Israel became a historical reality.

Again, we discern a similarity with Job: Satan intended his downfall, but God his resurrection. It is the same with Israel; as Susman wrote (near the end of the Holocaust!),

> Below consciousness, in the deeper, more original certainty of being, lives this certainty in the hearts of the people [of Israel]: the destruction that, on behalf of Satan, aims at its downfall, on behalf of God aims at its existence and survival. It is the secret that can hardly still be uttered, that the dark circle of fate in which God, today, has locked his people, is the circle of his love itself.[92]

Susman uses this picture: the *Shoah* is the pupation through which Israel has arrived at the butterfly stage.[93]

To be sure, we cannot second-guess God's doings. That is, we may never say that the Holocaust was the only way to reach this goal, and that no other way would have been possible. On the contrary, we keep wondering whether the almighty God could not have chosen an easier path leading to the state of Israel than through the *Shoah*. The question is

---

92. Susman (1948 165).
93. Ibid., 194.

entirely comparable with that other painful question: Could God not have chosen an easier path leading to the salvation of believers than the horrendous way of the cross, the curse, the abandonment?

We humans do not seem to be able to circumvent this consideration: without the Holocaust, a new Jewish self-awareness as well as a longing for the Jews' own, safe land seems hardly conceivable. Without this new Jewish awareness, there would have been no state of Israel. And in particular, without the state of Israel no ultimate Messianic restoration of peace and justice in the Promised Land, with Zion at the center of the Messianic kingdom, seems imaginable.

This is all purely human reasoning. But it fits well with this famous word from the Midrash: "When King Ahasuerus gave his signet ring to Haman [Est. 3:12], and in this way sealed the latter's horrendous persecution of the Jews, he did more for Israel than all the prophets."[94] This is a profound thought! Here, a Jewish tradition offers an explanation of the meaning—if we dare to use this word—of all the persecution of the Jews, a persecution that, in the view of so many people, was and is so terribly meaningless. Nothing has had greater effect than this to guarantee that Israel has kept its Jewish identity and self-awareness by clinging to the Torah, and has not become lost in the Gentile sea.

Time and again, the prophets exhorted Israel to return to the Torah. It seemed to be of little avail. However, the "Christian" persecutions, aimed at destroying the nation, repeatedly drove Israel, unconsciously and unintentionally, back to this: to its own deepest identity, that is, *to the Torah*. "A cord of three strands is not quickly broken" (Eccl. 4:12), and here is one way to understand this: the Tanakh calls Israel the apple of God's eye (Deut. 32:10; Zech. 2:8; cf. Ps. 17:8), and he gave to his people the Torah to be the apple of *their* eye.[95] And in

---

94. Quoted in ibid., 147; more accurately (Megillah 14a): ""The removal of the ring did more than forty-eight prophets and seven prophetesses who prophesied in Israel: none improved the people's conduct, but the removal of the ring did."
95. Cf. Prov. 7:2, where the father says to his son, "Keep my commands and you

the midst of this triangle—God, Israel and Torah—stands the Messiah, who is both the true personficiation of Israel and the true embodiment of the Torah.

---

will live; guard my teachings [sing., *torah*!] as the apple of your eye."

Chapter 4
Theological Supersessionism

[Regarding Israel and the Promised Land,] "There are only two solutions left," sniggered a young man with the sweet features of a girl under a distinctly military crewcut, "the natural solution, which would be for the Messiah to turn up on a cloud and take us there with a flap of his wings, and the supernatural solution, which would be for civilized nations to actually do something, however small."

André Schwarz-Bart[1]

4.1 Back to the Torah
4.1.1 The Eternal Torah

AT THE CLOSE of the previous chapter, I wrote that Israel is the apple of God's eye (Deut. 32:10; Zech. 2:8; cf. Ps. 17:8), and he gave—if we may apply Proverbs this way—to his people the Torah to be the apple of *their* eye.[2] This forms a triangle, so to

---

1. Schwarz-Bart (2011, 66); André Schwarz-Bart was a Jewish Polish-French author, who became world famous for his novel, *The Last of the Just* (1985).
2. Cf. Prov. 7:2, where the father says to his son, "Keep my commands and you

speak: God – Israel – Torah. And at the center of this triangle stands the Messiah, who is both the true personification of Israel and the true embodiment of the Torah.

I have a good friend in Israel who is a descendant of Rabbi Isaiah (Yeshaya) Horowitz (ca. Prague 1565 – Tiberias 1630; cf. §8.2.1). This famous Rabbi, called a *nasi* ("prince") in the land of Israel, wrote a prayer, called *Tefillat haShelah*, "Prayer of the Shelah,"[3] in which he apparently read the first word of the Hebrew Bible, *Berēshit* ("in [the] beginning"), as follows: first, the letter *Bēt*, then the word *Rēshit*, "beginning."[4] The *Bēt* is the second letter of the alphabet, and stands for the number two. Therefore, the prayer says: "Because of two (*Bēt*) things called beginning (*Rēshit*) God created the world: because of the Torah and because of Israel. For they are your people and your inheritance that you have chosen from all nations; you have given them your Holy Torah; and you have drawn them close to your holy name."[5] Here, we have the triangle: the *one* God created the world with a view to *two* objectives: Israel and the Torah. Therefore, the prayer continues with asking God for two things: first, give me many children, Oh God, so that Israel may be multiplied and continue to exist; and second, let them learn and keep your Torah!

Here, the fourth component—which turns the triangle into a quadrangle or pyramid—is not mentioned: the Messiah. But it is mentioned in so many other prayers and writings, such as in the *Amidah* (or the *Shemonēh 'Esrēh*), which is prayed three times a day, and which says, "The offspring of your servant David may you speedily cause to flourish, and

---

will live; guard my teachings [sing., *torah!*] as the apple of your eye." See further in §5.1.

3. *Shelah* was the nickname of Rabbi Yeshaya Horowitz; it is the acronym of his best-known work: *Sh'nē Luchot haB'rit* ("Two Tablets of the Covenant"), published by his son in Amsterdam (1648).
4. This homiletical reading of the first word of the Torah is actually much older. It is a midrash that appears, e.g., in *BeReshit Rabbah*, one of the oldest of the Aggadic Midrashim (from the early Talmudic period). Both Rashi (R. Sh'lomoh Yitzchaki) and Nachmanides cite this midrash in their commentaries.
5. https://images.shulcloud.com/32/uploads/Rabbi/prayerforworthychildren.pdf.

enhance his pride through your salvation, for we hope for your salvation all day long."

The prayer of Rabbi Yeshaya speaks of the beginning of Israel's history, whereas the Messiah points to the great apotheosis of that history. This point deserves our further attention. Something occurred to Israel about which the nation itself was unaware and that remains a secret to many Christians. It is this: by repeatedly being cast back upon the Torah, Israel was unconsciously also kept near to him who in his own person is the *eternal Torah*.[6] Recently, a rabbi repeated this tragic misunderstanding: the Jews could not accept Jesus because they wished to remain faithful to the Torah. This mistaken notion has been perpetuated throughout the centuries: the Jews must choose between Jesus and the Torah. Indeed, most Jews think they can have the Torah without Jesus, just as most Christians think they can have Jesus without Israel and the Torah. Both are mistaken.

Some have said that some Jews chose Christ, while other Jews stayed with the Torah—as if there is a bifurcation here, where the Jew has to choose, or even an antithesis between Jesus and the Torah. Rather, it is better to say that earlier Jews consciously chose him who is the Eternal Torah, even though they have usually chosen other words to express this truth. Later Jews, insofar as they belonged and belong to the true core of Israel—the "Israel of God"—preferred to stay with the Mosaic Torah. Thereby they unconsciously remained intimately connected with him who is the Eternal Torah. No true Jew can ever be disconnected from the Messiah. The former (Jesus-believing) Jew is connected with him in a conscious, intentional, manifest way; the latter (Jesus-rejecting) Jew is connected with him in an unconscious, unintentional, hidden manner—but a manner that one day will be brought to light.

Recall that remarkable verse in 2 Corinthians 3:3, "[Y]ou show that you are a letter from [or, of[7]] Christ delivered by us, written not with ink but with the Spirit of the living God,

---

6. See extensively, Ouweneel (1994, 247–48; 1997, 452–55).

7. I understand the phrase to mean a letter whose content is Christ.

not on tablets of stone but on tablets of human hearts." Paul was obviously thinking here of the *Torah*, specifically the Ten Commandments, which God had written on the two tablets of stone: "And he [i.e., God] gave to Moses, when he had finished speaking with him on Mount Sinai, the two tablets of the testimony, tablets of stone, written with the finger of God" (Exod. 31:18; cf. 32:16; 34:1, 4, 28; Deut. 9:10).

Now compare Matthew 12:28 ("it is by the Spirit of God that I cast out demons") and Luke 11:20 ("I drive out demons by the finger of God"), and you will discover that the Spirit of God and the finger of God are parallel. Then look back again at 2 Corinthians 3:3, where I find the following contrasts:

There were tablets of stone	–	there are now tablets of the hearts[8]
God wrote on them with his finger	–	God writes on them with his Spirit
They were delivered by Moses	–	they are delivered by Paul (and many others)
What is written is the Torah	–	what is written is Christ.

As soon as the Torah is not merely studied but is truly written in the Jew's *heart*, they are not far from having *Christ* written in their heart—even if, at first, they are unaware of it (see the example in the next section).

4.1.2 A Remnant "Seeing"

According to the prophetic Word, a "remnant" (Heb. *sha'ar*) will be formed at the core of Israel during the end time, a faithful segment that will recognize in Jesus of Nazareth the

---

8. Cf. Jer. 31:33, "I will put my Torah within them, and I will writeit on their *hearts*" (cf. Rom. 2:15; Heb. 8:10; 10;6).

Messiah of Israel.⁹ The prophecies concerning the end time presuppose a people of Israel restored in their land, with their own nation state, initially disbelieving in Jesus.¹⁰ Great experts of the prophecies predicted already before 1900 the establishment of such a Jewish state in disbelief, although in their days not a trace of this could be discerned.¹¹ As long as the mighty Ottoman Empire existed, such an Israelite state was politically unthinkable (the Ottoman Turks occupied Jerusalem from 1517 to 1917). Why then did these theologians believe in such a future state of Israel? Because they believed the prophetic Scriptures.

Today, since the establishment of this state in 1948—less than three years after the end of the Holocaust—we have become accustomed to this state, which at this point has existed for three quarters of a century. Human beings become accustomed to the greatest miracles. But we will never become accustomed to this bewildering fact: humanly speaking, the state of Israel became possible not only through the definitive fall of the Ottoman Empire (1922) but also through the Holocaust (1942-1945). What theologian in the eighteenth or nineteenth century could have presumed that the state of Israel would come into existence along this route?

Job 42 is not simply the recapitulation of the happy state of Job 1:1-5 (cf. 29:2-25). No, the bliss of the end far surpasses that of the beginning, for "I had heard of you by the hearing of the ear, / but *now my eye sees you*" (Job 42:5).¹² For Job, too, this final result could be reached only through a kind of *Shoah*. It was not *during* the *Shoah* that he saw God, but ultimately *as a consequence of* the *Shoah*. Similarly, numerous surviving Jews have complained that they had not seen God in Auschwitz—though many others have given different testimonies—but ultimately Auschwitz led to what James describes: "You have heard of the patience of Job, and you have

---

9. Ouweneel (1999, chapter 4, §5.4.2).
10. For the New Testament teaching on this, see volume IV/1a, chapters 13–14.
11. See ibid., chapter 4.
12. Cf. Job's own prediction: "[I]n my flesh I shall see God, whom I shall see for myself, and my eyes shall behold, and not another" (Job 19:26–27).

seen the *end of the Lord*, that the Lord is merciful and compassionate" (James 5:11). It is only in this "end of the Lord," as in the "end" of Job's story, that the eyes of those faithful ones of Israel will behold the king in his beauty (Isa. 33:17; cf. 35:2). Faith is by "hearing" (Rom. 10:17)—but I venture to say that, ultimately, there can be no true faith without "seeing." Paul prays for the Ephesian believers "that the God of our Lord Jesus Christ, the Father of glory, may give you the Spirit of wisdom and of revelation in the knowledge of him, having the *eyes of your hearts enlightened*" (Eph. 1:17-18). Blessed are those who are allowed to "see" the glory of the Lord *before* his glorious appearance.

Today, most Jews cannot see—and most Gentiles cannot either—because "whenever Moses is read a veil lies over their hearts. But when one turns to the Lord, the veil is removed" (2 Cor. 3:15-16).

In the novel *The Last of the Just*, we find such a man whose eyes were opened, very touchingly, to some extent.

> "Two thousand years of Christology," [the Judeo-Christian doctor] said dreamily, as if to himself. "And yet—I know it's absurd but I still believe, and I love the person of the Christ more than ever. Well, except that he's not the blond Christ of the cathedrals any more, the glorious Saviour put to death by the Jews. . . . He's *something else*," in a suddenly Jewish tone, the miserable tone of a prisoner.
>
> And then, surprising Ernie and the neighboring patients and perhaps himself, he raised his hands to his temples to hold his glasses firm, and broke into sobs.[13]

Nowhere in literature have I found a more beautiful and moving expression of what we find in Zechariah 12:10: "I will pour out on the house of David and the inhabitants of Jerusalem a spirit of grace and pleas for mercy, so that, when they look on me, on him whom they have pierced, they shall mourn for him, as one mourns for an only child, and weep bitterly over him, as one weeps over a firstborn."

---

13. Schwarz-Bart (1985, 354).

4.2 Again, Jesus and the Torah
4.2.1 "But I Say to You..."

Jesus and the Torah belong together. Jesus *is* the Eternal Torah; to put it this way, he in his person *is* God's commandment to humanity. But Jesus *is* the Torah also in the sense that he *is* the love that people are commanded to have for God and for their neighbors. When the Messiah said, "Your Torah is in my heart" (Ps. 40:8), he was basically identical with what *believers* have in their heart, as we saw in 2 Corinthians 3:3. When Paul prayed that Christ may dwell in believers' hearts though faith (Eph. 3:17), this was basically the same as what was said of the *tzaddiq* (the righteous one):

> The mouth of the *tzaddiq* utters wisdom,
>   and his tongue speaks justice.
> The Torah of his God is in his *heart*;
>   his steps do not slip (Ps. 37:30-31).

However, if this is true—if having the Torah in your heart is basically the same as having Jesus in your heart—how is it possible, as some Jews and some Christians assert, that at times Jesus *contradicted* the Torah? Especially in the Sermon on the Mount, Jesus gave the impression—at least to some—that he wished to correct certain parts of the Torah, or wished to reject them. We see this especially in the five-fold expression, "You have heard that it was said (to those of old) . . . but *I* say to you . . . ."[14]

It has been suggested that Jesus was here rejecting morality of the Tanakh in favor of a newer, higher morality. *In reality, however, Jesus never rejected or corrected any Mosaic commandment.*[15] Imagine, how such a thing would be possible, given that the Torah was designed and given by God himself, and has never been abolished by God? On the contrary, he calls his own Torah an "eternal (everlasting)" Torah:

---

14. Matt. 5:21-22, 27-28, 31-34, 38-39 and 43-44.
15. *Contra*, e.g., Weber (1981, 291). Thus, thoroughly incorrect is what Aafjes (1950, 28) wrote in reference to Matt. 5:31-32: "In this way, Jesus annuls Moses' Torah-giving in the book of Deuteronomy." And later: "Jesus radically puts an end to the oath" (106).

Your testimonies are my heritage *forever*,
>for they are the joy of my heart.
I incline my heart to perform your statutes
>*forever*, to the end (Ps. 119:111-12; cf. vv. 44, 98, 142, 144, 152, 160).

4.2.2 Jesus' Four Comments

Instead of correcting or rejecting God's commandments, Jesus did something very different, which is summarized here in four points.[16]

(1) He brought to light the *true depth* of the Torah. The Mosaic Torah said that a murderer deserves the death penalty. Jesus did not correct or annul this, but pointed out that a person is really a murderer already at the moment they "only" desire another person's death (Matt. 5:22). An adulterer deserves the death penalty, but one is really an adulterer already at the moment they "only" look at another with lustful intent (v. 28). When properly understood, the Torah reveals not just our *sins* but more profoundly, our *sinfulness*, our sinful *nature* (Rom. 3:20; 7:7). Jesus showed that our natural condition is really far worse than our initial superficial impression of the Torah. But by giving us this deeper impression Jesus was not correcting the Torah, but was bringing to light what had been *within the Torah when God gave it to Moses*.

(2) Indeed, Jesus uttered sharp criticisms in Matthew 5. However, these are never criticisms concerning the Torah as such, but rather concerning the mistaken Pharisaic interpretations of the Torah, the omissions from it or additions to the Torah that the Pharisees had invented. Such mishandling of the Torah actually robbed it of its spiritual strength. For instance, the Pharisees said that you must love your neighbor, and hate your enemies. The former phrase is entirely in line with the Torah (Lev. 19:18), but the latter phrase is not at all. Your "neighbor" is not only one of your relatives, your friends, your people, but it can also be one from a hostile nation. It is not simply a person close to you, but every person whom you encounter in life. Such a person must never be

---

16. Ouweneel (2001a, 123–29).

hated but must be loved, and therefore helped, if necessary. This is the magnificent truth that Jesus revealed in the parable of the good Samaritan (Luke 10:25-37).[17]

Jesus provided another example:

> . . . Moses said, "Honor your father and your mother" [Exod. 20:12; Deut. 5:16]; and, "Whoever reviles father or mother must surely die" [Exod. 21:17; Lev. 20:9; Deut. 27:16]. But you say, "If a man tells his father or his mother, 'Whatever you would have gained from me is Corban[18]" (that is, given to God)—then you no longer permit him to do anything for his father or his mother, thus making void the word of God by your tradition that you have handed down. And many such things you do (Mark 7:10-13).

The Torah was being circumvented in a vicious and disrespectful way: that portion of financial and material support to which your parents are entitled is being withheld from them on the pretext that it is being set aside as an offering to God, whereas in reality you are using it for yourself. This error was not the Torah's fault, but it was human (rabbinic) tradition that was transgressing the Torah at this point, and thereby offending the God of the Torah.

(3) Just as the apostle Paul did later, Jesus brought to light the real heart of the Torah by implicitly changing the negative commandments (prohibitions: "You shall *not* . . .") into their counterparts. For instance, the sixth commandment ("You shall not kill") *fundamentally* means that if you can prevent the death of your neighbor, then do it. Or this: "You shall love your brother so much that you are prepared to put your life at risk for him" (cf. 1 John 3:16). The seventh commandment ("You shall not commit adultery") *fundamentally* means this: "Husbands, love your wives, as Christ loved the church and gave himself up for her" (Eph. 5:25). That is, "You shall love your wife so much that you are prepared to

---

17. Notice, though, that in this parable it was not some Jew who must help a Samaritan in distress, but a *Jew* in distress who must *accept* help from a Samaritan.
18. A Hebrew loanword: *qorban*, from *q-r-b*, here "to bring near," hence "offering" (only in Lev., Num., and Ezek. 40:43).

put your life at risk for her." The eighth commandment ("You shall not steal") *fundamentally* means this: "Let the thief no longer steal, but rather let him labor, doing honest work with his own hands, so that he may have something to share with anyone in need" (Eph. 4:28; cf. 1 John 3:17). That is, "You shall love your neighbor so much that you are prepared to provide for his poverty." The ninth commandment (freely rendered, "You shall not lie") *fundamentally* means this: ". . . speaking the truth in love, we are to grow up in every way into him who is the head, into Christ. . . . Therefore, having put away falsehood, let each one of you speak the truth with his neighbor, for we are members one of another" (Eph. 4:15, 25). That is, "You shall love your neighbor so much that you are prepared to serve them with the truth." In this way, both Jesus and Paul showed that each of the Ten Commandments is a variety of the single Commandment of Love, a truth that had been made known in the Mosaic Torah itself (Deut. 6:5; Lev. 19:18; cf. Matt. 22:34-40): "You shall love your neighbor so much that you shall serve them in any possible way."

(4) Jesus explicitly declared that he had not come to "abolish" (annul) the Torah and the prophetic books of the Tanakh, but to "fulfill" them, that is, to bring them to their fulness, to fill them out (Matt. 5:17-20). As we have seen, various interpretations of this word "fulfill" have been offered, among them that Jesus himself, in his own person, is the fulness of the Torah. If one wishes to understand God's deepest intention with the Torah, look at Jesus, at his person and his life. To put if differently: by fulfilling Jesus' commandments, you become "conformed" to his image (cf. Rom. 8:20): to *do* as he did is to *become* as he was.

4.2.3 In Summary

In summary, Jesus never transgressed the Torah, including the Sabbath commandments. At most, he criticized he rabbinic tradition in cases where it shrewdly circumvented the original divine intention of the Torah *or* strictly intensified its commandments beyond that divine intention—in order to be wiser than God—for instance, by putting pressure on the crowds that followed the teachings of the Pharisees and the scribes. This is what these spiritual leaders did, for instance, regarding the Sabbath (cf., e.g., Matt. 23:1-33; Mark 7:6-13).

It is essential to make this distinction, especially when evaluating Matthew 5: Jesus never criticized the Torah as such, but he did criticize certain rabbinic *interpretations* of the Torah. Behind this lay his conviction, which belongs to the Protestant heritage, that God's written Word is perfect—for it is divinely inspired (2 Tim. 3:16)—but the interpretation of Scripture is always fallible human work. Many theologians seem not to understood this, for when they are criticized, they react in unwholesome ways: anyone who attacks *their theology* is attacking the Bible. The same reaction met Jesus in Matthew 5: his criticizing the rabbinic interpretations of the Torah was understood as criticizing the Torah itself.

The same happened to Martin Luther, who did not criticize the "doctrines of the [Roman Catholic] church" as such, as has often been asserted. He criticized only those elements in these doctrines that—in his opinion—deviated from the written Word of God, and thus, were only human inventions. The same reaction often meets theologians who criticize certain points in the Protestant creeds or catechisms: they are not necessarily criticizing the Scriptures as such, but only those elements in these creeds or catechisms that are thought to deviate from the written Word of God.

4.3 Damage Caused by Supersessionism
4.3.1 Historical Roots of Supersessionism

Let us now look at supersessionism from a somewhat different viewpoint. From a purely human perspective, it is not very difficult to understand why in church history so many have allowed themselves to be enticed by this disastrous doctrine. There were various sources for this. The first source was the very origin and existence of the "Christian" Roman Empire. It began with the "conversion" of the Roman Emperor, Constantine the Great (312), and was crowned with the elevation of Roman Catholicism to be the state religion of this Empire (under Emperor Theodosius the Great, 380). The four pagan world empires (Babylonian, Medo-Persian,

Greco-Macedonian, and pagan-Roman) were succeeded by the "Christian" empire of the Messiah, which emphatically was *not* a Jewish Empire. On the contrary, almost from its beginning with the Council of Nicaea (325)—so valuable in a Christological respect—this empire has oppressed the Jews.

According to early supersessionists, this political, worldly triumph of Christianity over both paganism and post-New Testament Judaism clearly showed that, from the viewpoint of redemptive history, Christianity was the successor of Judaism and Christians had become the "true people of God," the "true Israel," in the present era. Moreover, there was no room for any *other* "people of God," namely, tiny, inconspicuous ethnic Israel. On the contrary, Israel is *Lo-'Ammi*, "Not-My-People" (Hos. 1:9–10; 2:23), and it must be treated as such, claimed the Christian leaders.

With a certain disdain, church father Jerome, when dealing with Malachi 1:4–5, told his readers that, according to the Jews, "Edom" represents the Romans, and that the Jews flatter themselves with the idea that, when the Roman Empire is destroyed, world dominion will come to the Jews.[19] And in his commentary on Daniel 2:34–35 and 45, Jerome again ridiculed the idea that the successor of the four world empires will be a *Jewish* empire.[20] Well, this is exactly what I believe the Bible teaches: the future Messianic empire will, in a sense, also be an *Israelite* empire:[21] "[The kingdom and the dominion and the greatness of the kingdoms under the whole heaven shall be given to the people of the saints of the Most High; *their* kingdom shall be an everlasting kingdom, and all dominions shall serve and obey *them*" (Dan. 7:27 ESV note).[22]

---

19. Quoted in Kocken (1935, 7). Regarding the view that, with the fall of the "Edomite" (i.e., Roman) Empire, an Israelite empire will begin, cf. Flavius Josephus (*Jewish Antiquities*), 4 Ezra and 2 Baruch; see Kocken (1935, 6–7); Adamek (1938, 27–28).
20. Kocken (1935, 7).
21. Cf. passages showing how "Zion" (Jerusalem with the new temple) will be the center of the world (Isa. 2:3–4; 60:14; 62:1–2; Micah 4:1–2; cf. Zech. 14:14–17).
22. Translations differ: many have "them," which is thought to refer to the "people

Indeed, it seemed simply unthinkable, certainly after the insurgence of Simon bar Kochba (132–135), that an independent Jewish people would ever again dwell in the land of Israel, especially after the rise of the Ottoman Empire (see above). Even the great pioneer of Zionism, Theodor Herzl, initially did not consider that Palestine would be the homeland for the Jewish people. Was this because he, too, thought this to be inconceivable? In his famous work, *The Jewish State*, he did mention Palestine, but also Argentina as a possible homeland.[23]

All the more remarkable, then, that so many (non-supersessionist) Reformed pastors in the seventeenth and eighteenth centuries,[24] as well as some Evangelical pioneers in the nineteenth century,[25] believed on the basis of God's Word in a Jewish state in the ancient Holy Land. Imagine that we had lived two hundred years earlier: all supersessionists would have assured us that it was *unthinkable* that the people of Israel would return to its own country, in order to establish their own state, because God would never allow such a thing to happen. Some Christians claimed the same with respect to the idea of humans landing on the moon. Unthinkable—God would never allow it.[26] But it happened (1969). It is uncertain what is a greater miracle: astronauts landing on the moon (where there were no Turks or Arabs to stop them), *or* Jews establishing their own modern, independent state in the Holy Land.

It happened. I was too young to notice it, but I was born in—as some people have called it—the worst year of world history, namely, at the low point of the Holocaust (1944), and the state of Israel was founded just before my fourth birthday (May 14, 1948). Notice the quotation above this chapter!

---

of the saints" (Israel), others have "him," thought to refer to the Most High.

23. Herzl (1896).
24. See Van Campen (2007) and Ouweneel (2011, §13.4).
25. See Voorhoeve (1866), and the English commentaries of John Darby, Frederick W. Grant, William Kelly, and many others.
26. One simple argument was this: "The heavens are the Lord's heavens, but the earth he has given to the children of man" (Ps. 115:16).

Expressed in my own words: it was a natural thing for God to lead so many of his people back to the Promised Land because this is where Israel naturally belongs. But it was a supernatural thing that God worked in the hearts of the majority of the member states of the United Nations to vote *for* the "Partition Plan for Palestine" (November 29, 1947). Millions of Christians worldwide had their ears near their radios to experience the miraculous outcome of this voting. The positive outcome guaranteed the possibility of the establishment of the Jewish state.[27]

It could or should never have happened, the supersessionists tried to assure us. But it did happen. And if the written Word did not stimulate supersessionists to rethink their position, then *this event* led quite a few of them to rethink the matter: could there be truth in the literal-interpretation-of-the-prophecies after all?

4.3.2 Theological Roots of Supersessionism

In the previous section, we considered some historical aspects that help us to understand how supersessionism could have arisen. Of course, there are also purely theological arguments, many of which we have already examined in volume IV/1a.

The universalistic view of salvation envisions only one "people of God," existing from penitent Adam and Eve until the new heavens and the new earth. Whether this is called "church" or "Israel"—or both, or something else—is essentially irrelevant. Even Augustine saw room for a massive conversion of the Jewish people in the end time.[28] But this would mean nothing else than a mass of Jewish converts streaming into the Christian church. Many Protestant theologians to-

---

27. Also a Palestinian state, of course, but the Palestinians did not avail themselves of the opportunity because the Arab nations were convinced they would soon drive the Jews out of the land. The same God who guaranteed the establishment of the Jewish state prevented the established of a Palestinian state. For decades now, there has been much debate on the "two-state solution" in the Holy Land: a Jewish and a Palestinian state side-by-side—forgetting that the Palestinians could have had their own state already in 1948.
28. *De Civitate Dei* XX.30; *Enarrationes in Psalmos* on Ps. 14:7.

day fully agree with Augustine on this point. This is why they sometimes reject the term supersessionism because they believe that God has *not* done away with Israel forever. Indeed, terms like supersessionism and replacement theology may be quite confusing in this and several other respects.

Christians who believe that in the end a massive conversion of Jews will occur are nevertheless supersessionists if they do not accept the literal fulfillment of the Tanakh prophecies concerning future Israel and the Messianic kingdom. Let me mention three illustrations.

(1) An amillennialist is by definition a supersessionist because they do not believe in a future Messianic kingdom in which Israel will be the center of the world and the Messiah will sit on the throne of David.

(2) In supersessionist thought, the idea of a "Messianic" (i.e., Jesus-believing) Jewry, observing both the Torah of Moses (including circumcision, Sabbath, festivals, and food laws) and the Torah of Christ, is inconceivable, which is precisely the view of millions of Roman Catholics and Protestants today.

(3) For the most consistent supersessionist, the establishment of the state of Israel in 1948 has *nothing* to do with biblical prophecies. When the initial contours of a Jewish state were becoming visible, Herman Bavinck wrote: "However we may view these political combinations [viz., concerning the establishment of a state of Israel], the New Testament furnishes not the slightest support for such an expectation."[29] And J. Douma, another Reformed theologian in the Netherlands, reportedly remarked that the establishment of the state of Israel in 1948 had just as little to do with biblical prophecy as the establishment of the state of Belgium in 1830.

The spiritualist view with regard to biblical prophecies has one supposed advantage, namely, that the expositor need not exegete the many details of the texts. Israel, Judah, Jerusalem, Zion, the temple (mount), these all refer to precisely the same reality, namely, the church, even in passages where a clear distinction is made between these concepts, as we have

---

29. Bavinck (*RD* 4:665).

seen. Some have put it this way: the *this-worldly* character of the Tanakh is indeed recognized, but people believe this must be interpreted in an *other-worldly* way.[30]

Supersessionist exegesis speaks in very vague terms about the "glorious future" of the church, without feeling obliged to explain what the numerous details of the prophecies are telling us. It is the same with "Assyria," the "fourth beast," Gog, Edom, the "beast" in Revelation 13, and so on. They all mean the same: some vague eschatological world power, threatening "the church," and defeated by Christ at his second coming. When it comes to explaining the fulfillment of the prophecies in the Tanakh, supersessionists have an easy job; it all remains vague and unreal.

4.3.3 Theological Decline of Supersessionism

An exegete who has concluded that the church is the "spiritual Israel" will understand "the church" as the referent wherever Israel is mentioned in biblical prophecy. This due to viewing the church as existing since Adam, so that wherever the Tanakh speaks of the people of God, or of "Israel," we may insert "the church."

Until 1951, Christians in the Netherlands almost exclusively read the Dutch States Translation of 1637, just as English-speaking Christians until the middle of the twentieth century almost exclusively read the Authorized Version, that is, the King James Bible (1611).[31] For Dutch readers this meant that for centuries, their understanding of Scripture was shaped by the chapter headings and the Annotations that accompanied the States Translation. As far as the prophetic

---

30. See, e.g., Berkouwer (1972, 173).

31. The States Translation got its name from the States General of the Netherlands, which had commissioned this translation, just as King James had commissioned the KJV in Great Britain. Neither of these was an ecclesiastical initiative, but a political initiative, which tells us something about the relationship between religion and politics in those days. Such an initiative would have been unthinkable in, e.g., post-1776 America.

books are concerned, these Annotations teem with references to "the church" where the text was speaking about Zion, Israel, Judah, Jerusalem, and so on.[32]

Here are several salient examples.[33]

The Annotation on Isaiah 8:8 commented that Immanuel is Christ, "who is the head of his Church, which was at that time in the land of Judah."

On Isaiah 9:3 [2], this alternative translation was given: "Lord, thou hast increased the joy of the people, or made the peoples Joy great, (speaking of the state and condition of the Church of the New Testament) forasmuch as they (consisting of Israelites and heathen) shall praise thee with one accord for the great mercies afforded unto them in Christ)."

When Isaiah 11:14 told us that Judah and Ephraim will "swoop down on the shoulder of the Philistines," the Annotation explained:

> This is spoken in a spiritual way; namely so, as that the faithful Israelites shall by the preaching of the Gospel, suddenly fall upon the Gentiles, lay hold of them, and conquer them, because they shall bring some of them to the Christian faith, and shall convince the rest, so that they shall have no excuse in the sight and presence of God. However the Prophet doth here intimate by this comparison (taken from a bird of prey, or from a fox, that falleth upon poultry, and the like) the victory, which the Lord should grant unto his Church against her enemies, as the same was performed, or accomplished by the Apostles, and other Pastors and Teachers.

Such pious fantasy, bordering on absurdity, warrants no comment. Israel *violently* overcoming its hostile neighbors (at the beginning of the Messianic kingdom) is interpreted

---

32. The Dutch-language Internet website hosting the Kanttekeningen (www.statenvertaling.net/ kanttekeningen.html) makes the rather disingenuous, if not duplicitous, claim that "the Annotations had emphatically not been intended as interpretation. They involved mainly linguistic comments." The material provided in our discussion proves the very opposite.
33. For each Annotation cited in this discussion, see Haak (1918, ad loc.); the Annotation for Isa. 9:3 is linked in Haak with Isa. 9:2.

to portray the church *kindly* convincing the Gentiles of the gospel.

When Isaiah 11:12 said that the LORD will "gather the dispersed of Judah [dispersed all over the world because of their sins] from the four corners of the earth," the Annotation explained: "To wit, in *Christ*, who gathereth his Church from the four corners of the World, so that in him is spiritually fulfilled, that which God promised, Deut. 30.4." Again, this has nothing to do with exegesis: there

is an enormous difference between bringing *dispersed* people *back* after having chastised them, and bringing the good news to the unconverted.

When Isaiah 11:16 said, "[T]here will be a highway from Assyria for the remnant that remains of his people," the Annotation explained: "The meaning is, all things shall be smoothed and planted, and be without let or hindrance, when Christ shall gather his Church by the preaching of the Gospel." Another example of pure imagination.

The heading above Isaiah 60 commented: "The Lord exhorteth his Church to rejoice because of the blessedness purchased for her by Christ." Joel 3 presented "A Prophecy of God's judgment upon the Enemies of his Church, deriding their vain devices and preparations against the same." Zechariah 14 had this heading: ". . . Mention is also made of the rare gifts, which the LORD would pour forth upon his Church, of their blessed and glorious estate."[34]

This technique went on and on. If you want to understand the damage spiritualistic supersessionism has done to Calvinist Christianity, you need only study the Annotations to the Dutch States Translation. From the seventeenth century onward, entire generations have been saturated with them. It is all the more remarkable that, in the seventeenth and eighteenth century, there have been Reformed and Presbyterian pastors who clung to the literal meaning of the prophe-

---

34. I read such headings for the first time when I was about 10; I could not understand and believe them—and I still cannot today.

cies, and thus to the literal "land promise" for literal, ethnic Israel (see volume IV/1a, §14.3.2).[35]

4.4 Church and Heaven Cut the Line
4.4.1 The Underlying Logic

The logic that was followed in supersessionist exegesis was quite simple. It began with stating that, from a redemptive-historical viewpoint, the New Testament church replaces or absorbs the Israel of the Tanakh. Thus, the sole spiritual future for the Jews, whether on earth or in eternity, lies not only in their conversion to Christ but also in their incorporation into the Christian church. This was how things went for, say, seventeen hundred years: Jews converted—voluntarily or under pressure—to "Christianity," joined the Roman Catholic or the national Protestant church (Lutheran, Calvinist, Anglican) or one of their spin-off churches, *and surrendered their Jewish identity*. Committed supersessionists like Abraham Kuyper were interested in "missionary work" among the Jews—but for him this meant, implicitly or explicitly, that the Jews' hope lay in joining the Reformed churches.

The fact that the great majority of Israel "stubbornly" refuses to do so, and clings to its rabbinic practices, and even to the name "Israel"—which the supersessionist claims as belonging to the Christian church alone—is disturbing, irritating, despicable. Ethnic Israel is a perpetual thorn in the side of a thoroughly supersessionist church, and since Constantine the Great until, say, the nineteenth century, this church included almost all Christianity.

One theologian has identified the church's "fall into sin" to be the rise of militarism after the fourth-century Constantinian shift,[36] and understandably so. Before 312, Christians generally refused to serve in the Roman armies. But after 312, it became an *honor* for young Christians to join the armies of the now Christian emperor. This explains why people like Saint George, who fought the "dragon," and the warrior Saint

---

35. See Van Campen (2007); Ouweneel (2011, §13.4).
36. Heering (1953).

Theodore, who later became the patron saint of Venice, were highly venerated after 312.

However, the church's "fall into sin" after 312 might more reasonably and plausibly be identified with the rise of anti-Semitic supersessionism. Constantine had barely "converted" to Christianity—intending to turn Christianity into a *Gentile* religion more than ever before—when he began enacting laws against the Jews. In 315, these laws involved converts to Judaism and to Christianity; in 321 these laws involved the obligation of Jews to take part in city government (which was very unfavorable because in this case one had to provide surety of the payment of taxes to the state).[37] Constantine's Sunday Law (321) was a means to separate Jews and Christians from each other by replacing Saturday with Sunday as the day of obligatory rest. And the Council of Nicea (325), important in the battle against the Arians (those who denied the eternal pre-existence and deity of Christ), deliberately furthered the separation between Jews and Christians by changing the date of Easter, so that Jewish *Pesach* would rarely coincide with Christian Easter.[38]

Slowly and reluctantly, part of the Reformed world began to change its mind when God's special ways with Israel became visible in the establishment of the state of Israel (1948), and in Israel's victories over its hostile neighbors, including the conquest of ancient Jerusalem (1967). Leading Reformed theologians began, somewhat hesitantly, to talk about the possibility that these developments might have something

---

37. Smelik (2004, 153).
38. Constantine argued (Eusebius, *De vita Constantini* III.18): "[I]t appeared an unworthy thing that in the celebration of this most holy feast we should follow the practice of the Jews, who have impiously defiled their hands with enormous sin, and are, therefore, deservedly afflicted with blindness of soul. For we have it in our power, if we abandon their custom, to prolong the due observance of this ordinance to future ages, by a truer order, which we have preserved from the very day of the passion until the present time. Let us then have nothing in common with the detestable Jewish crowd; for we have received from our Saviour a different way" (https://documentacatholicaomnia.eu/03d/0265–0339,_Eusebius_Caesariensis,_Vita_Constantini_%5bSchaff%5d,_EN.pdf).

to do with biblical prophecy. However, this change of mind was seldom consistently developed. On the one hand, it was recognized again that God had a future for a converted ethnic Israel in its own land, which was a positive development. On the other hand, many of these theologians maintained such notions as the "church since Adam," kept believing that Gentile believers were the "spiritual Israel," continued to view infant baptism as the replacement of the Tanakh rite of circumcision, insisted that the Sunday is the new "Sabbath," and argued that Israel's future lay solely and ultimately within "the church" (see next section).

This sad state of affairs reminds me—and I say this with respect—of Hosea 7:8, "Ephraim is a cake not turned," or, "They are like a thin loaf of bread that is baked on only one side" (NIRV). You cannot have it both ways (a bit of supersessionism, and a bit of "Israelism"); or to say it with the prophet Elijah, "How long will you go limping between two different opinions?" (1 Kings 18:21), or "How long will you stagger around on two crutches?" (EHV), or "How long are you going to sit on the fence?" (MSG).

4.4.2 The Five Replacements

This helps us somewhat in our assessment of supersessionism. The theologians mentioned above do believe that the state of Israel in some way or another relates to the prophecies in the Tanakh. In other words, they reject what I would call "hard" supersessionism. Yet, what they do believe could be called "soft" supersessionism. For instance, if one maintains that circumcision has been replaced by infant baptism, they would consider as biblically unjustifiable the circumcision as it continues to be practiced among "Messianic" (Jesus-confessing) Jews. This is because one cannot both circumcise and baptize—as these Jews indeed do—if the two are identical. A person believing in the replacement of circumcision with baptism is a "soft" supersessionist, who differs only in degree from a "hard" supersessionist.

Precisely the same is true for those who maintain that Sunday is the "Sabbath" of the new (church) era. They cannot possibly approve of Messianic Jews keeping the Sabbath as God had instituted it in the Tanakh.[39] Perhaps we should say that the "land promise" is a touchstone for supersessionism, but that the phenomenon of Messianic Judaism is an equally important touchstone. Perhaps a third touchstone is the fundamental question whether we may expect an earthly Messianic kingdom, whose center will be Israel, and which will arrive before the new heavens and the new earth. And those who do believe that the present state of Israel is related to the prophecies in the Tanakh, yet place all their eschatological hopes primarily in the bliss awaiting them after physical death, are still "soft" supersessionists.

These, then, are the five great replacements that belong to replacement theology (i.e., supersessionism), all of which are equally objectionable exegetically and theologically.

(1) *The Infant's Ritual.* The circumcision of the Tanakh has been replaced by (infant) baptism—something that is taught nowhere in the New Testament, certainly not in Colossians 2:11-12, "In him [i.e., Christ] also you were circumcised with a circumcision made without hands, by putting off the body of the flesh, by the circumcision of Christ, having been buried with him in baptism, in which you were also raised with him through faith in the powerful working of God, who raised him from the dead."[40] The "circumcision of Christ" intended here is not the literal circumcision ("made with hands") that Jesus received when he was eight days old, but his death on the cross, which is applied to a person when they come to faith in Christ, as if that believer themselves had died on the cross.[41] Here "circumcision" referred to the inner renewal of the person: the "circumcision" of the *heart*.[42] This inner work of God finds its counterpart in the outer event of baptism. This does not at all point to a replacement, but far more to a parallel.

---

39. The same disapproval would pertain to Seventh Day Adventists and other Christian Sabbath-keepers, of course.
40. See extensively, Ouweneel (2011, §6.2).
41. Cf. Rom. 6:5-8; Gal. 2:20; 5:24; 6:14.
42. Cf. Deut. 10:16; 30:6; Jer. 4:4; Rom. 2:29.

(2) *The Sacred Week Day.* Saturday has been replaced by Sunday; that is, the Tanakhic Sabbath has been moved from the seventh day to the first day of the week. Again, this is taught nowhere in the New Testament.[43] The first day of the week may be marked as a special day for Christians, but this has nothing to do with the Sabbath, which was a day of mandatory rest. If supersessionists say that the Sunday now is the "Lord's Day," they have no basis for that claim. The New Testament has two Greek expressions for the "day of the LORD," namely, *hēmera [tou] kyriou*,[44] which has exclusively an eschatological meaning (referring to Christ's return and the Messianic kingdom), and *kuriakē hēmera*, "Lord's[45] day," which occurs only in Revelation 1:10, and needs an interpretation of its own.[46] Even if the latter expression referred to the first day of the week, this would show that this day is special, but not that it is the "Sabbath" of the new era.

(3) *The Throne.* The earthly throne of David has been replaced by the throne of God in heaven; in other words, the "throne of David"[47] has apparently moved to heaven, in order to coincide with the throne of God. The Bible never teaches such a thing; on the contrary, Jesus makes a clear distinction (Rev. 3:21): "The one who conquers, I will grant him to sit with me on *my* throne [future!], as I also conquered and sat down with my Father on *his* throne [past and present!]." Inconceivable is Meyer's suggestion that the two thrones referred to here are identical.[48] It not only conflicts with logic ("you will sit on *my* throne, as I sat down on *his* throne"), but it also betrays the underlying supersessionism: the conquerors will sit with Christ on a throne *in heaven*. And if Luke 1:32 is taken into consideration ("the Lord God will give to him the throne of his father David"), some expositors might not localize this throne in heaven, but they nonetheless spir-

---

43 See extensively, Ouweneel (2001a, Appendix 3).
44. Acts 2:20; 1 Cor. 5:5; 1 Thess. 5:1–2; 2 Pet. 3:10.
45. The Gk. word *kuriakē* is actually an adjective, something like "lordly."
46. The older expositors all applied it to the Sunday, but this is no proof.
47. Cf. 2 Sam. 3:10; 1 Kings 2:12, 24, 33, 45; Isa. 9:7; Jer. 22:30; Luke 1:32.
48. https://biblehub.com/commentaries/revelation/3–21.htm.

itualize it, as we find, for instance, in Gill's Exposition: ". . . his throne was typical of the Messiah's throne and kingdom; which is not of this world, but is in his church, and is set up in the hearts of his people, where he reigns by his Spirit and grace; and this is a throne and kingdom 'given' by the Lord God."[49] Notice the misunderstanding here that we have encountered several times now: if something is not "*of* this world," it may yet be *in* this world (John 17:11–15), just as the "kingdom of heaven" is an other-worldly kingdom *on earth*.

In supersessionism, Jesus' throne may mean all kinds of things, as long as the "throne of David" does *not* mean what it has always meant: "So Solomon sat on the *throne of David* his father, and his kingdom was firmly established. . . . King Solomon shall be blessed, and the *throne of David* shall be established before the LORD forever" (1 Kings 2:12, 45). *Which* throne was to be established forever? *That* throne, the one on which King Solomon was sitting—no spiritualized throne, and no celestialized[50] throne either. And in closing, I notice that both the heavenly throne of God and the earthly throne of Solomon are called "throne of the LORD" (Exod. 17:6; 1 Chron. 29:23), but this does not mean that they are identical.

(4) *The People of God.* Ethnic Israel has been replaced by the New Testament church; according to supersessionism, the church has annexed and spiritualized—a double error—the yet unfulfilled promises for Israel, such as the "land promise," while it left the announced curses to Israel. What could violate the spirit of both the Tanakh and the New Testament more than this? Again, we may appeal here to the common sense of expositors. Moses said, God "will gather you again from all the peoples where the LORD your God has scattered you...And the LORD your God will bring you into the land that your fathers possessed, that you may possess it" (Deut. 30:3-5). The text is perfectly clear: (a) formerly, Israel's forefathers possessed the land of Israel; (b) because of their sins, God has *scattered* the Israelites among the nations; (c) but in the end he will bring them back to that same land. How could this

---

49. https://biblehub.com/commentaries/luke/1–32.htm.
50. To celestialize is to turn something earthly into something heavenly.

ever be applied to the New Testament Ecclesia? (a) What is the land that the forefathers of the Christians formerly possessed? (b) In what sense, have Christians, because of their sins, been scattered among the nations? (c) In what sense will they be brought *back*? And to what "land"? Valid exegesis requires opening the biblical text, not arguing the text away for the benefit of one's own biases.

(5) *The "heavenly" destination.* One very important, but often overlooked and neglected form of replacement belonging to replacement theology is that the "kingdom of heaven" (a heavenly kingdom *on earth*, beginning with the second coming of Christ) is replaced by the expectation of "heaven" when the believer dies; or to put it differently, the "land promise" is replaced by the promise of a "heavenly country" (cf. Heb. 11:16), which is erroneously understood to be "heaven" as the place where believers go when they die.[51] This point is important enough to devote the next section to it.

4.5 Christian Expectation
4.5.1 The Kingdom of Heaven or Heaven?

Especially this fifth replacement deserves further attention; the biblical expectation of the coming Messianic kingdom is replaced by the supersessionist expectation of heaven.[52] This incredibly drastic replacement has been, and is, characteristic of both the Roman Catholic and the traditional Protestant eschatology (including that of some Evangelical leaders): when a believer dies, they go to heaven, and that's it. This is the content of the gospel ("believe, and you will go to heaven")—the rest is less relevant. Dying and going to heaven is the great end goal; in the spiritual expectation of numerous Christians the thought of the second coming of Christ as well as the resurrection of the body hardly plays any other role than a theoretical one. They believe in it as part of orthodox faith, but they do not *live by* it. They are not *waiting* for or *looking forward to* this coming. This is because, when you get to heaven, you will already have it all.

---

51. See extensively, Ouweneel (2012a, chapters 2–3).
52. See extensively, Ouweneel (2020b; 2022).

The German language of Martin Luther is an interesting example of this profoundly significant replacement. In German, the kingdom of heaven is *das Reich der Himmel*, or, *das Himmelreich* (Dutch: *hemelrijk*).[53] Much more easily than in English, such an expression could very easily come to mean *Himmel* (Dutch: *hemel*), which is "heaven," taken in the sense of the blissful abode of the deceased (see the next section).[54] As one theologian explained it, the faith of many Christians has been more heaven-oriented than land-oriented in contrast with the land-oriented Jewish faith; the biblical themes of land and city have been spiritualized, and applied to some other-worldly place rather than to this earth.[55]

Supersessionism has always gone hand-in-hand with this expectation of heaven, and suffered the concomitant loss of perspective regarding the end times, Israel, and the coming Messianic kingdom. Characteristically eschatological statements were changed into statements about heaven-where-you-go-when-you-die. For instance, every statement about "entering the kingdom of heaven" was understood to mean "entering heaven when you die": "Truly, I say to you, only with difficulty will a rich person enter the kingdom of heaven. Again I tell you, it is easier for a camel to go through the eye of a needle than for a rich person to enter the kingdom of God" (Matt. 19:23; cf. 5:20; 7:21; 18:3; 23:13). And the apostle Peter's statement, "For in this way there will be richly provided for you an entrance into the eternal kingdom of our Lord and Savior Jesus Christ" (2 Pet. 1:11), was understood to mean "entrance into heaven." A good example of this replacement is the highly regarded English expositor Matthew

---

53. An example is a hymn by Heinrich von Laufenberg: *Im Himmelreich sind Freuden viel ohn End und Ziel: dahin soll uns Verlangen* ("In the realm of heaven are many joys without end and goal: to there must our desire be").

54. See extensively, Ouweneel (2011, §13.6.1; 2012a, §1.1.2). This is also the tone in many Bach cantatas: laments about the present, craving for heaven, but very little about the second coming of Christ; an exception is Cantata 140, *Wachet auf, ruft uns die Stimme*. (Cantata 62, *Nun komm, der Heiden Heiland*, deals not with the second coming but with Advent.)

55. Holwerda (1995, 87).

Henry.[56] However, once again, in the Bible the "kingdom of heaven" always referred to a heavenly kingdom *on earth* (even though it will have an "upper story," where Christ will reign with his risen and glorified saints; cf. Matt. 8:11).[57] It means that "heaven rules" (cf. Dan. 4:26), but *on earth* (as Nebuchadnezzar found out [Dan. 4]). The kingdom of God is not "*from here*" (John 18:36 NKJV)—but rather from above—but it is definitely here: it is a heavenly kingdom on earth. As Jesus said, "The kingdom of God is in the midst of you" (Luke 17:20-21).

How could this kingdom be "heaven"? Has *heaven* ever "suffered violence," as has the kingdom of heaven (Matt. 11:12)? Or how could John the Baptist and Jesus say that the "kingdom of heaven" has "come near" (3:2; 4:17 HCSB), if instead they should have called repentant people to "come near" the "kingdom of heaven"?

So what are Jesus-believers looking for? They look for the manifestation of the "kingdom of heaven" in majesty and glory at the re-appearance of Christ. But the supersessionist believer who is looking for the "kingdom of heaven" is really looking for the heavenly paradise which they believes they will reach at physical death.[58] This matter of the "intermediate state"—the period between one's death and resurrection—is rarely discussed in the New Testament. When terms like "(a)waiting" are used, it is always the second coming of Christ and the Messianic kingdom that were being referred to,[59] and sometimes the new heaven and the new earth that will follow upon it (2 Pet. 3:13).

Abraham Kuyper wrote: "The great majority of Christians do not think much further than their own death."[60] Hendrikus Berkhof spoke of "the centuries-long concentration on

---

56. bible.cc/matthew/19-23.htm en bible.cc/2_peter/1-11.htm.
57. Cf. Hill (2001), who contrasted those church fathers who believed in an earthly kingdom of heaven (Lat. *regnum caelorum terrestre*) with those who believed in a heavenly kingdom of heaven (Lat. *regnum caelorum caeleste*).
58. Cf. Ouweneel (2020b).
59. Luke 2:38; Rom. 8:23; 1 Cor. 1:7; Phil. 3:20; Titus 2:13; Heb. 9:28; 10:13.
60. Kuyper (1905, 201).

the salvation of the individual soul.... The consummation of mankind, which would give a new bodily existence as well, could hardly add anything essential to the salvation already received.... The question how God will achieve his purpose for the world is thereby reduced to insignificance: This, too, is untenable."[61] The Roman Catholic School Catechism, which between 1920 and 1964 was a mandatory component of instruction at all Roman Catholic schools in the Netherlands, began with the by now famous question: "To what end are we on earth?" The answer was: 'We are on earth to serve God, and as a consequence to be happy here and hereafter."[62] The beautiful aspect of it—in fact more beautiful than Answer 1 of the Heidelberg Catechism because it is not anthropocentric but theocentric—is that it is not primarily focused upon one's own salvation but upon serving God. Less beautiful is that, here again, the future seems to be what lies beyond death, rather than the resurrection, the second coming, the Messianic kingdom, and the new heavens and earth.

4.5.2 Dante Alighieri and Thomas à Kempis

No doubt, some of the most widely read books throughout church history are *La Divina Commedia* ("The Divine Comedy") by Dante Alighieri (written ca. 1308-1321), *De imitatione Christi* ("The Imitation of Christ") by Thomas à Kempis (1441), and *The Pilgrim's Progress* by John Bunyan (1678) (see next section). It is remarkable to notice how, in all three works, blessed death is described as *the* joyful expectation of the Christian, (almost) entirely bypassing the second coming of Christ and the establishment of the Messianic kingdom (to say nothing of the promises to Israel). In *The Divine Comedy*, Dante describes purgatory, hell, and heaven as places where people might go after their physical death. In order to get to

---

61. Berkhof (1986, 529–30); he referred to Aalders (1969) as well, "who for the sake of the individual expectation of heaven has entirely dropped the line of earth and humanity."
62. There is a clear parallel here with the Westminster Shorter Catechism: "Q. 1. What is the chief end of man? A. Man's chief end is to glorify God (1 Cor. 10/:31; Rom. 11:36), and to enjoy him for ever (Ps. 73:25–28)" (Dennison, [*RC* 4:353]).

heaven, the soul must go through a certain cleansing ("purging") process in purgatory. Resurrection and Christ's second coming lie far outside Dante's purview (although, also in his days, the Nicene Creed said, "I expect the resurrection of the dead and the life of the age to come"). Interestingly, British theologian Alister McGrath, too, who refers extensively to Dante, mainly deals with hell, purgatory, and heaven.[63]

In *The Imitation of Christ* by Thomas à Kempis, we do not hear about the second coming either, but there *is* a section called "Of meditation upon death."[64] In this part, we are extensively told how a Christian must spiritually prepare themselves for the hour of their death and the bliss that awaits them afterwards. Thomas is a pioneer of what has been called the "art of dying" and the accompaniment of the dying, a theme that in the Reformed world had lasting effects for centuries,[65] whereas for the second coming of Christ there was hardly any interest,[66] and even less for the Israel prophecies.

In Thomas' book we find the following remarkable sentences: "Always be thou prepared, and so live that death may never find thee unprepared. Many die suddenly and unexpectedly. 'For at such an hour as ye think not, the Son of Man cometh' [Luke 12:40]."[67] Notice what happens here: the second coming of which Jesus speaks in Luke 12 is identified with the hour of a Christian's death! Apparently, underlying this is the view that, when a Christian dies, Christ "cometh" in person to gather to himself the deceased believer. But this is not at all the teaching of the New Testament. There is a clear distinction between physical death, when *angels* come to take the deceased believer with them (Luke 16:22), and the

---

63. McGrath (2007, 469–71, 477–78).
64. Book 1, § 23; https://www.gutenberg.org/cache/epub/1653/pg1653.txt.
65. See, e.g., the (in)famous *Consolation of the Sick* by Rev. Cornelis van Hille (sixteenth century), in which the sick are "comforted" with the notice that they probably will soon die, and that they must spiritually prepare themselves for meeting a holy God; regarding this, see Ouweneel (2004, 46). The consolation consists not of healing, or of the Lord's nearness, but of going-to-heaven-when-you-die.
66. Hoek (2010).
67. Book 1, § 23.3.

second coming when Jesus *himself* comes to collect the believers (John 14:3), such that deceased believers are raised (1 Thess. 4:13-17) and living believers are transformed (1 Cor. 15:51-54).

In the same section, Thomas said in a different passage: "Keep thine heart free, and lifted up towards God, for here have we no continuing city. To Him direct thy daily prayers with crying and tears, that thy spirit may be found worthy to pass happily after death unto its Lord."[68] The words, "here have we no continuing city," were an allusion to Hebrews 13:14, "here we have no lasting city, but we seek the city that is to come." In the entire context of the letter to the Hebrews, it is obvious that this referred to the heavenly Jerusalem, the celestial capital of the Messianic kingdom of peace and justice (12:28), the statement thus referring to the "(Messianic) age to come" (6:5) and the "world to come" (2:5), arriving at Christ's return.[69] Thomas à Kempis, however, was unmistakably referring to the place where Christians go after they have died, as thousands of other Christians have done as well.

4.5.3 John Bunyan

At the end of the previous section, we encountered an entire complex of biblical city metaphors, including the "city that has foundations" (Heb. 11:10; cf. v. 16), the "city of the living God, the heavenly Jerusalem" (12:22), and "the city that is to come" (13:14), to the "city of my God, the new Jerusalem, which comes down from my God out of heaven" and the "holy city, new Jerusalem, coming down out of heaven from God, prepared as a bride adorned for her husband" (Rev. 3:12; 21:2).[70] There is an ancient tradition that does not link these metaphors with the Messianic kingdom, as they should be, but rather with heaven in the sense of the intermediate state; the latter subject is not explicitly mentioned but must be derived from the context. Thus, for instance, the Annotations to the Dutch States Translation (1637) linked

---

68. Book 1, § 23.9.
69. Cf. Ouweneel (1982, 2:ad loc.).
70. Cf. Rev. 21:10; 22:19; see also Gal. 4:26, the "Jerusalem above."

the "city" in Hebrews with heaven, and in Revelation with the "abode of the blissful believers," *or* with the church. Matthew Henry referred the "city" in Hebrews 11:10 and 16 to heaven, in such a way that he was apparently referring to the intermediate state.[71]

John Bunyan made extensive use of the city metaphor in his work *The Pilgrim's Progress*. This book describes the life of the Christian, who is a pilgrim en route not to the kingdom of God, arriving at Jesus' second coming, but to the "celestial city," that is, the "heaven" of the hereafter, to the intermediate state.[72] The protagonist, representing every human being who is open to the gospel, comes from the "city of destruction," is freed from his burden of sins at the cross, and after many vicissitudes comes to the river of death.[73] After having safely crossed this river, he arrives in the city of heaven, "heavenly Jerusalem." Bunyan supplied an exhaustive description of the glories of heaven—but the resurrection and the second coming of Christ pay no role in his story, nor does the Messianic kingdom. Just as Thomas à Kempis linked the believer's death with the coming of the Son of Man, so too in Bunyan's work the believer's death and the return of Jesus are intermingled. At the moment the Christian enters the "celestial city," they are "transfigured,"[74] which clearly suggests the transformation that the believer's body undergoes only at Jesus' second coming (1Cor. 15:51; Phil. 3:20-21).

In Bunyan's presentation, after physical death the Christian enters heaven, and is immediately invited to the marriage supper of the Lamb (Rev. 19:6-9). Here again, we encounter the serious confusion of the intermediate state with the resurrection state. The "celestial city" is described in terms of

---

71. www.biblestudytools.com/commentaries/matthew-henry-complete/hebrews/11.html. Idem 12.html en 13.html.
72. http://www.samizdat.qc.ca/arts/lit/Pilgrims_Progress.pdf.
73. This "river" resembles the way "Jordan" occurs in several spirituals, where it is the boundary between physical life and the hereafter, e.g., "Roll Jordan, roll, I wanter go to heav'n when I die."
74. www.verselink.org/topics/pil/plgrm12032.html; in the KJV, the word "transfigure" is used in Matt. 17:2 (and par.), from the Gr. *metamorphoomai*; 1 Cor. 15:51 has Gk. *allassō* (KJV: "change").

the new Jerusalem, such as streets of gold,[75] and many other metaphors from Revelation are being used, which in that Bible book are *never* related to the believer's intermediate state but rather to the resurrection state.

It is no wonder that so few Christians are really interested in Israel and in the coming Messianic kingdom. Their entire gospel is this: If you believe in Jesus Christ, your sins will be forgiven, and when you die you will go to heaven. What more do you want? In reality, this is nothing less than a shocking reduction of the biblical message. We may quietly assume that such Christians don't have a clue about what is meant by the "gospel of the kingdom" (unless they understand the kingdom to be "heaven").[76]

4.5.4 Summary

To a great extent, Dante Alighieri, Thomas à Kempis, John Bunyan, and many other, less well-known authors were responsible for the eschatological perspective of most Christians having become so blurred and impoverished. The Christian's future supposedly lies in the "heavenly city," which is entered at physical death. In practical Christianity, the hope of Christ's second coming, of the resurrection of the body, of the restoration of Israel, of the Messianic kingdom, and of the new heavens and earth, disappeared. Or it was degraded to a safe orthodox statement, somewhere at the close of a confession ("from whence he shall come to judge the living and the dead"), a "safe" statement that did not at all affect the practical lives of the believers. The second coming was believed to be at the "end of times," and thus, to believers' minds, almost by definition still far away. But the Christian's physical death was always "near." Be prepared for it! And all the other future matters, leave them to the specialists, or to

---

75. A question such as "Will there literally be streets of gold in heaven?" (https://www.gotquestions.org/streets-of-gold.html) is already mistaken in its starting point.
76. Cf. Matt. 4:23; 9:35; 24:14; Luke 4:43; 8:1; 16:16; Acts 8:12; this includes passages that, in the Greek, speak of "evangelizing" (preaching the gospel of) the kingdom.

the hobbyists. Why bother yourself about the Messianic kingdom, or even the Israel prophecies?

In a time of strong individualism, the gospel is about *me* and *my* future, which follows upon *my* physical death. *Or* in certain forms of charismatic belief and practice, the emphasis is on what the power of the Holy Spirit means *for me* here and now. This is the Spirit as he manifests himself in miraculous healings, glossolalia, prophecy, and the like. But in such circles, the interest in post-second-coming and post-resurrection events is meager as well. I see three types of Protestantism here, depending on where the center of their spiritual expectations lie: (a) the *here-and-now* Protestants, the (b) *hereafter* Protestants, and (c) and the *post-second-coming* and *post-resurrection* Protestants. By now, it is no secret where my own preference lies.

Supersessionism managed to readily fill the gap that this individualistic eschatology had created: the prophecies in the Tanakh are *not* about ethnic Israel or some Messianic kingdom. They are about *you*, about the church, and about heaven.

4.6 Again, the Anti-Semitic Breeding Ground
4.6.1 Church Fathers

By leading Christians to believe that the gospel's main objective was certainty about going to heaven when they die, supersessionists could implicitly argue: Forget about the Jews; they play no role in your eschatology. This is why Roman Catholic, traditional Protestant, and Evangelical congregations can have service after service, sermon after sermon, without ever referring to Israel (except when a passage from the Tanakh is chosen, and then only the Israel of the Tanakh is dealt with). This is why the Reformed Forms of Unity hardly ever refer to Israel or the Jews (except in a few references to the Tanakh), simply because they don't function in Reformed theology. You can be a good Christian while fully ignoring the state of Israel, or Judaism, or the Jews in general.

Perhaps this is one of the most sophisticated forms of anti-Semitism: not scolding or threatening the Jews, but ignoring them. These are the people who, when they visit modern Israel, are interested only in stories from the Tanakh and the New Testament—not at all in the state of Israel, or in the people of Israel, whether religious or secular, or in the Arab inhabitants of Israel.

Classic supersessionism has undeniably been a breeding ground for anti-Semitism.[77] Take, for instance, the Latin writing *Adversus Iudaeos* ("Against the Jews") by Cyprian of Carthage (d. 258).[78] He argued that the Jews should blame only themselves, and no one else, for not understanding the Scriptures, for losing Jerusalem and the Promised Land, for the fact that, one day, their rites would disappear, and that the Gentiles would take the place of the Jewish people as the chosen people of God.

Another example is John Chrysostom, one of the main church fathers in the Eastern church, whose "golden mouth"—this is the meaning of his name—has not always produced gold. In the time when supersessionism had already become profoundly rooted in the church, Chrysostom wrote his Greek work *Kata Ioudaiōn* ("Against the Jews"), a series of sermons directed against the Jews as well as Judaistic Christians.[79] He urged Jewish Christians to choose definitively between Judaism and Christianity, and if they chose the latter, to fully surrender their Jewish identity. He held the Jews *en masse* responsible for the crucifixion of Jesus, called it *deicide* ("murder of God"), and asserted that the Jews continued to rejoice in the death of Jesus. He compared the synagogue to a pagan temple, called it a source of all vices and heresies, a place worse than a brothel and a tavern, a nest of scoundrels and wild beasts, a temple of demons, the refuge of crooks and criminals, a hiding place of devils, a secret gathering of the murderers of Christ. Finally, he declared that he hated both

---

77. See extensively, Brustein (2003); Laqueur (2006); cf. Berkouwer (1972, 325–26); Ouweneel (2000a, 275).

78. PL 4:col.703–810; see Jansen (1981, 513–14). Several authors have written a work with this title, "Against the Jews," which in itself is indicative of ati-Semitism in the sense of being "against the Jews."

79. Regarding him, see also "John Chrysostom," *Encyclopedia Judaica*; Ouweneel (2014a, 238–40).

the synagogue and the Jews, declared that "demons dwell in the synagogue, and also in the souls of the Jews," and described them as making themselves "fit" for "slaughter."[80]

Other well-known church teachers, who often are widely appreciated but have written negative things about the Jews, include:

(a) Tertullian also wrote a work with the title *Adversus Iudaeos* ("Against the Jews"), in which he, in a matter-of-fact way, argued that Israel as such no longer has any future with God since, and because, it has rejected its Messiah. Now the church, no longer Israel, is the people of God. The circumcision commandment, the Sabbath commandment, and many other ordinances have been annulled. The temple sacrifices have been abolished.

(b) Aphrahat, a Syriac Christian author,[81] nicknamed the "Persian Sage," wrote twenty-three *Demonstrations*, in which he developed his views of Christian doctrine. Number 19 is titled *Adversus Iudaeos qui Dicunt se Denuo Congregatum Iri* ("Against the Jews, Who Say that They Will Yet Be Gathered Together"). He, too, argued against many Jewish laws (ignoring the fact that these had been given by God himself "forever"), and assured his readers that Israel would never be rebuilt. Already in the Tanakh, Israel is compared with Sodom, and we know that Sodom has been overthrown forever.[82]

(c) Augustine, too, wrote a *Tractatus Adversus Judaeos*, "Tract Against the Jews,"[83] presumably a sermon from the last years of his life. In this sermon he provides an orderly exposition of supersessionism, basically as we know it today. The (New Testament) church has taken the place of Israel; Augustine argued for instance that, when the prophets spoke of the "house of Jacob," they meant ethnic Israel, but when they wrote "Israel," they meant the church.[84] The announcements

---

80. Kata Ioudaiōn (Lat.: Adversus Iudaeos) I.6.
81. Regarding him, see Neusner (1997).
82. Isa. 1:9–11; 3:8–9; Jer. 23:14; Lam. 4:6; Ezek. 16:46–56; Amos 4:11; cf. Matt. 10:15; 11:23–24.
83. PL 42:col.51–64; see Jansen (1981, 514).
84. How could this be, when "Jacob" and "Israel," in poetic parallelism, are men-

of judgment were for the Jews (because they have not accepted the Christ), whereas the announcement of salvation was for the church (for she is today the spiritual Israel). Yet, as we saw, Augustine believed in a massive conversion of the Jews in the end times (who in this way would lose their Jewish identity and join the Christian church). But as far as the Messianic kingdom is concerned, he was an outspoken amillennialist (virtually the inventor of it) (see chapters 11-14).

(d) Isidore of Seville wrote a work called *De fide catholica contra Iudaeos* ("On the Catholic Faith Against the Jews"), in which he pleaded for the presence of the Jews within Christian society in view of their expected role at the second coming of Christ. Yet, despite this plea, his criticism of the Jews was exceptionally sharp: he described their way of life as intentionally conniving.

4.6.2 Martin Luther

Both Martin Luther and John Calvin were thorough supersessionists. We know all too well what they thought of the Jewish people.[85] At first, Luther had sharply resisted the persecution of the Jews, in particular because of his conviction that he would be able to win the Jews to his new doctrine. Although the Jews showed him their gratitude for his brave support, they continued in the faith of their fathers. Luther was so deeply disappointed about this that he changed from a warm admirer and defender of the Jews into their bitter opponent. When in 1537 Elector Frederick of Saxony, the great friend and follower of Luther, banned all the Jews from his land, he received Luther's full support for this.

In subsequent years, Luther published several writings against the Jews.[86] In them, he repeated all the usual falsehoods and calumnies that for centuries had been spread concerning the Jews. He even gave the explicit advice to destroy

---

tioned in the same verses (e.g., Isa. 9:8; 10:20; 14:1; 27:6; 29:23 etc.)?
85. See Ouweneel (2003, 199–200).
86. Brief wider die Sabbather an einen guten Freund (1538), Von den Jüden und ihren Lügen (1543), Vom Schem Hamphoras und vom Geschlechte Christi (1544).

the Jews' synagogues and houses, to burn their religious books, and to silence their spiritual leaders. In this respect, unfortunately, Luther sided completely with the powers of the Counter-Reformation; according to many Luther experts, it was his most serious faux pas. Of course, many have assured us that we must evaluate Luther's attitude toward the Jews against the background of his time—which in itself is correct—and that so many good things that Luther did and said form a counterweight to it. But this does nothing to diminish the reality that, by the end of his life, Luther was an ardent anti-Semite.

The reformer of the Alsace, Martin Bucer, was an equally bitter hater of the Jews.[87] When the law that Philip I, landgrave of Hesse (a part of Germany), had issued for the protection of the Jews expired in 1538, he asked Bucer to come up with suggestions for a new policy. The landgrave himself was benevolent to the Jews, but Bucer advised him to keep the Jews out of all occupations except those that would allow them a minimal standard of living. Bucer's infamous writing, *Judenratschlag* ("Jewish Advice," 1538) was full of negative stereotypes of the Jews. Ultimately, Philip chose for a compromise, which was so severe that many Jews were forced to leave the land of Hesse.

Pardon the comparison, but I do see a remarkable similarity between Muhammad and Luther. Initially, both sympathized with the Jews, and both were convinced that the Jews would accept their new doctrine. British scientist of religion, Karen Armstrong, believed that the rejection by the Jews was probably the bitterest disappointment in Muhammad's life.[88] It led to one of Muhammad's worst atrocities. Whereas Luther *preached* violence against the Jews, which was bad enough, Muhammed *employed* violence against them (a fact that is bypassed by Armstrong[89]). If the story is correct, Muhammad accused the Jewish Banu Qurayza tribe

---

87. Greschat (2004, 156–58).
88. Armstrong (1993, 154).
89. This was perhaps because more recent investigators have cast doubt on this event; e.g., Donner (2012, 73).

of treason, and when they refused to convert to Islam, he had all the man of this tribe (seven to nine hundred) decapitated.

4.6.3 Calvinism

Did Calvinism fare any better in this respect? John Calvin's attitude toward the Jews was also bitter because they refused to accept Jesus as their Messiah. For instance, in his *Commentary on Genesis* (49:10) he wrote:

> ... when, through nearly fifteen centuries, they have been scattered and banished from their country, having no polity, by what pretext can they fancy, from the prophecy of Jacob, that a Redeemer will come to them? Truly, as I would not willingly glory over their calamity; so, unless they, being subdued by it, open their eyes, I freely pronounce that they are worthy to perish a thousand times without remedy.[90]

A relatively unknown work by Calvin is his *Ad Quaestiones et Obiecta Judaei Cuiusdam* ("Response to Questions and Objections of a Certain Jew"), in which he writes: the Jews' "depraved and indomitable obstinacy merits that none of them be pitied, as they all delight in their evils while being oppressed by a great mass of miseries without end or measure."[91]

We must add here, though, that from the end of the sixteenth century, Calvinist Netherlands became a safe haven for European Jews. At the time, the Netherlands was virtually the only country in Europe where Jews could live without oppression and persecution, and enjoy total freedom to practice their religion in their synagogues and their homes. However, this freedom was allowed to Jews by the more liberal city rulers, who were not very outspoken in their Calvinist convictions (to put it mildly). Their motives for allowing freedom to the Jews were less religiously motivated and more economically motivated: Jewish Spanish and Portuguese fu-

---

90. https://biblehub.com/commentaries/calvin/genesis/49.htm.
91. http://truesonsofabraham.com/Calvin_Response.pdf, 39. This website provides the full translation of this work but also a number of anti-Semitic quotations from Calvin's Bible commentaries.

gitives often brought with them a lot of capital. In Calvinist Netherlands, as the proverb goes, the purse has triumphed all too often over the pastor.

We know many examples of Dutch pastors in the seventeenth and eighteenth century who, on the one hand, were open to the idea of some form of eschatological restoration of Israel. On the other hand, however, they were unable to suppress (often fierce) anti-Semitic remarks about the Jews, like those that had been directed toward them from the first century until then.[92] Conspicuous examples of such anti-Semitically minded theologians were Gisbertus Voetius, Johannes Hoornbeeck, Jacobus Koelman, Simon Oomius, Jacobus Fruytier,[93] Campegius Vitringa, Joachim Mobachius, and Franciscus Burman Sr. (see chapter 8). Over against these, for instance Johannes Coccejus and in particular Hero Sibersma, and also Remonstrants such as Hugo Grotius and Simon Episcopius assumed a much more tolerant attitude toward the Jews—though Coccejus made comments that were outright anti-Semitic.[94]

As the pendulum has swung the other way, we have found examples of philo-Semitism or Judeophilia that go to the other extreme.[95] It seems challenging to assume a proper Christian middle position with respect to Jews. We hate them or we hug them; we poke them or we pet them; we cast them out, or we cuddle them to death.

The Dutch scholar Hendrik Brugmans wrote in his history of the Jews in the Netherlands:

> Regarding the relationship of the authorities to the Jews in the days of the [Dutch] Republic [seventeenth and eighteenth century], we can say: that of the authorities was benevolent and

---

92. Van Campen (2007, 53–54, 75, 165, 253, 258–59, 468–70, 515, 538).
93. One wonders, therefore, whether such pastors were the most appropriate figures to name Dutch schools after, such as Hoornbeeck College (Amersfoort) and Jacobus Fruytier School (Apeldoorn).
94. Van Campen (2007, 21, 309–11, 357–58).
95. See especially Schoeps (1952).

tolerant, that of the church disapproving as well as intolerant, and that of the population moderate and indifferent.[96]

The simple truth is that the sons of the Reformation in the Netherlands were not all that benevolent toward Jews; on the contrary, they were rather hostile. No wonder: the Dutch Reformed had uncritically adopted the Augustinian supersessionism of the Roman Catholic Church, which entailed that the church demanded for itself the blessings promised to Abraham, and left to the Jews the Sinaitic curses. Accordingly, the Dutch Reformed Church consistently viewed the Jews as the cursed ones. Several times, the Reformed synods and local consistories pressed the authorities to enact more severe measures against the Jews.[97] Actually, such appeals against Jews fortunately had little effect within the political constellation of the Netherlands; economic well-being triumphed over ecclesiastical positions.

The Dutch Counter-Remonstrant pastor Abraham Costerus wrote a *Historie der Joden* ("History of the Jews"),[98] which clearly brought to light his anti-Jewish attitude. When the Spanish *conversos* (Jews who had been forced to be baptized as "Christians") found refuge in the Netherlands, and there openly returned to their Jewish religion, the Dutch Reformed Church reacted exceptionally fiercely. Pastor Costerus depicted these Jews as an "unclean nation," which tried to build a public synagogue "in which they can perform their evil and foolish ceremonies, and can spit out their gross blasphemies against Christ and his holy Gospels, as well as their curses against the Christians and the Christian authorities."

But Costerus' work exerted little influence, at least in public life: again, the purse triumphed over the pastor.

---

96. Brugmans and Frank (1940, 642).
97. A comparable example from recent times: Christmas 2020, the general secretary of the Protestant Church in the Netherlands, René de Reuver, offered apologies to the Jews on behalf of the church. In May 2021, sentiment moved in the opposite direction when five pastors of this church tried to convince the entire church that apologies should also be offered to the Palestinians, who had been so badly oppressed by the Israelis.
98. Costerus (1608).

To be sure, supersessionism and anti-Semitism are not necessarily correlative; we should not make things worse than they actually are. However, because of the nature of supersessionism, unfortunately the two did go hand in hand all too often. In the course of European history, few countries have been more tolerant toward the Jews than the Netherlands. However, with a few happy exceptions this was not due to the influence of the country's Reformed leaders.

4.7 Who Are the Jews?
4.7.1 Nazis and Palestinians

One of the subtle forms of anti-Semitism is the denial that the Jews of today are the historical continuation of ancient Israel. Everyone can see for themselves that there are white, brown, yellow, and black Jews; an intermingling on a tremendous scale with other nations and other races must have occurred.

Actually, this intermingling goes back to the remote past. Today, the rabbinic rule says that a person is a Jew if their mother is Jewish; the father is irrelevant in this respect. However, when we consider the marriages of Jacob's sons, it is obvious that these involved Gentile women; these women were not descendants of Terah (Gen. 11:28–30), as Sarah, Rebekah, Leah, and Rachel had been. Think of Judah and Tamar (Gen. 38) and of Joseph and Asenath (Gen. 41). King Solomon had many Gentile wives, whose children would have received a place in Israel. In the genealogy of Jesus (Matt. 1), we find Ruth and Tamar, neither of whom was a descendant of Terah. In their day, Ezra and Nehemiah opposed the many mixed marriages in Israel (Ezra 10; Neh. 13). This was especially because the children behaved more like Gentiles than like Jews: "In those days also I saw the Jews who had married women of Ashdod, Ammon, and Moab. And half of their children spoke the language of Ashdod, and they could not speak the language of Judah, but only the language of each people" (Neh. 13:23–24).

In other words, intermingling was never a great issue among Jews as long as the children learned and followed the Jewish ways, not the pagan ways of the Gentiles. It is of no avail to assert that only Jews of "pure blood" can be considered to be Israelites. But the opposite is just as bad. In Nazi theology it was asserted, without batting an eye, that there is not the least proof that Mary and Jesus were Jews; Jesus was even called the greatest anti-Jew of world history (in spite of all the times that Jesus in the New Testament is even referred to as a descendant of King David and even as the "*King* of the Jews"). Very similar absurdities can be heard today among fiercely anti-Zionist Palestinian liberation theologians like Naim Ateek (an Anglican), Mitri Raheb (a Lutheran), and Yohana Katanacho (an Evangelical). Jesus is described as the "first Palestinian liberation theologian"; today's Jews are said to have nothing to do with biblical Israel, and thus to have no right to be in the Holy Land. Just as the Nazi theologians tried to identify Jesus as Aryan, modern Palestinian theologians attempt to identify him as a Palestinian, a man who, together with his people (the Palestinians) suffers under the Jewish occupation.[99] In this way, each author designs their own picture of history to suit them.

Clearly, if it were plausible that today's Jews have nothing to do with ancient Israel, then supersessionism will be shown to be right after all. For, in that case, the state of Israel indeed would have nothing to do with biblical prophecies, for these speak of an "Israel" that, in a purely ethnic sense, has not existed since centuries (if the critics are right). However, I assume that many supersessionists would have nothing to do with *this* absurd type of anti-Semitism, coming first from the Nazi "Christians," and now from "Christian" Palestinians. In that respect, they would join other supersessionists who reject the anti-Semitism of, for instance, Jerome, Chrysostom, and Martin Luther. However, this does not alter the fact that, throughout the centuries, a close link can be pointed out between supersessionism and anti-Semitism. The absurdity that modern Jews are not Israelites has turned out to be a powerful tool in this respect.

---

99. See extensively, the summaries and analyses by Kant (2015).

4.7.2 Other Theories

(a) A theory that is a bit older claims that the Ashkenazi[100] (i.e., Eastern and Middle European) Jews are mainly Khazars.[101] The Khazars were semi-nomadic Turkish people who built a mighty empire in the Caucasus from the seventh to the tenth centuries. According to tradition, this empire accepted the Jewish religion. When, in the tenth century, the Khazar empire was destroyed by the Russians, the Jewish Khazars spread across Eastern and Middle Europe, thus gradually constituting a substantial part of the Ashkenazi Jews. Especially since the nineteenth century, this theory was used by Western anti-Semites, including even the American Ku Klux Klan, to claim that the modern Jews have little in common with ancient Israel.[102] To a great extent, Jews are not Israelites at all, but a kind of Turkish group.

However, what is forgotten is that (a) the story does not apply to the many Sephardic (Spanish, Portuguese, and Middle Eastern Jews), that (b) all the Ashkenazi Jews have Abrahamic blood in their veins,[103] and that more importantly (c) they stand in the tradition of those Jews who honor the obligations relating to circumcision, Sabbath, *kashrut*, and Jewish festivals *in an uninterrupted line of Jewish traditional life*.

We may notice here that many Ashkenazi Jews bear German, or more correctly, Yiddish family names. This suggests that these names originated in the Yiddish linguistic region; they are seldom of Slavic, and rarely of Turkish origin. In fact, they often have a biblical background. For instance, my—originally possibly Jewish Swiss—foremother Dorothea Lieberman carried a German, or rather Yiddish, family name

---

100. Ashkenaz was a grandson of Japheth (Gen. 10:3); the Jews applied the name Ashkenaz first to Scythian, later to Slavic territories, and finally to Northern Europe and Germany.
101. See Ouweneel (2014a, 317–18); cf. https://en.wikipedia.org/wiki/Khazars#History_of_discussions_of_ Khazar Jewishness.
102. See https://en.wikipedia.org/wiki/Khazars#Use_in_anti-Semitic_polemics; see extensively, the studies by Harkabi (1987); Wexler (2007).
103. On the internet, many pedigrees of Jewish families can be found that go back to the early centuries of our era, or even further back.

(meaning "dear man, "beloved man"[104]). Among Jews, "Lieber Mann" was used as a nickname for beloved biblical figures such as Moshe (Moses), Eliakim, Yehudah (Judah), and so on.

(b) Today very few scientists take such theories as the Khazar theory scientifically seriously. These illusions are just as speculative as the so-called British Israelism (or Anglo-Israelism), which claims that the Celtic and Germanic tribes, especially those in Great Britain, are the lost ten tribes of Israel. (Although the Celts are ethnically totally different from the Anglo-Saxons, they must be included, too, because they constitute a considerable part of British ancestry.) At present, this incredibly a-historical view still has very few adherents;[105] nevertheless, it might still appeal to supersessionists who believe that "Ephraim" (say, the ten tribes) would be the church from the Gentiles (see volume IV/1a, §9.3.2).

(c) In connection with these theories, we must mention a hypothesis that has become known as integrationism (not a very clear name). This view claims that the population living in Palestine before the Zionists arrived there consisted partly of ethnic Jews who were no longer aware of their Jewish roots. The view has been described by the Israeli historian Shlomo Sand,[106] but is not his own invention. According to Sand, young David Ben-Gurion was an adherent of integrationism. The latter argued that after the Bar Kochba insurgence (132–136), the Jews living in the Holy Land had not all departed into exile. Many of these Jewish inhabitants supposedly joined Islam after the conquest of Palestine by the Arab Muslims (seventh century). Young Ben-Gurion and congenial men such as Yitzhak Ben-Zvi and Israel Belkind saw it as their task to make the indigenous Palestinians aware of these Jewish roots.

Ben-Gurion later abandoned this idea, but (much later) its appeal continued to attract Shlomo Sand. He argued that young Ben-Gurion was not far wrong. When a foreign power

---

104. See https://en.wikipedia.org/wiki/Liebermann.

105. See http://www.britishisrael.co.uk.

106. Sand wrote in Ivrit the book *When and How Was the Jewish Nation Invented?*; French version: Sand (2008).

conquers a country, it will begin mixing with the conquered population. The Assyrians did this after they had conquered the northern Israelite kingdom (2 Sam. 17). Similarly, when the Anglo-Saxons came to what we today call England, they intermingled with the Celtic population (and their collective genes mixed with those of the French after the conquest of England by William the Conquerer, 1066). Before this, a similar thing had happened with the Romans, who in Western Europe mixed with the local Celtic and Germanic tribes. Similarly, Sand suggested that an Arab inhabitant of Palestine, whose ancestors had lived for centuries in the Holy Land, might be more related to the earlier Jews of Palestine than many of the blond-haired and blue-eyed Jews from (or still in) the Western world.

Sand's book was on the bestseller list for weeks; nevertheless, his ideas have not enjoyed the endorsement of experts.[107] Yet, at least one intriguing element in his theory stands. If, during the seventh century, millions of Christians in North Africa and the Middle East joined Islam, why could the same not have happened with thousands of Jews in seventh-century Palestine? In other words, it is an intriguing but unanswerable question, on the one hand, how many original Israelite Jews belong to the indigenous Palestine population, and on the other hand, how many of such genetic traits may be found among the very European looking Ashkenazi Jews.

(d) Finally, there are people who believe that the true Hebrews were the Africans who had been made slaves. This theory is inspired by Deuteronomy 28:32 and 68:

> Your sons and your daughters shall be given to another people, while your eyes look on and fail with longing for them all day long, but you shall be helpless. . . . And the LORD will bring you back in ships to Egypt, a journey that I promised that you should never make again; and there you shall offer yourselves for sale to your enemies as male and female slaves, but there will be no buyer.

---

107. See, e.g., ttps://web.archive.org/web/20090816051432/http://www.isracampus.org.il/Extra%20Files/ Anita%20Shapira%20–%20Shlomo%20Sand%20book%20review.pdf.

This supposedly refers to Africans in the Diaspora (South America and North America). Some even include Native Americans involved in this group. Some members of this movement do acknowledge Jesus as the Messiah, but also wish to follow the ordinances of the Tanakh (e.g., Sabbath, the feasts, and so on.).[108]

4.7.3 Conclusion

We have considered a number of tribal-historical speculations: the Israelites of today are actually Palestinians (or the reverse: the Palestinians are partly Jewish by origin); or they are the Khazars and their modern descendants; or they are (some of) the African-Americans, with or without (part of) the Native Americans.

Over against this, we state that, basically, modern Jews (especially from the two tribes,[109] but including many from the ancient ten tribes) are the continuation of the Jews of former ages. These are the Jews who after AD 70 have dispersed throughout the world, but have maintained their Jewish religion throughout all these centuries. To be sure, they have intermingled with many different nations. Many proselytes from the Gentile world may have joined them and intermingled with them. Nevertheless, the Jews have preserved their social, cultural, and especially religious identity. They did so not by pursuing "racial purity" (whatever this misleading expression may mean), but by continuing to observe Tanakh ordinances regarding circumcision, Sabbath, festivals, and food.

We may assume that these Jews have the blood of Abraham, Isaac, and Jacob flowing in their veins, though perhaps not in *all* their ancestral lines. However, the most important component in their identity is not their race but their religion. *This* is the nation that called itself "Israel" when, in the first century of our era, it was dispersed among the nations

---

108. Regarding them, see Van der Kooye (2015) and https://www.thegospelcoalition.org/article/9–things-you-should-know-about-black-hebrew-israelites/.
109. The word "Jew" comes from *Yehudi*, that is, a person belonging to the tribe of Judah; today the term is used for all Israelites.

(and mixed with them). *This* is the nation, that, throughout all these centuries, continued to call itself "Israel," despite all the intermingling. And *this* is the nation of which a considerable part now lives in the ancient land of Israel, the Holy Land, *Ha'Aretz*, regardless of their racial appearance. The modern *charedim*[110]—in a somewhat derogatory way often called "ultra-orthodox" Jews—are the direct continuation of the "sect" (or party) of the Pharisees in New Testament time (Acts 15:5; 26:5). From these Pharisees direct line passes down through Mishnah and Gemarah, so to speak, to the Jewish orthodoxy of our days. No (pseudo-)historical and genetic studies can change anything substantial in this historical reality.

---

110. From Heb. *chared*, "[God-]fearing"; the *charedim* are *charedim lid'var Hashem*, "fearing (venerating, respecting, have reverence for) the Word of God."

Chapter 5
The Suffering of Israel

To whom do I offer them, these pages, written fully
   Of sorrow, suffering, and vicissitudes
Unfathomably deep, yet magnificently elevated?...
My brethren, almost stiffened, where this hand.
   ...
Stood over you, outcasts of the earth,
   Not yet a word of future was produced:
"They will see him whose law, whose heart they broke –
   (He never breaks his covenant!) –
"And kiss they will one day Him whom they pierced!"
   Grace will meet us from the wound.
Isaac da Costa (emphasis added)[1]

---

1. Da Costa (Dutch edition 1876, v–vi); this "Dedication to Israel's Dispersed" (Dutch *Toeëigening aan Israels verstrooiden*) was omitted in the 1849 English translation. Isaac da Costa was a well-known Dutch Jewish Christian poet, lawyer, and historian. I offer a somewhat clumsy rendering of part of his poem.

5.1. The Innocent
5.1.1. Two Apples of the Eye

READER, PLEASE CONSIDER THESE quotations from the Tanakh:

> "[The LORD] found him [i.e., Israel] in a desert land, and in the howling waste of the wilderness; he encircled him, he cared for him, he kept him as the apple of his eye" (Deut. 32:10).

> "Keep me as the apple of your eye; / hide me in the shadow of your wings" (Ps. 17:8).

> "For thus said the LORD of hosts, after his glory sent me [or, glory, he sent] to the nations who plundered you, for he who touches you touches the apple of his eye" (Zech. 2:8).

> "[K]eep my commands and live; / keep my teaching [Heb. *torot*, sing. *torah*!] as the apple of your eye" (Prov. 7:2)

The first three quotations tell us that Israel, or even the individual faithful Israelite, is the apple of God's eye. The fourth quotation tells us, if we interpret the father's teaching for his son as God's teaching for Israel, that the Torah is the apple of Israel's eye. It is the iris (the colored part) in what is outwardly visible of the eye that is called the "apple" of the eye. By instinct, we are extremely sensitive as to anything harmful that might happen to our eyes; in other words, the (apple of the) eye is very *precious* to us. It is very important to understand the metaphors just quoted: as the Ecclesia is the most precious possession of her heavenly Bridegroom, Israel is the most precious possession of the God of Israel. And the Torah is the most precious possession of Israel (see §4.1.1). God, Israel, and the Torah are a "threefold cord" that "is not quickly broken" (cf. Eccl. 4:12). "Not quickly"—but *can* it be broken at all? Is not all Christian theology that declares the Mosaic Torah to have been abolished not an attempt to rob Israel of its most precious possession, and thereby to "break the threefold cord"?

Let me quote some others words by Solomon; compare these three passages in his Song:

"My beloved is mine, and I am his" (2:16).

"I am my beloved's and my beloved is mine" (6:3).

"I am my beloved's, and his desire is for me" (7:10).

Notice the moral order in these statements (all made by the female protagonist of the book): her first joy is that the beloved is *her* possession (*her* "apple of the eye," so to speak), and then that she is *his* possession. In the second statement, we find the reverse: first comes that fact that she is the *beloved's* possession ("apple of the eye") before she speaks of her own possession. In the third statement, the latter element is even entirely left out. Israel can say, "God is *my* God"—but it is a deeper knowledge that she is the apple of *his* eye, and that his desire, his care, his love, his protective hand, goes out to *her*.

The young woman's own "apple of the eye" is especially what the beloved has given to her, as the apple of Israel's eye is the greatest gift that God has given to Israel: the Torah. The words of the Torah are the "sweet" words of his mouth (Song 5:16)—sweeter than honey. This demands some more of attention (see next section).

5.1.2 Stealing the Honey

God's eye, Israel's eye. Let me give another example of this mutuality. Israel sings,

> [T]he rules[2] of the LORD are true,
>   and righteous altogether.
> More to be desired are they than gold,
>   even much fine gold;
> sweeter also than honey
>   and drippings of the honeycomb (Ps. 19:9b–10).

---

2. Heb.: plural of *mishpat*, more lit., "act of justice, just ordinance"; a synonym for Torah.

The sayings of the Lord are honey to Israel, but this is reciprocal: the sayings of Israel are honey to her heavenly Bridegroom: "Your lips drip nectar, my bride; honey and milk are under your tongue; the fragrance of your garments is like the fragrance of Lebanon" (Song 4:11).

It could be stated this way: supersessionists rob God of *his* honey (the sweet words of his beloved, i.e., the remnant of Israel), and they rob Israel of *its* honey: the Torah (sweet instruction) of God (cf. Prov. 16:24; 24:13). Stop with your Torah, they shout, for it is obsolete (as the expiration date on the honey pot indicates). Stop with your God, they shout, for he has long ago stopped with *you*, guilty ones that you are. They shout like Shimei shouted to the fleeing King David: "Get out, get out, you man of blood, you worthless man! The Lord has avenged on you all the blood [you have shed].... See, your evil is on you, for you are a man of blood" (2 Sam. 16:7-8). Zophar overtly suggested that Job as a wicked man (Job 20:5, 29), and the words of Eliphaz implied the same (Job 22:15, 18). However, Job (read: Israel) replied by defending his faithfulness to the Torah: "I have not departed from the commandment of his lips; / I have treasured the words of his mouth more than my portion of food" (Job 23:12). Israel defends its faithfulness to God's commandments; therefore, it suffers all the more under the horrors that it must endure, not blaming the Gentiles for it, but God himself, as indicated by the sequel of Job's words:

> But he is unchangeable, and who can turn him back?
> What he desires, that he does.
> For he will complete what he appoints for me,
> and many such things are in his mind.
> Therefore I am terrified at his presence;
> when I consider, I am in dread of him.
> God has made my heart faint;
> the Almighty has terrified me (Job 23:13-16).

5.1.3 Direct and Indirect Government

Job remained faithful to the Torah ("instruction") that God had entrusted to him.[3] Yet, he realized that, in some way or another, God was against him. He cannot grasp the reason for this, just as, throughout the centuries, the Jews have wrestled with the question why God was targeting precisely *them*. For what reason? Is God arbitrary in his doings? Can that be true? No, it would be arbitrariness if the righteous and the wicked would be equally afflicted by God, but this is exactly what does *not* seem to be the case. Often, it seems that the wicked are prosperous and blessed, whereas the righteous fare very badly (Job 21:7-33).

This was also the problem with which Asaph wrestled (Ps. 73), and Jeremiah, too (Jer. 12:1-3). It is what has been called the *indirect* government of God: he allows evil to prosper and the good to suffer—until the day of judgment, when there will be *direct* government of God: the evil will suffer, and the good will prosper. To understand this, one must "discern their *end*" with eyes enlightened in God's sanctuary (Ps. 73:17). This is what James calls the "*end* of the Lord" (5:11 KJV), which brings to light "how the Lord is compassionate and merciful" after all.

For the time being, Job suffered innocently, Israel suffers innocently, and so many of those faithful to God in general suffer innocently. They may be sinners, like all of us, but they are not criminals, deserving the severe afflictions they sometimes receive. This was the great question with which Rabbi Harold S. Kushner also wrestled in his popular book.[4]

Job asked this question: "You say, 'God stores up their iniquity for their children.' Let him pay it out to them, that they may know it" (Job 21:19). I understand this to mean that the punishment for the iniquities of the wicked comes upon the innocent, in this case the children of the wicked. This is

---

3. It is irrelevant to our argument that the Mosaic Torah cannot be literally intended here. Interestingly, it is Eliphaz who told Job: "Receive *torah* from his mouth, and lay up his words in your heart" (Job 22:22).
4. Kushner (1981).

THE ETERNAL PEOPLE: GOD IN RELATION TO ISRAEL

not fair: Job desires that the wicked themselves bear the consequences of their actions. Here, we see faintly shimmering behind the text the profound question of substitution, that is, of vicarious suffering: the innocent must suffer for—this is, instead of, or for the benefit of—the guilty. Could it mean that Job is perhaps suffering vicariously, too? And could it be similar for Israel? This is probably one of the most profound questions that we could ask about the history of Israel.

5.2   The Holocaust
5.2.1 Terminology

It is remarkable that, when referring to the *Shoah* (Heb. for "ruin, destruction"; see, e.g., Isa. 10:3; 47:11), historians often use the term *Holocaust*. This word of Greek origin has been used not only in connection with Israel; earlier, all other large massacres were designated "holocausts," such as the Armenian genocide (by the Turks) during World War I. In the 1950s, the term was used more and more to describe the massacre of six million Jews during World War II. Today, the term "the" Holocaust (with the article) refers exclusively to the *Shoah*, that is, the destruction of almost six million Jews by the Nazis during World War II.

The term is quite remarkable because the Greek word *holokauston* means "burnt offering." In Leviticus 1:3 and many other passages, we find in the Septuagint the related term *holokautōma*, which literally means "that which is burned up entirely"; compare the Hebrew counterpart, *'olah*, which literally means as much as "that which goes up [in smoke]." The burnt offering was an animal sacrifice in which almost the entire animal (that is, without the blood, the skin, and the dung) was offered on the so-called altar of burnt offering in order to go up in smoke.

We should not exaggerate the sacrificial character of the Holocaust because the term was used for other massacres as we;;. Yet, this sacrificial character is the very reason why some prefer to avoid the term and use the term *Shoah* instead. It has been debated whether the term Holocaust should not also be used for the Nazi massacre of the gypsies (more correctly: Sinti and Roma), the Slavic peoples (including the Soviet war prisoners), homosexuals, and handicapped people (in total about five million victims). In practice, this virtually never happens: the term remains reserved for the *Shoah*. One reason may be that the Nazis had the explicit plan to only exterminate all the Jews, not necessarily all Slavic people, all handicapped, and so on. The *Shoah* was so massive and so unique that it is fitting to reserve the term "Holocaust" only for this massacre.

The extent to which we should understand the word "Holocaust" literally, that is, the extent to which the *Shoah* had a sacrificial character, is one of the topics of this chapter (which is an elaboration of §§3.1 and 3.2). Leviticus 1 (cf. 6:9–13) is about voluntary burnt offerings that Israelites could offer to God as an expression of worship and thanksgiving, and also of dedication. But Exodus 29:38–46 deals with the mandatory, daily burnt offering, each morning and afternoon, which was necessary as the holy foundation (a) on which God could meet with his people, (b) on which the people would be sanctified by God's glory, and (c) on which a holy God could dwell in the midst of his people. It is the sacrifice of an *innocent* animal, through which God can dwell among *guilty* humans. It seems inconceivable that we could say, in a similar way, that the Holocaust was the sacrifice of *innocent* Israel, through which God can have dealings with *guilty* humanity. And *if* we say such a thing, then at best only with a very specific meaning. This is what we must investigate in the next sections.

5.2.2 Israel's First Mass Destruction

Ever since Israel developed as a nation, it has suffered almost *continually*. In Egypt the descendants of the patriarch Jacob expanded to become a bona fide people. As soon as a Pharaoh "arose who did not know Joseph" (Exod. 1:8)—that is, had not heard of him *or* did not wish to acknowledge him—the persecutions began. Their cause was *fear*, apprehension toward these peculiar, unique people, who were always—or were always thought to be—superior to the Gentile nations: "Behold, the people of Israel are too many and too mighty for us. Come, let us deal shrewdly with them, lest they multiply, and, if war breaks out, they join our enemies and fight against us and escape from the land" (Exod. 1:9-10). The Israelites were not only pressed to do forced labor, but after the Hebrew midwives had refused to kill the newborn boys, all the Egyptians were called upon to throw all the newborn boys into the Nile (v. 22). Notice: the midwives "feared God," and because they refused to be Pharaoh's tools of murder, God "gave them families" (v. 21),[5] so the nation grew all the faster.

In the course of history, all the four elements of created matter have been employed against Israel. In Egypt, it was the *water* and death by drowning. During the Holocaust, it was the poisoned *air* in the gas chambers that the victims had to breathe, and the *fire* of the crematoria through which their bodies went up in smoke. And as to the *fire*, it was also intended to put an end to the lives of Daniel's three friends (Dan. 3). At other times, it was the *earth* in which Jews were buried after having been killed, and sometimes buried alive. Indeed, everywhere the created world turned against God's people: "I will break the pride of your power, and I will make your heavens like iron and your earth like bronze" (Lev. 26:19; Deut. 28:23).

Just as many Jews tried to escape the Holocaust by hiding, it was Moses who became the first "hider" in the history of Israel.[6] For three months, he was kept in hiding by his mother Jochebed. As Stephen tells us: "At this time Moses was born; and he was beautiful in God's sight.[7] And he was brought up for three months in his father's house" (Acts 7:20). At last, the mother "obeyed" Pharaoh by taking her son to cast him into the Nile, but then in such a way that he was enclosed by an "ark[8] of bulrushes" (Exod. 2:3 KJV; others: a "papyrus

---

5. Lit., "made them houses," which some have taken literally; but cf. 2 Sam. 7:11; 1 Kings 2:24.
6. Cf. Aafjes (1950, 51).
7. The Septuagint reads in Exod. 2:2 "fair to God"; a typically Hebrew superlative, as in Jonah 3:3, a "city great to God," i.e., a very large city. Perhaps Paul meant the same in 2 Cor. 10:4, lit. "mighty to God," i.e., exceedingly powerful.
8. "Ark" is here Heb. *tēbah*, i.e., an "ark" covered with pitch, like the one Noah had built (Gen. 6:14); not to be confused with Heb. *aron*, used for the "ark" of

basket"). The meaning of this was profound: here, "in" Moses as it were, an entire nation was safely guided through the waters, just as, about eighty years later, the same occurred to Israel in the Red Sea under the guidance of Moses himself (Exod. 13–14).

God was *with* Moses in the waters, as he was later *with* Israel in the waters (cf. Isa. 43:2, 16). He was *with* Israel in Auschwitz, even though many Jews as well as Christians might find this a despicable idea (cf. §3.5.2). The God who allowed the Israelite boys to be thrown into the Nile, and Israel to pass through the Red Sea, Daniel's three friends to be cast into the fiery furnace, allowed (part of) Israel to enter the gas chambers of the Nazi camps. Why he did so, we may not fully grasp, but we choose to maintain that these things did not occur "behind his back," yes, that he was *with* them in these sufferings, and even suffered with them: "In all their [i.e., Israel's] affliction he was afflicted, / and the angel of his presence saved them; / in his love and in his pity he redeemed them; / he lifted them up and carried them all the days of old" (Isa. 63:9).

5.2.3 Not Keeping *From* But Keeping *Through*

We have just discovered a very important biblical principle: God has never promised to keep his people away from all peril, but rather that he would be *with* them *in* all peril, and guide them *through* (even though many of them will perish in the peril).

* *Water:* Israel's passage through the Red Sea (Exod. 13–14) was described in this manner: "*Your* way was through the sea, *your* path through the great waters; yet your footprints were unseen" (Ps. 77:19).

* *Fire:* God did not prevent Israel from entering the "iron furnace" (Deut. 4:20), but he did come down from heaven (Exod. 3:8), and "dwell" with them in the fire of the bush that depicted this iron furnace (33:16).

* *Water:* God did not prevent Jonah from being cast into the sea and from being swallowed by the sea monster; but

---

the covenant.

deep down in the sea, God was so near that he heard Jonah's prayer, and commanded the fish to vomit Jonah out (Jonah 2; the rabbis interpreted the story as a picture of Israel's exile).

* *Fire:* God did not prevent Daniel's friends from being cast in the fiery furnace, but in that horrible fire the "Son of God" was *with* them (Dan. 3:25 KJV).

* *Water:* Jesus did not prevent his disciples from facing a terrible storm when they were on the lake, but he was *with* them in that storm, in their boat (Mark 4:37-39).

* God never promised his people that he would keep them from the fire and the water; but he did promise that he would be with them *in* the fire and the water:

> When you pass through the waters, *I will be with you*;
>> and through the rivers, they shall not overwhelm you;
> when you walk through fire you shall not be burned,
>> and the flame shall not consume you.
> For I am the LORD your God,
>> the Holy One of Israel, your Savior (Isa. 43:2-3).

5.3 Vicarious Suffering
5.3.1 What Is It?

One of the ideas with respect to Israel that Christians find difficult to accept is the matter of vicarious suffering (see earlier, briefly, in §3.2). In Isaiah 53, the servant of the LORD very clearly dies "for," or even "instead of" others:

> [H]e was pierced for our transgressions;
>> he was crushed for our iniquities;
> upon him was the chastisement that brought us peace,
>> and with his wounds we are healed (Isa. 53:5).

Many Christians have difficulty grasping how such words could ever be applied to Israel. Is there a sense in which Israel has "vicariously" suffered for the Gentiles? Or, recalling Job as a type of Israel, can we say that in some sense or another Job had "vicariously" suffered? If so, what could this be understood to mean?

The Jewish German philosopher Hermann Levin Goldschmidt wrote:

> Just like the servant of God in Second Isaiah [read, Isa. 42–53], and just like the twenty-second Psalm—of which the first words are the last[9] ones on the cross: 'My God, my God, why have you forsaken me?' (Ps. 22:1; Matt. 27:46; Mark 15:34), just like this, Job takes the suffering upon himself: his innocent and vicarious suffering.[10]

And Rabbi Israel W. Slotki (whose words may have been revised by Rabbi Abraham J. Rosenberg) says regarding Isaiah 53:4-6: "[These words are the] recognition that the servant's [i.e., Israel's!] sufferings were not due to his secret sins. It is now frankly acknowledged [by the 'us' speaking in Isa. 53] that he was the victim who bore the dire penalties which the iniquities of others have incurred."[11] In the opinion of Jewish expositor Joseph ben Abba Mari ibn Kaspi, the "us," referred to the "Babylonians, or their representatives, having known the servant, i.e. exiled Israel idealized, in his humiliation and martyrdom, and now seeing his exaltation and new dignity, describe their impressions and feelings."[12]

In §3.2 problem of "substitution" in Isaiah 53:8 was mentioned, where the servant of the LORD is described as having been "stricken for the transgression of my people." This expression, "my people," seems to conflict with the interpretation that the servant suffers for Gentiles. Rashi said of this that the "innocent servant" (Israel!) bore the "suffering that should have been inflicted upon the wicked members of the community."[13] I suppose that Rashi meant to say that the true "Israel of God" suffers for the transgressions committed by the unfaithful masses of Israel. No matter how this may

---

9. Actually this is the fourth to the last saying; but in Matt. 27 and Mark 15 they are indeed the last ones.
10. Goldschmidt, in Susman (1948, 53).
11. Slotki (1983, 262).
12. Ibid., 261.
13. Ibid., 263.

be interpreted, both interpretations see true Israel as vicariously suffering for others, whether Gentiles or the wicked in Israel itself.

Regardless whether the chapter is applied to Israel, or to the true core of it, it cannot refer to any form of substitution in the sense of *atoning* for the sins—that is, blotting out the sins—of others. Only Jesus Christ, through his self-sacrifice on the cross, was able to take upon himself sins of all those who believe in him, and to truly blot them out, so that they no longer exist before God. Only he is the Lamb of God who takes away the sin of the world (John 1:29). Even the true Israel, the "Israel of God," cannot blot out sins, either its own sins or those of the nations. However, there is also a secondary, derivative, non-atoning form of substitution: in its history, the Jewish nation has many times been the "scapegoat" of other nations. In Leviticus 16 we read that on the Day of Atonement, the "scapegoat" was part of the twofold sin offering; but in ordinary parlance, a "scapegoat" is a person who, or a group of people which, is blamed or punished for the faults or actions of other people (Cambridge Dictionary).

When, life utterly deteriorates in a land or society, people always look for a scapegoat. This has happened to Israel numerous times in world history. It was blamed for actions that the Gentiles had committed, or it was blamed for misery that happened to Gentiles, like a pestilence or epidemic. Either Israel suffered where others, the actual guilty ones, ought to have suffered; or it suffered for disasters for which it bore no responsibility at all. It suffered much more than other nations, as if it soaked up the guilt and the sufferings of others, whereas in reality it was often less guilty than the others.

5.3.2 The *Shoah* in Isaiah 53?

Let me quote here the Dutch theologian and cultural philosopher Frank de Graaff, an orthodox Christian, who—against much of Christian tradition—applied Isaiah 53 to the *Shoah*.[14] He saw especially verse 7 "very literally fulfilled in the

---

14. De Graaff (1987, 93–94).

thirties and forties of the twentieth century." He wondered how it was possible that, despite knowing the Bible so well, Christianity failed to recognize the *Shoah* in Isaiah 53 immediately. De Graaff wondered: "What cover lay over the heart of Christians during all those centuries?" Then he quoted Isaiah 53:7-8 and said, "Must I explain here? He who remembers something of those people, wearing their stars, who let themselves be quietly led to the trains, the camps, the gas chambers, must understand. My God, how did 2,000 years of Christian exegesis shut Scripture, and thus the hearts of the people? How the Christians abused Jesus by severing him from his people."

De Graaff was expressing here a kernel of truth—Jesus is, and remains, associated with his people, throughout its entire history.[15] Regrettably, De Graaff was guided too much by emotions and too little by careful exegesis. He did exaggerate when he said, "Israel suffers, does penance for the sins, trespasses, injustice of the *goyyim*. That is to say, Israel is the mediator between its God and the *goyyim*."[16] The term "mediator" can be used here only in the (limited) sense that we also encounter with Job, who mediated between his God and his friends (Job 42:7-9). In this derivative sense, Moses, too, has been a "mediator" between God and Israel (Gal. 3:19).

De Graaff wrote: "Atonement must be brought about through satisfaction.[17] Well, this is what Israel accomplished in its suffering for the nations. . . . For our transgressions, the plague was on the people of Israel. His suffering brought us atonement." He continued: "Vicariously, [the Jew] suffers for the sin and guilt of the *goyyim*." In my view, such statements go much too far. What is being overlooked is that in Isaiah 53 the lamb that is led to the slaughter is not just Israel, but first and foremost the Messiah of Israel, who—as De Graaff himself has expressed it—is the true personification of Israel. Isaiah 53 contains truths that, strictly speaking, cannot be

---

15. Ouweneel (1995, 112).
16. De Graaff (1987, 93–94, 97).
17. Here "satisfaction" means satisfying the demands of a holy and righteous God through an appropriate sacrifice.

said of Israel at all, but only of the Messiah of Israel. Israel is the scapegoat, the one who is always blamed for the sins and miseries of others, but it is not the one *atoning* for sin, that is, blotting out sins. When it comes to that, *Israel itself needs a sin offering*, which only the Messiah can bring to God; only he is the true mediator between God and humanity (1 Tim. 2:5; Heb. 9:15).

5.3.3 Counterarguments

First, in the New Testament, Isaiah 53 is never applied to Israel but exclusively to the Messiah:[18]

(a) "This [i.e., Jesus' miracle working] was to fulfill what was spoken by the prophet Isaiah: 'He took our illnesses and bore our diseases'" (Matt. 8:17; cf. Isa. 53:4).

(b) "[H]ow is it written of the Son of Man that he should suffer many things and be treated with contempt?" (Mark 9:12; cf. Isa. 53:3).

(c) ". . . Then Philip opened his mouth, and beginning with this Scripture [Isa. 53] he told him [i.e., the Ethiopian eunuch] the good news about Jesus" (Acts 8:32-35; cf. Isa. 53:7-8).

(d) Jesus "was delivered up for our trespasses" (Rom. 4:25; cf. Isa. 53:5a; 1 Cor. 15:3).

(e) "He committed no sin, neither was deceit found in his mouth" (1 Pet. 2:22; cf. Isa. 53:9)

(f) "By his wounds you have been healed" (1 Pet. 2:24; cf. Isa. 53:8b).

Second, notice Daniel 9:24 as well as the suggested link with verse 26 (NKJV): "Seventy weeks are determined / For your people and for your holy city, / To finish the transgression, / To make an end of sins, / To make reconciliation for iniquity, / To bring in everlasting righteousness, . . . after the sixty-two weeks / Messiah shall be cut off, but not for Himself; . . . ."

---

18. Other than the passages in which Jesus is called the "Lamb" (John 1:29, 35; 1 Pet. 1:19; thirty times in Rev.), reminding us of Isa. 53:7, but they could also be references to the Passover lamb (1 Cor. 5:7).

Third, notice Psalm 40:6-8:

> In sacrifice and offering you have not delighted,
>   but you have given me an open ear.
> Burnt offering and sin offering
>   you have not required.
> Then I said, "Behold, I have come;
>   in the scroll of the book it is written of me:
> I delight to do your will, O my God; . . . ."

This is not Israel speaking, nor David, as Jewish tradition wishes to have it[19]—but none other than the Messiah is speaking here, the "Man of God's counsel."[20] After saying that God cannot be satisfied by animal sacrifices, he then presents himself instead: "Behold, *I* have come." See the explanation of the passage in Hebrews 10:8-10:

> When he said above, "You have neither desired nor taken pleasure in sacrifices and offerings and burnt offerings and sin offerings" (these are offered according to the law), then he added, "Behold, I have come to do your will." He does away with the first in order to establish the second. And by that will we have been sanctified through the offering of the body of Jesus Christ once for all.

5.3.4 Derivative, Figurative

People writing about this subject must explain very carefully to unprepared readers in what derivative, figurative sense they speak of Israel supposedly being a "sacrifice" and a "mediator." These readers are familiar with New Testament thinking on atonement and substitution, and they would rightly argue that not only Gentiles but also Jews, even the most faithful among them, need the atoning death of *Christ*.

---

19. The "scroll of the book" could then have been the book of Ruth, where David's origins are described (4:18–22); but more probably it referred to the Torah—see Cohen (1985, ad loc.) and the Talmud: Yebamot 77a; Gittin 60a—or perhaps to the book of God's counsel (cf. Ps. 139:15–16).
20. Cf. Isa. 46:11, where this expression is used for King Cyrus, who was a type of the Messiah (cf. 44:28–45:1).

Another feature of Isaiah 53 is that the s/Servant is presented as the guiltless one. However, Israel was not the sinless one. In Psalm 44, Israel is the guiltless one, for it could say,

> All this has come upon us,
> > though we have not forgotten you,
> > and we have not been false to your covenant.
> Our heart has not turned back,
> > nor have our steps departed from your way (vv. 17-18).

But being guiltless is not the same as being sinless; Job was guiltless (when it came to the great crimes that his friends accused him of), but not sinless. Job and the true Israel of God have a sinful nature, but neither suffers a punishment for certain grave trespasses he/it had supposedly committed. The servant in Isaiah 53, the guiltless one in Psalm 44, and the innocent Job do not represent Israel in its entirety—which did go into exile because of its wicked sins—but only the faithful part of the nation, the core, the Daniels and Ezekiels who, in personal innocence, had to join the others in exile. This remnant always remained standing, like Daniel's friends who remained standing as the masses knelt down before the idol (Dan. 3:8-12). The true, faithful, ideal, "everlasting" Israel of God is not sinless but it is guiltless (see again Gal. 6:16).

The faithful core of Israel lived in innocence in Babylonia, having been exiled there along with the guilty ones. During the third exile, too, from the destruction of Jerusalem in 70 until now, there has been a faithful Israel—still blind to Jesus, but loving the God of Israel and observing the Torah, as best they could, and can. One day, Gentiles will be distressed to learn about all the evil they have perpetrated against all the *tzaddiqim* throughout the centuries. In this respect, this Jewish remnant resembles the true Servant—for the Servant *is* "Israel" (Isa. 49:3), the true personification of Israel. They are one with him, even if they do not yet know him. It was Nebuchadnezzar who perceived the Son of God being with Daniel's friends in the fiery furnace, but it is doubtful whether the friends themselves had perceived him. He was there with them nevertheless. God was with Job in his misery, but it took quite some time before he could say, "[N]ow my eye sees you" (Job 42:5).

One Jewish-Christian New Testament scholar wrote: "To the 'lamb of God', [the church] added numerous scapegoats from his own people; she laid on Jesus' brothers the cross that she herself did not want to bear[21]; she has intertwined its own fortune [viz., salvation] with the misfortune of his people."[22] That is, the church behaved as if its own salvation could not be realized without pouring mischief upon Israel. Jesus said, 'Deliverance comes *from* the Jews" (John 4:22), to which the church added: "Disaster[23] belongs *to* the Jews."

In 1948 (three years after the end of the Holocaust), the Council of Brethren of the German national Protestant Church proclaimed the thesis that God's judgment still rested upon Israel because it has rejected its Messiah). How could they dare saying such a thing! In 1962, the German scholars Dietrich Goldschmidt (of Jewish descent) and Hans-Joachim Kraus (pioneer of the Jewish-Christian dialogue) replied to this:

> In reality, the church laid the cross that she did not want to bear herself upon Israel, and Israel has accepted the cross. The church praised the "Lamb of God" who takes away the sins of the world, but at the same time she turned the Jew within her gates into a "scapegoat." In this manner, she pushed him on the road that Jesus had gone, and that she, following her Lord, should have gone herself."[24]

Jesus Christ the Lamb—Israel the scapegoat. These two are not theologically correlative, but they are often parallel historical realities.

---

21. Cf. Luke 9:23; 14:27 about the cross that Jesus' followers are called to take upon themselves, and not to put on the shoulders of others.
22. Lapide (1984, 68).
23. In German (and Dutch), the wordplay works even better: "deliverance" is *Heil* (*heil*), "disaster" is *Unheil* (*onheil*).
24. Goldschmidt and Kraus (1962, 250).

5.4 More on Job and Israel
5.4.1 Representation

Margarete Susman scrutinized the mystery of vicarious suffering most carefully. Regarding Job's purity, about which Job continually testified before God in order to be vindicated, she said that this contained more "than just the will to be personally pure":[25] this purity "involves human existence; it is at the same time vicarious purity; this is the meaning of the sacrifices that Job brings for his sons, for their possible guilt"[26] (Job 1:5). Susman argued that this is true also of the Jewish people: they live in a "sphere of vicarious purification and atonement, which in this way necessarily transcends its own existence." Thus, the people suffer in a double way: they suffer "for their own backsliding," but they also suffer for "the non-guilt of the human race, which they represent from the beginning."

"Non-guilt" [Ger. *Unschuld*] is a tricky word here. Apparently, Susman discerned in all humanity a core of people that were "not guilty," though not sinless, people serving God according to what they know of him from creation (Rom. 1:20) and their conscience (2:15). The apostle Paul argued that Gentiles who are oriented toward God, though not "having" *the* (Mosaic) Torah, are a "Torah" to themselves and have the "work of the Torah" written on their hearts (Rom. 2:13-15). That is, they do what the Torah commands, even though they do not know the Torah.

This is a vital point. The Jew who does not keep the Torah, and who is circumcised in the flesh but not in the heart, is not a true *tzaddiq*. However, the Gentile who does keep the Torah according to its deepest sense, and who is circumcised in the heart, though not in the flesh, is a *tzaddiq* in the true sense of the term. It is this latter group that Susman calls the "innocent" part of humanity: not sinless—"there is no one who does not sin" (1 Kings 8:46)—but guiltless as Job was, that is, neither apostate nor wicked. Of this, the true Israel of God,

---

25. Susman (1948, 59).
26. And one may add: brings for the friends (Job 42:7–9); Job's sons represent the multitude of the Jewish people, the friends represent the repentant Gentiles.

knowing more of God through the Torah than the *goyyim*, is the prototype: "The fact that the history of Israel can truly be understood only in this way, as primordial image and substitution of human history, is testified by all prophecy," says Susman.

Susman's argument can be summarized this way: the life of Job is not just some human life isolated from other lives, such as those of his children and his friends. This is even more true of Israel: its history as a nation is not just some national history isolated from other national histories. After Noah's Flood, when God allowed all the nations to walk in their own ways (Acts 14:16), and chose one nation, Israel, with this one nation he continued the *history of humanity as such*. To this one nation, he gave the Sinaitic Torah, which *in its deepest sense was intended for all humanity*. In receiving the Torah, Israel was a representative of (German: *Vertreter*) or substitute for (German: *Stellvertreter*) humanity. In its deepest sense, the covenant with Israel was intended for all nations; therefore, the LORD spoke of Gentiles who "hold fast his covenant," and thus will be allowed into his house (Isa. 56:3–7), and of the covenant that he had made with all the peoples (Zech. 11:10).

In summary, just as Job represented Israel, so Israel represents all humanity. Susman saw a connection between the "peculiar guilt with which the Torah charges the people from the beginning," and the "guiltless guilt of Job": "At Mount Sinai, Israel accepted the Torah, but it [i.e., the people] did not accept it [i.e., the Torah] for itself; it accepted it for *humanity*."[27] The "righteousness that this Law proclaims," is applicable "not only to one nation, but to humanity." This truth lies embedded in an ancient Jewish tradition: "If Israel had not accepted the Torah at Mount Sinai, God would have returned the world to chaos, or the angels would have destroyed the world."[28] This is a point of central importance: to "the acceptance of the Law and the faithfulness to the Law" is "bound

---

27. Susman (1948, 97).
28. E.g., Talmud: Abodah Zarah 3a; also *Nephesh Hachayyim* 4.1; see Finkel (2009, ad loc.).

not only the continued existence of Israel, but of the world." In other words, in giving the Torah, God "entrusted humanity to the people" (i.e., Israel). In short, not only Israelites but *all humans are called upon to be tzaddiqim*, according to the knowledge and understanding that each of them possesses.

According to Susman, on this fact "the ferocious anger of the prophets" was based: if Israel fails, all humanity will perish. But, it may be added, where Israel as the scapegoat takes upon itself the guilt of humanity—and allow me to ultimately think here of the One who is the true personification of Israel—*all* those in the Gentile world who truly humble themselves before God will be saved. "Salvation is from the Jews," because of him who, as the personification of Israel, has taken upon himself the guilt of all those who are "of a contrite and lowly spirit" (Isa. 57:15).

5.4.2 The *Tamidim*

It is true, the wrath of the prophets was heaped upon the Torah-disobedient people, since this disobedience affected all Torah-less nations, so that Israel is dispersed among all peoples of the world. But conversely, in the ultimate return of Israel to the Torah, *all nations* are blessed. God promised Abraham that in him and in his progeny all families of the earth would be blessed (Gen. 12:3). But when God came again to Abraham to renew this covenant, he said to him, "I am God Almighty; walk [habitually] before Me [with integrity, knowing that you are always in My presence], and be blameless and complete [in obedience to Me]" (Gen. 17:1 AMP). Blameless, complete (perfect, pure-hearted, sincere) is one Hebrew word: *tamid*. This is what Abraham, in his covenant relationship with the LORD, was supposed to be, this is what Israel is supposed to be, and this is what was testified about Job: "[T]hat man was blameless [Heb. *tam*[29]] and upright [Heb. *yashar*], one who feared God and turned away from evil" (1:1, 8; 2:3). Abraham and Job were prototypes of Israel, on the one hand, because of divine election, but on the other hand, because of their own "blamelessness, perfection, pure-heartedness,

---

29. The Heb. words *tamid* and *tam* are related, with roughly the same meaning.

The Suffering of Israel

sincerity." Thus, the blessing for all nations is made co-dependent on the faithfulness of Abraham and his offspring: if, through the failure of Israel's false shepherd, God's bond with Israel is broken, his bond with *all the peoples* is broken: "I became the shepherd of the flock doomed to be slaughtered by the sheep traders. And I took two staffs, one I named Favor [Heb. *noʻam*, Pleasantness], the other I named Union [Heb. *Chobʼlim*, Bindings]. And I tended the sheep. . . . And I took my staff Favor, and I broke it, annulling the covenant that I had made with all the peoples" (Zech. 11:7, 10).[30]

Of course, this thesis, namely, that the existence of the world depends vicariously on Israel's faithfulness to the Torah, can be maintained only in terms of human responsibility. However, the sovereignty of God renders Israel's calling as irrevocable (Rom. 11:29). If Israel is and remains unfaithful, the nation will perish, and with it the world will perish. Here we encounter again the full force of the statement, "Salvation is from the Jews" (John 4:22). One of the consequences of this is that *the salvation of not a single soul in the world can be severed from the ultimate salvation of the (true) Israel*. Thus, from the human viewpoint, the salvation of Job's children and of his friends is "from Job," namely, based upon his sacrifices for them (Job 1:5; 42:8-9). And please notice that Jobs offers this sacrifice for his friends *when he is still in his misery*, that is, before God "restored his fortunes" (Job 42:7-10).[31] In its *suffering*, Israel as the scapegoat takes the guilt of the world upon itself, or rather, as the scapegoat it is *blamed* for all the misery in the world. Thus, in all its suffering, Israel remains standing, in order that the world be saved.

Perhaps, the very *Shoah* is the most shocking and painful example of Israel as *vicarious* offering because of the fol-

---

30. Cf. Job 5:23; Hos. 2:18, God's covenant with all the world; however, the Heb. word for "peoples" here is *ʻammim*, not *goyyim*; many expositors therefore assume that, in Zech. 11, all the tribes of Israel were being referred to (cf. *ʻammim* in Deut. 33:3; Hos. 10:14).

31. De Graaff (1987, 107). "Restoring one's fortunes" is the well-known Heb. expression *shuv shʼvut*, which we encounter so often also in reference to Israel (e.g., Deut. 30:3; Ps. 14:7; 126:1, 4; Jer. 29:14; Ezek. 16:53; Hos. 6:11; Joel 3:1; Amos 9:14).

lowing consideration: "Hitler's war against the Jews had the priority over his war against all other enemies. [Heinrich] Himmler and [Adolf] Eichmann tirelessly insisted that, despite urgent needs of the armed forces, priority had to be given to the deportations."[32] As others have shown, Hitler's *Endlösung* (the final "solution" of the Jewish "problem," read: the extermination of the Jewish nation) was a tremendous hindrance to gaining the victory in the war against the allied forces.[33] It is not impossible that, without Auschwitz, Hitler would have won the war, and would have plunged Western Europe and other parts of the world into the horrendous Nazi slavery. Hitler had to choose: either give up Auschwitz (and the other death camps) in order to win the war, or give up the victory in order to be able to destroy as many Jews as possible. In other words, the six million Jewish victims could be viewed as the "sacrifice" that "had to" be offered in order to save the lives of hundreds of millions of Gentiles.

Israel realized that, in this respect, it had not always remained faithful. At the beginning of World War II, Jews on both sides were forced to take up arms in order to fight each other, French Jews against German Jews, and so on. In André Schwarz-Bart's novel, *The Last of the Just*, there is a *tzaddiq* who says,

> All this is happening . . . because Israel is tired of carrying the sacrificial knife in its own throat. The sacrificial lamb has gone out among the Nations, he no longer wished to live with God. Our unfortunate brothers have become Frenchmen, Germans, Turks and perhaps Chinese, imagining that I ceasing to be Jews they would cease to suffer. . . .[34]

In this striving for assimilation, Israel's responsibility was at stake. Christians had their own responsibility toward Israel. Many of them found an excuse for the *Shoah* in their belief that Israel had to suffer for its *own* sins; they sometimes

---

32. *Encyclopedia Judaica* (1971), s.v. "Holocaust"; quoted by Jocz (1981, 16).
33. Haffner (1979).
34. Schwarz-Bart (1985, 72).

even thought that they were called to cooperate in punishing Israel for these sins. Other Christians, in shame, considered that, if the Holocaust (i.e., burnt offering!) does have a sacrificial character, Israel had to vicariously suffer for *our* (Gentile) sins. The difference is enormous. Some appointed themselves to be Israel's executioners as alleged instruments of God. Others, beholding Israel's misfortune and beating their breasts (cf. Luke 23:48), humbled themselves before God. Some became Israel's tormenters in view of Israel's (real or alleged) sins, other tormented themselves because of Israel's misery.

5.4.3 Job and Joseph K.

Let me point here to the fascinating parallel that has been suggested between Job in the book of Job and Joseph K., the protagonist in the novel, *The Trial*, of the German-speaking Jewish author Franz Kafka.[35] There seems to be a large difference between the two: in the end, Job is restored, whereas K.[36] is ultimately put to death. However, one author who wrote extensively about the parallel between these two persons made the intriguing comment that the manner of Joseph K's death points more to a sacrifice than to an execution, which reminds the reader of the biblical *Aqēdah*, the "binding" of Isaac by Abraham (Gen. 22:9-13).[37]

Job offers a sacrifice, whereas K. dies as a sacrifice; but from the viewpoint of symbolism, is the difference all that great? Sure, K. dies in despondency; but are not both elements present in Israel's suffering: both the desperation of the nation wrestling with its invisible Judge (as well as its enemies) and the endurance of the "scapegoat"? As well as the ultimate restoration, not of Joseph K., but at least of Job/Israel?

This truth becomes most evident in the Messiah, because he is the true personification of Israel. In their suffering, the people of Israel remain standing, in order that the world

---

35. See Ouweneel (2000a, Intermezzo I.2); Kafka (2011).
36. Some have asked whether with this initial Kafka was perhaps referring to himself.
37. Wilk (1986, 155).

may be saved. If the Israel of the Tanakh had perished, for instance through Haman (as we read in the book of Esther), the Messiah would not have been born of Israel. If New Testament Israel would perish, the Messiah would not be able to come from Zion (Rom. 11:26). Israel suffers in order to bring forth the Messiah at God's time—not only at the beginning of the present era, but also in the end time. Remember how the Messiah is born of Israel's labor pains:

> ... O Bethlehem Ephrathah, ...
> from you shall come forth for me
> > one who is to be ruler in Israel [i.e., the Messiah], ...
> Therefore he [i.e., God] shall give them [i.e., the individual Israelites] up until the time
> > when she [i.e., ideal Israel] who is in labor has given birth;
> then the rest of his [i.e., Messiah's] brothers shall return
> > to the people of Israel (Micah 5:2-3).

Ultimately, everything depends on the Messiah. Therefore, ultimately it is only through the Messiah's sacrifice that the repentant from Israel as well as from the Gentiles will be atoned. However, *the Messiah can never be severed from his people*. When the Messiah suffers, Israel suffers; when Israel suffers, the Messiah suffers, for he is the true personification of Israel. If the Messiah is the burnt offering, in a certain sense Israel is too. If the Messiah is the scapegoat, in a certain sense Israel is too.

5.5 Various Types in the Tanakh
5.5.1 Prophets and Psalms

Indeed, salvation is not only from the Messiah, but from the Messiah in conjunction with Israel: "Salvation is from *the Jews*" (John 4:22). In this, we see the double function of the Messiah: he is not only the true personification of Israel, he is also the One who leads and carries Israel's history; or more briefly: he *"is"* Israel, and he is there *for* Israel, leading from the beginning to its glorious and divinely determined end:

> I am God, and there is no other;

> I am God, and there is none like me,
> declaring the end from the beginning
> and from ancient times things not yet done,
> saying, "My counsel shall stand,
> and I will accomplish all my purpose" (Isa. 46:9-10).

This is leading and bearing occurs "from above," so to speak, by the One who transcends all history. But the same prophet says that God is *in* the misery *with* Israel:

> In all their affliction he was afflicted,
> and the angel of his presence saved them;
> in his love and in his pity he redeemed them;
> he lifted them up and carried them all the days of old
> (Isa. 63:9).

The Messiah went, and goes, with the Israelites through their history, and he suffered, and suffers, passing through the waters and the fire along with them.[38] At a certain time—the "fullness of time"—he suffered vicariously *for* them—that is, for the repentant ones among them, the true *tzaddiqim*—and in their subsequent history, he also suffers *together with* them. No one can understand Messiah's sufferings without discerning his sufferings *for* Israel. But no one can understand Messiah's sufferings either without discerning his sufferings *together with* Israel.

The history of the Messiah is reflected in the history of Israel; in all of Israel's suffering, the Messiah is among them with his Spirit. As a consequence, in many Psalms the two voices, that of the Messiah and that of Israel, can hardly be distinguished. Take, for instance, Psalm 69: verses 4, 9a, 9b and 21 are referring to the Messiah,[39] but in verse 5 clearly Israel is speaking: "O God, you know my folly; / the wrongs I have done are not hidden from you." The Messiah and Israel—together they pass through history, until the great final result:

---

38. Deut. 33:16; Isa. 43:2; Dan. 3:25; Mark 4:35–41.
39. As is evidenced in, respectively, John 15:25; 2:17; Rom. 15:3; Matt. 27:34.

God will save Zion
and build up the cities of Judah,
and people shall dwell there and possess it;
the offspring of his servants shall inherit it,
and those who love his name shall dwell in it
(Ps 69:35-36).

Thus, Israel and the Messiah cannot be severed; and occasionally it is difficult to distinguish is in the foreground when considering the person of Job, or the faithful in the Psalms, or the s/Servant in Isaiah 42-53.

Margarete Susman, too, saw clearly that Israel cannot complete its own history but depends on its Messiah for that. Israel *knows* this, even if it does not yet *know* who its Messiah is. Israel has accepted the Torah, which was given for, and belongs to, all humanity, and in this way it has accepted its cumbersome destiny; as Susman says, "With this Law, the people have surrendered themselves to their destiny, which they cannot realize in the midst of historical life, that is, which can be fulfilled only at the end of history through him who completes creation unto kingdom [of God] and the nations unto [true] humanity."[40]

5.5.2 Esther and Mordecai

In this context, it is worthwhile to consider the figure of Esther; elsewhere, I have dealt with the typology of the book of Esther and argued that Esther is a type of true Israel.[41] In this view, Ahasuerus is a representation God in his world dominion, Mordecai is a type of the Messiah, and Haman, the "Jews' enemy" (Est. 3:10; 8:1; 9:10, 24), is a type of the Antichrist, and more broadly, of all anti-Messianic powers that have threatened Israel throughout the centuries. A remarkable detail is that, in Esther 2:5, Mordecai is called a "Benjaminite" (from *ben-Yamin*, "son of my right hand"), but literally it says, *ish yemini*, "man of the right hand." This expression reminds us immediately of Psalm 80:17, "[L]et your hand be on the

---

40. Susman (1948, 98–99).
41. See Ouweneel (1998a, §4.5.3). A Jewish tradition refers to Mordecai as a "prophet"; see Talmud: Megillah 15a.

man of your right hand, / the son of man whom you have made strong for yourself!" This referred to the Messiah, but, interestingly, others see it as a reference to Israel.[42] Recall the double meaning of Job and of the s/Servant in Isaiah, both of whom point to Israel *and* the Messiah of Israel.

The book of Esther ends with the triumph of Mordecai and Esther, and of the entire nation of Israel. It is hard *not* to discern in Mordecai (Est. 9-10) a type of the Messiah in the Messianic kingdom. His position may be compared with that of Joseph as the viceroy of Egypt—another important type of the Messiah: "Mordecai the Jew was second in rank to King Ahasuerus, and he was great among the Jews and popular with the multitude of his brothers, for he sought the welfare of his people and spoke peace to all his people" (Est. 10:3).

Thus, the book culminates in the glory of this pair: the Messiah and Israel in the midst of the nations, that is, the ultimate glory of Zion in the Messianic kingdom. One would almost think that Mordecai and Esther were married, just as the Messiah and Israel will one day be husband and wife.[43] Interestingly, there is a Jewish tradition that saw them as a married couple. Some rabbis read in Esther 2:7 not "daughter" but "wife."[44] The idea then is that Esther was taken away from Mordecai without their (supposed) marriage becoming known (cf. 2:10). This makes Esther's move in chapter 3 even more dramatic: until that point, she had been forced to submit to King Ahasuerus, also sexually, but this time she would voluntarily submit to him, on her own initiative. In this view, this would be equivalent to adultery. Therefore, according to the Torah, she would be forbidden to return to Mordecai. In turn, Mordecai could not divorce her, for fear that the marriage would become known to the court. If Mordecai and Esther were indeed married, this would intensify the typological significance of the book: the ancient marriage relationship between God and Israel ultimately culminates in that between the Messiah and his bride: the Israel of God.[45]

---

42. See volume IV/1a, §8.4.3; see also Cohen (1985, 266).
43. Cf., e.g., Isa. 54; Ezek. 16; Hos. 2; and especially Song 1–8.
44. Talmud: Megillah 13a.
45. In the typology of the Song of Songs, the "mother" (1:6; 3:4; 6:9; 8:1–2, 5)

One of the most moving moments in the book was when Esther went to the king in order "to beg his favor and plead with him on behalf of her people" (Est. 4:8). Notice Mordecai's words to her, "who knows whether you have not come to the kingdom for such a time as this?" (v. 14). It is the "fullness of time" for Esther, so to speak. It was like Job knowing when to offer sacrifices for his children. The notion of representing other *nations* does not clearly come to light in the book of Esther, although ultimately Esther and Mordecai were a blessing for all the kingdom, including many nations (cf. Est. 1:1). Yet, we find here a remarkable example of representation and substitution: "Go, gather all the Jews to be found in Susa, and hold a fast on my behalf, and do not eat or drink for three days, night or day. I and my young women will also fast as you do. Then I will go to the king, though it is against the law, and if I perish, I perish" (Est. 4:16)—namely, *perish for the benefit of the people*. This reminds us of the prophetic words of Caiaphas the high priest: "[I]t is better for you that one man should die for the people, not that the whole nation should perish" (John 11:50).[46] These words refer to Jesus dying "for the people"; in Esther 4, the Israel of God was figuratively dying for *its* people, and for all the kingdom: it is better that the true Israel should die than that the whole nation should perish. This is the same as saying that it is better that the true *personification* of Israel should die than that the whole nation, or even all humanity should perish.

5.5.3 Jonah and the Sea

In the Tanakh we also find typological examples of Israel functioning as a vicarious substitute for the Gentiles. The prophet Jonah is one of them, an unmistakable type, not just of the Messiah (Matt. 12:40-41; Luke 11:32) but also of

---

represents ancient Israel, whereas the daughter represents the future remnant of Israel, linked with the male protagonist of the book: the Messiah; see Ouweneel (1973).

46. For the difference between "people" (Gk. *laos*, Hebr. *'am*) and "nation" (Gk. *ethnos*, Heb. *goi*), see De Graaff (1987, 378–80): the Messiah dies for the actual *'am*, i.e., the true Israel, which in the end is for the benefit of the entire Jewish nation.

Israel,[47] similar to the s/Servant in Isaiah 42-53. Jonah is a remarkable example of how Israel and the Messiah can merge as types. Notice Jonah's important statement to the seamen in the midst of the tempest:

> "Pick me up and hurl me into the sea; then the sea will quiet down for you, for I know it is because of me that this great tempest has come upon you." Nevertheless, the men rowed hard to get back to dry land, but they could not, for the sea grew more and more tempestuous against them. Therefore they called out to the LORD, "O LORD, let us not perish for this man's life, and lay not on us innocent blood, for you, O LORD, have done as it pleased you." So they picked up Jonah and hurled him into the sea, and the sea ceased from its raging (Jonah 1:12-15).

Jonah surrenders himself in God's tempest to the billows of the sea in order that the Gentile seamen may be saved. A pure form of substitution! However, in this peculiar case, the emphasis lay on the guilt of Jonah/Israel, in contrast with other examples, in which an innocent sacrifice takes the place of the guilty one(s).

The notion of Israel's vicarious position is also encountered in the New Testament: "For if their rejection means the reconciliation of the world, what will their acceptance mean but life from the dead?" (Rom. 11:15). This is similar to saying that, *without Israel having been set aside, there could have been no reconciliation for the world.* This, in turn, is almost equivalent to saying that, as the scapegoat, Israel must die so that the world will live. Salvation is from the Jews, but to this end, it seems, salvation must be withheld from the Jews for a while. However, at the same time the text said that one day Israel will again be accepted, and that this will be like a resurrection from the dead. The notion of the physical or spiritual resurrection is well-known to the prophets in the Tanakh.[48] Jonah went down into the waters of death, into the "belly of *She'ol*" (Jonah 2:2), in order that the Gentiles would live. But

---

47. See Ouweneel (2000a, Appendix IV).
48. Isa. 26:19; Ezek. 37:11–14; Dan. 12:1–3; Hos. 6:1–3.

Jonah's "life" is "brought up from the pit" (v. 6); as Jesus commented, "[J]ust as Jonah was three days and three nights in the belly of the great fish, so will the Son of Man be three days and three nights in the heart of the earth" (Matt. 12:40). Jesus could say by the mouth of the prophet, "[Y]ou will not abandon my soul to *She'ol*, / or let your holy one see corruption. / You make known to me the path of life" (Ps. 16:10–11; cf. Acts 2:31; 13:35). Similarly, the true Israel will one day say,

> O LORD, you have brought up my soul from *She'ol*;
> > you restored me to life from among those who go down to the pit.
> Sing praises to the LORD, O you his saints,
> > and give thanks to his holy name.
> For his anger is but for a moment,
> > and his favor is for a lifetime.
> Weeping may tarry for the night,
> > but joy comes with the morning (Ps. 30:3–5).

And elsewhere:

> The snares of death encompassed me;
> > the pangs of *She'ol* laid hold on me;
> > I suffered distress and anguish.
> Then I called on the name of the LORD:
> > "O LORD, I pray, deliver my soul!"
> Gracious is the LORD, and righteous;
> > our God is merciful (Ps. 116:3–5).

5.6 Scapegoat and Exile
5.6.1 Shoah and Sacrifice

One of the most remarkable Jewish authors who viewed the *Shoah* as substitution, and saw it as a parallel with Christ, was Rabbi Ignaz Maybaum. He himself escaped the *Shoah* by emigrating in 1939 from Austria to England. In 1965 he published his book about "the face of God after Auschwitz."[49] In it, he used the crucifixion of Jesus as his model for interpret-

---

49. Maybaum (1965); see the discussion by Rubenstein and Roth (1987, 303–308). For a Christian view, cf. Marquardt (1990–91).

ing the *Shoah*. Just as Jesus was the innocent victim whose sacrificial death enabled the salvation of humanity, the six million innocent victims of the *Shoah* were divinely chosen, not only as "victims" (such as when we speak of the victims of a traffic accident), but also as "sacrificial offerings," persons who are sacrificially slaughtered.

Coming from a Jewish pen, such a comparison may sound astonishing, but Rabbi Maybaum believed that in the *Shoah* God used a "language" that the entire Christian world should have been able to understand—New Testament language. Precisely because the Jews were God's chosen people, they were "sacrificed" in the death camps: the Golgotha of modern humanity is Auschwitz; the cross—the Roman gallows—was replaced by the gas chamber.[50] Obviously, such a view encountered enormous resistance, among both orthodox and liberal Jews. And quite a few Christians would have great difficulty, too, accepting that the six million murdered Jews "died for the sins of others."[51] Therefore we hasten to underscore anew that this "dying for the sins of others" can never be equated with the vicarious sufferings and death of the Messiah, which, as a genuine sin and guilt offering, really *blots out* the sins of people. In this sense, Israel itself needs the Messiah's sacrifice. No matter how much we can apply Isaiah 53 to Israel, in the first place it is Israel itself confessing here that the chastisement for *their* sins was upon the Servant of the LORD (v. 5), and that *he* became for them the true guilt offering (v. 10).

However, in the secondary sense of the eternal "scapegoat," Israel suffered too, and did so very specifically for the benefit of the nations. As we have seen, in common parlance the "scapegoat" is still the figure that is blamed for the mischief and guilt of others. In this use of the picture, the point

---

50. Maybaum (1965, 36).
51. Ibid., 67; he argued that Western humans, with remorse, ought to say of the Jew what Isaiah said of the Servant (Isa. 53:4–5): "Surely he has borne our griefs and carried our sorrows; . . . he was pierced for our transgressions; he was crushed for our iniquities." Jewish martyrdom, argued Maybaum, shows what meaning the cross can have, and thus has an effect that is more fruitful than the Christian dogma from the Middle Ages.

is not the extent to which the scapegoat may be personally guilt as well. We know that the true core of Israel is indeed righteous, but never sinless. But when the discussion involves the metaphor of the scapegoat, this is not the point. The point of the discussion involves the guilt of *others* that is placed upon the scapegoat, entirely along the lines of the scapegoat in Leviticus 16:20–22. The others are guilty, but the scapegoat bears the consequences of that guilt. As the protagonist of Psalm 69:4 puts it, "Though I did not steal, I must repay" (CSB). Certain people "steal," but the scapegoat must make the restitution.

Only in this sense can there be substitution in the case of Israel. However, we must not underestimate this form of vicarious suffering, as if it were merely a type that we could easily eliminate from our theology. This is especially true because the things we have considered so far seem to suggest a solemn conclusion: historically speaking, *the nations can never arrive at full salvation without this role of Israel as scapegoat in history*, with the *Shoah* as the nadir. Let us consider this matter a little more closely.

5.6.2 The *Galut* As Atonement

Israel's sufferings *par excellence* are expressed in the Greek term *diaspora*, Israel's "dispersion" among the nations of the world, and the associated Hebrew term *galut*. In the Tanakh, we find the terms *goleh*, a person referred to as "exile" (KJV: captive; 2 Sam. 15:19), *golah*, "(captivity,) exile,"[52] and *galut* as a collective term: "exiles,"[53] or being carried away in exile, in brief: exile (as a condition).[54] The root *g-l-h* means here "to emigrate, to be carried away (deported)."

Jewish tradition has linked the *galut* with the notion of atonement, though not in the full, sacrificial sense of the term, but in the derived sense of penance. For the mass of the Jewish people, the *galut* was chastisement for their own sins,

---

52. 2 Kings 24:15; Ezra 8:35; Ezek. 12:4, 11; in other passages we find Heb. *sh'bi* and similar words.
53. Isa. 20:4; 45:13; Jer. 24:5; 28:4; 29:22; 40:1; Obad. 20.
54. 2 Kings 25:27; Jer. 52:31; Ezek. 1:2; 33:21; 40:1; Amos 1:6, 9.

as was the case in the first exile (in Egypt) and the second exile (in Babylon). However, the true Israel of God, which certainly is not sinless, definitely suffered guiltlessly—think again of the Daniels and the Ezekiels in exile—and thus are chastised not for their own guilt but rather for that of others. Suffering *through* the sins of others might be closer to suffering *for* the sins of others than we might suppose.

Jewish tradition says, "Galut is the atonement for everything."[55] To illustrate this, one could point to the example of Moses, who was kept out of the Promised Land because he had struck the rock (Num. 20:11-12), notwithstanding the most glorious testimony that was given of him.[56] Another example is David, the godliest king, who obeyed God in the most perfect way; see the glorious testimony given of him.[57] He was a truly Messianic figure. Yet, he was not allowed to build a house for the LORD because of all the blood that he had shed (1 Chron. 22:8; 28:3). As Susman wrote, "It is only in the atonement of the exile, in the life of the people severed from all visible form, that the bloody hands are atoned, and that the people return to the pure communion devoted to God alone, excluding state, war and violence."[58] This is a marvelous description of the Messianic kingdom.

This "atonement of the exile" implies that, under these circumstances, the people were, and are, *unable* to defile itself through wars, political suppression of others, or any forms of violence; rather, they themselves fall prey to war and violence. This state of non-violence fits Israel; throughout the centuries, it has been the lamb led to the slaughter. Therefore, in all the history of Israel, though it could not escape from raging wars, it nonetheless viewed war as a mortal sin.[59] We might be tempted to forget this when war has become so normal in Israel's history—but in the case of David

---

55. Susman (1948, 93).
56. Exod. 33:11; Num. 12:3; Deut. 34:10–12.
57. 1 Sam. 13:14; 1 Kings 9:4; 11:33–34, 38; 14:8.
58. Susman (1948, 101).
59. Ibid., 178.

we see that even the wars that he fought *for God* defiled his hands and rendered him unfit for building the temple.

It is true, in the Torah we find the death penalty for many—in our eyes sometimes even minor—wrongdoings. However, the Talmud tells us that, when the Jewish Council decreed a death penalty only once after seventy years, the judges were viewed as murderers.[60] The tract says that *it is impossible to abolish the death penalty, but it is criminal to apply it!* Don't kill, even as authorities. Israel must be the non-violent one, who does not shed blood. Rather, its blood *has been shed* during virtually the entire third exile.

5.6.3 Two Observations

Two observations are relevant at this point.

First, how shocking was the co-responsibility of Israel's *unfaithful* multitude for Jesus' death (that is, to the extent it was in Jerusalem at that time and took part in shouting for Jesus' condemnation). This implies a remarkable paradox. On the one hand, the mob of Israel was guilty, and all those in Israel who approve of what the mob in those days did, make themselves equally guilty. On the other hand, it is my impression that the main reason why Israel suffered throughout so many centuries has less to do with the *guilt* of the mob than with the *innocence* of the true remnant of Israel, the "scapegoat" of the nations.

Second, how great is the responsibility of the *state* of Israel, now that the people again constitute a nation state, and, when it comes to war and violence, is in danger of behaving like all other peoples, no matter how much it is trying to operate within the boundaries of international law (if it does indeed—does it always?). In the state of Israel, the *galut* in its political respect is over—not in the religious respect, as long as the temple has not been rebuilt—and this means that Israel is no longer the defenseless lamb, or scapegoat, which it has been for so many centuries. It defends itself rather powerfully and effectively, and in doing so runs the risk of committing the same violations of international law that the others

---

60. Makkoth 7a; see Levinas (1987, 58, 225).

nations do. The lamb runs the risk of becoming a slaughterer of lambs (see extensively, chapters 9–10).

It is futile to argue that Israel is nevertheless so much better than its neighboring countries. After all, Israel is a democratic nation, while the neighbors are not. It maintains—with some mistakes—human rights as defined in the Universal Declaration of Human Rights, and its neighbors rarely do so. It condemns terrorism—in the sense of *intentionally* killing innocent citizens to achieve certain political goals—whereas its neighbors harbor various terrorist organizations: Hamas, Hezbollah, Islamic Jihad. The state of Israel does not participate in terrorism.[61] However, such arguments are hardly relevant because of the unique position for which God had chosen Israel:

> [I]f you call yourself a Jew and rely on the law and boast in God and know his will and approve what is excellent, because you are instructed from the Torah; and if you are sure that you yourself are *a guide to the blind, a light to those who are in darkness, an instructor of the foolish*, a teacher of children, having in the Torah the embodiment of knowledge and truth—you then who teach others, do you not teach yourself? While you preach against stealing, do you steal? . . . . You who boast in the Torah dishonor God by breaking the Torah. For, as it is written, "The name of God is blasphemed among the Gentiles because of you" (Rom. 2:17–24, citing Ezek. 36:23; cf. Isa. 52:5b).

And compare the words of the LORD through the prophet Isaiah, in which (the remnant of) Israel and the Messiah wonderfully merge as both the s/Servant of the LORD:

> You are my servant,
>   *Israel*, in whom I will be glorified. . . .
> It is too light a thing that you should be my servant
>   to raise up [the rest of] the tribes of Jacob
>   and to bring back the preserved of Israel;
> I will make you as a *light for the nations*,

---

61. There was Jewish terrorism during the British period, though (§10.3.2).

that my salvation may reach to the end of the earth (Isa. 49:3, 6).[62]

Whether or not the secular part of Israel, along with the supersessionists, wish to see and acknowledge this truth, Israel remains the chosen people of God, with a tremendous responsibility toward all humanity.

5.7 More on the *Galut*
5.7.1 Penance in Patience

Israel is and remains a unique people after all, no matter how "normal" it attempts to be, also within its present nation state. Even the socialism of a large part of the Israelis is unique. Zionism as such is usually somewhat religious, but it is still rooted in a very idealistic socialism. This socialism, entirely in line with tradition, opposes violence and oppression, and is oriented toward the coming paradise, and therefore also easily assumes the form of communism.[63] Ethnic Israel cannot (entirely) deny this utopianism. The communism of the Jew Karl Marx, and of so many Jewish communists in his wake,[64] was seeking a "paradise"[65] that was nothing but a secularized form of the Messianic kingdom.

One aspect of this secularization of the kingdom is that humans themselves are actively endeavoring to usher in this "paradise." In this respect, such Jews resemble their forefather Jacob, who in his own way tried to hasten the Messianic blessing, with mischievous consequences. Yet, he is and remains Jacob, the vessel of God's covenant promises, who in the end does receive the blessing—along the road of repentance, confession, and faith. There is no other way, for Jew or Gentile, to receive *any* divine blessing. Israel sometimes represents the better side of Jacob, sometimes it represents

---

62. Cf. 42:6; 60:3; cf. also the New Jerusalem: "By its light will the nations walk" (Rev. 21:24).
63. Cf. Susman (1948, 114–19, 122).
64. Moses Hess, Ferdinand Lassalle, Eduard Bernstein, Leon Trotsky, and Israel Epstein (https://communismblog.wordpress.com/2014/12/11/list-of-communist-jews/) (cf. chapter 3 note 21).
65. Regarding the concept of "paradise," see Ouweneel (2020).

his less good side—but Jacob and Israel (originally one and the same!⁶⁶) remain the chosen vessel of God. Saying that no human being can be blessed apart from Abraham, Isaac, and Jacob, is the same as saying that no one can be blessed apart from Israel.

This is how the Jewish journalist Mau Kopuit formulated it:

> It was not David Ben Gurion, Israel's first prime minister, who made Jerusalem the capital of Israel. It was David, Israel's first king-singer. Jerusalem, Zion, became the center of Israel, long before the thought of any political Zionism could come up. However, it is political Zionism that, after so many centuries of dispersion, has brought back the Jews. It is Zionism that, with all political means, has strived for the Jews' own Jewish state. But political Zionism could take root only because, in the Jewish consciousness, religious Zionism is so deeply anchored.⁶⁷

In other words, no matter how secular Zionism was (and is), it is inconceivable without this *deeply religious* yearning for the land of the fathers. We could hardly imagine a Jew who is so strongly secularized that this longing has been entirely smothered within him.

In his conversations with the Roman Catholic theologian Karl Rahner, Orthodox Jewish New Testament scholar Pinchas Lapide spoke of the remarkable phenomenon of the "atheist Jew":

> When a person, with some Jewish atheists, has some more extensive conversations, it often turns out that, in fact, they are anti-theists: they are angry with God because, in their opinion, he allowed one and a half million Jewish children to be burned. . . . [What such Jewish 'atheists'] usually do not know is that, in their indignation, they remain faithful to one of the oldest Jewish traditions.⁶⁸ They argue with their Creator, just as once

---

66. See Gen. 32:28; 35:10; 46:2; 49:2; Isa. 14:1; 27:6; 29:23; 40:27; 41:8, 14; 43:1, 22, 28; 44:1, 5, 21, 23; 45:4; 46:3; 48:1, 12; 49:5–6.
67. Kopuit (1977, 7); for this problem cf. also Houwaart and Gerssen (1980).
68. Regarding this, see Laytner (1990), who mentioned the same and some other

Abraham argued about Sodom and Gomorrah [Gen. 18], just as once our progenitor Jacob did at the ford of the Jabbok [Gen. 32];[69] they rebel as once Jeremiah did [Jer. 20]. Israel, the new name that Jacob, in that nightly fight, could wring out of God, means "God's fighter"[70]—a feature that the patriarch Jacob, together with the new name, has passed on to all his descendants. But all this has nothing to do with atheism, for only a madman combats something of which, or someone of whom, he denies the existence. The Jewish fight with God is perhaps the highest degree of acknowledging God—a thorough, uncompromising taking the Lord of the world seriously, such that it does not wish to allow any injustice, any stain on the image of God.[71]

Even the so-called "atheist" Jews—I do not mean superficial, indifferent Jews, but Jews who continue to think and ponder profoundly—are religious in their heart of hearts, for basically many of them do not at all deny the existence of God; they are only *angry* with God. Actually, this anger is tragic enough; the godly Jew *bends* under their suffering—the angry Jew *barks* about their suffering. But perhaps such a distinction is too simplistic: Job was a godly man, but he too was angry with God. However, finally he had to say, "I repent . . ." (Job 42:6):

> I had heard about you with my own ears,
>   but now I have seen you with my own eyes.
> That is why I take back what I said,
>   and I sit in dust and ashes to show that I am sorry
> (Job 42:5–6 GW).

5.7.2 The Solitude of the *Galut*

The *Galut* consists in one long penance. It means no more fighting wars, only enduring wars; this is suffering. It means no use of violence, but repeatedly being led to the slaughter as a defenseless lamb. It is precisely this being exiles, this

---

examples: Abraham, Moses, Elijah, Jeremiah, and, of course, Job.
69. For a different interpretation of this episode, see volume IV/1a, chapter 2.
70. This is one possible interpretation; cf. volume IV/1a, §1.1.2.
71. Lapide and Rahner (1984, 74–75).

homelessness, this defenselessness of the Jews that evoked from the nations not pity increased aggression against them. It is the feeble (defenseless) kid at school, not the fighting kid, who gets bullied.

There is a German wordplay involved here: the fact that the Jews were *heimatlos* ("homeless") made them *unheimlich* ("scary, mysterious").[72] I would add: and made them look *homely* ("unattractive"). The Jews may be our neighbors, perhaps for centuries, yet you know they are never *really* part of us; they belong somewhere else. And their defenselessness makes them scary, even unattractive, and this enhances our Gentile aggression.

The great majority of the Jewish nation had made itself guilty of fornication, more correctly: adultery, sexual immorality, that is, apostasy from the true service of God and "whoring after" foreign gods.[73] In the *galut*, this unfaithful "woman," who ran after the wrong "men," is left to herself and her solitude. The prophet tells his wife, who had become an adulteress: "You must dwell as mine [i.e., as my wife] for many days. You shall not play the whore, or belong to another man; so will I also be to you" (Hos. 3:3). Then follows the application:

> For the children of Israel shall dwell many days without king or prince, without sacrifice or pillar [devoted to Baal], without ephod[74] or household gods [Heb. *teraphim*]. Afterward the children of Israel shall return and seek the LORD their God, and David their king [i.e., the Messiah], and they shall come in fear to the LORD and to his goodness in the latter days" (Hos. 3:4–5).

Many days left to itself: that implies, on the one hand, Israel's penance will occur apart from the Davidic king, the temple, and the sacrificial ministry; but on the other hand, there will be no more idolatry, but only the prayers, the deeds of

---

72. Rubenstein (1968, 22); both expressions contain the word *heim* ("home"), but the meanings are very different.
73. Cf. Exod. 34:15–16; Lev. 17:7; 20:5–6; Num. 15:39; Deut. 31:16.
74. The ephod may refer here to the priestly ministry in the temple (cf. Exod. 28:6–14), *or* to the priests of the idols (cf. Judg. 17:5; 18:14, 17–20).

love, the high festivals, and the days of fasting that would be left to them.[75]

A Jewish story tells how, shortly after creation, the lamb complained with God because it lacked horns, claws, jaws, tusks, and proboscis with which to defend itself. It felt helplessly exposed to the mistreatment by other animals. God offered to grant similar powerful weapons to the lamb as well. The lamb refused, however, because it did not wish to hurt or injure others. It asks only for the "weapons" that would help to forget the inflicted sorrow, and to make the suffering endurable. Thereupon, the Creator equipped the lamb with three "weapons" that produce peace even during its worst suffering: meekness, devotion, and patience.[76]

Compare these two passages: Job asked, "What is my strength, that I should wait? And what is my *end*, that I should be *patient*?" (Job 6:11). And the apostle James commented: "You have heard of the *patience* of Job, and you have seen the *end* of the Lord, that the Lord is merciful and compassionate" (James 5:11 DRA).

5.8 The *Lamed-Waws*
5.8.1 The Thirty-Six *Tzaddiqim*

A Jewish tradition tells about the thirty-six special righteous ones (Heb. *tzaddiqim*) thought to exist among the people of Israel in each generation.[77] They are called *Lamed-Waws* (in Slavic languages, *lamedwawniks*) because the numerical values of the letters *lamed* (30) and *waw* (6) add up to 36.[78] Ac-

---

75. Dan. 3:38–40 (apocryphal, DRA): "Neither is there at this time . . . holocaust, or sacrifice, or oblation, or incense, or place of firstfruits before thee, that we may find thy mercy . . . . As in holocausts of rams, and bullocks, and as in thousands of fat lambs: so let our sacrifice be made in thy sight this day, that it may please thee."
76. Told by Kanner (1990, 32–33, though the source is not found in Talmud or Midrash).
77. Susman (1948, 190–91). Only from Israel? The Gentile Oskar Schindler (known from Spielberg's movie *Schindler's List*) was buried in Jerusalem (1974) as one of the "thirty-six righteous ones" (from the nations?) (cf. next note: "The world . . . .").
78. See, e.g., Talmud: Sanhedrin 97b: "Abaye said: The world must contain no

cording to some Talmudists, the origin of the story goes back to the time of Isaiah.

> ... To understand this metamorphosis, one must be aware of the ancient Jewish tradition of the Lamed-Vov, a tradition that certain Talmudists trace back to the source of the centuries, to the mysterious time of the prophet Isaiah. Rivers of blood have flowed, columns of smoke have obscured the sky, but surviving all these dooms, the tradition has remained inviolate down to our own time. According to it, the world reposes upon thirty-six Just Men, the Lamed-Vov, indistinguishable from simple mortals; often they are unaware of their station. But if just one of them were lacking, the sufferings of mankind would poison even the souls of the newborn, and humanity would suffocate with a single cry. For the Lamed-Vov are the hearts of the world multiplied, and into them, as into one receptacle, pour all our griefs....[79]

In no respect can the *Lamed-waws* be distinguished from common mortals. Often, they themselves do not know that they belong to the *Lamed-waws*. According to a very old tradition, these are the most pitiful ones: "For those the spectacle of the world is an unspeakable hell."

> "When an unknown Just rises to Heaven," a Hasidic story goes, "he is so frozen that God must warm him for a thousand years between His fingers before his soul can open itself to Paradise. And it is known that some remain forever inconsolable at human woe, so that God Himself cannot warm them. So from time to time the Creator, blessed be His Name, sets forward the clock of the Last Judgment by one minute."[80]

[fewer] than thirty-six righteous men in each generation who are vouchsafed [the sight of] the *Shechinah's* countenance, for it is written, *Blessed are all they that wait for him* ['him' is Heb. *lo*, written as *lamed-waw*] ... [they are] those who see Him through a bright speculum" (cf. 1 Cor. 13:12).

79. Schwarz-Bart (1985, 4–5).
80. Ibid., 4.

The *Lamed-Waws* represent the true Israel, the faithful core of the nation, the "Israel of God"; according to the tradition, the *Shekhinah* rests upon them. In this sense, in his day Jesus was the *Lamed-waw* more so than any other Jew, for it was on him that the *Shekhinah* preeminently found its resting-place (see chapter 11). In note 79, I quoted the Talmud, where the *Lamed-Waws* are linked with the last line of Isaiah 30:18, in which the word "him" has the numerical value of 36:

> Therefore the LORD waits to be gracious to you,
>   and therefore he exalts himself to show mercy to you.
> For the LORD is a God of justice;
>   *blessed are all those who wait for him.*

That is, the *Lamed-waws* are those who put their confidence in the LORD, submitting themselves to him in faith, no matter through what misery they must pass. These are the *tzaddiqim* ("righteous"), of whom we find exactly seven examples in the New Testament: Zechariah and Elizabeth, the parents of John the Baptist (Luke 1:6); Joseph, the husband of Mary (Matt. 1:19); Simeon (Luke 2:25); John the Baptist himself (Mark 6:20); Joseph of Arimathea (Luke 23:50-51);[81] and in particular Jesus, concerning whose righteousness we have a seven- (or eight-?) fold testimony.[82]

One description of the *Lamed-waws* offered this portrait:[83]

> Who is Job-Israel? This is no doubt the Self or Essence of Israel. . . . These are the righteous ones. Each generation has the 36 public and the 36 hidden righteous. The public righteous know the meaning of guiltless suffering. They know that they suffer for the sin of the nations. The 36 hidden righteous do not know this. Therefore, their suffering is deeper. They suffer for the sin of the nations without knowing it. When they know, they enter

---

81. Luke 1:6; Matt. 1:19; Luke 2:25; Mark 6:20; Luke 23:50–51.
82. Matt. 27:19, 24; Acts 3:14; 7:52; 22:14; 1 Pet. 3:18; 1 John 2:1; perhaps James 5:6.
83. De Graaff (1987, 108).

the kingdom of God. They even do not know that they are righteous. These are the greatest in Israel.

Others have said about these righteous that for their sake God withholds his destroying wrath, and the rest of humanity receives grace.[84] In some reports, there must be thirty-six of such who are righteous; other reports say that even one is sufficient. Usually, the righteous are not conspicuous. They may be unknown even to themselves.[85]

5.8.2 The Last *Lamed-Waw*

Let me refer here again to the moving novel by André Schwarz-Bart, which I have already quoted several times: *Le dernier des justes*, in English: *The Last of the Just*.[86] The book is based upon the legend of the thirty-six *tzaddiqim*. The author was a young French Jew, who had lost his relatives in the Nazi gas chambers. The well-known Jewish theologian Pinchas Lapide called the book an "unforgettable monument for all Jewish martyrs," and wrote that this masterpiece, for which the author in 1967 received the "Prize of Jerusalem," was soon translated into Hebrew, along with fourteen other languages.[87] Reading this deeply touching novel forms a good spiritual preparation for grasping the book of Job as a foreshadowing of the suffering of the Jewish people, from the beginning until the gas chambers of the Nazi death camps.

One who can cry over the suffering of Israel, but also over the suffering of humanity in general, enters in this way into the profoundest mystery of Israel, and thus, to some extent, they themselves become a little bit of a Jew. "My teacher in Jerusalem always said, What is a Jew? A person who feels pain when in South Africa a black person is mistreated; whose stomach growls when in Biafra a child suffers hunger. He who is not able to suffer with all humans must not consider himself to be a true Jew."[88] Let me quote here again the words

---

84. Rubenstein and Roth (1987, 262–66).
85. Ibid., 262.
86. Schwarz-Bart (1985).
87. Lapide (1984, 13); in 1959, this book was awarded the Prix Goncourt.
88. In Lapide and Rahner (1984, 87).

about God himself: "In all their affliction he was afflicted" (Isa. 63:9). He is not only *with* his people in all their miseries, but he feels the pain they feel. Compare the poetic words that Julius Anton von Poseck wrote concerning the righteous: *Jeden Schlag, Spott und Schmach fühlst Du als Dein eignes Leid* ("Every blow, mocking and defamation you feel as your own sorrow").

One of Schwarz-Bart's protagonists, the righteous Mordecai Levy, says this:

> "... the Lamed-Vovnik takes our suffering upon himself.... And he raises it to heaven and sets it at the feet of the Lord—who forgives. Which is why the world goes on ... in spite of all our sins, ... [W]e'd have to know what goes in the heart of a Lamed-Vovnik, and he himself doesn't know, isn't aware that his heart is bleeding away. He thinks it's simply life passing through him. When a Just Man smiles at a baby, there is as much suffering in him, they say, as in a Just Man undergoing martyrdom."[89]

Later in the book, Mordecai explains to his young grandson, Ernie Levy—the main protagonist in the book—what a *Tzaddiq* is:

> "All right then, listen to me," Mordecai said after a bit more reflection. "Open both ears: If a man suffers all alone, it is clear his suffering remains within him. Right?"
>
> "Right," Earnie said.
>
> "But if another looks at him as says to him, 'You're in trouble, my Jewish brother,' what happens then?"
>
> The blanket stirred and revealed the sharp point of Ernie Levy's nose. "I understand that too," he said politely. "He takes the suffering of his friend into his own eyes."
>
> Mordecai sighed, smiled, sighed again. "And if he is blind, do you think that he can take it in?"
>
> "Of course, through his ears!"
>
> "And if he is deaf?"
>
> "Then through his hands," Ernie said gravely.
>
> "And if the other is far away, if he can neither hear him nor

---

89. Schwarz-Bart (1985, 57).

see him and not even touch him—do you believe then that he can take in his pain?"

"Maybe he could guess at it," Ernie said with a cautious expression.

Mordecai went into ecstasies. "You've said it, my love—that is exactly what the Just Man does! He senses all the evil rampant on earth, and he takes it into his heart!"[90]

Is there really such a "Jew" in each of us, who can cry with others, suffer with others, one who is able to vicariously take upon oneself the sufferings of others? What do we do with that "Jew"? Adolf Hitler must have said at one time to his confident, Hermann Rauschning (according to the latter's own report), "Each of us bears the Jew in himself; only, outside us he can be more easily persecuted than within us."[91] Exactly: either we persecute that Jew outside us in the bitterest way, if need be in the name of Jesus—or we develop that Jew within us: the *tzaddiq*, the truly godly one, the one who wholeheartedly loves God as well as his people.

---

90. Ibid., 174.
91. Quoted by Susman (1948, 115).

Chapter 6
The Rejection and Preservation of Israel

If men rise up to pursue you and to seek your life, the life of my lord shall be bound in the bundle of the living in the care of the Lord your God. And the lives of your enemies he shall sling out as from the hollow of a sling.

1 Samuel 25:29

Awake! Why are you sleeping, O Lord?
   Rouse yourself! Do not reject us forever!
Why do you hide your face?
   Why do you forget our affliction and oppression?

Psalm 44:23–24

6.1   Jesus and Israel—Who Killed Whom?
6.1.1   The Cruel Friends

JOB AND ISRAEL SUFFERED two calamities: one was what they lost, the other was what they received. First, Job lost his children, his possessions, his health (he was full of loathsome sores). During the *galut* Israel lost its king, its city, its temple, and its sacrificial ministry; Israel was (as the Gentiles said) "a man of sorrows [or, pains] and acquainted with grief [or, sickness], and as one from whom men hide their faces he was despised, and we esteemed him not" (Isa. 53:3).

However, their second calamity involved what Job and Israel received from others. In addition to the suffering mentioned, Job received all the vicious accusations and reproaches from his three "friends." The same occurred to Israel, in terms of all the similar accusations and reproaches from the Gentiles. Actually, the same occurred to the Messiah, who is the personification of Israel (cf. Matt. 27:40–43).

Those who vexed Job were not strangers but friends. The same was true for Israel (and for the Messiah):

> [I]t is not an enemy who taunts me—
>   then I could bear it;
> it is not an adversary who deals insolently with me—
>   then I could hide from him.
> But it is you, a man, my equal,
>   my companion, my familiar friend (Ps. 55:12-13).
> Even my close friend in whom I trusted,
>   who ate my bread, has lifted his heel against me (Ps. 41:10).

Who have been Israel's natural friends and brothers during the entire third exile? Christians. Who were the people who oppressed Israel most during the *galut*? Christians. Of course, I am not referring to the faithful core of Christianity;[1] these must be distinguished from the Christian masses, just as the true Israel must be distinguished from the Jewish masses. However, that faithful core was often very small, both among Christians and among the Jews. Broadly speaking, it was "Christian" nations that oppressed Israel, generally speaking much more than Islamic nations have ever done. (Remarkably enough, in the present time—after the Holocaust—the roles seem to have been reversed.)

---

1. An interesting example during the time of the Reformation was the humanist Johannes Reuchlin, who remained a Catholic. He was a great-uncle of Philip Melanchthon, an expert in Greek and Hebrew, and a defender of the Jews; regarding him, see Ouweneel (2014a, 389–90).

It belongs to the most profound and horrifying riddles of Israel's history that the greatest and most encompassing sufferings were inflicted upon this nation in the name of the *Jew* Jesus. How is this possible? Much has been written on this mystery. On the basis of the book of Job, I would say that the friends accuse Job of having a grave crime on his conscience, whereas Job is innocent. Similarly, throughout the centuries, the non-violent lamb Israel has been accused of the greatest act of violence in the history of humanity: the murder of Jesus of Nazareth. We heard Eliphaz say,

> [Y]ou have exacted pledges of your brothers for nothing
>   and stripped the naked of their clothing.
> You have given no water to the weary to drink,
>   and you have withheld bread from the hungry
>   (Job 22:6–7).[2]

This is the biting accusation: Israel robbed Jesus, Israel Jesus of his clothing, Israel refused to give water and bread to Jesus, Israel killed Jesus. When it comes to the mob in Pilate's court, shouting for Jesus' execution, this is correct. But when it comes to Israel in its entirety, the Israel down through all the Christian centuries, the accusation is just as false as the one addressed to Job by Eliphaz. For centuries, Christians have punished the masses of Israel for what the crowd in Pilate's court did—and they did so in the name of Jesus. They not only accused Israel, no, they appointed themselves to be the executioners of Israel.

Let me give two practical examples. We are told of the American evangelist Harry A. Ironside that, one day, he gave a Jewish bootblack in New York a considerable tip with the words, "I give you this in the name of Jesus." The man looked up and said, "I come from Eastern Europe. There, our goods were stolen in the name of Jesus, our women were raped in the name of Jesus, our houses were set on fire in the name of Jesus. You are the first person who does something good to me in the name of Jesus."

---

2. Compare this with Jesus' own statement: "[A]s you did not do it to one of the least of these, you did not do it to me" (Matt. 25:45).

The second example comes from my personal memory. A German Jewess of advanced age told us in a speech that, as a little girl in Nazi Germany, she had experienced how she with her family, and many other Jews, had been barricaded inside a synagogue, which was then set on fire. Outside, the people yelled the name of Jesus. I do not recall how she escaped, but I will never forget what she told us: "In the name of Jesus all my family was murdered—but in the name of Yeshuah I have found eternal salvation." She had discovered that the "Jesus" of the pogroms and the Nazis was not the same as, and actually had nothing in common with, the Yeshuah whom she had learned to know from the New Testament.

6.1.2 The Torah-Less

In the New Testament, Jews are blamed for having murdered Jesus. It is incorrect to reply that it was not the Jews but the Romans who executed him. Yes, the Romans bore an enormous share in the guilt for this atrocity; but the apostle Peter told Israel on the Day of Pentecost: "[T]his Jesus, delivered up according to the definite plan and foreknowledge of God, *you crucified* and killed by the hands of lawless men [i.e., the Torah-less Romans]" (Acts 2:23). Sometime later, Peter said to Israel: "*[Y]ou* killed the Author of life, whom God raised from the dead" (3:15) and: ". . . Jesus Christ of Nazareth, whom *you crucified*" (4:10). The disciples of Emmaus described ". . . how our chief priests and rulers delivered him [i.e., Jesus] up to be condemned to death, and crucified *him*" (Luke 24:20). And Stephen told the spiritual leaders of Israel: ". . . the Righteous One, whom *you* have now betrayed and murdered, you who received the law as delivered by angels and did not keep it" (Acts 7:52-53).

Three times we read here that the *Jews* crucified Jesus,[3] although none of them had had a hammer in his hand. It is like King Solomon who "built" the temple (1 Kings 6:1), although he, too, probably never used the hammer himself. You can be

---

3. When Jacob Revius wrote in a poem: "It was not the Jews, Lord Jesus, who crucified you . . . ," he did not mean to deny the Jews' guilt but rather to lay the guilt on ourselves: "It is me, Oh Lord, who did this to you . . . for alas! all this happened because of my sins."

responsible for *doing* a thing, even if the hands that actually carry it out are those of others.

6.1.3 Only the Crowd in Pilate's Court

The vital point here, however, is that the passages quoted refer to the mob and the leaders in Jerusalem standing in the court of Pilate; spiritually speaking, *these* were essentially just as Torah-less as the Romans were. First and foremost, it is *such* people whom Jesus calls "workers of Torah-lessness."[4] All the more painful was this Jewish statement: "*We have a law, and according to that law he ought to die because he has made himself the Son of God*" (John 19:7).[5] Jesus was condemned *on the basis of the very Torah of which he is the sense, the content, and the goal* (Rom. 10:4).

However, we must carefully consider here that all these passages refer particularly to the inhabitants of Jerusalem, and more specifically to those who shouted, "Crucify him!" To the Jews in Pisidian Antioch, the apostle Paul spoke very differently: the gospel is for

> . . . *those* who live in Jerusalem and *their rulers*, because *they* did not recognize him nor understand the utterances of the prophets, which are read every Sabbath, fulfilled them by condemning him. And though *they* found in him no guilt worthy of death, *they* asked Pilate to have him executed. And when *they* had carried out all that was written of him, *they* took him down from the tree and laid him in a tomb (Acts 13:27–29).

Notice the "they"; it is not "you" but "those in Jerusalem." This is the example for us. Nowhere in the New Testament is it "the" Jews in general, or all the Jews living around AD 30, who are declared guilty. Even less does the New Testament give us any basis for declaring all Jews guilty who have lived worldwide since the first century. *Only the crowd in Pilate's court was guilty.* It is a typical characteristic of anti-Semitism

---

4. Matt. 7:23; cf. 13:41; 23:28; 2 Thess. 2:7; 1 Tim. 1:9; Heb. 10:17; 1 John 3:4.
5. In Johann Sebastian Bach's *Johannes Passion* (*St. John's Passion*) these words resound very loudly in a chorus to which Susman (1948, 54, 89) referred twice.

to say, *"you Jews . . . ,"* as has been done throughout the Christian era. We should rather say, *"those in Jerusalem,"* as Paul did.

In 1 Thessalonians 2:14–16 as well, Paul limits his accusations to the Jews in Judea:

> For you, brothers, became imitators of the churches of God in Christ Jesus that are in Judea. For you suffered the same things from your own countrymen as they did from the Jews, who killed both the Lord Jesus and the prophets, and drove us out, and displease God and oppose all mankind by hindering us from speaking to the Gentiles that they might be saved—so as always to fill up the measure of their sins. But wrath has come upon them at last!

On the basis of this passage, the apostle has been accused of anti-Semitism,[6] but his statement must be counterbalanced by this other word by him: "I have great sorrow and unceasing anguish in my heart. For I could wish that myself were accursed and cut off from Christ for the sake of my brothers, my kinsmen according to the flesh [i.e., the Jews]. . . . Brothers, my heart's desire and prayer to God for them is that they may be saved" (Rom. 9:2–3; 10:1).

6.2 "His Blood Be On Us"
6.2.1 A Double Blunder

Words must be considered in their context. This is true especially regarding the (in)famous statement in Matthew 27:25, where the Jewish mob in Pilate's court is shouting: "His blood be on us and on our children!" Forty years after they had spoken these words, the blood of Jesus literally *came* upon the children of this generation *in Jerusalem*, namely, during the destruction of the city and the temple by the Romans.

But be careful here: did this disaster come upon Israel *because of* what they had said to Pilate? Does God hold people to every curse that they, in their folly, may pronounce upon themselves? The answer is a decisive No. The LORD himself declare,

---
6. Cf. Jansen (1981, ad loc.).

> If a woman vows a vow to the LORD and binds herself by a pledge, while within her father's house in her youth, ... If she marries a husband, while under her vows or any thoughtless utterance of her lips by which she has bound herself, and her husband hears of it and says nothing to her on the day that he hears, then her vows shall stand, and her pledges by which she has bound herself shall stand. But if, on the day that her husband comes to hear of it, he opposes her, then he makes void her vow that was on her, and the thoughtless utterance of her lips by which she bound herself. And the LORD will forgive her (Num. 30:3–8).

I believe that on the very same day the mob in Pilate's court pronounced this curse, the LORD "made void her vow that was on her, and the thoughtless utterance of her lips by which she bound herself." I believe that this happened when Jesus spoke these words on the cross: "Father, forgive them, for they know not what they do" (Luke 23:34). This is an important point, which I will elaborate in the next section.

Thus, the first blunder is that so many Christians have taken it for granted that God has held Israel to the curse they had uttered. But was it really "Israel" that uttered the curse? Here we have the second blunder. The curse could not be carried out any further than on those who pronounced it: *these* Torah-less Jews in Pilate's court, together with *their* children. What gives us the right to extend this curse that a small group pronounced on itself and their children to a curse of *God* on *all Israel*, from the first century until now? This is the double blunder: first, Israel's self-curse is not God's curse, and second, the self-curse of a small group is not the self-curse of an entire nation, throughout the centuries, all over the world.

This double blunder has had the most heinous consequences for the Jewish nation, despite the clear words of the prophet: "The soul who sins shall die. The son shall not suffer for the iniquity of the father, nor the father suffer for the iniquity of the son. The righteousness of the righteous shall be upon himself, and the wickedness of the wicked shall be upon himself" (Ezek. 18:20). This is not to deny that descendants sometimes must bear the *consequences* of their forefathers' sins, for the Ten Commandments clearly said,

"I the LORD your God am a jealous God, visiting the iniquity of the fathers on the children to the third and the fourth generation of those who hate me" (Exod. 20:5).[7] But this is something essentially different from the children being *punished* for the sins of their forefathers. And even less does any Gentile—"Christian" or not—have the right to appoint *themselves* as the executioner to carry out this punishment. What is worse: the stupidity that the crowd in Pilate's court pronounced on itself, or the hundreds of thousands of "Christians" who thought they had the right, or even the duty, to murder hundreds of thousands of Jews because of this stupidity?

6.2.2 The Effect of the Blood

There is yet a third blunder that we might make here. Do the words "his blood be on us" necessarily involve only a curse? Could not this statement reach far beyond what these Jews themselves might have imagined? Even the murderous statement by the high priest Caiaphas in John 11:50 was interpreted by the Holy Spirit as a prophecy that Jesus would die for Israel, that is, vicariously, in their place, and for their benefit. Could it not be the same with the murderous words of the crowd in Pilate's court? Compare their words with the profound words that the high priest spoke to the apostles: "We strictly charged you not to teach in this name, yet here you have filled Jerusalem with your teaching, and *you intend to bring this man's blood upon us*" (Acts 5:28). Primarily, this is equivalent to saying: you want to make us responsible for the death of "this man"[8] (indeed, cf. Acts 4:10). Yet, the high priest was making a strange statement, since the people had indeed shouted, "His blood be on us and on our children!" It was not the apostles who had "brought" Jesus' blood on these Jews, but rather they themselves had done this—unless

---

7. Cf. Exod. 34:7; Num. 14:18; Deut. 5:9.

8. It is worth noting that later Jewish tradition also refers to Jesus as "this man"; some orthodox Jews avoid mentioning his name, says Jocz (1949, 111). Lapide (1984, 19–22) pointed to a modern novel of the Jewish Nobel Prize winner Samuel Josef Agnon, in which the same occurs. I have the same experience with some Jewish guides in Israel.

the high priest wished to distance himself from the people. Regardless of the high priest's intention, on a deeper level he was touching the essence of the gospel: the apostles' message did intend to bring the as yet unbelieving Jews *under the blood of Jesus* (something very different from bringing *upon them* the blood of Jesus).

For twenty centuries now, the people of Israel, at least the true Israel of God, has been brought under the blood of Jesus by God's electing grace, even if they do not (yet) know this. Soon, the true high priest will return from the heavenly sanctuary; this involves his second coming, which will bring with it the atonement of Israel: "Seventy 'weeks' are decreed about your people and your holy city, to finish the transgression, to put an end to sin, and to atone for iniquity, to bring in everlasting righteousness" (Dan. 9:24). However, this is the same high priest who, already almost twenty centuries ago,

> entered once for all into the holy places, not by means of the blood of goats and calves but by means of his own blood, thus securing an eternal redemption. . . . Christ has entered, not into holy places made with hands, which are copies of the true things, but into heaven itself, now to appear in the presence of God on our behalf (Heb. 9:12, 24).

Whether (penitent) Israel is aware of this or not, *that* was the moment when the blood for their atonement was sprinkled before and on the "atonement cover" (NIV) that is on the heavenly ark (cf. Rev. 11:19). This was described in Leviticus 16:16–17:

> Thus he [i.e., the high priest] shall make atonement for the Holy Place [or, the sanctuary], because of the uncleannesses of the people of Israel and because of their transgressions, all their sins. And so he shall do for the tent of meeting, which dwells with them in the midst of their uncleannesses. No one may be in the tent of meeting from the time he enters to make atonement in the Holy Place until he comes out and has made atonement for himself and for his house and for all the assembly of Israel.

6.2.3 Under the Blood

The apostolic gospel preaching was directed toward bringing part of Israel under the blessing of this blood before the Great High Priest would return from the heavenly sanctuary (see previous section). Already when the Sinaitic Covenant was made, Israel was brought under the blood of the covenant (Exod. 24:7-8): Moses

> took the Book of the Covenant and read it in the hearing of the people. And they said, 'All that the LORD has spoken we will do, and we will be obedient.' And Moses took the blood and threw it on the people and said, "Behold the blood of the covenant that the LORD has made with you in accordance with all these words."[9]

This was precisely the way Jesus Christ offered his own blood, as he said regarding the cup at the institution of the Lord's Supper: "[T]his is my blood of the covenant, which is poured out for many for the forgiveness of sins" (Matt. 26:28). Jesus used the words as Moses had done, but applied them to himself: "*my* blood of the covenant." But there is more. Just as Moses brought the people under the covenant blood, Jesus brings his disciples under his *own* blood, even a great mass of people, for he says of it: "... which is poured out *for many* for the forgiveness of sins." We may wonder if Jesus meant with these "many" only Jews, or also Gentiles (cf. Matt. 20:28, "the Son of Man came ... to give his life as a ransom for many"). At any rate, Israel is included. Just as Moses, Jesus had the entire nation in view, even if he knew that "not all who are descended from Israel belong to Israel" (Rom. 9:6). Only the true "Israel of God" (Gal. 6:16) would receive a share in it, but also the "many" who among the Gentiles would believe in him. If some Jews shouted before Pilate, "His blood be on us and on our children," *they* thought of their co-responsibility

---

9. Some expositors see also a threatening aspect in this sprinkled of the blood on the people: if they would not keep their promise, and thereby break the covenant, judgment would come upon them.

for his death. But ultimately, the grace of God will bring the true Israel under the *blessing* of the blood of Christ.[10]

As far as the Jews are concerned who die before the return of the Messiah, that is, the Jews from whose eyes the scales have never fallen (cf. Acts 9:18; 2 Cor. 3:15–16), I think of this Pauline statement, which is true for all people, and therefore also for them: "[T]o those who by patience in well-doing seek for glory and honor and immortality, he [i.e., God] will give eternal life. . . . glory and honor and peace for everyone who does good, the Jew first and also the Greek" (Rom. 2:7, 10).[11] However, when considering this, we always keep in mind (a) that such persons are saved only on the basis of Christ's work of atonement, even if they themselves do not know this; (b) that no person is saved without true, repentant humbling before God; and (c) that this is not possible without the work of the Holy Spirit, even if the person involved is unaware of this.

6.3 Rejection and Preservation

6.3.1 The Bundle of the Living

The quotations in §5.1.1 present us with a wonderful metaphor: Israel is so precious that it is like the apple of God's eye. Israel is, if we may say so, God's "sensitive spot." Whatever we will have to say about Israel's being "rejected" for a while, this truth—don't touch the apple of God's eye!—will stand until the end. Nothing can affect Israel unless God allows Israel's enemies to affect the people to a certain extent. God's *rejection* of Israel does not interfere with his *protection* of Israel. I think of the constable who chased a group of rascals who had created mayhem. When he caught up with them, he seized one of the boys and gave him a good spanking. The bystanders shouted: "That's not fair! The other boys were just as naughty!" "Yes," he replied, "but this one is my son!"

---

10. Cf. De Graaff (1989, 432–35, 475–80), who in my view, however, makes the great exegetical mistake of elevating this deeper meaning of the statement of the people to their *deliberate intention*. In reality, the people were as little conscious of this deeper meaning as Caiaphas was in John 11.
11. See more extensively, Ouweneel (2009, §13.3.2).

When Israel is "naughty," it may seem that it receives more "spanking" than other nations, who may even more "naughty" than Israel. But Israel is God's firstborn son (Exod. 4:22). Do not look only at the spanking—look at the relationship that the father and the son enjoy when they are back home, and when the naughtiness has been confessed and forgiven. Look at the efforts of the father to save his son when the boy would get into real trouble. After all, the son is the apple of the father's eye. When the boy is naughty, the father may physically punish him.[12] But when the boy is in great danger, the father may be prepared to pay even the price of his own life in order to save the son.

Let me give the following illustration. In the state of Israel, I have seen many Jewish gravestones; especially the slopes of the Mount of Olives are full of them. On many of these stones, we find these five letters: t-n-tz-b-h (in Hebrew characters, of course). They stand for: *T'hē naphsho* [or, *naphshoah*] *tz'rurah b'tz'ror hachayyim*, that is, "May his [or, her] soul be bound in the bundle of the living." I am told that these words belong to the most frequent written words in all Israel! They paraphrase the words spoken by Abigail, the wife of Nabal and later wife of King David. This is what she said: "If men rise up to pursue you and to seek your life, the life of my lord shall be bound in the bundle of the living in the care of the LORD your God. And the lives of your enemies he shall sling out as from the hollow of a sling" (1 Sam. 25:29).

The picture is like that of a shepherd picking up stones and putting them in his shepherd's pouch (cf. the stones that David picked up in 1 Sam. 17:40). Some of them are so precious that they are carefully preserved in the shepherd's bundle; others are taken out—if they ever were *in* the bundle—and slung at predators or thieves threatening the shepherd's herd (cf. v. 49). Abigail says to David, *You* are a stone so precious to God that you will always be preserved and protected in the bundle of those who will live before him forever; but your

---

12. Of course, this is an old story; in many countries, the physical punishment of children is legally forbidden now, despite Prov. 13:24, "Whoever spares the rod hates his son, but he who loves him is diligent to discipline him."

The Rejection and Preservation of Israel

enemies are like stones that he will sling away. To the former, this means everlasting life, to the latter, everlasting death.

In our thinking, let us read "Israel" here for "David," who, later as king, represented the entire nation. The words then can be read as follows: if enemies rise up to pursue Israel and to seek the nation's life in order to exterminate it, the life of (the true) Israel shall be bound in the bundle of the living in the care of the Lord its God. To me, these are some of the most touching words in the Tanakh about God's protecting care: his people are "wrapped in the bundle of the living." Even if they have died, like the Jews who are in those graves, they "live to him" (cf. Luke 20:38). Alive or dead, they are what God says through the prophet:

> Because you are precious[13] in my eyes,
> and honored, and I love you,
> I give men in return for you,
> peoples in exchange for your life (Isa. 43:4)

Speaking about "rejection" in this chapter, imagine the condition David and his men in this story. David was fleeing before King Saul; in fact, his own people had turned their backs on him. He was banned from a normal life in society, he had little faith left, he was bitter and depressed, at the point of breaking down and becoming vengeful and violent. At this moment, one might think that this lonely outcast was the very opposite of a "man after God's heart" (1 Sam. 13:14). But then Abigail makes a feast for him and his men, and encourages him. Her name means "Joy of the father," and this fits in nicely with the illustration about the constable and his son. It is *David* who, at this critical moment, must learn that he is still the joy of his heavenly Father, and that this Father will never give up on him; he is safe in God's bundle.

---

13. The Heb. verb is *y-q-r*, "to be precious"; cf. Ps. 72:14 and 116:15, even the death of God's beloved ones is "precious" in his sight. Cf. also Heb. *s'gulah*, one meaning of which is "treasured possession," such as Israel was to the Lord (Exod. 19:5; Deut. 7:6; 14:2; 26:18; Mal. 3:17).

6.3.2 Similar Metaphors

Abigail spoke words of hope to this "rejected" outcast: you are "in the bundle of the living in the care of the LORD your God." No enemy and no mischief can change the fact that you are *forever* in God's "bundle." In Jewish tradition, it has become a consolation for those left behind: the deceased are forever in God's hands. But in our story, the words were spoken to a living man, not to tell him something about the hereafter, but to guarantee to him that, already *here on earth*, he is under God's special protection, no matter how dismissed by God and men he may feel.

The "bundle" is something in which valuable things[14] may be bound together, and in which these things are preserved and protected. In certain circumstances, the owner may *speak* as if the objects contained in the bundle are worthless to him, but be not deceived: look at the care with which he handles the bundle. God may speak as if he has set Israel aside, and to some extent, this may indeed be true. But look at the care with which he has preserved and protected Israel until this very day, despite the many victims in Israel that he has allowed to be slaughtered.

In certain passages, the mention of God's "hand" was already sufficient to express the same thought of protection and preservation. The LORD's s/Servant said of him, "[I]n the shadow of his hand he hid me" (Isa. 49:2), and a little later, the LORD said to all his people: "Behold, I have *engraved* you on the palms of my hands" (v. 16), which was a much stronger picture than just "holding." Still later: I have "covered you in the shadow of my hand" (Isa. 51:16). I like the expression "the hollow of his hand," even if in Isaiah 40:12 it is used in a different context. All the faithful are safe in the hollow of the LORD's hand.

At the end of his earthly life, Jesus prayed, "Father, into your hands I commit my spirit!" (Luke 23:46), clearly anticipating his imminent death. But in Psalm 31:5 ("Into your hand I commit my spirit"), this was a general statement, not

---

14. See the same word, *tz'ror*, in Gen. 42:35 and Prov. 7:20 (money), and in Song 1:13 (myrrh).

of a dying person, but of God's faithful living in the midst of all kinds of peril and oppression. This is what the faithful in Israel have been praying throughout the centuries: Let us be safe in the hollow of your hand! Fully reassured, the beloved young lady said of the beloved young man: "His left hand is under my head, / and his right hand embraces me!" (Song 2:6; 8:3). And later: "Keep me near you like a seal you wear over your heart, / like a signet ring you wear on your hand" (8:6 EHV).

6.4 Why the "Rejection"?
6.4.1 God's Punishment?

Time and again, the question must be asked: *Why* did Israel, apart from a "remnant" (Rom. 11:5), not accept Jesus?[15] How is it possible that today there are about 2.5 billion Gentile Christians, one third of the world's population? Even if we assume that among them there are millions of nominal hangers-on, that still leaves an enormous number. In comparison with these numerous Christians—genuine or not—the number of 0.5 to 1.5% "Messianic" (Jesus-confessing) Jews among Israel looks like nothing. Actually, this number must be distinguished from the "Hebrew Christians," Jesus-confessors of Jewish descent, who in doctrine and lifestyle cannot be differentiated from Christians of Gentile descent; but these, too, will not be more than a few percent of the Jewish nation.

This is a remarkable contrast: so *many* Gentiles and so *few* Jews confess the Jew Jesus as the Messiah of Israel and as their personal Savior and Lord. There is something mysterious in this contrast. How is it possible that millions of Gentiles have acknowledged Jesus as the Messiah of Israel, and virtually all Israelites have not?

After many Jews had not only rejected Jesus but, in the second century, also accepted the rebel Shimon bar Kochba—who was a nobody in comparison with Jesus—as their Messiah,[16] many Christians were definitively convinced that the

---

15. See Ouweneel (2000a, §7.3).
16. Even one of the greatest rabbis of those days, Aqiva, believed that Bar Kochba

Jews were totally corrupted and hopelessly lost. And when the Jews were chastised by the Romans, the Christians in those days could not see anything else in this than the punishing hand of God. The well-known apologist Justin Martyr was the first important representative of this view, in his *Dialogue with the Jew Trypho* (ca. 133). His argument sounded quite plausible: just as God had used the Babylonians to punish the Jews for their idolatry (Hab. 1:5-11; cf. also Isa. 10:5), God had used the Romans to punish the Jews for this murder of Jesus (Acts 7:52). Apparently, it did not occur to him that the Romans oppressed and persecuted Christians as well; for what crime on the part of Christians was *this* the punishment? Justin basically made the same mistake as the friends of Job: if you suffer, you must have done very bad things. Suffering *can* be punishment for the bad (as in the case of the Babylonian exile), but it can also be a test, a trial of the good. Job was tested, not punished; the early Christians were tested, not punished. Why would it have been different for the Jews who were oppressed by the Romans?

Nevertheless, the solemn question remains: Why *did* the Jews reject their Messiah? We do understand that the unfaithful, blind mass of the people did so—"this crowd that does not know the Torah" (John 7:49). But where was the true "Israel of God" in those days? Does this group coincide precisely with the Jews who did accept Jesus (cf. Rom. 11:5; Gal. 6:16)? Or should we say that, since Christ, there is still some "faithful Israel" *other than* the "Israel of God" that accepted him? Could there be *two* "true Israels": one that accepted Jesus and has become part of the Ecclesia of God—the body of Christ consisting of Jewish and Gentile believers—and one that has not (yet) accepted Jesus because of the "veil" that is over their hearts (2 Cor. 3:14-15), yet a company that was and is faithful to the Torah, to the calling of Israel, sincerely godly in its serving the true God, persistent in its expectation of the Messiah?

These are difficult questions, whose answers cannot be superficial. One superficial theory is that Israel has badly sinned by rejecting the Messiah, and that it has had to pay for

---

was the Messiah.

this for almost two thousand years. This theory was false in particular because those who held it were usually the same as those *through whom* the Jews had to suffer. These were the "Christians" who believed that Israel had deserved punishment, and therefore were all too happy to help inflict this punishment upon Israel. However, again, recall that those who touch Israel are touching God's very sensitive "spot": the apple of his eye. This is true also for the ethnic Israel as it has existed *since* the rejection of its Messiah, for it is *from this Israel*, and none other, that the Israel of the future Messianic kingdom will be built. As the LORD says through the prophet Joel:

> I will gather all the nations and bring them down to the Valley of Jehoshaphat. And I will enter into judgment with them there, *on behalf of my people and my heritage Israel*, because they have scattered them among the nations and have divided up my land, and have cast lots for my people, and have traded a boy for a prostitute, and have sold a girl for wine and have drunk it (Joel 3:2-3).

6.4.2 Ignorance and Unintentionality

Another theory is that Israel did certainly recognize and acknowledge the Messiah, but that it *simulated* rejecting him so that the Gentiles, too, might receive a share in the divine salvation.[17] In other words, Israel *consciously* rejected the One they knew to be the Messiah in order to render a service to the Gentiles, since now the gospel has come to *them*.

This cannot be possibly correct: does God need the help of such a conscious Jewish ruse? Israel's rejection of its Messiah occurred "according to the definite plan and foreknowledge of God" (Acts 2:23; cf. 4:28), but certainly not according to the definite plan and foreknowledge of Israel. On the contrary, the apostle Peter said, "[B]rothers, I know that you acted *in ignorance*, as did also your rulers" (3:17). Jesus prayed on the cross, "Father, forgive them, for they know not what they do" (Luke 23:34[18]). The apostle Paul, who with great fervor had

---

17. De Graaff (1987; 1989).
18. Perhaps Jesus was referring primarily to the Roman soldiers, but certainly also

persecuted the Christians, speaks of himself as one who "formerly was a blasphemer, persecutor, and insolent opponent. But I received mercy because I had acted *ignorantly* in unbelief, and the grace of our Lord overflowed for me with the faith and love that are in Christ Jesus" (1 Tim. 1:13–14).

Ignorance does not mean guiltlessness; under the Torah, a sin offering definitely had to be brought to God for sins that had been committed through ignorance (or unintentionally, or by mistake, or inadvertently).[19] However, ignorance does imply a refutation of the two theories mentioned, not only the idea of a conscious ruse on the part of Israel, but also the theory described in the previous section. Numbers 15:22–31 makes the important distinction between unintentional sin, for which there is no punishment but forgiveness, and sinning "with a high hand," that is, in a spirit of conscious rebellion (v. 30), with a hand lifted up toward heaven, so to speak. For such sinning there is no forgiveness, but only judgment.[20] Israel committed the former sin, and therefore there will eventually be atonement for the people, or at least for the true, penitent remnant of it.

Please note that it is *God* who brings judgment on the haughty and impenitent. No person has the right to bring punishment upon Israel on their own initiative and authority. On the contrary, people who have done, or do, so are like criminal witnesses, who have testified against Israel, and have asserted that the latter has sinned against the LORD "with a high hand." These are the people who insist that the full force of the Torah must be applied to Israel, so that the latter will be condemned as murderers and undergo the penalty of eternal death. Such false witnesses overlook the fact that the same Torah will be applied to *them* in all its force:

---

to the Jewish crowd that was standing there mocking him (Matt. 27:41–43).
19. Heb. *bishgagah* from the root *sh-g-g*, "to err, to fail"; see Lev. 4:2, 13, 22, 27; 5:15, 18; 22:14; Num. 35:22; Deut. 19:4; Josh. 20:3, 9.
20. Cf. the blasphemy against the Holy Spirit (Matt. 12:22–32), for which there is no forgiveness. either.

they will undergo the death penalty because of their wicked testimony, as we shall see.[21]

6.4.3 False Witnesses

An example of such a false testimony is found in the story of the vintner Naboth. There were two such false witnesses, described as "sons of Belial" (Heb. *b'nē beliyyal*) (1 Kings 21:10, 13 KJV), equivalent to "worthless men" (ESB). But Belial (or Beliar) is also the name of a demon, and even specifically a name for Satan; as the apostle Paul said, "[W]hat partnership has righteousness with lawlessness? Or what fellowship has light with darkness? What accord has Christ with Belial [Gk. *Beliar*]? Or what portion does a believer share with an unbeliever?" (2 Cor. 6:14–15).[22] If we realize that "sons of Belial" are servants of Satan, we are free to call the false witnesses who, throughout the centuries, have falsely witnessed against Israel, "servants of Satan" as well. No matter how noble their reputation in church history may have been, when it came to Israel, the apple of God's eye, they behaved as instruments of the devil.

This leads to an interesting question: Is it possible to be a great man of God in some respects, and an instrument of Satan in other respects? The answer is: absolutely. Compare the two solemn testimonies that Jesus gave of one and the same man, Simon Peter, in one and the same chapter, separated by merely five verses: "Blessed are you, Simon Bar-Jonah! For flesh and blood has not revealed this to you, but my Father who is in heaven. . . ." and "Get behind me, Satan! You are a hindrance to me. For you are not setting your mind on the things of God, but on the things of man" (Matt. 16:17, 23).

Satan (the devil) himself has acted as a false witness in several cases: in the cases of Job, of the high priest Joshua,

---

21. Exod. 23:1; Deut. 19:16–19; Prov. 6:16, 19; 19:5, 9; 21:28.
22. Cf. *Ascension of Isaiah* 2:4, "Manasseh turned aside his heart to serve Beliar; for the angel of lawlessness, who is the ruler of this world, is Beliar, whose name is Mantanbuchus. and he delighted in Jerusalem because of Manasseh, and he made him strong in apostatizing (Israel) and in the lawlessness which were spread abroad in Jerusalem" (http://www.earlychristianwritings.com/text/ascension.html).

THE ETERNAL PEOPLE: GOD IN RELATION TO ISRAEL

and of the body of Moses.[23] Generally speaking, he has been referred to as the "accuser of our brothers" (Rev. 12:10; cf. the meaning of the word "devil," from Gk. *diabolos*, "slanderer").

The apostle Paul said in an almost threatening tone: "Who shall bring any charge against God's elect?" (Rom. 8:33). The friends of Job accused him in the most false way possible, especially in Job 20 and 22, and God stood up for him in an unusual manner. Job is *God's man*. The point is not so much that the friends have wronged Job, but that they have wronged *God*. As God said to one of the friends, Eliphaz, "My anger burns against you and against your two friends, for you have not spoken *of me* what is right, *as my servant Job has*" (Job 42:7). This is an important principle: he who does not speak rightly about *Israel*, does not speak rightly about *God*. It is the same principle that we find with Jesus: acting badly against his followers is acting badly against *him*: "Truly, I say to you, as you did not do it [i.e., good things] to one of the least of these, you did not do it to me. And these [i.e., such people] will go away into eternal punishment, but the righteous into eternal life" (Matt. 25:45-46). Speaking badly of Israel is speaking badly of God, and acting badly against Israel is acting badly against God, for the true Israel is the *Israel of God*. We know that this refers only to the penitent, righteous, spiritual part of Israel, but *we* are not in a position to determine what Israelites belong to this true Israel, and what do not.

It is true that the majority of Israel has rejected its Messiah. However, no person may be so audacious as to pronounce a sentence upon this Israel, or even to function as God's executor. *Do not touch Israel in any way.* "Vengeance is *mine*, and recompense," says the LORD (Deut. 32:35; cf. Rom. 12:19; Heb. 10:30). The poet told us:

> When they were few in number,
>   of little account, and sojourners in it,
> wandering from nation to nation,
>   from one kingdom to another people,
> he allowed no one to oppress them;

---

23. Job 1–2; Zech. 3:1; Jude 9.

> he rebuked kings on their account,
> saying, "Touch not my anointed ones,
> do my prophets no harm!" (Ps. 105:12-15).

From the context, it is clear that the poet was thinking here (especially) of the patriarchs. Rabbi Abraham Cohen argued that the latter are called "anointed" because they had been designated by God to become the ancestors of a kingdom of priests[24] (Exod. 19:6; cf. Isa. 61:6). Because this anointing was done without literal oil, we are perhaps allowed to say that the patriarchs were anointed with the Holy Spirit.[25] At any rate, Abraham is called a "prophet" (Gen. 20:7), and Isaac and Jacob declared very significant prophecies.[26]

6.5 Ignorance Versus Responsibility

6.5.1 Tension

Again, Israel's ignorance regarding its Messiah does not eliminate Israel's responsibility. We are not in a position to judge Israel, but we *can* definitely conclude that Israel's rejection of its Messiah did not accidentally happen to the people, like a natural disaster happens to humans. Only a small part of Israel was responsible for Jesus' *death*, but a large part was and is responsible for his *rejection*. At the same time, there is in Israel's ignorance something unique, which emphatically points to God's sovereign ways with Israel.

To human reason, this triangle of Israel's ignorance, Israel's responsibility, and God's sovereign counsel is like an impregnable fortress, which we cannot penetrate with our human logic.[27] This tension between Israel's responsibility and God's sovereign counsel is encountered in various passages. Jews in Jerusalem made themselves culpable for Jesus death; yet it occurred according to God's counsel: ". . . this Jesus, delivered up according to the definite plan and foreknowledge of God, you crucified and killed by the hands of lawless men" (Acts 2:23). They killed Jesus, but they did so out of ignorance,

---

24. Cohen (1985, 346).
25. Cf. Isa. 61:1; Acts 10:38; 2 Cor. 1:21-22; 1 John 2:20, 27.
26. Gen. 27:27-29; 28:3-4; 48:15-16; 49:1-27; see especially v. 1.
27. This was the great subject of Ouweneel (2008).

in order that, in this way, the word of the prophets would be fulfilled (3:15-18). The rulers of Israel counseled against the LORD and his Anointed, but in all they did they were carrying out God's plan:

> "The kings of the earth set themselves, and the rulers were gathered together, against the Lord and against his Anointed"—for truly in this city there were gathered together against your holy servant Jesus, whom you anointed, both Herod and Pontius Pilate, along with the Gentiles and the peoples of Israel, to do whatever your hand and your plan had predestined to take place (Acts 4:26-28; quoting Ps. 2:2).

The Emmaus disciples emphasized Israel's responsibility; they described "how our chief priests and rulers delivered him up to be condemned to death, and crucified him" (Luke 24:20). But Jesus replied, "Was it not necessary that the Christ should suffer these things and [thus[28]] enter into his glory?" (v. 26). On the one hand, the rulers were responsible for Jesus' death; on the other hand, it was ordained by God that Jesus *had to* die.

This tension cannot be solved rationally. One imaginary escape is to emphasize the freedom of human choice, so that God's counsel is pushed to the background, or is reduced to mere foreknowledge.[29] Another imaginary escape is to emphasize God's absolutely sovereign counsel—*he* decides what is going to happen—so that virtually nothing is left of human responsibility. The only proper route is to accept both biblical truths—God is one-hundred percent sovereign, and humans are one-hundred percent responsible—surrendering the logical ideal of finding a common denominator.

6.5.2 The "Veil"

Consider the "veil" or "cover" that lies over the heart of Israel, as the apostle Paul explained: "[T]o this day, when they [i.e., Israel] read the old covenant [i.e., the Tanakh], that same

---

28. Or, "and enter like this" (JUB), or "and only then to enter" (AMP).
29. See the difference between "knowing beforehand" (foreknowledge; Gk. verb: *proginōskō*) and "destining beforehand" (predestination; Gk. verb: *prooraō*).

veil remains unlifted, because only through Christ is it taken away. Yes, to this day whenever Moses is read a veil lies over their hearts. But when one [or, he, or it] turns to the Lord, the veil is removed" (2 Cor. 3:14-16). Israel had blindfolded *itself*, yet believed that it could spiritually "see"; as Jesus said, "If you were blind, you would have no guilt; but now that you say, 'We see,' your guilt remains" (John 9:41).

No doubt, it was Israel's own responsibility that it was blind, that is, had this "veil" over their hearts. But it is equally clear that it was an *imposed* "veil," which one day is also going to be *removed*—not by Israel itself but by the Lord. Therefore, it is true to say that, viewed from Israel's responsibility, it first turns to the Lord, and then the veil is removed. But it is equally true to say that, viewed from God's counsel and sovereign grace, first the veil is taken away, and then Israel will be able to "see," and thus to turn to the Lord. So, what is first, Israel's conversion *or* God removing Israel's veil? This same question arises with *each* human conversion: Who is first in this process, the penitent human turning to God, *or* God turning that person around?

Many Evangelicals will answer: the former of course: a person must come to God before God can bless them (see, for instance, the prodigal son; Luke 15:11-23). Many (hyper-)Calvinists will answer: the latter of course: a person's total depravity implies that, by themselves, they *cannot* turn to God. The person is first—or God is first. In a sense, I believe both are equally true, depending on the viewpoint from which one considers the matter.

One thing must be certain to all: God's sovereign providence and Israel's responsibility must not be played off against each other.[30] Take for instance the example of Judas, one of Jesus' twelve disciples. He was entirely responsible for his treason; yet Jesus says of him: "I have guarded them [i.e., the disciples], and not one of them has been lost except the son of destruction, *that the Scripture might be fulfilled.*"[31] Similarly, every Israelite who had taken part in the rejection

---

30. See note 27.
31. John 17:12; cf. Ps. 41:9; 109:8 (Acts 1:20).

was entirely personally accountable for having rejected Jesus' Messiahship, while at the same time the Scripture was fulfilled in this rejection. It predicted what (the majority of) Israel would do—yet Israel was, and remained, fully responsible.

6.6 "What If ... ?"

6.6.1 "What If Israel Had Accepted Its Messiah?"

In order to focus a bit more on the aspect of God's counsel, let us try to answer two "what if" questions, although I admit that this is always a risky business. First, *what if* the great majority of Israel had indeed accepted Jesus Christ as its Messiah? The answer must be that immediately the Messianic kingdom would have arrived, and *there would never have been an Ecclesia gathered largely from the Gentiles*. Listen carefully to the apostle Peter's words:

> Repent therefore, and turn back, that your sins may be blotted out, that *times of refreshing* may come from the presence of the Lord, and that he may send the Christ appointed for you, Jesus, whom heaven must receive until the *time for restoring all the things* about which God spoke by the mouth of his holy prophets long ago (Acts 3:19-21).

In other words, because we know of God's counsel concerning the Ecclesia—the body of the glorified Christ and the temple of the Holy Spirit—we seem to be forced to conclude that, humanly speaking, Israel simply could not have accepted its Messiah.

Second, *what if* this Ecclesia indeed *was* gathered from the Gentiles, and eventually all Israelites would have accepted the Messiah? Then, according to the requirements of the church throughout the centuries, the Jews would have fully assimilated with the Gentile believers. Thereby Israel would have lost its national, ethnic character, *and there would have been no ethnic Israel that God could restore in the Promised Land, during the coming Messianic kingdom.* For this reason, too, we seem to be forced to conclude that, viewed *not* from Israel's responsibility but from God's counsel, the great majority of Israel simply could not have accepted its Messiah.

Someone has observed that, from the viewpoint of the preservation of a distinct Judaism, the forefathers were right in rejecting Jesus, when they lost their land and began their pilgrimage. The argument is that, if the Jews had accepted Jesus, they would have been dissolved in the sea of Christianity, and this would have been the end of the distinct, Jewish identity. Diaspora Judaism was forced to close its ranks and therefore established the Ritual Law that enclosed the Jewish community of the Ghetto.[32] Circumcision, Sabbath, festival times, food laws, and ritual prayers thereby gave Israel the unwavering identity through which it managed to maintain itself throughout all those centuries.

It is quite fascinating that some Jews, especially those with a high regard for Jesus, noticed this state of affairs surprisingly sharply, but were unable to discern the deeper reason why the Jews rejected Jesus as their Messiah. To argue that this is no surprise because the "veil" is over their heart is not intended to be derogatory, but rather the very opposite. It is a great miracle of God's gracious providence that, through this "veil," he has preserved a people of Israel until this very day, a people that managed to maintain its distinctive religious-ethnic character. It is a people among whom today we may sometimes find the greatest sympathy for Jesus, but who, by definition, *cannot* recognize him as their Messiah (apart from a limited number of exceptions). *Millions* of Gentiles did recognize Jesus, not only as their personal Savior but as the Messiah of Israel—and Israel itself cannot do so. Again, there is something profoundly mysterious in this. The "veil" is not only, or even primarily, a matter of Israel's guilt, but of God's counsel and providence.

Notice what we are saying here. Israel ought to have accepted its Messiah, who by hundreds of signs and marks proved that he *was* the Messiah. But they didn't. Millions of Christians did, but the Jews didn't. So they were, and are, guilty of failing to do the proper thing. But at the same time,

---

32. See the essay by Ferdynand Zweig included in Kac (1986, 64–65).

we notice that, *if* they had accepted their Messiah, there were two options. Either the Messianic kingdom would have begun immediately, and then there would have been no Ecclesia. Or the Messiah would have delayed his return in order to gather his Ecclesia from the nations, in which case Israel would never have been able to preserve its identity within the mass of Gentile believers. In other words, the actual course of events turned out to be the only way in which, ultimately, there could be both an Ecclesia and a restored Israel.

6.6.2 Stop Being a Jew?

Two more remarkable points deserve consideration. The first point is that some Jews in principle might be prepared to acknowledge Jesus as the Messiah, especially those who, when one day the Messiah will appear, will not be surprised if he turns out to have the facial features of Jesus of Nazareth.[33] Yet, they are prevented from recognizing Jesus *now* because of a deeply rooted and rather strange misunderstanding. It is this: today if a Jew confesses Jesus as the Messiah, they forfeit their Jewishness, leave the people to which they ethnically belong, and become part of almost entirely non-Jewish Christianity. This is the misunderstanding: *by becoming a Jesus-believer the Jew stops being a Jew*. Isn't this remarkable? Here is a Jew who reaches the very core of their Jewishness by not only living according to the Torah, but also by getting to know their Messiah and beginning to serve him. And this requires them to *stop* being a Jew? If Jesus is the Messiah of Israel, and Israel acknowledges this, how could Israel, in doing so, stop being Israel?

Of course, Christianity has significantly contributed to this sad and foolish misunderstanding insofar as it distinguished and distanced itself from Israel as much as possible. Moreover, it demanded of its Jewish converts that they surrender their Jewishness completely. The Jew who was considering accepting Jesus *could* receive no other impression than that, in this way, they would remove themselves from Judaism. They would be converting not only to *Jesus*, but

---

33. This is a subtle way of saying that he *is* Jesus; cf. §3.4.6.

they would be converting—in their imagination—from one religion to another: from Judaism to Christianity. In other words, they failed to recognize that they were accepting *not* the Jewish Jesus of the New Testament but rather the Christ of the Christian "establishment." The apostle Paul had warned: "[I]f someone comes and proclaims another Jesus than the one we proclaimed, or if you receive a different spirit from the one you received, or if you accept a different gospel from the one you accepted, you put up with it readily enough" (2 Cor. 11:4; cf. Gal. 1:6-9).

Must we not honestly say that the Westernized ("blond-haired and blue-eyed") and Greco-Romanized "Christ" of the established churches is hardly identical to the thoroughly Jewish Jesus of the New Testament? All the more remarkable, then, that today, almost eighty years after the end of the *Shoah*, we encounter a stunning phenomenon. The *Shoah* was one of the most powerful means for Jews to rediscover their Jewish identity, and I am sure this helped Jewish Jesus-believers to rediscover and maintain their Jewish identity as well. The "Messianic" movement began at the end of the nineteenth century, but it received its boost especially after World War II (1945), more specifically after the establishment of the Jewish state (1948), and, at least in the land of Israel, even more so after the reconquest of Old Jerusalem and the Western Wall (1967).

"Messianic" Jews are Jews who have come to recognize in Jesus of Nazareth their Messiah, as well as their Savior, yet strongly strive for maintaining their Jewish identity. Just as the Jews in the land of Israel, described in the book of Acts, they circumcise their baby boys, they observe the Sabbath and the great festivals (from *Pesach* to *Purim*), they observe the food laws (i.e., they eat kosher). In short, they are Jews and they wish to *remain* Jews. They even dislike being called "Christians"—because of all the misunderstandings that this appellation creates—and do not wish to be dissolved in the sea of the Christian establishment. They prefer forming their own "Messianic" (Jesus-believing Jewish) congregations, even though they realize very well that they are part of the

Ecclesia, that is, the body of Christ and the temple of the Holy Spirit.

Just like Gentile Christians, they exhibit a wide variety of views and habits. I know this from experience, because in the state of Israel I have attended the services of quite a few varieties of Messianic Jews. On the one hand, some of them can hardly be distinguished from common Evangelical congregations, except that they meet on the Sabbath. On the other hand, some of them can hardly be distinguished from Orthodox Jewish synagogues (until you come to the sermon, which is Yeshuah-centric).[34] In practice, these differences are less significant than it may seem: essential is that they all confess Jesus—or, as they would say, Yeshuah—as their Messiah, Lord and Savior.

6.6.3 The "Veil" Over the Gentile's Heart

The second remarkable point deserving consideration is that we can speak honestly about the "veil" over Israel's heart only if we keep in mind that from about 300 until 1900 a "veil" was over the hearts of Christians, too, with the exception of a handful of theologians, who actually thought in supersessionist terms after all. It was an act of God's providence to place the "veil" over Israel's heart, but can we say the same about the "veil" over the hearts of Christians? Israel itself was also responsible for the "veil" over its heart, but could this not be said with even more justification about the "veil" over the hearts of Christians?

Just as the majority of Israel had, and has, no eye for the true identity of Jesus, the majority of Christians had, and have, no eye for ethnic Israel and God's special plans with it. The great mass of Israel denied, and denies, its Messiah; the great mass of Christians denied, and still denies, ethnic Israel and its prophesied future. Some of them are quite friendly toward Jews and somewhat benevolent toward the state of Israel. But because of their explicit or implicit supersessionism, they deny—consciously or unconsciously—the special

---

34. Regarding their identity, see extensively, Schiffman (1996); Stern (1997, especially chapter 2); this summary is found in Stern (2009).

status and Messianic future of Israel. One could also put it this way: *both the majority of Israel and the majority of Christians deny Jesus in his specific quality of Messiah of ethnic Israel and its future King.*

Today, we live in a unique period of world history when the eyes of Israel are beginning to be opened to its Messiah, and this is a great miracle. At the same time, the eyes of Christians are beginning to be opened to (ethnic) Israel and God's future for it, and this, too, is a great miracle. Both are miracles *of God*, and both are intimately related. The rise of "Messianic" Judaism (but also the greater openness to Jesus among orthodox Jews) is related to the increasing rejection of supersessionism among orthodox Protestants. God is at work! Eyes are being opened—no matter how slowly—on both sides! I believe that the two developments are signs that we are living in the "end time," that is, the time shortly before the second coming of Christ and the establishment of the Messianic kingdom.

Jews as well as Christians may be looking forward to the fulfillment of the prophet's words:

> On this mountain the LORD of hosts will make for all peoples
>   a feast of rich food, a feast of well-aged wine,
>   of rich food full of marrow, of aged wine well refined.
> And he will swallow up on this mountain
>   the *covering* that is cast over all peoples,
>   the *veil* that is spread over all nations (Isa. 25:6–7).

Some expositors understand this "covering" or "veil" to refer to the nations' blindness regarding the God of Israel. But could it not refer to Israel as well? As Isaiah said, "[W]e esteemed him [i.e., the LORD's s/Servant] stricken, / smitten by God, and afflicted" (Isa. 53:4b)—but now we know better. As we have seen, this "we" is either Israel realizing that they were wrong, but now beginning to see who this "Man of sorrows" (v. 3) really is, namely, the Messiah. Or it is the nations realizing that *they* were wrong, but now beginning to see who this "man of sorrows" (v. 3) really is, namely, the Israel of God.

6.7 Israel's "Conversion"
6.7.1 What Is Conversion?

To state the matter with utmost clarity, the biblical conversion of a Jew *never* involves a kind of transition from one religion to another, from Judaism to Christianity. Such a transition from one religion to another occurs if a Jew became a Buddhist—as some Jews have[35]—for Judaism and Buddhism are two different religions. But Judaism and Christianity are not two different religions, because Christianity is essentially Judaism fulfilled. A Jew who becomes a Jesus-believer does not join another religion—Jesus was a Jew, not a "Christian"!—but thereby finds the core, the essence, of Judaism as such. Such a person has become more "Jew" than they ever were before, so to speak.

So then, what *is* a Jewish conversion? The Greek New Testament contains two different meanings of the term.[36] The first is "to turn around" (Gk. *epistrephō*; cf. Heb. *sh-v/u-b*, "return"), as in 1 Thessalonians 1:9-10, where certain messengers who visited the apostle Paul to "report concerning us the kind of reception we had among you, and how you *turned to God from idols* to serve the living and true God, and to wait for his Son from heaven, whom he raised from the dead, Jesus who delivers us from the wrath to come." This was an almost literal "turning away" from evil, and a "turning toward," and thus "returning to," God.

The second meaning of "conversion" is "repentance," that is literally, a "change of mind" (Gk. *metanoia*). It was the first recorded word out of Jesus' mouth after he had begun his public ministry: "Repent [change your inner self—your old way of thinking, regret past sins, live your life in a way that proves repentance; seek God's purpose for your life], for the kingdom of heaven is at hand" (Matt. 4:17 AMP; cf. 3:2; 11:20-21; 12:41).

Sometimes, these two aspects of "conversion"—turning around and repentance—appeared in one passage: "Repent

---

35. Cf. Kamenetz (1994).
36. In the Dutch States Translation of 1637, both meanings were expressed by the same word: the noun *bekering* and the related verb *zich bekeren*.

[Gk. *metanoēsate*] therefore, and turn back [Gk. *epistrepsate*], that your sins may be blotted out" (the apostle Peter in Acts 3:19). The apostle Paul told Jews and Gentiles "that they should repent [Gk. *metanoein*] and turn [Gk. *epistrephein*] to God, performing deeds in keeping with their repentance" (26:20).

In summary: "conversion" is a change of one's inner self, regretting one's sins, confessing them to God, very concretely turning away from the evils that characterized one's former life, and turning to God in order, from now on, to serve him alone. On the one hand, such a turning around is a matter of the person's responsibility; one is *guilty* if one does not do it. On the other hand, such a turning around is possible only through the power of the Holy Spirit, and is thus a sovereign work of God's saving grace.

6.7.2 Various Cases

In what cases is conversion necessary?

(1) Conversion presupposes that a person has departed from God's ways. Young Samuel did not have to "convert," for he had served the Lord from early childhood (1 Sam. 1-3). To be sure, by nature Samuel was a sinner, like all of us; and his sinful nature came to expression later in his life, when he showed a lack of wisdom regarding his sons (1 Sam. 8:1-3). But there is a difference between having a sinful nature and *practicing* sins by following evil ways (cf. Rom. 1:18-32; 1 Pet. 4:2-3). Apparently, through the Holy Spirit, God very early worked the life of new birth in Samuel, so that he did not have to be turned away from evil ways. It is exactly the same with young Christians who, at a very early stage, begin following and serving Jesus. Timothy seemed to be an example of this; Paul wrote, "I am reminded of your sincere faith, a faith that dwelt first in your grandmother Lois and your mother Eunice and now, I am sure, dwells in you as well" (2 Tim. 1:5).

(2) Where the Jew has fallen into an idolatrous or secularized condition, conversion (spiritual return) to the God of

Israel and his Torah *was*, and still *is*, mandatory. This is a conversion that could, and can, occur at all times, from the time of Israel's wilderness journey to the Promised Land until the time of its conversion at the coming of the Messiah. As God says through the prophet,

> Therefore I will judge you, O house of Israel, every one according to his ways, declares the Lord God. *Repent* and *turn* from all your transgressions, lest iniquity be your ruin. Cast away from you all the transgressions that you have committed, and make yourselves a new heart and a new spirit! Why will you die, O house of Israel? (Ezek. 18:30–31).

(3) From the time when the Messiah of Israel was revealed, "conversion" also implies the believing acceptance of Jesus Christ. As the apostle Peter said on the Day of Pentecost, "Repent and be baptized every one of you in the name of Jesus Christ for the forgiveness of your sins, and you will receive the gift of the Holy Spirit" (Acts 2:38).

Zechariah and Elizabeth were true Jewish *tzaddiqim*, for they sincerely served the God of Israel (Luke 1:6). But Rabbi Sha'ul of Tarsus, who later became the apostle Paul, gave evidence of his unconverted (blind) condition by combating Christ with all that was within him. He needed what so many Jews still need: the "scales fell from his eyes" (Acts 9:18).[37] His conversion (Acts 9:1–19) entailed recognizing and confessing what and who Jesus Christ really was, and surrendering to him in faith.

(4) Jews who know very well who and what Jesus Christus *truly* is can hardly be called "born again." But how many of them exist? Only Gods knows their hearts, as he knows ours.

(5) It is different with Jews who (still) have the "veil" over their hearts when it comes to Jesus—all the more so because of the terrible picture that so many Christians have given of

---

37. An orthodox rabbi with whom I wrote a publication on our differences said he believed that one day, the scales would fall from both our eyes. I agreed, but asked him if he knew where that expression came from: from a story about a rabbi whose eyes were opened when he met Jesus!

him throughout the centuries—but sincerely serve God and observe his Torah. I think of the *tzaddiq* of Psalm 1:

> Blessed is the man [or, person]
>   who walks not in the counsel of the wicked,
> nor stands in the way of sinners,
>   nor sits in the seat of scoffers;
> but his delight is in the Torah of the LORD,
>   and on his Torah he meditates day and night (vv. 1-2).

I would not dare to claim that some of these people could not have been converted and born again, even though God's work in them has not yet been completed (but in whom of us *has* God's work been completed?). We leave the judgment concerning such matters to him who "knows the hearts."[38]

6.8 Two Israels

6.8.1 Christ *or* the Torah?

An example of someone with the highest esteem for Jesus of Nazareth, *and* with a clear opinion as to why most Jews have not accepted Jesus as Messiah, *and* a profound understanding of the significance of Israel's distinct continuation, was the Jewish German poet and writer Margarete Susman. She wrote that the part of Israel that has accepted Christ no longer "lives" as "Israel" because it has merged with the Christian world. By contrast, "the part that has rejected Jesus continues to live its dark historical destiny as a community rejected by the world."[39] The significance of this decision to reject Jesus as Messiah "was, just as the acceptance of the Sinaitic Law, an event within the redemptive core itself." That is, "the Messianic message risen from the depth of the nation," as it has unfolded through Christian preaching in the world, yielded "a contrast with the message that the nation preserves within itself."

---

38. Acts 1:24; 15:8; cf. 1 Sam. 16:17; 1 Chron. 28:9; Ps. 7:9; 139:23–24; Jer. 11:20; 17:10; 20:12; Rev. 2:23.
39. Susman (1948, 104–106). Of course, this is no longer entirely true after the rise of the "Messianic" (Jesus-confessing) movement (perhaps 350,000 members worldwide, between 10,000 and 20,000 in the state of Israel).

How did this come about? And what exactly does it mean? Essentially, the Torah brought about the split: "The Law, which Jesus had come to fulfill, was burst apart by Christ." That is, the Torah seemed to fall apart in two pieces: a "part that died in the fulfilled truth of Christianity," and a "part that was preserved by the nation with all the more fervor, and that deployed itself in ever newer forms."

I understand this to mean that the part that died the Torah viewed from a negative standpoint: the Torah understood as a legalistic order of things, which came to an end with Christianity. The part that was preserved is the Torah according to its true spirit and intention, as it was kept and investigated among the Jewish people. In John's Gospel, we heard the shout of a Jewish crowd demanding the death of Jesus: "We have a law . . ." (John 19:7). This is the Torah in its first meaning: we hear in this shouting "the running out of the Law that died in Christ," "not the living, ever burning truth of the Law as preserved in the Jewish nation as in a sanctuary"—which is the Torah in its second meaning.

The things that Susman expresses here are fascinating; nevertheless, I perceive a certain tension in her argument. To be sure, it is prophetically certain that Israel will be restored in the Promised Land, and that even the temple ministry will be restored, entirely according to the Torah. And indeed, to this end a part of Israel must be preserved that keeps the Torah until the second coming of Christ. So where is the tension in Susman's argument? Notice how far she goes: she calls Jesus by his name "Christ," which means the same as "Messiah"; in him she perceives the Messianic message; she speaks of the "fulfilled truth of Christianity,"[40] and even of "the Law that died in Christ." Actually, the latter is inaccurate: it was not the Torah, in any sense at all, that died in Christ, but the Jesus-believer has died to the Torah (Rom. 7:4; Gal. 2:19-20), that is, to the order of things that makes a

---

40. Regarding Christ, see further Susman (1948, 103–105, 123, 150–60, 199). She spoke about his miracles, his resurrection, the salvation that he brought, and about Christ as Son.

person's everlasting salvation dependent on keeping the Torah in one's own natural strength. The Jesus-believer has *not* died to the Torah as the eternal Law of Love, which remains binding for every creature.[41] In other words, the Jesus-believer has not died to the *principle* of a Torah as such—they remain God's "servant" (more literally, God's "slave") in all eternity (cf. Rev. 22:3). Rather, they have died to legalism and ritualism, in which the Spirit of God is lacking.

6.8.2 Christ *and* the Torah

In the light of the foregoing, the claim that Christ "broke apart" (German: *gesprengt*) the Law is entirely mistaken. Rather he said, "Do not think that I have come to abolish the Law or the Prophets; I have not come to abolish them but to fulfill them. For truly, I say to you, until heaven and earth pass away, not an iota, not a dot, will pass from the Law until all is accomplished" (Matt. 5:17-18).[42]

First, Jesus himself always kept the Torah. At no time did he personally break the Torah, contradict the Torah, or annul (parts of) the Torah (cf. §4.2). The only things he contradicted were those traditions woven around the Torah that went against the Torah as such by rendering its commandments burdensome or its power ineffective. According to both the letter and the spirit of the Torah, he was completely faithful to the Torah.

Second, the claim that Israel has maintained the observance of the Torah is only partially true. After the destruction of the temple (AD 70) and the end of the sacrificial ministry, this was simply impossible: the majority of the six hundred and thirteen commandments could no longer be fulfilled. Most of the rules that are followed in rabbinic Judaism are not (explicitly) found in the Torah at all. As it developed, this Judaism gradually moved from studying the Torah as such to studying the rabbinic tradition contained mainly in the Talmud. Additionally, *within* Judaism, numerous people have

---

41. Rom. 3:31; 8:4; 13:8–10; Gal. 5:14; 6:2; James 1:25; 2:8, 12.
42. For a more extensive discussion of this passage, a summary of which is offered above, see Ouweneel (2000a, §§6.1.2, 6.2.3, and 6.3).

identified the differences between the spirit of the Torah and the spirit of the traditions woven around the Torah. Jesus was (one of) the first who criticized this "tradition of the elders."[43]

Here are my difficulties with Susman's argument. On the one hand, Jesus did not criticize, break, or annul (parts of) the Torah. On the other hand, Judaism to a great extent has lost itself in the admiration of its traditions. There is nothing wrong with traditions (Gk. *paradoseis*) as such, of course: "So then, brothers, stand firm and hold to the traditions that you were taught by us, either by our spoken word or by our letter" (2 Thess. 2:15; cf. 3:6; 1 Cor. 11:2). But the love for the Torah, that is, for the inspired Word of God, must always come first. And such Jews, who deeply loved the Torah first and foremost, have always existed in Judaism. An outspoken example of this in the New Testament—apart from Saul of Tarsus before he came to faith in Jesus—is no doubt Gamaliel, in Judaism known as Rabban Gamliel haZaqen (9 BC–AD 50). He was a grandson of Hillel the Elder and the grandfather of Gamaliel II. In Acts 22:3, Paul mentioned him (with a certain pride) as his teacher. Gamaliel rejected the persecution of Jesus-believers on the basis of an interesting motive: if these people were "of God," no persecution could ever destroy them; and if they were not "of God," their movement would disappear by itself (Acts 5:34–39).[44]

It is worth noting that the apostle Paul described himself— when he was still Rabbi Sha'ul, when he had not yet become a Jesus-believer—as being "zealous for God," just like the traditional Jewish judges before whom he was standing at that point: "I am a Jew, born in Tarsus in Cilicia, but brought up in this city, educated at the feet of Gamaliel according to the strict manner of the law of our fathers, being zealous for God as all of you are this day" (Acts 22:3). At another point, he said this about his pre-Jesus stage of life: "I was advancing in Judaism beyond many of my own age among my people, so extremely zealous was I for the traditions of my fathers"

---

43. Matt. 5:17–48; 15:1–20; 23:1–36; Mark 7:1–23.
44. No wonder that later Christians speculated that Gamaliel himself had subsequently become a Jesus-believer (Pseudo-Clemens, *Recognitiones* I.65).

(Gal. 1:14). There was and is nothing wrong with being "zealous for the traditions of the fathers," as long this zeal served being "zealous for *God*." Paul described his life, including the time before his conversion, this way: "Brothers, I have lived my life before God in all good conscience up to this day. . . . I always take pains to have a clear conscience toward both God and man" (Acts 23:1; 24:16). "I thank God whom I serve, as did my [not yet Jesus-believing] ancestors, with a clear conscience" (2 Tim. 1:3).

This was all quite impressive. Paul was not the type of convert that before his conversion had been "living in sensuality, passions, drunkenness, orgies, drinking parties, and lawless idolatry" (cf. 1 Pet. 4:3). On the contrary: before his conversion, Saul/Paul had been just as "zealous for God" as after his conversion, and he had always lived with a good conscience, both before and after his conversion, "righteous before God, walking blamelessly in all the commandments and statutes of the Lord" (cf. Luke 1:6).

Although we are no "heart-knowers" (cf. Acts 1:24 DLNT), we assume that there must be many such godly Jews today; they do not know their Messiah yet, but they wholeheartedly love God and his Tanakh. The teachers among them resemble Ezra the scribe, who "had set his heart [first] to study the Torah of the LORD, and [second] to do it and [third] to teach his statutes and rules in Israel" (Ezra 7:10).[45]

6.8.3 The Godly Jew

Can such a thing exist: a godly Jew who does not recognize Jesus? It can! Before Saul of Tarsus got to know Jesus, he was *the* prototype of the true, Christ-less but godly, devoted, Torah-loving Israelite, such as they exist until this very day. He testified about himself: ". . . circumcised on the eighth day, of the people of Israel, of the tribe of Benjamin, a Hebrew of Hebrews; *as to the Torah, a Pharisee*; as to zeal, a persecutor of the church; *as to righteousness under the law, blameless.*"

---

45. Notice the order: teach what you practice yourself. The false teachers "teach, but do not practice" (Matt. 23:3).

However, to be sure, he does add: "... But whatever gain I had, I counted as loss for the sake of Christ. Indeed, I count everything as loss because of the surpassing worth of knowing Christ Jesus my Lord. For his sake I have suffered the loss of all things and count them as rubbish, in order that I may gain Christ and be found in him, not *having a righteousness of my own that comes from the Torah, but that which comes through faith in Christ*, the righteousness from God that depends on faith" (Phil. 3:5–9).

The first part of the quotation shows that these two can go together: persecuting Jesus-believers *and*, according to the criteria of the Torah, being blameless. When the Heidelberg Catechism (Q/A 3) asked: "How do you come to know your misery?", the catechist obediently replies: "The law of God tells me." But when Rabbi Sha'ul looked into the mirror of the Torah (cf. James 1:23–25), and asked (so to speak), "Mirror, mirror, on the wall, who is the most righteous of us all?," the mirror would have replied, "You, Sha'ul, you are blameless, you are a genuine *tzaddiq*."

At the time, Rabbi Sha'ul did not make a mistake in giving this self-judgment; otherwise, the later apostle Paul would have written: "... as to righteousness under the law, I *seemed* blameless." No, Saul/Paul came to know his "misery" as a sinner not by looking into the mirror of the Torah, but by looking into the eyes of Jesus.[46] It was then that he discovered himself to be the "number one sinner' (1 Tim. 1:15 CJB)!

We can learn another thing from Paul's words: that "zeal" (godly devotion) does not always necessarily imply understanding; as he wrote to the Romans:

> Brothers, my heart's desire and prayer to God for them [i.e., Israel] is that they may be saved. For I bear them witness that they have a zeal for God, but not according to knowledge. For, being ignorant of the righteousness of God [as revealed in Jesus, cf. 1:16–17; 3:21–22], and seeking to establish their own [by

---

46. See Ouweneel (2018a, ad loc.). Cf. the case of that other Jew, Simon Peter: "[T]he Lord [Jesus] turned and looked at Peter. . . . And [Peter]. . . went out and wept bitterly" (Luke 22:61–62).

a legalistic Torah-keeping], they did not submit to God's righteousness. For Christ is the end [i.e., goal, fulfillment, meaning] of the Torah for righteousness to everyone who believes (Rom. 10:1-4).

Here we have the problem of Job all over again. The truly Torah-faithful *and* suffering Jew is being held in the same vise that once held Job in its grip: one side of the vise is that such a Jew is still without an Arbiter (Umpire, Mediator, Redeemer, Intercessor; cf. Job 9:33; 33:23-24), for they do not have Christ; the "veil" is still over their heart. The other side of the vise is that like Job, they try to maintain their own righteousness before God by pointing to their Torah-observance; Job said, "I have not departed from the commandment of his lips; / I have treasured the words of his mouth more than my portion of food" (Job 23:12). It is only when the Messiah appears that the true Israel will "take back" its self-righteous words, just as Job did: "[N]ow my eyes have seen You. / Therefore I take back my words / and repent in dust and ashes" (Job 42:6 HCSB).

Until that time arrives, Israel will continue living as the suffering Job did, "speaking correctly about God" (cf. Job 42:7 CEB), but also speaking correctly about itself, clinging to him, but also complaining about him: "Though he slay me, I will hope in him; / yet I will argue my ways to his face" (Job 13:15). Uninterruptedly he serves God, but he also challenges him—until God will give answer to this Israel of God. Then, this Israel will no longer declare its innocence—no matter how guiltless the true Israel may indeed have been—but it will "repent in dust and ashes."[47] In the case of Israel, this will occur in a much more dramatic way than with Job. God spoke to Job "out of a whirlwind" (Job 38:1). But when, in the end time, he deals with Israel, the celestial conditions will be far more severe:

> Behold, the day of the LORD comes,
>   cruel, with wrath and fierce anger,
> to make the land a desolation

---
47. Job 42:6; cf. Isa. 57:15-19; Ezek. 14:6; 18:30; Zech. 12:10-14.

and to destroy its sinners from it.
For the stars of the heavens and their constellations
    will not give their light;
the sun will be dark at its rising,
    and the moon will not shed its light (Isa. 13:9-10)

I will show wonders in the heavens and on the earth, blood and fire and columns of smoke. The sun shall be turned to darkness, and the moon to blood, before the great and awesome day of the LORD comes. And it shall come to pass that everyone who calls on the name of the LORD shall be saved. For in Mount Zion and in Jerusalem there shall be those who escape, as the LORD has said, and among the survivors shall be those whom the LORD calls (Joel 2:30-32; cf. Luke 21:24-27).

6.9   What Is Anti-Semitism?
6.9.1   No Hatred of Jews in the New Testament

At this point we must pause to clarify and discuss a term used several times already: anti-Semitism. Jews and Arabs are both Semites in the sense of descendants of Sem, or Shem (Gen. 10). Yet, in practice the term is used for Jews only; unfortunately, also Arab Muslims can be anti-Semites. A simpler, but harsher, term would be "hatred of Jews (judaeomisy, the opposite of judaeophilia). What is it exactly?

The claim of both non-Jesus-believing Jews and by liberal Christians is incorrect, namely, that the New Testament itself contains the seeds of anti-Semitism.[48] This cannot be true because the New Testament never condemned a Jew simply for being a Jew—but such condemnation is the essence of anti-Semitism, which involves prejudice, or discrimination against Jews, or even hostility or hatred to Jews as such. The New Testament condemns *certain* Jews, not because they are Jews, but because they did something evil, like the mob in Pilate's court that shouted for the death of the innocent Jesus. And it would have been just as bad if Muslims or (nominal) Christians had done this. Seven things the New Testament

---

48. See, e.g., Jansen (1999); cf. Küng (1967).

never does are the very things that characterize genuine anti-Semitism. (These points have been mentioned earlier, so the relevant Bible passages need not be repeated.)

(1) The New Testament never said that *all* Jews were guilty of the death of Jesus, nor all Jews of all time—*only* the Jews in Pilate's court and the Jews standing around the cross, scoffing and mocking Jesus.

(2) The New Testament never said that God has permanently set aside the Jewish nation in order to make room for the church gathered from the nations. "The" Jewish nation was never definitively rejected; it was only temporarily set aside. As surely as (ethnic) Israel has become *Lo-'Ammi*, so surely it will again become *'Ammi*.

(3) The New Testament never said that God has broken his covenant with ethnic Israel, and that it is no longer God's chosen people. God's calling of Israel is irrevocable; he can never regret it, or resent it, or repent having done so. His counsel is everlasting.

(4) The New Testament never said that Judaism as such is or was a religion of pure legalism, and that Jews in the time of the New Testament generally believed that they were able to enter the Messianic kingdom on the basis of their own achievement. On the contrary, when correctly understood, Judaism is a religion of pure grace, and of Torah-observance out of pure love.

(5) The New Testament never taught that Judaism is essentially a religion of revenge and judgment, whereas Christians allegedly emphasize love. In reality, the message of Judaism contains God's mercy, and the message of Christians contains God's judgment.

(6) The New Testament never said that, in the time of the New Testament, all Pharisees (read: all orthodox Jews) were hypocrites; to be sure, some of them were—as the later rabbis themselves have confirmed—but Pharisees like Nicodemus ("*the* teacher of Israel," John 3:10), Saul of Tarsus, and Gamaliel, certainly were not.

(7) The New Testament never taught that, the Torah was "abolished" or "annulled" in (or by) Jesus, thereby rendering Judaism superfluous.

In summary. The New Testament is not anti-Semitic. Moreover, this would be hardly conceivable, because

(a) it was written by at least seven Jews: Matityahu (Matthew), Mark, Yochanan (John), Sha'ul (Saul/Paul), Ya'aqov (James), Shimon (Simon Peter), Yehudah (Jude), and one Jewish proselyte (Luke);

(b) it is as much the inspired Word of God as "the other Scriptures" (2 Pet. 3:16), that is, the Tanakh (cf. Rom. 16:26; 1 Tim. 5:18);

(c) both Jesus and his apostles (emissaries, Heb. *sh'lichim*) were full of love for Israel, and by this love they tried to lead the nation to *t'shuvah* (conversion to God through Jesus) (see especially Rom. 10); and

(d) it is explicitly said that Jesus gave his own precious life for Israel (even Caiaphas expressed this in his way: John 11:50), and the apostle Paul was prepared to be cursed for the sake of Israel (Rom. 9:3).[49]

But of course, Jesus and the apostles had their complaints about some Jews of their day, like the hypocritical leaders of Israel, who said that Jesus was possessed by the devil. Jesus replied that this was quite illogical: he had explicitly come to destroy the kingdom of Satan—so how could he be possessed by Satan (Matt. 12:22-32; John 8:30-59)? If someone criticizes certain church leaders, must we then conclude that thereby such a person is anti-church? If someone criticizes certain Jews, must we then conclude that thereby such a person is an anti-Semite? Jesus and the apostles themselves were Jews, and continued to love Israel and to testify to Israel. If they leveled sharp criticism at certain Jewish leaders (see also Matt. 23; 1 Thess. 2:14-16), this does not at all mean they were anti-Semites.

---

49. Cf. the same attitude of Moses in Exod. 32:31–32.

6.9.2 Hatred of Jews in the Church

Although the New Testament itself is not anti-Semitic, nevertheless anti-Semitism ("hatred of Jews") became one of the worst sins of the Christian church. However, this does not necessarily mean that Christians criticizing certain Jews—or vice versa—constitutes hatred of Jews in general, or hatred of Christians in general. Surely civilized and benevolent Jews and Christians should be allowed to critique and even blame each other for certain things. As long as such reproaches have a plausible basis, or as long as the discussion of them is open and civil, such Jews are not anti-Christian, and such Christians not anti-Semitic.

Apart from the Christian reproaches already mentioned, later Christians laid other reproaches at the feet of the Jews. The Jewish Council in Jamnia, the place where the Council met after the fall of Jerusalem,[50] had pronounced a curse over the *minim*, "heretics," which, according to many (not all), also contained the Jesus-believing Jews, and had thrown them out of the synagogues.[51] In this way, the cleft between Jews and Christians has widened. Just as Jesus-believing Jews were no longer welcome in the synagogues, they were not welcome in the church either as long as they had not fully renounced everything that belonged to their Jewish identity. (Today, "Messianic" Jews are still continually in danger of being consigned to a religious no-man's land because they are accepted by neither orthodox Jews nor by many Christians.[52])

Another example: during the Roman persecutions Christians were required to pay homage to the deified emperor, whereas this was not required from Jews. Therefore, Christians who were of Jewish descent—and these were many—appealed to their Jewishness. The Roman authorities verified this with Jewish authorities, who claimed that Jesus-believing Jews were no longer Jews. In this way, Jewish leaders consciously contributed to the death sentence pronounced over such Jesus-believing Jews. Later, Jews could blame Christians

---

50. See Ouweneel (2014a, chapter 6).
51. Cf. John 9:34; regarding the *minim*, see §2.8.1.
52. See, e.g., Stern (1997, 12–16).

for having contributed to the murder or execution of numerous Jews. It is so regrettable that Abraham's spiritual children became each other's bitterest enemies—one of the most tragic things in religious history, if not in world history.

6.9.3 The Jewish Identity

In this respect both Jews and Christians have crossed the line.

(1) Jews asserted, and many still assert, that Jews who come to faith in Jesus are no longer Jews, no matter how Jewish their lifestyle remains. In my view, it is the very opposite: no Jew is more Jewish than the one who has found the Jewish Messiah. However, among Jews the opposite occurred: Jesus-believing Jews were unceremoniously excluded from the community.

(2) Christians basically made the same mistake, but then in the opposite direction: they asserted, and many still assert, that Jews who come to faith in Jesus *should not be allowed* to remain Jews any longer, that is, to maintain a Jewish lifestyle and a Jewish identity. In earlier centuries, Jesus-believing Jews who tried to maintain their Jewish identity could be executed for it.

(3) Christians have asserted that Jews who refuse to accept Jesus in faith were no longer "Jews" (in a certain sense), and that Gentiles who did accept Jesus in faith became "Jews" as members of the church, the "spiritual Israel" (even if this "Jewishness" was bereft of anything that might remind people of the Jewish identity).

Both Jews and Christians were utterly and tragically mistaken on these three points, with dramatic consequences.

Please note that incorrect theology with regard to Israel as such is not necessarily anti-Semitic. A person may be sincerely convinced that Israel as people of God in the ethnic sense has been replaced by the New Testament church, which does consist of Gentile Jesus-believers as well as Jewish Jesus-believers, and in which every Jew is welcome. This is not anti-Semitism. But if a person concludes from this that all non-Jesus-believing Jews are under the curse of God, and especially if they deduce from this the right to persecute, expel, or even kill the Jews, then they are anti-Semites. And this happens very easily! When, especially since the fourth century, the idea took root that the Ecclesia is the "true Israel," it could only arouse irritation if there was on earth still an ethnic people who claimed that *they* were Israel and were unwilling to join the church. Such a "nuisance" has repeatedly led to anti-Jewish measures and pogroms.

In this way, unfortunately the light was dimmed on both sides: most Jews were blind to the fact that Jesus is the Messiah, and most Christians were blind to the fact that Israel, despite its rejection of its Messiah, is and remains the people of God, and God's promises to these people are "irrevocable" (Rom. 11:28-29). Or, to state it even more succinctly: Jews are often blind for who Jesus really was and is, and Christians are often blind for what Israel really was and is. On both sides, by God's grace much light from him continues shining; but because of this blind spot, unfortunately the light has remained dim on both sides.

In the presence of such tunnel vision, on the pure mercy of God has ensured that on both sides the light was never extinguished completely. One day, among both parties the scales will fall from the eyes (cf. Acts 9:18). Christians will recognize their error when God fulfills his promises to Israel—something he has already begun to do, given the miraculous establishment of the state of Israel. Jews will recognize their error when, on the day the Messiah appears, God reveals in his face the features of Jesus of Nazareth. And although none of us has ever seen Jesus in the flesh,[53] we will "recognize" Jesus just as really as Peter, Jesus' disciple, "recognized" Moses and Elijah on the Mount of Transfiguration (Matt. 17:4), although he had never seen them before. In the same way, the wicked in Israel will "recognize" "Abraham, Isaac and Jacob, and all the prophets in the kingdom of God" (Luke 13:28), "reclining at table" (Matt. 8:11). And in fact, this too ("recognizing" in Jesus Israel's Messiah) has already begun, given

---

53. Cf. H. J. Schoeps, quoted in Kac (1986, 58).

the worldwide growth of the "Messianic" (i.e., Jesus-believing Jewish) movement (cf. Zech. 12:10). On the day of Jesus' return, *all* people will see him (Rev. 1:7) and know immediately who he is.

In short, one day, all Jews will have to acknowledge *Jesus* (with exceeding joy or with gnashing of teeth), and one day all Christians, and even all nations will have to acknowledge *Israel* (with exceeding joy or with gnashing of teeth). At *that* time the Messianic kingdom of "righteousness and peace and joy in the Holy Spirit" (cf. Rom. 14:17) will arrive. The true meeting-point of Jews and Christians lies not in the most benevolent and tolerant dialogue (no matter how commendable). It lies even less in the church. It lies in him who is both the King of Israel and the Head of the Ecclesia. Until that moment, Israel and the Ecclesia will have to move on separately—but they might begin practicing their future communion now by learning to talk to each other learning to understand and even accept each other.

Chapter 7
Earlier Jewish-Christian Relationships

Where a harlot has set herself up, that place is a brothel. But the synagogue is not only a brothel and a theater; it also is a den of robbers and a lodging for wild beasts. . . . [W]hen God forsakes a people, what hope of salvation is left? When God forsakes a place, that place becomes the dwelling of demons.

John Chrysostom[1]

If it is expedient to hate any men and to loathe any race I have a strange dislike for those of the circumcision. For up to the present day, they persecute our Lord Jesus Christ in the synagogues of Satan.

Jerome of Stridon[2]

---

1. http://www.tertullian.org/fathers/chrysostom_adversus_judaeos_01_homily1.htm.
2. Hieronymus, *Ep.* LXXXIV, 3; *Corpus scriptorum ecclesiasticorum latinorum* 55:123; see http://www.worldfuturefund.org/wffmaster/Reading/Religion/Antisemitism%20Early.htm.

7.1 Some Church Fathers

7.1.1 Chrysostom and the Jews

In his attitude toward the Jews, church father John Chrysostom,[3] archbishop of Constantinople, went further than quite a few other church fathers. In eight of his sermons, called *Kata Ioudaiōn* ("Against the Jews"), he turned against the Israelites. In a very inordinate way, he accused them of being collectively responsible for the death of Jesus, which is a serious error. He also raged against Christians who attended Jewish ceremonies. Apparently, such attendance frequently occurred on Sabbaths and at other Jewish festivals. It indicates that there must have been many Christians who sympathized with the Jews and with the *biblical* festivals.

Chrysostom also reproached Christians who showed some preference for Jewish physicians and Jewish judges, perhaps also for medical and judicial reasons—were they more clever and wiser than Gentile physicians and judges?— but primarily for religious reasons. Indeed, Chrysostom was aware that many Christians had great respect for the Jews, and viewed their ceremonies as sacred, and realized that some of them considered beginning to live like the Jews. Therefore, he did his utmost to exterminate the viewpoint of these Christians, which in his eyes was a pernicious one. To stop this Christian tendency, he did not shrink from calling the Jewish synagogues worse than brothels and bulwarks of Satan (see the quotation at the head of this chapter).

Unfortunately, Chrystostom's sermons have strongly contributed to the development of Christian anti-Semitism. It is not difficult to understand why: from scolding synagogues it was only a minor step to closing or even destroying these synagogues, as has happened many times. In the twentieth century, the German Nazis abused these sermons. As happened to Martin Luther in much later time (§4.6.2), they have sadly damaged the reputation of this great theologian. But these are symptoms of a much wider development, both within Eastern Orthodoxy and Roman Catholicism and within later

---

3. This nickname, Gk. *chrysostomos*, means "golden mouth," a reference to Chrysostom's eloquence.

Protestantism: an entrenched anti-Semitic theology, which in its effects has hurt the Jews more than any other hatred of Jews.[4] If pagans demonstrate such hatred it is bad; if respected Christians leaders do such a thing it is disastrous.

7.1.2 Jerome and the Jews

The church father Jerome,[5] who revised the extant Latin Bible translations, and as a result produced the important Vulgate (the authoritative Latin Bible translation, which still is the official Bible of the Roman Catholic Church), owed much to the Jews.[6] Talmud teachers taught him Hebrew, and he thoroughly investigated their traditions and writings. Without this knowledge of Hebrew, the Vulgate would never have been possible. Jerome's own Old Testament commentaries often tied in closely with Jewish expositions.

Despite all this, Jerome, too, vigorously reproached the Jews, described them as stubborn and hostile toward the Christians, pronounced curses over them, and rejoiced in their mishaps. In his Commentary on Zephaniah, he called them "miserable people, who yet deserve no pity" (Lat. *populum miserum et tamen non esse miserabilem*[7]), and expressed his abhorrence of them. See the second quotation at the head of this chapter: ". . . I have a strange dislike for those of the circumcision. For up to the present day, they persecute our Lord Jesus Christ in the synagogues of Satan." The latter expression is a reference to Revelation 2:9 and 3:9, ". . . those who say that they are Jews and are not, but are a synagogue of Satan," and ". . . those of the synagogue of Satan who say that they are Jews and are not, but lie."

The Jews to whom Jesus was referring in these passages were not "real" Jews, for, as the apostle Paul writes, "[N]o one is a Jew who is merely one outwardly, nor is circumcision

---

4. Cf. Wilken (1982); Michael (2015).
5. The Gk. form is *hieronumos*, which means "holy name," or "(person with) a holy name."
6. Regarding him, see Ouweneel (2014a, 256–59).
7. The wordplay, *miser – miserabilis*, is lost in the translation.

outward and physical. But a Jew is one inwardly, and circumcision is a matter of the heart, by the Spirit, not by the letter" (Rom. 2:28-29). Such false Jews, that is, Jews with "uncircumcised" hearts, may be offspring of Abraham, but they are not "children" of Abraham in any spiritual sense, but rather "children of the devil" (cf. John 8:39, 44). Therefore, their synagogues were called "synagogues of Satan[8]." Jerome's great error was that he applied one broad criterion to all the Jews, as if they were all unfaithful, insincere, and unrighteous.

This was the mistake of millions of Christians, including many leaders: *they never recognized the faithful remnant in Israel*—faithful, even though the "veil" lay upon their hearts, so that they did not recognize Jesus. They were, and are, like the Emmaus disciples: "While they were talking and discussing together, Jesus himself drew near and went with them. But *their eyes were kept from recognizing him*" (Luke 24:15-16).[9] Of course, there are important differences: the Emmaus disciples *had* believed in Jesus and were sadly disappointed about what had happened to him. Yet, the similarity is conspicuous. All these centuries, the faithful in Israel have been "talking and discussing together," and Jesus himself "drew near and went with them," but "their eyes were kept from recognizing him." They did not discern *Jesus*, and Chrysostom and Jerome, and so many others, did not discern the *faithful in Israel*, the Jews with the circumcised hearts. These are the Jews in whom, like Nathanael, "there is no deceit"; they sit under their fig tree, but no "Philip" has yet come to them telling them, "We have found him of whom Moses in the Torah and also the prophets wrote" (John 1:45, 47, 50). But Jesus saw early on what was in Nathanael. However, the "Chrysostoms" and "Jeromes" of Christianity did not have this discernment when it came to recognizing the faithful in Israel.

In his polemics, what Jerome had personally learned from Jews who had been benevolent toward him he used as

---

8. Heb. *satan* means "adversary"; its Gk. equivalent is *diabolos* (from which the word "devil" was derived), which means "slanderer" (cf. Rev. 12:10; Zech. 3:1–2; Job 1:10–11; 2:4–5).

9. Cf. similar cases of spiritual blindness in Gen. 19:11 and 2 Kings 6:18.

arguments against them. No one of the church fathers was more thoroughly familiar with Judaism than he was, and no one had learned more from Jews and Jewish writings than he had. No one knew them so intimately as he because of his nearly thirty-two years spent in the Holy Land, where he met them almost daily, and learned from them. Many fellow-Christians even blamed him for this, but Jerome himself was proud of it. He called them the "masters" and "artists," from whom he had directly learned the "art" of Bible study. However, all these things did not prevent him from writing such nasty things about, and against, the Jews. I am unaware of any investigator who has been able to solve this (not only theological, but also psychological) riddle.

7.1.3 Augustine and the Jews

It is difficult to overestimate the significance of the great church father Aurelius Augustine,[10] bishop of Hippo Regius in North-Africa.[11] His influence was so enormous that for several centuries after him, no theologian arose who could compare with him. More than a millennium later, Martin Luther became as an Augustinian monk, and John Calvin was inspired by Augustine more than by any other earlier theologian.

In spite of his greatness, Augustine carried out heavy attacks against the Jews. He did so for decades, marking as low points his Good Friday Sermon of the year 397, his *Tractates on the Gospel of John*, and the sermon from his last years: *Adversus Judaeos* ("Against the Jews"). He called the Jews wild, cruel, and wicked, and blamed them for having killed Christ "in their fathers." He described them as "wolves," "sinners," "murderers," and "torn up dirt."

Yet, Augustine did demonstrate nuance. He praised the Jews as God's chosen people, and as trailblazers of Christianity through the faithfulness with which they had kept and handed down the Scriptures, in line with Romans 3:1–2:

---

10. Lat., *Aurelius Augustinus*, the first part presumably coming from *aurum*, "gold," and the second part from *augustus*, "sacred, exalted, venerable."
11. Regarding him, see Ouweneel (2014a, 274–79).

"Then what advantage has the Jew? Or what is the value of circumcision? Much in every way. To begin with, the Jews were *entrusted with the oracles of God*"—that is, the words of God as contained in the Holy Scriptures. As witnesses of the age and authenticity of the Scriptures, the Jews remained of lasting value for the church, argued Augustine. Therefore, they ought not to be killed, nor forcibly converted.[12] He believed that, in the end time, many Jews would still be converted to their once disowned Messiah. However, in his thinking this was supposed to mean that these converted Jews would thereby join the Christian church and would need to forsake their former Jewish identity.

As we saw, the latter is, until this very day, the standpoint of Roman Catholics, Eastern Orthodox, and many traditional Protestants: Anglican, Lutheran, Calvinist, and Evangelical. That is, the Jew who comes to faith in Jesus thereby becomes a "Christian," and must learn to behave like all Christians by renouncing all that belonged to his earlier life: no more circumcision of the little Jewish boys, no more Sabbath-keeping, observing only the Christian, not the Jewish festivals, no more food laws. Refusing any of these changes rendered the converted Jew suspicious.

Forcing converted *Jews* to live like *Gentiles* (within established Christianity) is just as bad as forcing converted *Gentiles* to live like *Jews*; think of the modern rise of the Judaeophile congregations that, without being Jewish, adopt an identity that is as Jewish as possible. This has been referred to as "playing the Jew," both by Jews and by Christians. But if we do this, we should be consistent and refer to the opposite error as Jews "playing the Gentile." Both are grave mistakes. Please notice Galatians 3:28, "There is neither Jew nor Greek, there is neither slave nor free, there is no male and female, for you are all one in Christ Jesus." *In Christ* the distinction between Jew and "Greek" (Gentile) is annulled, but in practical daily life the distinction continues to function, just as much as the distinctions between" slave" and "free"

---

12. See extensively, Fredriksen (2010).

(or employee and employer) and between "male and female" continue to function.

Augustine's ambivalent attitude—severe reproaches mixed with great respect—was present among later Christian thinkers as well, such as with Pope Gregory I the Great (the well-known pope of the "Gregorian chant"[13]). The underlying error of these theologians was supersessionism, which strongly colored the view of Augustine and many later Christian thinkers. Augustine read the following passage negatively:

> O house of *Jacob*,
> > come, let us walk
> > in the light of the LORD.
> For you have rejected your people,
> the house of *Jacob*,
> because they are full of things from the east
> and of fortune-tellers like the Philistines,
> and they strike hands with the children of foreigners
> (Isa. 2:5–6; cf. 8:17).

Augustine thought that in such negative passages, "Jacob" referred to ethnic Israel, whereas in the restoration prophecies, "Israel" referred to the (New Testament) Ecclesia. This is a strange view, because in Isaiah's poetic language, "Jacob" and "Israel" were often parallel, both in negative (e.g., 9:8; 40:27; 42:24) and in positive statements (e.g., 10:20; 14:1; 27:6; 29:23; 41:8, 14).

Despite this, Augustine has nevertheless supplied us with a more nuanced picture of the Jews than many other church fathers have done. But, as things often go, little of the master's nuances found survived among his pupils.

---

13. It has been suggested that at the foundation of this church "chanting" lie very ancient Jewish synagogue melodies, just as the "canonical hours" have their roots in Jewish prayer hours, while the well-known threefold *Sanctus* ("Holy") goes back to the Jewish *Kedusha* prayer, which itself is rooted in Isa. 6:3.

7.2 Anti-Jewish Church Decisions
7.2.1 The Visigoths

From the fifth to the seventh centuries, no fewer than thirty synods or councils were held in Toledo, the capital of the powerful Visigothic kingdom, which was one of the Germanic successor states of the western Roman Empire, comprising modern Spain and southern France.[14] At some of these councils, the gathered bishops, perhaps under pressure from the king, adopted severe measures against the Jews. This was done not only against those who continued to adhere to Judaism, but also against those who had been forcibly baptized into Christianity. These were people who, out of pure fear, had promised the king that they wanted to have nothing to do with Judaism anymore, but were not taken very seriously. I mention in particular the eighth (653), the ninth (655), the twelfth (681), and the seventeenth Councils (694). Many Jews sought asylum abroad, especially in North Africa.

The successive kings and the council leaders failed to realize that their extremely cruel measures hastened the decline and fall of the Visigothic kingdom. The Jews who had fled to North Africa cooperated with the local Muslim leaders. Together, Jewish and Muslim fighters invaded the Visigothic kingdom in 711 and issued the Visigothic army a devastating defeat. The event was remarkable because it was one of the rare times that Jews took up the arms against "Christians" who had tormented them to the utmost. The actions of these Jews were partially responsible for the Christian Iberian Peninsula falling into the hands of the Muslims.

Let this be clear: without the "Christian" oppression of the Jews and their subsequent flight to Africa *it is questionable whether the Muslims would ever have been able to conquer Spain*. And please keep in mind: these Muslims would remain in the southern part of Spain for no fewer than seven centuries. The influences of this Muslim occupation are still

---

14. Toledo (Lat. *Toletum*) lies about 73 km or 45 miles south of Madrid; in the seventh and eighth centuries it was the capital of the Visigothic kingdom, which was also called the *Regnum Toletanum*, "kingdom of Toledo," one of the most powerful kingdoms of western Europe at the time.

visible everywhere in Spain, especially in its more southern regions, not least in architecture, and the Spanish language contains many words of Muslim (Arabic or Persian) origin.

Muslim influence extended further. The Muslims were not satisfied with Spain; they intended to conquer as much of Europe as they possibly could. In 732, their army collided with that of the Frankish ruler[15] Charles Martel ("Charles the Hammer")—grandfather of Charlemagne—in the Battle of Tours and Poitiers. Martel won, but had he lost, Europe might have been Islamic today. Therefore, this Battle has been called one of the most decisive events in European history. And it all began with the Muslim conquest of Spain, which would scarcely have been possible without the Jewish support. Imagine, if God had allowed it, Europe might have become Islamic as a consequence of all the horrors "Christian" Europe had inflicted upon the Jewish exiles in their midst.

As soon as the Muslims had seized power in Spain, the Muslim rulers abolished all the oppressive laws that the "Christians" had issued against the Jews. Moreover, in that same Islamic Spain one of Israel's most important "Golden Ages" began, a time of great flourishing, religiously, socially, economically, and culturally. We have spoken of mysterious things; here we have two more riddles. First, why were the Iberian Muslims so benevolent toward the Jews, far more than (most of) the "Christians" had ever been? And second, how can we explain the enormous contrast between that benevolence and the attitude of modern Muslims toward the Jews? Few will be able to give satisfactory answers to these riddles, which are of a metahistorical nature. That is, they involve factors that go beyond the common factors with which historians reckon in their investigations.

7.2.2 Other Powers

In the meantime, the Byzantine—or, eastern Roman—Empire easily matched the Visigoth kingdom. The Council of Trul-

---

15. More precisely, duke and prince of the Frankish kingdom ("Francia"), "mayor domus" of the Merovingian king.

lo[16] (or *Concilium Quinisextum*, "Fifth-Sixth Council"), held in Constantinople (692), prohibited Christians, on pain of excommunication, from associating with Jews or to consult Jewish physicians. In 722, the Greek Orthodox Emperor Leo III forced all Jews in his empire to become Greek Orthodox, and to abandon everything Jewish (clothes, objects, customs, rituals, festivals, food laws, etc.).

In the so-called Holy Roman Empire of the German nation,[17] the first persecutions began: in 1012, the Roman Catholic Emperor Henry II banned all Jews from Mainz, a city on the Rhine, where they had lived for so many centuries and had built up a flourishing Jewish life.

These were some of the political powers. The church, too, continued to adopt several measures against the Jews. In 1050, the Council of Narbonne prohibited Christians from living in Jewish houses. In 1078, the Council of Girona commanded that Jews pay just as much as Christians in support of the Roman Catholic Church. An even lower point was reached during the Third Lateran Council in Rome (1179), and under the (in)famous Pope Innocent III. He humiliated the Jews most of all, pushing them as pariahs down to the lowest level of society. Innocent III was the mightiest power in Europe; as it was said, without him no king or emperor (whom he viewed as his vassals) could lift their little finger. And this very man was the great persecutor of the Jews. Church laws from the time of the Merovingians (early Middle Ages) were revived, both in 1179 and during the Fourth Lateran Council in 1215.

Jews and Christians were strictly segregated. In public life, Jews had to clearly distinguish themselves from Christians. Jews wearing the Yellow Star (or Star of David), as they did in Nazi occupied countries, was a practice that was devised first not by Nazis but by "Christians." Jews would be dishonored for many centuries by this kind of requirements. Popes repeatedly ensured that these humiliating regulations

---

16. Trullo was the name of the imperial domed hall where the Council was held.
17. It lasted from the Emperor Charlemagne (800) until its dissolution by the French Emperor Napoleon (1806); it was a genuine "thousand-year-reign."

were strictly observed in *every* European country. To be sure, some emperors, like Frederick II, and some popes, like Gregory X, were made of better stuff. But the diabolical flood that Roman Catholics had unleashed upon European Jewry could not be contained.

In 1180, the French King Philip August imprisoned all the Jews in his country and demanded a ransom for their release. In 1811, he canceled all the loans that Christians had borrowed from Jews, and demanded a percentage for himself. In 1182, he confiscated all Jewish possessions and banned the Jews from Paris.

In 1190, first, almost all the Jews in the English town of Norwich, and later five hundred Jews in York, were massacred by "Christians." In 1222, the Council of Oxford prohibited Jews from building new synagogues, keeping slaves, or associating with Christians. In 1282, the archbishop of Canterbury ordered that all London synagogues be closed and prohibited Jewish physicians from treating Christians.

In 1267, the Synod of Breslau in Prussia (modern Wrocław in Poland) ordered that all Jews should live in a separate quarter.

In 1279, the Synod of Ofen[18] prohibited all real estate transactions between Christians and Jews.

In 1434, the Council of Basel prohibited Jews from obtaining academic degrees or functioning as mediators in contracts between Christians.

The horrendous list goes on and on.

7.3 The Popes

7.3.1 Pope and Emperor

The horrible persecutions of the Jews in the late Middle Ages cannot be severed from the supremacy of papacy in those days. These persecutions received an entirely new impulse through three disgusting "Christian" accusations, which were supported by the highest church authorities.

---

18. This was the German name of Buda, the city part of Budapest that lies on the western shore of the Danube and during the Middle Ages had a population that in majority was German.

(1) *"All Jews are guilty of 'deicide,' that is, the murder of God."* This is a double mistake. First, only the mob in Pilate's court was guilty of Jesus' death, not all Jews of all time. Second, "God" cannot be murdered. Jesus was murdered according to his human nature, not according to his divine nature. We have here the same mistake as in "The Crucified God,"[19] and in calling Mary the "mother of God."[20] What can be said of Jesus according to his human nature cannot be automatically transferred to his divine nature, and *vice versa*.

(2) *"The Jews commit ritual murders."* They allegedly do so in particular during the Passover feast,[21] because they need the blood for the preparation of their *matzes*—which is an absurdity, because it was strictly forbidden to the Jews to eat blood in any form[22] (see §7.8.3). Why would they be so religious as to celebrate the biblical festivals, and at the same time trample the divine commandment underfoot? Through Cardinal Humbert of Silva Candida, Rome had asserted that "bread and wine are not only sacraments, but the true body and the blood of the Lord. . . . [T]he body of the Lord is really broken, and ground by the believers' teeth."[23] Against the background of this doctrine—"chewing your own god"—it was rather hypocritical to the Jews that Rome accused them of "deicide" and ritual murders.

(3) *"The Jews violate the hosts (wafers) of the Eucharist, and thus desecrate this sacrament."* Of course, any evidence for this nasty accusation could never be supplied. The Jews felt safest if they stayed as far away from Christians as possible. Why would they provoke the latter's hatred and revenge by desecrating what was most holy to them (see §7.8.3)?

Was it mere coincidence that, first, the Jews experienced their greatest peace and prosperity in Europe during the Car-

---

19. Moltmann (1996).
20. See extensively, Ouweneel (2007).
21. See Ouweneel (2004, Excursus 37).
22. Gen. 9:4; Lev. 3:17; 7:26–27; 17:10–14; 19:26; Deut. 12:16, 23; 15:23.
23. Quoted in Mann and Heuss (1951, 382).

olingian[24] and Ottonian[25] emperors, that is, *when the supremacy was in the emperors' hands* (even though these were always Roman Catholics)? And that they experienced their most horrible time during the reform movement of Humbert of Silva Candida and Hildebrand of Sovana (Gregory VII),[26] that is, *when the supremacy passed to the popes?* It is difficult to believe that such was mere coincidence. It cannot be denied that the Carolingians and the Ottonians were full-blooded followers of Rome. But did they nevertheless constitute a certain counter-balance to the popes? A counter-balance that fell away when the actual power in Europe fell into the hands of the popes? It is difficult, if not impossible, to give a final judgment on this question. However, anyone who is prepared to accept the destiny of the Jews as a kind of indicator for the metahistorical developments in Europe will continue to ask such questions. It is not for nothing that during these very centuries, the thirteenth, fourteenth and fifteenth centuries, the papacy experienced its moral decline, and thus became one of the principal causes of the Reformation.

Speaking of the Reformation: Protestants do well to remember that before the sixteenth century the Roman Catholic Church was *their* church as well. After the Reformation, they can choose to distance themselves from certain Roman Catholic actions, but before that time, virtually *all* western Christians belonged to the Roman Catholic Church (aside from the few pre-Reformational movements). The atrocities of that church against the Jews were "our" atrocities. The popes were "our" leaders, who were supposed to have been in such intimate contact with God that they should have known what was appropriate toward the Jews. Protests on behalf of reform-minded movements within the church,

---

24. Descendants of the Frankish ruler Charles Martel; the greatest of them was the latter's grandson, Charlemagne (Emperor "Charles the Great," d. 814).
25. A Saxon dynasty (919–1024): Otto I the Great, his son Otto II, the latter's son Otto III.
26. Interestingly, Hildebrand had Jewish blood in his veins: an ancestor of his was Leo, son of the rich businessman Baruch, who lived in the Jewish ghetto of Rome; see Prinz (1966).

against the crimes that the church committed against the Jews, were very limited.[27]

7.3.2 Examples

Here are some painful examples.[28] Pope Innocent IV ordered the French King Louis IX (later canonized: "Saint Louis") to burn all copies of the Talmud that could be found. Louis obediently fulfilled the order.

Pope Clement IV appointed a committee that had to "purify" the Talmud of all (alleged) accusations against Jesus and Christians (1264)—an impossible task because it cannot be determined with certainty where the Talmud was referring to Jesus or Christians (see extensively §2.8).

Pope Nicholas III issued an edict forcing Jews to attend sermons aimed at their conversion (1278).

Pope Nicholas V established the Inquisition in order to trace Jewish "heresies" among the *marranos* (1463), that is, Jews in the Iberian Peninsula who converted or were forced to convert to Christianity (see §7.6). It must be noted that, formally, the Inquisition had no authority over Jews, but it did have such authority over Roman Catholics, and therefore also over Jews who had converted, or had been forced to convert, to Catholicism.[29]

Pope Julius III prohibited the printing of the Talmud, and gave an order to burn all the extant copies (1553); about 12,000 copies were destroyed throughout Italy.

Pope Paul IV, who has been called the most anti-Semitic of all the popes, wrote in his bull *Cum nimis absurdum* that it was absurd and inadmissible to show love to Jews whom God, because of their guilt, had condemned to everlasting slavery, and he imposed all kinds of restrictions on them (1555). With his support, a baptized Jew forced his way into the synagogue of Recanati (Italy) on *Yom Kippur* in order to deliver a conversion sermon there. The Jews threw him out,

---

27. See, e.g., the ambiguous attitude of the Hussites and the Bohemian Brethren: https://www.jewishvirtuallibrary.org/hussites.
28. en.wikipedia.org/wiki/Timeline_of_antisemitism.
29. See Ouweneel (2004, Excursus 40).

for which they themselves were all thrown out of Recanati (1558). This pope did allow the Talmud, but only after the text had been censored, and only if it had been printed by a Christian (1559).

Pope Pius V confirmed the bulls of Paul IV, and banned Jews (except those who lived in the Jewish ghettos of Rome) from the papal territories (1566).

Pope Sixtus V prohibited the printing of the Talmud (1586).

Pope Clement VIII wrote: "The entire world suffers under the usury of the Jews, their monopolies and deceit" (1596).[30]

Pope Pius VI published an *Edict Concerning the Jews*, in which he reauthorized all the measures against the Jews that had earlier been lifted (1775).

In 1786, the situation in the Jewish ghetto—near the Vatican—was so desperate that the inhabitants addressed a petition to Pope Pius VI, but to no avail.

Pope Pius VII restored the Jewish ghetto in Rome after the defeat of Napoleon (1815): the Jews were forced to leave their houses in the city, and to live again in the stuffy ghetto in the Trastevere quarter; they were also obliged to attend conversion sermons.

Pope Pius IX called the Jews "howling dogs": "at present, there are too many of them in Rome, and we hear them howling in the streets, and they disturb us at all places" (1871).[31]

We are glad to add that there were positive exceptions: Pope Innocent IV rejected the absurd complaint that Jews killed Christian infants (1247; enforced by Pope Gregory X in 1272).

In a bull, Pope Martin V reminded Roman Catholics that Christianity was rooted in Judaism, and warned the monks not to stir up the people against the Jews (1422).

---

30. See especially his 1592 decree *Cum saepe accidere*; see more generally about papal decrees against the Jews: http://www.jewishencyclopedia.com/articles/3822–bulls-papal-concerning-jews.
31. For this and other quotations, see Stowe (2007).

Pope Leo X permitted the Jews to have the Talmud printed in Venice (1520); this was done by a Christian from Antwerp, of Dutch descent: Daniel Bomberg (originally: Daniel van Bomberghen). Bomberg had moved from Antwerp to Venice, where he had learned Hebrew from the Catholicized Jew Felice da Prato (Felix Pratensis).[32]

7.4 Modern Amillennialism

7.4.1 Amillennialism and Two Millennialisms

All (a)millennialism involves a certain view of the "thousand years" mentioned in Revelation 20:

> Then I saw an angel.... And he seized the dragon, that ancient serpent, who is the devil and Satan, and bound him for a *thousand years*, and threw him into the pit, ... so that he might not deceive the nations any longer, until the *thousand years* were ended.... I saw the souls of those who had been beheaded for the testimony of Jesus and for the word of God... They came to life and reigned with Christ for a *thousand years*. The rest of the dead did not come to life until the *thousand years* were ended. This is the first resurrection. Blessed and holy is the one who shares in the first resurrection! Over such the second death has no power, but they will be priests of God and of Christ, and they will reign with him for a *thousand years*. And when the *thousand years* are ended, Satan will be released from his prison ..." (Rev. 20:1-7).

All anti-Semites mentioned in the previous sections were amillennialists, that is, people who do not believe in a future thousand-year Messianic kingdom. Of course, this statement must not be reversed: not all amillennialists are anti-Semites. Yet, we may wonder whether there is not a deeper connection between the two: amillennialists do not believe in a future *Jewish* kingdom, for this is what the Messianic kingdom is, along with many other things: it is Messianic in the specific sense of a *Jewish* kingdom (Dan. 7:18, 22, 25, 27), in which Jerusalem will be the center of the world (Isa. 2:2-3; 60:14).

---

32. Pratensis was one of those converted Jews who heavily attacked the non-Jesus-believing Jews; his nickname was "the Jews' Scourge."

Amillennialists do not believe in a future *Jewish* kingdom, and anti-Semites do not believe in a future *Jewish* kingdom, either. *Pre*-millennialists (those who believe Jesus will return *before* the Messianic kingdom) do believe in a future Jewish kingdom, and post-millennialists (those who believe Jesus will return *after* the future Messianic kingdom) sometimes do too, while pre- and post-millennialists, too, can sometimes be fervent anti-Semites when it comes to *modern* (that is, unconverted) Jews (see §8.1.2).

Elsewhere, I have written extensively about millennialism (the doctrine of the future thousand-year kingdom) in church history, within the wider framework of the kingdom of God (also see chapter 13 in the present book).[33] On the one hand, there is amillennialism ("there will be no future Messianic kingdom of worldwide peace and righteousness before the new heavens and the new earth"), and on the other hand, there is millennialism ("there will be a future Messianic kingdom of worldwide peace and righteousness, either before or after the second coming of Christ, but at any rate before the new heavens and the new earth").

Please note that the prefixes "pre" and "post" before "millennialism" are somewhat arbitrary: the second coming occurs before ("pre") or after ("post") the Messianic kingdom, but one could also say: the Messianic kingdom will arrive before ("pre") or after ("post") the second coming of Christ. But of course, we will employ the common parlance.

It is remarkable that twentieth century interest in the "millennial hope" (the hope of the future Messianic kingdom) occurred not only among orthodox Evangelicals but also among influential theologians like Karl Barth and Paul Tillich, who certainly cannot be assigned to the mainstream of orthodox Protestantism.[34] Thus, their millennial ideas only vaguely resemble those of what are usually called pre- and post-millennialists. Yet, their interest is a fascinating sign; neo-orthodox and Evangelical thinkers find each other in their rejection of the amillennialism of Augustine and

---

33. Ouweneel (2011, chapters 9–14; 2012a, chapter 9).
34. Bloesch (2004, 90–92).

the Reformers. However, this tells us nothing about their attitude toward Israel; a person can be a millennialist, and yet completely spiritualize the Israel prophecies—and at the same time defend the Jewish people of one's own day, as Karl Barth did in 1933-1945. The reverse was encountered with some pastors of the Second Reformation in the Netherlands: they interpreted the Israel prophecies literally, while speaking of contemporaneous Jews in an anti-Semitic way (see §8.1.2).

7.4.2 The Power Interests of Amillennialism

The earliest church fathers, *if* they wrote at all about the matter, were pre-millennialists. We think here of Justin Martyr, Irenaeus, Melito, Tertullian, Hippolytus, Victorinus, Lactantius, and others.[35] One gets the strong impression that this dominant pre-millennialism receded into the background as a consequence of the Great Shift in the fourth century: the Roman Empire became Christian, the world was supposed to be ruled by Christ, namely, through the emperor and the pope, so that people began to believe that the Messianic kingdom of peace and justice had arrived.[36] As this new view was received by the masses, in principle amillennialism was born: there *is* no longer any other Messianic kingdom that we are supposed to expect.

As we have seen, it was the church father Augustine who developed amillennialism.[37] His influence was so enormous that, until this very day, all Roman Catholics and the great majority of traditional Protestants—insofar as they give the matter any thought at all—adhere to his eschatology. He is the source of all the well-known amillennialist arguments, such as:

(a) The thousand-year kingdom of Revelation 20:1-7 is being fulfilled in the present age, more concretely within the Christian church.

---

35. Regarding these authors, see Froom (1950); cf. also Aalders (1985).
36. See extensively, Ouweneel (2003, chapters 4-5) regarding the coherence of the metahistorical and the theological developments in the fourth century.
37. Augustine, *De civitate Dei* XX.9: the church has entered the millennium.

(b) Satan was "bound" during the first coming of Christ,[38] not in the sense that he would no longer exert influence,[39] but rather that he is prevented from "deceiving the nations" (Rev. 20:3) to such an extent that spreading the gospel would be hindered.

(c) The "first resurrection" (Rev. 20:4–6) is the spiritual rebirth of believers (cf. John 5:25).

(d) Revelation 20:1–7 is a recapitulation of the previous chapters of the book,[40] not the description of a new stage after the second coming of Christ described in Revelation 19.

Supersessionists would do well to consider two things here. First, setting aside the pre-millennialism of the first centuries of church history, as well as the spread of Augustinian amillennialism, were the consequence not primarily of theological but of political-historical developments. Second, the rise of Augustinian amillennialism was a necessary mainstay for the rise of the papacy. *There is no papacy without supersessionism.*[41] This is because the pope was supposed to rule in the present ("thousand-year") kingdom as the deputy or substitute of Christ on earth. Therefore, absolute obedience was due to him; this is what I have called the Thyatira phase of the church (the "dark" Middle Ages).[42] Pope Innocent III in particular claimed to be the supreme feudal lord over all the rulers of Europe. The prophetic predictions about the glory of the Messianic kingdom were believed to be fulfilled in the dominion, riches, and beauties of the Roman Catholic Church. The reward and elevation of believers no longer depended on the second coming of Christ, but on the power that rested with the papacy.

Over against this doctrine, pre-millennialism was an explicit threat that had to be combated with all force. For

---

38. Cf. Luke 10:18; Heb. 2:14–15; 1 John 3:8.
39. Cf., e.g., 1 Cor. 7:5; 2 Cor. 12:7; Eph. 6:12; 1 Thess. 2:18; 2 Thess. 2:9; 1 Tim. 3:7; 2 Tim. 2:26; James 4:7; 1 Pet. 5:8.
40. So, e.g., Greijdanus (1965, ad loc.).
41. Of course, supersessionism does exist without the institution of the papacy, as traditional Protestants show.
42. See Ouweneel (2010b, 53–55).

this doctrine implies that Christ's Messianic kingdom in power and glory could not arrive before the second coming of Christ.[43] If this were true, both the Holy Roman emperors and the popes would lose the ground under their feet.[44] Moreover—and this is of enormous metahistorical significance—pre-millennialism would create space again for hated and despised Judaism: the future Messianic kingdom is specifically and explicitly a *Jewish* kingdom, as we have seen and will continue to examine.

It is interesting to see that the English King Henry VIII separated the church from Rome, shaping it into the (half-Protestant) Church of England, and was happy to exercise *both* dominions in his own person: the secular rule as king, and the spiritual rule as the Supreme Head, under Christ, of the Church of England. The changes were rather drastic, but a few important things remained the same: amillennialism and supersessionism were still the pillars of this new church, and as king *and* head of the church, Henry was still the representative of Christ on earth. Some Anglican theologians who came later may have become pre-millennialists, but given the history and character of the Church of England, it is *by nature* an amillennialist and supersessionist church, as is the Roman Orthodox Church, along with the various Eastern Orthodox Churches.

In Lutheranism and Calvinism, things are different, because here the secular supremacy was thought to lie in the hands of the political rulers, not in the hands of any church leaders. The local ruler was viewed as the representative of Christ on earth. Therefore, Martin Luther always sought the support of the (Lutheran) German rulers,[45] and in the Netherlands, it was not the church but the States General (the Parliament) that convened the Synod of Dordt (1618–1619) and

---

43. Peters (1952, 1:516–17).
44. There have been no Holy Roman emperors after 1806, but there are still Roman popes, although none of them made claims like those of Innocent III.
45. Germany was still a patchwork of many different counties, duchies, and princely states, which had been under the general supremacy of the Emperor, but after 1648 were formally all autonomous.

7.5 What Does Amillennialism Involve?
7.5.1 The Millennium

As we have seen, amillennialists do not believe in a future Messianic kingdom *before* the new heavens and the new earth, whether this kingdom is before (post-millennialists) or after the second coming of Christ (pre-millennialists). Either, the thousand years are entirely dismissed, or amillennialists believe that we are presently living in the thousand-year kingdom. In this case, the number thousand is interpreted figuratively (many post- and some pre-millennialists interpret this number figuratively). In this view, the beginning of the figurative "thousand years" could be understood as occurring in

(a) AD 30: the day of the resurrection (when Jesus rose from the dead), or the day of his ascension (when he took his place at the right hand of God in heaven), or the Day of Pentecost, the day when the Holy Spirit was poured out (Acts 2);

(b) AD 70: the destruction of Jerusalem, when the Roman Empire triumphed over Israel, city, temple, and over Judaism as such by destroying its heart;

(c) AD 313: the Great Shift inaugurated with the conversion of Emperor Constantine the Great, when the Roman Empire began to develop its "Christian" character; or

(d) the Edict of Thessalonica issued by Emperor Theodosius I (AD 380), in which Nicene Christianity became the state religion of the Roman Empire; thus, a Christian world empire was established, whereas Judaism was reduced to a (seeming) trifle. One of the most solemn questions to be asked about European history is this: Where was God's sympathy in those days, with the pomp and circumstance of the Vatican, or with the faithful ones, living among the Jews in the Jewish ghetto of Rome, nearby the Vatican? (Apart from the faithful ones, living within Christianity in those days, of course.)

Because the Millennium is thought to be the present age, some of these thinkers prefer other terms than amillennialism, such as "nunc-millennialism" (Latin *nunc* = "now": the Millennium is in the present), or "realized amillennialism" (this linguistically erroneous term means "doctrine of the realized Millennium"), or "pro-millennialism" (the doctrine that is "pro" Millennium, but not interpreted as something of the future).[46]

Some older post-millennialists complicated the subject still further by postulating a "double Millennium," one in the past or the present, and one in the future; thus, for instance, Thomas Brightman and Johannes Cocceius.[47] In this sense, their post-millennialist teaching overlapped with amillennialism. Cocceius localized the (first) Millennium in what I have called the Smyrna period[48] of the church (ca. 300 until far into the Middle Ages, but before the great supremacy of the papacy).

7.5.2 Who Has World Dominion Today?

From an amillennial perspective, Jesus Christ is reigning in the Millennium today, not so much in the political but rather in the spiritual sense, from his Father's throne. Or, if one wishes to bring in the political aspect as well: Christ reigned through the popes and the Holy Roman emperors (the emperors of a large part of Europe) between 962 (the coronation of Emperor Otto I)[49] and 1806 (the abdication of the last "Roman" emperor, Francis II, under the pressure of Napoleon), and through the successors of these "Roman" emperors in the various European countries. At the end of the present age, Christ will visibly return, the dead will be raised and will undergo the judgment unto life or the judgment unto death (cf. John 5:28–29). Then, the visible reign of Christ will begin, which coincides with the new heavens and the new earth. This will be the "eternal state" (Lat. *status aeternus*). Already today, Jesus Christ possesses all power in heaven and on earth (Matt. 28:18), so that his kingdom is not only future but also present.

---

46. Adams (1970); A. A. Hoekema in Clouse (1977); Spykman (1992, 540–43).
47. See Ouweneel (2012a, §9.4).
48. For this expression, see Ouweneel (2010b, 52).
49. Or 800, if one views this Empire as having begun the day Charlemagne was crowned by the pope to be the Frankish emperor of the "Romans" (read: all western and middle Europeans).

Amillennialists assume that the apostle Peter's quotation from Joel 2:28–32 (Acts 2:17–21) makes clear that the Messianic kingdom has already begun. In their view, other passages point in the same direction.[50] In reply to this, we emphasize that pre- and post-millennialists, too, acknowledge that the kingdom of God (the reign of Christ) exists already today. However, first, at present the kingdom of God is a *hidden* kingdom (if you do not want to see it, you don't see it; cf. "secrets" in Matt. 13:11; "hidden" in Col. 3:3; as long as Christ is still hidden, the kingdom is hidden as well). Second, at present the kingdom of God exists *alongside* the kingdom of Satan (Matt. 12:25–28), engaged in a continual struggle with each other (Eph. 6:10–12), in which Satan has seemed to triumph in many cases (think of the persecution and oppression of Jesus-believers in many countries throughout the centuries).

No, when we speak of the "Messianic kingdom" in the strict sense, we speak of Christ's kingdom of universal peace and righteousness and joy that will arrive with his second coming, when the kingdom of Satan will be definitively defeated and all war will be abolished.

Theoretically, amillennialism might certainly be combined with literal interpretations of the Tanakhic prophecies, in particular the belief in a national and spiritual restoration of ethnic Israel. But this is only theoretical. In practice, rejecting the notion of a future Messianic kingdom—established between Christ's return and the "eternal state"—virtually always seems to entail a figurative interpretation of the Israel prophecies. And this is understandable: of what use is a *national* restoration of *ethnic* Israel, as the prophecies predict, if the other parts of the prophecies are not taken literally as well: the arrival of the Messiah (Anointed King) who, in universal peace and righteousness, will rule over this restored Israel?

Amillennialism is still very strong in Roman Catholicism, Eastern Orthodoxy, and traditional Protestantism (Lutheran, Calvinist, Anglican), and even among certain Evangelical groups (insofar as all these Christians reflect on eschato-

---

50. Matt. 12:28; Luke 17:20–21; Rom. 14:17; 1 Cor. 4:20; Col. 1:13.

logical questions). From the seventeenth century until the earlier part of the twentieth century, amillennialism was challenged by rising post- and pre-millennialism; but in the second half of the twentieth century, it has found new defenders. The debate, not only concerning Revelation 20:1-7, but especially concerning the literary genre of the entire book of Revelation, plays a central role in this. Generally we may identify these four interpretive options: (1) Revelation is essentially allegorical poetry (concerning the past, or the future, or both), *or* (2) it is a kind of historiography of the future, *or* (3) it is a kind of historiography of the past, say, the first century, *or* (4) it covers all of church history.

In a certain respect, pre-millennialism and amillennialism are rather close (in contrast with post-millennialism), in that both tend to exhibit an inclination toward pessimism: in the present age, good and evil remain standing side by side, and evil may become stronger and push aside the good for a time. This condition is thought to end in a drastic way at the second coming of Christ. At the same time, it is true that both pre- and amillennialism can live quite well with belief in a future flowering period of the church—as does post-millennialism—in that, after the second coming of Christ, the Messianic kingdom will arrive before the "eternal state" (according to pre-millennialism), *or* the "eternal state" will begin immediately at that point, because we are already living now in the Millennium (according to amillennialism).

7.5.3 Why Is Amillennialism Attractive?

We can certainly understand why amillennialism is so attractive to many Christians. After pre-millennialism, it is the oldest Christian view of the "thousand years" of Revelation 20. Moreover, it bears the stamp of orthodoxy because it was advocated by men like Augustine, Jerome, Luther, and Calvin, and has been given approval in various venerable confessional documents.[51] It forms a simple, transparent eschatological

---

51. The Nicene-Constantinopolitan Creed says, *cuius regni non erit finis*, "... whose reign shall have no end"; this *might* be read as a rejection of a "thousand-year" kingdom—but pre-millennialists are aware of Daniel 7:14, too, where it is said of the Son of Man: "[H]is dominion is an everlasting domin-

system, with just one resurrection, one judgment, and hardly any prophetic program awaiting fulfillment. It does not contain such cumbersome problems as the debate between pre-, mid- and post-tribulationism (does Jesus return before, in the midst of, or at the end of the seven years of the Great Tribulation?).[52] It is especially suited for theologians who enjoy reminding us—somewhat dismissively—that the Bible is not a "puzzle book" or a "transportation timetable."[53]

This dismissiveness resembles that of some Christians who prefer to dismiss "complicated" theology in order to "just listen to what the Bible says." Theology is a difficult scholarly enterprise, and this is certainly true for eschatology. It is unavoidable that it is sometimes quite a "puzzle" to distinguish clearly among all the eschatological views, and to create some theological order from this chaos, but also some theological order from the biblical data.

Amillennialism is attractive also because it is very compatible with federalism (covenant theology), with its inclination to what is called covenant universalism ("all divine–human relationships are by definition covenantal").[54] Further, amillennialism easily succumbs to the perilous error of spiritualism; this is the view that likes to call the literal—or, as spiritualists say, "literalistic"—exegesis of the prophecies "carnal" or "earth-oriented." And amillennialism is very compatible with supersessionism (replacement theology), which imagines the (New Testament) Ecclesia to be some "spiritual Israel," which is supposed to have replaced ethnic Israel (though some supersessionists would prefer to formulate this somewhat differently).

---

ion, which shall not pass away, and his kingdom one that shall not be destroyed" (cf. 1 Cor. 15:28, where one day the *[Triune]* God will be "all in all," which includes the Son).

52. Cf. Ouweneel (2012a, chapter 10).
53. E.g., Boersma (1978); Verkuyl (1992, 463); terms like eschatological "program," "end time scenario," "puzzle book," and the like are derogatory terms that amillennialists often use in reference to pre-millennialists.
54. Regarding this, see Ouweneel (2011, chapters 1–4).

The serious dangers of amillennialism can be summarized as follows.[55]

(a) Spiritualism has a disastrous effect on the entire body of Christian doctrine, as modernism demonstrates, even though conservative amillennialists restrict their application of it almost exclusively to eschatology (without supplying us with the theological grounds for such a restriction). Supersessionists would react with indignation if we were to claim that, if they wish to be consistent, they should apply their spiritualizing method to, for instance, Christology (the doctrine of Christ) and soteriology (the doctrine of redemption) as well.

(b) But even within their eschatology, amillennialists are not consistent in the way they apply their spiritualizing method to biblical prophecies. For instance, they usually believe in a literal second coming of Christ and in a literal resurrection of the dead. But in cases where they feel the need to combat pre- or post-millennialism, or where they wish to support their supersessionism, they apply their spiritualizing method. Again, we are not supplied with any grounds for such an eclectic approach.

Note well: opposing this spiritualism does not entail employing literal*ism*: all sound exegesis accepts figurative language in the prophecies (cf. volume IV/1a, §9.7); for instance, what is "coming with the clouds of heaven" (cf. Dan. 7:14)? What is "every valley lifted up, every mountain made low" (Isa. 40:4)? But accepting figurative language in prophecy does not require declaring that "Israel," "Judah," "Ephraim," "Zion," "Jerusalem," "the land," and so on, must all be understood figuratively. In sentences such as "you will be removed far from your land, and I will drive you out" (Jer. 27:10) and "God will bring you [back] into the land that your fathers possessed" (Deut. 30:5), amillennialists mistakenly and unaccountably interpret the former sentence literally, and the second sentence figuratively.

(c) Amillennialists defend their spiritualist approach as a hermeneutical tool designed to avoid problems relating

---

55. Here I am borrowing from, and paraphrasing, Walvoord (1950, 49–50).

to the fulfillment of prophecies, without seeing that these "problems" exist only on the basis of the amillennialism itself. Thus, this spiritualizing method has arisen from an alleged need, *not* as a natural result of exegesis as such. Others rightly argue that amillennialism historically arose not so much through studying the prophecies, but rather by neglecting them. I concur with this judgment, though prefer to distinguish other historical causes for the rise of amillennialism (see volume IV/1a, chapter 4).

The most important theological consequences of amillennialism are the following.[56]

(1) *Soteriological:* amillennialism is mainly responsible for the Reformed reductionist covenant theology (federalism), which elevates one of the many topics of Scripture, the covenant, to the main issue of redemptive history, and understands all dispensations in biblical salvation as stages in the progressive revelation of the one covenant of grace. It should be added, though, that many other groups of Protestants have seriously *neglected* the subject of covenant;[57] they have their own hobbyhorses.

(2) *Ecclesiological:* amillennialism is also linked with the doctrine that the Ecclesia is the totality of all born again humans from Adam and Eve until the last day. Here, the essential differences between Israel and the Ecclesia are greatly neglected. It must be added, though, that classical dispensationalists have seriously neglected the *similarities* between believers in the Tanakh and believers in the New Testament. So often, theology is mainly reactive, moving from one extreme to the other, instead of walking the middle path of sound theological thinking.

(3) *Eschatological:* in spite of the mutual differences, conservative Protestant amillennialism is essentially identical with other forms of amillennialism, such as the Roman Catholic and liberal Protestant eschatologies. In the past, the spiritualizing method of amillennialism has been used to justify both conservative Calvinism, liberal modernism, and

---

56. Pentecost (1964, 389–90).
57. See extensively, Ouweneel (2011).

Roman Catholic theology, that is to say, very different, if not mutually hostile, views. Conservative amillennialists find themselves keeping the wrong company.

(4) *Christological:* Christ is formally acknowledged as the Messiah of Israel, but no longer in any Jewish sense: not the Anointed King of ethnic Israel, on the throne of David in Jerusalem, but rather the Anointed King of the world (or of the church, the "spiritual Israel"), on the Father's throne in heaven. He is King over Zion, but no longer over the literal Zion of Psalm 2:8; 9:12; 14:7; 20:3 and so on, but only over the figurative Zion of Hebrews 12:22 and Revelation 14:1. Emphasizing the Jewishness of Jesus can cause irritation among supersessionists, as I know from experience. Though it must be added that the Jewishness of Jesus can also be one-sidedly overemphasized at the expense of the redemptive significance that he has for all the nations of the world.

7.6 The Iberian Jews
7.6.1 What Are *Marranos*?

Amillennialism, combined with supersessionism, has done great damage to Israel. In addition, many "Christian" *practices* have caused great harm to the Jews. One of the saddest stories in the history of Jewry in its confrontation with Christianity is the story of the *marranos*. These were the Jews of the Iberian Peninsula who were baptized forcibly or under great pressure, but who, under the guise of Christianity, often surreptitiously kept practicing their Jewish religion. It is one of those disgraces of Spanish history that historians have strongly suppressed.[58] For the Dutch, the story of the marranos is important because many of the Iberian Jews, fleeing to the Netherlands after the late fifteenth century, had a marrano past.

Some wished to derive *marrano* from the Aramaic word *maranatha* ("Our Lord, come!," or, "Our Lord has come"; cf. 1 Cor. 16:22). But the Spanish word means "pig" (perhaps a

---

58. My Spanish guide in the Alhambra (Granada), a few years ago, claimed he had never heard the word *marrano* in the sense described here. He could tell me only that it means "pig."

sarcastic name for people who refused to eat pork), and if derived from the Arabic (*mucharram*) it means "cursed." In the fifteenth century, the number of these *conversos* ("converted ones") surpassed the one hundred thousand. They had achieved great prosperity and a high status, even within the Spanish and Portuguese court. The marranos married into Gentile noble families, and some of them obtained high church positions, such as those of bishops and cardinals. The marrano Tomás de Torquemada was even a grand inquisitor; through his decisions, thousands of Jews lost their lives at the stake. The marrano Hernando de Talavera was bishop of Granada, and Juan Pérez de Montalván was priest and notary of the Inquisition.

Among the marranos, there were Jews who had cared nothing about Judaism, and for whom their so-called "conversion" opened the door to brilliant careers. Their new "faith" meant nothing to them either, even though they pretended it did. Others, however, maintained their Jewish beliefs, but only in the utmost secrecy (*crypto-Jews*). Still others had been baptized, but confessed much more openly that they continued living according to their Jewish religion: they observed the Sabbath and *Pesach*, ate *kosher* as much as possible, and had their little boys circumcised. Ordinary Jews, that is, those who had escaped compulsory "conversion," were tolerant toward these *conversos*, because they knew very well that, under the Christian disguise, these people had remained ordinary Jews, practitioners of the Jewish religion.

The marranos suffered in various ways. Often, they suffered inwardly because they felt they had betrayed their ancestral faith. And they suffered outwardly because, as neo-Christians (Spanish: *cristianos nuevos*; Portuguese: *cristãos novos*), they fell under the direct supervision of the Inquisition, and often they were exposed as heretics.[59] They also suffered because many Jews no longer wanted anything to do with them, whereas many Spanish and Portuguese continued to view them as Jews, so they endured all the anti-Semitism, envy, and suspicion connected with that. They were hated

---

59. See Ouweneel (2014a, Excurse 38).

more than ordinary Jews because they were viewed as false Christians, as hypocrites (which in many cases was basically correct). Occasionally, in various Iberian cities (Toledo, 1467; Córdoba, 1473; Lisbon, 1506), riots broke out that focused on attacking the marranos.

Perhaps the deepest tragedy was that only one way of escaping persecution was to become, as a marrano, an anti-Semite oneself: a hater of the Jews. In addition to Tomás de Torquemada, another remarkable example was the archbishop Paul of Burgos, who had been born as Shlomo haLevi ("Solomon the Levite"), and was an influential rabbi and Talmud expert. In 1391, he was baptized (at nearly 40 years old) and became a fierce opponent of Judaism. This is a common psychological phenomenon throughout religious practice; for example, former fervent Catholics sometimes become the most fervent Protestants, former fervent Calvinists sometimes become the most fervent Evangelicals. Their beliefs may have changed, but not their fervor.

In modern times as well, leaders of Jewish origin have exhibited strong anti-Semitic tendencies, like the Austrian chancellor Bruno Kreisky. The worst example is Adolf Hitler, if the theory is correct that his father, Alois Hitler, had been fathered by a Jew with Adolf's grandmother, Maria Schicklgruber; at the time, this lady worked in a prosperous Jewish family. We also know now that the *bolshevists* (the early Russian communists) were anti-Semites, even though some of their earlier members, like Leon Trotsky, were Jews. Vladimir Ilyitch Lenin was one-quarter Jewish.

7.6.2 The Inquisition

The term "Inquisition" (interrogation, examination) is a collective name for various Roman Catholic judicial institutions tasked with tracking down "heretics," and judging them. The Inquisition began in the twelfth century in France with the aim of tracking Cathars, Waldenses, and Albigenses (who belonged to the Cathars), and later other pre-Reformational movements, and after the sixteenth century, Protestants. In the Napoleonic era, and in Spain in 1834, the Inquisition as a system tracking down and condemning heretics came to an end.[60]

In theory, the Inquisition dealt only with the judicial side of the matter. When a person had been sentenced by its tribunal, they were turned over to the secular authorities, which executed the sentence. In this way, the Roman Catholic Church could always maintain that she herself never killed heretics. However, it knew perfectly well what would happen to the extradited heretics, and explicitly intended this in delivering its verdicts. If one says that those Jerusalem people who condemned Jesus in AD 30 did not (literally) kill him but that it was the Roman soldiers who did this, one could also exonerate the Roman Catholic Church for never having killed heretics. However, just as Peter and Stephen told their Jewish audiences that *they* had killed Jesus, so too we can say that the Roman Catholic Church has killed thousands of Christians with diverging opinions.

Formally speaking, the Inquisition had nothing to do with religious movements outside the Roman Catholic Church, such as Judaism and Islam (or Hindus and Buddhists for that matter), but only with alleged heretics within its own walls. This group included the Protestants, as well as witches (women who had been baptized Roman Catholic). However, in countries where Roman Catholic authorities forced Jews and Muslims to be baptized, as in Spain, these "converts" (Spanish: *conversos*) automatically fell under the jurisdiction of the Inquisition. These where the *moriscos* ("converted" Muslims) and the *marranos* ("converted" Jews). To a large extent, these "converted" Muslims and Jews continued to confess their former religion surreptitiously, or they returned to it secretly. If they were caught, they fell into the hands of the Inquisition. Imagine such a system: the authorities compelled a person to become a Christian against their will, and subsequently the Inquisition condemned that person if they had secretly continued to practice Islam or Judaism.

Here again, the Church could maintain that it was not occupied with the persecution of Jews but had sentenced

---

60. See extensively, Lea (2016).

only Christian heretics. But this would be a very hypocritical standpoint: it was *Jews* whom they delivered to the authorities to be *executed*.

The Inquisition went to great lengths to demonstrate that a *marrano* continued secretly to practice Judaism. Those who prayed the Psalms without the addition, *Gloria Patri et Filio et Spiritui Sancto* ("Glory to the Father, the Son and the Holy Spirit"), those who avoided eating pork, even those who washed their hands before eating, or put on clean underwear before the Saturday, was suspected as heretics. During the winters, the Inquisitors needed only to stand on a roof or a tower to watch the houses where no smoke rose from the chimneys (cf. Exod. 35:3): *there* they would find those practicing Judaism in secret. Such indications were often sufficient to bring people to the stake.

Every Spanish person was encouraged to anonymously report suspected heretics. Thereupon, suspects were detained and tortured until they confessed their "crimes" *and* betrayed other marranos. In 1481, the first *autodafe* (Portuguese: *auto da fe*, "act of faith"; Spanish: *auto de fé*) was held; that is, the first six marranos were burned at the stake in the Spanish city of Sevilla. Thousands would follow them, both in Spain and in Portugal, and later in the colonies of these countries.

The Inquisition has been one of the most important reasons for Jews to take refuge in other countries where the Inquisition had little or no power. Even the few marranos who took their new Christian faith very seriously often emigrated for two reasons. On the one hand, they were never trusted by their fellow-Christians, and because the least suspicion was often sufficient to put them in the stocks, if not worse, despite their Christian devotion. On the other hand, they were hated by the Jews. The marranos were neither fish nor fowl (like the Messianic Jews in our present time).

7.6.3 Marranos in the Netherlands

Under all this pressure, not only non-baptized Jews but also many marranos fled from the Iberian Peninsula. After having arrived in other countries, they sometimes thought they could discard their masks and practice Judaism openly again. However, this sometimes met with resistance and misunderstanding from the local people. When, around 1593, the first marranos arrived in the Protestant Northern Low Countries—the present Netherlands—they were initially thought to be Iberian Roman Catholics. Therefore, when they held a meeting on *Yom Kippur* (1596), they were stopped by the constable and his men because the Roman Catholic service was forbidden. When the misunderstanding was cleared up, they received permission to live in Amsterdam as practicing Jews. This was not so much out of charity or sympathy, but rather because these Jews were wealthy people.[61]

Another encounter between marranos and the Dutch involved the many Portuguese marranos who had fled to the large Portuguese colony of Brazil, where they established large plantations (sugar cane, rice, cotton, tobacco). Almost all physicians in the colony were marranos, as well as the first governor-general, Thomé de Sonza (or Sousa, d. 1579). But the tentacles of the Inquisition reached deeply into Brazil, where many marranos, suspected of following Jewish practices, were arrested, tortured, and dispossessed. This changed when, through the Dutch West India Company, the Dutch began populating the colony (1642). Many Brazilian marranos chose the side of the Dutch, who not only conquered the colony, but also allowed the marranos to live like Jews again. Rabbis came from Amsterdam to lead the new Jewish congregations.

Alas, the Jewish joy lasted only briefly. From 1645 to 1654, the Portuguese waged war against the Dutch, until they had reconquered the entire colony. The Dutch had barely left when the Portuguese authorities ordered all Jews to leave the colony immediately. Some Jews returned to the Netherlands, but most of them resorted to various regions in the Caribbean territory: Curaçao,[62] Jamaica, Barbados, and not least

---

61. See further, Ouweneel (2014a, Excurse 45).
62. Some years ago, I visited the synagogue on the Caribbean island of Curaçao, the oldest of all the surviving synagogues in the Americas.

to Suriname, which in 1667 passed into Dutch hands.[63] They built large plantations there, and as the other white planters, owned thousands of black slaves. A strange situation, when one considers that many Jews were being oppressed at that same time in Europe.

In 1654, twenty-three of the Jews who fled from Brazil arrived at what in those days was called New Amsterdam, later called New York. They laid the foundation for what ultimately would become the largest Jewish community on earth (even today 1.1 million in New York City and 2 million in New York State). Even after the establishment of the state of Israel (1948), it took quite some time before there were more Jews living in the Holy Land than in that one city of New York. (At present, we are told that there are about 15 million Jews worldwide, of whom almost 7 million live in Israel, but there are still about 6 or 7 million Jews in the United States.[64])

7.6.4 Famous Marranos

Finally, let me mention some other of the most famous marranos, well-known people who had one or more close Jewish ancestors who had been baptized as Christians. None less that Saint Teresa of Ávila was one; she was one of the most amazing Christian women of the Middle Ages, and (centuries later) was declared to be a *Doctor Ecclesiae Universalis* ("Doctor of the Universal Church"). Until today, she is venerated even by Anglicans and Lutherans. Her father's father, Juan Sánchez de Toledo Cepeda, was a marrano, who because of his secret Jewish practices had fallen into the hands of the Inquisition. Teresa and "Santiago" (the apostle Saint James, the son of Zebedee) are the patron saints of Spain; for Roman Catholic Spain, which has fought the Jews for such a

---

63. I also visited the Jodensavanne ("Jewish Savanna") in Suriname, and saw there the ruins of one of the oldest synagogues in the Western hemisphere (1665–1671), and on the tombstones many Portuguese names of well-known Jewish families.

64. Numbers vary—depending on the method of counting—but it is still quite possible that, today, there are more Jews living in the United States than in Israel.

long time, it is interesting to have two Jewish protectors in the heavenly places.[65]

Teresa of Ávila reminds me of the German philosopher Edith Stein, who by origin was an orthodox Jewess. After reading the autobiography by Teresa of Ávila, she decided to become a Roman Catholic and a nun; nevertheless, she was brutally killed by the Nazis as a Jewess (1942).

The famous monk-poet, theologian, and academic, Luis de León had marrano roots. Presumably, the same was true for Miguel de Cervantes, author of the most famous Spanish novel of all times: *Don Quixote*. It has even been said that many of the most famous Spanish Christians had a marrano background.

Another was the famous French philosopher Michel de Montaigne,[66] who through his mother was of Jewish-Aragonese origin. And then there was the French Calvinist theologian (later converted to Roman Catholicism) Isaac de la Peyrère (Pereira). An interesting man! In 1643, he wrote a booklet entitled *Du rappel des Juifs* ("Appeal to the Jews"), in which he urged them to return to Israel; then, the Messiah would come, that is, Christ would return on earth. As far as we know, not a single Jew responded—apparently, he issued his appeal a few centuries too soon.

The well-known Jewish philosopher Baruch de Spinoza came from a family that, before it came to the Netherlands, consisted of marranos.[67] In Amsterdam, they began living as Jews again, and became so strict that they cast the more liberal Spinoza out of their synagogue.

If we take "marrano" in the broader sense of "Hebrew Christian" (traditional Christian with Jewish roots), then the United States has known quite a few marranos. Two recent American secretaries of state were both Roman Catholic. The one is Madeleine Albright (born 1937 as Marie Jana Korbelová), whose parents turned from Judaism to Christianity in

---

65. Cf. Poland, known for its anti-Semitism, but whose primary patron saint is the *Jewess* Mary, called the "Queen of Poland."
66. See Jama (2001).
67. See, e.g., Nadler (2001).

1941. The other one is John F. Kerry, whose paternal grandparents were Hungarian-Jewish immigrants who had converted to Catholicism.

The Anglican Benjamin Disraeli was also a marrano, who was prime minister of the United Kingdom in 1868, and later in 1874–1880. His Jewish parents converted to Christianity in 1817, after which they had all their children baptized as Anglicans.

Of course, many more western Jewish political leaders could be mentioned, like president Pierre Mendès-France of France, chancellor Bruno Kreisky of Austria, secretary of state Henry Kissinger of the United States, minister of foreign affairs Jevgeni Primakov of Russia, but as far as we can assess, these have all become a-religious. By contrast, the modern orthodox Jewish Jared Kushner, of pure Ashkenazy-Jewish descent, is the son-in-law of former president Donald Trump, and sometimes called Trump's "truest heir."[68]

7.7 The Disaster Year 1492

7.7.1 Columbus

The year 1492 likely leads us to think first of the re-discovery of the North American continent by Europeans. I say *re*-discovery because the Norse explorer Leif Erikson had discovered it about five hundred years before Columbus. (Of course, those whom we call "native Americans," coming from Asia, had discovered it much earlier still.) America's re-discovery had everything to do with the Jews. Christopher Columbus was probably of marrano origin. It is hard to provide definitive proof of this because it was in the best interests of Columbus to hide his Jewish descent from the Spanish *reyes catolicos* ("Catholic king and queen"), Ferdinand of Aragon and Isabella of Castilia. His actual family name was Colon,

---

68. https://www.vox.com/policy-and-politics/2016/11/21/13651942/jared-kushner-donald-trump. Other well-known Jewish American contemporary politicians are Michael Bloomberg, Eric Cantor, Joe Lieberman, Adam Schiff, Chuck Schumer, Bernie Sanders, and the present secretary of state, Tony Blinken, and the present secretary of the treasury, Janet Yellen. The husband of vice president Kamala Harris, Douglas Emhoff, is Jewish. Ruth Bader Ginsburg was the first Jewish female Justice of the Supreme Court.

Eariler Jewish-Christian Relationships

and this was a well-known Jewish name. This is only one of the many hints pointing to his Jewish origin. Presumably, his Spanish parents had emigrated to Italy as marranos, and he was born in Genoa.[69] Some historians believe that Columbus was actually a Portuguese Jew, whose real name was Salvador Fernandes Zarco. This was the son of Isabel Gonçalves Zarco, daughter of the Jewish Portuguese sailor João Gonçalves Zarco (the name Zarco might even go back to that of the great Kabbalist Joseph Ibn Sharga).

In 1968, the well-known Jewish Nazi hunter Simon Wiesenthal wrote the book *Segel der Hoffnung* ("Sails of Hope"),[70] in which he launched the theory that Columbus was a Sephardic Jew who had continued secretly to practice the Jewish faith. His quest for the New World was not inspired by lust for gold or land, but rather by the wish to find a safe home for the Jewish people. It is uncertain whether many scholars have accepted this idea.

The interpreter whom Columbus took with him on his journey, Luis de Torres, was a marrano who knew Hebrew. This skill was deemed necessary because presumably in the far "Indies" that Columbus hoped to reach, the ten tribes of Israel had settled, and of course these would have been speaking Hebrew. This Jewish interpreter was the first of Columbus' company to set foot on the American continent, in order to make the first contact with the natives.[71] The first words spoken by a Westerner in the Americas were...in Hebrew! In addition, the treasurer of the *reyes catolicos*, Luis de Santángel, who strongly supported Columbus' expedition, was a marrano.

Speaking of the "Disaster Year" 1492, we can hardly describe the discovery of America as a "disaster"—unless we think of the destiny of thousands of "Indians" who perished

---

69. See extensively, De Madariaga (1967).
70. Wiesenthal (1973).
71. See Goldberg (1993) for this and a number of other remarkable peculiarities of Jewish history.

through Spanish hands, hungry as the Spanish were to find gold and silver (not so Columbus, if we may believe Wiesenthal).

7.7.2 The Last Iberian Muslim Kingdom

At any rate, the conquest in that same year, 1492, of the last Muslim kingdom on the Iberian Peninsula, in the far south, *was* a disaster. It involved the downfall of the Nasrid dynasty in Granada. Of course, this was not a disaster for Christians, who, after so many centuries of Islamic dominion, finally had the entire Iberian Peninsula under their control again. No, it was a disaster for the *Jews*. Under the Nasrids, they had been able to lead a reasonably comfortable life in their own quarter in Granada: the Realego. However, when the Catholic king and queen reacquired hegemony, they immediately made short work of this Jewish quarter. This was because it was the year in which, in Granada, the Alhambra decree had been issued, requiring all Spanish Jews to either convert or leave the country. Presumably, the *reyes catolicos* thought that most Jews, to save their lives, would indeed convert; however, this occurred only to a limited extent. This was a matter not only of principle, but also of prudence: in Spain the marranos scarcely had a better life than ordinary Jews. In and after 1492, more than one hundred thousand Jews left the country and became wanderers in many European countries.

In Granada, this meant that everything in the Realego that was reminiscent of the Jewish presence was removed. Perhaps a synagogue was turned into a church—as happened in ten of twelve cases in all Spain—but most of them were simply destroyed. The names of the streets were stripped of their Jewish characteristics; today they still bear the name of various Catholic saints. Anyone walking through the Jewish quarter—as I myself have done in Spanish cities like Córdoba, Granada, Sevilla and Toledo—will scarcely be able to recognize anything specifically Jewish. In Sevilla, part of the old ghetto wall still exists, but it features no commemorative plaque. In the Realego (Granada), in April 2013 a tiny Sephardic museum was opened; if I had not known of its existence, I would have passed it by. Thus, the de-Islamization of Granada meant a triumph for the Roman Catholic Church, but a disaster not only for Muslims but also for Jews. Those of Granada had only these two options: either convert—becoming "marranos"—or flee.

To the fanatical king and queen, Ferdinand and Isabella, who through their marriage had united Spain, the pope gave this honorary title: *reyes catolicos*, as we have seen. There are still quite a few Spanish monuments on which their names appear as *Fernando el Católico* and *Isabella la Católica*. Fanatical they were—but fanaticism is rarely accompanied by wisdom. Driving out the Jews in 1492 meant for Spain an enormous brain drain: intelligence and capital left the country in a massive way. It is impossible to imagine that the king and queen, or their counselors, had not foreseen this. The situation was comparable with that of 1685, when King Louis XIV in France revoked the Edict of Nantes, which had guaranteed religious freedom to all his subjects. As a consequence, France lost masses of Huguenots, and along with them France lost skills, capital, and commercial contacts.

Those who visit Spain today will find only a handful of synagogues dating from before 1492: the Great Synagogue of Barcelona, two synagogues (in Sevilla and Toledo) that today function as churches, both carrying the same name: *Santa María la Blanca* ("Saint Mary the White"), another synagogue in Toledo: the El Transito synagogue, the synagogue of Córdoba, and that of Híjar (and perhaps a few others). I have visited four of the six myself, not as a tourist, but rather as a melancholic, meditating in sadness about what had been done to the Jews in Spain (and in the rest of Europe). Melancholic indeed. I sat in the *Santa María la Blanca* of Sevilla during the mass, because this was the only opportunity to visit the inside of the church. I sadly tried to imagine how the place had once been a synagogue; I visualized the *aron*, the alcove where the sacred scrolls had been preserved, and in my mind, I saw a few hundred Jews attending the service. At that moment I suddenly looked up to see a white pigeon flying along the ceiling of the building, roving about, looking for a "rest for the sole of her foot," so to speak (cf. Gen. 8:9). That enlivened me and filled me with hope and joy as I recalled Psalm 74:18-19:

> Remember this, O LORD, how the enemy scoffs,
>   and a foolish people reviles your name.
> Do not deliver the soul of your dove to the wild beasts;
>   do not forget the life of your poor forever.

7.7.3 Jews and Protestants

In the previous section, I mentioned the Jews and the Huguenots. No matter how different the two groups were, for Roman Catholic rulers like the kings of Spain and France they were all the same enemy. *Un roi, une foi, une loi* ("One king, one faith, one law") was the ideal of the French King Louis XIV. All those holding deviating opinions had to adapt to Roman Catholic teaching. In 1685, Louis XIV revoked the Edict of Nantes, which abolished the final remains of Huguenot religious freedom. Already two years earlier, King Louis had driven all Jews from the French islands, such as Martinique.

After the rise of Lutheranism, the response of the German Emperor Charles V had not been very different. At the Peace of Augsburg (1555) this slogan was applied: *Cuius regio, eius religio*, "Whose region it is, his religion it is": Lutheran princes would rule over Lutheran regions, Catholic princes over Catholic regions. (For Calvinists, and possible Anabaptist or Jewish rulers—assuming that these existed, or could exist—this principle was not applied.) As the king of Spain, Charles V maintained the Inquisition in that country, which was especially persecuting former Jews and former Muslims. But in Germany, at the Diet of Speyer (1544), Charles spoke in favor of protecting the Jews (*Große Speyrer Judenprivileg*, "Great Jewish Privilege of Speyer"). This was rather inconsistent; but in Germany, the Emperor may have assumed this attitude partly in opposition to Luther's anti-Semitic writing of the year before (1543).[72]

The general rule was that subjects ought to have the faith of their ruler, or else they should either convert or leave—or

---

72. Regarding the history of the German Jews, see Herzig and Rademacher (2007).

be killed. In fact, this was a typically medieval way of thinking. The year 1492 fell in a period when such self-evident "truths" were no longer generally accepted, and in 1555 this was even less the case. A new age had arrived—even if it take the French Revolution (1789) to spread modernity throughout the West: freedom and equality for all citizens, including the Protestants and the Jews. A person's religion was determined not by the ruler, but by that person's conscience. Truly a revolutionary insight, but today perfectly self-evident, even for the most counter-revolutionary Christians. It took no fewer than three hundred years of severe fighting on the part of Jews and Protestants in the Roman Catholic countries—but (let us not forget) also for Jews in Protestant countries.

7.8 Jewish-Christian Disputes and Processes
7.8.1 "Jesus Cannot Be the Messiah"

Throughout the centuries, Jewish rabbis had to continually defend themselves against the teachings of Christians, in order to protect their own people against them, and to rebut the constant criticisms of Christians. Well-known Jews who responded to Christians included Rabbi Abbahu, Maimonides, David Kimchi, and Nachmanides.[73] The never-ending question from Christians was: Why did you, and do you, Jews, not wish to accept Jesus as your Messiah? The Jewish answer consisted mainly of the following three elements (see earlier §3.4):

(1) We do not see that Jesus is indeed the fulfillment of the Messianic prophecies in the Tanakh; on the contrary, we believe that what you, Christians, do with the Tanakh is a form of ventriloquism: it does not say what you say it says.

Take the way some New Testament writers apply to Jesus verses from the Tanakh that have nothing to do with Jesus, or even with the Messiah in general; for instance, Matthew 2:15 (Hos. 11:1); 2:18 (Jer. 31:15); 2:23 (Isa. 11:1; 60:21), and so on.

Reply: Matthew and others often quote the Tanakh according to its deeper (midrashic) sense; other prophecies are

---

73. Regarding him, see Ouweneel (2014a, 358–60).

of a more direct nature, such as: the Messiah will be born in Bethlehem, as the rabbis told King Herod (Matt. 2:4-6; Micah 5:2).

(2) For us, the life and preaching of Jesus do not constitute any form of evidence, or even vague hints, that he satisfies the Tanakh's picture of the Messiah.

For instance, the Messiah will subdue all the enemies of God and all the oppressors of Israel (e.g., Micah 5; Zech. 14),[74] but Jesus never opposed the Roman occupying force that ruled Israel at the time. On the contrary, he allowed himself to be delivered to them, and to be crucified. It may have been harsh, but in fact the Jews around the cross were perfectly correct:

> You who would destroy the temple and rebuild it in three days, save yourself! If you are the Son of God, come down from the cross.... He saved others; he cannot save himself. He is the King of Israel; let him come down now from the cross, and we will believe in him. He trusts in God; let God deliver him now, if he desires him. For he said, "I am the Son of God" (Matt. 27:40-43).

Reply: But what *is* the picture that the Tanakh gives of the Messiah? Did not the rabbi, who rejected Jesus, develop a picture that would resemble Jesus as little as possible?

(c) If Jesus were the Messiah, we might expect on the basis of the prophecies in the Tanakh that Israel would have been set free, and universal peace and righteousness would have been established. However, in two thousand years this has never been realized, not even among the Christians themselves. And for Israel, their situation has never been worse than during the last two thousand years.

---

74. In the New Testament the priest Zechariah emphasized the same point: God "has raised up a horn of salvation for us in the house of his servant David, as he spoke by the mouth of his holy prophets from of old, that we should be saved from our enemies and from the hand of all who hate us; to show the mercy promised to our fathers and to remember his holy covenant, the oath that he swore to our father Abraham, to grant us that we, being delivered from the hand of our enemies, might serve him without fear, in holiness and righteousness before him all our days" (Luke 1:69-75).

Indeed, if Jesus is the child born, the Son given, of which Isaiah 9:6 spoke, why was the remainder of this passage not fulfilled:

> ... and the government shall be [or, is] upon his shoulder,
>   and his name shall be [or, is] called
> Wonderful Counselor, Mighty God,
>   Everlasting Father, Prince of Peace.
> Of the increase of his government and of peace
>   there will be no end,
> on the throne of David and over his kingdom,
>   to establish it and to uphold it
> with justice and with righteousness
>   from this time forth and forevermore (Isa. 9:6–7).

Reply: Many prophecies were not fulfilled precisely *because* the Jews in Jesus' day rejected him, and many of them had sought his death! But these prophecies will be fulfilled at his second coming.

In the Middle Ages, several public disputes occurred between Jews and Christians where these and other questions were raised. Interestingly, the Jewish rabbis were usually better prepared for these debates than the Christian theologians. One psychological reason for this is that a small minority is trained to continually and self-consciously distinguish itself from the large majority, not the other way around.

Remarkably enough, what occupied the focus of these medieval disputes not biblical exegesis as such, nor the person of Jesus, but rather the Talmud. Christians took the initiative for such disputes, and they blamed the rabbis who had contributed to the Talmud for having said—as the critics asserted—such nasty things about Jesus, Mary, and Christians. The focus never landed, for instance, on the writings of the church fathers in which they had said nasty things about the Jews! Christians were the attackers, and Jews had to defend themselves.

7.8.2 Three Disputes

Three disputes have become the best-known in history, in each of which, remarkably, the rabbis were opposed not by a long-standing Gentile Christian but by a converted (i.e., Jesus-believing) Jew. Apparently, it was assumed that converted Jews knew Judaism better than Gentile Christians did, and would perhaps be more aggressive toward the Jewish debaters than Christians of a Gentile background.

These are the three most (in)famous disputes:

(1) The *Dispute of Paris* (1240), namely, at the court of King Louis IX (after his canonization called "Saint Louis"[75]). Four rabbis challenged the "Christianized" Jew Nicolas Donin about the alleged blasphemies in the Talmud regarding God and Jesus. Rabbi Yehiel of Paris tried to prove that Jesus the son of Panthera (see §2.8.1) could not have been the same as the Jesus of the New Testament, and that the term *minim* ("heretics") in the Talmud does not refer to Christians in general, but only to Christians of Jewish descent. However, his argument did not prevent the king from ordering, two years later, that twenty-four truckloads of Talmud copies be burned.

(2) The *Dispute of Barcelona* (1263), where Rabbi Nachmanides, the famous Bible expositor, challenged the converted Jew and monk Pablo Christiani (notice the name: "Paul the Christian"!). Pablo tried to prove from the Talmud that the rabbis who contributed to it secretly believed that Jesus was the Messiah—an absurd viewpoint, as Nachmanides could easily demonstrate. Regarding whether the Messiah had already arrived, Nachmanides replied that he could not believe so, since the promised end of all wars had not yet arrived:

> The LORD "shall judge between many peoples,
>   and shall decide disputes for strong nations far away;
> and they shall beat their swords into plowshares,
>   and their spears into pruning hooks;
> nation shall not lift up sword against nation,

---

75. He was only one of many anti-Semites who have been canonized by the Roman Catholic Church (though not for their anti-Semitism as such, of course).

neither shall they learn war anymore
(Micah 4:3; cf. Isa. 2:4; Joel 3:10).

Nachmanides also made clear that the greatest difference between Jews and Christians concerned not so much the person of Jesus—Messiah or not?—but rather the being of God. According to the rabbi, Christians taught that God himself had become a human being through a Jewish womb, in order to return, through death and resurrection, to his "divine primordial state." Nachmanides said that, for Jews, this was inconceivable and unacceptable.

This, however, was a caricature of Christian teaching; this is not at all the Nicene (orthodox Christian) teaching, whatever the theologians of Nachmanides' day may have told him. Christians do *not* believe that God became a human being, thereby ceasing to be God for a time, and then became God again. Rather, Christians believe that God *the eternal Son* became a human being, *while at the same time remaining God,* and in all eternity will be both God and Man.[76]

Nachmanides' arguments were so successful that both his Jewish and Christian friends had to warn him against the threatened revenge of the order of the Dominicans if the latter were to lose the Dispute. Therefore, Nachmanides himself broke the Dispute off on the fourth day, before the bomb would explode. Thereupon, his opponents triumphantly claimed the victory. When Nachmanides published the statements that he had made at the Dispute, such that every reader could see how the debate had really occurred, he was forced to leave the country.

(3) The *Dispute of Tortosa* (from February 1413 to November 1414) was the most impressive medieval Dispute because of all the pomp and circumstance that accompanied it, and because of its duration. It was organized by Antipope Benedict XIII and attended by hundreds of ecclesiastical prelates. Josua Lorqui (Geronimo de Santa Fé), a Christian Jew, took upon himself to prove from the Talmud itself that Jesus is the Messiah—a foolish enterprise. Twenty-two Jewish opponents

---

76. See extensively, Ouweneel (2007, chapters 2–9).

had the task of either refuting this or becoming Christians.[77] No fewer than sixty-nine sessions were held, which in fact led to nothing. Lorqui could not prove his point (of course), and his opponents did not possess the courage of a Nachmanides to refute his folly with counterarguments. The ultimate outcome of the Dispute was a papal bull (May 1415), in which the study of the Talmud was prohibited, and various humiliating measures were issued against the Jews.

The problem with such Disputes was that, generally speaking, the Christians, even trained clergymen, could not handle the arguments of the much better educated Jews.[78] Therefore, in 1227 and subsequent years an entire series of orders was issued in the German-speaking countries prohibiting *sacerdotes illiterati* ("illiterate priests") from holding public disputes with Jews because the risk of their complete failure was far too great. Conversely, Pope Gregory IX ordered the *Jews* not to engage in disputes with Christians because the common people might be misled by such debates. The Jewish debaters might be so convincing that the untrained Christians might conclude that these Jews were right.

7.8.3 The Accusation of Ritual Murder

It is important to pay some special attention to one of the most foolish charges leveled by Christians against Jews throughout the centuries. For instance, Jews were accused of stealing sacred wafers in order to crush them as a form of sacrilege, or to slice through them, and thus to repeat the crucifixion of Jesus, as it were. In 1298, a witch hunt broke out in southern Germany against the Jews because of this silly accusation. Within that one year, many thousands of Jews were punished because of this perfidious allegation, and many lost not only their property but also their lives. From southern Germany, a wave of anti-Semitic hatred spread to other countries. In

---

77. It repeatedly amazes me how simple this "becoming a Christian" was considered to be: a person needed only to be baptized, that is, receive a few drops of water over which the baptismal formula was pronounced.
78. This sounds a bit like disputes between orthodox Christians and Jehovah's Witnesses, which are often won by the latter because *they* are trained to refute their adversaries, who are not.

1309, Jews in the towns of Sittard and Susteren, in the Dutch province of Limburg, sought refuge against their "Christian" enemies by fleeing to the castle of Born. This failed, because these enemies conquered the castle, burned it down, and one hundred ten Jews were burned alive. This was the first Jewish pogrom in the territory of modern Netherlands.[79]

The most frequent complaint was that Jews allegedly murdered Christians, in particular children, in order to use their blood for their ceremonies.[80] Even today, we can find Internet websites where people spread this lie of the ritual murder of Christians, especially very young Christians. One of the allegations was that Jews need this blood for the annual preparation of *matzes* during *Pesach* (the Jewish Passover). The folly of this is that the accusers should know that the Tanakh explicitly forbids not only murder but also the consumption of animal blood (and even more so human blood). God said to Noah, and through Moses and Ezekiel respectively, "[Y]ou shall not eat flesh with its life, that is, its blood" (Gen. 9:4). "It shall be a statute forever throughout your generations, in all your dwelling places, that you eat neither fat nor blood."[81] "You eat flesh with the blood and lift up your eyes to your idols and shed blood; shall you then possess the land?" (Ezek. 33:25).

Unfortunately, popular beliefs are unaffected by such biblical arguments. There is no point in showing that, if Jews wished to celebrate *Pesach*, they could not possibly accompany that celebration with the commission of the most heinous of sins.

"Blood libel," accusing the Jews of ritual murder, began in 1146 in the English city of Norwich, and reached its lowest point in the French city of Blois, where fifty-one Jews were

---

79. The only other pogrom in Europe that involved Dutch territory was that of 1348–1349. It was caused by the plague epidemic of 1346–1348. Entire Jewish communities were exterminated in Brussels, Basel, Frankfurt am Main, but also in the Dutch city of Zutphen.
80. See Dundes (1991); Van der Horst (2006); Johnson (2012).
81. Lev. 3:17; cf. 7:26–27; 17:10, 14; 19:26; Deut. 12:16, 23; 15:23; cf. 1 Sam. 14:33.

burned alive in a tower on the basis of a false allegation of infanticide. The event led to a kind of Christian mass psychosis. In 1181, three hundred Jews were burned in Vienna (Austria) because they had supposedly slaughtered three boys as sacrificial animals. Later, it became evident that the boys had drowned, and that the crowd had murdered innocent Jews. Things went from bad to worse: in 1199 Jews were killed in the German city of Erfurt because of a similar allegation.

In 1235, thirty-two Jews were killed in Fulda (Germany) without any legal process to deal with the allegation of ritual infanticide. Fortunately, Emperor Frederic II immediately appointed a commission of inquiry consisting of clergymen and noblemen. These gentlemen concluded that, on the basis of the Bible, it was highly unlikely that Jews would ever quench their thirst with human blood, and that therefore the Jews in Fulda must have been innocent. Thereupon, the emperor forbade all his subjects from ever launching such a complaint against the Jews again. It did not help very much: in numerous cases involving disappearances or the discovery of human corpses, Jews were blamed. In 1247, Pope Innocent IV repeated that those who knew anything about the Jewish religion had to acknowledge how ridiculous the allegation of ritual murder was. Therefore, he insisted that the Jews should be treated in a friendly and benevolent way.

Again, this did not help very much. It was a Flemish Dominican, Thomas of Cantimpré, who proclaimed in 1263 in his *Bieënboek* ("Book of Bees") the nonsense that Jews suffered from a strange diarrhea, which could be healed only in two ways: either the Jews so afflicted must convert to Christianity, or they must annually murder Christians in order to use their blood as a medicine.

In the fifteenth century, the "blood libel" emerged again. In 1475, in Trent the corpse of a three-year-old boy was found, named Simon. Immediately, without any basis a Franciscan penitentiary preacher and the local bishop accused the Jews of having martyred and murdered little Simon. A great number of Jews was taken captive, and a mock trial was organized against them. The Doge of Venice *and* the Duke of Tirol *and*

Pope Sixtus IV came to the defense of the falsely accused Jews. Nevertheless, the bishop had a number of Jews killed. Great pressure was put on the Pope in order to canonize little "Simon of Trent." Pope Sixtus refused, but later Pope Gregory XIII did canonize him. Centuries passed before, in 1965, Pope Paul VI removed him from the Calendar of Saints, so that this blot was finally erased. However, the imprint of this shameful blot cannot be removed so easily.

Many other examples of such disgraceful accusations could be mentioned. Let me limit myself to a relatively recent example, namely, from the nineteenth century. It is the so-called Damascus affair.[82] In 1840, in this city a physician disappeared, father Tommaso da Calangianus. Thereupon, his fellow monks began to spread the story that he had been ritually murdered by the Jews. Seven Jews were imprisoned and severely tortured; but they kept declaring their innocence. One died under torture, a second one was forced to join Islam, the remaining five "confessed" their "guilt" under the most severe pressure. The affair drew international attention, because the allegation had originated with Christians but had been processed by the Muslim authorities. Protesters from many countries traveled to Damascus, so that ultimately the authorities were forced to release all their Jewish prisoners. Most of them had been irreparably mutilated. In this crime, Muslims and Christians had been fraternally united.

---

82. See https://en.wikipedia.org/wiki/Damascus_affair.

Chapter 8
Later Jewish-Christian Relationships

The mission among the Jews must not intend to make a single proselyte—something for which no distinct mission is needed—but rather to attack the essence of rabbinism in its aortic center, and to this end, armed with thorough knowledge, to punish the arrogance of the Jews in this thorny terrain through the Law, and only when that arrogance is broken, to heal the wound through the Gospel.

Abraham Kuyper[1]

8.1 The Reformed and the Jews
8.1.1 The Second Reformation

The Anglo-Saxon Calvinists developed a rather unique relationship to the Jews. For example, the Puritans following Oliver Cromwell, who assumed a benevolent attitude toward the Jews, featured on their banner the phrase "The Lion of Judah," based on Revelation 5:5: "Weep no more; behold, the Lion of the tribe of Judah, the Root of David, has conquered,

---

1. Kuyper in *Acta* (1890, 5).

so that he can open the scroll and its seven seals" (cf. Gen. 49:9).

These Puritans also loved to adopt biblical names drawn especially from the Tanakh. They wished the Council of the State in England to consist of seventy members, like the ancient Sanhedrin (the Jewish Council). In 1649, the proposal was made in the Parliament to move the Sabbath back from Sunday to Saturday.[2] The Puritans who emigrated to America liked to compare their journey with the exodus of Israel, and they called the bay of Massachusetts the "New Jerusalem" (cf. Rev. 3:12; 21:2, 9). There was even a proposal to make Hebrew the official language of the colonies, and the Puritan John Cotton thought that the Mosaic Torah ought to be made the foundation for legislation.[3] To be sure, all these Jewish tendencies disappeared rather quickly.

As far as the Netherlands is concerned, we notice that mention of Israel is conspicuously lacking in the Reformed confessional documents, the so-called Three Forms of Unity. The Heidelberg Catechism makes no mention of Israel. The Canons of Dordt contain three brief references to Israel in the Tanakh. The Belgic Confession, too, contains three brief references, one of which is negative (Art. 9): the doctrine of the Trinity has always been maintained "against Jews, Muslims, and certain false Christians and heretics." There is not a single word about the special plans that God still has with Israel; contemporaneous and future Israel are totally outside the picture. This gives the thoroughly erroneous impression that biblical Christianity can exist without any connection with biblical Israel.

In this respect, these confessional documents fully reflect the views of millions of Christians worldwide, who, in their understanding of the gospel, see no need for including Israel in their system. To them, Christianity is about forgiveness now—or, for charismatics: about the power of the Spirit now—and heaven later. That's it—and for this, you need no

---

2. See especially the Puritan Thomas Shepard, *Theses sabbaticae* (1649).
3. See his *An Abstract of the Laws of New England* (http://reformed.org/ethics/index.html?mainframe=/ ethics/laws_of_new_england.html).

Israel. Ask such Christians for a brief summary of the gospel of God's grace for poor sinners, and they will quickly provide an answer. But then ask them for a similar brief summary of the "gospel of the kingdom" (Matt. 4:23; 9:35; 24:14); usually they scarcely know what to answer (except when they confuse the "kingdom of heaven" with "heaven"). Their gospel is *individualistic* and *heaven-oriented*, where the gospel of the kingdom is *collective* and oriented toward the *restoration of God's creation*. Their idea of the kingdom refers to the present, or perhaps to the new heaven and the new earth—but not to the Messianic kingdom of peace and righteousness that will be established here on earth when the Messiah returns; as the apostle Paul says, "I charge you in the presence of God and of Christ Jesus, who is to judge the living and the dead, and by his *appearing* and his *kingdom*" (2 Tim. 4:1).

Indeed, the narrow (individualistic, heaven-oriented) gospel of these Christians needs no Israel. But in the (collective, world restoration-oriented) gospel of the kingdom, the Messiah, Zion, Israel, and the throne of David occupy the central place. And *this* is the gospel that will be preached in particular in the end time (Matt. 24:14): "[T]his gospel of the kingdom will be proclaimed throughout the whole world as a testimony to all nations, and then the end will come"—"the end" meaning here "the end of the [present] age" (v. 3), that is, the age immediately preceding the "age to come" (Heb. 5:6), the Messianic age.

One theologian has written extensively about the views of many seventeenth- and eighteenth-century pastors of the Second Reformation with regard to Israel.[4]

(a) First, following Luther and Calvin, committed supersessionists ("replacement theologians") saw the church as the "spiritual Israel" that has replaced ethnic Israel, which as such no longer has a biblical future. Some examples were Samuel Maresius and Jacobus Fruytier.

(b) Second, some theologians believed that Romans 11:26 ("all Israel is saved") was definitely speaking about ethnic Israel, and not about some spiritual Israel. At the same time,

---
4. Van Campen (2007).

however, they spiritualized the prophecies in the Tanakh, and rejected the idea of a literal return to, and restoration of Israel in, the Holy Land. Some examples were Johannes Hoornbeeck and one of the best known of all: Gisbertus Voetius.

(c) The third group of theologians believed in de fulfillment of the land promise, but not in the rebuilding of the temple as described in Ezekiel 40–44. Some examples were Jacobus Koelman and Wilhelmus à Brakel.

(d) The fourth group of theologians believed in a literal rebuilding of the temple, and even in a restoration of the Jewish sacrificial ministry; a well-known example was Theodorus van der Groe, but he was quite exceptional. Modern Reformed supersessionists seem to completely ignore groups (b), (c), and (d). Personally I am quite sympathetic to the views of Van der Groe, this last representative of the Second Reformation in the Netherlands (seventeenth- and eighteenth century).

8.1.2 Anti-Semitism

Some supersessionists, like Jacobus Fruytier, made remarkably anti-Semitic statements about the Jews of their own time. Some theologians who saw that God had a tremendous future in store for Israel sometimes made such statements (Gisbertus Voetius, Jacobus Koelman, Simon Oomius) (see §7.4). Voetius, *the* leader and representative of Reformed orthodoxy at the time, called the Jews greedy and hypocritical, and viewed their virtues as nothing but carnal zeal and all their ostensibly good works as "glamorous sins." As great as his expectation was for the future of ethnic Israel, so harsh was his condemnation of the Jews of his time.

Theologically this can be understood to the extent that future Israel will consist of repentant and renewed Jews, whereas the Jewry of Voetius' day may have included greedy, hypocritical, carnal Jews, just as every religion includes nominal adherents. But Voetius was able to discern the truly righteous and godly people among the Reformed, so why then was he unable to discern the righteous and godly people among the Jews of his day? Is this not *the* characteristic of anti-Semitism to assert that *the* Jews are this or that? Apparently, it is possible to believe in a glorious future for ethnic (repentant) Israel, and at the same time be an anti-Semite toward one's contemporaneous Jews. Surprisingly, we encounter this phenomenon among the pre-millennialists of the nineteenth- and twentieth-centuries as well.

In opposition to this, theologians who are not considered part of the Second Reformation, like Johannes Coccejus and in particular Hero Sibersma, and also Arminians—who continued to call themselves Reformed![5]—such as Hugo Grotius and Simon Episcopius, assumed a very tolerant attitude toward the Jews of their day. However, even Coccejus could not avoid making occasional remarks that we today would call outright anti-Semitic. Grotius argued for a dialogue with the Jews, but on the condition that the Jews would first renounce the Talmud. (This is the same as saying to your opponent: I allow you to remain Reformed, but in view of our dialogue you must first renounce the Three Forms of Unity.) He also warned against an all too large expansion of Jewry because this could entail an economic threat for the legitimate interests of the Christian population of his own country.

Such examples illustrate that Christians have always had an ambivalent attitude toward Israel and Judaism. This is true of a-, post- or pre-millennialists, supersessionists or (as Steven Paas calls them) "Israelists," anti-Semites or philo-Semites. Zechariah 12:2–3 (DARBY) says,

> Behold, I will make Jerusalem a *cup of bewilderment* unto all the peoples round about, and also against Judah shall it be in the siege against Jerusalem. And it shall come to pass in that day that I will make Jerusalem a *burdensome stone* unto all peoples: all that burden themselves with it shall certainly be wounded.

As an application of this passage, we may say that Israel has always been a "cup of bewilderment" and a "burdensome stone" for Christians, and it will be so until the return

---

5. Cf. the dissertation by William den Boer (2008) on Arminius; the fact that he called Arminius "Reformed" caused a buzz among his Christian Reformed (Christelijke Gereformeerde) fellow church members.

of Christ. Most Jews did not and do, not discern who Jesus was and is; most Christians did not and do not discern who Israel was and is: they usually fail to discern the *tzaddiqim* in Israel, and they fail to realize that Jesus was not first and foremost *their* Savior, but *Israel's* Messiah: its Anointed King. Most Jews cannot imagine Jesus sitting on the throne of his Father in heaven; most Christians cannot imagine Jesus one day sitting on the throne of David in Jerusalem. Which group is worse?

One thing has improved: today there is more serious (and warm) dialogue between Jews and Christians than ever before. But Jews still do not feel *understood* by Christians. They appreciate the increased affection, but at the same time they are a little scared of it, thinking of all the past centuries. As one Dutch rabbi has put it: "Formerly, we were *hurt* to death by the Christians, today we are *hugged* to death by them.[6] We do not appreciate very much either the one, or the other." I can imagine their apprehension; I would be scared, too, if the lion suddenly sits before me and offers me his paw.

8.1.3 Abraham Kuyper

Let us now consider *the* leader of the Reformed world around 1900: the Dutch theologian, pastor, politician, and prime minister, Abraham Kuyper. During a "Mission Congress" in 1890, he made the following remarkable statement (see the quotation at the beginning of this chapter):

> The mission among the Jews must not intend to make a single proselyte—something for which no distinct mission is needed—but rather to attack the essence of rabbinism[7] in its aortic center, and to this end, armed with thorough knowledge, to punish the arrogance of the Jews in this thorny terrain through the Law, and only when that arrogance is broken, to heal the wound through the Gospel.[8]

---

6. In Dutch it sounds even better: *doodgeknuppeld – doodgeknuffeld*.
7. The term "rabbinism" refers to the totality of Talmudic-rabbinic Judaism.
8. See note 1; regarding this see extensively, Van Klinken (1996).

This statement does not suggest much love for the Jewish people, whereas love is, or should be, the condition for all true missionary activity. Instead, this statement displays a certain arrogance in suggesting that one can win over their opponent to their own position by breaking the opponent's arrogance. To be honest, this statement resembles more closely the arrogance of Job's friends than the warmth of the true gospel preacher's heart.

Kuyper did not believe in a biblical future for a (repentant) ethnic Israel in the Holy Land; he was a staunch supersessionist. Moreover, he adopted a negative posture toward the Jews of his day. Yet, he believed that one should try to win them for "the gospel," that is (in his view), for the Reformed Churches. In this respect, he differed from his more hyper-Calvinist coreligionists who had joined the Secession of 1834, and who had deep respect for the Jewish people, also for the Jews of their own day. Hyper-Calvinists and Kuyperian Reformed differ in this respect to this day. We must mention, though, that after the Holocaust the attitude of the latter has become milder, whereas among both groups supersessionism is equally strong today.

Unfortunately, during the Nazi period, the attitude of G. H. Kersten, the founder of the Netherlands Reformed Congregations, was too positive toward the Germans, and too negative toward the Jews.[9] In general, during the Nazi occupation (1940–1945), the Dutch hyper-Calvinists were more inclined to view the Nazi government as the legitimate government in the sense of Romans 13—"it is God's will that they are in power now because of our sins"—and therefore were less inclined to support the Dutch Jews. The Kuyperian Reformed, however, though staunch supersessionists, were magnanimous in helping the Jews, and vigorous in opposing the Nazi occupation. Although there were clear exceptions on both sides, we can see that the attitude of the Reformed toward the Jews was complicated and mixed; but things were not very different among Lutherans, Anglicans, and Evangelicals.

---

9. See, e.g., Golverdingen (1993); Van Beek (2007); https://www.reforum.nl/forum/viewtopic.php?t=6111.

Between the establishment of the Kuyperian Reformed Churches in 1886 and World War II, Kuyperians did their best to win Jews to their faith. At the same time, they sometimes displayed resentment when Jews advanced in the banking world and in the legal profession beyond the Kuyperians.[10] This was because, in their perception, the Jews did *not* belong to the Dutch nation, even though they had Dutch passports.[11] In the (in)famous ancient battle cry, *God, Neêrland en Oranje* ("God, Netherlands and Orange"), "Netherlands" was thought to refer specifically to the Dutch Calvinists, so in their view, adherents of false religions did *not* belong. That included Jews and Roman Catholics (not to mention Arminians, Mennonites, Baptists, etc.).

Moreover, the slogan "God, Netherlands and Orange" is supersessionist *par excellence* because "Netherlands" is here understood to refer to some (spiritual) "Israel," and (the house of) "Orange" to a kind of spiritual "house of David." You need only read the eighth stanza of the Dutch national anthem, in which prince William of Orange says,

> O David, thou soughtest shelter
> From King Saul's tyranny.
> Even so I fled this welter
> And many a lord with me.
> But God the Lord did save me
> From exile and its hell
> And, in His mercy, gave him
> A realm in Israel.[12]

The inference is that God would similarly give a kingdom to prince William (cf. volume IV/1a, §4.5).

Especially in the eighteenth and nineteenth centuries, this notion became very widespread in Calvinist Nether-

---

10. A common nickname for them was *mannen broeders*, lit. "men brothers" (Gk. *andres adelphoi*), as we find it in Acts 1:16; 2:29, 37.
11. Some of them had ancestors who had been living in the Netherlands for several centuries, whereas, for instance, only two of Kuyper's own eight great-grandparents were Dutch.
12. See https://en.wikipedia.org/wiki/Wilhelmus.

lands. The Dutch war of freedom against Spain was compared to the liberation of Israel from Egypt. Prince William of Orange was not only a kind of new David, but also a kind of new Moses.[13] In this romanticized picture, there was no place for Jews (neither for the non-Reformed Dutch, for that matter).

8.2 The Jewish Influx into the Netherlands

8.2.1 Sephardic Jews

At the Union of Utrecht (1579), the northern part of the Low Countries, which is more or less modern Netherlands, had declared freedom of conscience for all religions and convictions. This was a remarkably modern action, which showed great tolerance (except on the part of the strictest Calvinists, who had vigorously opposed such religious freedom). Even if the Dutch provinces had in view here especially Roman Catholics and Anabaptists, it was especially the Iberian marranos (see §7.6) who came to make grateful use of it. From about 1593, the first marranos arrived in the city of Amsterdam. Some of them came directly from Spain and Portugal. Others came from Antwerp, where many marranos had settled already in the beginning of the sixteenth century, shortly after the Disaster Year 1492. When the Spanish conquered Antwerp (1585), many marranos went to the northern Low Countries, especially to Amsterdam. But even after these left, to this very day, the city's *Haredi* ("ultra-orthodox") Jewish community is, relatively speaking, one of the largest among all the cities of the world.

At first, Amsterdam looked suspiciously at the Jews from Spain and Antwerp,[14] not so much because they were Jews but rather because the Eighty Years' War of the Netherlands against Spain (1568–1648) was still raging, and because the Dutch were suspicious of all those who came from the Iberian Peninsula. At first, the marranos attended mass, as they

---

13. See, e.g., W. Meijer, "Oranje en Israël," in A. J. Servaas van Rooijen (1898, 434–52); Huisman (1983).
14. Flemish Antwerp (now Belgium) belonged to southern Netherlands, which was still under Spanish rule.

had done in Spain and Portugal. However, with the so-called "Alteration" of 1598, Amsterdam joined the cities that after 1572 had been resisting the Spanish regime and deposed the Roman Catholic city government. From that moment, the marranos openly returned, with a feeling of relief, to the religion of their fathers. Their first (Ashkenazi) rabbi was Uri HaLevi, originally from Emden (Germany). Shortly after, the new city authorities gave permission to the Jews to openly live out their faith. This occurred not only because of the city's religious tolerance but also, as we saw, because the Portuguese Jews brought with them much capital and important commercial relationships, which led to increased prosperity for Amsterdam.

In the same year, 1598, the first synagogue was founded in Amsterdam. A few years later, a Sephardic rabbi arrived, Joseph Pardo from Venice, so that there was both an Ashkenazi and a Sephardic Jewish community in Amsterdam. In 1608, a second synagogue was founded, and in 1618 a third one. The Calvinist city government did tolerate other religious convictions, but preferentially in such a way that their meeting places (churches, synagogues) were not conspicuous. Therefore, it took until 1639 before the Portuguese Jews received permission to build a synagogue that was clearly recognizable as such from the street. In 1675, the famous Portuguese-Israelite Synagogue (called the *Snoge*) was completed, which is still standing at the Mr. Visser Square,[15] and at that time was the largest synagogue in the world. It was built according to a wooden model of Solomon's temple, made by Rabbi Jacob Juda Leon Templo (notice his name) on the basis of his fertile imagination. If there was any Jewish "temple" at the time, it must have been at Amsterdam!

8.2.2 "Dutch Jerusalem"

For a long time, three phenomena were increasing simultaneously in the Netherlands, especially in Amsterdam: the influx of ever newer groups of Jews, the flourishing of Jew-

---

15. Named after Judge Lodewijk Ernst Visser who, as president of the Supreme Court in the Netherlands, strongly opposed the oppression of the Jews during the Nazi occupation.

ish life, religiously and culturally, and the economic flourishing of the city. Amsterdam ought never to forget how much it owes its development as a world trade center to the Jews (besides other factors). The Sephardic Jews invested capital in the *Verenigde Oost-Indische Compagnie* (VOC, "United East India Company," in English better known as the Dutch East India Company), oriented especially to what is now Indonesia) and in the *West-Indische Compagnie* (WIC, West India Company, oriented especially to what is now Suriname and the Dutch Antilles). They also invested in rising industries, and in opening up overseas territories. The VOC was the first formally listed public company, the forerunner of modern corporations. Imagine what it would have been without the contributions of the Jews! Between 1585 and 1672, Amsterdam became the most important market in the world.

By and by, Amsterdam acquired no fewer than four nicknames, all four of which had a Jewish meaning: (a) the "Dutch Jerusalem," (b) *Em b'Yisra'ēl* ("Mother in Israel"),[16] (c) another Jewish name: *Mokum* (Ashkenazi pronunciation of Heb. *maqom*, "place" in the sense of dwelling-place[17]), and (d) the name *Hamehulloloh* ("the Highly Praised"). Important Portuguese-Jewish family names dating from those days and still present in the Netherlands are de Castro, Teixeira de Mattos, Nunes da Costa, Lopez Suasso and Lopez Cardozo, de Pinto, Querido, Belmonte, Coutinho, and Capadoce.[18]

Not only did Jewish religious studies flourish, but so did Jewish (natural) scientists, literary men, and artists who had found their way to Amsterdam. One of the most important scholars of marrano descent was Manasseh ben Israel (Portuguese name: Manoel Dias Soeiro), rabbi, kabbalist, diplomat, printer, and publisher. His portrait has been painted

---

16. Cf. Judg. 5:7 (the prophetess Deborah) and 2 Sam. 20:19 (the city of Abel-Beth-Maacha).
17. In Yiddish, many cities were referred to in this way, usually with an additional letter, such as *Mokum Beis* ("City B") for Berlin. In the end, the reference *Mokum* remained preserved for Amsterdam alone.
18. Poet-historian Isaac da Costa (see Da Costa [1849]), his wife Hanna Belmonte, and the physician Abraham Capadoce were well-known nineteenth-century Jews who joined the Dutch Reformed Church.

by Rembrandt van Rijn, who was also his friend. Rembrandt bought a house in the middle of the Jewish quarter, and was befriended by so many Jews that some thought that he was Jewish.

Speaking of publishers: in addition to Manasseh ben Israel, there were Jewish publishers like Immanuel Benveniste, David de Castro Tartas, and father and son Joseph, and Immanuel Athias. Influential books, sometimes written by Jewish scholars who lived far away, were printed in Amsterdam. One example is the encyclopedic ethical work *Sn'nē Luchot HaB'rit* ("The Two Tablets of the Covenant"), written by Rabbi Isaiah Horowitz[19] (see §4.1.1), which his son had published in 1648 by Benveniste.

It must certainly be called peculiar—and not a coincidence—that, since 1967, at least five mayors of Amsterdam had Jewish roots: Ivo Samkalden, Wim Polak, Ed van Thijn, Job Cohen, and Lodewijk Asscher (deputy mayor).

8.2.3 Ashkenazi Jews

During the Thirty Years' War (1618-1648) between Roman Catholics and Protestants in Central Europe, a very different group of Jews moved to Amsterdam (since 1635), namely, the much less prosperous Ashkenazy or German Jews, followed in 1648 by Polish Jews, and in 1655 by Lithuanian Jews. Because these poor Jews did not become citizens of Amsterdam, many professions remained closed to them; however, they could become diamond cutters, brokers, surgeons, pharmacists, booksellers and traders in old clothes (*voddenjood*, "trashy Jew"). In 1673, the Hungarian and the Polish Jews joined to become one German-Jewish congregation.

At the same time, there was and remained a considerable distance between the Sephardic and the Ashkenazy Jews in Amsterdam. Such was the case with respect to religious attitude (former marranos versus deeply pious Jews) as well as

---

19. Later in life, he became the Chief Ashkenazi Rabbi of Jerusalem; he was nicknamed the Sh'lah or Shalah, or even Shalah Qadosh ("Holy Shalah"), Sh-L-H being the acronym of *Sn'nē Luchot HaB'rit*. The work contains a chapter for each *parashah* (weekly Torah portion). The Shalah lists the commandments found in each parashah, and explains their stated and hidden meanings.

with respect to socio-economic status (rich versus poor) and cultural engagement (often strongly secularized versus ascetic).

Actually, many Portuguese Jews were certainly strict about doctrine, perhaps partly because many of them had been forced to be marranos. Therefore, it was understandable, yet very painful, that in 1665 the rabbis expelled the still young, brilliant philosopher Baruch de Spinoza[20] from the synagogue. Ultimately, he was to become one of the most famous Dutch thinkers, with worldwide renown.

It was especially the more liberal Protestant magistrates such as mayor Cornelis Pieterszoon Hooft (father of the well-known man of letters, Pieter Corneliszoon Hooft) who, partly out of self-interest, recognized the potential of the Jews, and granted them room to live and to function freely. As a consequence, the Jews in the Netherlands faced less persecution. However, in general, ardent Calvinists did not have a very positive attitude toward the Jews (§4.6.3). Even after the establishment of the so-called Batavian Republic (1795–1806) in the Netherlands (under French supervision), when the National Assembly granted the Jews complete equality, the latter occurred under the strong protests of the Utrecht theology professor IJsbrand van Hamelsveld. Nevertheless, after the fall of Napoleon, of all the countries that until 1814 had been under French supremacy, the Netherlands was the only country that continued to allow the Jews complete equality of rights after the liberation from the French.

8.3 The State of Israel

8.3.1 Three Miracles

Let us now jump to the twentieth century, which has been so dramatic for Israel. Two combinations of events stand out: first, the Holocaust; second, the establishment of the state of Israel, only three years after the end of World War II. A third important event was the rise of the Messianic movement,

---

20. Afterwards, he called himself Benedictus de Spinoza (Benedictus meaning the same as Baruch: "Blessed"); his main work, the *Ethica*, was published after his death.

that is, the Messiah-confessing (i.e., Jesus-believing) Jews—a process that, on a limited scale, had begun long before the war.

The state of Israel is a miraculous phenomenon. First, it is a miracle that, throughout the centuries, the people of Israel have never been completely assimilated into the Gentile world, but have preserved their own identity. No doubt, Israel has intermingled with many nations: there are white, brown, black, and yellow Jews, so to speak. However, due to the Tanakh and the Talmud, due to the Sabbath and the other Jewish calendar highlights, due to circumcision and food laws, and due to the indestructible Messianic hope, there is today a nation of Israel, which is religiously identifiable and genetically consolidated, even today (see §4.7). In Suriname, a former Dutch colony, it is assumed that, at one time, one-third of the white population was Jewish, and, like the other whites, they easily intermingled with the black population.

Second, it is a miracle that Israel was never completely exterminated, although many world powers, smaller countries, and individual malefactors had tried to do this, from the Pharaoh of Egypt to the *Führer* of Nazi Germany, and many other foes. We must realize how incredible this is. In the course of history, numerous people groups have either assimilated—so that they are no longer identifiable—or have been massacred or have died out. However, Israel, a people with its totally unique religious and ethnic identity, still exists after more than three thousand years. All those empires that have opposed Israel, from the ancient Egyptian kingdom of Pharoah to the Nazi empire, have drowned in the ocean of history. But Israel is still alive—(partly) living today in the very same country where it had lived for many centuries a long time ago.

Third, consider the miracle that, in 1918, and the end of World War I, the political situation in the Middle East had changed so much, especially through the fall of the Ottoman Empire, that a Jewish home in the Holy Land had suddenly become an option. For centuries, the well-known words from the *haggada* of the Seder night, *Shana haba'a birushalayyim*

("Next year in Jerusalem"), had seemed an impossible dream. Only a limited number of Jews had managed to sustain themselves throughout the centuries in *HaAretz*. However, on September 3, 1897, after the Zionist congress in Basel the Jewish journalist and leading Zionist, Theodor Herzl, wrote in his diary: "In Basel I founded the Jewish state. . . . Perhaps in five years, at any rate in fifty years everybody will see it."[21]

He turned out to be a secular prophet. Indeed, fifty years later, on November 29, 1947, the General Assembly of the United Nations approved by a two-thirds majority a division of the Holy Land between Palestinian Jews and Palestinian Arabs,[22] and thereby cleared the way for a Jewish state. Actually, this also made possible a Palestinian-Arab state, but the Arabs did not avail themselves of the opportunity. This was because they, as well as the rest of the Arab Muslim world, wanted to possess the *entire* country for themselves; they believed that, through war, it would not be too difficult to conquer all of Palestine.[23] No wonder: there were a hundred times more Arabs than Jews in the region! Driving out the Jews would be a piece of cake.

Since then, they have been saddled with the consequences of this foolish omission and of failing to destroy the Jewish state. They talk constantly about having their own Palestinian state, and they could have had it for three quarters of a century now. (To be sure, many Jews—religious and secular—would love to have the entire country, too, but they were pragmatic enough to be satisfied in 1948 with the possibilities available to them at that time.)

8.3.2 Two More Miracles

That approval by the General Assembly of the United Nations was the fourth miracle (and, humanly speaking, would

---

21. *Encyclopaedia Judaica*, 2003, 2nd edition, 9:66.
22. Not "Jews and Palestinians," for until that time the Jewish inhabitants of the Holy Land had been called "Palestinians" as well; any inhabitant of *HaAretz* is a Palestinian.
23. Saada (2016, 177–78) pointed to Matt. 5:5, "Blessed are the meek, for they shall inherit the earth [or, the land"— not "conquer" it. Actually, this is true for both Palestinian Arabs as well as Jews.

be totally inconceivable at the present time, now that the enemies of Israel are in the majority within that organization). It led to a series of events that is unknown in history: a nation that, thousands of years ago, lost its territory, managed to preserve its identity throughout the centuries, and returned to its ancient territory. It did so in order to establish a nation state there, as of old, and, since 1980, did so with Jerusalem, including Old Jerusalem (within its Turkish walls) as its "everlasting capital." There is an incredibly remarkable continuity—with interruptions—from the entrance of Israel into the Promised Land (see the book of Joshua) until this day, no matter how strongly Muslims and others have tried to deny this historical continuity.[24]

The fifth miracle is that the establishment of the state of Israel was proclaimed on May 14, 1948,[25] and that it managed to sustain itself until today, despite the enormous numerical preponderance of its Arabic opponents. Even supersessionists cannot avoid the conclusion that God's sovereign protection became visible here in an exceptional way. Israel had to face the War of Independence, beginning on May 15, 1948, in which it lost the ancient city of Jerusalem. Then, there was the Suez crisis of 1956, the Six-Day War of June 1967, the *Yom Kippur* war of 1973, the Lebanese Wars of 1982 and 2006, the First Intifada (1987-1993) and the Second Intifada (2000-2005), and the Gaza War (2008-2009). In the meantime, Israel has peace treaties with Egypt and Jordan, and in 2020 established diplomatic relationships with Bahrain, the United Arab Emirates, Sudan, and Morocco. But officially it is still at war with Syria, while Iran constitutes a permanent and increasing threat.

---

24. In the Camp David conference (2000), Yasser Arafat asserted that there had never been a Jewish temple in Jerusalem, but one *had* existed in Nablu (https://en.wikipedia.org/wiki/Temple_Denial).

25. On May 14, David Ben-Gurion read the Declaration of Independence, but on May 15, the British Mandate expired, so that this was the first day of the actual existence of the state of Israel. On the Hebrew calendar, May 14 (*Yom ha'Atzma'ut*, "Day of Independence") is 5 Iyyar, a date that in 2021 falls on April 14/15, in 2022 on May 4/5, and in 2023 on April 25/26.

Some Christians hailed the foundation of the state of Israel as a fulfillment of biblical prophecies, or at least the beginning of, or the run-up to, this fulfillment. Other, especially Reformed, Christians hastened to assure us that they were happy with this new state for the Jews, but that it had nothing to do with biblical prophecies.[26] For a long time, Vatican City, as a political entity, hesitated to acknowledge the state of Israel, but in 1993, forty-five years after the establishment of the state, it happened under Pope John Paul II. In this year, the two reached a "Fundamental Accord." In 1994, Israel received a Vatican *nuntius*, and Vatican City received an Israeli ambassador (which is nearly equivalent). For the rest, the official standpoint of the Roman Catholic Church is also that the establishment of the state of Israel is not a fulfillment of biblical prophecies. The ecclesiastical establishment, Eastern Orthodox, or Roman Catholic, or Protestant, maintains its supersessionism—but with an increasing number of exceptions.

Many orthodox Jews were, and are, also a bit reluctant to link this state with the biblical prophecies, and understandably so. As a rabbi told me, in principle it is possible that this state, too, will be destroyed, that the Jews will be dispersed again, and that they will return again to Israel at a much later time. Some *Haredi* ("ultra-orthodox") groups have completely rejected, and still reject, the state of Israel with the argument that it is the Messiah alone who may, can, and will grant such a state to his people, and that this will occur only after the repentance and spiritual restoration of the Jewish nation.[27] This is also the standpoint of Christians who do see in the establishment of the state of Israel the hand of God, and even the run-up for the fulfillment of the prophetic Word, but who also believe that this fulfillment requires the repentance and

---

26. Aalders (1949, 31): "What has happened in Palestine, and whatever may further happen there, has nothing to do with the divine prophecy offered to us in Holy Scripture."
27. See, e.g., https://chabadcurrents.wordpress.com/2016/05/12/chabad-zionism-complicated-relationship/.

spiritual restoration of Israel.[28] This matter will be dealt with in following chapters.

8.4 "Messianic Jews"
8.4.1 A New Movement

For some forty years now, we have been witnessing the rapid rise of an entirely new phenomenon, which began in the late nineteenth century: that of the so-called "Messianic" (Messiah-confessing, i.e., Jesus-confessing) Jews. This is a confusing appellation, for *all* orthodox Jews confess (the coming of) the Messiah. We are dealing here with a group of Jews who believe that *Jesus of Nazareth* was, and is, the expected Messiah; therefore, it would be more accurate to call this the movement of the "Jesus-believing" (or, "Yeshuah-believing") Jews. I can understand, however, why they wished to introduce that word "Messiah": they wish to emphasize that Jesus is not only their personal Lord and Savior, but also the Messiah of Israel.

These Jesus-believing Jews must be distinguished from what has been referred to as "Hebrew Christians." These latter are people of Jewish descent who have preserved very little of their Jewish identity, and usually are members of the established churches. They differ very little, if at all, from their Gentile fellow church members. Messianic Jews, however, wish explicitly and emphatically to retain their Jewish identity. They prefer not to call themselves "Christians" for at least two sets of reasons. First, there are historical reasons: the term "Christian" is loaded with too many negative connotations. Second, they do not wish to be confused with "Hebrew Christians" because they highly value their Jewish identity, which they (rightly and consistently) view as God-given. For similar reasons, they prefer the name "Yeshuah" to the name "Jesus." These Messianic Jews circumcise their sons, observe the Sabbath and the other Jewish festivals,[29] while the men often wear a *tallit* (a praying garment) as well as a *kippa* (or

---

28. See, e.g., Deut. 30:1–10; Ezek. 36–37; Zech. 12–14.
29. Regarding the Jewish festivals and Messianic Jews, see Van de Poll (2008, especially chapter 3).

yarmulke) and *tzitziyyot* (tallit edges; cf. Num. 15:38-39). In short, they live and function as ordinary orthodox Jews—or as Jews of a more conservative[30] or Reform type—with the tremendous difference that they believe that Jesus is the Messiah of Israel.

The group is very heterogeneous, just as orthodox Jews and orthodox Christian are. On the strictest side, we find orthodox Jews who, in their synagogues, do not differ in any respect from other orthodox Jews, except in their preaching, in which they confess their faith in Yeshua haMashiach (Jesus the Messiah).[31] More centrist are groups of people who are strongly attached to the Mosaic Torah, but do not feel bound to all the Talmudic expositions and applications of it. They are comparable to (non-Jesus-believing) Jews of the more conservative or Reform type. And on the other side, we find groups that are scarcely different from ordinary Evangelical congregations, except that they observe the Sabbath and other Jewish holy days, administer circumcision, and live according to the biblical food laws.

As far as the third type of Messianic congregations is concerned, the knowledge of Judaism seems occasionally rather limited here. Perhaps we might better call them Evangelical congregations with some Jewish fringe. This is not meant as a criticism; these congregations may determine for themselves what type of Jesus-believing lives and congregations they believe are most biblical and preferable.

8.4.2 The Jewishness of Messianic Jews

Neither Jews nor Christians have the right to deny Messianic Jews their Jewishness. This is because they are people born

---

30. Conservative Judaism is more liberal than (ultra-)orthodox Judaism; it endeavors to steer between retaining the ancient Jewish traditions and opening up to modern life; Reform Judaism constitutes an even more liberal form. What is decisive is the significance attached to what is called the "Oral Torah," thought to be contained in especially the Talmud: is it absolutely binding on all Jews, or not?

31. A conspicuous example is Joseph Shulam, well-known, e.g., from his commentary on the letter to the Romans (1998).

of Jewish mothers, and because they practice their Jewishness (circumcision, Sabbath, festivals, food laws) better than do many secular Jews. How could anyone claim, for instance, that a Jewish atheist or Buddhist is more Jewish than a Messianic Jew because the former does not believe in Jesus, and the latter does?

At best, we could say that these Jews are not adherents of rabbinic or Talmudic Judaism; but even this is not true for the most conservative of these Messianic Jews. To claim that Messianic Jews are no longer Jews is based on a circular argument: first, it is stated that a Jew can be orthodox or liberal, Buddhist or atheist, without losing their Jewish identity, but that they do lose it if they believe that Jesus of Nazareth is the Messiah of Israel.[32] By means of this—hardly consistent—statement it is subsequently "proven" that Messianic Jews are no longer Jews.

The reverse is just as inconsistent. This involves certain traditional conservative Christians who do not wish to recognize Messianic Jews as "Christians" (or, in this case, Jesus-believers). Their argument is this: true Christians know that Israel has been replaced by the church, circumcision has been replaced by infant baptism, Saturday observance has been replaced by Sunday observance as the sacred day of the week, and the earth has been replaced by heaven as the destiny of salvation. Thus, Messianic Jews have often come to inhabit a no-man's-land: rejected by both orthodox Jews and traditional Christians. The similarity between orthodox Jews and traditional Christians is that both rob the Messianic Jew of his Jewishness. The former say, You are no longer a Jew; the latter say, We do not allow you to be a Jew any longer.

The apostle Paul was perfectly right when, long after his conversion to Jesus, he said twice: "I *am* a Jew," and not, "I *was* a Jew" (Acts 21:39; 22:3). He remained "a Hebrew of Hebrews," he remained a Pharisee (Phil. 3:5; Acts 23:6; today we would say, an "orthodox Jew"). Jews who have found their

---

32. Was this claim ever made with regard to other pretended "Messiahs" of Israel? Were, for instance, the followers of Sabattai Zvi (Shabtai Tzvi) ever declared to have turned from being Jews into non-Jews?

Messiah (cf. John 1:45) do not cease being Jews, but have reached the very fullness of their Jewishness. Orthodox Jews say (as it were), Stay with us, or you will lose your Jewishness. Traditional Christians say (as it were), Come over to us, but first surrender your Jewishness. Jews say, Forget about Jesus, or you will lose your Jewishness! Christians say, Forget about your Jewishness, or you will lose Jesus! These are false choices: forcing Jews to choose between their Jewishness and Jesus!? Thank God, Messianic Jews do neither the former nor the latter. They remain what they were: Jews; and in a sense, they are more Jewish than ever before because they have found the *Jewish* Messiah. As one Jew told another Jew: "We have found him of whom Moses in the Law and also the prophets wrote, Jesus of Nazareth, the son of Joseph" (John 1:45).

Traditional Jews may disagree with this, but it is absurd to deny the Messianic Jew's Jewishness. The absurdity lies in the age-old falsehood that, when Jews come to faith in Jesus, they change religions, from Judaism to Christianity. They do not. Jesus is first and foremost the Jesus of *Jews*, not the Jesus of *Christians*. Believing Jews do not leave Judaism to embrace a Gentile Jesus, but believing Gentiles leave the idolatrous Gentile world to embrace the Jewish Jesus.

Conversely, traditional Christians from the Gentile world, with their established, totally "de-Jewishified" denominations, are just as absurd when they deny the Messianic Jew's Jewishness. Such an attitude goes back to the anti-Semitism and supersessionism of the ancient and medieval church, which was willing to accept Jesus-believing Jews only after these had fully denied their Jewish identity. Even after the Day of Pentecost (Acts 2), it could be said of the Jewish followers of Jesus: "You see, brother, how many thousands[33] there are among the Jews of those who have believed. *They are all zealous for the Torah*" (Acts 21:20). Who dares to tell modern Messianic Jews that they are no longer allowed to be "zealous for the Torah," that is, to live as a believing Jew?[34]

---

33. More literally, "myriads" (i.e., "tens of thousands").
34. See extensively, Ouweneel (2001a).

8.4.3 Judeophilia

By contrast, today many Christians of Gentile descent identify so strongly with Messianic Jews that they themselves have begun behaving like Jews. Here we encounter a fourth remarkable development in the twentieth century. This reflects the ancient error that believers from the Gentile world are supposedly incorporated into Israel. This error can move in two opposite directions, both of which are equally reprehensible because the underlying idea of incorporation is reprehensible.

The first direction is *anti-Semitic*. Jews will be accepted into the church if and only if they renounce their Jewish identity. On the one hand, this position views the church as the true Israel or spiritual Israel, while completely eliminating everything that is Jewish: Sabbath and festivals, circumcision and food laws. This is the absurdity of a totally *un*-Jewish Jewishness, or of an Israel that has nothing Israelite about it. It is like telling an Australian that they can remain Australian only if they renounce the English language and surrender their Australian passport.

The second direction is the opposite: it is the *philo-Semitic* position. This view entails that, if Jesus-believing Gentiles are indeed incorporated into the new, spiritual Israel, they must be consistent and must begin living as Jews. To be sure, Jesus-believing Gentiles are *allowed* to celebrate the Jewish festivals together with Jewish friends; they can even learn a lot from doing so. However, those who claim that Jesus-believing Gentiles are *biblically obliged* to do so are totally mistaken. Jews are under the Mosaic Torah, both if they do and if they do not believe in Jesus; their conversion to Jesus does not alter this fact in the least. We have seen in Acts 21:20 that Jesus-believing Jews were still "zealous for the Torah," just as they had been before their conversion.[35] In Christ, the Mosaic

---

35. Supersessionists have termed this a "weakness" on the part of these Jesus-believing Jews. But the text does not support this allegation at all. On the contrary, Acts 21 goes on t tell us how the apostle Paul himself showed his "zeal" for the Mosaic Torah (vv. 20–26). He called himself "zealous for God" in the same way as his Jewish accusers were (22:3).

Torah was not annulled, but fulfilled, as we have seen (Matt. 5:17).

Conversely, however, Jesus-believing Gentiles must not be put under the Mosaic Torah; this was wisely and correctly decided upon by the apostles under the explicit guidance of the Holy Spirit (Acts 15:28). The Jew, Jesus-believing or not, remains under the Mosaic Torah, whereas the Jesus-believing Gentiles never were under the Mosaic Torah, and were never placed under it. They are *allowed* the celebrate the bible festivals with the Jews, they are *allowed* to live according to the biblical food laws, and so on—why would they not?—but they are not *obliged* to do so (§1.5). They are under the "Torah of Christ" (Gal. 6:2), which is basically the great Love Commandment (cf. John 13:34-35). This is what the Mosaic Torah and the Messianic Torah have in common—but the Messianic Torah for believing Gentiles does not include the Sabbath and other festivals, circumcision and food laws.

The (psychological) difficulty of many Christians is that they live out of a kind of reaction theology: from a fully understandable aversion to supersessionism, some Jesus-believing Gentiles move to the other extreme, and assume a (pseudo-)Jewish identity. However, extreme standpoints will not help us. Instead, we must follow this fundamental principle: Jews—Jesus-believing or not— remain under the Mosaic Torah, whereas Gentiles never come under the Mosaic Torah (unless they decide to join [non-Jesus-believing] Judaism, with all the consequences that this entails).

One result of this confusion is that often both orthodox Jews and traditional Christians do not know how to deal with Messianic Jews. On the one hand, the (Jewish) erroneous view claims that Messianic Jews are no longer Jews. On the other hand, another (Christian) erroneous view insists that Messianic Jews ought not to live as Jews anymore. Notice the similarity between these two errors: Jesus-believing Jews are simply Christians; they should cease living as Jews and begin to live like Gentile Christians do. Both groups view Messianic Jews as a kind of *contradictio in terminis*, something like a square circle.

Today, a third error is added: some orthodox Christians of Gentile descent now wish to live like Jews. Some Jesus-believing Jews seem to like this very much (while others do not like this at all). What a chaotic situation: Jesus-believing Jews are urged to live as Gentiles, and Jesus-believing Gentiles are urged to live as Jews.

8.5 Jewish Cultural Blessing

8.5.1 Jewish Pioneers and Founders

Let us now look at some modern developments among Jews. Since many in the Jewish world are to a large extent secularized, they have obtained crucial positions within Western culture.[36] Some remarkable examples are found in the natural sciences and related medical sciences. Of course, Jewish natural scientists have achieved notoriety in the past; in the Middle Ages, this involved in particular astronomers/astrologers (at the time, the two could still hardly be distinguished), especially Mar Samuel, Sa'adiah Gaon, Abraham ibn Ezra, Moses Maimonides, and Levi Gersonides. The latter refuted geocentrism (the earth is the physical center of the universe) long before Nicholas Copernicus and Galileo Galilei did so; Gersonides was a thoroughly biblically thinking man. We must add, though, that after 700 this almost always involved Jewish scholars working under an Islamic regime, first on the Iberian Peninsula, later in the Ottoman Empire. In Christian countries, Jews rarely achieved success within the sciences. How many talents have remained unused in this way we will never know.[37]

Not only Christian resistance prevented Jews from devoting themselves to the natural sciences. Just as with certain Christians, sometimes their own traditional worldview—such as the geocentrism just mentioned—constituted a hindrance.

---

36. Cf. Ouweneel (2014a, Excursus 46).
37. Of course, this is also true of women; if Marie Curie had lived earlier, she would have had no chance of success. The combination of being *Jewish* and a woman is even more remarkable: in 1947, the Jewess Gerty Theresa Cori-Radnitz received the Nobel Prize for medicine together with her husband and a third person. The Jewess Rosalyn Sussman Yalow received the same prize in 1977, and Rita Levi-Montalcini did so in 1986.

Later Jewish-Christian Relationships

This was more prevalent among the much more strongly isolated Ashkenazy Jews than among the much more integrated Sephardic Jews. Not only did Christians refuse to admit Jews into their universities, but many Ashkenazy Jews rather preferred to study in their own *shuls* (synagogues) or *yeshivas* (Talmud schools).

Especially due to men like the Jewish philosopher Moses Mendelssohn (grandfather of the composer Felix Mendelssohn Bartholdy), the door to Western society was opened for Jews, even if for the time being it was only ajar. As soon as this occurred, many Jews soon managed to reach the top. If the Nobel Prize, presented for the first time in 1901, may be a good indicator, then the following is noteworthy: the first Nobel Prize for a Jew was presented in 1905, namely, to the chemist Adolf von Baeyer, in 1906 to the chemist Henri Moissan, in 1907 to the physicist Albert Abraham Michelson, in 1908 to the physiological/medical scientists Élie Metchnikoff and Paul Ehrlich and to the physicist Gabriel Lippmann, and so on. In the course of time, the Nobel Prize has been awarded to more than eight hundred people, at least 20% of whom were Jews, whereas Jews constitute only 0.2% of the world's population.

Expanding our field of vision beyond the natural sciences, we encounter thinkers who have deeply influenced modern culture (whether one agrees with them or not): the naturalist Charles Darwin,[38] the political economist Karl Marx, the politician Vladimir Lenin, the psychoanalyst Sigmund Freud, and the physicist Albert Einstein. At least three of these five were Jewish (Marx, Freud, and Einstein), and Lenin was one-quarter Jewish (§7.6.1). The point is that (adapted, secularized) Jews rose easily to the top, whether in the positive or in the negative sense.

Because of—among other things—prejudices against the Jews, various Western inventions have been attributed to

---

38. In anti-evolutionist Turkish school books, Darwin seems to have been branded a Jew as a form of scolding (https://www.abqjew.net/2013/01/charles-darwin-mot.html; see this site for [speculative] arguments that Darwin had Jewish blood).

Christians, whereas it was Jews who invented these things (if we may believe Hirsch M. Goldberg, who here and there might have been a little too nationalistic).[39]

* The invention of the zeppelin is attributed, naturally, to German Count Ferdinand von Zeppelin, but the real inventor was the Hungarian Jew David Schwarz.

* The invention of the airplane is attributed to the American brothers Wilbur and Orville Wright, but the real inventor was the German Jew Otto Lilienthal.

* The inventor of the gramophone was not the American Thomas Alva Edison, but the German-American Jew Emile Berliner.

* The inventor of the telephone was not the Scottish-American Alexander Graham Bell, but the German Jew Johann Philipp Reis; he also named the apparatus a "telephone."

* The inventor of the radio was not the Italian Guglielmo Marconi, but the German Jew Heinrich Rudolf Hertz, after whom the unit of frequency called the "hertz" was named.

In all these cases, a Jew was the inventor while a non-Jew received the honor.

8.5.2 Jewish Medical and Natural Scientists

In the Middle Ages, famous Jewish physicians included Chasdai ibn Shaprut,[40] Juda Halevi,[41] Maimonides, Gersonides,[42] Nachmanides, and Obadyah Sforno.[43]

For modern health care, Jewish scholars have been of inestimable value. John de Sequeyra showed that tomatoes are not poisonous, as Americans at first believed.

During the American Civil War, both the Union and the Confederacy appointed Jewish physicians as heads of their medical departments: Phineas Jonathan Horwitz and David Camden de Leon, respectively.

---

39. Goldberg (1993).
40. Regarding him, see Ouweneel (2014a, 296–97).
41. Regarding him, see ibid., 329–30.
42. Regarding him, see ibid., 375–76.
43. Regarding him, see ibid., 387–89.

Jewish Abraham Jacobi was the father of American pediatrics. The Jewish Simon Baruch performed the first successful appendectomy. The Jewess Aletta Jacobs was the first female physician in the Netherlands.

The Jewish Casimir Funk opened an entirely new field of research, namely, that of the vitamins; he also coined the term "vitamin."

The Jewish Paul Ehrlich found the medicine against syphilis. The term "antibiotics" comes from Jewish Selman Abraham Waksman. Jewish Jonas Edward Salk developed the first polio vaccine.

In 1965, the Nobel prize for medicine or physiology went to three men for their groundbreaking biological research. Two of them were Jews: André M. Lwoff and François Jacob. Even more remarkable is that the Nobel prize for physics in 1988 was awarded to three Jews: Leon M. Lederman, Melvin Schwartz, and Jack Steinberger for their neutrino research.

Three Jewish physicists provided initial research for the atomic bomb: Albert Einstein, Niels Bohr (Nobel Prize for physics in 1922), and Robert Oppenheimer.

During my own brief biological career (1966–1976), I attended lectures given by three Jewish natural scientists of world significance: Sydney Brenner (Nobel Prize 2002, with the Jewish H. Robert Horvitz and a non-Jew), Ilya Prigogine (Nobel Prize 1977), and Lewis Wolpert (Royal Medal in 2018). At the last biological conference I attended (Andover, NH 1976), judging by their names, no fewer than ten percent of the attending biologists were of Jewish descent.

8.5.3 Jewish Philosophers

Twentieth-century philosophy would have been impoverished without the Jewish contribution. The following list is certainly not exhaustive.

Older thinkers (from after 1500): Isaac Abravanel, Isaac Luria, Michel de Montaigne, Baruch Spinoza, Moses Mendelssohn and Karl Marx.

Neo-Kantianism: Hermann Cohen and Ernst Cassirer.

Phenomenology: Max Scheler, Edmund Husserl, and Helmuth Plessner (Jewish father, non-Jewish mother).

Existentialism: Lev Shestov, Martin Buber, Gabriel Marcel, Hannah Arendt, Emmanuel Levinas.[44]

Neo-Marxism: Walter Benjamin, György Lukács, Ernst Bloch.

Philosophy of Life: Henri Bergson.

Vienna Circle ("Wiener Kreis"): Otto Neurath, Friedrich Waismann.

Linguistic philosophy, logical positivism, postmodernism: Ludwig Wittgenstein, Alfred J. Ayer, Jacques Derrida, Noam Chomsky, Saul Kripke.

Frankfurt School: Theodor Adorno (Jewish father, non-Jewish mother), Max Horkheimer, Herbert Marcuse.

Philosophy of Science: Imre Lakatos, Michael Polanyi, Karl R. Popper, Thomas S. Kuhn, Hilary Putnam.

Structuralism: Roman Jakobson, Claude Lévi-Strauss.

Other philosophers: Franz Rosenzweig, Edith Stein, Simone Weil, Abraham Joshua Heschel, Isaiah Berlin, Alain Finkielkraut, Martha Nussbaum.

Founders of psychology: Alfred Adler, Sigmund Freud, Max Wertheimer.

Pioneers of modern mathematics: Georg Cantor, Norbert Wiener, Alfred Tarski.

Other Jewish thinkers: Émile Durkheim (social scientist), David Bohm (physicist).

8.5.4 Jewish Composers and Writers

In the great majority of cases where Jews excelled, no matter in what science or scholarly discipline, we must conclude that, with respect to religion, they were very liberal at best. Orthodox Jews were, and are, excellent in religious matters;

---

44. By contrast, one of the best-known existentialists, the non-Jewish Martin Heidegger, was an outspoken anti-Semite. Another well-known existentialist, the non-Jewish Jean-Paul Sartre, extensively analyzed anti-Semitism; see Sartre (1946).

secularized Jews were, and are, excellent in all other disciplines, both of thought and of the arts.

As far as the latter are concerned, many have followed King David, who is described as an inventor of musical instruments. The prophet Amos (6:5) speaks of those who "like David invent for themselves instruments of music." The Jews have always—or at least after they had been admitted to Western society as equal members—been masters of classical music. Consider classical music with composers who are now dead but whose music we can still hear, such as especially Felix Mendelssohn Bartholdy, Giacomo Meyerbeer, Ignaz Moscheles, Jacques Offenbach, Charles-Valentin Alkan, Anton Rubinstein, Joseph Joachim, Gustav Mahler,[45] Karl Goldmark, Paul Dukas, George Gershwin, Kurt Weill, Artur Schnabel, Arnold Schoenberg, Emmerich Kálmán, Erich W. Korngold, Ernest Bloch, Fritz Kreisler, Ernst Toch, Mario Castelnuovo-Tedesco, Otto Klemperer, Darius Milhaud, Richard Rodgers, Nathaniel Shilkret, Alexander Tansman, Leonard Bernstein, Aaron Copland, Alfred Schnittke, György Ligeti, and Philip Glass.

In 1944-1945, Shilkret designed the plan for a *Genesis Suite*, a work for narrator, chorus, and orchestra on Genesis 1-11, in which seven composers collaborated. Six of them were Jewish: Schoenberg, Shilkret himself, Tansman, Milhaud, Castelnuovo-Tedesco, and Toch; the seventh composer was Igor Stravinsky.

Some of the very greatest orchestral conductors of the last hundred years who are now dead but whose music we can still hear, were Jewish, such as Bruno Walter, Pierre Monteux, Heunz Unger, George Szell, Otto Klemperer, Jascha Horenstein, Karel Ančerl, Kirill Kondrashin, Eugene Ormandy, Antal Doráti, Leonard Bernstein, Erich Leinsdorf, Sir-Georg Solti, Kurt Sanderling, Lorin Maazel, André Previn, Mariss Jansons, and James Levine.[46]

---

45. To me, Mendelssohn and Mahler belong among the very greatest.
46. Some of these *Jews*, Walter, Unger, Klemperer, Horenstein, Ančerl, Bernstein, and Jansons, were among the greatest interpreters of the music of the *Jewish* composer Gustav Mahler. Jewish composer and conductor Berthold Gold-

Some of the greatest violinists ever, who are now dead but whose music we can still hear, were Jewish, such as David Oistrakh, Jascha Heifetz, Nathan Milstein, Yehudi Menuhin, and Isaac Stern.

Some of the greatest pianists ever, who are now dead but whose music we can still hear, were Jewish, such as Artur Schnabel, Clara Haskil, Myra Hess, Julius Katchen, Artur Rubinstein, Emil Gilels, and Vladimir Horovitz.

Finally, I mention here some Jewish men of letters who have received the Nobel Prize for literature (the year of the prize in parenthesis): Henri Bergson (1927), Boris Pasternak (1958), Nelly Sachs (1966), Saul Bellow (1976), Isaac Bashevis Singer (1978), Harold Pinter (2005), and Bob Dylan (= Robert A. Zimmerman, 2016).

In addition to them, I mention the following novelists: Marcel Proust, Franz Kafka, Stefan Zweig, Franz Werfel, Arthur Koestler, Isaac Bashevis Singer, Chaim Potok, André Schwarz-Barth, and Amos Oz.

When it comes to secularization, the situation among the "Christians," that is, the Western Gentiles with Christian roots, is in fact not much different. That is, today there are still very few orthodox Christians who belong to the top class in the field of philosophy, and the natural and medical sciences, and the arts (painting, composition, literature). Unfortunately, the combination religious-scientific, which was self-evident during the Middle Ages and in early modernity is no longer obvious. This is true for both Jews and Gentiles.

8.6 Christian Misunderstandings About Jews
8.6.1 Five Misunderstandings

In the final part of this chapter, here is the question at hand: What were and often still are the chief misunderstandings that Jews and Christians have with respect to each other? This is a rather subjective question, and has been answered at various points already. But here is a coherent summary of the answers.

---

schmidt conducted in 1964 the Deryck Cooke edition of Mahler's Tenth (and last) Symphony.

Please remember that not *all* Christians evidence *all* the following misunderstandings with regard to Jews, nor do the latter evidence *all* the following misunderstandings with regard to Christians. Absurd allegations about ritual infanticide and the like are countenanced by very few Christians, but are found only among Muslims.[47]

Here are some of the misunderstandings already discussed.

(1) "Ever since Good Friday to this day, all Jews are co-responsible for the death of Jesus, and if they do not come to faith in him, they will be lost forever."

Reply. Every sinner is responsible only for their own sins. Only the Jewish mob screaming for Jesus' death in the court of Pontius Pilate is co-responsible for the death of Jesus.

(2) "As a nation, ethnic Israel has been set aside forever as the people of God; the individual Jew will be saved only if he or she joins what is now, and from now on, the people of God, that is, the Christian church (surrendering his or her Jewish identity)."

Reply. The prophecies in the Tanakh and the New Testament show that ethnic Israel has *not* been set aside forever; one day, the Israelites will repent and spiritually return to the God of Israel, and physically to the land of Israel, and then be accepted again as people of God.

(3) "In Christ, the Mosaic Torah, or at least the civil and ceremonial laws in that Torah, that is, including the entire sacrificial ministry, has been abolished."

Reply. This is not correct; the Mosaic Torah will remain in force as long as the present earth exists; Jesus did not come to annul the Torah, but to fulfill it.

(4) "The God of the Jews is a God of violence and revenge, whereas the God of Christians is a God of love and mercy."

Reply. The God of the Tanakh is as much a God of love and mercy as the God of the New Testament is a God of violence and revenge.

---

47. Harkabi (1972); very extensively on the hatred of Jews among Muslims: Jansen (2006).

(5) "Because Gentile Jesus-believers have been incorporated into 'Israel,' they must adapt as much as possible to the Jewish way of life: circumcision, Jewish festivals, food laws, and the like."

Reply: They must *not* do this. Gentile Jesus-believers are never placed under the Mosaic Torah; this claim is just as erroneous as the claim that Jesus-believing Jews are no longer bound to the Mosaic Torah.

8.6.2 Three More Misunderstandings

Here are several misunderstandings requiring additional comments.

(6) "Jewish are legalistic: they think that, by keeping the Torah in their own strength, they can receive an inheritance in the Messianic kingdom. They do not live by grace, but by works."

Reply. Godly Jews have always been aware of the fact that a person can live with God only by grace: "Noah found favor [or, grace] in the eyes of the LORD" (Gen. 6:8); "The LORD, the LORD, a God merciful and gracious, slow to anger, and abounding in steadfast love and faithfulness . . ." (Exod. 34:6); ". . . the LORD make his face to shine upon you and be gracious to you" (Num. 6:25). Godly Jews have always believed that good works proceed only by power granted by God himself: "Surely goodness and mercy shall follow me all the days of my life" (Ps. 23:6); "Not by might, nor by power, but by my Spirit, says the LORD of hosts" (Zech. 4:6).

This is the reverse of what we find among Christians, who have learned that they may live with God only by grace, but must follow the commandments of Christ.[48] And if any legalistic Jews believe they can attain ultimate salvation by their own strength and faithfulness, numerous Christians believe the same thing. Both groups suffer the same error, which was never part of any God-given regulations but is an abuse of them (see §1.8). The religion of Israel was revealed by God himself, and therefore was never legalistic in nature; on the

---

48. 1 Cor. 9:21 (cf. 7:19); Gal. 6:2; cf. Matt. 28:19; John 14:15, 21; 15:10; Rom. 13:8–10; 1 John 2:3–4; 3:22–24; 5:2–3; 2 John 1:6; Rev. 12:17; 14:12.

contrary, "[T]he Torah is holy, and the commandment is holy and righteous and good" (Rom. 7:12). "Now we know that the Torah is good, if one uses it in a Torah-like way" (1 Tim. 1:8).

In summary: the Torah is of God, and legalism is of the human (sinful) flesh.

(7) "Jews still administer circumcision, which is enough reason why they will have no part in God's salvation, for Paul says, 'Listen! I, Paul, tell you that if you allow yourselves to be circumcised, it means that Christ is of no use to you at all' (Gal. 5:1 GNT)."

Reply. In his letter to the Galatians, the apostle was speaking explicitly about preachers who were teaching that, in addition to believing in Christ, Gentiles were also obligated to be circumcised, and to observe the entire Mosaic Torah. Such heretics defile Christianity in its very significance for the Gentiles. However, for Jews it is a very different matter. Neither Jesus nor Paul set aside the Mosaic Torah and the Jewish customs rooted in the Torah; on the contrary, it was said of Paul, and to him, that "you yourself [i.e., Paul] also live in observance of the Torah" (Acts 21:24), just as he told the Jewish leaders in Rome that he "had done nothing against our people or the customs of our fathers" (Acts 28:17). This is why he felt free, or even obligated, to circumcise his assistant Timothy because the latter had a Jewish mother (Acts 16:3). Today, Messianic Jews still circumcise their newborn sons, *not* because they think that this is a necessary condition for salvation, but as a sign of the covenant that God has made with Abraham and his physical descendants (Gen. 17).

(8) "The Jews, or at any rate *some* Jews, have murdered God."

Reply. It cannot be denied that the Jewish mob in Pilate's court that delivered Jesus to the Roman authorities and demanded the death penalty against him in this way made themselves culpable of Jesus' death. Stephen called these Jews outright murderers.[49] This was because Jesus' death was a judicial murder, in which the false accusers were just as guilty as the false judges.

---

49. Acts 7:52; cf. 2:23; 3:15; 10:39; 13:28.

However, this does not mean that they committed "deicide," that is, that they "murdered *God*"; God is "immortal" (1 Tim. 6:16), that is, he cannot die, and thus cannot be killed. The Son of *God* became Man (John 1:14), in order to surrender his human body unto death (Heb. 2:14). In other words, Jesus died according to his human nature, but not according to his divine nature,[50] even if these two natures at the same time are inseparable. We must simply leave this Christological mystery for what it is,[51] and simply maintain that—if I may express the matter in this human way—Jesus is one hundred percent divine, and one hundred percent human.[52] As God, Jesus cannot die; as a human, he is not omnipresent. As God, he can grant forgiveness (Mark 2:7), accept worship (Matt. 2:2, 11; 14:33; 28:9, 17), and raise the dead (cf. 2 Kings 5:7). As Man, he could be tired (John 4:6), hungry (Matt. 4:2), and thirsty (John 19:28).

8.7 Jewish Misunderstandings About Christians
8.7.1 Three Misunderstandings

These are some misunderstandings that many Jews have about Christianity:

(1) "Jesus and his apostles transgressed the Mosaic Torah, especially the Sabbath commandment, and this is sufficient reason for orthodox Jews to reject them and their teachings."

Reply. As far as we can gather from the New Testament, Jesus never contradicted or transgressed the Mosaic Torah, although he did contradict or ignore certain *rabbinic additions* to the Torah, which he judged not to be according to the spirit of the Torah. For instance, the Mosaic Torah does not forbid plucking heads of grain on the Sabbath (cf. Matt. 12:1-8), or healing the sick on the Sabbath (vv. 9-14).

(2) "If a Jew would come to faith in Jesus as Messiah and Savior, they would, in this way, join the Christian church, and thus lose their Jewish identity."

---
50. *Contra*, e.g., Moltmann (1993: "The Crucified God").
51 See Ouweneel (2007, chapters 8–9; 2014a, Excursus 12).
52. Not 50% human and 50% divine, as I once heard a Mormon guide say in the Mormons' Visitor's Center in Salt Lake City.

Reply. If a Jew comes to faith in Jesus as Messiah and Savior, they do not "change religions"; on the contrary, they reach the heart and essence of *their own* religion: Judaism. It has been the folly of many Christians to force Jesus-believing Jews to join a Christian denomination and to completely surrender their Jewish identity. Among Messianic Judaism, it has finally become evident how Jews can both believe in Jesus and remain what they always were: Jews.

(3) "It is quite conceivable that Jesus was sent by God in order that the Gentile nations, too, through him would find the way to the Father (John 14:6); but Jews do not need this because they *already are* with the Father."

Reply. (a) When God the Son refers to the Father, he speaks of him who was *his own Father* since eternity (see, e.g., John 1:1–18; 17:1–5); not of the Father who is the Creator of, and Provider for, his people (cf. next section).[53] (b) Just as the prophets had done, both John the Baptist and Jesus told the people to repent, humble themselves, and turn to God. Jews belong to the chosen people of God on earth, but this does not mean that they automatically share in God's eternal salvation.

8.7.2 The Fourth Misunderstanding

The misunderstandings that follow in §§8.7.2–8.7.6 demand additional explanation.

(4) "Christianity has fundamentally separated from Judaism by its introduction of the Trinity doctrine, which is radically at odds with the Tanakh and rabbinic teaching."

Reply. Nothing in the doctrine of the Trinity fundamentally conflicts with Judaism. Christians, too, are strict monotheists; that is, they believe in one God, and therefore can whole-heartedly chant the *Sh'ma* together with the Jews: *Sh'má, Yisra'el, Adonai Elohēnoe Adonai echad:* "Hear, Israel, the LORD your God is a sole LORD," or, ". . . the LORD is one," or, ". . . is the only one" (Deut. 6:4; see §3.4.5). Remarkably, when Jesus was asked to summarize the Torah, he also included this *Sh'ma* in his summary (Mark 12:29–31; not mentioned

---

53. Ps. 103:13; Isa. 63:16; 64:8; Mal. 2:10; also cf. Deut. 14:1; Hos. 1:10.

in Matt. or Luke): "The most important [commandment] is, 'Hear, O Israel: The Lord our God, the Lord is one. And you shall love the Lord your God with all your heart and with all your soul and with all your mind and with all your strength.' The second is this: 'You shall love your neighbor as yourself.' There is no other commandment greater than these."

Following Jesus himself, Christians do not believe in three gods; speaking of three divine "persons" may be misleading given the modern meaning of the word "person" as an independently acting individual. The German-American theologian Paul Tillich had a point when he emphasized that we should speak instead of the three *personae* of the Trinity, *not* the persons, apparently so that the early Christian term *persona* not be confused with the modern psychological "person."[54] In order not to cause confusion, it is better to say, not that God "has" a Son but rather that God *is* Father, Son, and Holy Spirit. This not is evident from the Tanakh, but is based on the ongoing divine revelation in the New Testament—"ongoing," because it could not have been revealed any earlier than after the coming of the Son of God into this world. At the same time, this further revelation does not conflict with any truth given in the Tanakh; rather, it makes a number of statements in the Tanakh much clearer, such as:[55]

> Your throne, *O God*, is forever and ever.
> > The scepter of your kingdom is a scepter of uprightness;
> > you have loved righteousness and hated wickedness.
> Therefore God, your God, has anointed you
> > with the oil of gladness beyond your companions
> > (Ps. 45:6–7).

The text speaks of a person who is addressed as "God" *and* who *has* a God: "your God." Then there is this text: "Who has established all the ends of the earth? / What is his name, and *what is his son's name?*" (Prov. 30:4). Here are two more:

---

54. Tillich (1968, 2:166); cf. Barth (2009, 56–57); Kasper (1983, 285–90); Van de Beek (1987, 294–308).
55. See extensively, Ouweneel (2007, especially chapters 2 and 8).

For to us a child is born,
> to us *a son is given*;
and the government shall be upon his shoulder,
> and his name shall be called
Wonderful Counselor, *Mighty God*,
> *Everlasting Father*, Prince of Peace (Isa. 9:6).

One will come from you [i.e., Bethlehem]
to be ruler over Israel for Me.
His origin is *from antiquity*,
from eternity (Micah 5:2 HCSB).

This latter text refers to a King of Israel who is born in Bethlehem, but whose origin lies in past eternity. In New Testament language: this is person, divine from all eternity, is born as a human being in the fullness of time in Bethlehem.

8.7.3 The Fifth Misunderstanding

(5) "Christianity justifies itself through many improper expositions of the Tanakh, in particular by trying to read Jesus into the Tanakh, and through all kinds of allegorical interpretations that neglect the literal exegesis of the text."

Reply. The underlying question is, of course, who has the proper key to understanding the Tanakh: the orthodox Jew or the orthodox Christian? Is it self-evident that the average rabbi knows and understands the Tanakh better than the average Christian Old Testament professor? Or should we not say instead that the Jew and the Christian simply have a "different" Tanakh open before them? This is to say, the Jew reads the Tanakh through the glasses of the Talmud, whereas the Christian reads the Tanakh through the glasses of the New Testament. Both claim to be holding revelation in their hands: the Talmud is the written record of the Oral Torah, which God gave to the Israelite Moses on Mount Sinai, as orthodox Jews believe. And the New Testament is revelation of God that God gave to the Jewish emissaries (apostles) of Jesus. As the apostle Peter put it, the apostle Paul wrote letters that are just as much "Scripture" as "the other Scriptures" (2 Pet. 3:15).[56]

The matter is even more complicated. Throughout the centuries, the Jewish and the Christian interpretations of the Tanakh have (negatively) influenced each other. Christians applied to Jesus passages in the Tanakh that the rabbis had initially interpreted in a Messianic way. This led later rabbis to reject the Messianic interpretation of such passages.[57] Some important examples are Psalm 22:16b, Isaiah 52:13-53:12, and Zechariah 12:10, which formerly were all interpreted in a Messianic way, but after Christian applied them to Jesus, the Jews abandoned the Messianic interpretation.

Let me add here that for Christians, too, the grammatical-historical exegesis (what Jews often call the *p'shat*) always comes first. Moreover, Christians are familiar with typological exegesis, but are easily silenced in such explanations by the Jews with their allegorical (aggadic, midrashic, kabbalistic) interpretations. The simple truth is that both (orthodox) Jews and (orthodox) Christians are, or ought to be, familiar with both grammatical-historical and midrashic exegesis.

8.7.4 The Sixth Misunderstanding

(6) "Jesus cannot be the Messiah, first because, according to Christians themselves, he was not a physical son of Joseph, and second, because not a single legitimate authority has ever given him the *s'michah* ("laying on of hands") or has anointed him with oil (Messiah = Anointed One)."

Reply. First, Joseph was the legitimate father of Jesus because Jesus was born of Joseph's marriage with Mary (Miriam). Therefore, Jesus was called the "son of Joseph,"[58] who himself was called "son of David" (Matt. 1:20). Thus, Jesus enjoyed all the rights of his earthly, legitimate father, and there-

---

56. Cf. 1 Tim. 5:18, "[T]he *Scripture* says, . . . 'The laborer deserves his wages,'" which is a quotation from Luke 10:7. See also the "prophetic *Scriptures*" in Rom. 16:26 (NKJV), which, in my view, are the apostolic writings of the New Testament.
57. See Ouweneel (2014a, Excursus 33).
58. Luke 3:23; 4:22; John 1:45; 6:42; cf. Matt. 13:55, "the carpenter's son."

fore was legitimately entitled to the throne of David (cf. Matt. 1:1–16).

Second, the question about Jesus' authority was already asked by Jesus' opponents in his own day: "[W]hen he entered the temple, the chief priests and the elders of the people came up to him as he was teaching, and said, "By what authority are you doing these things, and who gave you this authority?" (Matt. 21:23). Notice Jesus' reply: he did not defend himself, but demonstrated that his opponents were unable or unprepared to recognize true divine authority, wherever they saw it, if it did not suit them. So what use was it to point out to them his *s'michah* or anointing?[59]

Third, Jesus had definitely been anointed, though not with ordinary oil but with what the oil symbolizes: "[Y]ou yourselves know. . . . how God anointed Jesus of Nazareth with the Holy Spirit and with power. He went about doing good and healing all who were oppressed by the devil, for God was with him" (Acts 10:37–38). This refers to the event described in Luke 3:21–22, the baptism (*mikweh*) of Jesus by John the Baptist: "[W]hen Jesus also had been baptized and was praying, the heavens were opened, and the Holy Spirit descended on him in bodily form, like a dove; and a voice came from heaven, 'You are my beloved Son; with you I am well pleased.'" God himself anointed Jesus with the power of the Holy Spirit;[60] no earthly anointing with oil can beat this!

The Tanakh spoke of this anointing with the Spirit: "The Spirit of the Lord God is upon me, / because the Lord has anointed me" (Isa. 61:1). In the synagogue of Capernaum, Jesus applied this verse explicitly to himself (Luke 4:18–21). Indeed, Jesus received from no one a *s'michah* (rabbinic consecration)—but which earthly authority would have had the

---

59. A similar example: after having seen several miracles of Jesus, the spiritual leaders "asked him to show them a sign from heaven" (Matt. 16:1). That is, they saw with their physical eyes, but did not discern with their spiritual eyes (cf. Jesus' reply, vv. 2–4).

60. Cf. 1 Sam. 16:13, which speaks of an anointing with oil, but where the effect is power, too: "Then Samuel took the horn of oil and anointed him [i.e., David] in the midst of his brothers. And the Spirit of the Lord rushed upon David from that day forward."

right or ability to do so? The same question can be asked with regard to Moses, the prophet (and according to some rabbis,[61] "king in Yeshurun," Deut. 33:5): Who would have had the authority or the ability to anoint him, or lay hands on him? Moses functioned with such divine power and authority that nobody would have thought of asking: Where is your anointing or *s'michah*?[62] It is the same with the Messiah: he will come on the clouds of heaven with such power, glory, and majesty that no Jew or Gentile will ask him for his papers. Or, to use a trivial image: one does not ask a world-renowned composer, singer, or instrumentalist for their conservatory diploma. Another trivial image: we do not ask the sun by what authority it is shining.

Interestingly, even if Jesus had not received the *s'michah* from anyone, this did not prevent the Jews, both his friends and the outsiders, from giving him the honorary title of "rabbi"; this Hebrew loanword appears in the Greek text of John 3:2, 26 and 6:25. Recall as well the Greek equivalent *didaskalos* ("Master, Teacher") in Matthew 12:38; 19:16; 22:16, 36. People used this term not because they believed that Jesus had received a certain education or anointing but because they acknowledged him as an authoritative Torah-teacher: "[W]hen Jesus finished these sayings, the crowds were astonished at his teaching, for he was teaching them as one who had authority, and not as their scribes" (Matt. 7:28–29).

8.7.5 The Seventh Misunderstanding

(7) "Christians worship a human being, and this is not only unbiblical—it is blasphemy: robbing God of the homage that belongs to him alone."

Reply. This is the exact opposite of the allegation, and just as unjustified, that Jews have murdered "God," or the Protestant allegation that Roman Catholics worship something

---

61. See Cohen (1983, ad loc.).
62. Only *before* his return to Egypt did some Israelite have the audacity to ask him, "Who made you a prince and a judge over us?" (Exod. 2:14).

that is merely a tiny piece of bread.[63] Roman Catholics worship *Christ*, and therefore they also worship the wafer, because, according to the doctrine of transubstantiation, the bread has been changed into the body of Christ. One need not agree with this, but one is still obligated to doing justice to the intentions of the other.

In the same way, Christians worship *God*, and therefore also Christ because, according to the New Testament, Christ is none other than "God manifested in the flesh" (2 Tim. 3:16); the *Logos* ("Word") was God and, in the fullness of time, has become flesh (John 1:1, 14). Christians do not worship humans as such, but they do worship God the Son; they worship Christ not according to his human, but according to his divine nature, so to speak, even though they believe that, since the incarnation of the Word, the two natures are inseparably connected. How much Christians are against worshiping humans, or even angels, may be clear from the following passages: "When Peter entered, Cornelius met him and fell down at his feet and worshiped him. But Peter lifted him up, saying, 'Stand up; I too am a man'" (Acts 10:25-26). Jesus could have said, too, "I too am a man"—but he was so much more than that, which Peter was not: a divine person. "I [i.e., John] fell down at his [i.e., the angel's] feet to worship him, but he said to me, 'You must not do that! I am a fellow servant with you and your brothers who hold to the testimony of Jesus. Worship God'" (Rev. 19:10).

8.7.6 The Eighth Misunderstanding

(8) "Jesus cannot be the Messiah because the Messiah establishes a kingdom of peace and righteousness, and this kingdom evidently has not yet arrived. Christians could have known this from the Tanakh, and thus we must conclude that they are ignorant because they nevertheless insist that Jesus of Nazareth is the Messiah."

Reply. The Tanakh itself distinguishes between a Messiah born as a little child in Bethlehem (Micah 5:2) and a Messiah triumphantly descending on the clouds of heaven (Dan.

---

63. E.g., Moerkerken (2004, ad loc.).

7:13). This distinction seems related to another distinction, which we do not find in the Tanakh but only in Jewish tradition. This is the distinction between the suffering Messiah ben Joseph and the triumphant Messiah ben David.[64] Jesus had first been born on earth, and suffered and died as Messiah ben Joseph; that is, at his first coming, he fulfilled Isaiah 53. At his second coming, he will descend on the clouds of heaven, and establish his kingdom of peace and righteousness as Messiah ben David—a kingdom to which Isaiah 53:12 alluded. For instance, compare the transition from Isaiah 9:6 ("a child is born") to verse 7 (the Messiah on the throne):

> *[First coming]* For to us a child is born,
> to us a son is given;
> and the government shall be upon his shoulder,
> and his name shall be called
> Wonderful Counselor, Mighty God,
> Everlasting Father, Prince of Peace.
> *[Second coming]* Of the increase of his government and of peace
> there will be no end,
> on the throne of David and over his kingdom,
> to establish it and to uphold it
> with justice and with righteousness
> from this time forth and forevermore.
> The zeal of the Lord of hosts will do this.

We find a similar contrast between Micah 5:2 (the Messiah born in Bethlehem) and verses 4–5 (the Messianic kingdom):

> *[First coming]* But you, O Bethlehem Ephrathah,
> who are too little to be among the clans of Judah,
> from you shall come forth for me
> one who is to be ruler in Israel,
> whose coming forth is from of old,
> from ancient days. . . .
> *[Second coming]* And he shall stand and shepherd his flock in the strength of the Lord,

---

64. https://en.wikipedia.org/wiki/Messiah_ben_Joseph.

> in the majesty of the name of the L%%ORD%% his God.
> And they shall dwell secure, for now he shall be great
> > to the ends of the earth.
> And he shall be their peace.

In the dialogue between Jews and Christians, it would be enormously helpful if both groups would take an important step. Christians should recognize that the Messianic founder of the promised universal kingdom of peace and righteousness *must still come*. And it would help if Jews would recognize that Jesus was at least a "Messianic rabbi"—perhaps one of the four "Craftsmen" mentioned in Zechariah 1:18-20:

> And I lifted my eyes and saw, and behold, four horns! And I said to the angel who talked with me, "What are these?" And he said to me, "These are the horns that have scattered Judah, Israel, and Jerusalem." Then the L%%ORD%% showed me four *craftsmen*. And I said, "What are these coming to do?" He said, "These are the horns that scattered Judah, so that no one raised his head. And these have come to terrify them, to cast down the horns of the nations who lifted up their horns against the land of Judah to scatter it" (italics added).

Interestingly, in the Talmud,[65] these Four Craftsmen are identified as "Messiah ben David, Messiah ben Joseph, Elijah [cf. Mal. 4:5-6], and the Righteous Priest [Zech. 6:13]."

Another Jewish tradition says that in each generation a person is born from the tribe of Judah with the potential of being a Messiah, if the world is ready for him.[66] Even many Jews will readily admit that during the first century of our era, no single Jew satisfied this qualification as well as Jesus of Nazareth did.

---

65. Talmud: Sukkah 52b.
66. Rabbi Obadyah of Bartenura (or, Bertinoro) in his Commentary on Ruth; see https://www.chabad.org/ library/article_cdo/aid/101679/jewish/The-Personality-of-Mashiach.htm.

8.8 Peace and Its Bringer
8.8.1 Varieties of Peace

After the earthly appearance of Jesus Christ, universal peace and righteousness on earth in any political sense has not yet arrived, but there *is* peace in the hearts of millions of people who have accepted the divine gospel of, and concerning, Jesus Christ:

(a) *Objective peace in general:* "[I]n him all the fullness of God was pleased to dwell, and through him to reconcile to himself all things, whether on earth or in heaven, *making peace* by the blood of his cross" (Col. 1:19–20).

(b) *Specifically, peace between Jews and Gentiles:* Christ "is our peace, who has made us [i.e., Jewish and Gentile Jesus-believers] both one and has broken down in his flesh the dividing wall of hostility [that existed between them] (...). And he came and preached *peace* to you who were far off [i.e., Gentiles] and *peace* to those who were near [i.e., Jews]" (Eph. 2:14, 17).

(c) *Subjective: positional peace* (i.e., the peace that characterizes the believers' position before God): "Therefore, since we have been justified by faith, we have *peace with God* through our Lord Jesus Christ" (Rom. 5:1).

(d) *Subjective: practical peace:* "And the *peace of God*, which surpasses all understanding, will guard your hearts and your minds in Christ Jesus" (Phil. 4:7). "[L]et the *peace of Christ* rule in your hearts, to which indeed you were called in one body" (Col. 3:15).

(e) *Collective peace:* "[T]he kingdom of God is not a matter of eating and drinking but of righteousness and *peace* and joy in the Holy Spirit" (Rom. 14:17). That is to say, already within God's kingdom in its *present* form, there is peace—insofar as the Holy Spirit is allowed to work there—not peace in any political, but peace in the spiritual sense.

8.8.2 The Bringer of Peace

The Messiah is, and will be, the great Bringer of Peace: "[T]his One shall be peace" (Micah 5:5 NKJV). At his coming into the world, when the angels proclaim: "Glory to God in the highest, and on earth *peace* among those with whom he is pleased!" (Luke 2:14), the latter phrase[67] means either "in people with whom he is pleased" (ESV), or (cf. Vulgate: *hominibus bonae voluntatis*): "in people of good will" (cf. CJB, DRA; ERV: "people who please him"). The former rendering emphasizes God's sovereign and electing grace; the latter translation emphasizes the human responsibility: Jesus' disciples are those who perform God's will (cf. Mark 3:35).

It is especially for Israel, and more specifically for Jerusalem, that the Messiah has sought this peace. He wept over the city saying: "Would that you, even you, had known on this day the things that make for *peace*! But now they are hidden from your eyes" (Luke 19:42). Peace in the Messianic kingdom entails an irrevocably *deep contrast* between those who choose the side of the Messiah and those who reject him:

> Do you think that I have come to give *peace* on earth? No, I tell you, but rather division. For from now on in one house there will be five divided, three against two and two against three. They will be divided, father against son and son against father, mother against daughter and daughter against mother, mother-in-law against her daughter-in-law and daughter-in-law against mother-in-law (Luke 12:51-53).

As long as sin is in the world, this contrast will always remain. Even in the Messianic kingdom that will arrive at the second coming of Christ, there will be the contrast between the true subjects of the Messiah and those who will (falsely, hypocritically) "come cringing to him" (cf. 2 Sam. 22:45; Ps. 18:44; 66:3).

---

67. At least in the translation being followed here; cf. the NKJV for another reading: "goodwill toward men."

Chapter 9
Israel and the Palestinians

*"I love the Bible, the book of the God of Israel, and I love Jesus, the Messiah of Israel. But the Israelis themselves make it very difficult for us to love **them** too. ..."*
Christian Palestinian in Galilee
       (personal conversation; emphasis added)

*An old Franciscan monk on Mount Tabor told me after I had saluted him with "Shalom": "Shalom!? Why do you adopt that word from the Israelis? They do not **want** peace at all with the Palestinians. ...*

9.1   Introduction
9.1.1 Black and White

THE ISSUE OF THE state of Israel and the Palestinians involves many misunderstandings and deceptions. Among orthodox Christians, too, various sensitivities and standpoints regarding Israel are circulating that I consider to be unbiblical and even harmful. I have in mind not only supersessionism, but also views that fawn over the state of Israel and depict the relationships between Palestinians and Israelis in black-and-white terms. In both cases, I feel that essentially an unbiblical view of the prophetic word is at stake. Additionally, many non-Christian views, are increasingly shifting in sympathy from the Jewish side to the Palestinian side.

Here is one example. The Dutch former diplomat and political activist, Jan J. Wijenberg, wrote in 2011:

> Zionism is de facto the national ideology of Israel. Its highest aim is the establishment of Eretz-or Great-Israel, preferably without, but if necessary with as few as possible, subjugated Palestinians. Therefore, Israel is busy conquering the West Bank of the Jordan River and East Jerusalem, all the while as the Palestinians in Gaza are being kept under control in a strangling, medieval siege. The social life of the "remaining" Palestinians is being systematically destroyed. With its spare-nothing-and-nobody cruelty, the Zionist regime can compare with many regimes in the region.[1]

Here, the negative features of the state of Israel, which no doubt exist, are magnified in an almost absurd way. In August 2020, Jewish Dutch writer and columnist Arnon Grunberg wrote a public letter to Wijenberg, in which he called him an anti-Semite.

Some critics make a somewhat more serious impression. One such example is the book written by the Dutch Roman Catholic former prime minister Dries van Agt, in which he spoke up for what he calls the "tragedy of the Palestinian people."[2] On his website he wrote:

> I have put myself to writing because, in our land and elsewhere too, there is still much ignorance as to what really happened with the Palestinians after World War II, as to the immense injustice that is still done to these people, and the deep distress in which they have landed. To a large extent, this ignorance is the result of prejudice. This is also caused and nourished by

---

1. Wijenberg (2011, 7).
2. Van Agt (2009, subtitle); website id driesvanagt.nl.

distorted information, and leads to indifference to, or even abhorrence of those driven out and oppressed.

Notice the prejudicial terms "ignorance," "injustice," "prejudice," "driven out and oppressed." They show that Van Agt himself was not without prejudice either. In itself this is not a problem, for none of us is without prejudice, certainly in a sensitive, explosive issue—religiously and politically loaded—like the Israeli-Palestinian problem. Van Agt, too, has often been called an anti-Semite by his opponents, an allegation which he rejects with indignation.

In 1970, the Roman Catholic Bible teacher Lucas H. Grollenberg wrote: "No future for Zionist Israel."[3] In a sense, this is correct. In the Messianic kingdom, "Zionist" Israel will no longer exist, but only a repentant, humbled, and believing Israel—although this was not at all what Grollenberg meant, of course.

The political activist Gretta Duisenberg, wife of the Dutch former finance minister Wim Duisenberg, asserted in a 2010 speech that the state of Israel was only a "temporary phenomenon."[4] On her website, people could find such historical nonsense as "an exclusively Jewish state in originally Palestinian territory."[5] Yes, "Palestine" is no doubt "Palestinian territory," just as France is French territory. But Duisenberg clearly meant "territory that belongs, or has belonged, to the Palestinians," that is, Arab Palestinians. This is a historical absurdity. Never in history has Palestine belonged to the people who are today called, after the time of Palestine Liberation Organization leader Yasser Arafat, "Palestinians." Even if Duisenberg meant that Arabs have always lived in Palestine, she would have had to admit that Jews have always lived in Palestine, too; they were there more than thousand years earlier than any Arabic-speaking people. But such considerations are lost on Gretta Duisenberg.

---

3. Grollenberg (1970, 171).
4. Mentioned on https://nl.wikipedia.org/wiki/Gretta_Duisenberg, but no longer available at www.stopdebezetting.org.
5. stopdebezetting.org.

And then there is the Dutch historian Chris van der Heijden, who wrote a book with the remarkable title (translated): *Israel: An Irreparable Mistake.*[6] Irreparable? In his book, things turn out to be not that bad. And no wonder: the Israeli–Palestinian question is far too complicated to be caught in a few cheap, popular headlines.

9.1.2 Irreparable?

It seems as if in this entire debate, giving even the appearance of objectivity and neutrality is hardly possible, or even attempted. There seem to be only two diametrically opposed parties: a fiercely pro-Israeli one and a fiercely pro-Palestinian one. In such matters, it seems possible to discern certain fashionable trends. In 1967, during the Six-Day War, the Netherlands almost unanimously stood behind the Israelis. Many young people, including myself, donated blood for those "poor Israeli soldiers." Today, the sympathies are completely reversed. If a war broke out today, Western students would likely give their blood for those "poor Palestinian fighters" rather than for the Israelis. The question is fascinating: What historical (if not metahistorical) and psychological changes have taken place in the thinking of many Western people?

Christians are naturally involved in these debates, too, and probably far more so than Hindus, Buddhist, and atheists, because of our links with biblical history. But let us not think that the issue is any less complicated for Christians. Many of them are quite unfamiliar with the details and history of the Israeli-Palestinian conflict. Because Israel is involved, their natural sympathies may extend to the Jews—until they find out that there are many Christians among the Palestinian Arabs (though, every year there seems to be fewer, as a consequence of Muslim pressure). I have personally preached in several Christian Arabic-speaking churches in Israel, both in Galilee and on the West Bank.

So then, where should my "natural" sympathies lie? With my Christian brothers and sisters, or with my older brother Israel? Or with both? But how does this third solution

---

6. Van der Heijden (2008).

work in practice? I have spoken with people from all parties involved: orthodox Jews, secular Jews, Arab Christians and Arab Muslims. Speaking purely politically speaking (if such is even possible), there are two main views: *all* the land should belong to "us" (Jews or Muslims), or, we prefer the two-states solution, at least for the time being (in which ancient Jerusalem should, of course, be on "our" side—Jewish or Muslim). In fact, these are four different solutions. And here is a fifth pragmatic political solution, which, strangely enough, is rarely mentioned: a *one state* solution, satisfying the following conditions:

(a) This state would be neither specifically Jewish, nor specifically Arab-Muslim, but *strictly democratic*, with strict equality of civil rights for all its citizens, and for all its religions.

(b) The Gaza Strip, the ancient land of the Philistines, would not be part of this state, but brought under Egyptian control again (with a nod to the Jews: in this way, in this new state a Jewish majority would be guaranteed).

(c) Only those Arab-Palestinian refugees would be allowed to return who can prove that their ancestors live in the land before, say, 1920; the others are integrated in the countries where they have been living for several generations.

(d) There would no longer be a Jerusalem-problem: the city will be the capital of this new state, in which all factions peacefully tolerate each other.

Of course, a multitude of objections against this plan would arise from the Jewish side and from the Arab side. Yet, I think that it is a much better plan than any two-states plan.

Ultimately, there is a sixth solution, proposed to me by an Arab taxi driver: "Only Jesus can solve the problem." I carefully hugged him, although this was very dangerous in Jerusalem traffic. When Jesus comes, he *will* establish this one state, of which he will be the head, and in which Jews and Arabs will have equal rights (cf. Ezek. 47:21–23!).

It is high time that (orthodox) Christians begin to collectively develop a balanced view of the Middle East conflict, a safe middle-way between, on the one hand, an uncritical philo-Semitism and, on the other hand, the present-day fashion to depict the state of Israel only as a bad bogeyman and the Palestinians as the poor, oppressed outcasts. Or have the minds been so heated already that we mainly encounter the two extreme viewpoints? It is like the "good guys" and the "bad guys" in an old-fashioned Western movie or in a Karl May novel: there is only black and white. The good guys are *very* good, and the bad guys are *very* bad. However, opinions are hopelessly divided today on the question *who* in *Ha'Aretz* belong to each group.

9.1.3 A Middle Course

A middle course is preferable. On the one hand, the biblical truth teaches that one day, in God's time, he will give all the Holy Land to (a repentant, humbled, believing) Israel, under the blessed rule of the Messiah. On the other hand, another biblical truth teaches that this time has not yet arrived as long as the Messiah has not yet come, and as long as Israel has not yet massively repented and believed. Therefore, it is a mistake, both in a theological and in a judicial-political respect, to assert that Israel is biblically entitled to any part of *Ha'Aretz*.

One must also follow a middle course between various aspects, none of which must be emphasized at the expense of the other aspects.

(a) International law demands that in exchange for a solid peace treaty, Israel must return the disputed territories (Judea and Samaria, or "the West Bank," and East Jerusalem). *This* is something with which people such as Van Agt and Duisenberg will happily agree.

(b) However, it is not at all clear *to whom* these territories must be returned. In the last five hundred years, they have been under the hegemony of Turks, British, and Jordanians, *but never of "the" Palestinians*. Such an entity did not even exist. So, who is entitled to them?

(c) The political reality is that although a peace treaty as intended under (a) may look solid on paper, the safety risks for Israel will always be too large. As a consequence, no peace proposal can ever be realistic. *This* is something that people such as Van Agt and Duisenberg presumably will never be prepared to acknowledge.

(d) The religious reality is that orthodox Islam is unable or unwilling to accept the rights of the state of Israel within ancient Palestine. From its religious standpoint, this is impossible: land that for such a long time—since the seventh century—has belonged to Allah, can never be given up, least of all to Jews.

(e) For the same reason, Muslims is unable or unwilling to give up East Jerusalem.[7] We can only wonder about the shocking naïveté of people like Van Agt and Duisenberg, and many others, who seem unable or unprepared to recognize points (d) and (e). The matter is viewed from the standpoint of politics and international law, but little or no attention is being paid to the religious dimension (which is actually also true for many Israelis and Palestinians themselves). The cultural distance between East and West Jerusalem is far greater than that between the American city El Paso and the Mexican city Ciudad Juárez. The latter two form one urban area, with enormous cultural differences, but no religious dimension is involved, as in the case of East and West Jerusalem.

To whom does East Jerusalem belong? Many Palestinians live in and around the old city, and these cannot be ignored or expelled. However, let us be clear about this: *Old Jerusalem has never belonged to those who are now called Palestinians.* It once belonged to the Jews, for many centuries since the city of Jebus[8] was conquered by King David:

---

7. If one prefers, a distinction can be made between East Jerusalem (the entire Jerusalem city territory east of the demarcation that existed until 1967) and Old Jerusalem (the city between the Turkish city walls plus the adjacent Temple Square).

8. Jebus was the name of the city at the time, but before that, the names were Salem (Gen. 14:18; cf. Ps. 76:2; Heb. 7:1–2) and Jerusalem (from Josh. 10 to 1 Sam.); in Judg. 1:8 we read, "And the men of Judah fought against Jerusalem and captured it and struck it with the edge of the sword and set the city on fire."

David and all Israel went to Jerusalem, that is, Jebus, where the Jebusites were, the inhabitants of the land. The inhabitants of Jebus said to David, 'You will not come in here.' Nevertheless, David took the stronghold of Zion, that is, the city of David... And David lived in the stronghold; therefore it was called the city of David (1 Chron. 11:4–7).

In Jerusalem, the Israelites built what is called the First Temple (the temple of Solomon), and after the Babylonian captivity the Second Temple (the temple of Zerubbabel, later that of Herod). But the Muslims also have their sanctuaries there: the Dome of the Rock (the Dome that was built over the rock where Abraham and David, respectively, built their altars; Gen. 22:9 and 2 Sam. 24:24) and the Al Aqsa Mosque.[9] Without perceiving this religious dimension, people can speak of returning (to whom? whose was it before?) only in a naïve way, or speak of "placing Old Jerusalem under international authority"—which would lead to massive insurrection among both Israelis and among Palestinians.

9.2 Critics of Israel

9.2.1 Jewish and Christian Critics

Critics of Israel have occasionally included religious Jews. One example is the psychologist Mark Braverman, whose grandfather was a Jew born in Jerusalem. In his book, Braverman wished to connect with the "Jewish prophet" Jesus, who criticized the political and religious Jewish powers of his days, just as Braverman wished to do.[10] He blamed the anti-supersessionists for making the Jews "hostages of their history," a feature of supersessionism as well. Thus, starting from Israel's supposed chosen position, they do not have a realistic view of the state of Israel. In Braverman's view, both Jews and Christians ought to have more regard for international law and the duty of social justice. These are not purely secular matters, argues Braverman, for basically they go back

---

9. This is the mosque allegedly referred to in the Quran, Sura 17: Al-Isra' ("The Night Journey") as "the farthest [Arab. *al aqsa*] mosque."
10. Braverman (2010).

to the Bible as well, or more generally to divine righteousness.

A similar critic is the Jewish liberation theologian Marc H. Ellis, who became known through critical studies like *Judaism Does Not Equal Israel: The Rebirth of the Jewish Prophetic*.[11] This title means that the essence of Israel is not "the land," and even less the state of Israel, but the prophetic voice that resounds time and again throughout history: the voice against social injustice. Ellis discussed extensively why Jews, who had to suffer under "Christians" for so many centuries and now are in the reverse position, inflict the same sufferings upon the Palestinian people. This question arises today from various sides.

Another kind of critic, but with comparable views, is the Palestinian Evangelical theologian Yohana Katanacho, dean of the Bethlehem Bible College. He has argued that "the land" does not belong to Israel, but to Christ.[12] His views are a-millennialist and purely supersessionist, and therefore are no great help in assessing the prophetic significance of the state of Israel. Generally speaking, it is not easy for Palestinian Christian theologians to take a millennialist viewpoint, according to which Israel, in its own land, will be the center of the Messianic kingdom. An exception is the Palestinian millennialist Naim Khoury, pastor of the First Baptist Church in Bethlehem. His position is not easy: he has been criticized for his theological position on Israel by both Jews and Muslims, and by supersessionists of many different Christian denominations.

Another group of Palestinian theologians is associated with the Sabeel Institute for Palestinian Liberation Theology,[13] and the Kairos document of 2009, a Christian Palestin-

---

11. Ellis (2009; see also 2011).
12. Katanacho (2012); for a discussion see http://www.evangelicalreview.com/01–2018_flashman_'yohanna,_the_ land_of_christ'.pdf; regarding him, see Kant (2015, 182–94), who deals also with the Palestinian liberation theologian Naim Ateek (133–63).
13. See Katanacho (2012, 164–67).

ian manifesto;[14] these are all examples of certain forms of supersessionism. Since then, what is called Sabeel-Kairos theologians are found also in Western countries (for an example, see the next section).

In May 2021, a typical form of disinformation was exposed, which may serve as an illustration of the "fake news war" going on today. One reason that Hamas gave for the hundreds of missiles that it fired at Israel during that month was what the Israeli government was supposedly doing in Sheikh Jarrah, a neighborhood just northeast of ancient Jerusalem (i.e., in the disputed territory!): trying to evict Palestinians from houses where they had lived for centuries, in order to settle Jewish families there. What a shame!

But the reality is quite a bit different. Sheikh Jarrah is religiously important for orthodox Jews because it supposedly is the burial site of Simeon the Just, a Jewish high priest of the Second Temple in Jerusalem (third century BC). Therefore, in 1875, two rabbis purchased the land from Arabs, as was registered in Turkish records of the time. In 1946, two Jewish organizations had the registration confirmed with the British, but in 1948, the Jordanians occupied Sheikh Jarrah, and expelled all the Jews. In 1956, the Jordanian authorities leased the property to twenty-eight Palestinian families. In 1967, Sheikh Jarrah, as well as the rest of eastern Jerusalem came under Jewish authority again. In 1973, the registration of the Jewish ownership was re-confirmed. In 1982, the Jewish owners granted the Palestinians living there "protected tenant" status, consenting that they could continue to live there as long as they paid rent. In 1993, the Palestinian Authority told the tenants no longer to pay no rent to the Jews because such payment would confirm the Jewish ownership. In February 2021 an Israeli court decided that, if the Palestinians kept refusing to pay rent, they could be evicted. The fate of the Palestinian tenants was set to be determined on May 10 by the Israeli Supreme Court, but the Court has delayed its decision. But the entire procedure gave Hamas one argument among others to attack Israel.

---

14. Ibid., 168–76.

9.2.2 Dutch Kairos-Sabeel Critics

A group of theologians known as Kairos-Sabeel Netherlands, belonging to the Protestant Church in the Netherlands,[15] are also critics of Israel policy. In May 2021, five pastors of this church wrote a public letter addressed to "the Palestinian people." In this letter, they wrote among other things:

> ... As a church, we wish to offer your people our apologies. For centuries, your people have lived under various regimes in the land that we call "the land of the Bible." You have suffered severely under the decision of the great Western powers in the previous century to put your land at the disposal of the Jewish people, subsequently [you have suffered] under the support for your violent expulsion. The state of Israel was recognized by the then newly formed United Nations under guarantees of international law for your people. However, in the past decades, still other parts of your land have been occupied, and even incorporated, your population was discriminated against, chased away, and cut off from sources of life. Your people have been split up, divided, and dispersed.[16]

It is astonishing to see how few of these statements are historically correct. Consider just these few components, which will be examined in the remainder of this chapter and of this volume.

1. There never was such a thing as a "Palestinian people," having lived in the Holy Land for "centuries." The ancestors of a large portion of modern Palestinians did not live in *Ha'Aretz*, say, 120 years ago, and for a large part were not even of Arab descent. And those Arabic-speaking people who did live there never understood themselves as an independent ethnic entity, "the Palestinians"; this contrasts with the Jewish nation, an ethnic nation for over three thousand years, which lived in the Holy Land for many centuries, though later was largely dispersed over the world.

---

15. This denomination was formed in 2004 from the Dutch Reformed Church and the Kuyperian Reformed Churches in the Netherlands.
16. https://kairos-sabeel.nl/excuus-aan-palestijnen/.

2. The Holy Land *never* was *"your"* (i.e., the Palestinians') land. This was first because of all those regimes that the five pastors mention; there never ever was such a thing as a Palestinian state. Second, Palestine never was exclusively "of the Arabs" because of the considerable number of Jews who lived in the land during those same centuries. They themselves were even called "Palestinians," because a "Palestinian" is anyone whose homeland is Palestine.

3. It is not true that the Western powers gave land that belonged to "Palestinians" to the Jewish people. First, it was not the Western powers but the majority of the United Nations. Second, the growing number of Jewish immigrants *bought* land in *Ha'Aretz*, land that from that point forward legally belonged to them. Third, because of growing tensions between the increasing Jewish and Arab populations, the United Nations devised a plan, not to "make land of Palestinians available to the Jews," but to divide the land as fairly as possible among the two growing groups. The Jews accepted the plan, the Arabs did not, because they wanted the *entire* land, as they still do today.

4. It is not true that, in more recent times, Jews have "occupied" *"your"* (i.e., the Palestinians') land. The West Bank had never belonged to the Palestinian Arabs. In earlier times, it had been "occupied," successively, by the Turks, the British, and the Jordanians, without any theologians in the world complaining about this. No international law can possibly decide, once and for all, that the Palestinian Arabs are more entitled to Judea and Samaria than, for instance, the Jews.

5. Are the Palestinian Arabs being "oppressed" by the Israelis? Are they not being oppressed by their own corrupt and undemocratic leaders? And do they not "oppress" the Jews with their terrorist actions, whereby they *purposely* kill citizens (which the Israelis in principle never do)? And if Palestinians are "chased away" and "dispersed," did their Arab Muslim brothers in the neighboring countries not do the same to the Jews in their midst, who had lived there for many centuries? Why this naïve speaking as if the Jews are the bad

guys, and the Arabs just poor victims? Long before the foundation of the state of Israel, the Arabs were stirred up by their leaders to kill the Jews. The leaders keep proclaiming that the "Zionists" must be destroyed—something that the Jews have never said of the Palestinian Arabs.

More points could be mentioned but they will be examined in this and subsequent chapters. How sad it is when Christian leaders, like these Dutch pastors, call the Palestinians (of whom the great majority is Muslim, who claim the entire Holy Land for Allah) their "brothers," and turn their back on the Jews, who deserve the term "brothers" far more than Muslim Arabs. "Salvation is from the Jews," not from the Muslims.

9.2.3 An Arab Critic

Quite different from the Jewish critics and the Palestinian and Christian supersessionists just mentioned is the story of the Palestinian Taysir Abu Saada (in short: Tass Saada).[17] By origin, he is not a theologian at all, not even a Christian, but a Muslim terrorist. He was born in a refugee camp in the Gaza Strip, and grew up in Saudi Arabia and Qatar. Among other things, he was Yasser Arafat's driver, and a sniper in the PLO (Palestinian Liberation Organization). In this capacity, he killed several Israeli opponents. However, in the United States he found the love of his life: Jesus Christ, the Jew who loves Arabs just as much as he loves Jews, who turned Saada's entire upside down. Saada experienced a radical conversion, got the opportunity to explain the gospel to his own relatives, and even to Yasser Arafat, as Tass himself told me.[18] He began helping and supporting the poor and the needy in Gaza and in the West Bank, and explained to them the gospel of Jesus Christ.

Something happened that he could never have expected earlier: he asked Israelis to forgive what he and other Palestinians had done to them, and learned to pray: "O God, bless

---

17. Saada (2008; 2016).
18. Saada himself told me this, at a conference in the Netherlands where we shared the podium.

your people Israel. O Lord, lead them back to their Promised Land. Let them see you as their God."[19] Over against the "spirit of terror" in the Middle East, Saada learned to be a bringer of peace, and to pray for those who sow death and destruction, no matter on what side these people may be. What a difference from all those Western critics who have put all the blame on Israel, and have depicted the Palestinians as the poor victims of Jewish terror. It is not that Saada does not see the crimes that sometimes have been committed by the Israeli side. But he has learned to see the dangers of both Muslim and Zionist extremism, as well as the special prophetic position of Israel.

Indeed, the same God who has converted Arafat's chauffeur in such a miraculous way has also opened his eyes to the historical truth. He wrote: "I realized I had been fighting the wrong kind of war. You Israelis do have a right to this land, and I had been trying to take what rightfully belongs to you."[20] And:

> I am convinced, from my reading of Scripture, that God wants the Jews to be living in this land. He promised it to them long ago through his prophets, and he has never changed his mind on that. So to try to throw them out is to fight against God. That is why we Arabs, in spite of our larger numbers, our petrodollars, and all the rest, have never been able to defeat Israel.[21]

But he continued: "The truth is, God loves both Arabs and Jews—and wants to bring us both to a higher perspective. He is not 'anti' either one of us. He wants the people of the Middle East, *all* of us, to realize that Jesus is our Savior and Reconciler."[22] Tass Saada is one of *many* Muslims who, especially after September 11, 2001, have come to faith in Jesus Christ. Altogether the number of these converts is said to be greater than ever before in the history of Islam.[23] One Joel

---

19. Saada (2008, 108).
20. Ibid., 179.
21. Ibid., 198.
22. Ibid., 199.
23. J. Rosenberg in Saada (2008, xi).

Rosenberg made that claim, and is the founder of the *Joshua Fund*, a humanitarian organization with the mission to bless both Israel and its neighbors in the name of Jesus on the basis of Genesis 12:1-3:

> Now the Lord said to Abram, "Go from your country and your kindred and your father's house to the land that I will show you. And I will make of you a great nation, and I will bless you and make your name great, so that you will be a blessing. I will bless those who bless you, and him who dishonors you I will curse, and in you *all the families of the earth shall be blessed*" (italics added).

Saada himself is the founder of *Hope for Ishmael*, an organization that seeks to reconcile Arabs and Jews. Saada's story is, as it were, the key to this present chapter: the *sole* solution for the Israeli-Palestinian conflict is Jesus Christ—not only (subjectively present faith in him, but (objectively) his imminent return on the Mount of Olives. That is, he will come again, not in Tel Aviv or West Jerusalem, but within the disputed territories of modern Palestine.

The primary solution to be sought is not the reconciliation of Jews and Arabs to *each other*, for under the present circumstances, apart from a few very enlightened exceptions,[24] this is virtually *impossible*. The true solution is that Jews and Arabs are each reconciled *with God*, in Jesus Christ:

> ...All this is from God, who through Christ *reconciled us to himself* and gave us the ministry of reconciliation; that is, in Christ God was reconciling the world to himself, not counting their trespasses against them, and entrusting to us the message of reconciliation. Therefore, we are ambassadors for Christ, God making his appeal through us. We implore you on behalf of Christ, be reconciled to God (2 Cor. 5:18-20).

---

24. Perhaps the most remarkable exceptions have been deeply secret meetings between Messianic Jews and Evangelical Palestinians: united in the same Lord in and in the same faith. I myself have been at such a meeting, held in the Netherlands.

Then, the reconciliation to each other will follow automatically:

> But now, you who were once far off have been brought near through the shedding of the Messiah's blood. For he himself is our *shalom* — he has made us both [i.e., Jewish and Gentile believers] one and has broken down the *m'chitzah* which divided us by destroying in his own body the enmity occasioned by the *Torah*, with its commands set forth in the form of ordinances. He did this in order to create in union with himself from the two groups a single new humanity and thus make *shalom*, and in order to reconcile to God both [groups] in a single body by being executed on a stake as a criminal and thus in himself killing that enmity (Eph. 2:13-16 CJB).

9.3 Historical Aspects[25]
9.3.1 The Palestinians

A thorough analysis of the Israeli-Palestinian conflict would require an entire volume.[26] But we have room only for a few concise comments.

At the beginning of the twentieth century, the Jews living in the Holy Land were called "Palestinians" as well. This is no wonder: all the people whose homeland is Palestine are Palestinians. Therefore, we should rather speak of Jewish Palestinians and Arab Palestinians (or, Palestinian Jews and Palestinian Arabs). Today the term "Palestinians" refers to the Arabic speaking inhabitants of *Ha'Aretz*. Even the word "Arabic" is here more a linguistic than a national or ethnic notion: it refers to all people in *Ha'Aretz* who speak Arabic, irrespective of what part of the Middle East or southeastern Europe from which they, or their ancestors, have come, and irrespective of their religion: Christian, Islamic, or Druze. Some Palestinians are of ethnically Arab origin, but also of Greek, Turkish, Armenian, Central Asiatic, North African origin, and so on. Today, "Arabs"—apart from those living in

---

25. See more extensively, Ouweneel (2002, chapter 3).
26. What I present here is a summary of Ouweneel (2002) together with additions about more recent developments.

the Arab heartland, Saudi Arabia—have very few, if any, ethnic and historical bonds; in fact, they have only one thing in common: the Arabic language.

Thus, historically speaking, there never was such a thing as a Palestinian nation with its own distinct identity. Those whom we today call "Palestinians" are Arabic speaking people in Palestine, mixed with many other people—especially since the beginning of the twentieth century—who until 1920 lived in the Ottoman Empire (under the Turks), until 1948 in the British Mandate, and until 1967 in the Palestinian part of the Kingdom of Jordan. Formerly, they would scarcely have viewed themselves as a distinct nation. Moreover, the Palestinians living in the Gaza Strip had Egyptian nationality, those on the Golan Heights had Syrian nationality, and those on the West Bank had Jordanian nationality.[27] Ask any Arabic-speaking person in the Holy Land, living before 1967, what his nationality was, and he would have answered: "Jordanian," or "Egyptian," or "Syrian." It is a historical fact that never in history had a Palestinian state existed, and until 1967, neither had a Palestinian people as such existed. Only romantics and history forgers and fakers could assert anything other than this.

Just for clarity: of course, the *name* "Palestinians" is thousands of years old, for the word is nothing but a variation of the biblical word *P'lishtim* ("Philistines") (who definitely were not Arabs[28]). Once they learned that in the past, the Philistines had been the Jews' worst enemies, the Romans gave the name *Palestina* to the entire land just to harass the Jews. The Arabs call the land *Falastin*. After Roman times, a Palestinian was an inhabitant of Palestine, whether they were Jewish, Greek, Turkish, Armenian, Arab, or something else. Before the state of Israel was founded, the Arab inhabitants

---

27. Some of the latter have shown me their Jordanian passports, decades after 1967; they had no other passport.
28. Neh. 13:24 speaks of the "language of Ashdod" (one of the Philistine cities), as opposed to the "language of Judah" (probably Hebrew). The languages were presumably related to each other and to Aramaic, but others have argued that the Ashdodite language was a Phoenician or an Aegean or Anatolian one; see Yamauchi (1988, 765–66).

of Palestine had never claimed an identity of their own, and might even have laughed at the idea of a distinct Palestinian "people." Palestinian nationalism arose only after the establishment of the state of Israel, and especially after the Six Day War, in particular through the propaganda of Yasser Arafat, leader of the PLO (Palestinian Liberation Organization, founded in 1964).

On November 29, 1947, the General Assembly of the United Natiod a Jewish area, whereas Jerusalem was to receive an international status. A number of Jews was not happy because they wanted *all* the land; but most Jews were clever enough to accept the partition plan, and did so with great enthusiasm, because it opened the door to founding their own Jewish state within the Holy Land, which became reality on May 14, 1948 (5 Iyyar 5708).

The Arab part of the Palestinian population did not wish to cooperate with a partition for at least three reasons: (1) they claimed the entire land for themselves; (2) the Egyptians, Syrians, and Jordanians, who at the time ruled parts of the country, simply prohibited them from accepting the plan; and (3) the Palestinian Arabs thought that, with the help of neighboring Arab countries, they could easily drive out the Jews. If, at that moment, the Palestinian Arabs had immediately founded their own state (with the support of their neighbors), they could have spared themselves a lot of misery. All the complaints about Palestinians wanting their own state, and Jews preventing them from obtaining one for the last two-thirds of a century, crash against this rock: *Palestinians could have had their own state, but rejected the idea at the time* (or were prohibited from entertaining this idea at all). Any discussion of the Israeli-Palestinian conflict that ignores this essential fact is by definition unfair, one-sided, and ahistorical. If the Arab world had accepted the plan, humanly speaking Jerusalem would probably have been under international supervision right now.

Both the Arabs and the Jews played a role that was unfair. As to the Jews, the situation was aggravated by the fact that many Israelis were happy to hasten the flight of hundreds of thousands of Palestinians.²⁹ But here, too, every discussion of the Israeli-Palestinian conflict is unfair and one-sided if it ignores the essential fact that, over against the hundreds of thousands of Palestinians who were chased out of *Ha'Aretz*, there were *at least as many Jews who were chased out of Arab countries* (and found refuge in the new state of Israel).³⁰ Moreover, the Arab neighboring countries refused to integrate those fleeing Palestinians into their midst, but put them in miserable refugee camps, and have viewed them as second-class citizens until this very day. In this way, they have artificially propped up the so-called "Palestinian problem" in order to have a stick with which to beat the young state of Israel. The Arabs in the Jewish state of Israel, although actually (though not formally-judicially) being second-class citizens too, fare unspeakably better than the Palestinians in the refugee camps (and better than most Arabs in neighboring countries).

9.3.2 No Peace Possible

We must emphasize again that much of what in 1948 would have belonged to an Arab Palestinian state, if they had cooperated with the UN proposal, after 1948 was under the control of Egypt and Jordan. None of these two countries undertook any steps to establish a Palestinian state: Jordan annexed the West Bank, and kept its inhabitants under rigid repressive control (it even withheld from them the right to vote), and Egypt kept the Gaza Strip under military command.³¹ In other words, apparently no one in the Arab world was really interested in any Palestinian state. *In reality, this is not the issue*

---

29. Regarding Jewish misdeeds at this point, see extensively the Christian historian Christopher Sykes, in Laqueur (1969, 317), and the "New Historians" of Israel such as Melman (1992), Shlaim (1999; 2009), and Morris (2000; 2007; 2009); see Bouman (1998, 285–87). We must realize, though, that such a wholesome self-criticism would be unthinkable in Muslim countries! This is the nobility that is proper to Israel in comparison with its neighbors. Two other critics of the Jews are Flapan (1987), and Finkelstein (2005).
30. Some speak of 700,000 expelled Palestinians, and more than 700,000 expelled Jews.
31. So B. Maoz in Walker (1994, 167).

that is actually at stake. The real goal is not a Palestinian state as such, but the destruction of the state of Israel. This can be easily demonstrated. In recent decades, Israel has offered Palestinians their own state; they have offered to withdraw from the largest part of the West Bank. But both Yasser Arafat and Mahmoud Abbas have rejected all such proposals.[32] In 1948, they wanted the *entire* country and the destruction of Israel—in 2021 they still want the very same.

Thus, when it comes to Israel, we find among Arab Muslims only two interests: first (temporarily!) profit from Israel; second, that the state of Israel disappear from the scene, and all Israeli Jews be driven into the sea. If the Muslim Arabs are interested in a Palestinian state, then it can only be a state that contains all Palestine. In other words, the Arabic world is not and *cannot* be really interested in peace between Jews and Palestinians, or at best an (outward) peace as a temporary transition measure, if this is for the benefit of Arab Muslims. This is the great similarity between (extreme) Zionists and (extreme) Palestinians Muslim Arabs: *both want to have the entire country exclusively for themselves.* More moderate Israelis and Arabs would already be happy with a peaceful *status quo.* And orthodox Jews—as well as many orthodox Christians—are convinced that it is only the Messiah himself who can, and will, give all the land to a (repentant, believing) Israel.

Since 1948, the situation in *Ha'Aretz* has hardened because of constant battle. During the War of Independence (1948–1949), the Arabs lost the battle. The Jordanians did conquer East Jerusalem, though, and drove the Jews out of the city. The possibility of an international status for Jerusalem had now likely disappeared forever. Next, in 1956 a new war broke out—the Suez Crisis, or the Second Arab-Israeli

---

32. One shocking example: in 2000, during the Camp David negotiations led by U.S. President Clinton, Israeli prime minister Ehud Barak issued a far-reaching proposal to the Palestinians: an independent and sovereign Palestinian state on 98% of the West Bank, without any Jewish villages left behind. But Yasser Arafat refused; instead, he instigated the Second Intifada. In 2008, Israeli primeminister Ehud Olmert proposed still more concessions; again, the Palestinians, now led by Arafat's successor, Mahmoud Abbas, refused.

War—and in June 1967, a third one: the Six Days War. During the latter war, Israel occupied the Golan Heights, East Jerusalem, the West Bank (biblical Judea and Samaria), and the Gaza Strip, plus the part of the Sinai Desert that belonged to Egypt. As a consequence of their own aggression, the Arabs now had to cede East Jerusalem to the Jews; by their own doing, they had again rendered impossible achieving any international status for the city. There was this difference: the Jordanians had driven the Jews out of the old city, the Israelis did *not* drive the Arabs out of the old city.

In 1973 followed the Yom Kippur War. In 1979, Israel made peace with Egypt, and on this occasion obtained the occupied part of the Sinai Desert.[33] In 1982, Israel occupied Lebanon, after having been continually attacked by that country; from 1985, Israel occupied only the southern part of Lebanon. In 2000, it withdrew from this country. From 1987 until 1993, the First Intifada took place, that is, the insurgence of the Palestinians in the disputed territories (Judea, Samaria, Gaza, Golan). In 2000 there was a Second Intifada. In 2004, Israel withdrew from the Gaza Strip. In 2006, Israel was at war with Lebanon. Since 2012, there has been an ongoing conflict with the terrorist organization Hamas, which acquired hegemony in the Gaza Strip at the expense of Al-Fatah. A recent low point was the bombs and missiles that Israel and Gaza (Hamas) exchanged in May 2021, with hundreds of casualties.

The international community identifies Israel as the reproach of "colonialism" and "imperialism." This is an absurd falsification of history. It was *Israel* that, in 1947, agreed to a partition of the land and an international status for Jerusalem. Instead of agreeing to this partition plan, the Arabs have repeatedly made war against Israel. It is pure Muslim Arab imperialism that wishes to incorporate all Palestine into some Muslim Arab empire, in which the Palestinian Jews are indeed tolerated, but only as *dhimmis*: second-class citizens.

---

33. The Egyptian president, Anwar al-Sadat, had to pay the price for this: he was murdered in 1981.

Under normal circumstances and in ordinary relationships between neighbors who have a conflict, it must be possible to find a solution together. Unfortunately, human speaking, peace between the Israelis and the Palestinian Arabs is virtually impossible because it is quite doubtful that both parties (the conservative government of Israel and the Palestinian Authority) are prepared to pay the price for any form of peace:

(a) For *Israel*, this price would be to give up its settlements policy, that is, to stop building Jewish settlements in the disputed territories, or even to abandon the many settlements that have already been built. And almost even worse than this, Israel would *never* be prepared to give up Old Jerusalem (including the Temple Square); doing so would lead to an insurgence among the Israelis.

(b) For the *Palestinians*, the price would be to help construct borders between the Israeli and the Palestinian states such that the safety of both states is sufficiently guaranteed. And even worse that this: the Palestinians would have to acknowledge the state of Israel's legitimacy and right to exist. So far, they have *never* shown any willingness to do this. Please notice, as said before, some Palestinians would be prepared to acknowledge the state of Israel as an *accomplished fact*, if such a willingness would contribute to an agreement; but this is something very different from acknowledging Israel's *right* to have its own state in the Holy Land. And almost even worse than this, the Palestinians would *never* be prepared to give up Old Jerusalem (including the Temple Square[34]); doing so would lead to an insurgence among the Palestinians. What in 1947 was still theoretically conceivable—at least in the eyes of the United Nations—namely, East Jerusalem being placed under international supervision, by now has become unthinkable.

---

34. Called by Palestinians Haram ash-Sharif ("The Noble Sanctuary"); they generally deny that there ever was a Jewish temple at that site.

9.3.3 A Preliminary Theological Question

The discussion about having one or two states in *Ha'Aretz*, and about the status of East Jerusalem, is not only a matter of international law. For Jews as well as Christians, there is also a basic theological question that must be answered: Is it true that, biblically speaking, Israel has the right to claim the entire Holy Land, or at least certain parts of it? Several answers have been given to this question.

(a) The *supersessionist* answer (also given by Palestinian Christian supersessionists *and*, of course, by Muslim Arabs): "Israel does *not* have that right." There is this difference: in general, Christian supersessionists (perhaps with the exception of some Palestinian Christians) are happy for the Jews that they can live in the Holy Land, but Muslims are not. But when it is a matter of *rights*, both groups are likely to agree about the important *political* decision of the United Nations (Nov. 1947), but not that Israel has any *theological* right to claim *Ha'Aretz*. The "land promise" of the Tanakh must be spiritualized.

(b) The Muslims have an additional problem, though. The Quran says,

> Pharaoh sought to scare them [the Israelites] out of the land [of Israel]: but We [Allah] drowned him [Pharoah] together with all who were with him. Then We said to the Israelites: 'Dwell in this land [the Land of Israel]. When the promise of the hereafter [End of Days] comes to be fulfilled, We shall assemble you [the Israelites] all together [in the Land of Israel].[35]

Shaykh Abdul Hadi Palazzi, secretary general of the Italian Muslim Assembly, commented:

> God wanted to give Abraham a double blessing, through Ishmael and through Isaac, and ordered that Ishmael's descendants should live in the desert of Arabia and Isaac's in Canaan. The Qur'an recognizes the Land of Israel as the heritage of the Jews

---

35. Surah 17 ("Night Journey"), 102–10, as rendered in http://www.templemount.org/quranland.html.

and it explains that, before the Last Judgment, Jews will return to dwell there. This prophecy has already been fulfilled.[36]

In the light of these Qur'an statements, Muslims should have a religious difficulty denying Israel's title to the land.

(c) The Zionist answer (both Jewish and Christian): "The biblical promise of the Land must be understood literally; through God's governmental dealings, we see today how this promise is indeed being fulfilled. In 1967, God returned the land to Israel, and therefore, Israel must not return that land, or even parts of it, to the Arabs, for these are not entitled to it." The difficulty with this position is that matters of theology and of international law are being intermingled here, which is not very practical. But unfortunately, this impracticality seems to have been inevitable in the Israeli-Palestinian conflict. The real, diehard Zionist (both Jewish and Christian) can maintain their extreme standpoint only by ignoring international law, or by arguing it away.

(d) Is there still another option? There is (and again, it is one that orthodox Jews and orthodox Christians could easily have in common):[37] the biblical "land promise" must be understood literally, and will be completely fulfilled in the "end time," that is, the time just prior to Messiah's coming, and the time of this coming itself. However, promises on God's part do not necessarily imply claims and titles on the part of humans. On the one hand, God always fulfills his promise, but on the other hand, on the side of his people, true repentance, humbling, and confession of sins are needed. Compare Daniel 9: Daniel did not claim God's promise involving the return from the Babylonian exile, but confessed the guilt of the people, and God did the rest:

> I, Daniel, perceived in the books the number of years that, according to the word of the LORD to Jeremiah the prophet [Jer. 25:11-12; 29:10], must pass before the end of the desolations of Jerusalem, namely, seventy years. Then I turned my face to the

---

36. http://www.templemount.org/quranland.html.
37. Douma (2008) dealt too superficially with this option.

LORD God, seeking him by prayer and pleas for mercy with fasting and sackcloth and ashes (Dan. 9:2-3).

Unfortunately, such a confession on the part of the greater (secularized) portion of modern Israel seems a long way off. In God's time, that is, the time of Messiah's coming and of Israel's spiritual restoration, he will give all the land to Israel, but not before that time. God passively *allowing* Israel to conquer the West Bank is not the same as God actively *giving* this part of the land to Israel. As God said through the prophet Zechariah: "This is the word of the LORD to Zerubbabel: 'Not by might, nor by power, but by my Spirit,' says the LORD of hosts" (Zech. 4:6). In the course of time, God has allowed Israel to do many things, without this implying that God *approved* of all these things. Without repentance there can be no true restoration of Israel, and thus no definitive fulfillment of the "land promise." However, this does not diminish the claim that the establishment of the state of Israel is undeniably the *run-up* to, and the preparation for, this ultimate, complete fulfillment. It is not yet the real thing, but it *is* a necessary preliminary condition for this real thing. Those who assert that current events have nothing to do with biblical prophecy are wrong. Those who assert that current events are the fulfillment of biblical prophecy are wrong, too. In my view, the truth lies somewhere in between: current events in *Ha'Aretz* are the run-up to the full realization of biblical prophecy. The latter lies in God's hands who, on the one hand, will change the hearts of his people and, on the other hand, will send the Messiah, who will usher in the Messianic kingdom.

9.4 Political Aspects[38]

9.4.1 The Attitude of Israeli Politics

All the important political parties of Israel strive for a democratic state, which also implies that it is a state that has room for, and takes care of, an Arab or any other ethnic minority, as long as the majority in the country will be Jewish. All the important parties also strive for safe borders, and for peace

---

38. See extensively, Ouweneel (2002, chapter 4).

with their Arab neighbor countries. However, the "Left" (the Labor party) and the "Right" (the Likud[39] party) do not agree about the best way to achieve this peace and safety. The Labor party is more pragmatic, and therefore more prepared to make certain concessions. The Likud party pleads for a harsher attitude toward the Palestinians; therefore, Christian Zionists generally sympathize more with Likud than with Labor.

All of the most recent governments of Israel were led by the Likud party: Menachem Begin, Yitzhak Shamir, Ariel Sharon, and Benyamin Netanyahu. Important leaders of the Labor party were Golda Meir, Yitzhak Rabin, Shimon Peres, and Ehud Barak.

Both the Likud party and the Labor party have cooperated in the construction of Jewish settlements in the disputed territories, among Palestinian inhabitants. In this way, the Israelis at least gave the impression that they were not really interested in achieving peace in the sense of international law. This is because such a peace can be made only if (under strict conditions) the disputed territories (or at least a considerable part of them), including the settlements, would be handed over to certain international authorities, which in practice means: to the Palestinians, who wish to establish a Palestinian state there with the help of their Arab neighbors. Of course, the Palestinians themselves would also have to meet conditions that for them seem unfeasible, as we have observed.

Such Jewish settlements exist only in the so-called Area C, that is, since the Oslo Accords (1993–1995),[40] the area where Israel has complete civil and military control. Area C contains about 60 percent of all the disputed territories. In addition, there is Area B under common Israeli-Palestinian control (about 22%) and Area A (exclusive Palestinian control; about

---

39. The Heb. word *likud* means something like "consolidation."
40. The Oslo Accords between Israel and the PLO, no. I (1993 signed in Washington, DC), and no. II (1995, signed in Taba, Egypt), was the result of negotiations that had secretly started in Oslo. Prime figures were Israeli Prime Minister Yitzhak Rabin and PLO leader Yasser Arafat.

18%);[41] Areas B and A naturally do not contain any Jewish settlements. That Israelis and Palestinians agreed in Oslo to such a partition into three areas helps explain why the Israelis believe they have legitimately built their settlements in Area C. This point is often overlooked in foreign commentary on Israeli politics.

In some places, the presence of Jewish settlements, often inhabited by ultra-orthodox Jews and/or Zionist extremists, is most painful. In 2002, 80 percent of the city of Hebron was inhabited by more than 120,000 Muslims, and 20 percent (where 20,000 Muslims live) by only four hundred colonists. These Jewish colonists had to be protected by a disproportionately large number of soldiers, involving enormous costs. The reason for this trouble and these expenses is that Hebron is one of the four "holy cities" of Israel, along with Jerusalem, Tiberias, and Safed (Tzfat) (see §9.7.2). Hebron is a holy city because the tombs of the three patriarchs and three matriarchs are there: Abraham and Sarah, Isaac[42] and Rebekah, Jacob and Leah (not Rachel; she was buried near Bethlehem, Gen. 35:19; not Joseph, wh'o was buried at Shechem, Josh. 24:32).

9.4.2 The Attitude of Palestinian Politics

The Palestinians do not cease using violence, first because extremist Islamic Palestinians want to control all of Palestine, and therefore do not expect anything useful from negotiations with the Israelis. Second, more moderate Palestinians seem to believe now that they will gain more from the Israelis through violence than through negotiation. An important precondition for any Palestinian negotiation is that Israel must promise not to extend the Jewish settlements, or rather to restrict them.

But the Israelis will never make such a promise if the Palestinians, on their part, refuse to acknowledge the state of

---

41. Typical Area A cities are Bethlehem, Hebron, Janeen, Jericho, Nablus, and Ramallah.
42. Not Ishmael, as my Muslim guide told me when I visited the place for the first time.

Israel's right of existence within the Holy Land. More moderate Palestinians are prepared to accept the actual existence of Israel—as has been expressed already in the Oslo Accords—as long as they can get their own state. What is hidden in their agenda we can only guess—but the same is true about the agenda of the "hawks" among the Israelis. We do know, however, that in many Arabic speeches by leaders of the Palestinian Authority, they still tell their constituency that "all Palestine must be liberated," that is, rid of its Jewish inhabitants. It is all a matter of religion. Humanly speaking, without Judaism and Islam, the political controversies between Jews and Palestinian Arabs might be easily solved. However, on the basis of the Tanakh, orthodox Jews will always claim all the Holy Land—and on the basis of the Quran, orthodox Muslims will always do the same.

Already in the Ottoman Empire, it was the common practice that Muslim leaders, when their political power was inferior to that of non-Islamic powers, strived for *müdara*, the "cats' gentleness," until the power balance changed again in their favor, after which they again showed their true faces. Islam also propagates the practice of the *iham*, the systematic misleading of the "enemies of Allah" in dealing with them. The Oslo Accords were nothing but a temporary interruption of the hostilities (a *hudna* or a *muwada'a*) as a tactical means in political weakness.[43] Thus, after Arafat had signed these Accords, he reportedly said: "I view this agreement as nothing more than the agreement that was signed between our prophet Muhammad and the Koraish."[44] This is an allusion to what happened in Muhammad's days: two years after Muhammed had signed a peace treaty (Treaty of Hudaybiyya, 628) with the anti-Islam minded Koraish, he attacked this tribe fiercely and thoroughly defeated it.

---

43. This was the view of Scholl-Latour (2000, 276); this book by a preeminent German political scientist, Arabist, and journalist, who travelled throughout the Middle East for fifty years, is a must read for everyone who wishes to be informed in this field.
44. Ibid.; cf. Saada (2008, 195–98).

According to *Shariah* (Islamic law), the Oslo Accords cannot be taken seriously; Muslims have a religious duty to break them as soon as they find an opportunity to do so. During the Fourth Conference of the Islamic Research Academy in Cairo (1968), the highest Jordanian authority in the field of Islamic law said this: "Peace decrees are allowed only in order to, in times of weakness, recollect power for coming conflicts. The holy war [*jihad*] must be the basis of the relationships between Muslims and non-Muslims. Muslims have the freedom to break any agreement with non-Muslims."[45] Here, we see clearly that, in the Middle East, we are dealing with a spiritual battle between the God of Israel and Allah, the god of Islam. This makes the Israeli-Palestinian problem even much more serious. Ultimately, this is a battle in the heavenly places: "[W]e do not wrestle against flesh and blood, but against the rulers, against the authorities, against the cosmic powers over this present darkness, against the spiritual forces of evil in the heavenly places" (Eph. 6:12).

9.4.3 The Living Conditions of the Palestinians

It is true that the living conditions of the Palestinians are often bad. But this is not something for which Israel can be blamed—as has been done so often—or can be blamed *alone*. For centuries, the Palestinians have lived under miserable living conditions, for which the Israelis cannot possibly be blamed because at the time there were no Israeli authorities in *Ha'Aretz*. Moreover, what is "bad"? Some Palestinians, if they dare to openly admit it, will happily (or reluctantly) testify that, under the Israelis, they live more safely and prosperously than anywhere else in the Middle East. To the extent this might interest them, they would have to admit that Israel is the only truly democratic land in the Middle East. Democracy by definition means that democratic governments take into consideration the interests of minorities under their supervision, and this is generally what the Israelis have done with *their* country (though not as much as the latter might perhaps wish).

---

45. Quoted in Schrupp (1992, 63).

Of course, this is just one aspect of the matter. For many people, including Palestinians, living in relative prosperity is always worse than living in freedom coupled with the greatest poverty. A Hebrew Christian in Israel, pastor Baruch Maoz, wrote that the West Bank and the Gaza Strip were governed under a rigid, military hand; yet, this Israeli military government was the most enlightened, the most generous of all military occupations that the world has ever seen. Within twenty years, the standard of living on the West Bank and in the Gaza Strip reached the highest average in the Middle East, with the exception of the state of Israel. New industries were founded, agriculture improved, and the agricultural yield advanced by leaps and bounds. Tens of thousands of Arab Palestinians were employed within the state of Israel, and the government undertook continual attempts to end illegal employment, to end paying poverty wages, and to promote offering social security. However, the rising Palestinian national(istic) self-awareness had no outlet. Moreover, extensive contact with Israeli Jews exposed many Palestinians to a kind of arrogance that one would have thought that Jews could never display toward other people.[46]

It is true, at all times Christians must support the people of Israel because it is the apple of God's eye (Deut. 32:10; Zech. 2:8), and because Israel has been persecuted for centuries in particular by "Christian" Europe, with the Holocaust as absolute low point. Therefore, every Christian should assist in guaranteeing Israel a safe state in the ancient land of Israel. However, support for the people of Israel does not mean that Christians must approve of all decrees and actions of the government of Israel, or of fanatic ultra-orthodox and Zionist Jews. On the contrary, it is their duty to point out to their friends what is going wrong for the very reason that they are *friends*, even if friends must sometimes "hurt" each other (Prov. 27:6a). It is to be regretted that some Christian writers hardly seem to make the latter distinction.

---

46. Maoz in Walker (1994, 169); in a footnote, he added that the Israeli military administration provided enormous educational and medical benefits.

9.5 Deeper Backgrounds
9.5.1 Racism? Fascism?

As long as there is no all-inclusive peace plan for *Ha'Aretz*, Israel cannot one-sidedly annex the disputed territories; that would be suicide. Therefore, it must maintain the occupation of the disputed territories, even though this is not possible without a certain measure of oppression of rebellious Palestinians. However, Israel has also perpetrated forms of a severely humiliating oppression that surpass the minimum of inevitable oppression. The average Israeli, whatever their political and religious views may be, often exhibits remarkably little understanding for the position of the Palestinians. I hear this especially from Palestinian biblical Christians from the West Bank, but also from enlightened, moderate Israelis. The Jewish nation, which for thousands of years has itself been oppressed, should exhibit a little more sympathy for people that at present feel oppressed by the Israelis.[47]

However, to speak of racism here would be absurd; such an allegation is another typical example of unnuanced one-sidedness with which the various parties approach the Israeli-Palestinian problem. Jews and Arabs belong to the same race; according to their origins, both are Semites, descendants of Shem (Gen. 10:21-31; 11:10-32). Actually, what is usually meant by racism is that only immigrants of Jewish descent can obtain Israeli citizenship. However, this is a form of discrimination (favoring A above B), not of racism. All racism is discrimination, but not all discrimination is racism.

However, this definitely involves a problem of international law, all the more so because not only non-Jews but also Messianic (i.e., Jesus-confessing) Jews are excluded from Israeli citizenship. This occurs despite the "Law of Return" (*choq hash'vut*) of 1950, which says that *every* Jew—that is, each person who has a Jewish mother—has the right to emigrate to Israel. The painful reality is that, for instance, atheist and Buddhist Jews are in principle welcome to the state of Israel, but Messianic Jews are not.[48] The abhorrence toward

---

47. Cf. Reitsma (2006; see also 2017).
48. In practice, only those Messianic Jews who manage to hide their faith in Jesus

Jesus-believing people, including the Jewish ones, exists not only among many Muslim Palestinians, but also at the immigration service and by Israelis in general. Several times, ultra-orthodox Jews have damaged the synagogues or meeting-places of Messianic Jews in Israel.

Speaking of discrimination and racism: in November 1975, the United Nations branded Zionism as a form of racism. Or, to use another irritating word, indicating how sick the debate has become: the Israeli (!) historian Uri Davis has called the state of Israel an "apartheid state." This is absurd, because under the apartheid regime in South Africa non-whites were compelled to live together in their own territories; the various races literally had to live "apart." Such a situation is unquestionably non-existent in Israel, at least not to an extent that vaguely resembles the situation in South Africa since 1900. One-fifth of Israeli citizens are Arab.

In June 2018, the Turkish president, Recep Tayyip Erdogan, claimed that Israel is the most racist and fascist state in the modern world.[49] The reason for his statement was that a week earlier, the Israeli Parliament had adopted a law in which Israel is described as the "nation state for the Jewish people." Erdogan said he saw no difference between Hitler's obsession for the Aryan race and the law that had been newly adopted by the Israeli Parliament. "The spirit of Hitler, who led the world to the precipice, has found acceptance with a number of Israeli leaders," the Turkish president declared. He also criticized the missile attacks of the Israeli army against Hamas targets in the Gaza Strip: "With tanks, artillery and missiles on Palestinians, Israel has demonstrated that it is a terror state." He appealed to Muslims, Christians, politicians, NGOs, and journalists worldwide to undertake action against Israel. Erdogan "forgot" to mention that, for months already, Israel had been plagued by fire flyers and missile attacks from the Gaza Strip. And speaking of apartheid: no Jew is allowed to live in Gaza anymore.

---

are allowed to immigrate into Israel.
49. The Times of Israel, July 25, 2018.

The comparison with Hitler greatly offended the Israeli prime minister Netanyahu; on Twitter he said: "The fact that Erdogan attacks the nation state law is the greatest compliment that he can give this law." Apparently, what he wished to say is that if a law is attacked by a *bad* person it must be a *good* law. Netanyahu also underscored the fact that Erdogan had put tens of thousands of Turkish citizens into prison, and that his country is "a dark dictatorship."

In this totally one-sided and exaggerated "fake news war" with regard to Israel, there is something enigmatic or mysterious, which will be examined more closely in the following sections.

9.5.2 Palestinian "Sojourners"

If Israelis and Palestinians ever wish to arrive at a two–statestion,[50] then one of the troublesome questions will be whether the hundreds of thousands of Palestinian refugees must (be allowed to) return to Israel. Three solutions are conceivable, which can, or ought to, be put into practice at the same time by Israelis and Palestinians together.

(1) Refugees should partly integrate into the Arab countries where they have lived now for more than a century, and have produced a second and a third generation that, for the greater part, has never been in Palestine. These are Arabs who have long been part of society in these countries, even though they are still tucked away in camps.

(2) Refugees should partly be incorporated into the Palestinian territories, that is, in the Palestinian state that might be founded.

(3) Refugees should partly be incorporated into the state of Israel, especially those refugees who (or whose ancestors) have come from the territory of the present state of Israel.

One point often overlooked but requiring consideration is that the great majority of the Palestinian families had lived

---

50. In recent times, no one has shown more clearly that a two-states solution is an illusion than the Irish peacemaker, professor in Boston, Padraig O'Malley (2015). Yet, many countries continue to insist on such a solution because they see no alternative.

in the Holy Land for only a few generations; most of them were immigrants just as were most of the Jews. A second point is that the so-called Palestinians have the very same language, history, and culture as the Arabs in the neighboring countries. As we have seen, there never was a Palestinian nation as a distinct ethnic and cultural entity. If they had not been stowed away in camps, they would have integrated into the neighboring countries within a short time. However, those few Palestinian families whose ancestors have lived, sometimes for centuries, in *Ha'Aretz* before the Zionists arrived should certainly be allowed to return to their former dwelling-places in the land. As God said to Israel in view of the Messianic kingdom:

> You shall allot it [i.e., the land] as an inheritance for yourselves *and for the sojourners who reside among you* and have had children among you. They shall be to you as native-born children of Israel. With you they shall be allotted an inheritance among the tribes of Israel. In whatever tribe the sojourner resides, there you shall assign him his inheritance, declares the Lord God (Ezek. 47:22–23).

However, it seems as if the discussion of such issues is taboo in Israel. The truth is that many Israelis hate the Palestinians. This irrational hatred goes far beyond the understandable response to the Palestinian terrorist actions against Israel. This irrationality existing on *both* sides contains a mystery: it demonstrates to us that the entire conflict is occurring on a metahistorical level, the existence of which many Jews, Muslims and Christians are perhaps hardly aware. I once said to an Israeli friend: "The Muslims' hatred against Israel is a proof for the existence of a metahistorical reality, and thus indirectly a proof for the existence of God." The friend was clever enough to immediately understand the comment. However, today I would—and should—add that the Jesus-hatred of many Israelis is a proof for the present blinding of Israel, and thus indirectly a proof for the existence of God, too. Let the one who is able to receive this receive it.

At the end of the nineties, the leftish-liberal Israeli newspaper *Haaretz* spoke of a "cold civil war" within Israel itself because of the immense chasm between opposing opinions concerning the Palestinians. An inquiry of those days pointed out that no fewer than 27% of the students at the orthodox Jewish university Bar Ilan had some understanding about, or even approved of, the murder of the Israeli prime minister Yitzaq Rabin (1995) by their radical fellow-student Yigal Amir.[51] Apparently, they believed that someone who negotiated with the Palestinians deserved to die. In my view, such Israelis are no better than extremist Palestinians. Both views are rooted in hatred, or more accurately, in religion: ultra-orthodox Judaism and extreme Islam, respectively.

9.5.3 Criticizing Israel

Christians who love God, the Bible, and Jesus must also love the people of that God, the people of that Book, and the people of Jesus. They love Israel because God has testified of his love for no other people as he did with Israel:

> It was not because you were more in number than any other people that the LORD *set his love on you* and chose you, for you were the fewest of all peoples, but it is because the LORD *loves you* and is keeping the oath that he swore to your fathers, that the LORD has brought you out with a mighty hand and redeemed you from the house of slavery, from the hand of Pharaoh king of Egypt (Deut. 7:7–8).[52]

Christians cannot but stand behind God's beloved at all times and under all circumstances. However, we must also have the courage, as good friends, to point out to the *state* of Israel certain matters in which the authorities, in our view, cross the line. Therefore, I find it deeply saddening that certain Christian writers in the West immediately dismiss any form of criticism of the politics of Israel as anti-Semitism,

---

51. Scholl-Latour (2000, 461).
52. This is very different from John 3:16, "For God so loved the world . . . ." We care for all people because God cares for them; but one's loving poor beggars is not the same as loving one's "firstborn son" (Exod. 4:22) or one's "wife" (Isa. 54:5–10).

and doubt a person's faithfulness to the Bible if the latter dares to use the expression "occupied territories" (usually simply employing common parlance).

The truth of the matter is that it is more correct to speak of "disputed territories" because there is no reason—either from the viewpoint of history or of international law—why Israel's claims on especially the West Bank would be less valid than the claims of "the" Palestinians, who were "invented" as an ethnic entity " merely a few decades ago (to say nothing of the Romans, the Byzantines, the Arabic Muslims, the Crusaders, the Kurds, the Mamelukes, the Turks, the British, or the Jordanians, who, at times, all of whom had supervision over the West Bank). In other words, *whose* territories did the Israelis "occupy" in 1967? Those of "the Palestinians"? But these have *never ever in history* governed the West Bank. Those of the Jordanians? But these just poached that territory in 1948–1949; they, too, had no historical or legal right to possess it. At the time, there were no massive international protests against Jordan, like those against Israel many times after 1967. It seems that *any* nation can claim these territories as long as they are not Jews, who had lived there for many centuries.

Here again, we encounter the metahistorical riddle mentioned earlier. Why are the Israelis the last to have their rights respected by the international community? Strictly speaking, within the boundaries of international law, modern Israelis are not "entitled" to the "disputed" areas. But why are the protests so massive and so frequent? Why were there, as far as I can assess, never massive, international, legal protests against the Mamelukes, who "occupied" the land from 1260 to 1516? Or against the Turks, who "occupied" the land from 1516 to 1917? Or against the British, who "occupied" the land from 1917 to 1948? Or against the Jordanians, who "occupied" East Jerusalem and the West Bank from 1948 to 1967? It seems as if every nation is allowed to possess or "occupy" Judea and Samaria, *except the only nation on earth that ever had an independent ethnic existence there*, namely, Israel. This irrational, unreasoned, and mysterious abhorrence of

Israel's rights demonstrates the existence of a metahistorical, supernatural reality, of "powers behind the scenes," and thus indirectly of God—the God who is the *God of Israel*.

And yet, despite our full support of the people of Israel and of their legal and historic rights, it *must* be possible to criticize certain actions of the Israeli authorities, as, by the way, many Israelis themselves do. Such criticism does not come from enemies, so many of whom populate the General Assembly of the United Nations, but from Christian *friends*, and therefore, such criticism should be welcome to the authorities of Israel. A genuine friend is not someone who always wishes to please you, but who points out your mistakes and weaknesses to you: "Faithful are the wounds of a friend; / profuse are the kisses of an enemy. . . . / Oil and perfume make the heart glad, / and the sweetness of a friend comes from his earnest counsel" (Prov. 27:6, 9).

9.6 Religious Aspects[53]
9.6.1 The Temple Mount[54]

In the entire Israeli-Palestinian conflict, the Temple Mount[55] plays an essential role. First, for religious Jews, the Temple Mount is the most sacred place on earth because the First Temple (that of Solomon; 969–586 BC, i.e., 383 years) and the Second Temple (that of Zerubbabel; 516 BC–AD 70, i.e., 585 years) have stood there. This is a total of 968 years. Moreover, the *Shekhinah* (the divine presence) dwelt in the First temple (a fact that is not mentioned for the Second Temple).

Second, the Temple Mount is of essential importance for the Muslims, who refer to the place as Haram ash-Sharif ("the Noble Sanctuary"); to them, it is the third most sacred

---

53. See extensively, Ouweneel (2002, chapter 5).
54. Its Hebrew name is *Har haBayit*, "Mountain of the House," i.e., *har bēt-YHWH* ("mountain of the house of the LORD," Isa. 2:2), the Temple; it is also called Mount Moriah (2 Chron. 3:1; cf. Gen. 22:2).
55. This northeastern mountain is sometimes identified as Mount Zion (e.g., Isa. 2:3), which originally was the southeastern mountain—the mountain of the City of David (2 Sam. 5:7)—whereas today "Zion" has become the name of the south*western* mountain, just outside the Turkish walls, near the Zion Gate (see §13.3).

place, in addition to Mecca and Medina. The latter two cities are closely linked with the history of Muhammad and early Islam. Haram ash-Sharif is important because, according to Muslim interpretation, the Quran in Surah 17 describes how Muhammad made a nightly journey to heaven from *this* mountain.

Third, the mountain is historically important for Christians, too, because Jesus preached here so often, and because here the New Testament Ecclesia was born (Acts 2). Moreover, Jesus died and rose again very near this mountain (about 500 meters or 1500 feet away).

Fourth, by now the Temple Mount/Haram ash-Sharif has become a nationalistic prestige object also for less religious Israelis and Palestinians.

On the one hand, humanly speaking, it is totally inconceivable that Israelis and Palestinian Arabs would or could ever reach an agreement on the Temple Mount/Haram ash-Sharif. On the other hand, between 1948 and 1967, when the Jordanians occupied the West Bank and East Jerusalem, they exhibited very little (religious) interest for East Jerusalem and the Temple Mount. As far as I know, not a single Arab leader ever came to Haram ash-Sharif for instance to pray in the Al-Aqsah Mosque, or in the Dome of the Rock (sometimes mistakenly referred to as the Omar Mosque). Even the Charter of Yasser Arafat's PLO (Palestinian Liberation Organization) does not mention the Temple Mount/Haram ash-Sharif. Only after the Temple Mount had been conquered by the Israelis in 1967 did the Palestinians suddenly exhibit great political and religious interest in the place.

It is indeed a remarkable site. I remember sitting one morning, at 7 a.m., on the slopes of the Mount of Olives, praying and Bible reading, and quietly considering the site. It dawned upon me that I was looking at the most significant and most disputed square kilometer in the entire world. I have visited the Temple Mount many times, with my wife, or with one of my sons, or as the tour leader of a group of Christians, and often alone. Once, I visited the place with a Jewish guide, and once with a Muslim guide. When I got out my little Bible to check something my Jewish guide said, she almost fainted; both the Israeli and the Palestinian authorities do not allow any religious utterances on the Temple Mount (except for a loud *Allahu Akbar*,[56] which I heard shouted by dozens of Muslims when they saw a handful of orthodox Jews walking along the borders of the square[57]).

Conversely, when I was at the site with the Arab guide, and accidentally used the word "Temple Mount," *he* was the one who became terribly upset, and shouted at me: "There never was a temple here!" Yasser Arafat reportedly once said, "If there were ever a temple on this mountain, then the Quran would certainly have mentioned it." He forgot that the Quran does not mention the word "Jerusalem" (or *Al-Quds*, the "Holy Place," as the Arabs call it).

Throughout the years (from 1982 until today), I have always experienced the Temple Mount as the most highly charged, contradictory, bizarre, absurd place that exists on our globe. I often look at it, and I think: "This is the place where it is going to happen!" As it has been prophesied, "On that day *his feet shall stand on the Mount of Olives* that lies before Jerusalem on the east, . . . Then the LORD my God will come, and all the holy ones with him" (Zech. 14:4-5).

> It shall come to pass in the latter days
> that the *mountain of the house of the LORD*
> shall be established as the highest of the mountains,
> and it shall be lifted up above the hills;
> and peoples shall flow to it,
> and many nations shall come, and say:
> "Come, let us go up to the mountain of the LORD,
> to the house of the God of Jacob,
> that he may teach us his ways
> and that we may walk in his paths.'
> For out of Zion shall go forth the Torah,
> and the word of the LORD from Jerusalem"

---

56. "Allah is great," or as many wish to render it, "Allah is greater" (than any other "god," especially the God of Jews and Christians).
57. This must have been exceptional: most orthodox Jews do not tread the Square because they are afraid to enter the site where the Most Holy Place was, whose location is no longer precisely known (cf. Num. 4:18–20).

(Micah 4:1–2).

Notice these two key mountains: the Mount of Olives and the Temple Mount (or Mount Moriah) (other key mountains are mentioned in §14.7.4)! The Lord will come *to* the former mount, and the Torah will go forth *from* the latter mount. How near in time could these events be! And in our minds, how far are they still removed from us! And sometimes I think: How easy do supersessionists have it: for them, these places have only historical significance, and not the least theological significance.

9.6.2 The Two-Ways Doctrine

Another religious aspect to be dealt with is the "two-ways doctrine." The *concept* of this doctrine is certainly not very clear. There are some who believe that a dialogue between Jews and Christians, in which the two parties accept each other's positions *a priori*, already implies some kind of a two-ways doctrine: a Jewish and a Christian way to God. Others believe that taking the land promise literally already implies some kind of a two-ways doctrine: the way of the earthly Jerusalem and the way of the heavenly Jerusalem. This is how the meaning of the term "two-ways doctrine" has been eroded. A meaning that seems to make more sense is this one: a two-ways doctrine teaches that Jews, or any other people, can be saved through another way than *through Jesus Christ*.

In its strictest form, the Christian-Zionist two-ways doctrine implies that Christians from the Gentile nations ought not to bring the gospel of Jesus to Jews because God ostensibly has another way for Israel to be saved. David Stern, a leader among Messiah-believing Jews and one of the most learned among them, rightly stated that this is (unintentionally) a form of anti-Semitism, for what is worse than keeping the gospel of Christ from the Jews (of all people), to whom it belongs in the first place?[58] In every stage of redemptive history, there is only one way of salvation: forgiveness on the basis of Christ's work of atonement (in anticipation or in retrocipation), together with all the blessings founded upon it.

---

58. Stern (1997, 253–61); cf. extensively Van der Wolf (2010).

There is only one way, never two ways. However, we should not confuse this with the fact that God traveled a different way with the patriarchs than with Israel; he traveled with ancient Israel a different way than with post-Pentecost Israel; and he travels with the Ecclesia, the New Testament body of Christ, a different way than with Israel in the Diaspora, and in the end time, with Israel in *Ha'Aretz*.

The Bible says that God is, and always remains, the same: regarding the old heavens and earth, "They will perish, but you will remain; / they will all wear out like a garment. / You will change them like a robe, and they will pass away, / but *you are the same*, and your years have no end (Ps. 102:26-27). Jesus Christ is *the same* yesterday and today and forever" (Heb. 13:8). But it would be a great mistake to conclude from this that God always *acts* in the same way. He always acts according to the *same* great features of his being—love, light, holiness, grace, mercy, and so on—but he does *very different* things. Supersessionists love to emphasize the former, dispensationalists love to emphasize the latter. However, although God acts differently in subsequent redemptive-historical eras, some principles always remain the same, as expressed, for instance, in the following two passages: "Jesus said, 'I am the way, and the truth, and the life. *No one* comes to the Father except through me'" (John 14:6). And: "[T]here is salvation in *no one* else [than Jesus], for there is no other name under heaven given among humans by which we must be saved."

It is altogether different discussion, however, as to whether non-Jewish Christians who reject the two-ways doctrine are the most appropriate people to evangelize the Jews in Israel[59] (apart from the fact that evangelizing is forbidden in that country). By far the most appropriate people to bear witness to the gospel among Israelis are the Messianic Jews and their non-Jewish Jesus-believing companions there. Gentile Christians have two enormous disadvantages:

---

59. In my view, Douma (2008, 45–49) pays too little attention to this point, although I agree with him that evangelizing (witnessing about Christ) must be possible in Israel, if it is done in a wise and modest way (see the text).

(1) They can hardly avoid the false impression that they have come to preach to the Jews a foreign, non-Jewish religion, and thus to urge the latter to move from Judaism to this different religion ("Christianity"). Jews who come to believe in Jesus have not changed their religion, as I have emphasized time and again; rather, they have reached the culmination point of *their own* religion.

(2) After many centuries of persecuting Jews ("in the name of Jesus"!), and thus of heaping guilt upon themselves, Gentile Christians can and must assume an attitude of the greatest modesty and reluctance (see chapter 5). But it is true as well that numerous modern Messianic Jews witness with gratitude that they heard the gospel for the first time from Gentile Christians.

9.6.3 Recognizing the State of Israel?

Today, *Haredi* Jews refuse to recognize the state of Israel because they believe that such a state can be founded by the Messiah alone. The well-known anti-Zionist rabbi Moshe Teitelbaum even called the state of Israel "an invention of the devil."[60] Usually, Christian Zionists have paid little attention to the—in some respects quite relevant—arguments of people like Teitelbaum. Just ask them this question: Is the state of Israel from the Israelis' flesh, or from the Spirit?

Another category is comprised of those Jews who do recognize the state of Israel, but reject the notion of a Palestinian state, and on religious grounds claim the entire land. Even the great Jewish thinker and writer, Martin Buber, wrote before the foundation of the state of Israel, pleading for cooperation with the Arab population, that, as far as the autonomy was concerned, it was not necessary at all—as the majority of the Jewish population thinks—that all this (living and working in *Ha'Aretz*) should lead to a Jewish state or to a Jewish majority.[61]

Some people have compared the "conquest" of Palestine in 1948 and 1967 with the Israelite conquest of Canaan in

---

60. See Ten Berge (2011, 104).
61. Quoted in Houwaart and Gerssen (1980, 8).

the fifteenth or thirteenth century BC, though in a positive or in a negative sense.[62] However, such a comparison is entirely unjustifiable. First, in the time of Joshua, Israel stood explicitly in a covenant relationship with God, and it was God himself who gave orders to the people to conquer Canaan. In the twentieth century, there was no question of such orders—most Zionists would not even have been interested in them—and operating within the framework of a covenant relationship is possible only after repentance and humble return to the God of Israel.

Second, the conquest of Canaan did not—as has been asserted—entail a relentless, violent action against innocent inhabitants: ". . . the Kenites, the Kenizzites, the Kadmonites, the Hittites, the Perizzites, the Rephaim, the Amorites, the Canaanites, the Girgashites and the Jebusites" (Gen. 15:19–21). On the contrary, God allowed his people of Israel to be oppressed for centuries in Egypt while he was exercising generous patience with those wicked Canaanites. He had told Abraham: your descendants "shall come back here in the fourth generation, for the iniquity of the Amorites [i.e., the chief Canaanite people] is not yet complete" (Gen. 15:16). In other words, God was telling Abraham that it would be four generations before his descendants would come back here in Canaan. This was because he would not drive out the Amorites until they had become so wicked that they had to be punished (GNT). In the comparison just made, it is impossible to claim that the Jews of, say, before 1940, had been oppressed by the Palestinian Arabs. Rather, both had been oppressed by the Turks. There was no "conquest" of Canaan by the Israelis, nor was there, at the same time, any "punishing" the "wicked" Palestinian Arabs. What is worse in God's eyes: a pious Muslim Arab or a wicked Jew?

As to the Amorites, let us not assert to easily that they could hardly have known anything other than the idolatry to which they were accustomed. This is not true. In their midst, a person had lived like the king-priest Melchizedek, who had rejected the idols and had served *El 'Elyon* ("God Most High")

---

62. Cf. Chapman (1985, 166–69); Grenke (2008).

(Gen. 14:18–20). In his day, the city of Salem, most likely identical with the later Jerusalem,[63] apparently served this God, who was also the God of Abraham (see v. 22). Therefore, the Amorites were without excuse. However, the comparison with the Palestinian Arabs does not work. It could hardly be maintained that, in the twentieth century, the "godly" Israelis were the "rod of God's anger" (cf. Isa. 10:5) against the "wicked" Palestinians! Think of the many Christians among the Palestinians![64]

9.7 On Rights and Promises
9.7.1 Who Has the "Oldest Rights"?

If we forget about the distinct Canaanite tribes before Joshua,[65] the only independent and unified state that ever existed in *Ha'Aretz* was ancient Israel, under the central government of the successive kings Saul, David, and Solomon. After the latter king, the one state divided into two states: Israel (the northern kingdom of the ten tribes, also called "Ephraim," after the most prominent tribe) and Judah (the southern kingdom of the two tribes: Judah and Benjamin, called "Judah," after the most prominent tribe). After AD 70, an independent and unified state no longer existed in the Holy Land.

From 1516 until the nineteenth century, the land had been part of the Ottoman Empire. Around 1880, no more than 150,000 or 200,000 Arab Muslims, and a small number of Arab Christians, lived in a barren, impoverished, and abandoned Palestine. Between 1922 and 1929 alone, the non-Jewish population (those of Arab, Greek, Armenian, Turkish descent, etc.) increased by more than 75 percent.

In a 1931 census, the Muslim population of Palestine identified no fewer than twenty-four different countries of origin. In other words, most so-called "Palestinians" did not at all

---

63. In Ps. 76:3, "Salem" is parallel with "Zion," the poetic name of Jerusalem.
64. In an Arabic-speaking town like Kfar Yasif in Galilee, about half the population is (or at least was) Christian, and the other half was Muslim (with a few Druze), who had lived together in peace before the state of Israel was founded, and also long after this.
65. Notice the many Canaanite "kings" (city and tribal chiefs) referred to in the book of Joshua.

possess any centuries-long history in Palestine. The most important reason why masses of non-Jewish immigrants began flowing to Palestine was that the Jews drained the swamps, plagued by the malaria-carrying mosquitos, and developed the land and made it flourish. In this way, they provided work and prosperity to the non-Jews—even if the latter often responded only with jealousy and abhorrence. More than 90 percent of modern Palestinians come from families who arrived in "the land" after the first Zionists had arrived. The myth of a "Palestinian nation" arose first *after* the Six Days War (1967) and was a strategic weapon in the battle against Israel. This is widely known, but recognized and emphasized, among others, by the Arab American journalist Joseph Farah.[66] There never was such a thing as a Palestinian identity, a Palestinian language, a Palestinian culture, or a Palestinian national history.

Former prime minister Golda Meir (Labor party; d. 1978) reportedly once said that it was *not* as if there was some Palestinian nation in Palestine, that the Jews expelled and whose land they stole. There simply *was* no Palestinian nation.[67] This may sound a little exaggerated, but the central claim is entirely correct. And Golda Meir's successor, Menachem Begin (Likud party; d. 1992), once said that if this were Palestine and a Palestinian nation were living here, then the Jews are simply intruders.[68] The implication of this is that when Jews began flowing into this country, there *was* no large number of Arabs whom they could have expelled. There was room enough for the Jewish immigrants; the majority of the so-called "Palestinians" came *after* them, from both Arab and non-Arab countries. The only two things that bind these Palestinians together is that they live within the boundaries of the Holy Land—as do the Israelis—and that they have all learned to speak the same language as the one spoken by hundreds of millions of people in the various Arabic-speaking countries.

---

66. In 2002 his material appeared at www.worldnetdaily.com.
67. *Sunday Times*, June 15, 1969.
68. *Yediot Aharonot*, Oct. 17, 1969, and in Bober (1972, 77).

9.7.2 Who Has the Solution?

"Palestinians do not exist"—is it really that simple? Arabic-speaking people have lived in the country for at least twenty-five hundred years, even if they did not call themselves "Palestinians"; as Nehemiah tells us: "[W]hen Sanballat and Tobiah and the Arabs and the Ammonites and the Ashdodites heard that the repairing of the walls of Jerusalem was going forward and that the breaches were beginning to be closed, they were very angry" (Neh. 4:7; cf. 2:19; 6:1).[69]

When I once visited the crusaders' castle in Akko, the Arab guide rightly told me that for many centuries, Persians, Greeks, Romans, Turks, Egyptians, Crusaders, Kurds, Mamelukes, and so on, had ruled Palestine, and all of them disappeared after a while—but during *all* those centuries, Arabs lived in the land. What does it matter what they were called? They were there. And at any rate, after 1948, or after 1967, something like an Arab-Palestinian nationalism has existed, an Arab-Palestinian ethnic self-awareness, no matter how recent, with which the Israelis must reckon, whether they like it or not.

Forty years ago, I was staying in the home of an Arab Roman Catholic family, in the heart of the West Bank (today it is Area A!). What nice people, and what nice kids they had! I still see those boys before me, and hear the enthusiasm in their voices as they spoke of their great leader, Yasser Arafat! I felt a little uncomfortable, but it was a helpful experience. This is how nationalism and great national leaders—whether the outsiders like them or not—affect people. No historical analyses can diminish this. Why would these Palestinian boys—they were not even Muslims!—not be entitled to their own nationalism, even though Jewish nationalism is far older than theirs?

This is one side of the story, and it is an important one. But as always, there is another side to the story. Apart from some minor interruptions due to violent oppression, Jews also have *always* lived in the land—something my friendly Arab guide in Akko "forgot" to mention. The Israelites may

---

69. Even in those days, there was a conflict between Jews and Arabs.

have been called "intruders" in the fifteenth (others: thirteenth) century BC, but certainly not in the twentieth century. They had been there long before the rise of Islam, even though in the past centuries they were much less numerous than the Muslims. These Jews were found especially in the four "sacred cities": *Jerusalem*, site of the former temple; *Safed* (or *Tzfat*) in Galilee, famous for its Kabbalist rabbis and synagogues since the sixteenth century; *Tiberias*, where the Mishnah and the "Palestinian" (or Jerusalem) Gemarah were composed, and where the tombs of great rabbis are located (Yochanan ben Zakkai, Akiva, Meir, Maimonides, and many others); and *Hebron*, the place where the three patriarchs and three matriarchs had been buried (§9.4.1).

So, from a purely judicial point of view, what would have been the fairest solution for the future of *Ha'Aretz* at the moment this land was salvaged from the hands of the Turks (1917) and of the British (1948)?

(a) A Jewish state with a contingent of Arab inhabitants? Could the latter, especially given the power of Jewish (ultra-)orthodoxy, expect equal rights in such a state?

(b) An Arab state with a contingent of Jewish inhabitants? Could the latter, especially given the power of Islamic *Sharia*, expect equal rights in such a state?

(c) A neutral state, strictly democratic, in which all the ethnic groups and religions would have equal rights? But would such a state answer the Zionist ideal of a *Jewish* state in the Holy Land?

(d) Or, as a fourth option, partitioning the land into a Jewish state and an Arab state?

If anyone knows a useful political-judicial answer that solves all the problems, let them declare it. And let them also offer a solution for (Old) Jerusalem: should it be under Jewish, Islamic, or international supervision? For each of these three solutions there will be insurgence, either among the Palestinians, or among the Israelis, or among both.

9.8 Claiming the Holy Land
9.8.1 Whose Is It Anyway?

Who actually is the rightful "owner" of *Ha'Aretz*? God himself gives the answer: "The land shall not be sold in perpetuity, for *the land is mine*. For you are strangers and sojourners with me" (Lev. 25:23). "Strangers and sojourners"—this is an interesting expression. Usually it indicates that the people involved are *not* at home, but in a foreign country, either Israel in Egypt or in the Diaspora, or foreigners living among the Israelites in *Ha'Aretz*.[70] But the passage just quoted emphasized that what we call the "Holy Land" belongs to God; it is *his* land. Seen from this viewpoint, when the Israelites themselves were living in the Promised Land, they were "strangers and sojourners" with God, as if they are his "house guests" staying in his "home." Now the point is that, if the land is *his*, he grants it to whomever he wishes. He determines to whom he grants lodging, so to speak.

This point is so vital because it implies that, strictly speaking, even Israel cannot make any claims to the land. The land is the LORD's, and in his grace, he has outsourced it forever to the people of Israel; as we read,

> He is the LORD our God; . . . .
> He remembers his covenant forever,
>   the word that he commanded, for a thousand generations,
>   the covenant that he made with Abraham,
>   his sworn promise to Isaac,
> which he confirmed to Jacob as a statute,
>   to Israel as an everlasting covenant,
> saying, "To you I will give the land of Canaan
>   as your portion for an inheritance" (Ps. 105:7–11).

According to God's promises, it is also absolutely certain that God will one day bequeath the entire land to Israel. But it is a very different question *when* and *how* God will bequeath all the land to his people. The central question is this: If all Palestine belongs to Israel forever and ever, why have so many centuries passed during which Israel did *not* possess the land? Why, during all these centuries, was there

---

70. Cf. Gen. 15:13; 23:4; Exod. 2:22; 6:4; 12:19; Acts 7:6; 1 Pet. 2:11.

never a moment when Israel came back to *Ha'Aretz* with the message, "Here we are again, this is the land that our God has given to us, we have come to reclaim it"? Because the Jews did not have the power to do so. But if the land belongs forever and ever to Israel, why did *God* not give them this power during the past nineteen centuries? Why did he allow a situation in which Israel could not reclaim the land for so long? Or must we say: This does not matter, in 1967 God *did* give them the power to make the entire country their own? Is that the answer? So now they can claim it? Is it really that simple? The Philistines shouted, "Our god has given our enemy [i.e., Samson] into our hand" (Judg. 16:24)—but was this really the case? The supposed prophet Hananiah said, "Thus says the LORD of hosts, the God of Israel: I have broken the yoke of the king of Babylon" (Jer. 28:1-2)—but was this really the case? People can claim what they want.

9.8.2 Repentance and Confession

Or take the reverse situation; in Jeremiah's day, some Jews said, "... the LORD our God has doomed us to perish / and has given us poisoned water to drink, / because we have sinned against the LORD" (Jer. 8:14b). When during the twentieth century did we hear Israel, when hit by disasters, say, God afflicts us because we have sinned against him? During their horrible war against the Jews, the Nazi soldiers wore on their belts this text: *Gott mit uns* ("God with us"), and their "successes" during the twelve years of Nazi rule seemed to prove indeed that God was on their side, and not on the side of the Jews. But today, the Nazi empire has been destroyed, and the Jews have their own, very powerful state. It teaches us to be careful to claim God (or "god") for our case. This is true for Christians, Muslims, and pagans, but also for the Jews themselves.

What *mighty spiritual change* occurred in Israel that makes us believe that would lead God, after all these centuries, to suddenly give the entire land to the Israelis? Has the massive return to the land been associated with a massive return to the LORD?⁷¹ Again, God *allowing* Israel to occupy the West Bank is not the same as God *returning* this land to Israel. Actually, what does "returning the land" mean? The parts of the land that the Jews claimed in 1948 were assigned to them by the General Assembly of the United Nations but were also seized by them by expelling many Arabs from them. Did God give the entire land to Israel partly by means of illegitimate actions on the part of a largely a-religious Israel?

No, in the prophecy of Joel we obtain a very different picture; Joel 3:1-3, describing God judging the nations, followed Joel 2:27-32:

> You shall know that I am in the midst of Israel,
> and that I am the LORD your God and there is none else.
> And my people shall never again be put to shame.
> And it shall come to pass afterward,
> that I will pour out my Spirit on all flesh; . . . .
> And it shall come to pass that everyone who calls on the name of the LORD shall be saved. For in Mount Zion and in Jerusalem there shall be those who escape, as the LORD has said, and among the survivors shall be those whom the LORD calls.

9.8.3 Restoration of the Land and of the Hearts

This is the message of the prophetic word: by calling on the name of the LORD, and by receiving his Spirit, Israel will receive the fulfillment of the promises. Or, as the prophet Zechariah says, the day on which the LORD will protect the inhabitants of Jerusalem, and will destroy all the nations that come against Jerusalem, will be the day when he

> will pour out on the house of David and the inhabitants of Jerusalem a spirit⁷² of grace and pleas for mercy, so that, when they

---

71. Cf. such a link in Deut. 30:2–5, when you "*return* to the LORD your God, . . .with all your heart and with all your soul, then the LORD your God will *restore* your *fortunes* and have mercy on you, and he will gather you *again* from all the peoples where the LORD your God has scattered you. . . . And the LORD your God will bring you into the land that your fathers possessed, that you may possess it" (the words in italics render the Heb. *shub*, "to return").

72. Many others render, "the Spirit," which suggest a very special name for the Holy Spirit: he is *Ruach Chen weTachanunim*, the "Spirit of grace and of supplications" (as various renderings have it).

look on me, on him whom they have pierced, they shall mourn for him, as one mourns for an only child, and weep bitterly over him, as one weeps over a firstborn (Zech. 12:10-14).

Or listen to the prophet Ezekiel:

I will bring you out from the peoples and gather you out of the countries where you are scattered, with a mighty hand and an outstretched arm, and with wrath poured out. And I will bring you into the wilderness of the peoples[73], and there I will enter into judgment with you face to face. . . . I will purge out the rebels from among you, and those who transgress against me. I will bring them out of the land where they sojourn, but they [i.e., the trespassers] shall not enter the land of Israel. . . . For on my holy mountain, the mountain height of Israel, . . . there all the house of Israel, all of them, shall serve me in the land. There I will accept them, and there I will require your contributions and the choicest of your gifts, with all your sacred offerings. As a pleasing aroma I will accept you, when I bring you out from the peoples and gather you out of the countries where you have been scattered. And I will manifest my holiness among you in the sight of the nations. And you shall know that I am the LORD, when I bring you into the land of Israel, the country that I swore to give to your fathers. And there you shall remember your ways and all your deeds with which you have defiled yourselves, and you shall loathe yourselves for all the evils that you have committed (Ezek. 20:34-43).

As long as this conversion, and this spiritual restoration (Heb. *tiqqun*, as the rabbis called it) has not yet occurred—and it will occur only when the Messiah arrives—it is totally unbiblical and unspiritual to say that a *largely secular (a-religious) Israel,* which hardly cares about the LORD, *could claim rights to even the smallest parcel of the Promised Land.* On what grounds? On historical grounds ("this was our land two thousand years ago")? On theological grounds ("we believe in God and his promises")? On judicial grounds ("we have more le-

---

73. i.e., presumably, on your way to the Promised Land, when you will have to travel through many countries.

gal rights to this land than the Palestinians")? People may appeal to God's promises, but God fulfills them only in the way he himself has predicated: through repentance, confession, and conversion.

9.9 Taking and Giving
9.9.1 Do Not Steal Your Presents

Up tot his point, the Israelis have partially *received* the land (through the 1947 decision of the United Nations), but have partially *taken* the land, namely, the territories occupied in 1967. No doubt, this occurred under God's permission, and no doubt it is a forecast of the end time, a foretaste of the great *spiritual* restoration that God will work afterward among Israel through his Holy Spirit. But only when the latter will have occurred, will God *give* the land to Israel, the *entire* land, as he promised to Abraham, ". . . from the river of Egypt [i.e., the Wadi Al-Arish] to the great river, the river Euphrates" (Gen. 15:18).

A simple comparison may help clarify the underlying principle. We read in Genesis 27 that Jacob *stole* the patriarchal blessing from his father Isaac. There is a lot that could be said about this. First, this undoubtedly occurred under God's allowance. Second, Isaac himself was wrong for actually intending this blessing for Esau, despite God's own prediction (cf. Gen. 25:23b, "the older shall serve the younger"). Third, afterward Isaac confirmed the patriarchal blessing to Jacob (28:1). Fourth, in God's time Jacob and his progeny received the fulfillment of God's promises (see the books of Joshua and Judges). Fifth, part of this blessing is this: "Nations will be your servants and bow down to you. You will rule over your brothers, and they will kneel at your feet" (27:29), a matter that will be fully realized only in the Messianic kingdom.

However, one thing we are *not* allowed to say upon reading Genesis 27 is that God *gave* the blessing to Jacob. God must not be said to "give" people something when these people steal it. He can employ such actions, he can make good use of *our* sinful deeds. But this does not change the fact that these deeds *are* sinful, and that we are fully responsible for them.

And nothing that a person illegitimately takes can ever be said to be "given" by God. Consider David: God did not *give* Bathsheba to David (2 Sam. 11), but he *stole* her from Uriah, her husband. Yet, God *allowed* this sin, and even the killing of Uriah. After David's confession and restoration, God *allowed* Bathsheba to remain David's legitimate wife, and even made her the mother of Solomon and eventually of Jesus. Only after his confession and restoration could David say that God had *given* him Bathsheba to be his lawful wife.

Exactly the same is true for the territories that Israel illegitimately took for its own. First, this undoubtedly occurred under God's allowance. Second, the neighboring Arab countries themselves were wrong in that their belligerent threats gave the Israel the opportunity to make the disputed territories their own. Third, God will ultimately give Israel also the West Bank, namely, in the Messianic kingdom. However, one thing we are *not* allowed to say is that in 1967 God *gave* the disputed territories to Israel. This is wrong from both a logical and a theological viewpoint as well as from the viewpoint of international law.

Moreover, even in the Messianic future, Israel will not be in a position to claim for itself (parts of) the Promised Land, but only to receive the land in humility, from God's gracious and generous hand. This will not be taking but receiving. Only in the Messianic kingdom will Israel truly be able to say that the Lord has *given* them the entire land.

9.9.2 Biblical Evidence

Let us listen here to the clear statements of God's Word:

- First, come to the LORD, then, receive the land: "[H]e who takes refuge in me shall possess the land / and shall *inherit* my holy mountain" (Isa. 57:13b). "How blessed are the meek! for they will *inherit* the Land!" (Matt. 5:5 CJB).
- First, become a *tzaddiq*, then, inherit the land: "Your people shall all be righteous; / they shall *possess* the land forever" (Isa. 60:21).
- First, receive a new heart, serve the LORD, then inherit

the land:

> I will gather you from the peoples and assemble you out of the countries where you have been scattered, and I will *give* you the land of Israel. And when they come there, they will remove from it all its detestable things and all its abominations. And I will *give* them one heart, and a new spirit I will put within them. I will remove the heart of stone from their flesh and *give* them a heart of flesh, that they may walk in my statutes and keep my rules and obey them. And they shall be my people, and I will be their God (Ezek. 11:17–20; cf. 36:24–28).

- First, be revived through the Spirit of God, then inherit the land: "I will put my Spirit within you, and you shall live, and I will *place* you in your own land. Then you shall know that I am the Lord; I have spoken, and I will do it" (Ezek. 37:14).

There is no true, God-worked possession of the entire land without humbling, repentance, rebirth, and renewed dedication to the Lord, the God of Israel. Only the meek, the righteous, the godly, those who fear the Lord, those who love his name, will inherit the land.[74] No secular (unrepentant) Israel can ever claim the land; those who assert otherwise ignore the Word of God.

---

74. Ps. 25:12–13; 37:9, 11, 22, 29, 34; 69:36.

Chapter 10
Zionism and Islam

[T]he founding of a Jewish State, as I conceive it, presupposes the application of scientific methods. We cannot journey out of Egypt today in the primitive fashion of ancient times. We shall previously obtain an accurate account of our number and strength. The undertaking of that great and ancient gestor[1] of the Jews in primitive days bears much the same relation to ours that some wonderful melody bears to a modern opera. We are playing the same melody with many more violins, flutes, harps, violoncellos, and bass viols; with electric light, decorations, choirs, beautiful costumes, and with the first singers of their day.
. . .
  Politics must take shape in the upper strata and work downwards. But no member of the Jewish State will be oppressed, every man will be able and will wish to rise in it. Thus a great upward tendency will pass through our people; every individual by try-

---

1. This refers to Moses; *gestor* is a judicial consultant or mediator.

> *ing to raise himself, raising also the whole bodyof citizens. The ascent will take a normal form, useful to the State and serviceable to the National Idea.*
>
> Theodor Herzl[2]

10.1 Zionism and Religion
10.1.1 Dividing Up God's Land

IN A LETTER WRITTEN by a genuine philo-Semite, I read the words, "G'd is an extreme Zionist."[3] Such a statement points to great ignorance with regard to Zionism, and borders on sacrilege. God loves Zion, and Zionists love Zion, but this is just about the only similarity. Their love is of quite a different nature. God says, "I bring near my righteousness; it is not far off, / and my salvation will not delay; I will put salvation in Zion, for Israel my glory" (Isa. 46:13). But Zionists usually do not speak of God's salvation, and their ideas of righteousness and glory are quite different from God's ideas of them. I do realize that the Zionists formed, and form, a very heterogeneous company, but to assert that they were very religious, and cared about God's prophetic Word, would be an exaggeration. One only has to read *The Jewish State* by Theodor Herzl[4] to have the confirmation of this; he wrote, "I think the Jewish question is *no more a social than a religious one*, notwithstanding that it sometimes takes these and other forms. It is a national question, which can only be solved by making it a political world-question to be discussed and settled by the civilized nations of the world in council" (italics added).[5]

The Zionists were liberal, in particular socialist, Jews with political, social-economic, and nationalist motives, but hardly prophetic intentions. The Jewish historian and edu-

---

2. https://www.jewishvirtuallibrary.org/quot-the-jewish-state-quot-theodor-herzl, chapter 5.
3. Quoted in Ouweneel (2002, 48).
4. Herzl (1896).
5. See note 4; also quoted in Laqueur (1969, 6).

cator Jacob Katz said that the movement known as Zionism purified the Jewish Messianic faith of its miraculous eschatological elements, and embraced only its political, social, and some spiritual goals.[6] Thus, the Israeli Declaration of Independence of May 14, 1948, is totally secular, except for the obligatory (?) final formula: "Placing our trust in the Al.mighty, ..." Or should we rather take this in a positive sense, and argue that there was at least a modicum of faith in God among modern Israel's founding fathers?

To align God with Zionism is offensive, and almost blasphemous. Regrettably, some Christians like to call themselves "Christian Zionists." These are people who, for instance, sometimes refer to the prophecy of Joel: "I will gather all the nations and bring them down to the Valley of Jehoshaphat. And I will enter into judgment with them there, on behalf of my people and my heritage Israel, because they have scattered them among the nations and *have divided up my land*" (Joel 3:2). These "Christian Zionists" believe that, according to this verse, God forbids any "dividing up" of *his* land, and that, therefore, the Israelis should never agree to any partitioning of the land. Thus, a two-states solution is out of the question. In other words, *all* the Holy Land is for Israel. However, in 1947 it was the Jews themselves who agreed with the United Nations plan to divide the land into two parts, because they were well aware that if they refused, they would end up with nothing. The Arabs in turn desired one Palestinian state in which Muslims, Jews, and Christians would live together in peace (but under Islamic *Shariah*, of course, which rules out democracy). Apart from their deeper intentions, "Christian Zionists" will have to admit that the 1947 plan *did* divide up the land, but with good political intentions.

Moreover, Joel 3:2 is about the *nations* having scattered the Jews among the nations, and having divided God's land among themselves. This was something very different from what was going on in *Ha'Aretz* in 1947–1948, and later. Such a sloppy way of dealing with the prophetic Word overlooks whether Palestinian Arabs in Palestine are still allowed to

---

6. Katz (1973, 3).

have their own little place under the sun, in freedom, and not under the yoke of some occupying force. Some Jews do *not* allow the Palestinians such a place, even though some Palestinian families had lived in the Holy Land centuries before these Jewish families had arrived there. Who can fail to see the enormous difference between this situation and Joel's prophecy?

Speaking of "Christian Zionists," consider this biblically sober word of the Hebrew Christian Baruch Maoz, who leads a congregation in Israel. He argued that a territorial compromise is not a religious trespass. The Bible shows that Israel seldom had the entire promised territory under their control.[7] Nor is there any hint in Scripture that Israel is today called upon to seize it, or that it is allowed to do so without reckoning with the moral consequences of such a seizure. With regard to territories, Israel's duty toward God is first a moral one. If the Lord of history would grant Israel the possession of more territories than the Peace Accords of Oslo permitted, he can guide events in such a way that this will happen despite Israel's generosity. The divine promises can and should not serve as the basis for a political platform. God does not need any human help in order to realize his goals. Israel's moral and religious duty is not to insist on its right to the land, but on its obligation to love and honor the Palestinians—just as the Palestinians must honor Israelis. Selfishness is never a valid or wise guide to moral duty. Nor can this, in God's eyes, be an acceptable basis for national policy, as Maoz observed.[8]

10.1.2 "Occupied" Territories?

From the safety of our armchair, we can chatter easily about the Israeli-Palestinian issue. Who wants to be in the shoes of the Israeli prime minister, whether he/she is a leader of the Likud or of the Labor party? It is true, Western Christians should be reluctant to criticize Benyamin Netanyahu,

---

7. Think of the Philistines ("Palestinians") within *Ha'Aretz*, and other territories still in Canaanite hands (Judg. 1); think also of the partition of the land after King Solomon.
8. Maoz in Walker (1994, 182).

or Ehud Barak, or Ariel Sharon. But Western Christians should also be careful about shouting from a distance that Israel must *never* return the occupied territories. It is easy for them to say this—just as it is easy for the Christians who shout that Israel "must return these territories *as soon as possible.*" Again, the simple question remains: Return to whom? To the Palestinians? But they have never governed this land! To the Jordanians, who had occupied the area in 1948? To the British, who occupied the area in 1917? To the Turks, who had occupied the area in 1516-1517?

One might simply assert that the disputed territories should be given to the Palestinians. It is true, they have never governed this area, but at least they are the people living there. Alright, but there were also always Jews living there, at least in East Jerusalem. Why did no one shout after 1948 that the Jordanians, who had occupied the city, should return it to the Jews? Why is it self-evident that Old Jerusalem belongs to Palestinian Arabs? Why not to the Jews, whose capital Jerusalem was for over a thousand years?

At the same time, I ask Christian Zionists: Is it really that reprehensible to speak of "occupier" and "occupied territories"? I realize very well that these are emotionally loaded terms, but from the viewpoint of international law they are hardly objectionable. I have been arguing repeatedly that, spiritually speaking, Israel cannot simply claim the entire land as its own. Only through repentance and conversion that Israel, at God's time, that is, at the coming of the Messiah, will Israel receive all *Ha'Aretz*. But also from a political-judicial viewpoint, Israel cannot claim as its own the West Bank and the Golan Heights.[9] This is because the *state* of Israel never legitimately possessed these territories, but occupied them in 1967. To be sure, they had been conquered on the Jordanians, who had also illegitimately occupied the area, but this does not change the fact that Israel has no political-judicial rights to the area, either.

---

9. In the Tanakh, the "West Bank" is Judea and Samaria, the heart land of Israel; but Golan lay beyond the Jordan, in the area of the two and a half tribes (Deut. 4:43; Josh. 20:8; 21:27; 1 Chron. 6:71).

According to Merriam-Webster, "to occupy" means (among other things) "to take or hold possession or control of [a territory]," as in the sentence "enemy troops occupied the ridge."[10] This is precisely what Israel did with the West Bank and the Golan Heights after 1967. It is perfectly true that Israel occupied these territories during a war that Israel itself had not wanted, and that it occupied these areas in a war in which it stood over against an enormous force majeure. And it is true, the Palestinians have no political-judicial rights to the West Bank, either.[11] Therefore, it is an absurd historical falsification to assert that Israel "continues to occupy Palestinian territory." However, this does not change the fact that Israel has no political-judicial right to the West Bank and the Golan Heights (nor any theological right; see the previous chapter). The formal status of property is *undecided*—even if it is true that the United Nations (and what other judicial authority would have to decide it?) have for years had a Palestinian state in mind for the West Bank.

I admit that the United Nations does not seem very impartial. This organization has already voted on many anti-Israeli resolutions, but it has *never* proposed a resolution condemning the anti-Jewish terrorism. So, would Israel, under the guidance of the United Nations, be forced to hand over territories to an organization whose goal it is to destroy Israel? This is an enormous and insoluble problem. When two parties have made war against each other, and subsequently make a peace treaty in the true sense of the term, the territories that may have been occupied must be returned to the other party. International law obligates Israel to do this. However, in this case the peace treaty involved must be genuine and sincere. It must absolutely guarantee the newly determined borders and the safety of the two parties. But this is the very thing that is impossible if one of the two parties still describes in its Charter as its ultimate goal the destruction of the other party.

---

10. https://www.merriam-webster.com/dictionary/occupy.
11. With the Golan Heights it is a different story: they were Syrian territory.

10.1.3 The PLO Charter

The 1994 version of the PLO's National Charter contains the following phrases, which have never been amended despite promises to do so.[12] Article 15 says, "The liberation of Palestine, from an Arab viewpoint, is a national (*qawmi*) duty and it attempts to repel the *Zionist and imperialist aggression against the Arab homeland, and aims at the elimination of Zionism* in Palestine" (italics added).

Article 22 of the Charter says,

> Zionism is a political movement organically associated with international imperialism and antagonistic to all action for liberation and to progressive movements in the world. It is *racist* and fanatic in its nature, aggressive, expansionist, and colonial in its aims, and *fascist* in its methods. Israel is the instrument of the Zionist movement, and geographical base for world imperialism placed strategically in the midst of the Arab homeland to combat the hopes of the Arab nation for liberation, unity, and progress. Israel is a constant source of threat vis-a-vis peace in the Middle East and the whole world. Since the liberation of Palestine will *destroy the Zionist and imperialist presence* and will contribute to the establishment of peace in the Middle East, the Palestinian people look for the support of all the progressive and peaceful forces and urge them all, irrespective of their affiliations and beliefs, to offer the Palestinian people all aid and support in their just struggle for the liberation of their homeland.

How could peace ever exist between Palestinian Jews and Palestinian Arabs as long as the PLO maintains this Charter? And even if it would alter its Charter, this would be little more than a smokescreen: as we have seen, Muslims are constantly allowed to break their promises made to non-Muslims if this would serve the cause of Islam. This is the central point: strictly speaking this entire controversy involves not the "Palestinian situation," but Islam—a point shrewdly omitted from the Charter.

---

12. http://www.mythsandfacts.org/Conflict/statute-treaties/PLO_charter.htm.

For the sake of clarity and fairness, let me add that the PLO is strongly against the "Zionist" state of Israel, not necessarily against Jews as such. The Charter says in Article 6: "The Jews who had normally resided in Palestine until the beginning of the Zionist invasion will be considered Palestinians." But the same Charter makes these stupendous remarks (Art. 20): "Claims of historical or religious ties of Jews with Palestine are incompatible with the facts of history and the true conception of what constitutes statehood. Judaism, being a religion, is not an independent nationality. Nor do Jews constitute a single nation with an identity of its own; they are citizens of the states to which they belong." Really? The "facts of history"!? Israel never was a genuine state!? Jews are not a nation, only a religion!? One can hardly believe what is being claimed..

Should we remind the PLO of their own Quran (§9.3.3)? The Quran says,

> Pharaoh sought to scare them [the Israelites] out of the land [of Israel]: but We [Allah] drowned him [Pharoah] together with all who were with him. Then We [Allah] said to the Israelites: 'Dwell in this land [the Land of Israel]. When the promise of the hereafter [End of Days] comes to be fulfilled, We [Allah] shall assemble you [the Israelites] all together [in the Land of Israel].[13]

10.2 Terrorists or Liberators?
10.2.1 Who Are the Terrorists?

Today, we notice the tendency to distinguish between the terrorism of Al Qaeda, Taliban, and ISIS, and organizations like Hamas and Hezbollah, which allegedly are not terrorist organizations but liberation organizations. Some Western leaders also seem to be operating with this distinction when they occasionally associate with Muslim leaders who have openly expressed their support for organizations like Hamas and

---

13. Surah 17 ("Night Journey"), 102–10, as rendered at http://www.templemount.org/quranland.html.

Hezbollah, organizations that hate Israel with a deadly hatred. Some of these leaders are Abdurahman Alamoudi, the president of the American Muslim Council, and Muzammil Saddiqi of the Islamic Society of Orange County.

The notion that a person can be against Al Qaeda and for Hamas is a consequence of the lack of clarity about the term "terrorism." Since the Muslim attack on the World Trade Center and the Pentagon in New York on September 11, 2001, I have heard many people express the need for a well-honed description of "terrorism," but seldom have I encountered an attempt at an exhaustive description.[14] So let me make my own attempt. A non-terrorist liberation organization fights exclusively against military forces, even if in the process unfortunately there may be civil casualties. In contrast with this, terrorists also deliberately carry out violent actions against civilians, including the elderly, women, and children, and do so, unlike common criminals, for political, ideological, and/or religious reasons. Those who intentionally kill civilians are war criminals (when a regular war is involved), or terrorists (when a guerrilla war is involved), or common criminals (when the only goal is robbery and a murder spree).

On the basis of this description, there is no shred of doubt that Hamas, Hezbollah, the Taliban, the Islamic Jihad, the Islamic State (ISIS), the various Muslim Brotherhoods, and the like, are all terrorist organizations.[15] This means that, in the fight against terrorism, some of the United States' allies in the Middle East are themselves terrorists, or sympathizers to terrorist organizations.

Of course, the Palestinian terrorists vigorously and totally reject this description of terrorism. They dislike the negative term "terrorist" because, according to their religious conviction, they are occupied with a holy battle, ordered by

---

14. Some good recent examples of such attempts are Schmid (2011) and Williamson (2013).
15. Cf., e.g., the US Department of State List of Foreign Terrorist Organizations (https://en.wikipedia.org/wiki/ United_States_Department_of_State_list_of_Foreign_Terrorist_Organizations), or the organizations designated as terrorist by Canada (https://en.wikipedia.org/wiki/Organizations_designated_as_terrorist_by_Canada).

Allah himself. Moreover, because in Israel, each man and every woman is conscripted in principle, Hamas and Hezbollah view every Israeli citizen as a future, or active, or former soldier. Therefore, in their view, killing any Israeli civilian is nothing but part of a military conflict. As a Hamas leader reportedly said in an interview, the Geneva Convention[16] protects civilians in occupied territories, not civilians who in fact are themselves occupiers. All Israel, including Tel Aviv, is "occupied Palestinian territory." Therefore, we are not actually targeting civilians—that would violate Islam. That is the argument of Hamas.

In this way terrorists wash their hands of the matter. It is like someone saying: It is against my principles to kill humans; however, that person is not a human, but a pig; and under some circumstances, it is permissible to kill pigs. In other words, you accept a certain rule as binding for you—but in your special case, you declare the rule to be inapplicable.

10.2.2 What Is the Opinion of the Muslim Majority?

It is also a gross deception to claim that the large majority of Muslims abhor the crimes of Osama bin Laden and his Al Qaeda, and later abhorred of the crimes of ISIS. A bit of Internet surfing will yield numerous exclamations of joy about the actions of extremist leaders. The most conspicuous are those in which, at the time, Bin Laden was called a model Muslim and a representative *par excellence* of *Jihad*. Those who saw in him a forerunner of the Antichrist, should listen to that police officer of the Palestinian Authority who called Bin Laden "the greatest man in the world and our Messiah" (if we may believe the press).[17] Of course, there are also moderate and peace-loving Muslims, who, at least outwardly, do not seem to endorse the strong statements of Muslim fundamentalism. Yet, at the beginning of this century, the fervent support for Al Qaeda was estimated to involve at a minimum 10 percent, and at a maximum 50 percent of the Muslim

---

16. The Geneva Convention of 1949 describes the rights, among others, of civilians in war time, of war wounded, and of prisoners of war.
17. *The Independent*, Oct. 11, 2001.

world. This maximum amount consists of no fewer than six hundred million Muslims.

How does this relate to the Holy Land? We must assume that the percentage of Muslims who ardently desire the destruction of the state of Israel and who ardently support any form of Palestinian terrorism is no less—and this is a shocking thought. Imagine only one percent of these people with an AK-47 or a Kalashnikov in their hands, and you can easily imagine what a fear the Muslim masses can instill in the Jews living in the Middle East.

Who would like, or believe they have the wisdom, to lead the state of Israel under such circumstances? If Israel will not return the occupied territories, to any Muslim group, almost the entire Western world will ultimately turn against Israel. For Israel to return these territories, partially or entirely, is like inviting a murderous neighbor to live in the other half of their house. Prime minister Ariel Sharon chose the first option, with all the political risks that went along with it. Prime minister Ehud Barak was inclined to the second option, and fell on his face. This was because Yasser Arafat did not really want a compromise solution for Old Jerusalem—and the hundreds of thousands of Jews who demonstrated in the streets to protest against the policies of Barak did not wish such a compromise, either.

10.3 A Political or a Terrorist Solution?
10.3.1 A Hopeless Political Situation

The conclusion to be drawn seems inevitable: whatever Israel does—apart from destroying itself—will be wrong in many eyes. From a human viewpoint, the problems of the Middle East, and especially the Jerusalem question, are insoluble. This is odd, for one would expect that *no single* political problem is really and permanently insoluble. But the point is that the problems mentioned *are not essentially political*. No one can form a good picture of the dilemmas of the Middle East without taking into consideration the religious dimension. Most journalists and political commentators, however, refuse to consider such an elusive, intangible aspect.

Back in 1997, when Netanyahu was the Israeli prime minister, the great German-French Middle East expert, Peter Scholl-Latour, expressed it as follows:

> Either Israel accepts the utopian peace proposals of a Shimon Perez [d. 2016], evacuates not only the Golan but also ninety percent of the West Bank, opens the borders of the completely sovereign Palestinian state to all sides, and thereby heads toward its own downfall. Or the present government maintains the fragmentation of the Palestinian territories, cuts off all accesses to this autonomous area, denies the PLO the final decision-making authority, and condemns the Arabs to an undignified existence in some Eastern "homeland."[18] Also in this case, an intolerable situation arises, the conflict perpetuates, and Israel becomes increasingly the target of international disapproval.[19]

How could the situation be described any better? Strictly speaking, only two options exist: either the state of Israel effectuates its own downfall, or it steadfastly maintains its impossible position, and the international community will cause its downfall. In other words, from a human viewpoint, the situation is hopeless. Normally, one should not say such things too easily, for negotiators are extraordinarily inventive in finding "impossible" solutions, which, due to their creativity, suddenly turn out to be possible. However, in this unique case I believe we must make the following seven observations.[20]

(1) Israel would hermetically surround and contain a possible Palestinian state with its police and army—the Palestinians would vigorously disagree with the very thought of this.

(2) The Palestinians would insist on the return of all Palestinian-Arab refugees and their descendants—the Israelis

---

18. The reference is to the (non-white) "homelands" in South Africa under the apartheid regime: a Palestine state under the control of an all-powerful Jewish neighbor.
19. Scholl-Latour (2000, 429).
20. Cf. Scholl-Latour (2000, 406–407).

would vigorously disagree with such a return of what in principle would amount to millions of refugees.

(3) With a possible Palestinian state, Israel would demand complete control over the Western strip along the Jordan River (as they have today)—the Palestinians would vigorously disagree with this.

(4) The Palestinians would insist that the paramilitary units of the Palestinian Authority keep their heavy weapons—the Israelis would vigorously disagree with this because such weapons might be easily used against Israel.

(5) Israel would decline any discussion about its arsenal of nuclear arms—the Palestinians would vigorously disagree with this.

(6) The Palestinians would insist on the evacuation and transfer of the Jewish settlements on the West Bank—the Israelis would vigorously disagree with this, and would insist on free, militarily guaranteed access to these settlements.

(7) Now imagine that, through a series of miracles, some agreement could be reached on the previous six points; *everything would break down on this seventh point*. Without the slightest compromise, both Israelis and Palestinian Arabs would claim (Old) Jerusalem (the old city between the Turkish walls plus the Temple Square/Haram ash-Sharif) as their undivided and perpetual capital. Each of the two parties would do so partly on political grounds, partly on nationalistic grounds, partly for reasons of prestige, but especially on purely religious grounds: orthodox Judaism versus extreme Islam: Jerusalem belongs to Adonai or to Allah, respectively.

10.3.2 Palestinian As Well As Jewish Terrorism

Palestinian terrorism is often dismissed as pure anti-Semitism. There is a kernel of truth in this. The complete name of the Palestinian leader Yasser Arafat was Mohammed Abdel Rahman Abdel Raouf al-Qudwa al-Husseini. He had abridged his name in order to conceal his relationship to his uncle (or close relative) Muhammad Said Haj Amin al-Husseini, who in his time was the Mufti (highest Muslim legal expert) in Jerusalem. This man was involved in the bloody riots against the Jewish settlements in 1929 and 1936. During World War II, al-Husseini was very active in obtaining support for Nazi Germany, and in intermingling Nazi ideology with Islam. After the war, he was pursued for slaughtering Jews in Bosnia.

This uncle, Al-Husseini, with his militant, anti-Semitic variant of Islam, was an influential example to Yasser Arafat. The same was true for the Iraqi dictator, Saddam Hussein, who was raised in the house of his uncle, Khayrallah Tulfah. The latter was a leader in the pro-Nazi coup of the Mufti in Iraq (May 1941). The politics of Arafat and Saddam Hussein is understood on a much more profound level when one learns about these Nazi roots of their thinking. The same spiritual powers of darkness that we observe today with Muslim leaders had governed these former leaders as well. To cover this up, the Muslim leaders often choose to go on offense by accusing their opponent, Israel, of a Hitlerian, Nazi mentality (cf., e.g., the Turkish president in §9.5.1 and the PLO Charter in §10.1.3, and later in this chapter).

It is fair, though, to add that Israel also had its own terrorist organizations before the state of Israel had been established. The Irgun Zvai Leumi, an underground, illegal Jewish organization in the final days of the British military rule in Palestine and during the War of Independence (1948–1949), entirely satisfies the description of terrorism given above. Its leader was Menachem Begin, the very prime minister who later made peace with the Egyptian president, Anwar al-Sadat. The Irgun and its smaller affiliate branches, the Stern Gang and Lechi, dreamed of a Great Israel, and in order to reach this goal, did not hesitate to murder innocent citizens.[21] In 1944 Lechi killed the British minister of state in the Middle East, Lord Moyne (Walter Guinness), and in 1948 the Stern Gang killed the peace envoy of the United Nations, the Swedish diplomat Count Folke Bernadotte.[22] They were murdered because they represented British imperialism, which

---

21. Collins and Lapierre (1993, 109–11, 125–36, 362–14).
22. Bernadotte (b. 1895) was a grandson of King Oscar II of Sweden. In World War II, this man had negotiated the release of about 31,000 Nazi prisoners, including 450 Danish Jews, from the Theresienstadt concentration camp.

supposedly was responsible for thousands of Jewish casualties.

The mass murder of Palestinian citizens by Lebanese "Christians" in the Sabra and Shatila Camps, under the personal responsibility of the Israel defense minister (later prime minister), Ariel Sharon, was an act of pure terror (1982).

Although such matters have been sharply condemned by many Zionists, they are stains on the Israeli historical record, which many admirers of Israel prefer to forget. Anyone fighting a guerrilla war who kills civilians—or allows them to be killed—in order to reach their political goals are terrorists, whether they are Jews, or Christians, or Muslims.

10.4 Israel and Islam
10.4.1 Jerusalem and the Quran

It is noteworthy that Jerusalem, allegedly the third sacred city of Islam, is not mentioned anywhere in the Quran. Moreover, as a *city*, Jerusalem—even though called in Arabic *Al Quds* ("the Holy One")—is not at all important for traditional Islam. The only holy (sacred) and therefore important feature is the rock in the Dome of the Rock on the Temple Mount, for two reasons. First, here Ibrahim (Abraham) offered his son (according to Muslims: his son Ismael; see below); second, from this place Muhammad allegedly made a nightly journey to heaven.

It is assumed that the Quran alludes to this latter phenomenon in Surah 17:1, "Glory be to the One Who took His servant [i.e., Muhammad] by night from the Sacred Mosque [in Mecca] to the Farthest Mosque."[23] For world history, this alleged night journey is very highly significant because Muslims began to understand the "Farthest Mosque" as a mosque located far away in Jerusalem. No wonder: what was more beautiful than to imagine that the religion brought by Muhammad had triumphed especially over Judaism, and that therefore the Temple Mount belonged in Muslim hands? Especially because of this pure speculation Jerusalem became

---

23. https://quran.com/17.

the third city of Islam—with enormous political consequences until this very day.²⁴

However, this was not the only reason why Jerusalem occupies a very special place in the Islam. For Muhammad himself, the city was so important that he initially ordered his followers to say their prayers in the direction of Jerusalem, according to the example of Daniel (Dan. 6:10); only later was this direction for prayers changed toward Mecca.²⁵ Additionally, the Quran tells the story of Abraham sacrificing his son (Surah 37:102-107); the story does not say which son this was, but according to the most important Islamic tradition this was Ishmael. In the Bible, this occurred on a mountain in the "land of Moriah" (Gen. 22:2), that is, the Temple Mount, called Moriah (2 Chron. 3:1). Thus, this story might have added to the special significance of Jerusalem; but in the Quran the site is not mentioned; the impression is given that the event occurred near Mecca.

After Muslims conquered Jerusalem (638), Caliph²⁶ Omar visited the Temple Mount; in 691/692, at that site the Dome of the Rock was built, sometimes erroneously called the Omar Mosque. Around 711, Caliph Abd al-Wahd turned the church that Christians had built on the Temple Mount (sixth century) into a mosque. He named it Al-Aqsa Mosque in order to suggest thereby that this was the "Farthest Mosque" (*Al-Masujidi al-Aqtza*) mentioned in Surah 17 (see above). He did so despite the fact that in Muhammad's day there was no mosque (Muslim "prayer house") in Jerusalem! It is therefore impossible that Surah 17 could be referring to Jerusalem; presumably, Muhammad was thinking of Medina,²⁷ the second sacred city of Islam.

No matter what the proper exegesis of Surah 17 may be, by building the Dome of the Rock and by establishing the

---

24. See Ouweneel (2000b, 233–34).
25. Cf. Surah 2:127.
26. A Caliph is a person who is viewed as a politico-religious successor to Muhammad and a leader of the entire Muslim world.
27. The etymology of "Mecca" is obscure, but "Medina" is a common Arabic word for "city."

Al-Aqsa Mosque, the convictions of Islam about Jerusalem are clear: in this way, Islam has triumphed over both Judaism and Christianity. It triumphed over Judaism by claiming and incorporating the important rock on Mount Moriah (the older name of the Temple Mount). And it triumphed over Christianity by turning its church on the Mount into a mosque. It did the same in Istanbul with the Aya Sophia, but no transformation was more significant than the one on the Temple Mount.[28]

Despite this significance, throughout the centuries Muslims have cared very little about the Temple Mount. The great majority of (Arab) caliphs and (Turkish) sultans have hardly busied themselves with Jerusalem, or with the Temple Mount in particular; in the nineteenth century, the place had deteriorated to a filthy, impoverished site.

Remarkably, *in every period of history* (since the seventh century) *there were more Jews than Muslims living in Jerusalem*. In 1860, there were 11,000 Jews and 6,500 Muslims, and in 1906 there were 40,000 Jews and 7,000 Muslims. Throughout the centuries, Jerusalem has been more a Jewish than an Arab city. Yet, we are dealing with the bizarre fact that the Jews have no claim to (Old) Jerusalem other than through a totally mistaken appeal to the Tanakh (for no divine promise becomes a reality without repentance and conversion). However, the Palestinians have no claim to (Old) Jerusalem either, for the city has never been their possession, nor was it ever the *capital* of any kind of Palestinian nation or Palestinian state.

Who, then, has any claim to Jerusalem? Only the One who has said, "The land is mine" (Lev. 25:23), and: "It is I who by my great power and my outstretched arm have made the earth [or, land],[29] with the men and animals that are on

---

28. Interestingly, on the Iberian Peninsula the opposite had happened: after the time of Arab occupation, many mosques were turned into churches, the most famous one probably being the Mezquita (Spanish for "mosque"), the impressive cathedral of Córdoba.
29. The Heb. *eretz* or *aretz* can mean both "earth" and "land," which sometimes creates difficulties for translators. In the well-known expression *Ha'Aretz*, the meaning is unambiguously "the land."

the earth [or, in the land], and I give it to whomever it seems right to me" (Jer. 27:5). And even when the LORD has promised the land to a certain person, or a group, he lends it to them exclusively *for his time and under his conditions*, while the land always remains his possession. What his time is, we do not know (although since 1967, it can hardly take another century, one would presume). What his conditions are, we know very well: repentance, self-humbling, confession of sins, conversion. In the end, there can be no *t'shuvah* ("return") to *Ha'Aretz* without genuine *t'shuvah* to the LORD (see below).

10.4.2 Islamic Eschatology

Just because tiny Israel has won repeated skirmishes against the enormous forces of the Arabs, one should not conclude too easily that "God is on the side of Israel." To say that God is "on the side" of the secularized and largely a-religious Israel is a bit daring; or should we say that this Israel is carried by the prayers of the growing numbers of religious Jews? Nonetheless, it seems to be undeniably true that God has protected the people and the state against the spiritual powers of darkness.[30] What the New Testament says of the spiritual battle of Jesus-believers, seems to be applicable to the people of Israel was well. Jesus, who is the Personification of true Israel, said, when he was taken captive: "When I was with you day after day in the temple, you did not lay hands on me. But this is your hour, and the *power of darkness*" (Luke 22:53). And the apostle Paul wrote, "[W]e do not wrestle against flesh and blood, but against the rulers, against the authorities, against the *cosmic powers over this present darkness*, against the spiritual forces of evil in the heavenly places" (Eph. 6:12).

These "dark powers" can manifest themselves in many ways: sometimes even in the most extreme (violent) forms of Zionism (both Jewish and Christian), but obviously most clearly in the violent segments of the Islamic world. At it deepest level, the battle between Israel and the Islamic world

---

30. It is somewhat comparable to Jesus who prayed for Peter although—or *because*—he knew that Peter would deny him (Luke 22:31–32).

is a religious battle between (the godly core of) Israel and the "powers of darkness."

Muslim eschatology involves a worldwide Islamic empire, in which all "unbelievers," that is, including Jews and Christians, will either perish *or* will ultimately submit to Allah and the Quran (the Arabic word *islam* means "submission"). In order to attain this world empire, many territories must still be conquered. However, in the entire world no place can be found where the Islam's urge for conquest manifests itself more strongly than the city of Jerusalem, for historical, religious, and political reasons that are less obvious than it might seem. As the prophet said,

> Behold, I am about to make Jerusalem[31] a cup of staggering to all the *surrounding* peoples [think of the Arabic neighboring countries!].... On that day I will make Jerusalem a heavy stone for all the peoples. All who lift it will surely hurt themselves. And all the nations of the earth will gather against it (Zech. 12:2–3).

Even the most convinced supersessionist today cannot overlook that such passages exhibit a striking similarity to our own time.

10.4.3 What Is "Extreme"?

If we wish to understand Muslim eschatology more accurately, we encounter the difficult question of who and what are true Muslims. Are these moderate Muslims, who like to depict Islamic terrorists as extremists, or who assert that, for instance, the Al Qaeda and ISIS are not genuine Muslims? Or are the extremists the true Muslims, those who do nothing but carry out to the letter what the Quran and *hadith*[32] order them to do? If the latter is true, then "extreme Islam" is a pleonasm, like the term "round circle": Islam would be extreme by nature. Genuine Muslims would be not the moderates but the so-called extremists.

---

31. The supersessionist Annotations to the Dutch States Translation say, "Here, Jerusalem means the Christian church, as in Gal. 4:26; Heb. 12:18, 22."
32. The term *hadith* refers to the alleged statements of Muhammad that have been handed down orally.

But what do Quran and *hadith* order the Muslims to do? To quote from the Quran only belligerent passages is just as unfair as judging Jews and Christians on the basis of texts in the Torah that call for a merciless battle against the Canaanites. For instance, the Quran also says, "Let there be no compulsion in religion" (2:256).

Since September 11, 2001, Surah 5:32 has often been quoted:[33] "[W]hoever takes a life—unless as a punishment for murder or mischief in the land—it will be as if they killed all of humanity; and whoever saves a life, it will be as if they saved all of humanity." Therefore, anyone who asserts that Muslims are spreading Islam with the sword must also acknowledge that Charlemagne Vladimir the "Saint," and many other "Christian" leaders forcibly imposed Christianity upon their subjects. The Quran speaks of voluntary conversion, especially when Jews and Christians are involved; see, for instance, Surah 3:64, "Say, [O Prophet,] 'O People of the Book [i.e., Jews and Christians]! Let us come to common terms: that we will worship none but Allah, associate none with him, nor take one another as lords instead of Allah.' But if they turn away, then say, 'Bear witness that *we* have submitted [to Allah alone].'"

However, this generosity is only one side of the story. In the so-called "Verse of the Sword," the Quran says (9:5), "[K]ill the polytheists wherever you find them, capture them, besiege them, and lie in wait for them on every way," unless they allow themselves to be Islamized. Surah 48:16 tells Muslims with regard to non-Muslims (Jews, Christians, pagans): "Say to nomadic Arabs, who stayed behind, 'You will be called [to fight] against a people of great might, who you will fight unless they submit [i.e., join Islam[34]]. If you then obey, Allah

---

33. This statement is remarkably similar to one in the Talmud (Sanhedrin 37a), which is older than the Quran(!): "Whosoever destroys a single soul [of Israel], Scripture imputes [guilt] to him as though he had destroyed a complete world; and whosoever preserves a single soul [of Israel], Scripture ascribes [merit] to him as though he had preserved a complete world." The words "of Israel" are absent in some manuscripts.

34. Remember that the term *Islam* means "submission"; the name *Muslim* (derived from the same Arabic root as *Islam*) means "submitted one."

will grant you a fine reward. But if you turn away as you did before, he will inflict upon you a painful punishment." And in verse 28, Allah "is the One who has sent his Messenger [i.e., Muhammad] with [right] guidance and the religion of truth, making it prevail over all others."

Surah 3:85 says, "Whoever seeks a way other than Islam, it will never be accepted from them, and in the hereafter they will be among the losers." And Surah 9: "Those who do not believe in Allah. . . . fight against them" (v. 29), and: "Believers! Fight against the unbelievers who live around you; and let them find in you sternness" (v. 123).

10.5 The Goals of Islam
10.5.1 Islam and Peace

In the light of these considerations, we understand that, according to the letter of the Quran, friendship between Muslims and non-Muslims is fundamentally impossible. Surah 5:51 says, "Believers! Do not take the Jews and the Christians for your allies. They are the allies of each other. And among you he who takes them for allies, shall be regarded as one of them. Allah does not guide the wrong-doers" (also see 9:123 in the previous section). These and other passages in the Quran are often explained away by Muslims who wish to present a gentle image of Islam. In reality, these passages show what *Jihad* belongs to its essence is: the ultimate goal of Islam is to bring all the world to *islam* ("submission," to Allah, to the Quran, to the powers that represent Islam), *whatever the cost*.

Peter Scholl-Latour, the German journalist and Middle East expert mentioned several times already, wrote in a very telling way:

> I had often been accused of demonizing Islam and exaggerating it as a danger to the West. Significantly, these allegations were put forward mostly by theorists who had fabricated an extremely liberal ideal of the Koranic doctrine and, due to their own agnostic, often deeply pacifist convictions, were not in a position to grasp the existence of a religion that was aware of its exclusive correctness. In strictly Muslim circles, on the other

hand, I have always met with broad approval with my theses. . . What people in certain German faculties or institutes wanted to attribute to Koran believers was a relativization, a criminal belittlement, a rationalization of the holy and immutable revelation. The Koran should be adapted to the secular zeitgeist, an intolerable sacrilege even for non-fundamentalist Muslims.[35]

These words seem to me very sound and relevant for those Christians—or Jews, for that matter—who seek dialogue with Islam. It is a widespread misunderstanding, if not deception, that *islam* means "peace," in the sense of rest and harmony between two parties.[36] If an element of "peace" is contained in the term, then that kind of peace that is the effect of "submission," total surrender to Allah. In practice this means surrender to those opponents of yours who allegedly represent Allah and the Quran. On French television, an Arab Sheikh openly said, "How long must we still preach the Islam to you? The time will come when we will no longer warn you, but will subject (Islamize) you."[37]

If we take the term *islam* ("submission to God") in its widest sense, we can understand why Muslims also call the biblical Ibrahim (i.e., Abraham) a Muslim, because he submitted to the will of God. In this sense, all godly Jews and Christians are Muslims, too, because they submit to the will of God. But, of course, this is not what Muslims mean. Since the time of Muhammad, being submitted to God means being submitted to God (Allah) in the way the Quran describes him, and in the way the Quran is expounded by Muslim scholars. In my view, a Jew who embraces Jesus in faith does not change religions; they have found the deepest essence and goal of Judaism. But a Jew who becomes a Muslim—and please notice, who learns to venerate the prophet Isa (i.e., Jesus as the Islam portrays him)—definitely *has* changed religions, and thus has lost their Jewish roots and background.

---

35. Scholl-Latour (2000, 273).
36. See, e.g., http://www.peaceandislam.com.
37. Quoted in Schrupp (1992, 72).

Today, the world is still divided into two large territories: the *dar al-islam*, the "house of the Islam," in which the majority of the inhabitants are Muslim, and the *dar al-harb*, the "house of the war," in which the majority of the inhabitants are not yet Muslim. The former "house" has the duty of submitting (Islamizing) the latter "house," if possible with peaceful means, or otherwise in a violent way. When, ultimately, all people have become Muslims, the world will be *dar al-salaam*, the "house of peace." This is the Islamic view of "peace": it consists of all opponents having been Islamized, that is, brought to slavish submission to Allah, the Quran, *shariah*, and Muslim leaders.

10.5.2 Islam and Patience

When it comes to the great goal just described, Muslim leaders have much patience. President Hafez al-Assad of Syria, father of the present Syrian president (Bashar al-Assad), said after the Yom Kippur War (1973): "The Arabs lost five wars against Israel. We can afford to lose ninety-nine wars—we only need the hundredth one."[38] He continued: "We Arabs[39] have waited for two hundred years to kick the crusaders out of 'the land.' The Israelis have been here only fifty years—so we can still wait another hundred and fifty years." And also: "Each person who gives up one inch of Arab land (Jerusalem) will be considered a traitor, and we all know what is the destiny of traitors in the Arab world [read: the Muslim world]."[40]

Even though moderate Palestinians may say that they would be satisfied with a partition of the land, a genuine Muslim can never really mean this. Or at best they could accept such a partition as a transitional step toward the complete Islamization of the land. Territory once conquered for

---

38. Quoted in Mordecai (1995, 53–54).
39. We remember here, first, that five percent of these "we Arabs" in the Middle East and North Africa (more than 300 million people throughout nineteen countries!) are *not* Muslim. Second, it was by no means the Arabs who drove out the crusaders, but rather Turkish Seljuks, the Kurdish warlord Saladin, and finally the Egyptian Mamelukes (former military slaves from the Caucasus).
40. *Time*, Nov. 23, 1992.

Allah can never be abandoned.[41] The same principle functions where an individual who has become a Muslim (as a child, or at a later stage) can never change to another religion. This is why, in certain Muslim countries, Muslims who come to faith in Christ are murdered. For the same reason, such countries have few or no Christian churches, and have no genuine democracy (even where "elections" are organized simply to give a good outward appearance): where the Islam has received the upper hand, it reigns with a heavy hand, and suppresses all minorities.[42] Countries where persecution of Christians is most severe are a few communist countries (North Korea, China), and an entire range of Islamic countries (Afghanistan, Somalia, Libya, Pakistan, Eritrea, Yemen, Iran, Nigeria, Iraq, Syria, Sudan, and Saudi Arabia).

Given these facts, imagine what it means when Jews penetrate a supposedly Islamic territory, and manage to establish their own state in that region. For all serious Muslims, this is pure horror. Therefore, when referring to the state of Israel, they speak of the "erosion" of the territory of the Islam[43]—territory that for almost fourteen centuries (twice as long as Spain) has been a part of the *dar al-islam*! In contrast with Spain, Palestine, together with Saudi Arabia, is considered to belong to the heartland of the Islam: the first two sacred cities are in Saudi Arabia, the third one, Jerusalem (Arabic *Al Quds*, "the Holy One"), is in Palestine.

It is no wonder that we read in the Charter of the fundamentalist Hamas movement, dating from August 1988, first in Article 11:

---

41. Amazingly, Muslims do not follow the same reasoning with regard to Spain, where Muslims once exercised power for seven centuries. But perhaps the blood of the ("Arab") Middle East is thicker than the water of the Iberian Peninsula after all.
42. Less bad, but still bad, is the situation in strongly secularized Muslim countries like Turkey and Indonesia. Notice the numbers there: officially, only about 8% of Indonesians are Christians, but missionaries report than the real number is closer to 20%, a large part of whom are covert Christians.
43. Laffin (1989, 58).

The Islamic Resistance Movement believes that the land of Palestine is an Islamic Waqf[44] consecrated for future Moslem generations until Judgment Day. It, or any part of it, should not be squandered: it, or any part of it, should not be given up. Neither a single Arab country nor all Arab countries, neither any king or president, nor all the kings and presidents, neither any organization nor all of them, be they Palestinian or Arab, possess the right to do that. Palestine is an Islamic Waqf land consecrated for Moslem generations until Judgment Day. This being so, who could claim to have the right to represent Moslem generations till Judgment Day?"[45]

In Article 13 we read:

. . There is no solution for the Palestinian question except through *Jihad* [i.e., religious warfare]. Initiatives, proposals and international conferences are all a waste of time and vain endeavors. The Palestinian people know better than to consent to having their future, rights and fate toyed with.

10.5.3 "Where Was God/Allah?"

Seen in this light, it is understandable that, for each true Muslim, the Jewish state is a totally unacceptable and horrific reality. Imagine, in this state there are a few million Jews—enjoying the support of the "Christian" West—who still remain on their feet over against more than three hundred million Arabs in the region, not to mention perhaps the greatest enemy of the moment: Iran! How terribly humiliating for Allah, and for the international Islamic world. It is therefore no wonder that, when Osama bin Laden spoke of the "humiliations" inflicted upon the Islamic world, he was referring first and foremost to the presence of the Jewish state in Islamic territory [46] If world leaders fail to understand the *Islamic* standpoint

---

44. A *waqf* is a kind of religious foundation (in this case a piece of land) according to Islamic law.
45. http://avalon.law.yale.edu/20th_century/hamas.asp.
46. Subsequently, this came to include the Golf War and the ongoing "humilia tion" of Iraq, as well as the American military bases in the Middle East—es pecially in Saudi Arabia, the sacred heartland of the Islam—not to mention the

regarding Palestine, we will continue to be treated to more naïve peace proposals from America and Europe. In this way, the conflict in the Middle East will simply escalate.

Please note that the problem does not consist of Jews living in Palestine. The Charter of the PLO says that such Jews are simply "Palestinians," that is, inhabitants of Palestine. Indeed, under the British Mandate, the Jews had a "P" on their passport, indicating that they were "Palestinians." For at least thirteen centuries, hundreds of thousands of Jews have been living in the Islamic world, who possessed the so-called *dhimmi*-status.[47] This means that they were submitted to strongly restrictive and humiliating regulations, but nevertheless they were tolerated as being "people of the Scripture."[48] However, in 1948, after exactly 1310 years, the tables were turned in Palestine: the *dhimmis* got the upper hand, established their own state, and subjected to this also the Muslim inhabitants within this state, who in turn, were partially subjected to restrictive and humiliating regulations. For every genuine Muslim, this was absolutely intolerable and inadmissible.

However, just as Jews question how the LORD could ever have allowed the city and the temple to be destroyed in AD 70, Muslims the equally tormented by how Allah could have allowed Islam to lose its hegemony in Palestine. In the AD 70, the Roman gods seemed to triumph over the God of the Jews; in 1948 and 1967, the God of the Jews seemed to triumph over Allah. Unbearable. For Jews, the answer to *their* question can only be: God allowed it because so many Jews at the time had become unfaithful to the God of Israel. For Muslims, the answer to *their* question can only be: God allowed it because, in the last centuries, so many Muslims had become

---

exploitation of the Muslim countries during the colonial period (in particular with respect to their oil) and the poisoning of Muslim countries by Western, especially American, decadence (junk food, drugs, immorality, organized crime, pushing aside ancient traditions).

47. See Laffin (1989, 85–86).
48. Surah 2:105, 109; 3:64, 69–72, 75, 98–99, 113; 57:29; 4:153, 159, 171.

unfaithful to the pure teaching of the Islam.[49] Thus, the establishment of the state of Israel has inadvertently become one of the most important causes of the revival of Islamic fundamentalism. The idea was that, if the Muslims would return to pure Islam, the state of Israel would automatically disappear.

Unfortunately, the majority of Israel has not (yet) drawn a similar conclusion regarding itself: if we return to the God of Israel, our future as a nation and as a state will be assured.

10.6 Moses, Jesus, Muhammad
10.6.1 Similarities Between Judaism and Islam

(1) Both (pious) Jews and (pious) Muslims worship the God who has revealed himself to, and through, Adam, Noah (Nuh), Abraham (Ibrahim), Isaac (Ishaq), Jacob (Yaqub), Joseph (Yusuf), Moses (Musa), Aaron (Harun), David (Daud), and so on.

* There is this great difference, though: Jews believe that this God has revealed himself in the Tanakh, whereas Muslims believe that God has revealed himself much more perfectly through Muhammad and the Quran.

* It is absurd to claim, as some Christians do, that Allah is an idol or a demon; Muhammad was sharply against any form of idolatry. At the same time, it cannot be denied that the Allah of the Quran only vaguely resembles the God of the Tanakh.[50]

(2) Both (pious) Jews and (pious) Muslims have great respect for the Torah (Tawrah),[51] the revelation of God given through Moses, as both Jews and Muslims (and Christians) confess.

---

49. Please notice that orthodox Christians often give the same answer when something goes wrong in the "Christian" world (wars, pandemics, famines, earthquakes, etc.): God is punishing us for our sins.
50. We must remember here that Muhammad received all the knowledge that he had of God through Jews and Christians he met on his travels. From them, he likely also adopted the hatred of idolatry.
51. The Tawrah or Tawrat is mentioned eighteen times in the Quran.

* The difference is that Muslims read the Torah from an Islamic perspective—in the light of the Quran and the *hadith*—whereas Jews read the Torah from a Talmudic perspective (and Christians read it from a New Testament perspective).

(3) Both (pious) Jews and (pious) Muslims believe in the coming Messiah (Masih[52]).

* The difference is that, according to Muslims, Isa Al-Masih (Jesus Christ), has sojourned in this world earlier, as Christians believe, too. But some orthodox Jews, denying that Jesus was the Messiah, do reckon with the possibility that the coming Messiah will have the face of Jesus.

* Another difference is that Jews believe that the Messiah will establish the Messianic kingdom, and that peace and righteousness will fill the earth, whereas Muslims believe that Jesus will return to the world only for a short time.

(4) Both (pious) Jews and (pious) Muslims believe that they are called upon to serve God/Allah, and that God/Allah will reward those who have truly submitted to his will (think of the meaning of *islam*: submission).

* Of course, Jews and Muslims differ in the criteria for serving God: the Tanakh (and Talmud) and the Quran (and *hadith*), respectively.

* Another difference is that the average Muslim seems to be more focused on rules as such, whereas the godly Jew seems to know more of God's grace and mercy, and realizes that no genuine reconciliation with God can occur apart from a *repentant* heart and apart from a *sin offering* prescribed by God.

The greatest difference between Jews and Muslims is basically the same as the greatest difference between Christians and Muslims: *the person of Jesus Christ as the Son of God*.[53]

---

52. Masih (Messiah, Anointed, Christ) is a common name for Jesus in the Quran (Isa Al-Masih, Surah 3:45; 4:172), but without specific Jewish or eschatological significance attached to it. About his coming again, see Surah 3:45; 43:61. Jesus was taken to heaven by God (Surah 4:158), Muhammad was not. (Moses was not either, but Elijah was; 2 Kings 2.)
53. Cf. one of the inscriptions in the Dome of the Rock, speaking with great re-

10.6.2 Jesus Versus Muhammad

Here follows a survey of some of the strong differences between Jesus and Muhammad, with some collateral remarks about Moses. Muslims revere Muhammad as the greatest of prophets, and Jews revere Moses as the greatest of prophets, yet Jesus clearly demonstrated authority, teaching, and miracles that were greater than those of Moses and Mohammed, as is shown by the Tanakh and the Quran themselves, respectively.

(1) Jesus fulfilled biblical prophecy about being the Messiah. - Muhammad did not fulfill any biblical prophecy except the ones about false teachers.[54] (Moses could not fulfill any biblical prophecy because no Scripture had yet been written.)

(2) Jesus was virgin born of the most exalted woman (cf. Surah 19:20-22). - Muhammad and Moses were not virgin born.

(3) When Jesus heard the word of God, he went to the desert to be tempted and began his ministry with boldness (Mark 1:14-15). - When Muhammad heard the word of God (supposedly through an angel) he cowered, was uncertain, and wanted to commit suicide (Surah 74:1-5) (cf. the fears and reluctance of Moses in Exod. 3-4).

(4) Jesus received his instructions from God the Father (John 5:19). - Muhammed received them allegedly through

---

spect of Jesus, but adding: "God is only One God. Far be it removed from his transcendent majesty that he should have a son" (https://www.islamic-awareness.org/history/islam/inscriptions/dotr).

54. Muslims claim that Jesus himself announced the coming of Muhammad. They base this on a Quran verse where Jesus speaks of a messenger to appear after him named Ahmad, i.e., Muhammad ("praiseworthy") (Surah 61:6). Muslims also assert that evidence of Jesus' pronouncement is present in the New Testament, citing the mention of the Paraclete whose coming is foretold in John 14-16. Muslim commentators claim that the original Greek word used was *periklutos*, meaning "famed, illustrious, or praiseworthy," rendered in Arabic "Ahmad," and that this was substituted by Christians with *paraklētos* ("advocate, counselor, intercessor").

an angel. (Moses had direct access to God,[55] although he, too, is said to have received the Torah through angels[56]).

(5) Jesus never sinned (cf. Surah 19:19). – Muhammad was a sinner (Surah 40:55; 48:1-2). (Moses was also a sinner, so that he was not even allowed entrance into the Promised Land.)

(6) Jesus never fought. – Moses and Muhammad fought many times (though Moses did so at the command of the God of the Bible).

(7) Jesus never killed anyone; no one ever died in Jesus' presence; on the contrary, he raised people from the dead. – Muhammad killed many; many people died in Muhammad's presence because he killed them. (Moses killed an Egyptian [Exod. 2:12], but this was in his immature years, before he was called by God.)

(8) Jesus claimed to be divine (John 8:24; 8:58) as well as human. – Moses and Muhammad claimed to be only human.

(9) Jesus never married. – Muhammad had over twenty wives, including a nine-year old girl. (Moses married one wife, Zipporah, and perhaps two, if the Cushite wife [Num. 12:1] was another one than Zipporah.)

(10) Jesus spoke well of women. – Muhammad said women were half as smart as men (Hadith 3:826; 2:541), that the majority in hell will be women (Hadith 1:28, 301; 2:161; 7:124), and that women could be mortgaged. (The Law of Moses is not yet as positive on the position of women as later revelation in the Tanakh [Mal. 2:13-16!],[57] but much more positive than the pagans of his time.)

(11) Jesus owned no slaves. – Muhammad owned slaves. (The Law of Moses contains strict laws on slavery.)

(12) Jesus performed many miracles including healing (cf. Surah 3:49; 5:110) and miraculously feeding a crowd of peo-

---

55. Exod. 33:11; Num. 7:89; Deut. 34:10.
56. Acts 7:53; Gal. 3:19; Heb. 2:2.
57. Cf. the Tenth Commandment: adultery with a woman is hurting that woman's husband (Exod. 20:17; cf. Lev. 18:20; 20:10 etc.); Mal. 2: adultery is hurting your own wife.

ple, calming a storm with a command, and raising people from the dead. – Muhammad's only alleged miracle was the Quran. (Moses did many miracles, too, both in connection with the plagues of Egypt and during the wilderness journey.)

(13) Jesus received God's assistance by the Holy Spirit (cf. Surah 2:253) – This is not said of Muhammad.

(14) Jesus voluntarily laid down his life for God's people. – Muhammad saved his own life many times and had others killed. (Moses was *prepared* to lay down his life for God's people [Exod. 32:32].)

(15) Jesus died and rose from the dead. – Moses and Muhammad died and remain dead to this very day.

The Quran ascribes to Jesus a position above all other persons, and exalts him to a level no human being ever reached. Can a Muslim really maintain that Jesus is merely another prophet? To be sure, all prophets had some unique features, but with Jesus, his uniqueness is personal to himself. There is no comparison here with any other prophet. All these unique features, including the origin of his life, its conclusion and final destiny, are found in him alone. These unique features of Jesus are due to his being the Son of God.

10.7 Jews and Muslims
10.7.1 Islam and Judaism

As we have seen, the Middle East conflict is dominated by religious motives. From the standpoint of Islam, the Muslim world can never accept a Jewish state, in any form. It is as simple as that. Muslims have sometimes agreed to accept the presence of such a state in the Holy Land for the time being, but this is something very different from accepting the *right* of such a state to exist in that land.

According to international law, and in order to have a minimal chance of peace (in the political sense), Israel would have to return the disputed territories to the Arab world. Please notice: Arab, not Palestinian. This is because a Palestinian state has never existed. Nor did the disputed territories before 1967 belong to the Palestinians; therefore, in the literal sense, there can be no question of "returning" these territories to the Palestinians. However, it is equally clear that Jordan will never reclaim these territories for itself, but fully cooperates in striving for a Palestinian state. And it is equally clear that the United Nation' partition plan (1947) provided for an Arab part of Palestine—a plan with which Israel at the time agreed.

In this respect, Israel has no choice; this is the opinion of the entire international community, including Israel's largest ally, the United States. However, the enormous difficulty is that, were a part of the Holy Land to come under Arab Muslim autonomy, Israel would be seriously weakened. The threat of being overwhelmed by the Arab world would become all the stronger, for the Islamic world will *always* try again to destroy the Jewish state. This belongs to its religious convictions. Israel is thus confronted with a terrible dilemma: either continued intolerance *toward* the Palestinians or destruction *by* the Palestinians (and their allies).

Let no one think that this threat against Israel proceeds only from extreme Muslims. When it became clear that the Jews refused to accept his message, Muhammad himself began taking revenge on them, especially on the Banu Qurayza tribe. In 627, he presented them with two options: accept his message or be killed. After a siege of twenty-five days, they surrendered on the condition that their lives would be spared. Muhammad gave them a choice to name one of their members as their judge. This man's verdict was decapitation. In May 1627, seven to nine hundred Jewish men of this tribe were decapitated; their wives and children were sold as slaves.[58] At the same time, we know of Jewish tribes, such as Banu al-Harith, who retained their Jewish religion, yet were considered to be allies of Muslims. But other Jews were driven away, others were plundered and turned into taxpayers. In 640, Caliph Omar drove the lasts Jews out of Arabia. No Muslim—and actually no Jew either—can ever forget the oppressive attitude of the early Muslims toward the Jews. Even

---

58. The historicity of this massacre has been questioned by both Eastern and Western scholars.

though Islam has known times when Muslims and Jews lived together reasonably peacefully, where Jews get in the way of the Muslims, as today in *Ha'Aretz*, the old hatred arises again. Just as, nine hundred years later, Martin Luther did not respond well when the Jews refused his message, Muhammad did not tolerate Jews who refused to become Muslims.

The American historian and journalist, John Laffin, wrote that, if it is supposedly true that Muhammad rightly put Jews to death, the same could be said of Muammar al-Kaddafi, Yasser Arafat, and President Sadat,[59] former presidents of Libya, of the Palestinian Authority, and of Egypt, respectively. These, among many others, are the ones of whom the apostle Paul said, "In their case, the god of this world has blinded the minds of the unbelievers, to keep them from seeing the light of the gospel of the glory of Christ, who is the image of God" (2 Cor. 4:4).

10.7.2 Kill the Jews, or Tolerate Them?

Although there are some benevolent words about the Jews in the early parts of the Quran,[60] the main tenor is one of severe condemnation of the Jews: "The fact is that Allah has cursed them because of their denying the Truth. So, scarcely do they believe" (2:88). Allah is "wroth" with them (58:14), and: "As for the hereafter, the chastisement of the fire awaits them" (59:3). At the end of the nineteenth century alone, throughout the entire Muslim world thousands of Jews were murdered, simply because they were Jews.[61] In the period in and around World War II, in Muslim countries more than a thousand Jews were murdered during anti-Jewish riots.

It is no wonder that, on the collective-political level, peace between Jews and Muslims is in principle inconceivable.[62] Tolerating Jewish *dhimmis* under a Muslim government is

---

59. Laffin (1989, 18).
60. According to the Islamic view of the Quran, earlier verses in the Quran are overruled by later verses that teach something else (cf. Surah 13:39 and 17:86).
61. See Littman (1975).
62. I am not speaking here of the individual level; see wonderful examples in Saada (2016).

what is maximally reachable, and even this situation was often not realized. But permanent peace between a Jewish state, in a previously Islamic territory, and its Muslim neighbor states is simply unthinkable. Hamas representative Ibrahim Ghoseh in Amman wrote in 1992 that a compromise is not possible: the Muslims do not recognize the Zionist entity (notice the wording!), whatever forms it assumes.[63] Only Westerners who are ignorant or naïve, or both, fail to discern the religious dimension of this conflict. Only such people can believe in a compromise. These are either non-religious people, or Christians who wish to look at the matter only from the standpoint of international law and politics while ignoring the metahistorical dimension.

To be sure, Israel has made peace treaties with Egypt (1979) and with Jordan (1994), and in 2020 strengthened diplomatic relationships with Bahrain, the United Arab Emirates, Sudan, and Morocco. In themselves, these are positive developments. However, given the nature of Islam, we must fear that these treaties and relationships are of a purely pragmatic character. This is underscored by the fact that each time they tend to demand a life: in 1981, the Egyptian president Anwar al-Sadat was murdered by fundamentalist military forces (members of the Islamic *Jihad*), and in 1995, the Israeli prime minister Yitzhak Rabin was murdered by Yigal Amir, a Jewish extremist, because of the Oslo Accords made between Rabin and Arafat.

However, there is also another form of naïveté, namely, demonizing all individual Muslims. We may attribute Islam, as a religious order of things, to the prince of darkness,[64] and call it a bellicose, violent system. However, this should not close our eyes to the many individual *peaceful* Muslims. A human being must not be judged according to the ideological or religious system to which they adhere, but according to their own personal attitude and actions. Many Muslims do not take their own faith so seriously that they follow the letter of the Quran and the orthodox interpretation of it. And even if

---

63. Quoted in Bouman (1998, 280).
64. See Ouweneel (2000b, §8.4.3).

all Muslims did take their faith very seriously and consistently, even then we ought to see Muslims first and foremost as people whom God loves, and whom we should love as well. The fact that Israel is, and remains, God's people, does not mean that we should love Israelis—believing or not—more than Palestinian Muslims (or any other people in the world, for that matter). Today, we should do so even more as we hear of thousands of Muslims coming to Christ in our times.[65] In the face of every Muslim—as in the face of every Jew, or any other person—we should learn to recognize the person who one day might meet Jesus Christ, and become his follower and servant.

10.7.3 Foes or Friends?

As a religious system, Islam is by definition our opponent, since the Quran first and foremost has stamped *us*, Christians, as the opponent of Muslims—but the individual Muslim is *never* our opponent. I remember a city in the Netherlands where I gave monthly lectures on eschatology. Before each lecture, I had a light dinner at a Muslim restaurant, across from the church where I was to lecture. One of the lectures was on "The Future of Islam," and I told the Muslim restaurant owner about it. (In the remainder of this chapter, the reader can see more or less what I told my Muslim host.) He was very interested! From that moment forward, every month I told him about the subject for that evening's lecture, and we gradually developed a warm relationship. He was a serious Muslim—as far as I can assess—but there was not a grain of hostility in our conversations. I know, not all Muslims are like him. But that does not alter my point: we may not identify the Muslim person we encounter as our enemy.

One day, I visited the city where I had attended primary school, to see that the residents of almost the entire neighborhood were Muslims (mainly Turks and Moroccans). It was a warm summer day, and in front of their house, on

---

65. See, e.g., https://www.gospelherald.com/articles/59309/20151030/thousands-muslims-northern-iraq-converting-christianity-witnessing-isis-horror-ministry.htm.

the street, a Turkish family was having a meal. They called me, and kindly asked me whether I wanted to join them. I was surprised, but was happy to say yes. They told me it was some Islamic holiday on which they were supposed to hand out food to the poor. But because there were no poor in the Netherlands [?], they had chosen me. A most pleasant conservation followed, in which I spoke especially with the adolescent children, whose Dutch was much better than that of their parents. They went to a Christian school, and I asked them about the relationships between Christianity and Islam. We spoke in the friendliest way; how in the world could the thought have occurred to me that these people were my enemies? Similarly, I have met the friendliest Muslims in the Holy Land, not only in Galilee, but also on the West Bank and in East Jerusalem.

Islam, as a religion, is as far from me as I can imagine. The Muslims I have come to know were often the friendliest people. And *were* I to meet a Muslim who would call *himself* my enemy, I trust I would be reminded of this statement of Jesus: "You have heard that it was said, 'You shall love your neighbor and hate your enemy.' But I say to you, Love your enemies and pray for those who persecute you, so that you may be sons of your Father who is in heaven" (Matt. 5:43-45).

Sometimes, conflict seems to be inevitable, as in the case of the retributions that the Americans exacted in Afghanistan. However, to describe this action, President George W. Bush could have chosen no more unfortunate word than the term *crusade*. Was there no one around him to remind him of what this term evokes in the Muslim mind? It is the picture of the murdering, robbing, and raping "Christian" crusaders from the Middle Ages, on their way to, and within, the Holy Land, killing the Muslims and Jews they met. I do not dispute the right of the United States to exact retribution, but nonetheless, the first and foremost thing we should bring Muslims is not a "crusade"—a term derived from the Latin word *crux*, "cross"[66]—and especially not cruise missiles ("cruise" is

---

66. To be more precise: a "crusade" was a military expedition under the banner of the cross, i.e., the cross of Christ. In this way, the cross could provoke only

derived from *crux* as well) but the gospel of the *crux Christi*, the "cross of Christ."

10.8 Return to God and to the Land
10.8.1 The Essence of Believing

Here we must return to a remarkable paradox, with which we have been wrestling. On the one hand, what is occurring in the state of Israel is (largely) the work of humans. However, this does not mean that God has nothing to do with it. Here, we bump into the mystery of, on the one hand, human responsibility and, on the other hand, God's counsels and his providential dealings. Undoubtedly, until now God has been protecting his people and the state of Israel against the spiritual powers. What has occurred under God's protection in the last three quarters of a century is indeed miraculous. However, this does not mean that God is simply recognizing a people as "his people" while they are still largely Torah-less.

Here, we must pay attention again to the enormous spiritual difference between the conquest of Canaan under the spiritual champion Joshua and the "conquest" of Palestine by socialist Zionists—some of them terrorists—who were little concerned with God. To be sure, the Israel that conquered Canaan was a sinful people, yet it was a believing people: "*By faith* the people crossed the Red Sea as on dry land, but the Egyptians, when they attempted to do the same, were drowned. *By faith* the walls of Jericho fell down after they had been encircled for seven days" (Heb. 11:29-30; italics added). However, the state of Israel was established through a very different faith: faith in one's own strength, in the power of weapons. The godliest Jews sharply opposed the establishment of the state of Israel on such grounds. In addition, the people who, under the guidance of Zerubbabel and that other Joshua (or Jeshua), returned from Babylon, were a sinful, yet believing people: "Then rose up the heads of the fathers' houses of Judah and Benjamin, and the priests and the Levites, everyone whose spirit God had stirred to go up to rebuild the house of the Lord that is in Jerusalem" (Ezra 1:5);

---

negative emotions in the Muslims.

"as one man" they served God in the land (3:1). And through the prophet Zechariah, the LORD said to the returned exiles: "This is the word of the LORD to Zerubbabel: Not by might, nor by power, but by my Spirit, says the LORD of hosts" (Zech. 4:6).

It is impossible to claim that modern Israel was built by modern Joshuas and Calebs, or by modern Zerubbabels and Joshuas/Jeshuas. Were the largely socialist, a-religious Zionists people "whose spirit God had stirred to go up"? Were they modern heroes of faith who understood that their goal could be reached, not by might, nor by power, but only by God's Spirit? There were certainly praying people among them, but the majority seems to have put their confidence in their own strength.

The Bible teaches us differently: *God's Spirit works only (a) in people to lead them to repentance and faith,* and *(b) in people who already have repented and come to faith.* Exceptions are Balaam (Num. 23) and Saul (1 Sam. 10:10; 19:23),[67] but who would like to compare the founders of the state of Israel with such men? Unrepentant people are enemies of God, whether they are Jews or Gentiles—and God's Spirit does not work acts of faith in such people. To be sure, enemies of God can *become* children of God: "And you [i.e., Jews and Gentiles], who once were alienated and hostile in mind, doing evil deeds, he has now reconciled in his body of flesh by his death, in order to present you holy and blameless and above reproach before him" (Col. 1:21-22). However, as long as people are not children of God, they are still enemies of God; there is nothing in between. Therefore, what is our message to these people (Jews and Gentiles) who are still enemies of the gospel (cf. Rom. 11:28)? This is, first and foremost, not political or financial support, but exactly this: the preaching of the gospel.

---

67. And perhaps Judas, who in the end turned away, but must have belonged to those *twelve* who were sent out by Jesus, and of whom we are told: "[T]hey cast out many demons and anointed with oil many who were sick and healed them" (Mark 6:13).

10.8.2 The Paradox

But the paradox remains: God is with his people, but sometimes they can hardly be called his people—and yet he seems to be on their side. Here again, we encounter the unsolvable riddle of the relationship between human responsibility and God's councils and providence. The apostle Paul says, "For though we walk in the flesh, we are not waging war according to the flesh. For the weapons of our warfare are not of the flesh but have divine power to destroy strongholds" (2 Cor. 10:3–4).

Is *this* what we should tell modern Israel: Put away your "weapons of the flesh" and trust God alone? Actually, this is not a biblical principle at all. Only once did God tell his people: "The LORD will fight for you, and you have only to be silent" (Exod. 14:14), and this was at the one-of-a-kind redemption from Egypt.[68] However, shortly after this, Israel definitely had to take up its weapons against Amalek (Exod. 17), and again when they had to fight Midian (Num. 31), and again when they captured the Promised Land (Josh. 10–11).

On each occasion, it was God *and* their weapons. God can work *without* our weapons, and on other occasions he works *through* our weapons. But then, is he not with his people and their weapons *only* when there is faith on their side? Or should we show a bit more clemency with modern Israeli fighters? Who can tell how many prayers are sent up in Israel when it gets involved in battle, and what these prayers accomplish in heaven? And conversely, were the Israelites in the Tanakh always so full of confidence in God, whereas God still gave them the victory? Was there never any false self-confidence, as in Israel's first fight again the city of Ai (Josh. 7:2–5)? Or the reverse, was there never any fear when the Israelites were confronted with a mighty adversary?[69] In

---

68. Typologically, this means that Christ fought once *for* his people on the cross, but since then, fought and fights many times *in*, *with*, and *through* them against the spiritual powers; see Ouweneel (1998b).

69. Josh. 7:3; 11:6; 1 Sam. 7:7; 17:11; 28:5; 2 Kings 10:4; 19:6; 25:24–26; and 2 Chron. 20:3, 15, 17.

other words, perhaps we should not exaggerate the difference between a (largely) unbelieving army and a weak army of little faith. I venture to say there has been, and there is, always *some* faith in the army of Israel, which is blessed by the LORD. He is always with his people, not only when they are highly spiritual, highly confident, and completely unafraid. Jesus once said to his own followers: "O faithless generation!" (Mark 9:19). Yet, he told them: "I am with you always, to the end of the age" (Matt. 28:20).

Apparently, in some cases modern Israel has no choice but to take up their weapons, while the godly among them—as well as many fearful—also employ the "weapon of prayer" (Eph. 6:14-20), somewhat like Moses praying on the mountain, and Joshua and the army fighting in the valley (Exod. 17).

Let us not forget that, even when the Messiah comes, we read about Israel literally fighting against its enemies, apparently with their weapons in their hands:

> [T]hey shall swoop down on the shoulder of the Philistines in the west,
>> and together they shall plunder the people of the east.
> They shall put out their hand against Edom and Moab,
>> and the Ammonites shall obey them (Isa. 11:14).

> On that day I [i.e., the LORD] will make the clans of Judah like a blazing pot in the midst of wood, like a flaming torch among sheaves. And they shall devour to the right and to the left all the surrounding peoples, while Jerusalem shall again be inhabited in its place, in Jerusalem (Zech. 12:6).

10.8.3 Infidelity and Repentance

It is time to pay a closer look at the Hebrew word *t'shuvah* (*t'shubah*), derived from the root *shv(u)-b*. The verb means "to return," and the noun means "turn," "return," "conversion." In Jewish thinking, *t'shuvah* plays an important role. It can be understood in the spiritual sense, in which case *t'shuvah* refers to Israel's "return" or "conversion" to the God of Israel.

It can also be understood in the literal sense: the *t'shuvah* is then Israel's "return" to the Promised Land. It is quite significant that in 1839 Rabbi Judah Alkalai, a forerunner of Zionism, launched the revolutionary idea that the *t'shuvah* first and foremost must be understood in the literal sense as the return to *Ha'Aretz*.[70] But such a return can never become full reality unless it is accompanied, or followed, by the "return" (repentance, conversion) to God.

Clearly, in a deeper sense Israel always remains God's people, for "the gifts and the calling of God [with regard to Israel] are irrevocable" (Rom. 11:29). Therefore, God never delivers his people completely to their enemies. He keeps it, protects it, and today, too, he will not allow his people to be exterminated by their adversaries. However, God will acknowledge and accept his people overtly again as *his* people *only* when they have repented and returned to the God of their fathers, and returned to the Tanakh, and ultimately returned to their Messiah. Until this happens, Israel cannot claim any part of *God's* land as its own. I venture to say that in this context terms like "claims," rights" and "titles" belong to the carnality of sinful human nature; humans have the *duty* to humble themselves before God, and to live according to his commandment by his Spirit. That is, God's *promises* find their counterparts not in human *rights* but in human *duties*. Therefore, viewed from this standpoint, there are no unconditional covenants; every covenant involves the condition of repentance, conversion, and faith.[71]

In Hosea 1-2, the metaphor of marriage is used. At Mount Sinai, Israel had been accepted by the L ORD as his bride and wife (Jer. 2:2; Ezek. 16:1-14). Because of the spiritual adultery of the people—worshiping the idols of the Gentiles—God had to send his wife away, just as a husband divorces his wife and gives her a "certificate of divorce."[72] As we saw, the time when Israel is *Lo-'Ammi*, "Not-My-People," is the time during which

---

70. See M. Brearley in Walker (1994, 114).
71. See Ouweneel (2001a, §2.1).
72. Deut. 24:1–4; Isa. 50:1; Jer. 3:1–10; Ezek. 16:35–52; 23:1–49; Hos. 2:2–5.

God has sent away his wife. Now imagine that one day a divorced wife, who had received a certificate of divorce from her husband, simply steps into the house of her husband, establishes herself there, and acts as if nothing has happened. What will the husband say? Can he accept this? He can do three things. First, he may gladly receive her as if nothing had happened (an unlikely option). Second, with indignation he can again send her away. Third, he may just wait and see what the woman will do: just settle in the house again, or—perhaps after some time—confess her adultery, humbling herself before her husband, and begging him for his forgiveness.

In the twentieth century, Israel has settled again in *Ha'Aretz*, for a large part without confession, self-humbling, or praying for forgiveness. It acts as if nothing has happed, without wondering why God did not allow her back into her "house" for almost nineteen centuries. Yes, Israel even comes "claiming" parts of the house as its own. Now it is true that the LORD intensely loves Israel; he terribly regretted that he had to "send his wife away." Therefore, he does not angrily throw his unfaithful wife out of the house. But his heart does cry, and fervently looks forward to the time when his wife will finally humble herself before him. We happily believe that this time will come soon; see especially Isaiah 54:4-10 (and the last chapters of this book).

When will Isaiah **54** be fulfilled? Only after Israel speaks the confession of Isaiah **53**:4-6 (italics added):

> Surely he [i.e., the Messiah] has borne *our* griefs
>   and carried *our* sorrows;
> yet *we* esteemed him stricken,
>   smitten by God, and afflicted.
> But he was pierced for *our* transgressions;
>   he was crushed for *our* iniquities;
> upon him was the chastisement that brought *us* peace,
>   and with his wounds *we* are healed.
> All *we* like sheep have gone astray;
>   *we* have turned—every one—to his own way;
> and the LORD has laid on him
>   the iniquity of *us all*.

10.9 Ishmael and the Palestinians
10.9.1 Promises for Ishmael

It has often been asserted that Ishmael is the forefather of the Arabs. This is too simplistic. An Arab is someone speaking Arabic; for the rest, they might be of a very different ethnic origin. The early Egyptians were Hamites, that is, descendants of Noah's son Ham; the word Mitzrayim in Genesis 10:6 (CJB)—a son of Ham—is the common Hebrew word for "Egypt" (as some translations render it). Today, the Egyptians speak Arabic, after having strongly mixed with Shemitic tribes. At the same time, we remember that Hagar was an Egyptian woman (Gen. 16:1, 3), and that she chose for Ishmael an Egyptian wife (21:21). Thus, Ishmael's descendants were three-quarter Egyptian.

When we further consider the Bedouin tribes of the Arab peninsula, that is, "the people of the East" (Judg. 6:3; tent-dwellers, Isa. 13:20; desert-dwellers, Jer. 3:2; 25:24), these were certainly not all Ishmaelites. The sons of Keturah[73] (Zimran, Jokshan, Medan, Midian, Ishbak, and Shuah, and *their* sons, e.g., Sheba and Dedan; Gen. 25:2-3) also contributed to their genetic constitution. Other Bedouin tribes went back to Edom (i.e., Isaac!), such as the Amalekites (Gen. 36:12,16), and to Moab and Ben-Ammi (the Moabites and Ammonites, descendants of Abraham's nephew Lot; Gen. 19:36-38), not to Ishmael. They were all Abrahamites, though. Presumably, the Hagrities (1 Chron. 5:10, 19-20) did descend from Hagar (and Ishmael).

Actually, in the end, that population of the Arabian peninsula will have intermingled so strongly that each inhabitant will certainly have had Ishmaelite blood in their veins. In Isaiah 21:13-17, a direct link is suggested between, on the one hand, "Arabia," and, on the other hand, Dedan (from Ham *or* Keturah; Gen. 10:7; 25:3; Jer. 49:8) plus Tema and Kedar (from Ishmael; Gen. 25:13; Ps. 120:5; Ezek. 27:21). In Ezekiel 27:21, the link between Arabia and Ishmael is even clearer: "Arabia and all the princes of Kedar."

---

73. Rashi viewed her as identical with Hagar, but Rashbam and Ibn Ezra rejected this interpretation; see Cohen (1983, 132).

The matter is important because the Bible attributes a clearly historical as well as eschatological significance to Ishmael, such that Ishmael can hardly be defined other than as referring to the Arab nations of the Middle East. Already before Ishmael's birth, God made this promise to Hagar:

> I will surely multiply your offspring so that they cannot be numbered for multitude.[74] . . . Behold, you are pregnant and shall bear a son. You shall call his name Ishmael [i.e., God hears][75] because the Lord has listened to your affliction. He shall be a wild donkey[76] of a man, his hand against everyone and everyone's hand against him, and he shall dwell over against all his kinsmen (Gen. 16:10-12).

The latter phrase can be taken to mean that Ishmael lives in perpetual conflict with his brothers (i.e., Isaac and his descendants), but ultimately, they will live together in peace and harmony (i.e., in the Messianic kingdom).

In a certain sense, Ishmael could be viewed as a type of Israel according to the flesh (cf. Gen. 17:20; 25:13-16: twelve tribes!). Ishmael is a "donkey" (a wild, lawless man; 16:12), which, according to the Torah, ought to be redeemed by a Lamb (Exod. 13:13). But on the one hand, in his providential mercy, God takes care of this "wild donkey" (Exod. 17:20; 21:17), and in the end leads him to his destination through the blood of the Lamb. And on the other hand, when Israel

---

74. Today, there are about four hundred million Arabs (i.e., people whose first language is Arabic) in contrast to perhaps fifteen million Jews.
75. Ishmael was one of the few whose name God announced before the person's birth; see also his counterpart, Isaac (Gen. 17:19), as well as Solomon (1 Chron. 22:9), Josiah (1 Kings 13:2), Cyrus/Kores (Isa. 45:1–7), John the Baptist (Luke 1:13), and Jesus (Matt. 1:21; Luke 1:31). The first four were all types of the Messiah (even the Gentile Cyrus), and this puts Ishmael in a very special company.
76. The text probably refers to the onager (*Equus hemionus*), the Asiatic wild ass, found in the Arabic deserts, among other places; it is a picture of Ishmael's proud nomadic independence.

had incurred profound guilt, it is also compared to a "donkey" (Isa. 1:3; Jer. 2:23-24; Hos. 8:9), and thus needs the atonement through the Lamb just the same.

Remarkably, Rashi believed that Sarai spoke from the Spirit when she advised Abram to take Hagar to be his wife, because, when a wife has remained childless for ten years, the husband is entitled to take another wife in addition to the first one.[77] And another great medieval Jewish expositor, Nachmanides, emphasized that Genesis 16:3 die not say that Hagar became Abram's "concubine" (Heb. *pilegesh*, cf. Gen. 22:24; 35:22; 36:12), but his "wife" (Heb. *ishah*).[78] In the light of these considerations, Ishmael was definitely intended by God for his peculiar position. He was a full-fledged son of Abram, though subordinate to Isaac because the latter was intended as God's covenant partner (cf. Gen. 16:9). Therefore, God later told Abraham: "As for Ishmael, I have heard you [i.e., Abraham]; behold, I have blessed him and will make him fruitful and multiply him greatly. He shall father twelve princes, and I will make him into a great nation. But I will establish my covenant with Isaac" (Gen. 17:20-21). The reader can (rightly) emphasize the latter phrase, but could just as well underscore the former part of the statement: God also has a plan for Ishmael—very different from what we read, for instance, with regard to Moab, Ammon,[79] Edom, and the sons of Keturah. It is the same when Hagar with her son Ishmael is sent away from Abraham's house: one could emphasize that "through *Isaac* shall your [i.e., Abraham's] offspring be named," but also underscore what follows: "And I will make a nation of the son of the slave woman also, *because he is your [i.e., Abraham's] offspring [lit., seed; or, son]*" (Gen. 21:12-13; italics added).

---

77. I had a Christian Arab friend in *Ha'Aretz* who was born to a young wife, whereas his father's (childless) first wife lived in a small but tidy cottage on his father's property, and was well cared for.
78. See Cohen (1983, 75–76).
79. See, though, the remarkable phrase in Jer. 48:47 and 49:6, "Yet I will restore the fortunes of Moab/Ammon in the latter days," which is going to be fulfilled in the Messianic kingdom.

10.9.2 Isaac and Ishmael

For the identification of Ishmael this passage is relevant:

> These are the names of the sons of Ishmael, named in the order of their birth: Nebaioth, the firstborn of Ishmael; and Kedar, Adbeel, Mibsam, Mishma, Dumah, Massa, Hadad, Tema, Jetur, Naphish, and Kedemah. These are the sons of Ishmael and these are their names, by their villages and by their encampments, twelve princes according to their tribes. . . . They settled from Havilah to Shur, which is opposite Egypt in the direction of Assyria. He settled over against all his kinsmen (Gen. 25:13–18).

The twelve tribes of Ishmael contain, among others, these three: Nebaioth (cf. Isa. 60:7), Kedar (cf. Song 1:5; Isa. 21:16; 42:11; 60:7), and Duma (cf. Isa. 21:11).

Concerning Genesis 25, Rashi and Nachmanides pointed to three remarkable aspects. First, Ishmael was apparently reconciled with Isaac, for together, of one mind, they buried their father Abraham. Second, Ishmael's age at the time of his death is mentioned (137 years; Gen. 25:17); in the time of the patriarchs, mention of age was made for Abraham, Sarah, Isaac, Jacob, Joseph, and Levi only. And third, we are told that Ishmael "breathed his last," which elsewhere in Genesis is said only of Abraham, Isaac, and Jacob (Gen. 25:8; 35:29; 49:33; Heb. g-w-^{c} mot). According to the rabbis, this shows that, after his repentance, Ishmael was a *tzaddiq* ("righteous one").[80] These things (especially the announcement of the name, the mention of his age, and the description of his death, plus the two prophecies about him) place Ishmael on the same level with the patriarchs, though he never was God's covenant partner. This makes him a much more important figure than many Jews and Christians might like to accept (partly because of their understandable resistance to Islam).

Typologically, this is very important. It points forward to the great reconciliation between Israel and Ishmael (Jews and Arabs) in the latter days (see next section). Not through

---

80. See Cohen (1983, 133–34).

war, terror, or (deceitful) political treaties, but through repentance and self-humbling, as can be brought about only in the Messiah, by the power of the Holy Spirit. Not in a spirit of hatred and mutual distrust, but of love and mutual confidence.

For the fulfillment of this, Isaiah 60 is of great interest because here three (grand)sons of Ishmael are mentioned by name. This chapter prophesies about restored Israel:

> A multitude of camels shall cover you,
>   the young camels of Midian and Ephah;
>   all those from Sheba shall come.
> They shall bring gold and frankincense,
>   and shall bring good news, the praises of the LORD.
> All the flocks of Kedar shall be gathered to you;
>   the rams of Nebaioth shall minister to you;
> they shall come up [as sacrifices] with acceptance on my altar,
>   and I will beautify my beautiful house [i.e., the temple]
> (Isa. 60:6-7).

What is described here is how, precisely from the Arab world, long caravans will come to restored Israel: from the sons of Keturah (Midian, Ephah, Sheba [i.e., Yemen?]) and the sons of Ishmael (Sheba, Kedar, Nebaioth). They will come not only to support the new Israel, but especially to bring sacrificial animals that are be offered in the new temple (see below).[81]

Of the Messiah (the true Solomon) in the restored Israel we read:

> He shall have dominion also from sea to sea,
> And from the River to the ends of the earth.
> Those who dwell in the wilderness[82] [i.e., the Bedouins] will bow before Him,
> And His enemies will lick the dust.

---

81. In his poem *Hagar*, the Dutch Jewish-Christian poet Isaac da Costa quoted extensively from Isa. 60, where Hagar's descendants are mentioned, in order to describe Israel's glory during the Messianic kingdom (Dutch version: http://cf.hum.uva.nl/dsp/ljc/da.costa/hagar.htm).
82. Heb. *tziyyim*, in Ps. 74:14b and Isa. 23:13 "creatures of the wilderness," be it humans or wild beasts.

The kings of Tarshish[83] and of the isles [or, (Mediterranean) coastlands] Will bring presents;
The kings of Sheba and Seba
Will offer gifts.
Yes, all kings shall fall down before Him;
All nations shall serve Him" (Ps. 72:8–11 NKJV).

10.9.3 Summary

By way of summary, these are the seven remarkable biblical similarities between Isaac and Ishmael, each of which underscores the eschatological significance of the latter.

(1) Both were sons of Abraham, born of a legitimate marriage (difference: Sarah was a free woman, Hagar a slave woman; Gal. 4:21–31).[84]

(2) Both received their name from God himself before their birth: "God hears" (Ishmael), and hence: "[humanity] laughs" (Isaac; cf. Gen. 17:17; 21:6, 9).

(3) Both received, like their father Abraham, the sign of circumcision (Gen. 17:23; 21:4; difference: the actual covenant line was perpetuated with Isaac, not with Ishmael).

(4) Regarding both we read the exceptional expression that they "breathed their last" (Gen. 25:17; 35:29). This places Ishmael on that same level as the three patriarchs.

(5) Regarding both we are told how old they were when they died (180 and 137, respectively).[85] This, too, links Ishmael in Genesis with Abraham, Isaac, and Jacob (as well as Joseph, and the progenitors in Gen. 5 and 11).

(6) Both had precisely twelve sons, who in both cases expanded into twelve tribes. Hardly anything could underscore

---

83. Crete? Sardinia? South-east Spain?
84. The name "Sarah" comes from Heb. *sar*, "prince, ruler"; the name "Hagar" means "stranger" because she came from Egypt, *or* "reward." According to a Midrash (Gen. Rabbah 45), she was a daughter of the Pharaoh, given to Abram (cf. Gen. 12:16). Thus though she was indeed a slave, she was of high birth.
85. But notice that 137 is a prime number, whereas 180 (= 5×6^2) fits nicely on the patriarchal line (Abraham: 7×5^2; Isaac: 5×6^2; Jacob: 3×7^2; Joseph: $5^2 + 6^2 + 7^2$).

the similitude between Ishmael and Isaac/Jacob more than this.

(7) In the end, both will receive an inheritance in the Holy Land, and a unique position in the Middle East during the Messianic kingdom (see next section).

10.10 Arabs in the Messianic Kingdom
10.10.1 Ha'Aretz

In this section, we understand the word "Palestinian" to have the meaning it had before the establishment of the state of Israel: a Palestinian is an inhabitant of Palestine, irrespective of whether he/she has Jewish, or Arab, or Armenian, or Turkish, or Greek roots, and so on. In the Messianic kingdom, *Ha'Aretz* will be divided among the "Palestinians," that is, among the nations that have lived there for generations (let us say, from at least before 1900 or 1920). We remember that the land does not belong to people or people groups, neither to the Jews, nor to the Palestinian Arabs; it belongs to the LORD. He once spoke through Moses, not to Arabs or Turks, but to Israelites: "The land . . . is mine. For you are strangers and sojourners with me" (Lev. 25:23).

Against this background, we read the following prophecy about the future partition of *Ha'Aretz*:

> This [see vv. 13-20] is the territory you are to divide among the tribes of Isra'el. You are to divide it by lot as an inheritance both to you and to the foreigners living among you who give birth to children living among you; for you they are to be no different from the native-born among the people of Isra'el—they are to have an inheritance with you among the tribes of Isra'el. You are to give the foreigner an inheritance in the territory of the tribe with whom he is living (Ezek. 47:21-23 CJB).

This is a remarkable prophecy. *Ha'Aretz* belongs to the LORD, and he grants it to whomever he wishes. In this case, this means: he gives it to those who have lived there for generations. These are Jews as well as Arabic-speaking people. There will no longer be any dispute—military or judicial— about whose land it is, and whose land it has been in past centuries. During all that time, it belonged to the Lord, and he will give it to all "Palestinians," to the twelve tribes as well to those non-Jewish people whose ancestors have lived in the same land for many generations. It will *never* happen that the Arab world will drive the Israelis into the sea. And it will *never* happen that the Zionists will drive all Arabs from *Ha'Aretz*.

What a time shall that be! *Together* they will learn to know the God of Abraham through the Book of that God, and through the Messiah of that God. Together, that is, just as Ishmael and Isaac harmoniously buried their father Abraham (Gen. 25:8–10). As "foreigners" or "strangers" the Arab brothers will dwell among the tribes of Israel, something that will work only if the twelve tribes always remember that they themselves are "strangers and sojourners" with the Lord. *The land belongs, and will forever belong, to him.*

10.10.2 From Egypt to Assyria

In the Messianic kingdom, it is not only Israel but the entire region from Egypt to Assyria[86] that is blessed (Isa. 19:16–25). Today, the Egyptians are an Arabic-speaking mixture of Hamites and Semites, and the Assyrians are an Arabic-speaking mixture of all the nations that ever lived in that area (think of the ancient Assyrians and Babylonians). "In that day" (Heb. *bayyom hahu*, in Isaiah consistently a reference to coming Messiah and his kingdom), Egypt as well as Judah will fear the Lord because it is there that the Messiah has appeared (Isa. 19:16–17). "In that day there will be five cities in the land of Egypt that speak the language of Canaan [i.e., Hebrew] and swear allegiance to the Lord of hosts. . . . In that day there will be an altar to the Lord in the midst of the land of Egypt, and a pillar to the Lord at its border" (Isa. 19:18–19). Thus, there will at least be this other altar, in addition to the restored altar in Jerusalem (Ezek. 43:13–27). So Egypt, too, will be a center of the Messianic kingdom (Isa. 19:23–25). Egypt will call to the Lord, and he will send a Savior (v. 20); that is, Egypt, too, will accept Christ as their Savior, and serve him.

---

86. The term "Assyria" must refer to the entire region that, today, contains Syria, Iraq, Lebanon, and Jordan, perhaps even Saudi Arabia; in short: "Egypt and Assyria" may contain the entire Arabic-speaking Islamic heartland.

Isaiah 19:21-22 are quite remarkable:

> And the LORD will make himself known to the Egyptians, and the Egyptians will know the LORD in that day and worship with sacrifice and offering, and they will make vows to the LORD and perform them. And the LORD will strike Egypt, striking and healing, and they will return to the LORD, and he will listen to their pleas for mercy and heal them.

In these verses, it almost seems as if the word "Israel" has accidentally been replaced by the word "Egypt" because the language is so Messianic. To be sure, first there will be "striking," but this will be followed by "healing":

> In that day there will be a highway from Egypt to Assyria, and Assyria will come into Egypt, and Egypt into Assyria, and the Egyptians will worship [the LORD] with the Assyrians. In that day Israel will be the third with Egypt and Assyria, a blessing in the midst of the earth, whom the LORD of hosts has blessed, saying, "Blessed be Egypt my people, and Assyria the work of my hands, and Israel my inheritance" (Isa. 19:23-25).

Apart from Israel, no community of nations will receive such an important place in the Messianic kingdom as that of Middle Eastern Arabs—we may quietly say, *because of Ishmael*. "In that day," the heart of the Messianic kingdom will be formed by a kind of "Triple Alliance"[87] of Assyria, Israel, and Egypt: all three together will serve the LORD (Isa. 19:23), that is, the entire Middle East. "In that day," this threefold cord—at the "navel" of the earth" (Ezek. 38:12 JUB)—will be a blessing for the entire world (Isa. 19:24): "Egypt *my* people," "Assyria *my* handiwork," "Israel *my* inheritance" (Isa. 19:25 NIV).[88]

The following was told us as well about the Messianic kingdom:

---

87. This was the name of an old alliance between Germany, Austria-Hungary, and Italy (1882).
88. Rabbi Ibn Ezra saw in this an increase in affection; see Slotki (1983, 93).

> Sing to the LORD a new song,
> > his praise from the end of the earth,
> you who go down to the sea, and all that fills it,
> > the coastlands and their inhabitants.
> Let *[the dwellers in] the desert* and its cities lift up their voice,
> > the villages that *Kedar* [representative of Ishmael] inhabits;
> let the habitants of *Sela* sing for joy,
> > let them shout from the top of the mountains.
> Let them give glory to the LORD,
> > and declare his praise in the coastlands (Isa. 42:10-12).

Here "Ishmael" is being directly invited to join in singing the new hymn of salvation in the Messianic kingdom. Of course, this is true of *all* who will receive a share in the Messianic kingdom, but the dwellers of the desert (the Bedouins) and the Kedarites (Ishmaelites) are mentioned here in particular. I cannot doubt that, in the Messianic kingdom, the Ishmaelites will be second in rank after the people of Israel, ahead of all the other nations of the world.

The conditions to receive a heritage in *Ha'Aretz* during the Messianic kingdom are essentially the same for the Jew and the Arab: *on God's part*, his sovereign electing grace and unshakable promises. There are such for Israel, but also for Ishmael. *On the human part*, there must be repentance, self-humbling, confession of sins, and faith in the once-dead, risen, and returned Jesus, the Christ, Savior and King; in Hebrew *Yēshuah haMashiach*, in Arabic *Yassua* (or *Isa*) *Al-Masih*.[89] The latter condition (repentance and faith) is true for all humanity; but, apart from Israel, no non-Ishmaelites have ever received such promises as the Ishmaelites have received.

---

89. Actually, the last letters of *Mashiach* and *Masih* are the same sound; it is neither a common *h*, nor a *ch* (as in Loch Ness), but a sound in between these. Only the Yemenite Jews can make this very original Semitic sound; the other Jews pronounce it as *ch*.

Chapter 11
Supersessionism and Millennialism

When I am in Europe and speak of these [eschatological] things, I say: Pray for your government, for one day your young people will be in that army [of the Beast, Rev. 16:13-16), and will be called upon to put an end to "the problem of the Jews," those stubborn Jews who do not want peace, and who treat those poor Palestinians so badly. It is the David and Goliath story, but now it is the reverse: Goliath is the army of Israel, and little David are the stone throwing Palestinian youngsters. For years, a gigantic brainwashing has been going on. Don't be mistaken, Hitler could mislead an entire nation, but the Antichrist will do it with the entire world.

Messianic Jew Daniel Yahav[1]

---

1. Quoted in Hoekendijk (2001, 49–50).

11.1 Modern A- and Post-Millennialism[2]
11.1.1 Reformed A-Millennialism

IN GENERAL, WE NOTICE that supersessionism and a-millennialism are fraternally related. I know few pre-millennialists who are also supersessionists, and I can hardly imagine such a person. Post-millennialism adopts an intermediate position here: it can be easily combined with supersessionism, but also with a view that interprets the Israel prophecies literally. Therefore, it is incorrect to link the view that interprets the Israel prophecies literally exclusively with pre-millennialism, and even with pre-tribulationism (the doctrine that the Ecclesia is raptured before the Great Tribulation[3]), and even with the highly speculative eschatology of Hal Lindsey.[4] Refuting pre-millennialism and pre-tribulationism is not the same as refuting the literal approach to the Israel prophecies.

To avoid any misunderstanding, let me add two points of clarification. First, the term "millennium" as used in this chapter means precisely the same as what is being termed elsewhere in these volumes the "Messianic kingdom." And because Israel, with the Messiah in its midst, will occupy the central position in this kingdom, a study of millennialism is indispensable. Second, the term "millennium" means a period of thousand years; since 2001 we have been living in the third millennium after Christ. "The" millennium, in the sense of the (future) Messianic kingdom, will last a thousand years, leaving aside whether these will be a thousand literal years, or, more figuratively, a (very) long period.

In the Reformed world we encounter post-millennialists, especially among the theologians of the Second Reformation (seventeenth and eighteenth centuries) and their spiritual descendants, but the great majority of them advocated a-millennialism. Well-known Reformed Dutch a-millennialists

---

2. See Hamilton (1942); Berkhof (1949, 708–19); Feinberg (1961); Clouse (1977); Hoekema (1979, chapter 14); Boettner (1990); W. Balke in Van 't Spijker et al. (1999); Doyle (1999, chapter 8); Erickson (1999); Bloesch (2004, chapter 5); Hoek (2004, 178–99); and Larkin (2009).
3. See Ouweneel (2012a, chapter 10).
4. *Contra* Douma (2008); cf. Lindsey (1970).

in the twentieth century were Abraham Kuyper, Herman Bavinck, and Gerrit C. Berkouwer; and those with Dutch roots who emigrated (especially to the United States): Geerhardus Vos, Louis Berkhof, and Anthony A. Hoekema.

Remarkably, in 1872, the Christian Reformed Church in the Netherlands—in 1947 it became Churches—decided that as a denomination, it "will not allow anyone to teach or the spread the notion that Christ will reign visibly and bodily for a thousand years."[5] At that time, millennialism was apparently considered to be a fundamental heresy. For why else would one quarantine its teachings involved with such vigor? This must have meant that the Christian Reformed brothers and sisters believed that this doctrine in some way touched upon the foundations of Christian faith, even though it is difficult to see how this is the case.

In 1933, one well-known and esteemed pastor left the Christian Reformed Church because of the opposition within that denomination against his millennialist views.[6] Fortunately, today the situation in those churches is quite different.

11.1.2 Abraham Kuyper

A special place was taken up by the a-millennialist Abraham Kuyper. As we will see below, Revelation 19-22 presented an uninterrupted series of visions that, if interpreted without exegetical biases, would be viewed by all expositors as a chronological series (see below). The implication is that, in Revelation 19-20, the "thousand years" mentioned in 20:1-6 no doubt *follow upon* the second coming of Christ in 19:11-16. It is quite remarkable that a fervent a-millennialist like Kuyper *freely admitted* this point. He wrote:

> For a long time now, every view that this "thousand years" referred to a much earlier period has proven to be untenable. Three views have supplied samples of those entirely deviating interpretations [viz., that the thousand years began with Jesus'

---

5. See *Handelingen*, 1988, ad loc.
6. See Berkhoff (1929); regarding this matter, see Van der Schuit el al. (1933); Van 't Spijker et al. (1992).

death, *or* with Constantine the Great (fourth century), *or* with Charlemagne (around 800)]. . . . Over against all such proposals the Chiliasts [millennialists] were undoubtedly right when they properly maintained, though with different interpretations, that the thousand years did not lie behind us but were still to be expected.[7]

Subsequently, he wrote that what we find in Revelation 20:1–21:19, "not only stands in a mutual coherence, but begins only after the beginning of the Parousia [i.e., the return of Christ]."[8]

These were remarkable words by Kuyper, which all a-millennialists should take to heart. But how, then, could Kuyper still be an a-millennialist? Simply by subsequently reducing the thousand years to zero. He spoke of *tijdvervluchtiging* ("volatilization of time"), and said that the thousand-year period is "only the expression of the fullness of the divine action."[9] He defended this, as has been done repeatedly throughout the centuries, by appealing to 2 Peter 3:8: "[D]o not overlook this one fact, beloved, that with the Lord one day is as a thousand years, and a thousand years as one day" (quotation from Ps. 90:4). Kuyper made this appeal without realizing that although a thousand years with the *Lord* may be *as* a thousand years, for human beings these thousand years definitely consist of ten literal centuries. He also claimed that "in Revelation the term 'thousand' is *nowhere* taken literally," apparently without realizing that (a) the number thousand never occurs elsewhere in Revelation in other than composite numbers, and (b) where it does occur in composite numbers ("thousands of thousands," "144,000," "seven thousand"), the opposite of what Kuyper asserted is in fact the case: there is no compelling reason *not* to interpret these numbers literally.

Kuyper's argument amounted to this: being unaware of the purpose of those ten centuries in Revelation 20:1–7, he

---

7. Kuyper (1931, 336).
8. Cf. the quotation from Kuyper in Feinberg (1961, 169).
9. Kuyper (1931, 332–33).

argued them away. This is the way it works in theology, and in any other science: whatever does not fit into the paradigm (the investigator's underlying scientific und pre-scientific presuppositions) is simply ignored. From the viewpoint of Kuyper's eschatology this was certainly understandable: *a priori* he had no room for a physical kingdom of a visible[10] Christ down here on earth, after his second coming. His biases prevented him from taking Revelation 20:1-7 as it presented itself, *something Kuyper himself honestly admitted.*

The same can be said of the extensive work of the Reformed theologian K. Dijk,[11] which is replete with misconceptions about millennialism,[12] and is disfigured from start to finish by supersessionism and spiritualism. Thus, he wrote: "For the Jews as Jews there is no future anymore. See, your house is *left* to you desolate. There is no reference of a restoration," with a reference to Matthew 23:38.[13] This is quite incredible. Apparently, he had overlooked the words in the text immediately following: "O Jerusalem, Jerusalem, ... See, your house is left to you desolate. For I tell you, you will not see me again, *until* you say, 'Blessed is he who comes in the name of the Lord'" (Matt. 23:37-39, with reference to

---

10. Please note that Scripture does not say that Christ will be present on earth visibly during the entire Messianic kingdom; he will occupy the throne of David *on earth*, but as the risen and glorified Man his actual place is in heaven, at the right hand of God.
11. Dijk (1933); also Dijk (1952, 16–42 ["The Millennialist Expectation"], and 1953, 48–50, where he lumped "Darbyistic Adventism" together with the "Adventism" of William Miller, who was a forerunner of Seventh Day Adventism, and exerted great influence upon Charles T. Russell, forerunner of the Jehovah's Witnesses). This is a logical fallacy: put all the views with which you do not agree on the same line, without noticing the essential differences between them, so that the bad aspects of view P are automatically transferred to views Q and R as well.
12. Unfortunately, the same was true for Bavinck (*RD* 4:657); thus, e.g., the absurd suggestion that, according to the British Bible teacher J. N. Darby, father of classical dispensationalism, there would be no visible return of Christ (657); or that millennialism attributes "a temporary, passing value to Christianity, the historical person of Christ, and his suffering and death, . . ." (662). What a shame. Had he ever read Darby?
13. Dijk (1933, 499; italics original).

Ps. 118:26). If a matter is left in a certain condition *until* X happens, the strong implication is that, after X happens, the matter will change. Jesus told the inhabitants of Jerusalem that their temple would be destroyed, and that they would not see him again *until* they themselves would welcome him with the words of Psalm 118. So where is the evidence that Jesus said that the "house" of Jerusalem would be left desolate *forever?* This one point of criticism of Dijk's work must suffice for now.

In an English pamphlet Kuyper wrote:

> Reading this passage [i.e., Rev. 20:1-7] as if it were a literal description would not only tend to a belief in the Millennium but would settle the question of Chiliasm for all who might be in doubt concerning the same....
>
> If we take it for granted now, that these thousand years are to be taken literally, that these thousand years are still in the future, and that this resurrection was meant to be a bodily resurrection, why then we may say, that at least as far as Rev. 20 is concerned, the question is settled. Then we must admit that Rev. 20:1-7 is a confession of Chiliasm with all it contains.[14]

Thus, Kuyper honestly admitted that Revelation 20 as it presents itself must be interpreted the way he described in the quotations given. However, then his supersessionist biases took over and prevented him from reading the text in this way. Thereby the straightforward conclusions were simply argued away.

11.1.3 H. Berkhof

In the earlier work of the Dutch Reformed theologian, H. Berkhof, we clearly find a certain sympathy for millennialism, namely, for the post-millennialist variant, especially because post-millennialism cherishes hope for this earth, and does not look forward only to heavenly bliss.[15]

Similar notions are also encountered with K. H. Miskotte,

---

14. Kuyper (1934, 9).
15. See Berkhof (1986, 144).

and with O. Cullmann and H. Bietenhard.[16] Our Christian expectations cannot be restricted to our individual salvation, to going to heaven and to our eternal state. Salvation is above all a collective matter; Christ wished "to purify for himself a *people* for his own possession who are zealous for good works" (Titus 2:14), ". . . a holy *nation*, a *people* for his own possession" (1 Pet. 2:9; also cf. Acts 15:14). And even more than this: not just an entire *nation* or *people*, but the restoration of heaven and earth, "the time for restoring *all the things*" (Acts 3:21): ". . . waiting for and hastening the coming of the day of God, because of which the heavens will be set on fire and dissolved, and the heavenly bodies will melt as they burn! But according to his promise we are waiting for new heavens and a new earth in which righteousness dwells" (2 Pet. 3:12-13; cf. Rev. 20:11; 21:1).

11.2 Other Reformed Theologians
11.2.1 G. C. Berkouwer

G. C. Berkouwer gave an extensive description of the pros and cons of millennialism, and emphatically chose a-millennialism.[17] The consequence of this choice was a total confusion of the Messianic kingdom (the "seventh day" of world history, when sin will still be on the earth, but righteousness will *reign*) and the new earth during the "eternal state" (the "eighth day" of world history, when sin will have been removed from the cosmos, and righteousness will *dwell*;[18] see the quotation at the end of the previous section). Thus, Berkouwer took many passages from the Tanakh that clearly referred to the Messianic kingdom, and applied them to the "new earth," even though these passages (especially Isa. 65) still presuppose procreation[19] as well as sin and death (which unfortunateBerkouwer did not discern).[20]

---

16. Miskotte (1945); Cullmann (1941; 1963); Bietenhard (1955).
17. Berkouwer (1972, chapter 10).
18. "Reigning" could imply suppressing counter-powers (though not necessarily; cf. Rev. 22:5); "dwelling" suggests rest and harmony.
19. Cf. Ps. 22:30–31; 48:13; 78:4, 6 (if these Psalms are interpreted according to their Messianic dimension).
20. Berkouwer (1972, chapter 7).

Berkouwer also referred to a debate between E. Thurneysen and E. Brunner, a debate that could occur only among a-millennialists themselves. Thurneysen wrote: "The world in which we will enter in the future of Jesus Christ is therefore no other world, it is this world, this sky, this earth, but both perished and renewed. These forests, these fields, these cities, these streets, these people will be those that will be the scene of salvation."[21] To this Brunner replied that these statements were unbiblical, and argued that the form of this world will pass away (cf. 1 Cor. 7:31; 1 John 2:17).[22] Notice what is happening here: Thurneysen referred to the Messianic kingdom, and Brunner to the new heavens and the new earth. But because *both* of them failed to discern the distinction between these two matters, they spoke past one another.

When Berkouwer entered this debate, he began from the same error of failing to discern between the Messianic kingdom and the eternal state. He asked Brunner if what the latter had said was also true of Jesus' statement: "I tell you I will not drink again of this fruit of the vine until that day when I drink it new with you in my Father's kingdom" (Matt. 26:29)—apparently not realizing that Jesus' words referred to the Messianic kingdom (which is the Father's kingdom, Matt. 13:43), but not to the eternal state. In this way, the three partners in this conversation were deaf toward what the others were claiming. This is like people talking about the seventh day of the week, which for Jews and Christians refers to Saturday, but for modern Westerners with their modern calendars refers to Sunday. Thurneysen, Brunner, and Berkouwer were all imprisoned in the inner contradictions of the paradigm shared by all of them.

Given the great contradiction between the present era (the "sixth day" so to speak: the "human day"[23]) and the era of the Messianic kingdom (the "seventh day"), it is quite astonishing what Berkouwer stated that millennialism "contains a passionate expectation with its own color and content, be-

---

21. Thurneysen (1931, 209).
22. Brunner (1953, 222).
23. So literally in 1 Cor. 4:3, but with a different meaning.

cause it is oriented to what is to be realized in this present dispensation."²⁴ He wrote also about the expectations of millennialism "... within the boundaries of this dispensation"²⁵ in terms of its "... future realization *within this dispensation.*"²⁶ Is not Berkouwer confusing not only the "seventh day" and the "eighth day," but also the "sixth day" and the "seventh day"?

Only later does it become clear that Berkouwer was referring to *post*-millennialism.²⁷ He scarcely discussed pre-millennialism, and failed to define it properly. He described a- and post-millennialism as church-historical and end-historical categories," and believed that these two are "closer to one another than is often thought."²⁸ According to Berkouwer, the point is not at all a choice between these two views, but between an extremely vague "apocalyptic comfort" and "a strictly chronological narrative account." However, these are two errors that are both equally objectionable, but errors to which *all* forms of millennialism are susceptible.²⁹

11.2.2 J. A. Heyns

Indeed, a-millennialists have often seriously damaged the entire debate through the astonishing things they have asserted about millennialism. We face the irritating situation where an opponent describes a view in a way that demonstrates they have not begun to understand it, or have listened to others who have spread misinformation about that view.

For example, J. A. Heyns believed that, according to millennialism, Christ will return twice, once before and once after the Messianic kingdom, the second time on the clouds of heaven, and that at the end of the Messianic kingdom, before this alleged second (actually third) coming, Christ will

---

24. Berkouwer (1972, 291).
25. Ibid., 293.
26. Ibid., 294 (italics original).
27. Ibid., 296–97.
28. Ibid., 313.
29. Ibid., 315.

ascend to heaven with the resurrected believers.[30] I know no pre-millennialist who has ever taught this nonsense. Perhaps one source of all this confusion was Heyns' intermingling of post- and pre-millennialism. He interpreted millennialism in such a way that both the rapture of the Ecclesia and the Great Tribulation would occur at the end of the Messianic kingdom. One rarely finds so many misunderstandings living together.

When it comes to refuting millennialism, Heyns was remarkably brief: millennialism does not agree with the book of Revelation, for the thousand years began at the cross. But this is the very point that must first be demonstrated (see §11.6.1). Heyns could just as well have argued that the thousand years are yet to come since they will apparently (see Rev. 19) begin at the second coming of Christ.

Heyns was also able to tell us where millennialism originated: "As far as the historical origin of millennialism is concerned, it has been ascertained [!?] that its deepest roots lie in a compromise between the expectations of an earthly and a heavenly salvation."[31] Who was this authority who has ascertained this once and for all? It is a fascinating misunderstanding because, as I have argued elsewhere,[32] classical Roman Catholic and Protestant tradition was mainly oriented toward a "going to heaven when the believer dies." This is a one-sided thinking that is entirely at odds with the ongoing expectation of the New Testament, which is always oriented toward the second coming of Christ and the establishment of the Messianic kingdom.

11.2.3 J. van Genderen

J. van Genderen has also dismissed millennialism—the belief in a future Messianic kingdom, preceding the new heavens and the new earth—all too easily. He asserted that the chronological interpretation of the book of Revelation is not tenable. In certain details, this is sometimes correct, but not necessar-

---

30. Heyns (1988, 417–18).
31. Ibid., 418; cf. Van Genderen and Velema (1992, 847–53).
32. Ouweneel (2022).

ily in the main lines of the book. Here again, we encounter a circular argument, begging the question, taking as one's starting point precisely what must first be demonstrated.

In his discussion, Van Genderen criticized chiliasts for deviating from the chronology of Revelation "when it is to their advantage, namely, by referring to certain sections as inserts, digressions, or lengthy clauses."[33] In my own commentary, I argued as carefully as possible why Revelation itself urges us at many place to interpret its narrative chronologically, and also indicates where, by way of exception, this is not the case.[34] Revelation 12 is a clear example because the text refers back to the birth of Jesus Christ, and works forward from there.

Van Genderen did not engage these arguments, and limited himself to an apodictic assertion. Not surprising, when you recall that he and W. H. Velema were writing a *Reformed* dogmatics for Reformed students; in such a work space is limited for entering very deeply into non-Reformed teachings.

It served Van Genderen's purpose to claim that the order of things in Revelation is not chronological. In this way one can entirely ignore the order of the events in Revelation 19-21 (a chronological order that was acknowledged as such even by Kuyper). There is a repeated "Then I heard . . ." and "Then I saw . . ." in these chapters, powerfully underscoring the historical order of things here: *first* the second coming of Christ, *then* the thousand years, *then* the new heavens and the new earth. Only when the expositor rejects this clear order of events can they alter the order: first the thousand years, then the second coming of Christ, then the eternal state. At this point, the bias of a-millennialism declares the proper chronological order of events, regardless of what the apostle John may have to say about it.

---

33. Van Genderen and Velema (1992, 851); the author specifically refers to my commentary entitled *De openbaring van Jezus Christus*, 2:61ff., 145.
34. See extensively, Ouweneel (1988, 1990, at relevant places).

11.3 Modern Post-Millennialism
11.3.1 Classical and Dominionist Post-Millennialism

Post-millennialists believe in a flourishing period of the church as history has never known before. This period will last (literally or figuratively) a thousand years.[35] Especially those who do not interpret the thousand years literally see a very smooth transition between the present dispensation and this coming flourishing period, or they believe that this flourishing period has already begun. Thus, in this view, the distinction between the present era and the coming millennial kingdom is far less drastic than in the view of the pre-millennialists, where the second coming of Christ marks the drastic transition. According to post-millennialists, there is not such a dramatic intervention: rather, the power of Satan is gradually limited as the church, or the kingdom of God, comes to greater flourishing. Linked with this is the fact that pre-millennialists often expect a great decline (apostasy) within Christianity just before the second coming of Christ, whereas some post-millennialists believe that the "apostasy" mentioned in 2 Thessalonians 2:3 refers not to Christendom but to Jewry.[36]

Because of this expectation of a great flourishing period for the church, some post-millennialists like to call themselves "opti-millennialists," in contrast with what they call "pessi-millennialists" who are a- and pre-millennialists. We must note here, though, that a- and pre-millennialists are not necessarily pessimists, as if the last stage of church history should necessarily involve only apostasy and degeneration. In my own (very moderate) progressive dispensationalism I clearly see possibilities for opti-millennialistic notions.[37]

Important post-millennialists in the pre-modern period were Matthew Henry, Jonathan Edwards, and J. Wesley; in

---

35. Verkuyl (1992, 466) made the strange mistake of defining post-millennialists as people who believe "that the millennial kingdom is already behind us." The opposite is the case: post-millennialists believe that the millennium lies ahead of us, but before the second coming of Christ.
36. Warfield (1952).
37. See Ouweneel (2010b, chapter 14).

the modern period, C. Finney, B. B. Warfield, L. Boettner, F. N. Lee, and in the present time for instance K. A. Mathison[38] and H. R. Eberle.[39] As far as the Reformed in the Netherlands are concerned, I believed to hear post-millennialist sounds with pastors and theologians such as G. A. Zijderveld, C. Graafland, P. den Butter, and W. van Vlastuin.[40]

A separate place is occupied by the controversial school of the strictly supersessionist dominionism (dominion theology), or reconstructionism, or kingdom theology; among others, with G. L. Bahnsen, K. L. Gentry, and D. Chilton.[41] This movement does not necessarily adhere to post-millennialism—theoretically, it could even be combined with pre-millennialism—but it is definitely its natural ally because both look forward to the realized kingdom of Christ on earth, before the second coming of Christ.[42] It is rooted especially in the theonomic ideas of R. J. Rushdoony and G. North (Christian reconstructionism).[43] Their post-millennial dream is that, overall, the world will be Christianized (which does not mean that every individual will be Christian), and that in this way paradise will arrive on earth, and the Law of Moses will be in force again. This involves biblical theocratic republics everywhere (Chilton), minimal state interference, and social work through the church. There will be no democracy, but a Christian totalitarian system. I find it hard to avoid the prospect, in this view, that Christians will be fighting each other about *which* and *whose* Christianity will determine the character of this Christian totalitarian system.

To a limited extent, we see a similar approach in (branches of) Pentecostal eschatology because it strongly emphasizes overcoming the dark powers already today. Just as much

---

38. Warfield (1929); Boettner (1990); Lee (2006); Mathison (1999).
39. Eberle (2002); Eberle and Trench (2007).
40. Cf. Zijderveld (n.d.); Graafland (1978; 1979); Den Butter (1978); Boogaard et al. (1992); Van Vlastuin (1989).
41. Bahnsen (1999); Gentry (2009a,b); Chilton (2007).
42. Therefore, Pawson (1995, 252–58) distinguishes between spiritual and political post-millennialism.
43. Rushdoony (1973); North (1991).

passive eschatology, with its duality of the "already" versus the "not yet," places all the emphasis on the "not yet," so Pentecostal eschatology prefers to emphasize the "already." Already in the present age, all things are put under Christ's feet; during this time, Christ is waiting until his followers have completed this task.[44]

11.3.2 Re-Introduction of the Mosaic Torah

In particular, the way dominionists wish to apply the Mosaic Torah is remarkable. In a view in which the church will one day experience its time of glory on earth, and in which there will be no redemptive-historical place for ethnic Israel, this introduction of the Law of Moses is rather paradoxical. Apparently, the Mosaic Torah will not have been done away with at all. However, this view severs the Law entirely from the people to whom it had actually been given, and has been given *exclusively*. Of course, supersessionists deny this, for in their view the church *is* the (true, spiritual) "Israel." In reality, Acts 15 tells us explicitly that the Law of Moses was *not* to be imposed on Gentile Jesus-believers, and not on the entire world.

Evidently, these re-introducers of "the" Mosaic Torah do not intend to introduce *all* the Torah. They know exactly what in this Torah has been fulfilled, which to them also implies brought to an end, namely, the entire priestly and sacrificial ministry. In contrast with this, I do believe that *all* the Mosaic Torah is still in force, *but only for Israel*, as will become reality during the Messianic kingdom, including the priestly and sacrificial ministry.

Some adherents of an extreme kingdom theology suggest that the death penalty is to be applied—would this also require the method of stoning, as in the Tanakh?—not only for murderers, but also for adulterers and homosexuals, and even for breakers of the Sabbath, which to them of course is now Sunday.[45] It must be terrible to live under such a man-

---

44. An example is C. Peter Wagner (2008).
45. Regarding this error that the Sabbath has moved from Saturday to Sunday, see chapter 2.

made regime, which, unfortunately, is too similar to the kind of regime that we find in totalitarian Islamic countries. These extremists wish to reintroduce the wearing of Jewish garments, and to impose on all Christian churches and congregations the Presbyterian system of church government. Elsewhere, I have argued that the Presbyterian system of church government is not necessarily more biblical than the Episcopalian or the Congregationalist systems.[46] Moreover, what (political or other) authorities in this coming kingdom will decide that the Presbyterian system of church government is preferable?

This view of returning to the Tanakh, ignoring the New Testament "Law of Christ" (Gal. 6:2)—the Messianic Torah—is self-refuting. The actual problems of this extremist view lie not only in the field of theology, but also in the fields of Christian ethics and philosophy of the state.[47]

Over against such a view, which attempts to realize the millennial kingdom from above, that is, through political and judicial institutions, many post-millennialists prefer an approach from below: changing the hearts of people through the gospel, after which the institutions will automatically follow (?). One could speak here of a *revivalist* post-millennialism. This movement denies that the judicial and political structures of the ancient Israelite theocracy could or should be reintroduced.

In fact, the difference between a- and post-millennialism is not that great. In both views, the traditional (Augustinian) belief is maintained, entailing that the eternal state (the new heavens and the new earth) follow immediately upon the second coming of Christ. This is the same as saying that the thousand years, no matter how this phrase is interpreted, do not follow upon, but necessarily precede, this second coming. The only difference left is that (many) a-millennialists believe that we are living during the thousand years today, whereas post-millennialists view this as a future period. The latter differ among themselves about such questions as: Who

---

46. Ouweneel (2010a, chapters 7–8).
47. Cf. Ouweneel (2018b, §12.6.2).

will establish this millennial kingdom? What exactly will be Christ's relationship to this kingdom? What will be the precise nature of this kingdom? What will be the time of Christ's second coming in relationship to this kingdom?

11.3.3 A-Millennial Differences of Opinion

A-millennialists also differ among themselves, specifically about these matters:

(a) Do the thousand years—insofar they are interpreted to be an indeterminate period of time—refer to believers on earth (so Augustine[48]), or are they fulfilled among the—deceased, not yet risen—saints in heaven, who reign there with Christ (thus most modern a-millennialists)?

* Our response must be, of course, that the Bible says nothing about deceased, not yet risen saints reigning with Christ.[49]

(b) Is there something like a literal Messianic kingdom of peace to be expected for ethnic Israel, or are the promises concerning this kingdom fulfilled in the Ecclesia, whether on earth or in heaven?

* Our response to the first part of the question is, of course, in the affirmative; but I do not think many a-millennialists would agree.

(c) If the phrase "thousand years" is interpreted as an indeterminate period of time, when exactly did this period begin? Most a-millennialists say: at the death, or resurrection, or ascension of Christ. However, several interpreters have believed that the "first resurrection" (Rev. 20:5-6) refers to the liberation and revival of the church at the time of the Emperor Constantine the Great (fourth century).[50] Others thought of Charlemagne (Emperor Charles the Great, around 800), the first Frankish *and* Christian emperor of the restored "Roman" Empire.

* In a sense, one could just as well call these views post-millennialist, since in this view the Messianic kingdom suppos-

---

48. De civitate Dei XX.7.
49. See the extensive refutation in Ouweneel (2022).
50. Swete (1951).

edly arrived only a few centuries after the beginning of the New Testament Ecclesia. During the Roman persecutions of Christians, the Messianic kingdom was supposedly still a matter of the future.

Regarding the "first resurrection" (Rev. 20:5–6), a- and post-millennialists have different views. In addition to the interpretation just mentioned, the two most common interpretations are the following. First, it is interpreted as referring to the believer's rebirth or "being made alive" (Eph. 2:5; Col. 2:13). Second it is thought to refer to the believer's death, viewed as the entrance into eternal life, which supposedly is the entering into heavenly bliss.[51] In both cases, the expressions "first resurrection" and "second resurrection" in Revelation 20 are *not* consistently understood as *both* referring to being made alive *physically*. Only pre-millennialism is consistent here in understanding the "first resurrection" to refer to the bodily resurrection of believers, before the Messianic kingdom (at the second coming of Christ), and the "second resurrection" to refer to the bodily resurrection of unbelievers, after the Messianic kingdom (see the next sections).

11.4 Modern Pre-Millennialism[52]

11.4.1 Its Rise

Pre-millennialism continued to be advocated prior to the Reformation. The Waldenses, the Cathars, the Albigenses, the followers of John Wycliff, and the Bohemian Brethren adhered to the belief of the apostles.[53] Unfortunately, this apostolic belief was not held by the Reformers. Two possible reasons may be mentioned for this, both of which are valid.

First, the Reformers preferred to connect with mainstream Christianity rather than with various sectarian movements of prior centuries; as one might say, the Reformers preferred to remain catholic, though not Roman Catholic.

Second, the Reformers put the greater emphasis on soteriology (the doctrine of salvation) and ecclesiology (the

---

51. Ibid.
52. See much more extensively, Ouweneel (2012a, chapter 9).
53. Ibid., 521; Ryrie (1953, 27–28).

doctrine of the church), and other priorities in theology and church polity. As a consequence, they paid little attention to the difficult matters of eschatology. For instance, it is remarkable that John Calvin wrote commentaries on every Bible book except the Song of Solomon and the book of Revelation. Apparently without giving it much critical thought, the Reformers simply retained Augustinian supersessionism and spiritualism. This was one of the examples of the imperfections (incompleteness) of the works of the church in what I have called elsewhere its new Sardis stage (Rev. 3:2).[54]

Yet, indirectly and inadvertently, the Reformers contributed to the revival of pre-millennialism through their radical return to the literal method of Bible interpretation, including the exposition of the Israel prophecies. Here lies the enormous importance of pre-millennialism for our present discussion. In our view, the thousand-year kingdom, starting at the second coming of Christ, is *identical with what we have called the Messianic kingdom* throughout our discussion of Israel, the kingdom in which Israel will occupy the prominent place on earth, while the glorified Ecclesia will reign with Christ from heaven.

The first return to millennialism within Protestantism was a halfway measure in terms of the broad acceptance of post-millennialism, tying in with Joachim of Fiore (or Floris, d. 1202).[55] Especially in the Netherlands, during the period of the Second Reformation (sixteenth and seventeenth centuries), many theologians adhered to post-millennialism.[56] The great system builder of post-millennialism, however, is considered to be the English liberal unitarian Daniel Whitby, who, in addition to developing conservative post-millennialism, also developed a liberal evolutionistic system, rooted in an optimistic faith in progress. The events of the twentieth century, in particular World War II, along with the develop-

---

54. Ouweneel (2010b, 55–57).
55. Regarding the more modern developments that will now be discussed in the text, see the extensive series of articles by Walvoord (1949–1951); cf. Ouweneel (2011, §14.2.3).
56. See Ouweneel (2011, §13.5).

ments within liberal and neo-orthodox theology, have virtually ended this optimism. Many Protestants, both liberals and conservatives, returned to the a-millennialist viewpoint, a step that was not all that big.

Together with the rise of many new denominations in the nineteenth century, the interest in pre-millennialism was growing. We see this in various very different movements such as the more orthodox Apostolic movement (Edward Irving) and the Plymouth Brethren (J. N. Darby, H. C. Voorhoeve, F. W. Grant, and W. Kelly), and the more eccentric Seventh Day Adventists (W. Miller) and the Jehovah's Witnesses (C. T. Russell). In the rising Evangelical movement—taken in the broadest sense of the term—pre-millennialism became the most widely held eschatological view. In 1884, leaders in eleven denominations in the United Stated included no fewer than three hundred and sixty pre-millennialists, and four hundred sixty pre-millennialist leaders in Europe.[57] The *Scofield Reference Bible* (1909) what very influential in its development and spread of dispensationalism and pre-millennialism.[58]

The first centuries after the Reformation featured the following pre-millennialist theologians: J. Mede, especially *Clavis Apocalyptica* ("Key to Revelation"), J. H. Alsted, T. Brightman in his exposition of Daniel and Revelation, the well-known J. A. Bengel in his exposition of Revelation, and further the writings of R. Maton, J. Piscator, W. Sherwin, T. Goodwin), P. Jurieu, D. Cressener, R. Fleming, C. Daubuz, T. Hartley, M. F. Roos, J. J. Hess, and many others.[59] These expositors restored pre-millennialism to prominence.

Among these pre-millennialists, we encounter some of

---

57. Peters (1952, 1:542–46).
58. Whereas Plymouth Brethren Darby and Kelly were still reluctant to present a full system of so-called "dispensations," the *Scofield Reference Bible* presents the well-known system of seven dispensations: the dispensations of (1) innocence, (2) conscience, (3) human government, (4) promise, (5) law, (6) grace, and (7) the millennial kingdom. Today, very few scholars accept the Scofieldian system in this form.
59. Ibid., 538.

the greatest Bible expositors that the Ecclesia has ever seen.[60] In addition, this group included B. Keach, J. Gill, H. Olshausen, H. Alford, S. P. Tregelles, J. N. Darby, J. P. Lange, J. H.A. Ebrard, F. Delitzsch, A. A. Bonar), C. H. Mackintosh, J. C. Ryle, B. F. Westcott, J. A. Seiss, C. J. Ellicott, A. R. Fausset), F. B. Meyer, H. A. Ironside, L. S. Chafer,[61] and W. R. Newell .

H. Alford wrote that the majority (both in number and in learedness) of Evangelical scholars inf his day accepted the second coming before the millennial kingdom, following the simple and straightforward sense of the sacred text.[62] In South Africa there was a Reformed pre-millennialist, pastor C. W. M. du Toit.[63] In the Netherlands, within the Dutch Reformed Church (today, Protestant Church in the Netherlands) there were J. de Heer, and pastors such as W. Glashouwer,[64] and his son, W. J. J. Glashouwer Jr.[65]

11.4.2 Its Spreading

The amillennialist O. T. Allis stated that the movement of the Christian Brethren (or Plymouth Brethren) was chiefly responsible for the modern spread of pre-millennialism.[66] The publications by J. N. Darby[67] made pre-millennialism universally known. In this way, it became common knowledge among millions of Evangelicals, and was recently represented especially by non-Brethren like C. L. Feinberg, M. J. Stanford, J. F. Walvoord, J. D. Pentecost, T. F. LaHay, C. C. Ryrie, and N. L. Geisler. In Germany, we must mention especially the work of Brethren representative E. Sauer (of the Bible school, today theological academy, of Wiedenest).[68] In the

---

60. This according to Pentecost (1964, 390–91).
61. See Chafer (1983).
62. Alford (1958, 2:350).
63. Du Toit (1948).
64. De Heer (1934); Glashouwer and Verweij (1985).
65. Glashouwer (2016).
66. Allis (1945, 9).
67. Darby (*SYN* 8; *CW* 2:165–265; 5:1–106; 11:206–332; 28:336–59; 30:316–408).
68. Sauer (1951; 1952; 1955).

Netherlands, pre-millennialism became known through the writings of Brethren representative H. C. Voorhoeve,[69] and after him, J. de Heer.

The standard pre-millennial expositions of the book of Revelation, which remain foundational for all modern pre-millennialist commentaries, are those by two Brethren W. Scott and W. Kelly),[70] in addition to other commentaries by Brethren, which often build upon the previous ones.[71] All these commentaries are rooted in the literal interpretation of the Israel prophecies.

We are dealing here with the remarkable phenomenon that pre-millennialism was the dominant view during the first three centuries of church history, and has become so once again among orthodox Christians during recent centuries. The great majority of new Evangelical congregations established in Asia, Africa, and South America are committed to pre-millennialism. In other words, among today's active, churchgoing Christians worldwide, pre-millennialism is the dominant view. The greatest resistance comes from the Roman Catholic Church and traditional Protestant denominations insofar as they continue to cling to the a-millennial view. This is the view that, since Augustine, has been dominant in Western Christianity, while the Eastern churches are a-millennial as well.

In the Reformed world dominated by covenant a-millennialism, pre-millennialism is too easily discarded as a modern invention and sectarian in nature. As to this latter point: pre-millennialists have never organized themselves, have never formed sectarian denominations.[72] Also the Brethren movement, which exerted such an enormous influence

---

69. Voorhoeve (1922; 1969).
70. Scott (1920); Kelly (1868; 1870; 1904).
71. See especially Snell (1878); Baines (1879); Whybrow (1898); Grant (1902, n.d.-a, n.d.-b); Chater (1914); Ironside (1930); Burton (1932); Jennings (1937); Lang (1945); Tatford (1947); Van Ryn (1960); Rossier (1961, 1967); Bruce (1969); Coates (n.d.); Dennett (n.d.); Hoste (n.d.-a); Smith (n.d.); Stanley (n.d.).
72. See Chafer (*ST* 4:282).

within modern pre-millennialism, originated for reasons having to do not with eschatology, but with ecclesiology. Throughout the world, pre-millennialism occurs in virtually *all* Protestant denominations without having ever given rise to church divisions. Hundreds of Bible schools and theological academies, and thousands of local congregations, adhere to pre-millennialism. The great missionary movements are pre-millennial, as are the thousands of missionaries whom they have sent out. The great majority of evangelists worldwide are pre-millennial.

Not all pre-millennialism is the same. It makes a great difference whether one posits a single people of God throughout the centuries, identifying Israel and the Ecclesia. One can be a full-fledged supersessionist, adhering to the notion of a spiritual Israel, and yet believe in a thousand-year kingdom appearing after the second coming of Christ, which does or does not entail a national and spiritual restoration of Israel. This is sometimes called a historic or covenant pre-millennialism.[73] In the nineteenth century, adherents of this view were H. Alford, F. Delitzsch, R. C. Trench, J. P. Lange, C. H. Spurgeon, F. Godet, and G. N. H. Peters,[74] and in the twentieth century G. E. Ladd, G. R. Beasley-Murray, and M. J. Erickson.[75]

Over against them, we find dispensational pre-millennialism, which generally interprets the Israel prophecies in the Tanakh literally. This view goes back especially upon J. N. Darby[76] and his most important pupils: W. Kelly[77] and F. W. Grant,[78] and many other Brethren,[79] and thinkers sympa-

---

73. See recently Blomberg and Chung (2009) (especially their opposition to pre-tribulationism, which is inherent to dispensational pre-millennialism).
74. See Spurgeon (1969; many sermons in 1982); Peters (1952).
75. See Ladd (1974; 1977, 27–28); Beasley-Murray (1974); Erickson (1998, 1215–18, 1224–31).
76. See especially the volumes in Darby (*CW*) dealing with the prophets.
77. See his commentaries, largely contained in Kelly, *BT*; also Kelly (1868; 1870; 1970).
78. See especially Grant (1931; n.d.-a; n.d.-b).
79. See note 68, plus Bland (1890); Ritchie (1912); Scott (1920); Pache (1968); Ouweneel (1988–90); Bellett (n.d.); Trotter and Smith (n.d.); Hoste (n.d.-a,

thetic with them, such as B. W. Newton, A. C. Gaebelein, C. I. Scofield, and L. S. Chafer,[80] and later Hal Lindsey[81] and the *Left Behind* series by T. LaHaye and J. B. Jenkins.[82]

Well-known twentieth-century representatives of dispensational pre-millennialism were, or are, M. R. DeHaan, C. L. Feinberg and his son, J. S. Feinberg, D. G. Barnhouse, J. F. Walvoord, J. D Petecost,[83] C. C. Ryrie,[84] J. F. MacArthur, and N. L. Geisler.[85] As far as I know, none of these theologians belongs, or has belonged, to the (Plymouth) Brethren.

11.4.3 Millennial Dispensationalism

Within dispensational pre-millennialism, we distinguish between classical and progressive dispensationalism.[86] This amounts to three main views: historic, classic, and progressive dispensational millennialism. The principal differences between historic and dispensational pre-millennialism are the following.

(a) In its approach of the Tanakh, historic pre-millennialism does not differ that much from the a-millennialism because it views the Tanakh prophecies entirely or largely fulfilled in the (New Testament) Ecclesia. What J. F. Walvoord wrote about the rapture of the Ecclesia (before or after the Great Tribulation?) is also true for the difference between historic and dispensational pre-millennialism (cf. point [b]):

---

n.d.-b); Hoste and M'Elheran (n.d.).

80. Newton (1913); Gaebelein (1961); Scofield (1967); Chafer (*ST*, especially 4, 5, and 7).
81. Lindsey (1970). It is unfortunate that many authors (understandably) find the speculative Lindsey to be a useful target in combating a literal interpretation of the Israel prophecies, as, e.g., Douma (2008, 30).
82. LaHaye and Jenkins (2010).
83. DeHaan (1944); C. L. Feinberg (1961); Barnhouse (1985); J. S. Feinberg (1988); Walvoord (1949–1951; 1966; 1974; 1991); Pentecost (1964); Geisler (2005).
84. See Ryrie (1965) and his marginal notes in Ryrie (1995).
85. For Calvinists: MacArthur, *Why Every Calvinist Should Be a Premillennialist* (www.gty.org/Resources/Sermon+Series/300).
86. Ouweneel (2011, §14.4.3).

one's view is determined more by ecclesiology than by eschatology.[87]

(b) According to historic pre-millennialism, during the Millennium the Ecclesia will be on earth at the center of God's ways and blessings; restored Israel will be part of this Ecclesia. According to dispensational pre-millennialism, during the Millennium Israel will be on earth at the center of God's ways and blessings, while the Ecclesia will be with Christ glorified in heaven.

Here is a summary of the differences mentioned earlier between classic (or traditional) and progressive (including so-called revised) dispensationalism. The term "progressive" refers to the ideas that the successive dispensations exhibit a certain progression. Classic dispensationalism views the present dispensation (or simply, era) as a parenthesis or intermezzo between the earlier ways of God with Israel, which on the Day of Pentecost gave way to his totally new ways, namely, with the Ecclesia.[88] After the rapture of the Ecclesia (before the Great Tribulation), God "picks up the thread with Israel again," as a common formulation puts it. This means that the boundaries between the consecutive dispensations are rather sharp. From the classic dispensationalist standpoint, it is inconceivable that God would pick up the thread with Israel again while the Ecclesia is still on the earth.[89]

In progressive dispensationalism, the transitions are much more fluid, both with regard to the period described in the book of Acts and with regard to the last stage of the present dispensation. Thus, in Acts 2 the history of the Ecclesia on earth begins, but the thread with Israel has not (yet) been dropped at all. We read throughout the book of Acts various

---

87. Walvoord (1957, 16).

88. Van der Kooi and Van den Brink (2017, 375) wrote: "[With this] the complete redemption at the end of time is separated [Dutch *onderscheiden*; better: distinguished] from the opening of the way to God that has been realized through Jesus Christ. These two events are not simultaneous; an interim lies between them, [omitted from the English translation: the time of the Spirit]."

89. Thus, Voorhoeve (1922) described in 1866 extensively how Israel would return to its land and would establish its own state there, but located this all *after* the rapture of the Ecclesia from the earth.

specific appeals that are still being made to Israel.[90] Only in Acts 28:23-28 does there seem to be a (preliminary) farewell to Israel. In a similar way, one might imagine that, at the end of the present dispensation, there can be a similar transitional period, which, as in Acts, might last several decades. Again, today there is a Messiah-confessing Jewry in the land of Israel, as in Acts, and worldwide there is also a restoration of the wonders and signs of the Holy Spirit, as in Acts.[91]

Progressive dispensationalism acknowledges that the members of the Ecclesia are sons and daughters of Abraham, too, and have been welcomed to dwell under the roof of the New Covenant, which is made with Israel. According to classic dispensationalism, the Ecclesia has nothing to do with the New Covenant, and according to revised dispensationalism, there are two covenants: one for the Ecclesia and one for Israel. According to progressive dispensationalism, there is only one covenant, with a present partial fulfillment and a future complete fulfillment for Israel.

According to classic dispensationalism, Jesus' Sermons in Matthew 5-7 and Matthew 24-25, as well as the Great Commission (28:18-20), are meant for (the remnant of) Israel only, whereas the Ecclesia has nothing to do with the "gospel of the kingdom" (24:14). According to progressive dispensationalism, however, the Ecclesia, too, is intimately involved with the "gospel of the kingdom"; it puts great emphasis on the meaning of the kingdom of God in its present form,[92] and in this way, Israel and the Ecclesia—no matter how distinct—come together much more closely. This also means that, when prophecies of the Tanakh are quoted in the New Testament, we must not think only of their applications, as classic dispensationalism does.[93] No, we may think of genuine fulfillment, although a preliminary, incomplete one. In this way, new understanding has arisen with regard to the

---

90. See especially Acts 3:13–26; 7:2–53; 13:17–41; 17:2–3, 10–12.
91. See more extensively, Ouweneel (2010c).
92. See Ouweneel (2010c; 2011, chapters 9–12).
93. In this respect, I am more at home with classic dispensationalism than with progressive dispensationalism.

meaning that the prophecies in the Tanakh have for the Ecclesia as well, without the need of first declaring the Ecclesia to be the spiritual Israel.

11.5 Evaluation

11.5.1 Comparison

When we compare a-, post-, and pre-millennialism, we can identify the following strong and weak points of each.

A. A-Millennialism

(1) Strong Points

(a) The statement of Jesus that we read in Matthew 28:18, "All authority in heaven and on earth has been given to me," might be interpreted to suggest that the world rule of Christ has already begun, and will become reality not only in the future, but also in the present.

(b) The New Testament applied various aspects of the Messianic kingdom to the present time. A striking example is found in Hosea 1:10; things said about God's people in that passage were linked with the Messianic kingdom (also see Hos. 2:14-3:5), but in Romans 9:25-26 were applied to the Ecclesia. Therefore, it seems obvious to view the Messianic kingdom as realized in the present dispensation.

(c) Many aspects of the Messianic kingdom in the Tanakh appear to have been meant in a symbolic way (see, e.g., Isa. 11:6-8; 40:4; 65:25). So why could we not assume that all these prophecies, completely or partially, were meant to be interpreted symbolically?

This is closely related to whether the Ecclesia can be considered to be the "true" or "spiritual Israel."

(2) Weak Points

(a) In Revelation 19-20, in a part of the book that obviously makes a strictly chronological impression (through the repeated "And I saw . . . and I heard . ."), the Christ's thousand-year rule follows Christ's second coming, not the other way around, as a-millennialists like Abraham Kuyper have admitted.

(b) In an unbiased approach (to the extent such is possible), the two resurrections in Revelation 20:4–6 can be understood only in an equivalent sense: the two phrases refer to a physical resurrection of physically dead people, one before and one after the thousand years.

(c) In Daniel 7, the Messianic kingdom follows the coming of the Son of Man on the clouds of heaven, not the other way around.

B. Post-Millennialism

(1) Strong Points

(a) There is important evidence for a conversion of ethnic Israel and a period of the church's flourishing in the last days.[94]

(b) The strong points of a-millennialism mentioned are relevant here: if the Ecclesia is the spiritual Israel (which does not exclude the possibility of a massive conversion of ethnic Israel in the last days!), no need exists to make a sharp division between the present time and the Messianic kingdom later: the former smoothly flows into the latter.

(c) The prophecies in the Tanakh are often interpreted in a predominantly literal way.

(2) Weak Points

(a) The same as those of a-millennialism.

(b) The Great Tribulation, the apostasy, and the appearance of the Antichrist (2 Thess. 2:1–12) are viewed as past events, whereas the fall of the Antichrist will occur at the appearance of Christ.

(c) The danger "of a religiously colored progressive optimism, which does not come from biblical sources"[95] (although it is difficult to draw the boundary between this and

a *sound* expectation of the church's flourishing in the last days).

---

94. Cf. Ouweneel (2010b, chapter 14).
95 Van Genderen (1984, 46).

C. Pre-Millennialism

(1) Strong Points

(a) Pre-millennialism maintains the order of Daniel 2 and 7, and of Revelation 19-21: first the appearance of Christ, then the Messianic kingdom, then the new heavens and the new earth.

(b) It interprets the two resurrections in Revelation 20:4-6 in an equivalent sense: the physical resurrection of the righteous before, and that of the wicked after, the thousand years.

(c) The Great Tribulation, the apostasy, and the appearance of the Antichrist (2 Thess. 2:1-12) are viewed as events that occur in the last days, which come to an end with the appearance of Christ.

(2) Weak Points

(a) Revelation 20:1-7 does say that the glorified saints will reign with Christ during the thousand years, but it does not speak of a kingdom *on earth*. It does not spend any time describing the entirely new situation on earth (against which one might argue that this is not necessary because the Tanakh had already dealt extensively with this matter).

(b) Many argue that after the appearance of Christ, no separate Messianic kingdom, distinct from the new earth, is needed (see below).

11.5.2 Integration

It is obvious that a- and post-millennialism are more closely related than post- and pre-millennialism (not to mention a- and pre-millennialism, especially classic dispensational pre-millennialism, which are farthest removed from each other). The boundaries between the three views are often rather fluid, and perhaps they are becoming more and more fluid, which some might call a positive development. Here are examples of such fluid boundaries.

(a) A view that assumes a period of the church's flourishing before the second coming of Christ, along with a national and spiritual restoration of Israel, *and* believes in a Messianic kingdom of peace *after* the second coming and *before* the eternal state, has features that are both pre- and post-millennial. In other words, it is possible to be pre-millennial, and yet not to be a pessimist, to believe in a Messianic kingdom after Christ's second coming, and at the same time to harbor great expectations concerning what God does, or might do, in this world before the second coming.

(b) A view that minimizes the differences between the Messianic kingdom after Christ's second coming and the subsequent eternal state has features that are both pre- and a-millennial. In classic pre-millennialism, the boundary between the Messianic kingdom and the eternal state was very sharp (between what we have elsewhere called before the "seventh" and the "eighth" day of world history). Today, more emphasis is put on the fact that the dominion that the Son of Man receives is an everlasting dominion,[96] and that even the glorified saints "will reign forever and ever" (Rev. 22:5). Thus, the transition to the eternal state (Lat. *status aeternus*) has become more smooth. If therefore the phrase in the Nicene Creed, "whose kingdom shall have no end" (Lat. *Cuius regni non erit finis*) could ever have been used as an argument against pre-millennialism, then certainly no longer today. Notice 1 Corinthians 15:28, where Paul wrote, "When all things are subjected to him [i.e., Christ], then the Son himself will also be subjected to him who put all things in subjection under him, that God may be all in all." This seems to refer to a limited reign of Christ because in the end he surrenders his reign to God. However, we must keep in mind that in such an expression—"God will be all in all"—God is always the *Triune* God. That is, the Son will not be excluded from this everlasting dominion; what comes to an end is his reign as the *Son of Man*.

(d) A view that assumes something resembling *two* returns of Christ, one before and one after the thousand years—

---

96. Dan. 2:44; 7:14; Luke 1:33; cf. Isa. 45:17; 51:11; 55;3; 61:7; Jer. 32:40; Ezek. 16:60; 37:26. Consider also the fact that the "new heavens" and the "new earth" are mentioned in Isa. 65:17 (cf. 66:22), whereas the description that follows is obviously that of the Messianic kingdom.

held, for instance, by W. à Brakel[97]—has features that are both pre- and post-millennial. Such an assumption might seem strange: will there be a second *and* a third coming of Christ? However, perhaps we should speak instead of two "interventions" by Christ. In my view, the former is the actual *parousia* ("[second] coming," e.g., 2 Thess. 2:1), or *epiphaneia* ("appearing," e.g., 1 Tim. 6:14), or *apokalupsis* ("revelation, manifestation," 1 Pet. 1:7, 13) of Jesus Christ on the clouds of heaven. Whatever view one prefers, an "intervention" by Christ is always involved—no matter how this is understood—ushering in the eternal state.

(e) A view that assumes that the thousand years are already ended, and that yet expects a future period of the church's flourishing before Christ's second coming—as apparently Dutch pastors of the Second Reformation did, like J. Coccejus and D. F. van Giffen[98]—has features that are both a- and post-millennial.

11.6 Objections Against A-Millennialism
11.6.1 Satan Bound

Various objections against a-millennialism have been discussed already; I summarize them here, and add some new objections, plus some counterarguments.

We begin with some observations about Revelation 20:1-3:

> Then I saw an angel coming down from heaven, holding in his hand the key to the bottomless pit [or, the abyss] and a great chain. And he seized the dragon, that ancient serpent, who is the devil and Satan, and bound him for a thousand years, and threw him into the pit, and shut it and sealed it over him, so that he might not deceive the nations any longer, until the thousand years were ended. After that he must be released for a little while.

Is it correct to say, as a-millennialists do, that Satan has been bound since the work of Christ was completed on the

---
97. Van Campen (2007, 203).
98. Ibid., 294–95,427.

cross of Calvary? Although various Bible verses are quoted as proof, we must note the following.[99]

First, in John 16:11 (AMP), Jesus said that Satan *has been* judged and condemned already, that is, even before the cross.

Second, why is an angel mentioned in Revelation 20, and not Christ himself?

Third, if Satan has been definitively defeated on the cross, what does it mean that, after the thousand years Satan will be released again for a little while?

Fourth, how could anyone claim that today Satan has been rendered completely powerless? Passages speaking of the judgment on Satan can speak only of the *basic* victory over Satan on the cross. Thus, sin (Rom. 6:6), death (2 Tim. 1:9-10), and the devil (Heb. 2:14-15) have basically been "brought to nothing" or "abolished" or "destroyed" (in Greek always the same verb: *katargeō*), although their effects are still prominently visible until this very day.

Fifth, Revelation 20:1-3 was not speaking only of Christ's victory. Here, Saran is bound *and* thrown into the abyss, *and* the latter was closed above his head *and* sealed above him.

Sixth, most decisive is that the aim of this binding of Satan was that he will no longer "deceive the nations." In no way can the thesis be defended that, in the *present* time, Satan is no longer able to deceive the Gentiles. On the contrary, the Bible teaches us the reverse: "Be sober-minded; be watchful. Your adversary the devil prowls around like a roaring lion, seeking someone to devour" (1 Pet. 5:8).[100]

11.6.2 First and Second Resurrection

Let us now consider Revelation 20:4-6:

> I saw the souls of those who had been beheaded for the testi-

---

99. Especially Matt. 12:29; John 12:31; Col. 2:1; Hebr. 2:14–15; 1 John 3:8. Matt. 12:29 speaks of Christ's triumph over Satan during the temptations in the wilderness, or of his casting out demons—a heavy blow for Satan, but not one that impeded his free movements.
100. Compare Acts 5:3; 2 Cor. 4:3–4; 11:14; Eph. 2:2; 6:11–16; 1 Thess. 2:18; 2 Tim. 2:26; see also James 4:7: a "fleeing" devil does not comport with a "bound" devil.

mony of Jesus and for the word of God, and those who had not worshiped the beast or its image and had not received its mark on their foreheads or their hands. They came to life and reigned with Christ for a thousand years. The rest of the dead did not come to life until the thousand years were ended. This is the *first resurrection*. Blessed and holy is the one who shares in the first resurrection! Over such the *second death* has no power, but they will be priests of God and of Christ, and they will reign with him for a thousand years (italics added).

This passage refers to a "first resurrection," which obviously implies a "second restoration." However, this second resurrection is called here the "second death." This is because it involves the resurrection of unbelievers, who, after the judgment before the great white throne, are cast into the lake of fire together with their resurrection bodies (see 20:14; 21:8). Compare Jesus' statement about God "who can destroy both soul and body in hell" (Matt. 10:28). The wicked will rise from physical death and will be given over to eternal death in the lake of fire.

In light of Revelation 20:12-13, this second resurrection is understood by every expositor as a real physical resurrection from physical death. Because it is parallel with this second resurrection, the first resurrection must also be understood as a real physical resurrection from physical death, in the sense of Romans 8: "He Who raised up Christ from the dead will also restore to life your mortal (short-lived, perishable) bodies through His Spirit Who dwells in you" (v. 11 AMPC). Revelation 20 was speaking explicitly of "dead" people who come to "life" again. If in a passage where *two resurrections* are mentioned, the first one can be taken to be a *spiritual* resurrection with Christ, whereas the second one means *literal* resurrection from the grave, then all meaning in language has evaporated, and Scripture is swept away as a decisive testimony for any matter.[101] In other words, Revelation 20 taught undeniably that there will be *two* physical resurrections, one at the beginning and one at the end of the thousand years. The first resurrection involves believers exclusively, for these

---

101. Alford (1958, 4:732).

are called "blessed and holy," "priests of God and of Christ," reigning with the latter for the thousand years. At the second resurrection, after the thousand years, the wicked will be raised in order to be cast into hell "soul and body" (cf. Matt. 10:28). Their "coming to life" exclusively involves their receiving a body with which they will be cast into the lake of fire. Therefore, although they have been raised, they stand before the great white throne as the (spiritually) "dead" (Rev. 20:11–15).

In a general sense, the Bible often speaks of the "resurrection of the dead," in order to underscore the fact that ultimately every dead human will rise from death.[102] However, this expression must be carefully distinguished from the expression "resurrection *from* the dead,"[103] that is, the first resurrection, at which a part of the dead, namely, the righteous, rise from the midst of the totality of the dead, while the wicked stay behind in their graves.[104]

John 5:28 seems to create difficulties because this verse said, "[A]n hour is coming when all who are in the tombs will hear his voice and come out, those who have done good to the resurrection of life, and those who have done evil to the resurrection of judgment." This might be interpreted to suggest that all the dead, both the righteous and the wicked, will rise at the same time. However, look at the "hour" in verse 25: "[A]n hour is coming, and is now here, when the dead will hear the voice of the Son of God, and those who hear will live." This is the "hour" of the gospel preaching, through which the hearers, if they believe, receive spiritual life (cf. Eph. 2:1, 5; Col. 2:13). Today, we can say that this "hour" al-

---

102. Matt. 22:31; Acts 17:32; 23:6; 24:21; 26:23; 1 Cor. 15:12–13, 21, 42; Heb. 6:2.
103. "From [the] dead," Gk. *ek nekrōn*, "out of [the company of] the [physically] dead" (leaving other dead people behind in the graves); not to be confused with "from death" (Gk. *ek [tou] thanatou*, cf. John 5:24; Heb. 5:7; 1 John 3:14). All bodily resurrection is "from death," but not all of it is "from the dead."
104. Luke 20:35; Acts 4:2; 1 Cor. 15:20; Phil. 3:11; for the newness of this doctrine (resurrection *from* the dead) for the Jews of that day, see Mark 9:9–10; appar ently, for supersessionists this doctrine is still new.

ready comprises almost two thousand years. So why could the "hour" of verse 28 not comprise a thousand years, at the beginning of which the righteous are raised, and at the end of which the wicked are raised? In simpler terms: the text does not necessarily imply that the good and the evil ones will be raised at the same time. There is a "resurrection of the just" (Luke 14:14), distinct from the resurrection of the unjust (Acts 24:15). There is a "resurrection of life" (i.e., with everlasting life in view) and a "resurrection of judgment" (i.e., with everlasting judgment in view) (John 5:29).

In my view, 1 Corinthians 15, too, implicitly distinguishes between the two resurrections. In verse 23, we see that, at the coming of Christ, only "those who belong to Christ" are raised, that is, not the unbelievers (cf. the "dead in Christ," 1 Thess. 4:16). Apparently, the resurrection of unbelievers will occur only when, at the end of the Messianic kingdom, Christ will subject this kingdom to God the Father. At that moment, all enemies will have been defeated, *including death as such*. Christ "must reign until he has put all his enemies under his feet. The last enemy to be destroyed is death" vv. 25-26). This must necessarily be at the end of the Messianic kingdom, as we find in Revelation 20. Here, at the end of the thousand years, death and *hades* (the realm of the dead) will be thrown into the lake of fire, after *hades* will have "returned" its unbelieving dead.

11.6.3 Three Court Hearings

Since Augustine, the church's has acknowledged one resurrection only; likewise, it acknowledges one judgment only. However, when we investigate the Bible more closely on this point, we discover that there is indeed one judgment seat and one Judge (cf. Acts 10:42; 2 Tim. 4:1), but the Bible distinguished between several quite different *court hearings*, at different times and places, and with different people appearing before the judgment seat. Let me mention three such court hearings.

(a) First Hearing.[105]

* *defendants:* believers of the Tanakh and of the New Testament Ecclesia;
* *categories:* one (believers);
* *time:* at the second coming of Christ;
* *place:* in heaven;
* *criteria:* demonstrated faithfulness and devotion on earth;
* *judgment:* different reward in view of co-reigning with Christ and the person's position in eternity.

(b) Second Hearing (Matt. 25:31-46).[106]

* *defendants:* the nations living on earth;
* *categories:* three: righteous (the "sheep") and unrighteous Gentiles (the "goats") and the King's "brothers" (in my view, the first and third category overlap);
* *time:* immediately after the second coming of Christ, at the beginning of the Messianic kingdom (see vv. 31, 34);
* *place:* on earth;
* *criteria:* the Gentiles' attitude toward the King's "brothers";
* *judgment:* entering into the kingdom or into the eternal fire (in my view, this means that the "goats" die first, are raised after the thousand years, and appear before the great white throne; see [c]).

(c) Third Hearing (Rev. 20:11-15).[107]

* *defendants:* the dead wicked ones;
* *categories:* one (wicked ones);
* *time:* after the thousand years;
* *place:* not indicated ("between heaven and earth");
* *criteria:* judged according their (evil) works;
* *judgment:* the lake of fire.

---

105. Rom. 14:10; 2 Cor. 5:10; see also 1 Cor. 1:8; 4:3–5; 5:5; 2 Cor. 1:14; Phil. 1:6, 10; 2:16; 2 Thess. 1:10; 2 Tim. 1:18; 4:8; for details see Ouweneel (2012a, §11.4.1).
106. Ibid., §12.6.2.
107. Ibid., §14.3.

11.7 The Messianic Kingdom
11.7.1 The Kingdom in Glory

Another point of debate between millennialists and a-millennialists involves the biblical testimony concerning the kingdom that Christ will establish on earth at his second coming. Some a-millennialists have objected that Revelation 20 did not speak at all of a rule of Christ on earth. My first reply is: what then is the meaning of the following expressions: "Also I saw the souls of [the martyrs]. They came to life and *reigned with Christ* for a thousand years" (v. 4); ". . . they will be priests of God and of Christ, and they will *reign with him* for a thousand years" (v. 6)?

Twice the Greek verb *basileuō* is used here: "to reign as a king [Gk. *basileus*]."[108] Now, if the risen saints reign as kings together with Christ, does this not imply that Christ himself will reign as King? Already now, he has received all power in heaven and on earth (Matt. 28:18), but no Bible passage tells us that he actually reigns already now *as Son of Man*, or that he reigns *on earth*.[109] On the contrary, we are told: "[W]hen Christ had offered for all time a single sacrifice for sins, he sat down at the right hand of God, *waiting* from that time until his enemies should be made a footstool for his feet" (Heb. 10:12-13; italics added). Jesus Christ is now still sitting in the throne of his Father, just as, during the Messianic kingdom, he will sit on his own throne, that is, the throne of David (Rev. 3:21; cf. Isa. 9:7; Luke 1:32-33)—a distinction that, generally speaking, has been honored far too little.

We can speak of the kingdom of the Son of Man only after he has descended to earth on the clouds of heaven (Dan. 7:13-14), that is, at the "end [conclusion, completion, consummation, Gk. *synteleia*] of the [present] age." As the angel says, "The kingdom of the world *has become* the kingdom of our Lord and of his Christ, and he shall reign forever and ever" (Rev. 11:15).

This kingdom will arrive at the end of the "forty-two

---

108. Actually, "to reign" would suffice because this word comes from Latin *rex*, "king."
109. *Contra* Hoek (2004, 192–93).

months" or "1,260 days" (vv. 2-3), which is the last half of the seventieth "week" (period of seven years) of Daniel 9:24-27, a period immediately preceding the "consummation of the age."[110]

In the New Testament, this order of events—first Christ's second coming, then the establishment of the Messianic kingdom—is clearly confirmed. First and foremost, this confirmation is found in Jesus' End Time Sermon (Matt. 24-25; Mark 13; Luke 21), which we have sufficiently discussed in volume IV/1, chapter 13. In Matthew 25:31, the Son of Man will descend in his glories, and all the angels with him, and *then* the time comes when he will allow the "sheep" into "the kingdom prepared for you from the foundation of the world" (v. 34). In Luke 21:24, Jerusalem is trampled underfoot until the "times of the Gentiles" are fulfilled, and this turns out to coincide more or less[111] with the second coming of Christ: *then* the time of the "redemption" will arrive (v. 28).

11.7.2 Acts and Revelation

In Acts 1:6-7, after the resurrection of Jesus, the disciples asked him: "'Lord, will you at this time restore the kingdom to Israel?' He said to them, 'It is not for you to know times or seasons that the Father has fixed by his own authority.'" The disciples' question was perfectly understandable and correct, if we view it in the light of all the kingdom teaching that the disciples had received from the Master (see again volume IV/1, chapter 13). Many expositors have suggested that this was a misguided question, and that Jesus rejected it. But this is supersessionist wishful thinking: the text said nothing of the kind. That is, Jesus does not deny at all *the fact that* the kingdom will be restored to Israel, but states only that the disciples were not entitled to know at what "time" (Gk. *chronos*) or "season" ("opportunity," Gk. *kairos*) this was going to

---

110. Of course, he is always involved in the universal rule exercised by the *Triune God*; see Ouweneel (2012a, §6.5).
111. More or less—for since 1967, Jerusalem is no longer trampled underfoot by the Gentiles; however, there are still the two Gentile sanctuaries on the temple mount, which will, I assume, find their end at the second coming of Christ, *or* be consecrated to him.

happen. In brief he said: It will indeed happen, but in the Father's time.

Just a few weeks or months later, the apostle Peter preached this very point in saying to Israel,

> Repent therefore, and turn back, that your sins may be blotted out, that times [Gk. *kairoi*] of refreshing may come from the presence of the Lord, and that he may send the Christ [i.e., the Messiah] appointed for you [i.e., the Jews], Jesus, whom heaven must receive until the times [Gk. *chronoi*] for restoring all the things about which God spoke by the mouth of his holy prophets long ago (Acts 3:19-21).

Here we learn three things:

(1) At the second coming of Christ, the eternal state does not begin immediately, but first *times* of refreshing and of restoration of all things will arrive.[112]

(2) This restoration involves first of all Israel itself and its return to the LORD; it is thus first and foremost a spiritual restoration.

(3) The announcement of these wonderful "times" does not involve some new apostolic revelation; no, they refer to nothing other than the Messianic kingdom of which so many prophets had already spoken in the Tanakh.

Finally, let us also listen to the further testimony of the book of Revelation:

(a) In 2:26-27, Christ spoke of the *future* reign of the believers together with him, over the nations, with expressions about himself that can be applicable only *after his second coming* (19:15).

(b) In 3:21, Christ spoke in the *future* sense of his sitting on his own throne, and of believers sitting, and thus reigning, together with him in the *future*.

(c) In 5:10, the twenty-four elders spoke in the *future* sense of the saints reigning; not a single believer reigns with Christ

---

112. *Contra* Berkouwer (1972, 241): Jesus will return "at the end of the times"; the Bible text says the opposite: at Jesus' return, certain special "times" will arrive, but *not* yet the eternal state; see Ouweneel (2012a, §2.3).

now,[113] for no saint has already been glorified, for none of them has been raised and been given the glorious body belonging to the resurrection state (Phil. 3:20–21).

(d) In 11:15–18, we find a very important proclamation of the kingdom (almost at the end of the Great Tribulation, that is, shortly before the second coming of Christ). All events that will occur at the second coming are summarized here: (1) the coming of the (Messianic) kingdom, and thus the beginning of Christ's dominion; (2) the judgment on the nations; (3) the judgment of the dead (which, according to Rev. 20, will occur only after the thousand years); and (4) the retribution for both the righteous and the wicked.

(e) In 15:3–4, just before the second coming of Christ, the overcomers proclaim that the LORD God ("in" the person of Jesus Christ) is the King of the nations, and that all nations will come and bow down before him. Apparently, this is not the case before the second coming. Thus, the text was referring not to the nations coming near because of gospel preaching, or something like this, but to the nations coming to subject themselves, sincerely or hypocritically, to the Ruler of the earth.

11.7.3 The Jewish Kingdom

In his commentary on the book of Malachi, church father Jerome referred to the *Jewish* view of the Messianic kingdom. Malachi 1:4–5 spoke of Edom's destruction, and the glorification of the LORD far beyond the borders of Israel. With some disdain, Jerome mentioned that the Jews saw in Edom a representation of the Romans, and that they flattered themselves with the thought that, once the Roman Empire had been destroyed, world dominion would come to the Jews.[114] And in his commentary on Daniel, he said regarding chapter 2:40, in a derogatory way, that according to Jewish expositors the Messianic kingdom will be a *Jewish* kingdom, arriving af-

---

113. See Ouweneel (2020b, 2022) regarding deceased believers.
114. https://sites.google.com/site/aquinasstudybible/home/malachi/st-jerome-on-malachi--latin.

ter the destruction of the Roman Empire.[115]

Indeed, this is a thoroughly Jewish interpretation, which is encountered already in Flavius Josephus in his *Antiquities of the Jews*,[116] and in apocryphal Jewish books like 4 Ezra 2:10–13

> These are the words of the Lord to Ezra: "Tell my people that I will give to *them* the kingdom of Jerusalem which once I offered *to Israel*.... Ask, and you shall receive; so pray that your short time of waiting may be made shorter still. The kingdom is ready for you now; be on the watch!"[117]

This thought comports with the disciples' question to the risen Jesus: "Lord, will you at this time restore the kingdom to *Israel*?" (Acts 1:6).

Some modern expositors venture to say that this Jewish interpretation differs entirely from "the" Christian view. Thereby they call the supersessionist view "the Christian" one; apparently, there is no room in their thinking for other Christian views.[118] In reality, the Jewish interpretation contains exactly what millions of Christian millennialists believe, too. Like other supersessionists, Jerome was unable to see that the "people of the saints of the Most High" (Dan. 7:27), which during the Messianic kingdom will form the center of the world,[119] cannot be anything other than what Daniel necessarily understood by it, namely, (the faithful ones of) Israel. The Son of Man, to whom world dominion is entrusted at his coming (Dan. 7:13–14), is the Messiah. Christians recognize in him Jesus of Nazareth, to whom the New Testament

---

115. http://www.tertullian.org/fathers/jerome_daniel_02_text.htm.
116. Book I.19.6: God wanted to give the [Messianic] kingdom to Jacob, not to Esau; in book X.10.4, Josephus discussed the vision of Dan. 2, but he did not wish to enter in the meaning of the "stone" (vv. 34–35, 45), probably because he did not wish to offend the Romans ("I do not think proper to relate it, since I have only undertaken to describe things past or things present, but not things that are future.").
117. https://www.scribd.com/doc/2019085/4-Ezra-Revised-English.
118. See more extensively, Ouweneel (2003, §10.2, including footnotes).
119. Isa. 2:2, 3 [= Micha 4:1, 2]; 56:1–8; 60:8–16; Zech. 8:23.

applied Daniel 7 (see Matt. 24:30; 26:64). Thus, the Messianic kingdom is identical with the kingdom of the Son of Man (cf. Matt. 13:41; 16:28). At the same time, it is also definitely an *Israelite* world empire: the kingdom (or kingship) is given to the Son of Man, but also to the "(people of) the saints of the Most High" (Dan. 7:18, 22): the saints were oppressed "until the Ancient of Days came, and judgment was given for the saints of the Most High, and the time came when *the saints possessed the kingdom*" (Dan. 7:22).

> And the kingdom and the dominion
> and the greatness of the kingdoms under the whole heaven
> shall be given to the people of the saints of the Most High;
> their kingdom shall be an everlasting kingdom,
> and all dominions shall serve and obey them (Dan. 7:27, ESV note).

In this respect, the Jewish expositors—in contrast with what Jerome believed—were perfectly correct. One day, the last of the four empires in Daniel 7—the Roman Empire, in Revelation the *restored* Roman Empire of the end time, led by the Beast[120]—will be destroyed. This will occur when the Son of Man descends (Dan. 7:13). Then, the Messianic kingdom will begin. Its King will be the Messiah (the Anointed One) *of Israel*, and Zion will form the center of it (see below); these two points suffice to call this an Israelite empire. The Babylonian and Roman empires covered large parts of the ancient world, but they were named after their capitals: Babylon and Rome. The Messianic kingdom will cover the entire world, but could be called after its center: Jerusalem, Zion, Israel.

Like virtually all church fathers from before 300–350, and like the Jewish expositors, millions of Christians today believe again that the Messianic kingdom will be a kingdom on, and over, the present earth, and therefore must be distinguished from the eternal state of the new heaven and the new earth.[121] The glorious and powerful kingdom of the Son

---

120. See Ouweneel (2012a, chapter 6).
121. See extensively, Ouweneel (2012a).

of Man will be established *after* his coming "with the clouds of heaven" (Dan. 7:13), and not at his birth or his ascension, or on the Day of Pentecost, or at the conversion of Constantine the Great.[122] The establishment of that kingdom will involve the destruction of all diabolical powers that throughout the centuries have dominated the world empires, and above all have threatened Israel (Rev. 19-20). This kingdom will be the empire of the Messiah of Israel, who at the same time will be King of the entire world. In the end time, he will be manifested in power and majesty, and will *visibly* establish his kingdom on earth, with *Israel* (Jerusalem, Zion) as its center.

Jews and Christians, and Christians among themselves, may differ in their opinions on the precise interpretation of the Messianic prophecies concerning this kingdom. But Christian expositors, too, believing in a future Messianic kingdom on the present earth, in order to better understand its character, will have to consult, in addition to the book of Revelation, the prophetic books of the Tanakh; we already considered many examples of this.

11.8 The Torah Is Still Functioning!
11.8.1 The Restored Sacrificial Ministry

For many Christians, the thought that, during the Messianic kingdom, the sacrificial ministry will be restored, is one of the most shocking aspects of the view that I am defending here. This is due mainly to an important misunderstanding to which the Christian establishment has fallen prey over the centuries. This is the erroneous idea that the ceremonial laws of the Mosaic Torah, especially the sacrificial laws, or the Saturday Shabbat, have been annulled.[123] This is asserted despite Jesus' emphatic saying that he did *not* come to abolish (annul, cancel, do away with, Gk. *kataluō*) the Torah or the prophets, but to fulfill (Gk. *plēroō*) them (Matt. 5:17). This is precisely the core of the misunderstanding being alleged.

---

122. Today, the kingdom does exist, but only in a hidden form, and includes the totality of Jesus' followers; many parables of Jesus, but also Pauline references such as Rom. 14:17–18; 1 Cor. 4:20; Col. 1:13, refer to the kingdom in its present form (hidden because the King is hidden; cf. Col. 3:3).
123. See Ouweneel (2014a, Excursi 19 and 22).

In Jesus, the sacrificial ministry has been fulfilled: all the sacrifices of the Tanakh find their fulfillment in the one true sacrifice that he has brought.[124] But fulfilling is essentially different from abolishing. *This is why the apostles Peter, John, and Paul could still participate in the sacrificial ministry, after Calvary and Pentecost.*[125] Apparently, they still valued such sacrifices, despite the finished work of Jesus.

After the temple in Jerusalem had been destroyed in AD 70, the sacrificial laws remained completely in force, even though it was no longer possible to implement them. This would be done only after the temple will had been rebuilt, namely, the temple in the Messianic kingdom, as announced by the prophet Zechariah:

> Behold, the man whose name is the Branch [i.e., the Messiah]: for he shall branch out from his place, and *he shall build the temple of the* LORD. It is he who shall build the temple of the LORD and shall bear royal honor, and shall sit and rule on his throne. And there [or, he[126]] shall be a priest on his throne, and the counsel of peace shall be between them both (6:12–13).

The construction and the structure of this temple of the Messianic kingdom is extensively described by the prophet Ezekiel.[127]

This is a verry strange thought for many Christians, schooled as they have been in the notion that the ceremonial laws have been abolished. "Once for all," Jesus rendered the only sacrifice that truly takes away the sins of his people (Heb. 7:27; 9:12; 10:10); how then is it possible that, during the Messianic kingdom, animal sacrifices will be offered again? One of two realities emerges: either they ignore that the apostles Peter, John, and Paul apparently had no difficulty with the continuation of these sacrifices, *or* they declare that this par-

---

124. Cf. 1 Cor. 5:7; Eph. 5:2; Heb. 7:27; 8:3; 9:14, 23–28; 10:8–13.
125. Acts 3:1; 21:20–26; 24:17; 28:17.
126. The text either supposes a royal figure alongside a priestly figure, or a single Priest-King.
127. Ezek. 40:38–43; 42:13; 43:18–27; 44:11, 27–30; 45:9–25; 46:1–20; cf. Isa. 2:2; 60:7; Hos. 3:4; Joel 3:18; Micah 4:1; Zech. 14:20–21.

ticipation in temple sacrifices demonstrated weakness on the part of these apostles. After two thousand years, these critics know what Jesus meant better than these apostles, who sat at the feet of Jesus! These apostles understood very well that the animal sacrifices of the Tanakh *as such* were incapable of taking away any sins (Heb. 10:4). But this did not mean that these sacrifices were worthless. Their value lay in the fact that they *pointed forward* to the one, true sacrifice of Christ. In exactly the same way, it was possible to continue these animal sacrifices, both in the book of Acts and in the coming Messianic kingdom. These sacrifices remain incapable of taking away any sins; yet, the value of these sacrifices consisted and consists in their *pointing back* to the one, true sacrifice of Christ. This is comparable with the way the Lord's Supper does this, even if this is not an animal sacrifice.

Also among modern Messianic (i.e., Jesus-believing) Jews, we encounter believers who look forward to the reconstruction of the Third Temple, and to the sacrifices that will be offered there. This is not because they ignore the finality of the one, true sacrifice of Christ, which alone can take away sins, but because they do acknowledge this finality How enriching it will be for Israel when it becomes aware again of all these various sacrifices. There will be burnt offerings, grain offerings, peace offerings, sin offerings, and guilt offerings, all of which shed light upon certain specific aspects of the atoning work of Christ.[128]

Jesus perfectly and completely *fulfilled* the Mosaic sacrificial laws—but these have never been *abolished*. They will retain their function as a continual reference pointing to the one, true, all-sufficient sacrifice of Christ.

11.8.2 Attempts to Rebuild the Temple

As to this future reconstruction of the temple during the Messianic kingdom, let me add a few comments. During all of Christian antiquity and the Middle Ages, it was unthinkable that Christian leaders, including the Christianized Roman emperors, would have ever cooperated in the reconstruction

---

128. See extensively, Ouweneel (2009, chapter 4).

of Jerusalem and the temple. This was due to a combination of anti-Semitism and supersessionism. There was no future for ethnic Israel; the Diaspora was the Jews' deserved reward. So why contribute to a reversal of this divine punishment? Interestingly, such a reconstruction would definitively have been possible until the Islamic period, when the Muslims began to occupy the Holy Land (seventh century).

Interestingly, it was an emperor who had rejected Christianity, called Julian the Apostate (he ruled from 361 to 363), to whom the idea of such a reconstruction occurred. In an open letter to all Jews (362), he expressed his regret that his Christian (!) predecessors had given the Jews so much trouble. He abolished all the burdensome decrees of his predecessors, and even promised that, after conquering de Sassanids (i.e., the Persian rulers), he would order the rebuilding of both the city of Jerusalem and the Jewish temple, at his own expense.

Julian began immediately, even before his campaign against the Persians had come to an end. The first groups of workmen were already cleaning up the ruins, when suddenly flames burst up from them, which killed some of the laborers. Apparently, deeply under the ruins, gases had accumulated that now had caught fire. The people saw a sign in this: God had spoken! Immediately, the work was stopped. Julian himself did not return from his campaign; his apocryphal dying words were: *vicisti, Galilaee*, that is, "Galilean, you have won!"[129]

As far as we know, none of Julian's successors—surely not the successive Muslim rulers—ever revived the plan to rebuild the city and the temple. It simply was not yet God's time for such a reconstruction; this time can arrive only when the Messianic kingdom has come near, or arrives. In the meantime, during the twentieth century, sixteen centuries later, Jerusalem *has been* rebuilt, and since 1980 it is the official capital of the state of Israel. And one day—after the second coming of Christ—the new temple will also arise, a fact that numerous Jews as well as Christians do not doubt for a second (Ezek. 40–44).

---

129. Cf. the phrase "Jesus the Galilean" in Matt. 26:69.

Let the reader try to imagine how he/she would have felt if he/she had lived around 1880. Would anyone in those days have been able to believe that one century later, Jerusalem would be in the hands of the Jews, and would even be the capital of a Jewish state? Yet, it happened. Do we think that it is more difficult to believe that one day, sacrifices will be offered again in a Jewish temple? I do not know whether this will have to wait another hundred years—but it will happen. The "Temple Institute" in Jerusalem has already prepared a number of objects that are to be used in the Third Temple. And with respect to the sacrifices, for a long time, the institute was busy looking for a red heifer that satisfied all the conditions of Numbers 19:1-22, and it seems it has found it.[130]

11.8.3 Other Mosaic Elements

One of the most remarkable proofs that the Mosaic Torah was never abolished is that, according to the prophecies in the Tanakh, it will fully function during the Messianic kingdom. Try to imagine the difficulties of the supersessionists, who have chosen to spiritualize *all* the examples that we are going to consider, in order to apply them to the Ecclesia. If they believed in the verbal inspiration, and thus in the importance of every detail in the prophecies, their job would be very difficult. Elsewhere, I distinguished between the three forms of the one, eternal Torah of God: the Mosaic, the Messianic, and the Millennial forms of the Torah, which basically are fully one.[131] The distinction is important because, in Ezekiel 40-48, we find certain (minor) points in which this Millennial Torah seems to deviate from the Mosaic Torah. At this moment, these differences do not concern us: I am referring only to the clearly Mosaic elements that will be encountered in Israel when the nation will function during the Messianic kingdom.

(a) In the previous sections, mention has been made of the two most conspicuous examples: the *rebuilding of the lit-*

---

130. See http://www.templeinstitute.org; see also https://www.breakingisraelnews.com/113483/red-heifer-candidate-born-israel/.
131. Ouweneel (2001a; 2020a).

eral temple and the *literal altar*, as well as the *restoration of the literal sacrificial ministry*. Here are some other remarkable Mosaic elements during the Messianic kingdom.

(b) *The Sabbath*. As pointed out earlier, during the Messianic kingdom the Sabbath will be observed throughout the entire earth.[132] Anyone wishing to identify this as the weekly Sunday must not expect to be taken very seriously (see chapter 2). This must be an interesting point for all kinds of supersessionists: *in those days, all the earth will again celebrate the Sabbath*. As to those Christians who wish to observe the Sabbat already today, they remind me of that Seventh Day Adventist at my doorstep, decades ago, who asked me, "Why do *you* not keep the Sabbath?" My reply was: "Because I am not under the Mosaic Torah."

(c) *The food laws*, which Jews refer to as *kashrut*, a word that is related to *kosher*. Isaiah speaks very disapprovingly of those who eat pork (65:4; 66:3, 17). At God's glorious appearance at the beginning of the Messianic kingdom, he will target especially such non-kosher-eating people (Isa. 66:15–17). This clearly shows that, during the Messianic kingdom, the food laws will be in force: not only no pork, but apparently no eel, no clams, no shrimps, no oyster, and so on.

(d) *The biblical festivals*. Ezekiel 45:18–46:3 mentions specifically *Pesach/Matzot* (the Passover and the Feast of the Unleavened Bread) and *Sukkot* (the Feast of Booths), plus the New Moon's Day (the first day of every biblical month, which begins with the new moon). *Shavu'ot* (the Feast of Weeks or Pentecost) and *Yom Kippur* (Atonement Day) are not mentioned, but this does not necessarily imply that they will not be celebrated.

(e) *Circumcision*. Isaiah 52:1 says, "Awake, awake, put on your strength, O Zion; put on your beautiful garments, O Jerusalem, the holy city; for there shall no more come into you the uncircumcised and the unclean." Throughout the centuries, the Jewish people have preserved their identity especially through the four points mentioned here: the Sabbath, the *kashrut*, the *mo'adim* (the biblical appointed festivals),

---

132. Isa. 56:2–7; 66:23; Ezek. 44:24; 45:17; 46:1, 3, 4, 12.

and circumcision. Often, Sabbath and the Festivals were neglected first, while elements of *kashrut* (no pork, no shrimp) and circumcision were observed far more sporadically. Only those among them who had fallen away most radically—idolaters, atheists—abandoned the circumcision of their little sons. In the Jerusalem of the Messianic times, it will be inconceivable that uncircumcised Jewish males would be a part of the restored Israel.

Of course, Jews know very well that circumcision has a symbolic meaning; compare the "circumcision of the heart,"[133] and the "circumcision of the lips" (Exod. 6:12, 30).[134] However, this symbolic meaning does not imply that literal circumcision does not matter, or no longer matters. Romans 2:28-29 argues that a real Jew is circumcised not only in his flesh but also in his heart. But this statement could just as well be reversed: a real Jew is circumcised not only in his heart but also in his flesh. In coherence of all proclamations concerning the Messianic kingdom, God tells his people: "O house of Israel, enough of all your abominations, in admitting foreigners, *uncircumcised in heart and flesh,* to be in my sanctuary, profaning my temple, when you offer to me my food, the fat and the blood. You [or, They] have broken my covenant, in addition to all your abominations" (Ezek. 44:6-7). During the Messianic kingdom, such behavior will not be tolerated any longer, either among the Jews or among the Gentiles.

---

133. Lev. 26:41; Deut. 10:16; 30:6; Jer. 4:4; 6:10; 9:26; Ezek. 44:7,9; cf. Acts 7:51.
134. In 1982, a rabbi told me as we were standing at the Western Wall that his flesh *and* his heart *and* his lips had been circumcised, to show me that he was one step ahead of me (a Gentile): if my heart and lips were circumcised at all, then at least my flesh was not.

Chapter 12
God's Dwelling Place

*R[abbi] Hiyya ben Abba: "All the prophets prophesied only for the Messianic age, but as for the world to come, **the eye hath not seen, O Lord, beside thee [what he hath prepared for him that waiteth for him, Isa. 64:4].**"*
Talmud: Shabbath 63a (emphasis added)

The conception of the future world is rather vague in the Talmud. In general, it is the opposite of ʽolam hazzē, this world. In Berakoth I, 5, "this world" is opposed to the days of the Messiah, and this in turn is differentiated here from the future world.
Footnote to the foregoing quotation, Soncino edition of the Talmud

"[W]hoever speaks a word against the Son of Man will be forgiven, but whoever speaks

> against the Holy Spirit will not be forgiven, either in *this age* or in the *age to come.*"[1]
> Matthew 12:32 (italics added)

12.1 Jerusalem: Dwelling Place of God
12.1.1 Earthly Versus Spiritual

IN DIALOGUES WITH SUPERSESSIONISTS, it seems clear that their views sometimes have a subtle undertone that betrays a lack of respect toward the Bible, especially toward the Tanakh. I do not know how I could better describe this than with terms like "primitive" versus "lofty." It amounts to this: in anti-supersessionist pre-millennialism, the Messianic kingdom contains an *earthly* country, namely, *Ha'Aretz*, with an *earthly* city (Jerusalem), an *earthly* mountain, and an *earthly* temple (on Mount Moriah), with a Messiah sitting on an *earthly* throne, namely, the throne of David. Such a view is considered to be more "primitive" (more material, more tangible, more down-to-earth) than the "loftier" view of a *spiritual* kingdom, in a *spiritual* country, with a *spiritual* city, a *spiritual* mountain, and a *spiritual* temple, with a Messiah sitting on a *heavenly* throne. The latter is viewed as being more in tune with the "spirit" of the New Testament.

In short: the supersessionist idea is that prophetic literalism, which emphasizes the earth, is more primitive, perhaps even more carnal (flesh-inspired) than prophetic spiritualism, which emphasizes heaven. This also means that heaven-oriented supersessionists view themselves as more spiritual than the primitive and earth-oriented, perhaps carnal, Israelists. Supersessionists prefer the more ideal, mystical approach than one in which we are dealing with a concrete land, a concrete city, a concrete mountain, a concrete temple, and a concrete throne. They may not like to hear this, but in this respect their spiritualizing has more in common with liberal theology than with the orthodox theology of the

---

1. Gk. *aiōn* is rendered as "age" or "world" (this world – the world to come; cf. the same verse in KJV (but NKJV has "age").

first three centuries (and the orthodox theology of anti-supersessionist pre-millennialism). This is entirely comparable with the difference between liberal and orthodox Jews: the former view themselves as less primitive (even though they may prefer different terms) in their thinking than orthodox Jews, especially ultra-orthodox Jews. For modern humans—or rather, modern*ist* humans—the liberal and the supersessionist views are far more attractive than the primitive views of orthodox Jews and Christians, respectively.

Now, we know very well, of course, that there is indeed a "heavenly country" (Heb. 11:16, in contrast with the earthly country of Israel), as well as a spiritual city,[2] a spiritual mountain,[3] and a spiritual temple,[4] which is the (New Testament) Ecclesia of God, or is connected with it. But it is a logical error of the first order to conclude that therefore the eschatological land of Israel, the city, the mountain, and the temple of Israel, as well as the throne of David during the Messianic kingdom, must be spiritualized, too. We also know that, at present, the Messiah is sitting at the right hand of God on high.[5] But it is a logical error of the first order to conclude that therefore the (heavenly!) throne of the Father and the (earthly!) throne of David are identical. The Bible speaks of an earthly country and a heavenly country, an earthly city and a heavenly city, an earthly mountain and a heavenly mountain, an earthly temple and a heavenly temple, an earthly throne and a heavenly throne. They exist alongside each other, without the one excluding the other. The Bible never confuses or identifies them, as supersessionism does.[6]

---

2. Gal. 4:26; Heb. 11:10; 11:16; 12:22; 13:14; Rev. 3:12; 21:2, 9–10.
3. Cf. Rev. 21:10; see also "Zion" in Heb. 12:22 and Rev. 14:1, and implied in Gal. 4:27.
4. 1 Cor. 3:16; 2 Cor. 6:16; Eph. 2:20–22.
5. Matt. 26:64 and parallels; Acts 2:25, 33–34; 5:31; 7:55–56; Rom. 8:34; Eph. 1:20; Col. 3:1; Heb. 1:3, 13; 8:1; 10:12; 12:2; 1 Pet. 3:22.
6. Paas (2015, 22) mentions Israel's four elements: (a) the people, (b) the king, (c) the land, and (d) the temple (he omits the city and the throne), and applies them all to the Ecclesia, thus not properly distinguishing between Israel and the Ecclesia.

Please notice that Acts 7:47–48 is *not* a counterargument here. In this statement made by Stephen to the Jewish leaders, he said: "[I]t was Solomon who built a house for him. Yet the Most High does not dwell in houses made by hands." Stephen did not say, "*From now on,* the Most High does not dwell in houses made by hands," as if there were a difference between the situations of the Tanakh and the New Testament. Stephen, and later the apostle Paul on the Areopagus (Acts 17:24), did nothing but express the very same thought that King Solomon had uttered in 1 Kings 8: "But will God indeed dwell on the earth? Behold, heaven and the highest heaven cannot contain you; how much less this house that I have built!" (v. 27).

In other words, both the Tanakh and the New Testament teach that God is too great to be contained in any human-made building. Nevertheless, God has chosen to dwell in the tabernacle, the First and the Third Temple (for the Second Temple, see below).

12.1.2 Why Not "Primitive"?

There is nothing "primitive" in this way of thinking, for two very important reasons. The first reason is this. At Mount Sinai, God himself made known to Moses that he desired to dwell among his people: ". . . let them make me a sanctuary, that I may dwell in their midst" (Exod. 25:8); "I will dwell among the people of Israel and will be their God" (29:45), and that he was not ashamed that this dwelling place was nothing but a "primitive" tent: "He forsook his dwelling at Shiloh, / the tent where he dwelt among mankind" (Ps. 78:60).

Later, his dwelling was an earthly building; constructed by humans: the temple of Solomon, later the temple of Zerubbabel/Herod—but still very down-to-earth, "primitive" if one prefers. Throughout the time of the Tanakh, God was not ashamed to be enthroned between two man-made golden cherubim on the human-made lid on a human-made wooden chest.[7] King Solomon was quite aware of how special this

---

7. 1 Sam. 4:4; 2 Sam. 6:2; 2 Kings 19:15; 1 Chron. 13:6; Ps. 80:1; 99:1; Isa. 37:16.

condescension of God was (1 Kings 8:27; see next section), but indeed, condescension it was, and apparently God was not ashamed of this.

If, in ancient times, it was not beneath God's dignity to dwell among his people in a tent or an earthly building, why would it be beneath his dignity to dwell in an earthly home during the Messianic kingdom? Has God changed? Has he, in the meantime, become less primitive, more spiritual, less earth-oriented and more heaven-oriented? Did he perhaps, by and large, acquire more dignity or spirituality? We should realize how absurd this entire contrast between earthly and spiritual actually is. It is not even a proper contrast: earthly is not the opposite of spiritual but of heavenly; and spiritual is not the contrast of earthly but of literal or physical. This is the key: *earthly things can very well be very spiritual*, if they are invested with the glory of God.

I have argued extensively that Ezekiel 40-44 necessarily speaks of a literal, earthly temple. How else could one explain the multitude of architectural technological details of this new temple? What would be the purpose of these details, if in the end we were supposed to explain this temple spiritually? We are even informed about its geographical location. Ezekiel 48:21-22 speaks of a "holy portion" of land, in whose midst the "sanctuary of the temple" shall be, and which "shall lie between the territory of Judah and the territory of Benjamin," that is, in or near Jerusalem (cf. Josh. 15:8; 18:16, although the boundaries between the tribes in Joshua differ from those in Ezekiel).[8] It is of *this* temple that God himself said: "Son of man, this is the place of my throne and the place of the soles of my feet, where I will dwell in the midst of the

---

8. Lightfoot (1823, chapter 1) referred to a Jewish tradition teaching that the altars and the sanctuary of Solomon's temple stood in the territory of Benjamin, while the courts were in the territory of Judah. In the wilderness, the sons of Rachel (Ephraim, Manasseh, and Benjamin) camped on the west side of the tabernacle, and thus lived closest to the *Shekhinah*. Psalm 80:1–2 seem to aim at this: "You who are enthroned upon the cherubim [of the ark], shine forth./ Before Ephraim and Benjamin and Manasseh, stir up your might / and come to save us!"

people of Israel forever" (Ezek. 43:7)—"forever" always meaning as long as the present earth exists. (In the eternal state, after the Messianic kingdom, the situation will be different; see chapter 14 below).

It has been argued that, in Ezekiel, Israel received no divine command to build this new temple, and this is taken as an argument that we are dealing here with an ideal presentation of spiritual realities. The answer to this, of course, is that it will be the Messiah himself—without needing any divine command—who will build this temple:

> Thus says the LORD of hosts, "Behold, the man whose name is the Branch:[9] for he shall branch out from his place, and he shall build the temple of the LORD. It is he who shall build the temple of the LORD and shall bear royal honor, and shall sit and rule on his throne. And there [or, he] shall be a priest on his throne, and the counsel of peace shall be between them both (Zech. 6:12-13).

12.1.3 Symbolic Dwelling

The second reason why the notion of God dwelling on earth in a tent or building is not primitive is this. During the time of the Tanakh believers were very well aware that this dwelling by God in an earthly tent or building had a largely symbolic significance. They were not so primitive as to think that the God of heaven and earth could be contained in a tent or a building, or could be restricted to the square foot on the ark of the covenant, between the cherubim. In other words, they were quite conscious of the spiritual dimension of this notion of dwelling. At the consecration of the temple, King Solomon said in his great prayer: "But will God indeed dwell on the earth? Behold, heaven and the highest heaven cannot contain you; how much less this house that I have built!" (1 Kings 8:27). Even the largest building on earth, even the earth in its totality, could not contain him "who fills all in all" (Eph. 1:23). God said through Jeremiah: "Can a man hide

---

9. The Branch or Shoot (Heb. *tzēmach*) is a well-known designation of the Messiah: see 3:8; Isa. 11:1; Jer. 23:5; 33:15.

himself in secret places so that I cannot see him?... Do I not *fill* heaven and earth?" (Jer. 23:24; italics added).

The God of Israel exists beyond his own created world, but at the same time he fills this very same world with his presence. Both truths are equally important: stressing the former point will keep us from pantheism in any form (whereby God and cosmos are identical), and stressing the latter point will keep us from deism in any form (whereby God is so far beyond the world that he has nothing to do with it).

As David said about God's omnipresence:

Where shall I go from your Spirit?
    Or where shall I flee from your presence?
If I ascend to heaven, you are there!
    If I make my bed in Sheol [the realm of death], you are there!
If I take the wings of the morning
    and dwell in the uttermost parts of the sea,
even there your hand shall lead me,
    and your right hand shall hold me (Ps. 139:7–10).

God is so great that, when the prophet Isaiah beholds his glory within the temple of Solomon, the temple is just large enough, so to speak, to contain only the hem of God's robe ("the train [or, hem] of his robe filled the temple," Isa. 6:1). This is a splendid picture of God's greatness: no room or space can contain him. God himself said through the same prophet:

Heaven is my throne,
    and the earth is my footstool;
what is the house that you would build for me,
    and what is the place of my rest? (Isa. 66:1).

If the entire earth is so tiny that can serve at most as God's footstool, how could a tent, or even the square foot between the cherubim, ever be an adequate dwelling place for God? And yet, we take it completely seriously that the God of heaven and earth has chosen to dwell in the tabernacle, and later (a) on this earth, (b) in Israel, (c) in Jerusalem, (d) on Mount

Moriah, (e) in the temple, (f) in the Most Holy place, (g) on the atonement lid of the ark of the covenant.[10]

In short, we must interpret this dwelling of God in a tent or a building in a literal, but not in a literalist way. Speaking of tents, Isaiah referred to him "who sits above the circle of the earth, and its inhabitants are like grasshoppers; who stretches out the heavens like a curtain, and spreads them like a tent to dwell in" (40:22). It is equally true that God dwells in the vast "tent" of the sky—or, the universe—as that he dwelt in the (relatively speaking) tiny tent that was constructed at Mount Sinai. (See further in §12.3.2 about this "dwelling" of God in a celestial "tent.")

12.2 Concrete Reality
12.2.1 Concrete Dwelling

During Israel's wilderness journey, God dwelt in two "tents" at the same time, so to speak (see previous section): the earthly tabernacle, and the heavens—and, as we just learned from Solomon, even the "heaven of heavens" is too small a place for God to dwell in (see further in the next section). These are three "levels" of divine dwelling: in the earthly tabernacle (later an earthly building), in the sky, and beyond the heaven of heavens. Each of these three levels is concrete reality; no one of them possesses any more reality than the others.

One consequence of this truth is that, on the one hand, there is no place in the creation where God is *not* (Ps. 139:5-12). On the other hand, the tabernacle and later the temple were undoubtedly and definitely places of his very *special*, sacred, and even life-threatening presence (see §12.2.2).

In a special way, God's glorious presence filled the tabernacle, and later the temple. He who fills the universe (see previous section), is the One who also fills the sanctuary. The water that fills the ocean, also fills the bucket in which the water is drawn from the ocean. As we read of the consecration of the tabernacle: "Then the cloud covered the tent of meeting,

---

10. These have been referred to as seven concentric circles, with increasing degrees of sanctity (holiness): Jerusalem is holier than the rest of Israel, the temple is holier than the city, and so on.

and the glory of the LORD *filled* the tabernacle. And Moses was not able to enter the tent of meeting because the cloud settled on it, and the glory of the LORD *filled* the tabernacle" (Exod. 40:34-35; italics added). And at the consecration of Solomon's temple: "[W]hen the priests came out from the Holy Place, a cloud *filled* the house of the LORD, so that the priests could not stand to minister because of the cloud, for the glory of the Lord *filled* the house of the LORD" (1 Kings 8:10-11; 2 Chron. 5:13-14; 7:1-2; italics added).[11] If this was the case in the time of the Tanakh, it will be the case also in the temple that will exist during the Messianic kingdom: "As the glory of the LORD entered the temple by the gate facing east, the Spirit lifted me up and brought me into the inner court; and behold, the glory of the LORD *filled* the temple" (Ezek. 43:4-5; cf. 44:4).

12.2.2 Life-Threatening Sanctity

The glory of the LORD as a concrete reality in the tabernacle, and later in the temple of Solomon (the First Temple), is illustrated by the fact that entering the Holy Place, inside the veil, or even coming too near to the place, or even touching the "holy things," brought the death penalty on the intruder. In fact, this was already the case when Israel had arrived at Mount Sinai, and the glory of the LORD was on that mountain:

> [O]n the third day the LORD will come down on Mount Sinai in the sight of all the people. And you [i.e., Moses] shall set limits for the people all around, saying, "Take care not to go up into the mountain or touch the edge of it. Whoever touches the mountain shall be put to death. No hand shall touch him, but he shall be stoned or shot [with an arrow]; whether beast or man, he shall not live" (Exod. 19:11-13).

After the tabernacle had been built—but before it had been consecrated and the glory of the LORD had descended upon it—God said through Moses,

---

11. Interestingly, the phrase, "the glory of the LORD *filled* the" place, is used not once, but twice, and the identical phrase is repeated in 1 Kings 8:10–11 and in 2 Chron. 5:13–14 and 7:1–2, as if to underscore the importance of the event.

And it [i.e., his high priestly robe] shall be on Aaron when he ministers, and its sound [i.e., that of the golden bells on the robe] shall be heard when he goes into the Holy Place before the LORD, and when he comes out, *so that he does not die.*[12] ... You shall make for them [i.e., the priests] linen undergarments to cover their naked flesh. They shall reach from the hips to the thighs; and they shall be on Aaron and on his sons when they go into the tent of meeting or when they come near the altar to minister in the Holy Place, *lest they bear guilt and die* (Exod. 28, 42–43; cf. 30:20–21; italics added).

At later times, similar warnings were given:

Tell Aaron your brother not to come at any time into the Holy Place inside the veil, before the mercy seat that is on the ark, *so that he may not die.* For I will appear in the cloud over the mercy seat. . . . [the priest shall] put the incense on the fire before the LORD, that the cloud of the incense may cover the mercy seat that is over the testimony, so that he does *not die* (Lev. 16:2, 13; italics added).

[T]he sons of Kohath shall come to carry these [i.e., covered holy things], but they must not touch the holy things, *lest they die.* . . . [D]eal thus with them [i.e., the Kohathities], that they may *live and not die* when they come near to the most holy things: Aaron and his sons shall go in and appoint them each to his task and to his burden, but they shall not go in to look on the holy things even for a moment, *lest they die* (Num. 4:18–20; cf. 18:22; italics added).

12.2.3 God's Most Concrete Dwelling

To complete this introduction about the concrete reality of God's dwelling on earth, let me add that the most genuine

---

12. According to a Jewish tradition, this was the reason why a rope was tied to the ankle of the high priest when he entered to Most Holy place so that, in case he died, his body could be pulled out (see *Zohar* XVI.34, Yom Kippur §251: "Rabbi Yitzchak said, 'A chain was tied to the feet of the high priest, when he entered the Holy of Holies, so that if he dies there they will take him out, since it is forbidden to enter there.'" But see §12.5.3 below.

form of such divine dwelling on earth is possible only if God shares flesh and blood, that is, becomes human: a Man who at the same time remains God—God and Man in one person—and therefore can truly serve as a dwelling place for God. In the end, God can genuinely dwell only in the Man who *is* God. And, as we will see, here again the metaphor of the "tent" becomes relevant: "And the Word (Christ) became flesh (human, incarnate) and tabernacled (*fixed His tent of flesh*, lived awhile) among us" (John 1:14 AMPC; italics added; see §12.6.1). As life-threatening as touching Mount Sinai and the holy things in the tabernacle was, it was so impressive that Jesus *could* be touched. However, touching Jesus could have a very specific—one could say, sacred—significance: it was associated with *power*. The most conspicuous example of this is the story of the woman with the discharge of blood, who "touched the fringe of his garment" (Luke 8:44):

> Jesus said, "Who was it that touched me?" When all denied it, Peter said, "Master, the crowds surround you and are pressing in on you!" But Jesus said, "Someone touched me, for *I perceive that power has gone out from me*." And when the woman saw that she was not hidden, she came trembling, and falling down before him declared in the presence of all the people why she had touched him, and how she had been immediately healed. And he said to her, "Daughter, your faith has made you well; go in peace" (Luke 8:45–48; italics added).

This touching of Jesus brought forth power from him. But it was not the power that *killed*, as in the case of Sinai and the tabernacle, but the power that *healed* (lit., *saved*). This is a highly significant difference: when one comes into contact with the power of God, this power can destroy them, but it can also save them.

A comparable example is this. When Moses said to Israel, "I AM has sent me to you" (Exod. 3:14; emphasis added), this was a positive blessing for the people. When Jesus told his followers, "I AM (the bread of life, the light of the world, etc.),"[13]

---

13. John 6:35; 8:12; 9:5; 10:7, 11; 11:25; 14:6; 15:1.

this was, in all cases, a blessing for them, too. But when Jesus' enemies came to take him, and they told him that they sought Jesus of Nazareth, and Jesus literally answered, "I AM" (John 18:6; emphasis added), they drew back and fell to the ground. The same power can be both a redemptive blessing and a destructive force.

12.3 Dwelling Places of God
12.3.1 Introduction
When we peruse the Bible, we encounter a total of *twelve* dwelling places of God, or, in other words, twelve places where the *Shekhinah* (the glorious presence of God) stayed, or will stay, or ought to have stayed, either in the form of the pillar of the cloud, or of some other outward, physical manifestation of the glory of God: clouds, winds (tempest), fire (see this and the next sections), or in the person of the Holy Spirit. A brief survey of these is very fitting in this volume because one of the peculiar aspects of these seven dwelling places is that they are all related to Israel in some way or another, and more specifically with Jerusalem.

Of course, the activity of dwelling is broader than a definite (permanent) dwelling *place*. Take this example: "[T]hus says the One who is high and lifted up, who inhabits eternity, whose name is Holy: 'I *dwell* in the high and holy place, *and also with him* who is of a contrite and lowly spirit, to revive the spirit of the lowly, and to revive the heart of the contrite'" (Isa. 57:15; italics added). Or consider God's "dwelling" on Mount Sinai (Exod. 24:16), which was temporary, because God intended to come and dwell in the tabernacle that was to be built (Exod. 25:8; 29:45). Sometimes, the activity of dwelling referred to a temporary resting, sojourning, not to a specific dwelling *place* that God had chosen.

When it comes to the land of Israel specifically, we find various concentric circles so to speak:

(a) *The land*. God dwelt in the land of Israel (Num. 35:34).

(b) *The city*. God promises to dwell in Jerusalem forever (1 Chron. 23:25; Zech. 8:3).

(c) *The mountain.* God dwelt, and will dwell, on Mount Zion.[14]

(d) *The temple.* God dwelt, and will dwell, in the First and the Third Temple, respectively.[15]

(e) *The ark.* God dwelt upon the cherubim, namely, the two human-made figures on the atonement-lid that covered the ark of the covenant.[16]

12.3.2 God's Heavenly Abode

No fewer than eight of the twelve dwelling places have the character of a tent (Heb. *ohel*, Gk. *skēnē*), literally or figuratively; these eight tents will be indicated and numbered separately (see the summary in §12.8.2).

(1) *Heaven* (Heb. *shamayyim*), which is the first tent. In §12.1.3 we read in Isaiah 40:22 about God "who stretches out the heavens like a curtain, and spreads them like a *tent* to dwell in." This is God's first dwelling place, his first tent, prepared before the creation of the first human beings. It is the sky (Heb. *raqia'*, "expanse, canopy, firmament, dome") that we find nine times in Genesis 1.[17] It is the easiest divine tent to understand: we look outside the window, and we see it.

Heaven is sometimes even called *heaven of heavens* (Heb. *shamayyim hashamayyim*),[18] in order to distinguish this meaning of "heaven" from the physical heavens (*raqia'*): the sky with its clouds and its stars. In 1 Kings 8:29-49 and 2 Chron. 6:12-42 (Solomon's prayer at the consecration of the newly built temple), we find four times the expression "heaven your dwelling place," literally, the "place of your dwelling [i.e., the place where you dwell], [viz.] heaven" (Heb. *maqom*

---

14. Ps. 68:16; 74:2; Isa. 8:18; Joel 3:17.
15. 2 Sam. 7:5; 1 Kings 8:13; 1 Chron. 17:4; 2 Chron. 6:2; Ps. 26:8; Ezek. 43:7.
16. KJV: 1 Sam. 4:4; 6:2; 2 Kings 19:15; 1 Chron. 13:6; Ps.80:1; 99:1; Isa. 37:16 (alternative rendering: "to sit [enthroned]," from the root *y-sh-b*; see note 23).
17. In Gen. 1:14–15, 17, 20; in v. 8 the *raqia'* is called *shamayyim*, but in v. 1 *shamayyim* has a wider, cosmic meaning.
18. Deut. 10:14; 1 Kings 8:27; 2 Chron. 2:6; 6:18; Neh. 9:6; Ps. 68:33; 148:4 (KJV). Such a construction, like "servant of servants" (Gen. 9:25) or "holy of holies" (Exod. 26:34 DRA) is a typical Hebrew superlative: the "highest of heavens" or "highest heaven" (or the "lowest servant," "the most holy").

shibtekha hashamayyim). Here, heaven is not the sky, it is not even heaven as a cosmic designation, but heaven as the dwelling place of God.

Psalm 115 spoke of the different dwelling places that were divinely assigned to God himself and to humanity, respectively:

> Our God is in the heavens;
>> he does all that he pleases...
> The heavens are the LORD's heavens,
>> but the earth he has given to the children of man
> (vv. 3, 16).

The earth is the common dwelling place assigned to humanity by the Creator. In the book of Revelation, we find the peculiar expression "those who dwell on the earth,"[19] the "earth-dwellers," here in a negative sense. They are those who cling to the earth in the sense that they wish to have nothing to do with heavenly things. Such in contrast to Jesus-believers, who are described in 1 Corinthians 15 as "heavenly": "[A]s is the man of heaven [i.e., Christ], so also are those who are of heaven [viz., the believers]. Just as we have borne the image of the man of dust [i.e., the first Adam], we shall also bear the image of the man of heaven [i.e., the last Adam]" (vv. 48–49; cf. vv. 45–47].

The connection between God's heavenly dwelling place and Israel is that the Bible speaks of a heavenly temple,[20] of which the temple at Jerusalem apparently is a counterpart or reflection (mirror image). Similarly, the altar at Jerusalem (Rev. 11:1) reflects the heavenly altar.[21] Revelation 11:19 even speaks of a heavenly "ark of the covenant" as a counterpart of the earthly ark of the covenant (Heb. 9:4). Just as there is an earthly Jerusalem, there is also a heavenly Jerusalem.[22] Just

---

19. Rev. 3:10; 6:10; 8:13; 11:10; 13:8, 14; 14:6; 17:2, 8.
20. Ps. 11:4; 29:9; Rev. 3:12; 11:19; 14:17; 15:5; 16:17; Heb. *hēkhal* means both "temple" and "palace"; in each case, translators must choose, for instance, in Ps. 11:4 "temple" (ESV) or "palace" (GNT).
21. Heb. 13:10; Rev. 6:9; 8:3, 5; 9:13; 14:18; 16:7.
22. Cf. Gal. 4:26; Heb. 12:22; Rev. 3:12; 21:2, 10.

as there is an earthly "throne of the LORD" (1 Chron. 29:23; cf. Jer. 3:17), there is a heavenly "throne of the LORD" (Ps. 11:4); and we remember that the mercy seat on the ark of the covenant is also described as a throne of God (cf. 1 Sam. 4:4; 2 Sam. 6:2; 1 Chron. 13:6[23]).

During the time of King David, the LORD could be said to have dwelt in three tents at the same time: heaven, the tabernacle, and David's tent on Zion (see §12.4.3). Moreover, the LORD could be said to have possessed three thrones in those days: the throne in heaven, the throne between the cherubim on the ark (see note 23), and the throne of David.

Please note that in none of these cases does this mean that the heavenly counterpart *replaced* the earthly counterpart, as if, after the heavenly temple, altar, city, or throne has arrived, the earthly temple, altar, city, or throne no longer has any importance. If A is the *counterpart* of B, why and how should this necessarily mean that A has *replaced* B?

Let me conclude this section with a more general statement about God's dwelling from eternity, and for all eternity: ". . . the blessed and only Sovereign, the King of kings and Lord of lords, who alone has immortality, who dwells in unapproachable light, whom no one has ever seen or can see. To him be honor and eternal dominion. Amen" (1 Tim. 6:15-16).

12.3.3 The Tabernacle

(2) The *tabernacle*. It is quite remarkable that, after Moses had climbed Mount Sinai the first time, the very first thing that God discussed with him was his dwelling in the midst of Israel. The Most High God desires to dwell among the people whom he was making his own at that very time. It is like a man who has purchased a piece of land with the express purpose of building a house on it: God purchases a people with the express purpose of building a house in their midst.

---

23. The Heb. verb in these passages is *y-sh-b*, "to sit" (see, e.g., Gen. 13:6; 36:7), which sometimes means "to sit on a throne" (Ps. 9:4; Isa. 28:6; 1 Kings 1:46), but also "to dwell": in Isa. 40:22 (quoted in §12.1.3), "to sit" and "to dwell" is the same Heb. verb *y-sh-b*.

Please notice that the Bible did not say that God dwelt with Noah or Abraham. This is because the notion of God's dwelling is never a matter of his personal relationships with certain individuals. It is a collective notion: it is always a "dwelling *in the midst of.*" God dwells in the midst of a redeemed *people*:[24] "[L]et them make me a sanctuary, that I may dwell in their midst" (Exod. 25:8). "I will dwell among the people of Israel and will be their God. And they shall know that I am the Lord their God, who brought them out of the land of Egypt that I might dwell among them. I am the Lord their God" (Exod. 29:45–46). Here the Hebrew verb for "to dwell" is not *y-sh-b* (see notes 16 and 23) but *sh-kh-n*, a root from which also the Hebrew words *mishkan*, "tabernacle," and *Shekhinah* (literally, the "dwelling," the glorious presence of God) have been derived.

After reading about the tents of the patriarchs in Genesis, and the tents of Israel during their wilderness journey, we now hear about God's tent—this time not the sky, but a tent on earth—for the first time in Exodus 26:7: "You shall also make curtains of goats' hair for a tent [Heb. *ohel*] over the tabernacle [Heb. *mishkan*]; eleven curtains shall you make." This sounds a bit strange because "tabernacle" (from Lat. *tabernaculum*) means "tent" as well; but we remember that the Hebrew *mishkan* literally means "dwelling [place]." Thus, God's command involves a tent of goats' hair to be built as a roof over God's dwelling place. In Exodus 27:21 and later, the word "tent" was used for the tabernacle in its totality. It is the second in our list of eight "tents," divine dwelling places that are described as tents.

Of course, God cannot dwell among his people without a holy and righteous foundation.[25] Such a foundation was to be supplied, not only by the annual *Yom Kippur* ("Day of Atonement"), but by the daily burnt offerings, in the morning and

---

24. Notice that the tabernacle as such is said to "dwell in the midst" of the people (Lev. 16:16), and that God "dwells in the midst" of Israel's camp (Num. 5:3), and of the land (Num. 35:24).
25. Cf. ". . . the tent of meeting, which dwells with them in the midst of their uncleannesses" (Lev. 16:16).

in the evening, at the entrance of the tent of meeting (i.e., the tabernacle). Both *Yom Kippur* and the daily burnt offerings in the Tanakh point to the New Testament sacrifice of Christ:

> ... It shall be a regular burnt offering throughout your generations at the entrance of the tent of meeting before the LORD, where I will meet with you [plural: Israel], to speak to you [singular: Moses] there. There I will meet with the people of Israel, and it [or, they] shall be sanctified by my glory. I will consecrate the tent of meeting and the altar. Aaron also and his sons I will consecrate to serve me as priests. *I will dwell among the people of Israel* and will be their God. And they shall know that I am the LORD their God, who brought them out of the land of Egypt that I might dwell among them. I am the LORD their God (Exod. 29:42-46; italics added).

At the consecration of the tabernacle, while still at Mount Sinai, the glory of the LORD appeared and came to rest on and in the tabernacle:

> And he [i.e., Moses] erected the court around the tabernacle and the altar, and set up the screen of the gate of the court. So Moses finished the work. Then the cloud covered the tent of meeting, and the glory[26] of the LORD filled the tabernacle. And Moses was not able to enter the tent of meeting because the cloud settled on it, and the glory of the LORD filled the tabernacle (Exod. 40:33-35).

12.3.4 Tabernacle and Torah

A Jewish tradition in the Midrash supplies us with a particularly striking reason for the descent of the *Shekhinah* on the tabernacle:

> This is like a king who had an only daughter. There came one of the kings, and took her [to be his wife]; he wanted to go to

---

26. Heb. *kabod*, from the root *k-b-d*, literally "to be heavy," and hence "to come to honor" (Job 14:21); cf. the expression "man of weight (or, substance)"; the apostle Paul was probably alluding to this basic meaning: "[T[his *light* momentary affliction is preparing for us an eternal *weight* of glory beyond all comparison" (2 Cor. 4:17).

his land, and take his wife with him. The king said to him, "My daughter whom I have given to you, is my only daughter. I cannot separate from her. Nor can I say to you, 'Don't take her with you,' for she is your wife. Show me therefore this goodness that, wherever you go, you prepare a room for me, so that I can dwell with [the two of] you; for I cannot let my daughter go." Similarly, God said to Israel: "I have given you the Torah. I cannot separate from her. Nor can I say to you, 'Don't accept it.' But at all places where you will go, prepare for me a place in which I can dwell."[27]

The beautiful point of this analogy is that the Torah is here, first and foremost, a kings' daughter (daughter of God), and second, a queen, which she became by marrying a king, namely Israel. As to the former point, indeed, God addresses the Torah as "my daughter." (Heb. *bati*). This occurs in a famous Talmudic passage, in which the Torah is personified.[28] According to Rabbi Meir, the Torah-giving at Sinai is described by God as the "nuptial joy of my daughter," that is, of the Torah. This joy was endangered when Nadab and Abihu brought strange fire and had to be killed by the LORD (Lev. 10:1–2). God is compared here with a king, giving his daughter in marriage to Israel, at which the sons of Aaron functioned as groomsmen. Thus, Israel is here the bridegroom (God's "son-in-law"), while the Torah is the bride.[29] This notion ties in with the apocryphal Wisdom 8:2, where Wisdom (Heb. *chokhmah*) is called the bride of king Solomon

---

27. Exodus Rabbah 33 (94a); see Strack and Billerbeck (1924, 2:356) and Ouweneel (1998a, 55).
28. Sanhedrin 101a; Strack and Billerbeck (1924, 2:353–56) also refer to Lev. Rabbah 20, 10 on Lev. 16:1. This is similar to the Jewish Hellenistic thinker, Philo of Alexandria. However, he also spoke of Wisdom (which is essentially identical with the Torah) as God's spouse, through whom he created the world, and as the mother of the godly; see Wilckens (1971, 500–502); Schipflinger (1998).
29. Cf. *Zohar* (2:99a-b): the Torah reveals her mysterious beauty only to her lovers, who, if they follow her, eventually become her consorts; cf. Scholem (1960, 77–79). At *Simchat Torah* ("Joy of the Torah"), the second day of the *Atzeret* festival (immediately following upon *Sukkot*), one of the members of the congregation is honored as the "bridegroom of the Torah."

as the representative of the whole nation: "I [i.e., Solomon] loved her [i.e., Wisdom] and sought her from my youth, and I desired to take her for my bride, and I became enamored of her beauty" (RSV).

In the Talmud, the heavenly origin of the Torah is emphasized: "The following have no portion in the world to come: [first,] He who says that the Torah is not from Heaven," and so on.[30] Chokhmah/Torah is the Lady through whom God has created all things, a Lady who has descended from heaven to this earth,[31] to dwell among the people of Israel. The descent of this Lady was necessary because God wanted to marry his daughter to Israel. This marriage occurred at Mount Sinai. However, because he was unable and unwilling to separate from her, God descended to dwell in Israel, in a special "room" that had been prepared for him, and that travelled everywhere that Israel and the Torah moved. The queen from heaven became incarnate, so to speak, in the two stone tablets that God had given to Moses, and that were kept at the front of the sanctuary, within the ark of the covenant (Deut. 10:1-5; 1 Kings 8:9). Or she became incarnate in the book of the law that Moses wrote,[32] and that was to be put by the side of the ark of the covenant (Deut. 31:24-29; in 1 Kings 8:9, they were found *in* the ark).

Strangely enough, we must conclude here that rabbinic tradition features two more or less opposite metaphors. In the one just described, Israel was viewed as the bridegroom of the Torah, which is its bride. However, according to a very different metaphor Israel itself is the bride of God.[33] In this imagery, Israel is not God's son-in-law, that is, a male figure, but rather a female figure. The Torah is a treasure, but Israel, as God's bride, is too, as is expressed in the Hebrew term *s'gulah* in Exodus 19:5, "peculiar treasure" (KJV), "treasured possession" (ESV) (cf. Deut. 7:6; 14:2; 26:18). Here, the Torah

---

30. 'Avodah Zarah 18a.
31. See extensively, Ouweneel (1998a, 50–54).
32. Deut. 28:58, 61; 29:20–21, 27; 30:10; cf. Josh. 8:31; 23:6; 2 Kings 14:6; 2 Chron. 25:4; 34:14; Neh. 8:1.
33. Cf. Isa. 49:18; 54:6; 61:10; 62:5; Jer. 2:2; Ezek. 16:8–13; Hos. 2:19–20.

can be viewed as the written prenuptial agreement (Heb. *k'tubah*), but also as the dowry that God grants his wife at the wedding at Mount Sinai (cf. Jer. 2:2). Thus the psalmist said:

> [T]he rules of the Lord are true,
>   and righteous altogether.
> More to be desired are they than gold,
>   even much fine gold (Ps. 19:9–10).
> The *Torah* of your mouth is better to me
>   than thousands of gold and silver pieces (Ps. 119:72)
> I love your commandments
>   above gold, above fine gold (Ps. 119:127).

12.4 From the Tabernacle to the Temple
12.4.1 The Tabernacle in the Holy Land

After Israel had arrived in the Promised Land and had conquered it, the people camped at Shiloh, and set up the tabernacle there, for the time being, Shiloh became Israel's religious capital in *Ha'Aretz*.[34] In the time of the judges, "the house of God was at Shiloh," and Israel celebrated the "yearly feast of the Lord" there.[35] In 1 Samuel 3:3, this "house" was called "the *temple* [Heb. *hēkhal*] of the Lord, where the ark of God was" (cf. 1:9).

It is not clear whether Shiloh was the permanent place of the

tabernacle until the time of David. For instance, we read in Judges 20

> Then all the people of Israel, the whole army, went up and came to Bethel and wept. They sat there before the Lord and fasted that day until evening, and offered burnt offerings and peace offerings before the Lord. And the people of Israel inquired of the Lord *(for the ark of the covenant of God was there in those days)* (vv. 26–27; italics added).

---

34. Josh. 18:1, 8–10; 19:51; 21:2; 22:9, 12.
35. Judg. 18:31; 21:19; 1 Sam. 1:3, 24.

Had the ark been (temporarily) moved from Shiloh to Bethel? Or does the word "there" (read, "in the neighborhood") actually refer to Shiloh, which was only ten miles away?

In 1 Samuel 21, we read of the town of Nob, where the priest Ahimelech stayed at the time, of whom we read: he gave David "the holy bread, for there was no bread there but the bread of the Presence, which is removed from before the LORD, to be replaced by hot bread on the day it is taken away" (v. 6). This must have been the so-called "showbread" (Num. 4:7; 1 Chron. 9:32 etc.), suggesting that the "table for the showbread" (2 Chron. 29:18; cf. Exod. 25:23-30), as well as the rest of the tabernacle,[36] had moved from Shiloh to Nob (which lies much farther away from Shiloh than Bethel does).[37] In King David's time, we find the tabernacle again at a different place, this time at Gibeon:

> Zadok the priest and his brothers the priests [served] before the tabernacle of the LORD in the high place that was at Gibeon to offer burnt offerings to the LORD on the altar of burnt offering regularly morning and evening, to do all that is written in the Law of the LORD that he commanded Israel (1 Chron. 16:39-40).

"[T]he tabernacle of the LORD, which Moses had made in the wilderness, and the altar of burnt offering were at that time [of King David] in the high place at Gibeon" (1 Chron. 21:29). Young King Solomon went to this same place to consecrate himself to the LORD: "And the king went to Gibeon to sacrifice there, for that was the great high place. Solomon used to offer a thousand burnt offerings on that altar" (1 Kings 3:4; cf. 2 Chron. 1:3). After King Solomon had built the temple at Jerusalem, the tabernacle was transported to that new place, so that this ancient tent received a close connection with Jerusalem as well:

---

36. Mark 2:26 and Luke 6:4 say that David at the occasion entered the "house of God."
37. See §13.2.2 for passages suggesting that Shiloh had been destroyed by the Philistines.

[A]ll the men of Israel assembled before the king at the feast that is in the seventh month [*Sukkoth*]. And all the elders of Israel came, and the Levites took up the ark. And they brought up the ark, the tent of meeting [i.e., the tabernacle], and all the holy vessels that were in the tent; the Levitical priests brought them up [to Jerusalem] (2 Chron. 5:4-5; cf. 1 Kings 8:4).

Thus, the tabernacle began its history at Mount Sinai, and ended up in Solomon's temple on Mount Moriah (or, Zion), after an almost uncountable number of residences, both in the wilderness (cf. the long list in Num. 33) and in the Holy Land. On Mount Moriah/Zion it found its final destination: a place of rest.

12.4.2 The Ark in the Holy Land

The foregoing description is not the complete story because, since the days of the priest Eli, the ark of the covenant *had not been in the tabernacle*. This is important when we consider that God did not dwell simply in the tabernacle, but more concretely on the ark of the covenant, between the two golden cherubim, as we have seen. In 1 Samuel 4:4, we read how Eli's sons, the priests Hophni and Phinehas, took the ark out of the tabernacle. Did these men enter the Most Holy Place in order to take out the ark—and survive? How can this be in light of the passages quoted in §12.2.2? Or was the ark not being kept at that time in the Most Holy place? Or, if it was, can we say that for a long time the place had lost much of its glory, and therefore of its sanctity and restrictedness?

No matter the answer, they carried the ark with them in their battle against the Philistines. To Israel's utter dismay, the enemies captured the ark, and killed the two priests who had carried it. When the wife of Phinehas heard this, she was in the process of giving birth to a son:

[S]he named the child Ichabod [Heb. *Ikabod*], saying, "The glory [Heb. *kabod*][38] has departed from Israel!" because the ark of God had been captured and because of her father-in-law and her

---

38. See note 26; the woman could also have said, "The *Shekhinah* has departed from Israel" (but the word *Shekhinah* does not appear in the Tanakh).

husband. And she said, "The glory has departed from Israel, for the ark of God has been captured" (1 Sam. 4:21-22).

The ark was carried, first, to the Philistine city of Ashdod, then to Gath, then to Ekron.[39] After seven months of mischief that the ark brought upon the Philistines, they decided to send it back to the land of Israel. There, the men of Beth-shemesh looked upon (another rendering: into) the ark, and were punished for it (1 Sam. 6:19). What they did was comparable to what the LORD forbade in the passages mentioned in §12.2.2. If Hophni and Phinehas escaped God's judgment—only to be killed later by the Philistines—the men of Beth-shemesh did not.

Then the ark was sent on to Kiriath-jearim: "And the men of Kiriath-jearim came and took up the ark of the LORD and brought it to the house of Abinadab on the hill. And they consecrated his son Eleazar to have charge of the ark of the LORD" (1 Sam. 7:1). It is likely that Abinadab and Eleazar were Levites, or even priests; at any rate, their names were similar to those of two sons of Aaron: Nadab and Eleazar (Exod. 6:23). The ark stayed about twenty years in the house of Abinadab (v. 2), so that during this entire period it remained separated from the rest of the tabernacle. In 1 Samuel 14:18, King Saul demanded that the ark be brought to him, apparently to assist him in his battle; did he venture to make the same mistake that Hophni and Phinehas had made earlier?

This period is followed again with silence around the ark, until the time of King David:

> And David arose and went with all the people who were with hifrom Baale-judah to bring up from there the ark of God, which is called by the name of the LORD of hosts who sits enthroned on the cherubim. And they carried the ark of God on a new cart and brought it out of the house of Abinadab, which was on the hill (2 Sam. 6:2-3).

---

39. These were three of the five Philistine cities; the other two were Ashkelon and Gaza; all five were mentioned in 1 Sam. 6:17 (see also Josh. 13:3; Jer. 25:20); in addition to the Gaza Strip, four of these five cities are now part of the state of Israel. For more about this episode, see §13.2.2.

This first attempt to bring the ark to Jerusalem was a disaster, because David transported the ark on a cart instead of on the shoulders of the Kohathite Levites, as the LORD had commanded (cf. Num. 4:1-15). This is the more astonishing because no such judgment had fallen upon Hophni and Phinehas, or upon King Saul, when they took the ark to use it for their own purposes. Perhaps this is an illustration of the principle described in Leviticus 10:3, "Among those who are near me I will be sanctified," which might be taken to mean: "I will show myself as the Most Holy (or, in the most holy way) to those who are nearest to me." David was nearer to God than Eli's sons or Saul, and therefore he experienced God's holiness more than the other men did.

After this failure, the ark stayed in the nearby house of Obed-edom for three months (2 Sam. 6:10-11). Then, a no doubt trembling David tried again to carry out his plan, this time in the right manner:

> So David went and brought up the ark of God from the house of Obed-edom to the city of David with rejoicing. And when those who bore the ark of the LORD had gone six steps, he sacrificed an ox and a fattened animal. . . . So David and all the house of Israel brought up the ark of the LORD with shouting and with the sound of the horn. . . . And they brought in the ark of the LORD and set it in its place, inside the tent that David had pitched for it. And David offered burnt offerings and peace offerings before the LORD (2 Sam. 6:12-17).

12.4.3 The Third Tent

(3) The third tent mentioned in the Bible as a place that was linked with God's presence was the tent that David set up near the "city of David" (southeast of the present Turkish walls), presumably on Mount Moriah (northeast of the present Turkish walls), where later the temple of Solomon would be built. The purpose of the tent was to place the ark of the covenant there, after David had fetched it from the house of Abinadab (see previous section). As we saw, interestingly he did *not* put it in the tabernacle again, which at the time stood

in Gibeon and had not been brought to the same place in Jerusalem.

Notice that there were now *two* tents: one in Gibeon, namely, the tabernacle (without the ark), and one on Mount Moriah: a plain tent that contained the ark of the covenant.[40] Why did King David not bring the tabernacle to Mount Moriah as well, in orders to join the tabernacle and the ark again? The reason could hardly have been that David intended to have a temple built soon on Mount Moriah, as someone has suggested,[41] because after the temple was finished, the tabernacle was taken there anyway. Or must we think here of a modest tent, whereas the tabernacle with its court would occupy a large space on the Mount, and would obstruct the building of the temple?

This matter is related to another: During all these years, where did the glory of the LORD dwell: in the tabernacle, or on the ark? Let us keep in mind that the sacrifices to God were being offered not on Mount Moriah but on the altar of burnt offering: "[T]he king [Solomon] went to Gibeon to sacrifice there, for that was the great high place.[42] Solomon used to offer a thousand burnt offerings on that altar" (1 Kings 3:4).

When David expressed the desire to "dwell in the house of the LORD all the days of my life to gaze upon the beauty of the LORD" (Ps. 27:4), one may wonder whether he was referring to the tabernacle at Gibeon, or the tent on Mount Moriah (forerunner of the temple). It was easy for David to go to Moriah because the mountain was near his palace. (But notice that young King Solomon went not to Moriah, but to Gibeon, where the altar was! See above.) Also compare other passages in Psalms that are explicitly called Psalms *of David*:[43] "I . . . will

---

40. Notice the word "dwell" here: ". . . the ark of God *dwells* in a tent" (2 Sam. 7:2): God dwelt on the ark, the ark dwelt in David's tent.
41. https://biblehub.com/commentaries/2_samuel/6–17.htm.
42. This is in contrast with so many other "high places" where the Israelites used to bring their sacrifices, even Solomon himself (see v. 3); possibly: "that was the greatest of the high places," because here were the tabernacle and the altar of burnt offering.
43. Or must we assume, as some expositors do, that the reference "of David" means only that a certain psalm is part of a collection that David began, but to

enter your house. / I will bow down toward your holy temple" (5:7). "O LORD, I love the habitation of your house / and the place where your glory dwells" (26:8; also cf. 23:6).

Only after King Solomon had finished building the temple were the tabernacle and the ark joined again (after two-thirds of a century[44]): he brought both into the newly built temple (2 Chron. 5:4-5). No doubt could exist any longer about where exactly the dwelling of the LORD had to be located: in the tabernacle at Gibeon, or on the ark at Jerusalem. Actually, the Bible is quite silent on the matter; from the time Israel entered the Promised Land until the time of the new temple, we hear nothing about the pillar of cloud, or about the glory of the LORD dwelling in the midst of his people.

12.5 The Two Temples
12.5.1 Seeking the Place

(4) The fourth dwelling place of God was a building of wood and stone (1 Kings 5): the *temple*, the sanctuary that King Solomon had built in Jerusalem. We have seen that sometimes the same word is used for both "temple" and "palace," namely, Hebrew *hēkhal* (see, e.g., 1 Kings 21:1, where the word is used for the palace of King Ahab). Often, the word used for both "temple" and "palace" is simply the word *bayyit*, "house," as in the following verse: "Now Solomon purposed to build a temple [Heb. *bayyit*] for the name of the LORD, and a royal palace for himself [lit., a house (*bayyit*) for his kingdom]" (2 Chron. 2:1; cf. KJV). The LORD has his own house (which we call a "temple"), and the king has his own house (which we call a "palace"). Notice the literal parallelism here:

> a house – for the name – of YHWH
> a house – for the kingdom – of Solomon.

In addition to the many ordinary houses in Jerusalem, there were two special houses: one for the LORD, and one for

---

which other poets contributed?

44 I.e., at least twenty years in Abinadab's house, thirty-three years of David's kingship (2 Sam. 5:4; 1 Kings 2:11; 1 Chron. 29:27), and eleven years of Solomon's kingship (1 Kings 6:1, 37–38).

the king, which are not too different, for the king is *God's* king, king over his people in his land and city. One could put it this way: a royal palace for the king, *and a royal palace for the King of kings*.[45] Both the heavenly King, and his earthly representative, the son of David, dwelt in earthly houses or temples or palaces. And, if I may put it reverently, they were close neighbors: it was a short walk from the city of David to the temple.[46]

After Israel had just passed through the Red Sea, and thus had been delivered from Egypt, it was already looking forward to this dwelling place of God. This was possible only through the Spirit of God, for the people themselves were certainly not that spiritual:

> You have led in your steadfast love the people whom you have redeemed;
>   you have guided[47] them by your strength to your holy abode. . . .
> You will bring them in and plant them on your own mountain,
>   the place, O LORD, which you have made for your abode,[48]
>   the sanctuary, O Lord, which your hands have established
> (Exod. 15:13, 17).

Some see in this passage a reference to the Promised Land as a whole, but I prefer the interpretation that finds here an anticipation to the temple of Solomon. In my view, this is corroborated by the seven times that Deuteronomy refers to the future dwelling place of God in the Promised Land:

---

45. 1 Tim. 6:15; Rev. 17:14; 19:16; the title "king of kings" was also used for the head of the Babylonian (Ezek. 26:7; Dan. 2:37) or Persian empire (Ezra 7:12).
46. Today, the path to walk would go through the Davidson Center (Jerusalem Archeological Park), where the stairs are found that lead to the temple square.
47. Notice the imperfect tense of the Heb. verb, which is called a prophetic imperfect: the matter is so certain that it is viewed as already fulfilled; cf. Enoch's words: "Behold, the Lord has come with many thousands of His holy ones" (Jude 14 NASB).
48. The former word for "abode" is Heb. *navēh*, "dwelling, habitation" (from a root *n-v-h*, "to settle, to rest"), the latter word for "abode" is from the verb *y-sh-b*, "to dwell."

> [Y]ou shall seek the place that the LORD your God will choose out of all your tribes to put his name and make his habitation there. There you shall go, and there you shall bring your burnt offerings and your sacrifices. . . . to the place that the LORD your God will choose, to make his name dwell there, and so on (Deut. 12:5-6, 11).[49]

In fact, Israel apparently did not take very seriously this "seeking" the place where the LORD wished to dwell. He did not tell them in straightforward terms: You will have to build my temple in Jerusalem, namely, there and there. Rather, it was a "seeking" with the heart: the development of the desire to find this place, and to be led by God's Spirit in finding it.[50] This took several centuries after the entrance into the Promised Land; all the leaders (Joshua, the judges, King Saul) seemed to have different priorities. It was a matter of waiting for the right man, who would undertake this spiritual "seeking" as well as the "finding." This man was King David. He

> swore to the LORD
>   and vowed to the Mighty One of Jacob,
> "I will not enter my [own] house
>   or get into my bed,
> I will not give sleep to my eyes
>   or slumber to my eyelids,
> until I *find* a place for the LORD,
>   a dwelling place for the Mighty One of Jacob."
> Behold, we heard of it in Ephrathah;
>   we found it in the fields of Jaar.
> "Let us go to his dwelling place;
>   let us worship at his footstool!" (Ps. 132:2-7).

---

49. See also Deut. 14:23; 16:2, 6, 11; 26:2; cf. 23:16, "He shall dwell with you, in your midst, in the place that he shall choose within one of your towns, wherever it suits him."
50. This spiritual "seeking" is comparable to the "where" of Song 1:7-8 ("Tell me . . . where you pasture your flock?" "If you do not know, . . . follow in the tracks of the flock") and the "where" of John 1:38-39 ("Rabbi . . . , where are you staying?" He said to them, "Come and you will see").

The name "Jaar" (Heb. *ya'ar*) stands here for Kiriath-jearim[51] ("jearim" [*y'arim*] being the plural of *ya'ar*); this was the place where King David "found" the ark (see above). He set up a tent for it in Jerusalem, presumably on Mount Moriah, a tent that served as a forerunner for the temple of Solomon, which was to be built at the same spot.

The LORD helped David identify this spot because, after the three days of pestilence, the angel of the LORD appeared to him and gave him precise instructions:

Now the angel of the LORD had commanded [the prophet] Gad to say to David that David should go up and raise an altar to the LORD on the threshing floor of Ornan the Jebusite [which apparently was on the top of Mount Moriah]. So David went up at Gad's word, which he had spoken in the name of the LORD. . . . And David built there an altar to the LORD and presented burnt offerings and peace offerings and called on the LORD, and the LORD answered him with fire from heaven upon the altar of burnt offering. . . . Then David said, 'Here shall be the house of the LORD God and here the altar of burnt offering for Israel (1 Chron. 21:18–19, 26; 22:1).

Implicitly, this was a mighty confirmation on God's part that David had "found" the place that the people had had to "seek," and where God had wished "his name to dwell," as he had told the people already through Moses: here, on the top of Mount Moriah (2 Chron. 3:1), the temple was to be built.[52]

12.5.2 The Shekhinah in the Temple of Solomon

After King Solomon had finished building the temple and consecrated it to the service of the LORD, the pillar of the cloud is mentioned once again, the sign of the *Shekhinah*, the glorious presence of the LORD in Israel: "[W]hen the priests came out of the Holy Place, a cloud *filled* the house of the LORD, so that the priests could not stand to minister because of the

---

51. Kiriath-jearim means "town of the woods"; some translations read in Ps. 132:6, ". . . the fields of the wood," i.e., the fields around the "town of the woods."
52. Notice that the name "Moriah" appears in the Tanakh only twice: Abraham had to sacrifice his son Isaac on a mountain in the land of Moriah (Gen. 22:2), and Solomon built the temple on Mount Moriah (2 Chron. 3:1); it is generally assumed that the same mountain is meant.

cloud, for the glory of the LORD *filled* the house of the LORD" (1 Kings 8:10-11; cf. 2 Chron. 5:14). Israel never forgot how spectacular this was: God's glory visibly dwelling in their midst, in the house prepared for it, on the "mount of the LORD" (cf. Gen. 22:14).[53] What a blessing it was—until the unhappy time when the *Shekhinah* had to withdraw from the temple. This was when the sins of Judah became so numerous that God's judgment, including the destruction of the temple, had drawn near. No matter how evil the people of Judah had become, they could not imagine that the LORD would ever withdraw from them. They protested: "This is the temple of the LORD, the temple of the LORD, the temple of the LORD" (Jer. 7:4); in other words: Jeremiah, stop with your gloomy prophecies (see vv. 8-15; 26:4-9)! It is unthinkable that God would ever give up his *own* temple, his *own* city, and the Davidic dynasty that he himself had instituted. And yet, it happened. Not long before the city and the temple were to be destroyed by the Babylonian King Nebuchadnezzar, the time arrived when, in the visions of the prophet Ezekiel, the *Shekhinah* departed from the temple, slowly, almost hesitantly, but surely: "Now the glory of the God of Israel had gone up from the cherub on which it rested to the threshold of the house" (Ezek. 9:3).

> Then the glory of the LORD went out from the threshold of the house, and stood over the cherubim. And the cherubim lifted up their wings and mounted up from the earth before my eyes as they went out, with the wheels beside them. And they stood at the entrance of the east gate of the house of the LORD, and the glory of the God of Israel was over them (Ezek. 10:18-19).

> "Then the cherubim lifted up their wings, ... and the glory of the God of Israel was over them. And the glory of the LORD went up from the midst of the city and stood on the mountain that is on the east side of the city" (Ezek. 11:22-23).

---

53. Both Mount Sinai and Mount Moriah/Zion are called *har YHWH*, "mount(ain) of the LORD" (see also Num. 10:33; Isa. 2:3; Micah 4:1-2; Zech. 8:3).

It was a dramatic moment in Israel's history, for the questions burning in the hearts of the righteous were these: How could this ever have happened? Will the *Shekhinah* ever return to Jerusalem? If so, when will this occur? The answer is: *until this present day, it never did.* This is because it is highly questionable whether we could say that the glory of God dwelt in the Second Temple as well (see next section). Ezekiel had seen how the *Shekhinah* withdrew from the First Temple, but it was also given to him to behold how it would return—not in the Second Temple but—in the days of the Messianic kingdom (43:1-4; see §12.7.1).[54]

12.5.3 The Temple of Zerubbabel and Herod

(5) Of course, the Second Temple—the temple built by Zerubbabel and Jeshua—was intended to be a dwelling place of God just as much as the First Temple had been. Yet, rabbinic tradition states that the *Shekhinah* was not present in the Second Temple.[55] This is indeed the impression that we get when we read such passages as Ezra 6:13-18 (the dedication of the new temple) and Haggai 2:1-9 (Haggai's prophecy of the future glory of the temple). God said through Haggai to Zerubbabel (from the Davidic dynasty) and Joshua (or Jeshua) the high priest: "Who is left among you who saw this house in its former glory? How do you see it now? Is it not as nothing in your eyes? . . . [Only in the end time, the time of judgment] I will fill this house with glory, says the LORD of hosts" (Hagg. 2:3, 7). The "former glory" may refer to the outward splendor of the former temple of Solomon. But the link with verse 7 suggests that God is also, more or less implicitly, referring to the absence of the *Shekhinah* in the temple of Zerubbabel. The least we can say is that any reference to the descent of the "cloud," or to the glory of LORD "filling" the house, as occurred with, both the tabernacle and the First Temple, is completely lacking with the dedication of the Second Temple.

---

54. On the (presumed) metahistorical consequences of this withdrawal worldwide, see Ouweneel (2000b, chapter 4; 2014a, 87–90), where it is linked with the *Achsenzeit* ("Axis Period") discerned and described by Karl Jaspers (1953).

55. Talmud: Yoma 21b.

A remarkable fact linked with this absence of the *Shekhinah* is that, during and after the Babylonian exile, and after the construction of the Second Temple, God is often called the "God of heaven" (Heb. *Elohēy hashamayyim*), far more than ever before this period.[56] The Holy Spirit seems to have created the impression that God had withdrawn from the earth into heaven, at least for the time being, until the next event (see next section) at least five hundred years later.

Let me add two comments here. First, King David said, "The LORD, the God of Israel, has given rest to his people, and he dwells [or, will dwell] in Jerusalem forever" (1 Chron. 23:25)—as if, since God dwelt in the temple of Solomon, he would never leave the place.[57] However, we are forced to assume that the text was saying merely that (a) God will dwell in Jerusalem as long as the present earth lasts (this relativizes the "forever"), and (b) such "dwelling forever" did not exclude the possibility of interruptions.

Second, in Ezra 1:3–5, several expositors have claimed that many translations are mistaken in that they render the text as follows: "Whoever is among you of all his people, may his God be with him, and let him go up to Jerusalem, which is in Judah, and rebuild the house of the LORD, the God of Israel—he is the God who is in Jerusalem. . . . the house of God that is in Jerusalem." The mistake that is claimed to exist here is that after the Babylonian exile, people could *no longer* speak of "the God who is [i.e., dwells] in Jerusalem."[58] Other translations give what in my view is the correct rendering: ". . . build the house of the LORD God of Israel (He is God), which is in Jerusalem" (NKJV). That is, what "is in Jerusalem" is not God—as if he still dwelt there—but the house of God, the temple. A strong argument for this rendering is that those verses

---

56. 2 Chron. 36:23; Ezra 1:2; 5:11–12; 6:9–10; 7:12, 21, 23; Neh. 1:4–5; 2:4, 20; Dan. 2:18–19, 37, 44; Rev. 11:13; 16:11; in earlier times: Gen. 24:3, 7; Jonah 1:9; also cf. Ps. 136:26.
57. Interestingly, others read, ". . . that *they* may dwell in Jerusalem forever" (KJV).
58. The matter of God's omnipresence is not at stake here at all; the point is that God no longer dwelt in Jerusalem in the way he had done during the First Temple period.

speak of "the house of God (or, the LORD) that is in Jerusalem,"[59] that is, omitting the phrase "He is God."

The *house* had been rebuilt, but the *Inhabitant* was absent. One of the reasons why the "curtain of the temple was torn in two" at the death of Jesus (Matt. 27:51) may have been to show to the priests something they must have known all along, but which they now saw with their own eyes. No matter how much King Herod had ornately decorated the outside of the temple, its inside was an empty shell: the ark of the covenant was no longer there (cf. Jer. 3:16), and the *Shekhinah* did not dwell there, either.

King Solomon said, "Like a gold ring in a pig's snout / is a beautiful woman without discretion" (Prov. 11:22). I think of this verse when I hear the disciples say of the temple of Herod (the embellished form of the plain temple of Zerubbabel) "how beautiful it looked with its fine stones and the gifts offered to God" (Luke 21:5): a magnificent shell, but without any real substance.

In footnote 12 mention was made of the Jewish tradition that a rope was tied to the ankle of the high priest when he entered to Most Holy place so that in case he died, hid body could be pulled out. No matter how cynical this may sound, with the Second Temple the high priest had nothing to worry about: *there was no divine presence in the Second Temple*, and thus no danger of the high priest to dying in that Most Holy place.

12.6 Christ and the Ecclesia
12.6.1 Jesus Christ

(6) The sixth of God's twelve dwelling places is nothing less than the person of Jesus Christ himself, viewed as a human person in a human body. Two Bible passages must be mentioned in particular. The first one is the well-known verse in John 1: "[T]he Word (Christ) became flesh (human, incarnate) and tabernacled (fixed His tent of flesh, lived awhile) among us; and we [actually] saw His glory (His honor, His majesty),

---

59. Ezra 1:4; 2:68; 3:8; 4:24; 5:2, 16–17; 6:3, 5, 12; 7:16–17, 27.

such glory as an only begotten son receives from his father, full of grace (favor, loving-kindness) and truth" (v. 14 AMPC).

The "Word" is the *logos* mentioned in John 1:1-3. The verb "to tabernacle" (to fix one's tent, to dwell in a tent) is the Greek verb *skēnoō*, related to *skēnē*, "tent."[60] Jesus' human body was like a tent, in which the glory of God—we may no doubt say, the *Shekhinah*—dwelt ("tabernacled") on earth. This verse clearly suggests a connection with the tabernacle of the Tanakh, all the more so because, in the Septuagint, the Greek word for this tabernacle is *skēnē* (Heb. 8:5; 9:2, 6, 8, 21).[61] Thus, we can say that the body of Jesus was the fourth "tent" mentioned in the Bible as a dwelling place of God.

The second statement, corroborating the interpretation just given, came from Jesus' own mouth, as he was standing in Jerusalem next to the temple of Herod: "'Destroy this temple,[62] and in three days I will raise it up.' The Jews then said, 'It has taken forty-six years to build this temple, and will you raise it up in three days?' But he was speaking about the temple of his body" (John 2:19-21). The latter phrase is the explanation supplied by the apostle John of the enigmatic words of Jesus. The reference was to Jesus' own body, which, one day in the near future, the spiritual leaders of Israel would "destroy" ("break down"), but which Jesus himself, after three days, would raise from the dead through his own divine power (cf. John 10:17-18).

The significance of Jesus' words is quite remarkable. Because Jesus was standing next to the temple of Herod, listeners could hardly understand his words other than as a reference to this temple. But what Jesus was really saying was that, at that moment, the *Shekhinah* was not at all dwelling in the temple of Herod, *but in Jesus' own body*. At a later time,

---

60. This is not a common Greek verb for "to dwell"; more common words in the New Testament are Gk. *kathēmai, (kat)oikeō,* and *menō*.
61. The Heb. word for "tabernacle" is *mishkan*, literally "dwelling (place)," but the Lat. word is *tabernaculum*, "tent," and this is the word that, through the Vulgate, has entered our modern Bible translations.
62. Gk. *naos*, the actual temple house; not *hieron*, which is "temple" in the broader sense: the temple complex (e.g., Matt. 4:5).

most rabbis did admit the correctness of the former phrase, but unfortunately not that of the latter phrase.

Here we must point to another very relevant Bible verse; the angel Gabriel told Mary: "The Holy Spirit will come upon you, and the power of the Most High will overshadow you; therefore the child to be born will be called holy—the Son of God" (Luke 1:35). The verb "to overshadow" is Greek *episkiazō*, which is the same verb that, in was used in the Septuagint of Exodus 40: "Then the cloud covered the tent of meeting, and the glory of the LORD filled the tabernacle. And Moses was not able to enter the tent of meeting because the cloud *overshadowed* it, and the glory of the LORD filled the tabernacle" (vv. 34–35). When we read this verse together with John 2:19, we conclude that the *Shekninah* first "overshadowed" Mary in order to beget in her the holy Child Jesus, and subsequently came to dwell in the Child itself.

We find the same Greek verb, *episkiazō*, in Luke 9, during Jesus' transfiguration on the mountain, of which we read: "As he [i.e., Peter] was saying these things, a cloud came and *overshadowed* them, and they [i.e., the three disciples] were afraid as they *entered* the cloud" (v. 34). Here, the *Shekhinah* is associated not only with Jesus, but with the three disciples as well: not only Jesus (and Moses and Elijah) were in the cloud, but Peter, John, and James were, too. If we may view these disciples as foreshadowing the Ecclesia, this brings us automatically to the next section.

12.6.2 The Ecclesia

(7) Several times the *Ecclesia* is called the (spiritual) temple of God. "Do you not know that you [i.e., the believers] are God's temple and that God's Spirit dwells in you? If anyone destroys God's temple, God will destroy him. For God's temple is holy, and you are that temple" (1 Cor. 3:16–17). "[W]e are the temple of the living God" (2 Cor. 6:16). "[You are] built on the foundation of the apostles and prophets, Christ Jesus himself being the cornerstone, in whom the whole structure, being joined together, grows into a holy temple in the Lord.

In him you also are being built together into a dwelling place for God by [or, in] the Spirit" (Eph. 2:20-22).

The history of the Ecclesia began—again—in Jerusalem (*contra* the supersessionists: not in the Garden of Eden). There, the *Shekhinah*, now in the form of the Holy Spirit (cf. again Luke 1:35), descended upon her in order to dwell in this newly formed company. Again, we hear of remarkable external (atmospheric) phenomena, just as in the case of the tabernacle and the temple:[63] "[S]uddenly there came from heaven a sound like a mighty rushing wind, and it filled the entire house where they were sitting" (Acts 2:2). Just as, at the consecration of the tabernacle and later the temple, the glory of the LORD "filled" the tent, and later the building, it is here a "mighty rushing wind"[64] that "fills" the house. Cloud (think of the pillar of the cloud) and wind are some external characteristics of the *Shekhinah*, here in the special form of the Holy Spirit.[65]

Where the Ecclesia gathers, Jesus himself is in the midst of believers, according to his promise: "[W]here two or three are gathered together in My name, I am there in the midst of them" (Matt. 18:20 NKJV). This verse reminds us of two passages in the Tanakh. First, the tabernacle where the *Shekhinah* dwelt was called the "tent of meeting"[66] (another rendering: "tabernacle of the congregation"). The point is not so much that the tabernacle is the place where *believers* meet together, but rather that it is the place where *the* LORD—under the form of the *Shekhinah*—meets with his people. It is not primarily a "horizontal" but a "vertical" meeting.

---

63. Cf. the thick cloud, the fire, and the smoke in Exod. 19:9, 16, 18, and especially the fire coming down from heaven, about which we read in Lev. 9:24 and 2 Chron. 7:1–3.
64. The word "wind" is Gk. *pnoē*, related to Gk. *pneuma*, a word that can also mean "wind" (John 3:8), but usually is rendered as "s/Spirit."
65. To prevent the pagan notion that God would be a fire god, or a wind god (a god of the storm or the thunder), it is important to discover that sometimes things were reversed: when Elijah was at Mount Horeb, the Lord was *not* in the strong wind, the earthquake, or the fire, but in "the sound of a low whisper" (1Kings 19:11–12).
66. Heb. *ohel mo'ēd*, found in Exod. 27:21; 28:43; 29:4, 10–11, 30, 32, 42, 44.

Second, we read in the prophets: "Then those who feared the LORD spoke with one another [lit., a man with his neighbor; cf. the two of three in Matt. 18:20]. The LORD paid attention and heard them, and a book of remembrance was written before him of those who feared the LORD and esteemed his *name*" (Mal. 3:16). Based on this verse, the rabbis claimed that, where two or three God-fearing men sit together to study the Torah, or to render justice, or to pray—in short, are together in God's name—the *Shekhinah* is there in their midst.[67] Jesus probably knew this tradition, long before the Talmud had been written, and adapted it as follows: where two or three are gathered together in my *name*—to study God's Word, or to render justice, or to pray—there *I* am in their midst. Wherever he is, physically or in the Spirit, there is the *Shekhinah*; and because the Holy Spirit now dwells in the Ecclesia, we can say that the *Shekhinah* now dwells in the Ecclesia. Like the temple in the Tanakh, the New Testament temple is the dwelling place of the glory of God. This does not refer to what, unfortunately, the church often is in reality, but to what she is ideally in God's eyes.

12.6.3 The Individual Believer

(8) Also as far as the individual members of the Ecclesia are concerned, we are told with regard to their individual bodies: "[D]o you not know that your body is a temple of the Holy Spirit within you, whom you have from God?" (1 Cor. 6:19; cf. Rom. 8:9, 11; 2 Tim. 1:14).[68] To this, we may add a passage like Ephesians 3:17, where the apostle Paul prays that the believers may be strengthened with the power of the Holy Spirit, "so that Christ may dwell in your hearts through faith."

The body of every New Testament believer is a temple in which the Holy Spirit dwells. This dwelling place is sometimes called a "tent"; this is the fifth tent mentioned in the Bible as a dwelling place, not just of the human spirit but also of the Spirit of God: "[W]e know that if the tent that is

---

67. Talmud: Abot III.2 and 6; Berakoth 6a; Sanhedrin 39a; see Edersheim (1971, 2:124n2).
68. Cf. James 4:5 in some renderings: ". . . the Spirit whom He has made to dwell in us" (NASB; other renderings have "spirit," referring to the human spirit).

our earthly home is destroyed, we have a building from God, a house not made with hands, eternal in the heavens. For in this tent we groan.... For while we are still in this tent, we groan, being burdened" (2 Cor. 5:1-4). "I think it right, as long as I am in this tent, to stir you up by way of reminder, since I know that the putting off of my tent will be soon, as our Lord Jesus Christ made clear to me" (2 Pet. 1:13-14).

12.7   The Remaining Dwelling Places of God
12.7.1 The Millennial Temple

(9) The Millennial temple is the temple of the Messianic kingdom, as we have seen in Zechariah 6:12-13, quoted in §12.1.2. The text is quite explicit: no one less than the "Branch," that is, the Messiah, will build the "temple of the LORD," just as Solomon built the First, and Zerubbabel built the Second Temple. Many prophetic passages, describing the Messianic kingdom, simply take the existence of this Third Temple for granted.[69]

The construction of this building is described in detail in Ezekiel 40-44. Here, again, the (renewed) descent of the *Shekhinah* is concretely reported:

> "Then he [i.e., the angelic 'man' of Ezek. 40:3] led me to the gate, the gate facing east. And behold, the glory of the God of Israel was coming from the east [i.e., from the direction in which it had left; 10:19; 11:23]. And the sound of his coming was like the sound of many waters,[70] and the earth shone with his glory... And I fell on my face. As the glory of the LORD entered the temple by the gate facing east, the Spirit lifted me up and brought me into the inner court; and behold, the glory of the LORD filled the temple. While the man was standing beside me, I heard one speaking to me out of the temple, and he said to me, 'Son of man, this is the place of my throne and the place of the soles of

---

69. See, e.g., Isa. 2:2; 56:5,7; 66:20; Joel 3:18; Micah 4:1; Zech. 14:20–21.
70. A third metaphorical phenomenon: to the cloud (tabernacle, temple) and the mighty wind (Acts 2) is added now the roaring waters; all three express the overwhelming appearance of the *Shekhinah*. Notice the senses involved: seeing, feeling, hearing.

my feet, where I will dwell in the midst of the people of Israel forever'" (Ezek. 43:1-7).

Please notice how in this case the *Shekhinah* and the Holy Spirit are distinguished: the Spirit led the prophet, and what he saw and heard was the *Shekhinah*. Apart from this, the beginning of the Messianic kingdom is also characterized by a new outpouring of the Holy Spirit.[71]

The only hint about the location of this new temple is found in Ezekiel 48:21-22: it will be near the city of Jerusalem, that is, the region of Judah and Benjamin (see note 8). Presumably, this means that this Third Temple will be built at, or near, the place where the First and the Second Temples had stood, which is a quite obvious location.

12.7.2 The Immovable "Tent" Jerusalem

(10) The (earthly) Jerusalem of the Messianic kingdom in its totality is described as a city where the *Shekhinah* will dwell in the Third Temple. This city is presented as an immovable "tent," which is the sixth "tent" that is mentioned in the Bible as a dwelling place of God:

> Behold Zion, the city of our appointed feasts!
>   Your eyes will see Jerusalem,
>   an untroubled habitation, an immovable *tent*,
>   whose stakes will never be plucked up,
>   nor will any of its cords be broken.
> But there the LORD in majesty will be for us
>   a place of broad rivers and streams,
>   where no galley with oars can go,
>   nor majestic ship can pass (Isa. 33:20-21).

Jerusalem is indeed as movable and shakable as a tent, as history has demonstrated all too often. Many enemies have attacked this "tent," and have moved or shaken it, or have

---

71. Isa. 32:15; 44:3; Ezek. 36:27; 37:14; 39:29; Joel 2:28–29; please notice that Acts 2 cannot be the definitive fulfillment of Joel 2 because (a) not all the elements of Joel are found in Acts 2 (see vv. 19–20); (b) Peter expresses himself in a reticent way: "[T]his is what was uttered by . . ." (cf. the much stronger term "fulfilled" in 1:16; 3:18; 13:27, 33).

even made it to collapse; see, for instance, this passage, where the prophet complained:

> My tent is destroyed,
>   and all my cords are broken;
> my children have gone from me,
>   and they are not;
> there is no one to spread my tent again
>   and to set up my curtains (Jer. 10:20).

If, during the Messianic kingdom, Jerusalem can again be compared to a tent, this time it is an immovable and unshakable tent that offers its inhabitants a safe and unassailable abode: as long as the present earth exists, none of its tent pegs will ever be pulled up, and none of its ropes will ever be broken (ERV). Compare Isaiah 54:2, which was spoken to "Zion":

> Enlarge the place of your tent,
>   and let the curtains of your habitations be stretched out;
> do not hold back; lengthen your cords
>   and strengthen your stakes.

The city is described here as a "tent" presumably because the principal Inhabitant of this "tent" is the LORD himself, as suggested by verse 21. In Genesis 18, Abraham was sitting in the opening of his tent when the LORD with two angels came to visit him. In Isaiah 33, the LORD was sitting in his tent, and all the Abrahamites, even all the nations, came to visit him.

12.7.3 The "Booth" of David

(11) In Amos 9:11 we read:

> In that day I will raise up
>   the booth of David that is fallen
> and repair its breaches,
>   and raise up its ruins
>   and rebuild it as in the days of old.

This is the seventh "tent" mentioned in the Bible as a dwelling place of God.

(a) This "booth," or "hut," or "tent" (Heb. *sukkah*, Septuagint: *skēnē*; so also in the quotation in Acts 15:16), may refer to the Davidic kingdom (cf. NCV: "The kingdom of David is like a fallen tent," cf. CEV, GNT, ICB). In the last days (as in the days of the New Testament), this kingdom looks like a collapsed, broken, ruined "booth" or "tent," because for so many centuries no son of David occupied the throne of David.

(b) Or the "tent" is the city of David, if we take the "breaches" and "ruins" literally (cf. previous section). It is hard to imagine that, in the Jerusalem of the Messianic kingdom, the ancient city of David, now lying outside the Turkish walls, will not be part of restored Jerusalem.

(c) Or the "tent" is the "house" (dynasty) of David. During the Messianic kingdom, this "tent" will be restored: the Davidic kingdom will be restored through, and in the person of, the great Son of David, the Messiah.[72] If we link the notion of a "tent" with an Inhabitant, we may say that, during the Messianic kingdom, the Holy Spirit will rest upon the Messiah himself (cf. Acts 10:38).

12.8 Finally

12.8.1 The Eternal State

(12) The *temple* of the new heavens and the new earth—the eternal state—is none other than "the holy city, new Jerusalem, coming down out of heaven from God, prepared as a bride adorned for her husband. . . . the Bride, the wife of the Lamb" (Rev. 21:2, 9-10). Thus, the metaphor of God's dwelling place has now shifted from a temple building to an entire city (cf. 1 Chron. 23:25; Zech. 8:3), a spiritual city: the new Jerusalem in its totality. The text says, "Behold, the dwelling place [lit., tent, tabernacle, Gk. *skēnē*] of God is with man. He will *dwell* with them, and they will be his people, and God himself will be with them as their God" (Rev. 21:3). This is the (figurative) "tent" in which God will dwell among the people in the eternal state, the new heavens and the new earth (Rev. 21:3). It is the eighth "tent" mentioned in

---

72. Cf. Talmud: Sanhedrin 96b–97a, where Rabbi Nachman links the passage directly with the Messiah.

the Bible as a dwelling place of God. Perhaps we may say that the "tabernacle" (*skēnē*, "tent") that is first viewed in heaven (Rev. 13:6; 15:5) will ultimately stand on the new earth, in the midst of all God's people.

If one would still expect something of a temple in this city, the text tells us: "And I saw no temple in the city, for its temple is the Lord God the Almighty and the Lamb. And the city has no need of sun or moon to shine on it, for the glory of God gives it light, and its lamp is the Lamb" (Rev. 21:22-23). The image of the temple is used here in a double way: the city, the new Jerusalem as a whole, is as such the temple of the new world, *and* God himself is, so to speak, the temple of the new Jerusalem. Just as God dwelt in the midst of Israel, but then within the tabernacle, and later the temple, so God will dwell in the midst of the people in the new world—a world already holy in itself—but then in a Most Holy place, which was identified as the entire "holy city" (Rev. 21:2, 10; 22:19).[73]

12.8.2 Summary

Here are the twelve dwelling places, including the eight "tents," listed in summary fashion.

First abode	–first tent:	heaven (§12.3.2)
Second abode	–second tent:	the tabernacle (§§12.3.3-12.4.2)
Third abode	–third tent:	the tent of David on Zion (§12.4.3)
Fourth abode:		the temple of Solomon (First Temple) (§§12.5.1-12.5.2)
Fifth abode:		the temple of Zerubbabel (Second Temple) (§12.5.3)
Sixth abode	–fourth tent:	the body of Jesus Christ (§12.6.1)
Seventh abode:		the Ecclesia (§12.6.2)

---

73. Both the old Jerusalem (Neh. 11:1,18; Isa. 48:2; 52:1; Dan. 9:24; Matt. 4:5; 27:53; 11:2) and the new Jerusalem are called "holy city."

Eighth abode	–fifth tent:	the bodies of the believers (§12.6.3)
Ninth abode:		the millennial temple (Third Temple) (§12.7.1).
Tenth abode	–sixth tent:	the immovable "tent" Jerusalem (§12.7.2)
Eleventh abode	–seventh tent:	the "booth" (dynasty) of David (§12.7.3)
Twelfth abode	–eighth tent:	the tabernacle of God in the eternal state (§12.8.1)

Chapter 13
The Messianic Kingdom of Israel

Glorified and sanctified be God's great name throughout the world,

which he has created according to His will.

May he establish his kingdom in your lifetime and during your days,

and within the life of the entire house of Israel, speedily and soon. . . .

May his great name be blessed forever and to all eternity.

Blessed and praised, glorified and exalted, extolled and honored,

adored and lauded be the name of the Holy One, blessed be He,

beyond all the blessings and hymns, praises and consolations that

are ever spoken in the world. . .

> He who creates peace in His celestial heights,
> may He create peace for us and for all Israel.
> Qaddish[1] for the Dead

13.1 The Beginning of the Messianic Kingdom
13.1.1 A Jewish Kingdom

CONSERVATIVE EXPOSITORS HAVE NO doubt that the four world empires referred to in Daniel 2 and 7 are the Babylonian, the Medo-Persian, the Greek-Macedonian, and the Roman Empires. Two of these empires are named after cities, Babylon and Rome, and all four are named after nations: the Babylonians, the Medes and the Persians, the Greeks and the Macedonians, and the Romans. These empires are not named after mighty kings, although it is clear that the Babylonian empire is above all the kingdom of King Nebuchadnezzar, the Medo-Persian empire is above all that of King Cyrus the Persian, the Greek-Macedonian is above all that of King Alexander the Great, and the Roman Empire is above all that of the Emperor Augustus.

In both Daniel 2 and 7, these four empires are succeeded by a fifth empire: "[I]n the days of those kings the God of heaven will set up a kingdom that shall never be destroyed, nor shall the kingdom be left to another people. It shall break in pieces all these kingdoms and bring them to an end, and it shall stand forever" (Dan. 2:44).

> [A]s I looked, the [fourth] beast was killed, and its body destroyed and given over to be burned with fire. As for the rest of the beasts, their dominion was taken away, but their lives were prolonged for a season and a time [i.e., until their fall through the next beast]. I saw in the night visions, and behold, with the clouds of heaven there came one like a son of man, and he came to the Ancient of Days and was presented before him. And to him was given dominion and glory and a kingdom, that all peoples, nations, and languages should serve him; his dominion

---

1. *Qaddish* (Aramaic for "holy"; cf. Heb. *qodesh*) is a Jewish hymn in which God is praised, recited during Jewish prayer services.

is an everlasting dominion, which shall not pass away, and his kingdom one that shall not be destroyed (Dan. 7:11–14).

The fifth empire is that of the Son of Man, to whom is given "all power in heaven and on earth" (cf. Matt. 28:18). However, just as with the previous four empires, this kingdom could be named after the nation involved. Jesus called it "my Father's kingdom" (Matt. 26:29)—because the Father is the One who gives it to the Son of Man—but also the "kingdom of *their* Father" (Matt. 13:43), that is, the kingdom of "the righteous ones" (Heb. *tzaddiqim*) who share in this kingdom (cf. 25:34). In other words, it is the kingdom of the King, but also of his subjects, like the kingdom of the Netherlands is the kingdom of King Willem-Alexander just as much as it is the kingdom of the Dutch. Therefore, the Messianic kingdom can also be called a *Jewish* or *Israelite* kingdom (see earlier in §11.7.3). Just as the first kingdom was that of the Babylonians, and the fourth one was that of the Romans, the fifth one is that of the Israelites. The key verse is this (Dan. 7:27 ESV note):

> And the kingdom and the dominion
>   and the greatness of the kingdoms under the whole heaven
>   shall be *given to the people of the saints of the Most High*;
> their kingdom shall be an everlasting kingdom,
>   and all dominions shall serve and obey them.

In the Aramaic word used in the verse, *'am* ("people") is singular, but the English word "people" is a collective plural. If we replace it by "nation," the text says, "The kingdom . . . shall be given to the nation of the saints of the Most High; *its* [i.e., this nation's] kingdom shall be an everlasting kingdom, and all dominions shall serve and obey *it*," that is, Israel. As the ERV has it:

"Then God's holy people will rule over the kingdom and all the people from all the kingdoms of earth. This kingdom will last forever, and people from all the other kingdoms will respect and serve them [i.e., God's holy people]." We must not confuse this nation with the risen and glorified believers mentioned in Revelation 20:4-6, who will reign *together with* Christ from heaven. Daniel 7:27 referred to a nation *on earth*, people who will be no co-rulers with, but *subjects* to, King Messiah, while yet, at the same time, the kingdom is not just the King's kingdom, but *their* kingdom as well. When all the nations of the earth come and pay homage to the King, they will honor his nation as well. *All the nations will honor Israel.* In the vast Roman Empire, only a small part of its subjects were Romans in the proper sense: those of Rome and its surroundings. They were elevated above all the other subjects of the Empire, who were Romans at best in some secondary sense (cf. Acts 22:28). It will be the same in the Messianic kingdom: only a small part of its subjects will be the actual nation of the King, namely, Israel.

The Messianic kingdom is an Israelite kingdom because Israel will be its core nation, and Jerusalem will be the center of world dominion: *that* is where the throne of David will stand, and to *there* the nations will go up to learn about God:

> It shall come to pass in the latter days
>   that the mountain [Moriah/Zion] of the house [temple] of the LORD
> shall be established as the highest of the mountains,
>   and shall be lifted up above the hills;
> and all the nations shall flow to it,
>   and many peoples shall come, and say:
> "Come, let us go up to the mountain of the LORD,
>   to the house of the God of Jacob,
> that he may teach[2] us his ways
>   and that we may walk in his paths."
> For out of Zion shall go forth the law [Heb. *torah*, teaching],
>   and the word of the LORD from Jerusalem
>   (Isa. 2:2-3; cf. Micah 4:1-2).

13.1.2 A Cup and a Stone

The four world empires of history ought to play an important role in Jewish and Christian eschatology.[3] Elsewhere I have

---

2. The words for "to teach" *and* "law" (Heb. *torah*, see later in the verse) are both from the Heb. root *y-r-h*.
3. See Ouweneel (2003, chapters 3–6, 8–10; 2012a, chapter 6).

The Messianic Kingdom of Israel

attempted to demonstrate, on the basis of the book of Revelation and other sources, that the Roman Empire—the unifying principle inherent in Europe—has never ceased to exist. In the last days, it will rise again as the great (Western) world power, which will ultimately be defeated by Jesus Christ. The 144,000 "sealed ones" from all twelve tribes of Israel will be guided safely through these last days to the Messianic kingdom (Rev. 7).

The final battle, in which the ultimate victory is gained, will not happen in a moment. Christ will have returned, namely, "with the clouds of heaven." He will have destroyed the enemies who had gathered against him, and he will have redeemed his own (Rev. 14:17; 16:13-16; 19:11-21). He will have delivered the oppressed remnant of Israel, and will have raised the deceased saints from death. This is the beginning of the thousand years, as we see in Revelation 20:1-6. But this does not mean that, at this very moment, peace and justice enter immediately into the world. The armies of the Beast and the false prophets, as well as the armies of the "Assyrian,"[4] are not the only enemies whom Christ must defeat. Several other powers will obstruct the path to Christ's peaceful dominion; the perfect rest and peace cannot arrive until these enemies have been defeated as well.

Elsewhere I have explained the oppressive period through which Israel must pass before peace and justice arrive.[5] In this context, consider only the following verse, which, since 1967 (the year when, during the Six Days War, ancient Jerusalem was occupied by the Israelis), has become very relevant for our time:

> Behold, I am about to make Jerusalem a *cup of staggering* to all the surrounding peoples. The siege of Jerusalem will also be against Judah. On that day I will make Jerusalem a *heavy stone*

---

4. In my view, this is the same as Gog in Ezek. 38–39, because 38:17 tells is that "Gog" is the one of whom the prophets have earlier spoken, especially Isaiah.
5. See especially Ouweneel (2012a, chapter 12).

for all the peoples. All who lift it will surely hurt themselves. And all the nations of the earth will gather against it (Zech. 12:2-3).

Zechariah 12-14 forms a unity as one and the same oracle (Zech. 12:1, Heb. *massa*), which gives us a concise summary of events:

(1) 12:1-9: the siege (viz., by the "Assyrian" or Gog) and deliverance of Jerusalem.

(2) 12:10-13: the coming of Messiah and the outpouring of the "Spirit of grace and supplication" (v. 10 NKJV), and the subsequent mourning in Israel, when they will have recognized the returned Jesus as their Messiah.

(3) 13:1-4: the spiritual purification of the inhabitants of Jerusalem, and the destruction of the last forms of idolatry.

(4) 13:5-7: many older expositors read this as a Messianic prediction.[6] *God's* judgment on his "Shepherd/Companion" (13:7 NKJV).

(5) 13:8-9: the purification of Israel in order to render the remnant of the nation fit for the Messianic kingdom.

(6) 14:1-7: the LORD's appearance on the Mount of Olives (i.e., the second coming of Christ).

(7) 14:8-21: the Messianic kingdom.

13.2 Foreshadows
13.2.1 David and Solomon

What I wrote at the end of the previous section is beautifully depicted in the typology of the Tanakh. King David was undoubtedly one of the most splendid and straightforward types of the Messiah. The coming Messiah was called "Son of David,"[7] and sometimes even "David" for short,[8] as if he were a reincarnation of King David.[9] His son Solomon, the

---
6. See http://biblehub.com/zechariah/13-6.htm.
7. Cf., e.g., Jer. 23:5; 33:15; see also Matt. 1:20; 9:27; 12:23; 15:22; 20:30–31; 21:9, 15 and parallels.
8. Jer. 30:9; Ezek. 34:23–24; 37:24–25; Hos. 3:5.
9. Of course, this cannot be the case; the Bible does not teach reincarnation. Moreover, Jesus has already received his own glorified body; he will not, and

first "son of David" in a long line of Davidic "sons," is a type of the Messiah as well. David and Solomon form what has been called a "double type" of the dominion of Christ, just as, in a certain sense, Moses and his successor, Joshua, formed a "double type," as did Moses and Aaron, and much later Zerubbabel and Jeshua.

Before Christ will be able to reign as the true Solomon, the prince of peace[10] (cf. Matt. 12:42), he must first reign for some time as the true David. To be sure, the latter had been established as king in Zion, but he did not experience any rest until his death. Until the end, he remained involved in battle, particularly against the enemies within the Holy Land itself: the Philistines.[11]

In David—which means the "beloved"—we see the man "after God's heart" (1 Sam. 13:14), at first rejected and oppressed by the king who had been desired by the people, a type of the "man of lawlessness" (2 Thess. 2:3), the Antichrist.[12] This king, Saul, together with his subjects, persecuted the one who had been anointed as king over Israel, and also persecuted the latter's followers, the outcasts of the nation (1 Sam. 22:1-2). However, this rejected king was the one who delivered the people from the hands of the mighty giant Goliath (1 Sam. 17; type of Satan; cf. Heb. 2:14). We might extend the comparison a bit further, to discern a parallel between Samuel and John the Baptist—both prophets from the tribe of Levi—as forerunners of David and Jesus, respectively.

After this, Christ as the true David must do battle with all the remaining enemies (2 Sam. 5 and 8): he will be "destroying every rule and every authority and power. For he must reign until he has put all his enemies under his feet. The last enemy to be destroyed is death" (1 Cor. 15:24-26).

This destruction of death will occur only at the end of the Messianic kingdom. We must therefore conclude that this

---

cannot, return in the body of another person.
10. The name "Solomon" (Heb. *Sh'lomoh*) is derived from *shalom*, "peace" (cf. Isa. 9:6).
11. Cf. 1 Chron. 22:9, 18; 23:25; 28:2; 2 Sam. 21.
12. See extensively, Ouweneel (2012a, chapter 8).

kingdom will be a kingdom of peace only to a certain extent. It is a peace that will be brought about by subjugating enemies. However, in David's days this submission was to a large extent feigned (hypocritical): "As soon as they heard of me they obeyed me; foreigners came cringing to me [or, feigned obedience to me]. Foreigners lost heart and came trembling out of their fortresses" (Ps. 18:44-45; cf. 66:3; 81:15).

> The nations shall see and be ashamed of all their might; they shall lay their hands on their mouths; their ears shall be deaf; they shall lick the dust like a serpent, like the crawling things of the earth; they shall come trembling out of their strongholds; they shall turn in dread to the LORD our God, and they shall be in fear of you [i.e., Israel] (Micah 7:16-17).

In the Messianic kingdom as well, many will feign submission to Christ. This is evident from the end of the thousand years, when Christ's enemies, seduced by the liberated devil, will gather against him once more (Rev. 20:7-9). We must conclude that, both under David and under Christ, it was and will be a peace achieved by force. On the new earth, righteousness will *dwell* (2 Pet. 3:13), but during the Messianic kingdom, righteousness will *reign*, that is, be maintained under duress. Sinners may reach advanced age, but nonetheless, even sinners who reach one hundred years old, when they manifest themselves as rebels against the King, "shall be accursed" (Isa. 65:20b):

> No one who practices deceit
>   shall dwell in my house;
> no one who utters lies
>   shall continue before my eyes.
> Morning by morning I will destroy
>   all the wicked in the land,
> cutting off all the evildoers
>   from the city of the LORD (Ps. 101:7-8; cf. Zeph. 3:5).

Democratically-minded Westerners like us may be uncomfortable with terms like "force" and "duress." However, none of us should have any objection to an *autocratic* government, *provided* that its ruler would strictly satisfy at least two conditions: (a) they must be perfectly intelligent and wise, and (b) they must be perfectly selfless, that is, totally devoted to their subjects. This is what was formerly called an "enlightened despot," with the motto: everything done *through* the ruler, but everything done *for* the people.[13]

13.2.2 David and the Ark

One of the most important events in David's life was placing the ark on Mount Zion, in the city of Jerusalem that he had conquered. David was not allowed to build a temple, for he had blood on his hands; only Solomon could build the temple, when he ruled in Israel (1 Chron. 22). However, in principle the relationship between the people and God were established during this placing of the ark of the covenant on Mount Zion, which event was a type of the divine foundation of grace. It occurred while many enemies had not yet been conquered, the blessed rule had not yet been fully established, and a house for God had not yet been built. It happened because David believed in God's promise (Ps. 132): the ark established on Mount Zion was the guarantee that all the other blessings would arrive in due time as well.

Not only David, but the ark also was a type of Christ. The Messiah has been set as King over Zion, God's holy hill (Ps. 2:6; cf. 132:11-18). Before David brought the ark to Zion, no dwelling place of God existed any longer in Israel since the time when Shiloh had been rejected: in the days, of Eli the priest, God

> forsook his dwelling at Shiloh,
>   the tent where he dwelt among mankind,
> and delivered his power [i.e., the ark] to captivity,
>   his glory to the hand of the foe [i.e., the Philistines].
> He gave his people over to the sword
>   and vented his wrath on his heritage (Ps. 78:59-62).

---

13. Examples include Austrian Empress Maria Theresia and her son Joseph II, Prussian King Frederick the Great, Russian Czarina Catharine the Great, and the Dutch King Willem I.

The forsaking of Shiloh might be interpreted literally to mean that the place was destroyed (by the Philistines?), as the Lord seems to suggest through the prophet Jeremiah:

> Go now to my place that was in Shiloh, where I made my name dwell at first, and see what I did to it because of the evil of my people Israel. And now, because you have done all these things, ... and when I spoke to you persistently you did not listen, and when I called you, you did not answer, therefore I will do to the house that is called by my name, and in which you trust, and to the place that I gave to you and to your fathers, as I did to Shiloh (7:12–14; 26:6, 9).

In order words, Jeremiah told the people that it had happened before: the Lord had put an end to Shiloh,[14] and similarly he would put an end to the temple. First it was the Philistines (?), now it will be the Babylonians.

Typologically speaking, we might say that, when the Philistines captured the ark (1 Sam. 4), the "times of the Gentiles" began (cf. Luke 21:24). The ark went into exile, and in this way the *Shekhinah* went into exile, too. However, David's placing the ark on Mount Zion put an end to this, just as Christ would one day establish his kingship on Zion, and thereby definitively bring an end to the "times of the Gentiles." Although not all enemies will have been defeated, and the blessing, peace, and justice of the Messianic kingdom will not have fully arrived, Christ will establish his dominion on Zion, in a gracious relationship with his people, whom he has redeemed. This is the scene of Revelation 14:

> Then I looked, and behold, on Mount Zion stood the Lamb, and with him 144,000 who had his name and his Father's name written on their foreheads. And . . . they were singing a new song before the throne. . . . No one could learn that song except the 144,000 who had been redeemed from the earth. It is these who have not defiled themselves with women, for they are virgins. It is these who follow the Lamb wherever he goes. These have been redeemed from mankind as firstfruits for God and

---

14. i.e., the place (town) as such, for the tabernacle had been saved.

the Lamb, and in their mouth no lie was found, for they are blameless (vv. 1-5; cf. 7:1-8).

13.2.3 Christ on Mount Zion

In grace and glory, Christ will be enthroned on Zion, together with his faithful ones. The battle will commence against those who resist the full establishment of the Messianic blessings. As we read in Psalm 110:

> The LORD says to my Lord [i.e., King Messiah]:
>   'Sit at my right hand,
> until I make your enemies your footstool.'
> The LORD sends forth from Zion
>   your mighty scepter, [saying:]
>   "Rule in the midst of your enemies!" (vv. 1-2).

After this, the young men ("the dew of your youth," v. 3) go out to defeat the enemies, in particular "the head over a great country" (v. 6 DARBY), who—if this is a correct rendering—must be the Assyrian/Gog.[15] Putting their trust in their King, who is enthroned on Zion, they enter into battle:

> Those who trust in the LORD are like Mount Zion,
>   which cannot be moved, but abides forever.
> As the mountains surround Jerusalem,
>   so the LORD surrounds his people,
>   from this time forth and forevermore.
> For the scepter of wickedness shall not [forever] rest
>   on the land allotted to the righteous,
> lest the righteous stretch out
>   their hands to do wrong (Ps. 125:1-3).

"May all who hate Zion / be put to shame and turned backward!" (Ps. 129:5). This latter passage may have been referring to the Assyrian/Gog (cf. Isa. 37:22, 27).

---

15. See Ouweneel (2012a, §12.4.1).

13.3 The Place of Zion
13.3.1 The Holy Mountain

It is worthwhile to consider in a bit more detail the importance of Zion in the Bible. W. Dumbrell discerned a genuine "theology of Zion" in the Bible.[16] D. E. Gowan arranged his entire eschatology around the Zion concept: his first chapter deals with Zion as the center of eschatology in the Tanakh (with reference to Zech. 8), chapter 2 deals with peace in Zion: the transformation of human society, and chapter 3 deals with the people of Zion: the transformation of the human person.[17]

Let me clarify some geographical confusion. Zion has been the name of no fewer than three literal mountains at Jerusalem, and subsequently a poetic name for all Jerusalem, including all its mountains:

(1) At first, "Zion" was apparently the name for the mountain on which lay the "city of David," *or* the name of the fortress that originally stood there: "David took the stronghold of Zion, that is, the city of David."[18] This is the southeast hill of Jerusalem, outside the sixteenth-century Turkish walls, also called Ophel.[19] Zion *is* the "city of David" (1 Kings 8:1).[20]

(2) However, Mount Zion soon began to mean: the mountain where the LORD dwells, and where service is rendered to him.[21]

In this case, Mount Zion must be identical with Mount Moriah (2 Chron. 3:1), that is, the northeast hill, called the Temple Mount (a phrase not found in the Bible); the Muslims call the place Haram ash-Sharif ("the noble sanctuary"); they deny that there ever was a Jewish temple at that spot. Genesis 22 speaks of a mountain in the *land* Moriah; yet tradition

---

16. Dumbrell (1994, 75–95).
17. Gowan (2000).
18. 2 Sam. 5:7; 1 Chron. 11:5; cf. 1 Kings 8:1; 2 Chron. 5:2.
19. 2 Chron. 27:3; 33:14; Neh. 3:26–27; 11:21; Isa. 32:14; Micah 4:8.
20. Ancient Jerusalem shares the name "city of David" with Bethlehem, the city where David was born (Luke 2:4, 11).
21. Ps. 9:11; 65:1; 74:2; 76:2; 84:7; 99:2; 102:16, 21; 128:5; 132:13; 134:3; 135:21; Isa. 2:3; 8:18; Joel 3:17; Micah 4:2; Zech. 8:3.

assumes that the temple stood at the place where God had wished Abraham to sacrifice his son.

Consider the following quotation:

> "As for me, I have set my King
>   on Zion, my holy hill."
> I will tell of the decree:
> The LORD said to me, "You are my Son;
>   today I have begotten you.
> Ask of me, and I will make the nations your heritage,
>   and the ends of the earth your possession" (Ps. 2:6–8).

We may wonder here which mountain is meant: the first mountain mentioned ("city of David"), or the second mountain ("Moriah"), or should we think of the fourth meaning mentioned (see below)?

(3) Later Jews have erroneously considered the *southwest* hill (also just outside the Turkish walls[22]) to have been the original Zion, and this misunderstanding endures even today; think, for instance, of the Zion Gate in ancient Jerusalem. It is remarkable that today the tomb of King David is venerated on the southwest hill, although it is hardly conceivable that David was buried at any other place than *his* Zion: the "city of David" on the *southeast* hill (1 Kings 2:10).

(4) In the poetic and prophetic books of the Tanakh, Zion is very often identical with all Jerusalem, but then especially Jerusalem as the city where the LORD God has dwelt, and where his people serve him. Here are some examples.

> You will arise and have pity on Zion;
>   it is the time to favor her;
>   the appointed time has come.
> For your servants hold her stones dear
>   and have pity on her dust.
> Nations will fear the name of the LORD,
>   and all the kings of the earth will fear your glory.
> For the LORD builds up Zion;
>   he appears in his glory;

---

22. The story goes that Sultan Süleyman the Magnificent executed the builders of the walls because they had left "Mount Zion" outside them.

he regards the prayer of the destitute
and does not despise their prayer (Ps. 102:13-17).

Or consider these statements from the prophet Isaiah: "Behold Zion, the city of our appointed feasts!" (33:20). "[P]ut on your strength, O Zion; put on your beautiful garments, O Jerusalem, the holy city" (52:1). "City of the LORD, the Zion of the Holy One of Israel" (60:14).[23]

In a passage like Zechariah 8:3, the distinction between city and mountain seems to be still maintained to some extent: "I have returned to Zion and will dwell in the midst of Jerusalem, and Jerusalem shall be called the 'faithful city' [or, 'city of truth'], and the mountain of the LORD of hosts [shall be called] the 'holy mountain'."[24]

(5) In the New Testament, Zion has also become a spiritual designation for the new order of things that in Christ has become reality: "[Y]ou have come to Mount Zion and to the city of the living God, the heavenly Jerusalem" (Heb. 12:22). In Galatians 4:21-31, Zion was not mentioned, but was implied, first, in the expression "the Jerusalem above," second, in the contrast with Mount Sinai, and third, in the quotation from Isaiah 54:1, where, in comparison with, for instance, Isaiah 52:1-2, the reference was to Zion.

13.3.2 The Shekhinah in Exile

The first mountain of which we know that God manifested himself there to a *man* was Mount Moriah, where God spoke to Abraham (Gen. 22). The first mountain where God revealed himself to a *people* was Mount Sinai, in the desert of Sinai, where God granted to his people the Torah, the tabernacle, and the sacrificial ministry.[25] But God also announced to this people that in the Promised Land, they would receive

---

23. See also 2 Kings 19:31; Ps. 51:18; 102:21; 135:21; 147:12; Isa. 2:3; 4:3–4; 30:19; 31:9; 40:9; 41:27; 52:1; 64:10; Jer. 26:18; 51:35; Lam. 2:10, 13; Joel 3:16–17; Amos 1:2; Micah 3:10, 12; 4:2; Zeph. 3:14, 16; Zech. 1:17; 8:3; 9:9; notice in each case the Hebrew poetic parallelisms.
24. See also Isa. 10:12, 32; 24:23; 37:32; Joel 2:32; Zech. 1:14.
25. Regarding Sinai and Zion, see Ouweneel (1982b, 2:86–87; 1997, 292–99).

a fixed place of service,[26] which we now know would be on a third mountain. At that future place, they would be at rest from their enemies, and have an elevated center where God would dwell and rule in the midst of his people.

After Israel had entered the Promised Land, at the first Shiloh in the hill-country of Ephraim became the place where the tabernacle was erected and where God was served (see §12.3.1). As we saw, the place was dishonored by the sons of Eli the priest, Hophni and Phinehas, who were at the time members of the ruling priestly class. This was the offspring of Ithamar, the youngest son of Aaron.[27] They misbehaved so much that God had to judge the entire place (1 Sam. 2:30-34). This judgment came first upon Eli and his sons, but it continued until the last priest of the house of Ithamar was cast out, who was Abiathar. He had served David (see especially 2 Sam. 15), but was expelled by King Solomon because he sided with Solomon's half-brother and rival, Adonijah: "So Solomon expelled Abiathar from being priest to the Lord, thus fulfilling the word of the Lord that he had spoken concerning the house of Eli in Shiloh" (1 Kings 2:27). Abiathar was punished not just because he came from the "wrong" family but because of his own misconduct.

God then chose a new priestly family and a new place of worship: "I will raise up for myself a faithful priest, who shall do according to what is in my heart and in my mind. And I will build him a sure house, and he shall go in and out before my anointed forever" (1 Sam. 2:35).

This priest was Zadok, from the house of Eleazar, the third son of Aaron (2 Sam. 8:17; 1 Chron. 24:3; the first two sons had died, Lev. 10:1-3).[28] Zadok's priesthood would be everlasting: in the Messianic kingdom, it will be his "sons" (descendants) who will again fulfill the priestly service (Ezek. 40:46; 43:19; 44:15).

---

26. Deut. 12:5, 11; 14:23; 16:2, 6, 11; 26:2.
27. Exod. 6:23; 38:21; Lev. 10:6; Num. 3:2, 4; 4:28, 33; 7:8; 1 Chron. 24:1–6.
28. It is not clear how the fourth and youngest son of Aaron the priest, Ithamar, could have ever taken the first place instead of the third son, Eleazar.

Remarkably, when the wife of Phinehas the priest, Eli's son, gave birth to a son, whom she called *Ikabod*, "Gone is the glory," saying, "The glory [Heb. *kabod*] has departed from Israel ... for the ark of God has been captured'" (1 Sam. 4:21-22; see §12.4.2). The twice-mentioned word "departed" (Heb. *galah*) is of great interest here because it literally means "to be exiled, to go into exile." The related word *galut* is the well-known Hebrew term for the Jewish diaspora, Israel's dispersion over the nations of the world. What the wife of Phinehas was saying is that the ark had gone into exile: it had been taken from its homeland, and had to dwell in a strange land. If we may say that the *Shekhinah* still rested on the ark, it was the *Shekhinah* itself that had gone into exile; it wandered around in foreign parts of the world, as it had done during Israel's wilderness journey.

13.3.3 Four Exiles

In a certain sense, this exile of the *Shekhinah* was God's second exile. Four or five such exiles can be distinguished.

(1) *Egypt*. Already the time that Jacob and his descendants, the people Israel, spent in Egypt could be called an exile, away from the Promised Land. Please note that the patriarchs had an altar to offer sacrifices to God in *HaAretz*,[29] but not in Egypt. Israel had an altar again at Mount Sinai, in the wilderness, in the tabernacle, as they journeyed to God's "holy abode" (Exod. 15:13, 17).[30]

(2) *Philistia*. The second exile was in the land of the Philistines, when the ark of the covenant wandered from one city to another, and along with it also the glory of the LORD, the *Shekhinah*, had departed from the Holy Land. After the event recorded in Exodus 40:34-38, the *Shekhinah* had dwelt on the

---

29. Gen. 12:7-8; 13:4, 18; 22:9; 26:25; 33:20; 35:1, 3, 7.
30. It is remarkable that, during the Messianic kingdom, there will be an altar in the new temple at Jerusalem, but also one in Egypt: "In that day there will be an altar to the LORD in the midst of the land of Egypt, and a pillar to the LORD at its border. It will be a sign and a witness to the LORD of hosts in the land of Egypt" (Isa. 19:19-20).

ark,[31] but after the ark had been exiled to Philistia, we no longer hear about the *Shekhinah*, even after the ark had been carried back to Israel. The first time we hear about it again is in the temple of Solomon (2 Chron. 7:2).

(3) *Assyria and Babylon*. This is "the" exile (older renderings: captivity) reported in the Tanakh: for the ten tribes (the northern kingdom), this was in the Assyrian empire (since 722 BC), and as to the two tribes, this was in the Babylonian empire. This was the exile that had been often announced by the prophets, it was described by those who were in it (Ezekiel, Daniel), and later leaders looked back to it (Ezra, Nehemiah, Haggai, Zechariah). It began with the destruction of the temple (586 BC) and ended with the consecration of the new temple (516 BC). This was a period of seventy years, as had been predicted.[32]

(4) The longest exile was that of Israel since the destruction of Jerusalem (AD 70) until the reconquest and reconstruction of (ancient) Jerusalem (1967); this was a period of 1,897 years. Actually, this exile is still continuing; it will end only when the temple has been rebuilt, and the *Shekhinah* has returned to it (Ezek. 43:1-9). Throughout all these centuries, the people of Israel has been dispersed among *all* the nations, so that they will return from *all* the nations.[33]

Although part of Israel has returned to the Holy Land, they are not yet safe there. We might still identify a last small exile: that of the faithful ones in Judea, who, during the Great Tribulation, must flee to the mountains (Matt. 24:15-16), and from there to countries around Israel. We must think here especially of Moab (nowadays: the country of Jordan) (cf. Isa. 16:1-5; cf. historically Jer. 40:11-12). Interestingly, Moab was also the country where the family of David found refuge during the time when David was persecuted by King Saul (1 Sam. 22:3-4).

---

31. See also Exod. 25:22; Lev. 16:2; Josh. 7:6; 1 Sam. 4:4; 2 Sam. 6:2; 2 Kings 19:15; 1 Chron.13:6; Ps. 80:1; 99:1; Isa. 37:16
32. Cf. 2 Chron. 36:21; Jer. 25:11–12; 29:10; Dan. 9:2.
33. Deut. 28:37; Isa. 66:20; Jer. 29:18; 30:11; 43:5; 46:28.

13.3.4 Three Replacements

Shiloh was the place where the tabernacle had stood for such a long time. Because of the sins of Eli and his sons, and because the ark of the covenant had been carried away by these sons, Shiloh could no longer be the center of priestly ministry and of God's rule in Israel. In §13.2.2 I quoted Jeremiah 7:12–14 (cf. 26:6, 9), where the LORD himself explained without going into detail what he had done to the place. We are nowhere told what exactly happened to Shiloh; we can only presume that God allowed it to be destroyed. No matter what occurred, the point is that Shiloh was to be replaced by Mount Moriah. This was part of *three* replacements, as is explained in Psalm 78:

> [They] turned away and acted treacherously like their fathers;
> ....
> When God heard, he was full of wrath,
>   and he utterly rejected Israel.
> He *forsook his dwelling at Shiloh*,
>   the tent where he dwelt among mankind,
> and delivered his *power* [i.e., the ark] to captivity,
>   his glory to the hand of the foe. ...
> Their priests [i.e., Hophni and Phinehas] fell by the sword, ...
> Then the Lord awoke ....
> He built his sanctuary like the high heavens,
>   like the earth, which he has founded forever.
> He chose David his servant ....
>   to shepherd Jacob his people,
>   Israel his inheritance (Ps. 78:57–71; italics added).

Here we have all three replacements neatly arranged:

(a) *A new priesthood.* The unfaithful family of Eli, the father of Hophni and Phinehas, was discarded, and replaced (which is not mentioned here) by the family of Zadok. That is, the dynasty of Eleazar, the elder brother of Ithamar (sons of Aaron), re-obtained its legitimate place, which had been taken up by the dynasty of Ithamar.

(b) *A new sanctuary.* Substituting Eleazar for Ithamar also involved a tribal exchange because Shiloh was in Ephraimite territory, and Zion, which was going to be the new sanctuary, was in Judean territory:

> He rejected the tent of Joseph;
> he did not choose the tribe of Ephraim [son of Joseph],[34]
>
> but he chose the tribe of Judah,
> Mount Zion, which he loves (Ps. 78:67-68).

(c) *A new kingship.* The unfaithful King Saul, a Benjaminite, was replaced by the man after God's heart, King David, from Judah.

So too it will be in the Messianic kingdom: there, the new priesthood, the descendants of Zadok, will function; there, "David," the Messianic King,[35] will rule; and there Zion, the holy mountain of old, will be God's dwelling place. King, city, mountain, priest, and sanctuary—all part of one sacred totality, as it had been since ancient times.

13.4 Zion Restored
13.4.1 God's Dwelling Place Forever

The new priesthood and kingship and the new dwelling place of God are linked with Zion once and for all. Zion, the "city of David" (2 Sam. 5:7, 9) will forever be, and remain, the "city of our God" (Ps. 48:1). After David has conquered the fortress of Jebus, and has transferred the ark to Zion, Zion becomes forever—that is, as always, as long as the present earth exists—the city of God's dwelling *and* is forever linked with the house of David. God promises the latter in a proph

---

34. Ephraim was the leading tribe among the northern kingdom (sometimes in its totality referred to as "Ephraim"; so often in Hos.) of the ten tribes; leaders like Joshua and Jeroboam I were from Ephraim.

35. Robertson (2000, chapter 3) claims that, where Christ is priest after the order of Melchizedek, there is no place for the Levitical priesthood anymore. In contrast with this, I would identify David/Solomon, Judean Priest-King (see 2 Sam. 6:17; 24:25; 1 Kings 3:15; 2 Chron. 7:7), as a type of the Messiah, and

next to him, Zadok, who functioned as the Levitical priest, just as his descendants will do during the Messianic kingdom (Ezek. 40–44).

ecy that is first applicable to Solomon, but secondarily to *the great Son of David*:

> When your [i.e., David's] days are fulfilled and you lie down with your fathers, I will raise up your offspring after you, who shall come from your body, and I will establish his kingdom. He shall build a house for my name, and *I will establish the throne of his kingdom forever*. I will be to him a father, and he shall be to me a son [cf. Heb. 1:5!]. . . . And your house and your kingdom shall be made sure forever before me" (2 Sam. 7:12-16; italics added).

> Jesus Christ is *the* great Son of David, who will also literally fulfill all the predictions of Psalm 132:11-18.[36]

Thus, Zion becomes the last mountain that plays a role in Israel's redemptive history. On Mount Sinai, God gave the people a Torah that was magnificent, but *actually* only demonstrated that the people were sinful and accountable to God (Rom. 3:19). Zion, however, is the mountain where the ark of the covenant has been placed, the ark with the mercy-seat (or, more correctly, atonement-lid) (cf. vv. 20-25). The order of grace—which also contains laws—stands here over against the order of law—which also contains mercy (cf. 4:16; 5:20; 6:14). After Israel has broken the law, after both its priests (Eli and his sons) and its king (Saul) have failed, and when everything has come to depend on the grace of God, he chooses Mount Zion, the mountain of grace. Here, according to his gracious election, he makes a new beginning: a new priesthood, a new kingship, a new sanctuary, a new place of rest for God.[37]

From now on, Zion is permanently the place with which the faithful remnant of Israel is linked. This is the remnant that God forms in grace, time and again, in times of decline, after the people have failed under the Torah, and ought to be condemned in its totality. This *principle* of grace in the

---

36. That is to say, insofar as he has not already done so; compare Ps. 132:15 with Matt. 14:15–21.
37. Ps. 2:6–8; 1 Chron. 28:2; cf. Heb. 1:5; 5:5.

midst of apostasy is found already in Genesis 6: "So the LORD said, 'I will destroy man whom I have created from the face of the earth, both man and beast, creeping thing and birds of the air, for I am sorry that I have made them.' But Noah found grace in the eyes of the LORD" (v. 7-8 NKJV). This is what election is: *all* have deserved God's judgment, yet he wishes to save *some*, not because they are better than the others—although they *become* better than the others (see v. 9)—but because of God's sovereign grace.[38]

13.4.2 Sh'ar Yashub

The grace just described produces a remnant, that, according to its own responsibility, returns to him: "The remnant will return [Heb. *sh'ar yashub*[39]], the remnant of Jacob, to the Mighty God. For though your people, O Israel, be as the sand of the sea, a remnant of them will return" (Isa. 10:21-22 NKJV). As so often, "to return" has here the sense of both returning to the LORD and returning to the land of the LORD; the two events are inseparable (see especially the use of the verb in the Heb. text of Deut. 30:1-11; see §10.8). It does not mean that Jews cannot repent and return to the LORD outside the land, but it does mean that in the *ultimate* restoration of Israel the return to the LORD and the return to the land are inextricably connected.

In the New Testament, the spiritual side is expressed in the presentation of the spiritual Zion; see Hebrews 12:22, where we find the believing remnant or core of Israel (the true Israel, the "Israel of God," Gal. 6:16) at "Zion," that is, through grace in principle already brought to the rest of God (cf. Heb. 4:18), connected with Christ, the new Priest and the new King, the true Son of David, and with a new (heavenly) sanctuary, within the heavenly veil (10:19-22).

Thus, in the final days, there will be a new "Israel of God," as we found in Revelation 14:1-5 (see the quotation in

---

38. This has been emphasized in Reformed theology more than in most other theologies.
39. Notice that this was also the name of one of Isaiah's sons, as a witness to Israel (Isa. 7:3).

§13.3.2). They will have the character of those whom we find in the Psalms:

> Those who trust in the LORD are like Mount Zion,
>   which cannot be moved, but abides forever" (Ps. 125:1).

> When the LORD restored the fortunes of Zion,
>   we were like those who dream.
> Then our mouth was filled with laughter,
>   and our tongue with shouts of joy;
> then they said among the nations,
>   "The LORD has done great things for them."
> The LORD has done great things for us;
>   we are glad" (Ps. 126:1-3).

Thus, the literal Zion will form the center of the Messianic kingdom on earth, according to many promises of God.[40]

13.5 Blessing on Zion
13.5.1 Three Groups of Jews

In my view, we must clearly discern three groups of Jews:

(1) All Israelites who, since the Day of Pentecost (Acts 2) and *before* the second coming of Christ, have believed in Jesus as their Messiah, Redeemer, and Lord, belong to the Ecclesia, the body of Christ. At his coming, they will be taken up to heaven as glorified saints, together with all other risen and glorified believers (John 14:1-3; 1 Thess. 4:13-17).

(2) At the second coming of Christ, the wicked within Israel will be executed; they will have to wait until the end of the Messianic kingdom before they rise together with the wicked among the Gentiles and are judged before the great white throne (see above).

(3) Of special interest is a third group: these are righteous and pious Jews who still have the "veil" over their eyes (2 Cor. 3:14), so that they did not recognize Jesus as the Messiah;

---

40. See also Ps. 14:7; 50:2; 69:35; 87:2, 5; 102:13; 110:2; 133:3; 146:10; Isa. 2:2–4; 4:3–5; 10:24; 12:6; 18:7; 28:16; 29:8; 31:4–5; 33:5, 20; 35:10; 46:13; 49:14; 50:3, 11, 16; 52:1–2, 7–8; 59:20; 60:14; 61:1–3; 62:1, 11; Jer. 30:17; 31:6,12; Joel 2:15, 23; 3:21; Obad. 17, 21; Micah 4:7–8, 13; Zech. 2:7, 10; 8:2; 9:9.

however, they have sought God in sincerity, loved his Torah (Rom. 2:6-11), and have looked forward to the Messiah. At his coming, this "veil" will be removed (2 Cor. 3:16). Their eyes will be opened to Jesus the Messiah, such as happened to the brothers of Joseph (Gen. 45:1-15). With joy, they will enter the Messianic kingdom; their "eyes will behold the king in his beauty" (Isa. 33:17).

Notice where these three groups will be during the Messianic kingdom:

(a) *Heaven:* during the Messianic kingdom, the first group will be glorified with God in heaven, and experience the kingdom "from above," so to speak, as part of those who will reign over the universe with Christ in glory.

(b) *Hades:* the second group will be in *Hades* (Heb. *she'ol*, the realm of death, or of the dead), waiting to be condemned after their resurrection, and to be thrown in *Hell*, the lake of fire (Rev. 20).

(c) *Ha'Aretz:* the third group will dwell on earth, in their mortal bodies, in the Promised Land, as subjects of the great Messiah-King, who will be seated on the throne of David.

13.5.2 Return of the Dispersed to Zion

One of the first governmental acts of Christ will be to bring all the chosen of Israel who are still living among the Gentiles back to the land of Israel, and in particular to Mount Zion, where his grace and his glory will be established. Some Bible passages clearly speak of a being brought back to the Holy Land, a matter that involves all the twelve tribes of Israel:

> He will raise a signal for the nations
>   and will assemble the banished of Israel,
> and gather the dispersed of Judah
>   from the four corners of the earth (Isa. 11:12).In those days the house of Judah shall join the house of Israel, and together they shall come from the land of the north to the land that I gave your fathers for a heritage (Jer. 3:18).

For behold, days are coming, . . . when I will restore the fortunes of my people, Israel and Judah, . . . and I will bring them back to the land that I gave to their fathers, and they shall take possession of it" (Jer. 30:3).

I will strengthen the house of Judah,
    and I will save the house of Joseph.
I will bring them back because I have compassion on them,
    and they shall be as though I had not rejected them
    (Zech. 10:6).

As I live, surely with a mighty hand and an outstretched arm and with wrath poured out I [i.e., the LORD] will be king over you. I will bring you out from the peoples and gather you out of the countries where you are scattered, with a mighty hand and an outstretched arm, and with wrath poured out. And I will bring you into the wilderness of the peoples,[41] and there I will enter into judgment with you face to face. . . . I will make you pass under the [shepherd's] rod, and I will bring you into the bond of the covenant. I will purge out the rebels from among you, and those who transgress against me. I will bring them out of the land where they sojourn, but they shall not enter the land of Israel. . . .[42] For on my holy mountain, the mountain height of Israel, . . . there all the house of Israel, all of them, shall serve me in the land. There I will accept them, and there I will require your contributions and the choicest of your gifts, with all your sacred offerings. As a pleasing aroma[43] I will accept you, when I bring you out from the peoples and gather you out of the countries where you have been scattered. And I will manifest my holiness among you in the sight of the nations. . . . And there you shall remember your ways and all your deeds with which you have defiled yourselves, and you shall loathe yourselves for

---

41. Because of the addition "of the peoples," "wilderness" apparently has a figurative meaning here, just like "sea" (cf. Rev. 17:1–3, "waters" as well as "wilderness").
42. This is one of the phrases demonstrating that the passage applies far beyond the return from the Babylonian captivity.
43. Or "Because of the pleasing aroma," i.e., the aroma of the sacrifices, *or* of Israel itself as a sacrifice; cf. Isa. 66:20; Zeph. 3:10.

all the evils that you have committed" (Ezek. 20:33-43).

13.5.3 A Special Relationship

The special connection between the returned Jews and Mount Zion is describe in various passages:

> At that time tribute will be brought to the Lord of hosts from a people tall and smooth, from a people feared near and far, a nation mighty and conquering, whose land the rivers divide, to Mount Zion, the place of the name of the Lord of hosts (Isa. 18:7).[44]

> And the ransomed of the Lord shall return
>   and come to Zion with singing;
> everlasting joy shall be upon their heads;
>   they shall obtain gladness and joy,
>   and sorrow and sighing shall flee away (Isa. 35:10).

> He who scattered Israel will gather him,
>   and will keep him as a shepherd keeps his flock.
> For the Lord has ransomed Jacob
>   and has redeemed him from hands too strong for him.
> They shall come and sing aloud on the height of Zion,
>   and they shall be radiant over the goodness of the Lord,
> over the grain, the wine, and the oil,
>   and over the young of the flock and the herd;
> their life shall be like a watered garden,
>   and they shall languish no more (Jer. 31:10-12).

> In those days and in that time, . . . the people of Israel and the people of Judah shall come together, weeping as they come, and they shall seek the Lord their God. They shall ask the way to Zion, with faces turned toward it, saying, "Come, let us join ourselves to the Lord in an everlasting covenant that will never be forgotten" (Jer. 50:4-5).

A special prophetic phrase here is an expression found Jeremiah 30:3, namely, "restore the fortunes," (NKJV: "bring back from captivity," CJB: "reverse the exile"), that is, make the captives (exiles) return (Heb. *shub [et-]sh'but*; see vol.

---

44. See on this difficult chapter (Isa. 18), Vol. I, §10.7.2.

IV/1a, §5.6.1). The expression usually referred to ending the exile or oppression of the people of Israel, but sometimes it referred to the desolation of the land of Israel (Jer. 33:11; cf. 30:18). In many passages it referred to Israel.[45] As a prayer for Israel, it is related to the place where grace and redemption always come from: Zion: Oh, that salvation for Israel would come out of Zion! / When the LORD restores the fortunes [i.e., brings back the exiles] of his people, / let Jacob rejoice, let Israel be glad (Ps. 14:7; cf. 53:8).

In Psalm 126:1-4, quoted in §13.4.2, we clearly see the meanings of the expression *shub [et]-sh'but*. It involves the complete restoration of blessings in connection with Zion, but also bringing back the captives or exiles. Verses 1-3 speak of those who have already been brought back in connection with Zion: the redeemed remnant of Judah, exulting over its deliverance. But verse 4 speaks of those who must still return, in order to make the people of Israel complete again.

13.5.4 From Where Do the Dispersed Come?

The chosen from the twelve tribes of Israel will return from manyplaces on earth,. Some Bible passages say that they will come "from all nations"[46]—and not only they, but also the riches of these nations will come: "[Y]our heart shall thrill and exult, / because the abundance of the sea shall be turned to you, / the wealth of the nations shall come to you" (Isa. 60:5).[47] Here the "sea: is possibly a metaphor for the nations, mentioned in the following verses (vv. 6-9): Midian, Ephah, Sheba, Kedar, Nebaioth (these are parts of the Arabic world) and the "coastlands" of the Mediterranean.

The Bible mentions specifically Egypt (Heb. *Mitzrayyim*), Assyria (Heb. *Asshur*), and Ethiopia/Sudan (Heb. *Kush*).

Egypt: Just as happened in the old days during the exodus under Moses, "[T]hose who were driven out to the land of *Egypt* will come and worship the LORD on the holy moun-

---

45. Deut. 30:3; Ps. 85:1; Jer. 29:14; 31:23; 32:44; 33:7, 26; Ezek. 16:53; Hos. 6:11; Joel 3:1; Amos 9:14; Zeph. 2:7, 3:20; and prophetically in Job 42:10.
46. Isa. 66:20-21; cf. 11:12; 45:20; Ezek. 11:17; 20:34; 34:13; 36:24; 37:21; 38:8.
47. See also v. 11; 61:6; Isa. 17:12; Rev. 17:15.

tain at Jerusalem" (Isa. 27:13; italics added). They will be "recovered" from there, and the "tongue of the Sea of Egypt" (the Gulf of Suez or Aqaba?) will be "devoted to destruction" (11:11-15). "[A]ll the depths of the Nile shall be dried up" in order to let Israel pass (Zech. 10:10-11); "they shall come trembling like birds from Egypt" (Hos. 11:11).

Assyria: "[T]hose who were lost in the land of Assyria" will return (Isa. 27:13; 11:11, 16); the LORD will "gather them from Assyria" (Zech. 10:10-11); "like doves" they shall come from the land of Assyria (Hos. 11:11).

Ethiopia/Sudan: they will be brought back from the other sides of the rivers of *Kush* (Isa. 11:11); that can be both the Nile and the Euphrates.[48]

Further, the Israelites will return from the land of the Sinites (Heb. *sinim*, Isa. 49:12 ESV note). It has been claimed that this would be China.[49] However, the Dead Sea Scroll reads, "land of Syene" (ESV), and the NIV has "Aswan." In Latin, the Chinese are called *sinae*, and in Greek *sinai* (cf. sinology, Sinophile). The word "China" comes from *Qin* (pronounce: *Chin*). In Isaiah's time, Qin was one of the fourteen greater Chinese states; only in the third century BC did the Qin dynasty acquire hegemony over Middle China.[50]

Further, the Israelites will return from Pathros, Elam, Shinar, Hamath, and the coastlands of the sea, from the north, the west, the south and the east.[51] The ships from Tarshish will be the first to bring them back; Tarshish is a land that the rabbis identified as Tartessos in Spain.[52] The nations will bring the Israelites as a gift to the land of Israel. The chosen ones among them will be gathered together with the help of

---

48. See Isa. 11:15; 18:1–2, 7; 27:12; Zeph. 3:10; cf. Gen. 10:6–12.
49. Annotations to the Dutch States Translation; Gesenius (1829, ad loc.); Delitzsch (1975, ad loc.); Jamieson *et al.* (1934, ad loc.).
50. Regarding the hypothesis that the term "Sinim" referred to the Chinese, see extensively, Wang and Nelson (1998).
51. Isa. 11:11; 43:1–8; 49:12; Jer. 3:18; 23:8; 31:8; Hos. 11:11.
52. Others believe that the term "Tarshish" referred to Carthage (so the Septuagint), Rhodos (Julius Africanus), or a place on Sicily or Crete, or Sardinia, or in Great Britain, or in the Indian Ocean.

angels.⁵³

The Israelites will be threshed like grain from the river Euphrates to the Brook of Egypt. Only the chosen ones, those who have the seal of God on their foreheads, will arrive in the land, and dwell there in peace, safety and joy:⁵⁴ "In those days and in that time, . . . iniquity shall be sought in Israel, and there shall be none, and sin in Judah, and none shall be found, for I will pardon those whom I leave as a remnant" (Jer. 50:20). Please note that the word "chosen" that I just used applies to God's counsel. This must never be played off against human responsibility.⁵⁵ Therefore, with equal right we can say that only those who fear the LORD, the *tzaddiqim* ("righteous ones," cf. Isa. 45:25; 60:21), will be allowed to dwell in the land.

The faithful of the two tribes as well as of the ten tribes will be united unto one people of Israel: "In those days the house of Judah shall join the house of Israel, and together they shall come from the land of the north to the land that I gave your fathers for a heritage" (Jer. 3:18).

"Israel and Judah will unite and choose one leader. Then they will take back their land" (Hos. 1:11 CJB). This reunion is extensively described in Ezekiel 37:15-28: the Israelites from all twelve tribes will be gathered together in the land of Israel from all the nations, and there they will be made one people, never to be separated again. One King will rule over them, one from the house of David—this King is himself called "David" here—and God will make with them a covenant of peace. This does not necessarily mean that today the ten tribes are still hidden somewhere, as some have supposed. We may assume that, among the millions of Jews in New York alone, all twelve tribes of Israel are represented.⁵⁶

---

53. Isa. 14:1–2; 43:1–8; 49:8–12, 22; 60:9; Zeph. 3:10; Matt. 24:31; Mark 13:27.
54. Isa. 27:12–13; 35:3–10; Jer. 23:6; 31:1–14; Ezek. 28:25–26; 34:11–19; Matt. 24:31; Rev. 7:3–8.
55. See extensively, Ouweneel (2008).
56. To be sure, the word "Jew" comes from "Judean," but it has become the equivalent of "Israelite." In the ESV, Heb. *y'hudi* is rendered as "Judean" before the exile, and as "Jew" after the destruction of Jerusalem (586 BC); here it has al

13.6 The Restoration of Israel
13.6.1 Once More: Jacob and Esau

Some supersessionists try to discredit the literal interpretation of Zechariah 12 and 14 by emphasizing that these chapters spoke only of riders and horses, whereas modern armies use the most modern arms. First, we notice that, even if the eschatological armies use tanks and missiles, it is difficult to imagine that, and how, Zechariah would have mentioned them in his description.[57] However, there might be a more profound reason. In Zechariah 1 and 6, we find horses and riders, but there they turn out to be symbolic references to angelic powers.[58] Why could this not be the case in Zechariah 12:4 as well (not in 14:20): "'On that day,' declares the LORD, 'I will strike every horse with panic, and its rider with madness. But for the sake of the house of Judah I will keep my eyes open, when I strike every horse of the peoples with blindness.'" Is God concerned only with earthly nations and rulers? Is he not rather concerned with the spiritual powers behind them, described in figurative language? Take the rabbinic interpretation of Exodus 15:1: "I will sing to the LORD, for he has triumphed gloriously; / the horse and his rider he has thrown into the sea." The rabbis relate this horse and rider (singular!) not to Pharaoh, but to the angelic prince of Egypt.[59] Why could Zechariah 12:4 not primarily have been referring to the "horses and riders" of the *spiritual* powers being struck with madness and blindness? The most important opponent of Jacob is the angelic prince of Esau (see vol. IV/1a, chapter 2), as Balaam already prophesied.[60] One day, "a star shall come out of Jacob,

---

ready basically acquired the meaning of "Israelite."

57. Some have suggested that certain passages in Revelation (e.g., Rev. 9) do describe modern arms in language that was available to them; but here we have the opposite problem, namely, how could we be sure of this?
58. Ouweneel (2003, chapter 10); such powers are also meant in Rev. 9 (see previous note); see especially v. 11 there.
59. Mechilta Exod. 15:1 (43b).
60. Balaam has been called a false prophet, and false he was; but interestingly, the only prophecies from him that we know are divine and true.

and a scepter shall rise out of Israel" (Num. 24:17a). This obviously refers to the Messiah and the Messianic kingdom.

> [This scepter] shall crush the forehead of Moab
> and break down all the sons of Sheth.
> Edom shall be dispossessed;
> Seir also, his enemies, shall be dispossessed.
> Israel is doing valiantly.
> And one from Jacob [i.e., the Messiah] shall exercise dominion and destroy the survivors of cities! (Num. 24:17b-19).

According to a Jewish tradition, the "Edomite" (read, Western Christian) empire fights with "Jacob" (Israel) "until dawn," that is, until the end of Israel's exile, which ends with the arrival of Messiah's kingdom.[61]

I have argued elsewhere (vol. IV/1a, chapter 2) that Jacob/Israel has never given up Esau/Edom. It has never abandoned Western civilization, especially Europe and North America; on the contrary, it occupies crucial positions in that culture and society. It holds Esau tight, and will not let loose "until dawn," no matter how hard a blow it has received from Esau (Gen. 32:24-26). It does this not to destroy Esau/Edom, but rather in order that Esau/Edom will acknowledge Israel's birthright, and will convert to the God of Israel. "Salvation is from the Jews" (John 4:22). However, for the angelic prince of Rome—"the rider on his horse"[62]—there is no hope: his end is the lake of fire and sulfur (Rev. 20:10). For Western civilization as such there is no hope either: the (earthly) beast undergoes the same destiny as the (demonic) dragon who seduced him. However, the blessing that the angel gave to Jacob implies that, within Western culture, there are many who, in the last days, will acknowledge Israel as God's people, and acknowledge God as the God of Israel: "In those days ten men from the nations of every tongue shall take hold of the robe of a Jew, saying, 'Let us go with you, for we have heard that God is with you'" (Zech. 8:23).

---

61. Tanchuma wayyishlach 40b.
62. Cf. Rev. 6:1–2, and the contrast with that other rider on a white horse, Christ himself (19:11).

13.6.2 Judgment and Peace for Edom

When the angelic prince of Edom/Rome (the Western world) is judged, there will be condemnation for all "Edomites" who have continued to resist Israel and the God of Israel. And there will be peace for all "Edomites" who have put their confidence in the God of Jacob and his Anointed One. Both in the Bible and in rabbinic tradition, the restoration ((Heb. *tiqqun*) of Israel is linked with both the fall of the angelic prince of Edom/Rome and with the coming of the Messiah and the establishment of his kingdom, in which restored Israel will occupy the central position: "God will begin with expelling the angelic prince of the great city from his [celestial] dwelling place."[63] This "great city" is "Babylon," that is, Rome (cf. Rev. 16:19), *or* it is the "heavenly city." The Messiah will destroy Edom/Rome, and after this, will "have dominion from sea to sea" (Ps. 72:8, presumably from the Mediterranean to the Red Sea, Exod. 23:31); thus, wicked Edom will continue its rule until the Messiah comes.[64]

The glory of God will return to his temple at Jerusalem, as extensively described in Ezekiel 40-48, after he has repaid wicked Edom for all its evil deeds[65] (see the details Isa. 34:1-17 and 63:1-14). The Messiah will come when "Rome" falls in the thorns, which means: is torn apart.[66] Edom will fall by the hand of him who has been anointed for war, the descendant of Joseph.[67]

According to an ancient tradition, Messiah ben Joseph is the great warrior of the last days, and the forerunner of the actual Messiah: Messiah ben David. Thus, also in Jewish tradition, the insight lives on that one day, the Messiah will defeat the angelic prince of Edom/Rome, who will destroy the hostile powers, who will restore Israel to its land, who will restore the temple in which again the glory of the LORD will dwell, and who will establish his blessed dominion of peace

---

63. Pesikta R. 14, 15.
64. Pesikta R. 13, 2 (on Num. 24:18–19).
65. Pesikta K. Suppl. 5,3.
66. Song of Solomon Rabbah 2:17 (§1) (rabbi Levi).
67. Genesis Rabbah 99, 2.

and justice from sea to sea.

Seven world powers have consecutively oppressed Israel, as explained in Revelation 17:9-11:[68]

> [T]he seven heads [of the beast] are... seven kings [read, kingdoms], five of whom have fallen, one is [i.e., in John's days: the Roman Empire], the other has not yet come, and when he does come he must remain only a little while. As for the beast that was and is not, it is an eighth but it belongs to the seven [i.e., the revived Roman Empire of the end time, a revival of an earlier kingdom], and it goes to destruction.

That is, first there was the Egyptian kingdom, then the Assyrian, the Babylonian, the Medo-Persian, the Greek-Macedonian (with its successor kingdoms; see Dan. 11), and the Roman Empire (including the Western world power of the last days). The Pharaoh of Egypt committed the first holocaust by enslaving the people and massively murdering their sons (Exod. 1). Adolf Hitler committed the seventh oppression, the last and most horrible holocaust that Israel has experienced so far. And still the end has not come. There is still an eighth kingdom that must come, the revival of the empire of Edom/Rome. This is the empire of the Antichrist, that is, of the dragon and the beast (Rev. 12-13). This empire will again seek to exterminate the Jews. Once more, Edom will try to smash Jacob. Elsewhere, I have argued how, in this eighth kingdom, the traits of ancient Egypt become visible, how Assyria seems to revive, how characteristics of each of the four great world empires (Dan. 2 and 7) become visible in it, and how the beast will look like a new and greater Napoleon Bonaparte and Adolf Hitler.[69] But then the end will come. Then the ninth and last King will arrive; there will be no tenth. One day, Jacob's distress will be over.

---

68. For details, see Ouweneel (1990, ad loc.).
69. Ouweneel (2003, chapters 3–9).

13.7 The King and His Bride
13.7.1 A Heavenly and an Earthly Bride

Finally, there is rest, harmony, peace! Finally, the blessing arrives for which Jerusalem has waited so long. Finally, Messiah will reign on Zion, in perfect, undisturbed rest, in the midst of his beloved people. Will this not be the time when the inhabitants of Jerusalem will sing Psalm 45? There, we find first and foremost the glory of the King, but also that of Jerusalem, his earthly bride:

> [D]aughters of kings are among your ladies of honor;
>> at your right hand stands the queen in gold of Ophir.
> Hear, O daughter, and consider, and incline your ear:
>> forget your people and your father's house,
> and the king will desire your beauty.
> Since he is your lord, bow to him, ...
> All glorious is the princess in her chamber, with robes interwoven with gold.
> In many-colored robes she is led to the king,
>> with her virgin companions following behind her
>
> (vv. 9–14).[70]

With Eastern imagery, the glory of the Messiah is described, along with that of his (earthly) bride. Who is this bride? Does she come with various claims concerning her royal rights? Is she entitled to them because to her belong the "fathers" (cf. Rom. 9:5)? No. Her great guilt has robbed her of all her rights (Ezek. 16), and she can claim no more royal dignity than any other city could ever do: "[F]orget your people and your father's house" (v. 10b). She is accepted purely on the basis of sovereign grace, not on that of rights or promises. The King will desire her if she renounces all her rights, and acknowledges him as her Lord (Master). This election rests

---

70. Some believe that a princess from Tyre is here the bride (v. 12 ESV note: "The daughter of Tyre"), and render the text in this way; with many expositors, I believe this to be incorrect: cf. ESV: "The people of Tyre will seek your favor with gifts, the richest of the people."

on mercy (see the important teaching of Romans 9:1-29).[71] Jerusalem will be elevated above all cities on earth, including the other cities of Judah (Ps. 45:14).

The heavenly Jerusalem is the bride of the Lamb (Rev. 21:9-10), but the earthly Jerusalem is the bride of the King.[72] That is, the Ecclesia and restored Israel are redeemed companies that each have their own unique relationship with Christ. But we always remember that they have the most important relationship *in common*: they are both companies redeemed by the atoning work of Christ, and have been graciously accepted by his love and mercy. Grace is one of the great characteristics of the great King: ". . . grace is poured upon your lips" (Ps. 45:2). Compare the event in the synagogue of Capernaum: "[T]hey all were speaking well of Him, and were in awe and were wondering about the words of grace which were coming from His lips" (Luke 4:22 AMP; cf. Col. 4:6a).

13.7.2 The Wedding

Jesus Christ, the Son of God, is seated forever at God's right hand in heaven, as well as seated as the Messiah, the Son of David, on the throne of David (Ps. 45:6; cf. Isa. 9:7; Luke 1:32). As the true David, he will return to earth to go out into battle; his right hand will teach his awesome deeds, and peoples will fall before him (Ps. 45:3-4). After this, he will be enthroned as the true Solomon in uprightness (v. 6). Jesus Christ is the only Man who has ever perfectly and truly loved righteousness and hated wickedness. Therefore, his God has anointed him with the oil of gladness beyond your companions; that is the "Israel of God," associated with him (v. 7).

From the outset, the relationship between God and Israel has been that of husband and wife:[73]

> I remember the devotion of your youth,
>   your love as a bride,

---

71. See Ouweneel (2008, 240–41, and throughout).
72. Regarding this idea of two brides of Christ, an earthly and a heavenly bride, see Ouweneel (2007, 258).
73. See the extensive Epilogue in Ouweneel (1973).

how you followed me in the wilderness,
  in a land not sown (Jer. 2:2).

This was during the time after Israel's stay at Mount Sinai, where the marriage was officiated between God and Israel, complete with all the elements typical of a Jewish wedding:

(a) the *mikveh*, that is, the preparatory purification of the bride (Exod. 19:10–14; in the end time: Ezek. 36:25–27);

(b) the *chuppah*, that is, the "covering" under which the wedding takes place: the "thick cloud" over the mountain (vv. 16–17); since 40:34–35 it is the *Shekhinah* (end time: Ezek. 43:4–5);

(c) the *shadchen*, that is, the matchmaker (Moses, the marriage broker; also: the best man or groomsman) (in the end time, we may think of the eschatological "Elijah," Mal. 4:5–6, the more so because of the link between Elijah and John the Baptist, who presented himself as Messiah's "best man" in John 3:29);

(d) the *k'tubah*, that is, the wedding contract; in this case (and in the end time): the Torah (Exod. 20:1–17);

(e) the *Shabbat*, that is the "sign" of the matrimonial covenant (the engagement ring, as it were? Exod. 20:8–11; 31:16–17; end time: cf. Isa. 56:2–6).[74]

Centuries later, God said to Jerusalem about this period:

> When I passed by you again and saw you, behold, you were at the age for love, and I spread the corner of my garment over you and covered your nakedness; I made my vow to you and entered into a covenant with you, . . . and you became mine. Then I bathed you with water and washed off your blood from you and anointed you with oil. I clothed you also with embroidered cloth and shod you with fine leather. I wrapped you in fine linen and covered you with silk. And I adorned you with ornaments and put bracelets on your wrists and a chain on your neck. And I put a ring on your nose and earrings in your ears and a beautiful crown on your head. Thus you were adorned with gold and silver, and your clothing was of fine linen and

---

74. See, e.g., https://professorjt2012.wordpress.com/2013/10/03/wedding-vows/.

silk and embroidered cloth. You ate fine flour and honey and oil. You grew exceedingly beautiful and advanced to royalty. And your renown went forth among the nations because of your beauty, for it was perfect through the splendor that I had bestowed on you (Ezek. 16:8–14).

13.7.3 The Divorce

In each relationship, including every covenant between God and humans, there is a conditional element: "Now therefore, *if* you will indeed obey my voice and keep my covenant, you shall be my treasured possession among all peoples" (Exod. 19:5). The phrase "treasured possession" is one Hebrew word: *s'gullah*; it is a precious, highly esteemed possession, as a beloved wife is for her husband: a "darling." The word appears here for the first time, but later it is used more often for Israel.[75] Perhaps in no passage is its meaning expressed more beautifully than in Isaiah 43:4: "Because you are precious in my eyes, and honored, and I love you . . . ."

In a relationship that is so precious and affectionate, its rupture is all the more tragic. The greater the original love, the more horrendous is the infidelity, the adultery. Or also, the greater the love of the one partner, the greater is his/her pain over the infidelity of the other partner. The prophets point out that Israel, or Jerusalem, has become yoked with idols; this is spiritual prostitution:

> Plead with your mother,[76] plead—
>   for she is not my wife [anymore],
>   and I am not her husband [anymore]—
> that she put away her whoring[77] from her face,
>   and her adultery from between her breasts;
> lest I strip her naked
>   and make her as in the day she was born,
> and make her like a wilderness,
>   and make her like a parched land,

---

75. Deut. 7:6; 14:2; 26:18; Ps. 135:4; and for the future: Mal. 3:17; cf. the application to the Ecclesia: Titus 2:14; 1 Pet. 2:9.
76. The "mother" is Israel; the "your" refers to the individual Israelites.
77. Normally, the Heb. and Gk. words used are better rendered as "sexual immorality," but here, (spiritual) prostitution is clearly included.

and kill her with thirst.
Upon her children also I will have no mercy,
   because they are children of whoredom.
For their mother has played the whore;
   she who conceived them has acted shamefully.
For she said, "I will go after my lovers,
   who give me my bread and my water,
      my wool and my flax, my oil and my drink" (Hos. 2:2–5).

Therefore, God has sent away his people, just like a husband sends away his unfaithful wife with a certificate of divorce (in the sense of Deut. 24:1, 3):

If a man divorces his wife
   and she goes from him
and becomes another man's wife,
   will he return to her?
Would not that land be greatly polluted?
You have played the whore with many lovers;
   and would you return to me? . . .

. . . Have you seen what she did, that faithless one, Israel [i.e., the ten tribes], how she went up on every high hill and under every green tree, and there played the whore? And I thought, 'After she has done all this she will return to me,' but she did not return, and her treacherous sister Judah [i.e., the two tribes] saw it. She saw that for all the adulteries of that faithless one, Israel, I had sent her away with a *decree of divorce*. Yet her treacherous sister Judah did not fear, but she too went and played the whore. Because she took her whoredom lightly, she polluted the land, committing adultery with stone and tree. Yet for all this her treacherous sister Judah did not return to me with her whole heart, but [only] in pretense" (Jer. 3:1, 6–10; cf. Ezek. 23).

Malachi 2:16 told us that the Lord hates it when a husband puts away his wife. All the more remarkable, then, that the passage just quoted tells us that God has nevertheless sent his wife away with the "decree (certificate) of divorce." However, first, we notice that this can be explained only on the basis of Israel's "adulterous behavior," which was really outrageous. Second, that God hates certificates of divorce *must* imply that this "putting away" of God's own "wife" could never have been a permanent thing; one day, Israel will be accepted again (see next section). The *same* wife (the twelve tribes of Israel) will be graciously restored to her former position, and not, as supersessionism teaches, viz., that wife A (Israel) is put away, and wife B (the New Testament Ecclesia) is accepted in her place. Israel, even the true, spiritual Israel, is not the same as the Ecclesia, we must repeat. The "Israel of God" is *Jewish*, and is not a company of 99% Gentiles that has set aside *all* aspects of the Jewish identity. The Ecclesia is not Jewish and will never become Jewish (see vol. IV/1a, chapters 9–12). Therefore, it is unfair, if not outright absurd, to claim that the prophecies about disowning would refer to (ethnic) Israel, and the prophecies about re-acceptance would refer to the Ecclesia.

13.7.4 Re-Accepted

In the last days, Israel is restored, and then, so to speak, the certificate of divorce will be withdrawn:

> Where is your mother's certificate of divorce,
>   with which I sent her away?
> Or which of my creditors is it
>   to whom I have sold you?
> Behold, for your iniquities you were sold,
>   and for your transgressions your mother was sent away
>   (Isa. 50:1).

And later in the same book:

> Fear not, for you will not be ashamed;
>   be not confounded, for you will not be disgraced;
> for you will forget the shame of your youth,
>   and the reproach of your widowhood you will remember
> no more.[78]
> For your Maker is your husband,
>   the LORD of hosts is his name;
> and the Holy One of Israel is your Redeemer,

---

78. The text mixes two images: that of the widow and that of the divorced wife; in both cases, the wife has been "abandoned" by her husband.

> the God of the whole earth he is called.
> For the Lord has called you
>   like a wife deserted and grieved in spirit,
> like a wife of youth when she is cast off. . .
> For a brief moment I deserted you,
>   but with great compassion I will gather you.
> In overflowing anger for a moment
>   I hid my face from you,
> but with everlasting love I will have compassion on you (Isa. 54:4–8).

And as we read in Hosea,

> Therefore, behold, I will allure her,
>   and bring her into the wilderness,
>   and speak tenderly to her.
> And there I will give her her vineyards
>   and make the Valley of Trouble[79] a door of hope.
> And there she shall answer as in the days of her youth,
>   as at the time when she came out of the land of Egypt
>   [cf. Jer. 2:2].

And in that day, . . . you will call me "My Husband," and no longer will you call me "My Baal."[80] For I will remove the names of the Baals from her mouth, and they shall be remembered by name no more. And I will make for them a covenant on that day with the beasts of the field, the birds of the heavens, and the creeping things of the ground. And I will abolish the bow, the sword, and war from the land, and I will make you lie down in safety. And I will betroth you to me forever. I will betroth you to me in righteousness and in justice, in steadfast love and in mercy. I will betroth you to me in faithfulness. And you shall know the Lord (Hos. 2:14–20).

---

79. Or Achor; according to Eusebius and Jerome, as well as more recent investigators, this is a valley near Jericho; cf. Josh. 15:7; Isa. 65:10.
80. The word "Baal" (Heb. *baʻal*, "master") is an ambiguous term, for here it refers to the name of an idol (v. 17), but in Isa. 54:5 just quoted, *baʻal* is the word for "husband."

The prophet declared:

> For Zion's sake I will not keep silent,
>   and for Jerusalem's sake I will not be quiet,
> until her righteousness goes forth as brightness,
>   and her salvation as a burning torch.
> The nations shall see your righteousness,
>   and all the kings your glory,
> and you shall be called by a new name
>   that the mouth of the LORD will give.
> You shall be a crown of beauty in the hand of the Lord,
>   and a royal diadem in the hand of your God.
> You shall no more be termed Forsaken [Heb. *Azubah*],
>   and your land shall no more be termed Desolate [Heb. *Sh'mamah*],
> but you shall be called My Delight Is in Her [Heb. *Hephzibah*[81]],
>   and your land Married [Heb. *B'ulah*],
> for the LORD delights in you,
>   and your land shall be married.
> For as a young man marries a young woman,
>   so shall your sons marry you,[82]
> and as the bridegroom rejoices over the bride,
>   so shall your God rejoice over you (Isa. 62:1–5).

13.8 The Dominion of Christ

13.8.1 The King

Before discussing the Messianic kingdom further, let us first direct our attention to the King himself. In what an abundant and exhilarating way do the prophets speak of him, when they are beholding the glory that he will possess during the Messianic kingdom: "Your eyes will behold the king in his beauty" (Isa. 33:17). He who, as a Man, is the Son of David, the "root of Jesse"[83] (Isa. 11:1, 10; cf. Rev. 5:5; 22:16), is, accord-

---

81 Heb. *chephtzi-bah*; this (Hephziba) was also the name of King Hezekiah's wife (2 Kings 21:1).

82 Here we encounter a remarkable change of metaphors: God (re)marries Zion, but her children do the same, as it were. No biblical metaphor is more flexible than the bride metaphor (cf. note 77).

83 The traditional rendering "root" is misleading: A is the root (origin) of B,

The Messianic Kingdom of Israel

ing to his divine nature, the LORD of hosts (Zech. 14:5, 9, 17).

Each of these titles gives us food for thought because each of them shows us new aspects of the glory of Messiah.

(a) He is the promised *Branch* (Sprout, Shoot),[84] that is, the One who has sprouted from the house of David, the Son of David, sometimes himself referred to as "David."[85] King David was one of the greatest types in the Tanakh of the Messiah, and the Messiah was and is his greatest "Sprout."

(b) As David's great Son but also as God the Son, the Messiah is *King, Lawgiver,* and *Judge*: "For the LORD is our judge; the LORD is our lawgiver; / the LORD is our king; he will save us" (Isa. 33:22). As Judge, he is not just the Judge of Israel, but of all the living and all the dead (Acts 10:42; 17:31; 2 Tim. 4:1). He is *Priest-King* on his throne (Zech. 6:13), a picture that was already typologically presented in the person of Melchizedek (Gen. 14:18; cf. Heb. 7).

(c) We are moved especially by Messiah's love for, and loveliness with regard to, his people: he is their "everlasting rock" (Isa. 26:4; cf. 28:16; Zech. 3:9; 4:7) and their "everlasting light" (Isa. 60:19; cf. v. 1; Zech. 2:5), he who will be the *Shepherd* of his people: "I will set up over them one shepherd, my servant David, and he shall feed them: he shall feed them and be their shepherd" (Ezek. 34:23; cf. Isa. 40:11; Micah 5:4; Ps23:1). He will also be their *Keeper* (Isa. 27:3; 32:2; Jer.31:10).

(d) Secondarily, there is also Messiah's relationship to *all* nations worldwide: ". . . a light for the nations, / that my salvation may reach to the end of the earth" (Isa. 49:6b). Revelation 15:3 speaks of the *King of the nations*.[86]

---

but B is a shoot from A; the latter is applicable here.
84. Ps. 132:17; Zech. 3:8–10; 6:12; Isa. 4:2; 11:1; 42:1; 53:2; Jer. 23:5; 33:15.
85. Ps. 89:3–4; 132:11–18; Isa. 55:3; Jer. 23:5; 30:9, 21; 33:15–26; Ezek. 34:23–24; 37:24–25; Hos. 3:5; Amos 9:11; Luke 1:32–33.
86. Other manuscripts: "King of the ages (or, worlds)"; for the strange expression "King of the saints" (KJV), the manuscript testimony is very meagre.

13.8.2 Four Aspects

Here is a survey of the dominion that Christ will exercise as the true Solomon (cf. again Matt. 12:42), a rule extending into four concentric circles, so to speak.[87]

(1) *Inner circle:* he is *King over* (or *on*) *Zion*. This is important, for Zion is, spiritually speaking, the foundation of grace, both for Israel and for the nations. God himself said through the Spirit in his Word: "I have set my King on Zion, my holy hill" (Ps. 2:6). But even though his kingship rests on Zion, his power will extend to the ends of the earth (v. 8; see point 3 below). The prophets often speak of Zion as the foundation of Messiah's kingship.[88] And united with him, the remnant of Israel will also stand on that mountain of grace, accepted by him through this same grace (Rev. 14:1–5).

(2) *Second circle:* from Zion, Christ will *reign over Israel*. He will be the "sprig" that will be planted "on a high and lofty mountain," and will "bear branches and produce fruit and become a noble cedar" (Ezek. 17:22-23). Of the four Gospel writers, especially Matthew views him as the King of Israel (cf. points 3 and 4 below).[89] This will not be the land of Israel as it was before; rather, this will be larger than it was even during the reign of King Solomon. Then, it will have its actual boundaries as predicted:[90] Christ will rule over his people from the Brook of Egypt (Wadi al-Arish) to the River Euphrates. Here again, Solomon was a type of the Messiah.[91]

Only then will Israel really be the navel of the earth, when Christ rules over the world from the center of the world, that is, the intersection of Asia, Africa, and Europe: Israel.[92] Then, Jerusalem will shine throughout the earth as queen of all the cities, no matter how much larger London, New York, Lagos,

---

87. See Ouweneel (2007, chapter 5) for the personal titles of Jesus, e.g., Branch/Sprout, that are linked with the Messianic kingdom.
88. Isa. 24:23; 25:10; Obad. 21; Micah 4:7; Zeph. 3:15–17; Zech. 2:5–11; 9:9; Ps. 48:1–2; 99:2; 132:11–18; 146:10; 149:2.
89. Matt. 1:6, 21–23; 2:2, 6; 3:2; 4:17, 23; 5:3, 10, 19–20.
90. Gen. 15:18; Exod. 23:31; Micah 7:12; Zech. 9:10.
91. 1 Kings 4:21; 2 Chron. 9:26; Ps. 72:8.
92. Deut. 32:8–9; Isa. 19:24; Ezek. 38:12; cf. 5:5; Ps. 74:10–11; Isa. 10:23.

and Tokyo may be. The other cities of Judah (cf. Josh. 15:20–62) will be "her virgin companions following behind her" (Ps. 45:10, 14).

Apparently, there will be a (Davidic) "viceroy," called "the prince," who on behalf of the Messiah will rule over Israel.[93] The fact that this prince cannot be Messiah himself is evident from, among other things, the facts that this prince brings sin offerings also for himself, and that he has sons (Ezek. 45:22; 46:16–18).

(3) *Third circle:* Christ will not be King over Israel alone; he will also be the *ensign* [or, *banner*] *for the peoples* and the *light for the nations.*[94] He will reign over the ends of the earth, and be King over all the nations.[95] Compare here what was prophetically said of Solomon as type of the Messiah:

> He shall have dominion also from [the Mediterranean?] sea to [the Red?] sea,
> and from the River to the ends of the earth. . . .
> Yes, all kings shall fall down before Him;
> all nations shall serve Him" (Ps. 72:8, 11 NKJV).

He will judge the nations in righteousness and justice.[96] He is not only the "King of the Jews" (Matt. 27:37), he is also the Son of Man, whom "all peoples, nations, and languages shall serve" (Dan. 7:13–14). As such, Luke views him as the last Adam, the true Son of Man, who reveals to all humanity the grace and mercy of God. But he also views him as the One who will come in his kingdom and fill all people with fear.[97]

(4) *Outer circle:* when we speak of his title "Son of Man," we must think beyond the earth, for Psalm 8 relates this title to the entire universe. In Matthew 28:18, Jesus says, "All authority in heaven and on earth has been given to me." We

---

93. Ezek. 44:3; 45:9–46:24; cf. Jer. 30:21.
94. Isa. 11:10; 42:6; 49:6–7; 51:4; 55:4; Zech. 9:10.
95. Isa. 54:5; Jer. 10:7; Zech. 14:9; Ps. 2:8; Rev. 15:3.
96. Isa. 11:3–5; 32:1–2; 51:4–8; 60:17; Jer. 23:6; 33:15–16; Micah 4:3; Ps. 72:1–7, 12–17; 85:8–13; 96:10–13; 99:4; 101:6–8.
97. Luke 3:38; 4:22; 21:25–27; 23:4, 14, 42, 47.

see him here as the King addressing the remnant of Israel, represented by the eleven disciples, at the place of contempt (Galilee). At this very place, he appears to his own, gives them their royal commission, and promises to them his unshakable nearness until the end of the present age. What we find here goes further than point 3 above, for not only does the earth stand under his dominion but so do the heavens; he will reign over all creation, including the invisible creation: the world of the angels (Heb. 1:6; quotation from Ps. 97:7 LXX). God has made "known to us the mystery of his will, according to his purpose, which he set forth in Christ as a plan for the fullness of time, to unite all things in him, things in heaven and things on earth" (Eph. 1:9–10). The Son has been made "heir of *all* things" (Heb. 1:2), and those belonging to the Ecclesia have been made co-heirs, and will reign with Christ over "*all* things."[98] Christ has been given to the Ecclesia as "head over all things" (Eph. 1:22), which means that she herself does *not* belong to "all things" over which he will reign. She will be like Eve, who did not belong to the things over which Adam ruled; rather she ruled *with* him over all things (Gen. 1:26–28). Similarly, the Ecclesia will rule with Christ over the entire cosmos.[99] The (entire) creation "waits with eager longing for the revealing of the sons of God."[100]

13.8.3 The Basis: Christ's Redemptive Work

It is on the basis of his finished work on the cross that, one day, Jesus Christ will reign in glory. Sure, through him God has created all things, and as such, the Son is entitled to all creation and to dominion over it. This is because all things were created not only *in* (the power of) him, and *through* him, but also *for* him, that is, in his honor, with him as their goal.[101] However, Christ will not reign over creation as such, but over

---

98. Eph. 1:11; Rom. 8:17; 2 Tim. 2:12; Rev. 20:4, 6.
99. John 17:14, 16; 2 Cor. 5:17; Gal. 6:15.
100. Rom. 8:19–22; cf. Col. 3:4; 1 John 3:2.
101. John 1:3; Col. 1:16–17; Heb. 1:2, 10–12; Rev. 3:14.

a *cleansed* creation, where righteousness will reign.[102] Actually, this will not yet be the complete cleansing, for that will occur only when the new heavens and the new earth arrive. The cleansing begins with Christ's judgment over all the enemies of God and of God's people, and will be completed only when death will have been destroyed (1 Cor. 15:24-28).

This cleansing will not be carried out simply through a divine word of power. Indeed, God did call the worlds into existence simply by the power of his word.[103] But God's being makes it impossible for him to cleanse creation, groaning under the consequences of sin, merely by his word. Given God's own holiness and righteousness, he is obliged—if I may reverently use this word—to bring sin under judgment.[104] This is the "cannot" of God's moral being: he "cannot" lie (Titus 1:2 NKJV; Heb. 6:18), and similarly he "cannot" remove sin from creation without judging it. To this end, the Lamb was "foreknown before the foundation of the world" (1 Pet. 1:20), in order to "take away the sin[105] of the world" (John 1:29).

God made this judgment descend upon Christ, who was the only pure and sinless Man: "For in him all the fullness [of God] was pleased to dwell,[106] and through him to reconcile to himself all things, whether on earth or in heaven, making peace by the blood of his cross" (Col. 1:19-20). Creation has been estranged from God through unrighteousness. It is only through the blood of Christ, who was the perfect pleasure of the full Godhead (cf. 2:9), that creation can be, and will be, reconciled with God. Please notice:

---

102. Rom. 8:20–21; Isa. 32:1, 15–17; 65:17; 66:22.
103. Gen. 1:3, 6 etc.; Rom. 4:17; Heb. 1:3; 11:3; Ps. 33:9.
104. See extensively, Ouweneel (2009).
105. Singular! "Sin" as a power; not, as in the Roman Catholic mass, *qui tollis peccata* [sins] *mundi*, as if Christ has atoned all sins of all humanity; therefore, in my view we should not translate in 1 John 2:2, "for the sins of the whole world" (ESV), but "for the whole world" (NKJV); see Ouweneel (2009, §12.1.2).
106. *Not* "For it pleased the Father that in him should all fulness dwell" (KJV). The point here is not the eternal Father-Son relationship, but the relationship between the Triune (!) God and the Man Jesus Christ; see Ouweneel (2007, 290–91).

all things—not necessarily all humans. Compare the threatening "But" in Revelation 21:

> And he who was seated on the throne said, "Behold, I am making *all things* new." ... To the thirsty I will give from the spring of the water of life without payment.... ***But*** as for the cowardly, the faithless, the detestable, as for murderers, the sexually immoral, sorcerers, idolaters, and all liars, their portion will be in the lake that burns with fire and sulfur, which is the second death (vv. 5–8; emphasis added).[107]

Christ's *sufferings* involve the sufferings that he has endured *for* all who believe in him—in this, he is unique—as well as the sufferings (for the testimony of God) that believers share *with* him. In the latter, there is a strict order: first the sufferings, then the glory: "[H]eirs of God and fellow heirs with Christ, provided we *suffer* with him in order that we may also be *glorified* with him" (Rom. 8:17). "[I]f we *endure*, we will also *reign* with him" (2 Tim. 2:12). "[R]ejoice insofar as you share Christ's *sufferings*, that you may also rejoice and be glad when his *glory* is revealed" (1 Pet. 4:13). This is true for the Jesus-believers of our day, but was true throughout the history of Israel as well: "In all their affliction he was afflicted, / and the angel of his presence saved them; / in his love and in his pity he redeemed them" (Isa. 63:9)."[I]t is a time of distress for Jacob; / yet he shall be saved out of it" (Jer. 30:7). "[T]here shall be a time of trouble, such as never has been since there was a nation till that time. But at that time your people shall be delivered, everyone whose name shall be found written in the book" (Dan. 12:1).[108]

---

107. See Ouweneel (2012a, §§14.3 and 14.4).
108. The latter two passages seem to refer especially to the so-called Great Tribulation (Matt. 24:21; Rev. 7:14); see Ouweneel (2012a, §10.1).

Chapter 14
Tiqqun: Restoration of People, City, and Temple

> .... *Therefore, repent and turn to God, so that your sins may be erased; so that times of refreshing may come from the Lord's presence; and he may send the Messiah appointed in advance for you, that is, Yeshua. He has to remain in heaven until the time comes for restoring everything, as God said long ago, when he spoke through the holy prophets. For Moshe himself said,* **"Adonai will raise up for you a prophet like me from among your brothers. You are to listen to everything he tells you. Everyone who fails to listen to that prophet will be removed from the people and destroyed."** *[Deut. 18:15-16] Indeed, all the prophets announced these days, starting with Sh'mu'el and continuing through all who followed.*
>
> Acts 3:19–24 CJB (emphasis added)

14.1 Restoration of City and Temple
14.1.1 Rebuilding

WHEN WE THINK OF THE blessings of Christ's earthly bride, Jerusalem, one of the things that comes to mind is what exactly will happen to the city once the Messiah will have established the perfect peace. Jerusalem will be rebuilt, together with all the other cities of Judah: "God will save Zion / and build up the cities of Judah" (Ps. 69:35). "You will arise and have pity on Zion; / it is the time to favor her; / the appointed time has come. / For your servants hold her stones dear / and have pity on her dust" (Ps. 102:13-14).

This rebuilding is viewed from various aspects. First, it will be the work of the LORD himself: *he* will build Jerusalem (Ps. 147:2; cf. Jer. 33:4, 6), and "comfort" her ruins (Isa. 51:3; cf. Ps. 102:13-14). Sometimes the rebuilding is described in more general terms, but always with the blessing of the LORD in the background. The city will be rebuilt for him, even with a reference to her size: "Jerusalem shall remain aloft on its site from the Gate of Benjamin to the place of the former gate, to the Corner Gate, and from the Tower of Hananel to the king's winepresses. And it shall be inhabited, for there shall never again be a decree of utter destruction. Jerusalem shall dwell in security" (Zech. 14:10-11), and further the hill Gareb, Goah, the brook Kidron, the Horse Gate, the Benjamin Gate, and more.[1]

Second, Christ is presented as the builder of the city, as we see this typologically in King Solomon, and in King Cyrus the Persian.[2]

Third, of course, Christ will not be building the city by himself; his people will help him in this; they will even be called "the repairer of the breach, the restorer of streets" (Isa. 58:12; cf. 61:4).

Fourth, there will also be people from other nations coming to help in the rebuilding work: "Foreigners shall build up your walls, / and their kings shall minister to you" (Isa.

---

1. Cf. Jer. 30:16–18; 31:38–40; 2 Kings 14:13; 23:15; 25:23; 2 Chron. 26:9; Neh. 3:1, 28; 12:39; Jer. 20:2; 31:39; 37:13; 38:7; Ezek. 48:32; John 18:1.
2. 1 Chron. 22:6, 9–11; 28:6, 10; 2 Chron. 3:1; 36:23; Isa. 44:26–28; Ezra 1:2.

60:10). These foreigners will help in rebuilding not only the city, but also the temple (vv. 12-13; Zech. 6:15). This is very important, for the temple will occupy a chief position in the Messianic kingdom and will increase the radiance of Jerusalem even more. It is the counsel of the Lord that this temple will be rebuilt, and the Messiah himself will build it together with his people.[3]

How important his new temple will be was evident from the extensive description that we find of it in Ezekiel 40–43. Here, the prophet saw in the spirit successively the gates and the courts, then the actual temple house, the priestly dwellings, and finally the "law of the house" (Ezek. 43:12), referring to the territory around the temple. Ezekiel 44–46 deals with the priestly service in the new temple. There will again be an altar on which sacrifices will be offered. But the ark will be sought in vain, for it will no longer be needed: "[W]hen you have multiplied and been fruitful in the land, in those days, . . . they shall no more say, 'The ark of the covenant of the Lord.'" It shall not come to mind or be remembered or missed; it shall not be made again" (cf. Jer. 3:16).

This is because, when the Messiah comes, he will fill the house with glory, and the "latter glory of this house shall be greater than the former" (Hag. 2:7-9). This passage is interesting because it seems to admit implicitly that the *Shekhinah* did not descend on the Second Temple, and seems to offer an explanation for this (see §12.5.3). Haggai made the prophetic promise that, one day, the temple will yet be filled with the glory of God. For the longer term, the reference may be to the descent of the *Shekhinah* in Ezekiel 43, although this involved not the Second but the Third Temple. For the shorter term, Haggai may have been alluding to the coming of the Messiah, since in his person the *Shekhinah* would enter the Second Temple (see §12.6.1). This interpretation seems to be corroborated by Haggai's speaking (Hag. 2:7) of the "desire of all nations" (KJV), an expression that older expositors referred

---

3. Ezek. 37:26–28; Zech. 1:16–6:13; cf. Isa. 2:2–3; 44:28.

to the Messiah.[4] Among more modern translators and expositions, this interpretation is rarely found (ESV: "the treasures of all nations"; cf. "the wealth of the nations," Isa. 60:5, 11; 61:6).

G. E. Ladd was one of many who could not accept that, during the Messianic kingdom, bloody sacrifices would be offered again; it was unthinkable that God's redemptive plan would return to the age of the shadows.[5] But this is a tendentious way of putting things; I know of no expositor who asserts such a thing. It is essential to see that, also in the Tanakh, "it is impossible for the blood of bulls and goats to take away sins" (Heb. 10:4); their only value lay in *pointing forward* to the atoning sacrifice of Christ. In an entirely analogous way, we can imagine that, during the Messianic kingdom, bloody sacrifices will be offered again; they do not bring about any form of genuine atonement but *point backward* to the sacrifice of Christ (see §11.8.1).[6]

14.1.2 Descent of the Shekhinah

We know that the *Shekhinah*, the glorious presence of the LORD God, left the First Temple during the rule of the wicked King Zedekiah, when the sin of Judah had reached a climax (Ezek. 10:18–22; 11:22–23). From that moment, we nowhere read that God's glory ever filled the temple again, neither the First Temple, nor the Second Temple that, after the Babylonian exile, was built by Zerubbabel and Jeshua (Ezra 5–6). Actually, such a filling would hardly have been possible, for by this time Israel had become *Lo-'Ammi* (Hos. 1:9).

---

4. See, e.g., the Annotations to the Dutch States Translation: "Namely, *Christ*, whom all heathen and Nation should wish to embrace, coming to his church. Compare Gen. 49:10. Others thus: *and the wish of heathen shall come*: understanding it of the coming of the *Messiah*" (Haak [1918, ad loc.]).
5. Ladd (1978, 25); cf. Douma (2008, 66): "Thus, one who deems a new temple necessary . . . acts as if the work of Jesus Christ was *not* sufficient." If the work of Christ had indeed rendered the Second Temple superfluous, why did the apostles Peter, John, and Paul go there (after Pentecost) to participate in the sacrificial ministry there, offering animal sacrifices (Acts 3:1; 21:26; 24:17)?
6. See Ouweneel (2012a, §9.5.2).

Recall the important reality that now the dominion over the "prophetic earth"[7] lay in the hands of the heads of the nations, consecutively of the Babylonian, the Medo-Persian, the Greco-Macedonian, and the Roman Empires (Dan. 2:37–38; also see Dan. 7). As we saw, God had at this time assumed the character "God of heaven" more than before. Only when the "times of the Gentiles" are fulfilled (Luke 21:24) will the *Shekhinah* return to its temple, which will then be the Third Temple (see extensively, Ezek. 43:1–9).[8] From that moment, the temple will again be the earthly throne of the Lord, and the place of the soles of his feet, where he forever will dwell among the Israelites (i.e., as long as the present earth will last).[9]

As is obvious from the passages mentioned in note 9, the blessing of the Third Temple will extend to all the earth:

And the foreigners who join themselves to the Lord,
> to minister to him, to love the name of the Lord,
> and to be his servants,
everyone who keeps the Sabbath and does not profane it,
> and holds fast my covenant—
these I will bring to my holy mountain,
> and make them joyful in my house of prayer;
their burnt offerings and their sacrifices
> will be accepted on my altar;
for my house shall be called a house of prayer
> for all peoples (Isa. 56:6–7).

Yes, many will come "to beautify the place of my sanctuary" (Isa. 60:13; see vv. 7–13). The people will drink the new wine "in the courts of my sanctuary" (Isa. 62:9; cf. Deut. 14:24–26), and their sacrifices will be pleasing to the Lord

---

7. With "prophetic earth" I mean the earth as it exists within the prophets' field of vision: the Middle East, North Africa, and (Southeast and Middle) Europe.
8. If we identify a distinct "temple" of the Antichrist (cf. Matt. 24:15; 2 Thess. 2:4; Rev. 11:2; 13:14–17), the temple of the Messiah will actually be the Fourth Temple; one could also say that the Antichrist's sanctuary will be a false and precocious anticipation of the Messianic (Third) Temple.
9. Ezek. 43:7; Jer. 3:17; cf. Isa. 2:2–5; Micah 4:1–5; Hab. 2:20.

(Mal. 3:4; Ps. 51:18–19). The sacrificial ministry will be performed by Levitical priests (Jer. 33:18, 21–22; Mal. 3:3), namely, by the sons (descendants) of Zadok, as we have seen.[10]

In the Messianic and other prophetic Psalms, we hear of the rebuilding of the temple (Ps. 127:1, a psalm of Solomon, the "prince of peace"; and Ps. 132:13–18), and of the priestly nation (Ps. 133–134). Other passages deal with the blessing of individual believers in the new temple.[11] They will observe the law (Torah) and the word of the LORD that go forth from his sanctuary (Isa. 2:3; Micah 4:3). They will also celebrate *Sukkot* (the Feast of Booths), which in itself is such a wonderful type and anticipation of the Messianic kingdom.[12]

It is no wonder that, during the Messianic kingdom, Jerusalem will indeed be the "queen" of the earth, since the glory of the LORD will fill the temple, Messiah will establish on Zion the seat of his dominion, and the LORD will dwell in Jerusalem, in the midst of his people: "Shout, and sing for joy, O inhabitant of Zion, / for great in your midst is the Holy One of Israel" (Isa. 12:6). "[Y]ou shall know that I am the LORD your God, / who dwells in Zion, my holy mountain. / And Jerusalem shall be holy, / and strangers shall never again pass through it" (Joel 3:17). "Sing and rejoice, O daughter of Zion, for behold, I come and I will dwell in your midst. . . . And many nations shall join themselves to the LORD in that day, and shall be my people. And I will dwell in your midst" (Zech. 2:10–11). The nations will go up to Jerusalem to seek the LORD of hosts at Jerusalem, to entreat his favor (Zech. 8:20–22; cf. 14:16; Ps. 68:29).

14.2 The Grand City
14.2.1 The New Names of the City
The presence of the *Shekhinah* in the "beloved city" (Rev. 20:9) will give rise to magnificent new names for the earthly city of Jerusalem; as the prophet says,

---

10. Ezek. 40:46; 43:19; 44:15; 48:11; cf. 1 Sam. 2:35.
11. Ps. 65:4; 116:17–19; 135:1–4; 138:2.
12. Hos. 12:10; Zech. 14:16–21; cf. Exod. 23:16; Lev. 23:33–36; Num. 29:12–38; Deut. 16:13–15; Neh. 8:14–19; John 7:2, 37; cf. Ouweneel (2001b, 166–87).

> The nations shall see your righteousness,
>> and all the kings your glory,
> and you shall be called by a *new name*
>> that the mouth of the LORD will give (Isa. 62:2)

In the Tanakh we find no fewer than twelve such new names or appellations.

1. *Qiryat Melech Rav* (Gk. *Polis tou Megalou Basileōs*), "City of the great King" (Ps. 48:2; Matt. 5:35). Jesus himself calls Jerusalem this way, following the name that the sons of Korah had given her in David's time.

2. *Ir haTsedeq, Qiryat Ne'emanah*, "Righteous City, Faithful Town"[13] (Isa. 1:26 CEB). This is a name that God will give to the city once his divine justice will have been reestablished there.

3. *Ir YHWH Tzion Qadosh Yisra'el:* "City of the LORD, the Zion of the Holy One of Israel" (Isa. 60:14). This will be the name with which the former oppressors of Israel will designate the city when they humbly come to her.

4. *Chephtzi-bah*, "My Delight Is In Her" (Isa. 62:4); this is God's name for the city when he has restored the ancient bond of love with her (see chapter 13 note 80).

5. *Be'ulah*, "Married" (Isa. 62:4); see previous point.

6. *D'rushah*, "Sought Out" (Isa. 62:12): *God* seeks (desires, longs for) her blessing, or rather, seeks herself.

7. *Ir lo ne'ezabah*, "City Not Forsaken" (Isa. 62:12), that is, "not forsaken *anymore*," as she formerly had been (cf. v. 4, "You shall no more be termed Forsaken").

8. *Kissē YHWH:* "Throne of the LORD" (Jer. 3:17; cf. 1 Chron. 29:23, where this is the name for the throne that Solomon ascended). In the person of the Messiah, the LORD will again be enthroned in Jerusalem, and from there rule the earth. This throne must not be confused with the throne of God in heaven.

9. *YHWH Tzidkēnu:* "The LORD Our Righteousness" (Jer.

---

13. In Heb., adjectives are often expressed through substantives, e.g., "mountains of holiness" (Ps. 87:1 JUB) is "holy mountains" (KJV).

33:16 KJV), the name that the city receives when Judah is redeemed, and Jerusalem will be safe again.

10. *YHWH Shammah:* "The LORD Is There" (Ezek. 48:35). Here the Holy Spirit himself said that from now on this will be the city's name. It underscores the presence of the LORD himself, that is, of the *Shekhinah* in the city's temple.

11. *Ir haEmet, Har haQodesh:* "The faithful city, the holy mountain" (Zech. 8:3; JUB: "City of Truth, the mountain of holiness"). This is the name that the LORD will give to the city when he truthfully fulfills to her his promises, namely, to return to Zion, and to fill Jerusalem with his holiness, or also, when he praises *her* for *her* faithfulness.

12. *Ir-Elohim* (Ps. 46:4) of *Ir ha'Elohim* (87:3), that is, "City of God." In this series these are the simplest names. Both psalms have an eschatological meaning: "On the holy mountains is [the city's] foundation. / *Adonai* loves the gates of Tziyon [Zion] / more than all the dwellings in Ya'akov [Jacob]" (Ps. 87:1–2 CJB).

Six of the names mentioned point directly to the presence of the LORD-Messiah in Jerusalem, two point to his character as ruler in that city (King, throne), three point to his moral features (righteous, holy, truthful/faithful), and the four in Isaiah 62 point to his affection for her.

14.2.2 Living in the City

> It will be a special privilege to be allowed to live in Jerusalem. In those days, there will be no city on earth that is more desired as a habitation than this: "Jerusalem shall be inhabited as villages without walls,[14] because of the multitude of people and livestock in it. And I will be to her a wall of fire all around, . . . and I will be the glory in her midst" (Zech. 2:4–5).

---

14. Isa. 60:10 speaks of rebuilding the walls of Jerusalem, though. Should we perhaps construe this as a walled inner city, and a non-walled metropolis, like modern Jerusalem?

Old men and old women shall again sit in the streets of Jerusalem, each with staff in hand because of great age.[15] And the streets of the city shall be full of boys and girls playing in its streets. Thus says the LORD of hosts: "If it is marvelous in the sight of the remnant of this people in those days, should it also be marvelous in my sight . . . ? Behold, I will save my people from the east country and from the west country, and I will bring them to dwell in the midst of Jerusalem. And they shall be my people, and I will be their God, in faithfulness and in righteousness" (Zech. 8:4-8).

The LORD ardently longs to fulfill his promises, for his jealousy for this city is great (Zech. 8:2; cf. 1:12-17). He desires to clothe Jerusalem with great splendor, so that it will be an ornament for all the world: "You shall be a crown of beauty in the hand of the LORD, / and a royal diadem in the hand of your God" (Isa. 62:3; cf. 4:2; 46:13; Zech. 2:5). He will grant great power to the righteous people of Jerusalem. He will protect the city against inclement weather and against its enemies, so that it will be an untroubled habitation, an immovable tent.[16] He will fill its inhabitants with everlasting joy, and no sadness will ever have a grip on them again.[17] In those days, they will sing a song about Jerusalem: "In that day this song will be sung in the land of Judah: / 'We have a strong city; / he sets up salvation / as walls and bulwarks'" (Isa. 26:1-2). Yes, then that wonderful hymn will be sung that we find throughout the Bible, but that will be perfectly applicable only during the Messianic kingdom: "Praise the LORD, for his loving-kindness [read, covenantal faithfulness] is forever" (Heb. *Hodu l'YHWH, ki tov, ki le'olam chasdo*).[18]

The LORD will grant the people of Jerusalem all earthly blessings of which Moses had spoken; notice the seven occurrences of the root *b-r-kh* ("to bless") in this passage:

---

15. Cf. Isa. 65:20 speaks of a "young" man of hundred years.
16. Isa. 4:5–6; 33:20; 45:25; 60:21–22; Micah 4:8; Zech. 2:5.
17. Isa. 35:10; 51:11; 66:10–14; Jer. 31:12; 33:10–11; Zeph. 3:16–17.
18. 1 Chron. 16:34, 41; 2 Chron. 5:13; 7:3, 6; 20:21; Ezra 3:11; Ps. 100:5; 106:1; 107:1; 118:1–4; 136:1–26, and especially Jer. 33:11.

> [A]ll these [1] blessings shall come upon you and overtake you, if you obey the voice of the LORD your God. [2] Blessed shall you be in the city, and [3] blessed shall you be in the field. [4] Blessed shall be the fruit of your womb and the fruit of your ground and the fruit of your cattle, the increase of your herds and the young of your flock. [5] Blessed shall be your basket and your kneading bowl. [6] Blessed shall you be when you come in, and [7] blessed shall you be when you go out (Deut. 28:2-6).

Numerous Bible passages told us about the blessings of fertility and prosperity that the Israelites will enjoy during the Messianic kingdom; a number of them spoke in particular about the special blessings for the inhabitants of Jerusalem. The LORD

> will give rain for the seed with which you sow the ground, and bread, the produce of the ground, which will be rich and plenteous. In that day your livestock will graze in large pastures, and the oxen and the donkeys that work the ground will eat seasoned fodder, which has been winnowed with shovel and fork (Isa. 30:23-24).[19]

Such blessings make it very clear that such passages were notspeaking of heaven or of the eternal state. In other words, supersessionists can interpret them this way only by spiritualizing all these blessings (which is not easy, of course: what is the spiritual difference between the sheep, the cows, and the donkeys? And what does the "fruit of the womb" represent?).

14.3 Israel During the Messianic Kingdom (1)
14.3.1 Israel's Seven "Seasons": Introduction

As interpreters have long observed, the Song of Songs features not only the typological but also eschatological meanings.[20] One of the many magnificent passages in this Bible book is the following one, in which the bridegroom calls to his beloved:

---

19. Cf. Isa. 32:15–20; 51:3; 60:13; 66:12–14; Jer. 31:12; Joel 2:23–27; Ps. 72:16; 147:12–14.
20. See Ouweneel (1973, ad loc.).

> Arise, my love, my beautiful one,
>> and come away,
> for behold, the winter is past;
>> the rain is over and gone.
> The flowers appear on the earth,
>> the time of singing [or, pruning] has come,
> and the voice of the turtledove
>> is heard in our land.
> The fig tree ripens its figs,
>> and the vines are in blossom;
>> they give forth fragrance.
> Arise, my love, my beautiful one,
>> and come away (Song 2:10–13).

In these words we hear the sweet voice of the Messiah that, also in our day, echoes in the ears of Israel, even if only a minority of people respond to it. It is Israel's spiritual spring, already since the nineteenth century, but surely since the second half of the twentieth century. And this spring will be followed by summer, that is, the Messianic kingdom. This is the summer of which Jesus spoke, the summer beginning with the sprouting of the trees, Israel first, but also the neighboring countries: "From the fig tree learn its lesson: as soon as its branch becomes tender and puts out its leaves, you know that summer is near" (Matt. 24:32). This is what we are experiencing today: Israel's summer is approaching! Summer is marked by the lushest greenery:

> I will put in the wilderness the cedar,
>> the acacia, the myrtle, and the olive.
> I will set in the desert the cypress,
>> the plane and the pine together,
> that they may see and know,
>> may consider and understand together,
>
> that the hand of the Lord has done this,
>> the Holy One of Israel has created it (Isa. 41:19–20).

> [T]he LORD comforts Zion;
>> he comforts all her waste places
> and makes her wilderness like Eden,
>> her desert like the garden of the LORD;
> joy and gladness will be found in her,
>> thanksgiving and the voice of song (51:3).

> For you shall go out in joy
>> and be led forth in peace;
> the mountains and the hills before you
>> shall break forth into singing,
>> and all the trees of the field shall clap their hands.
> Instead of the thorn shall come up the cypress;
>> instead of the brier shall come up the myrtle;
> and it shall make a name for the LORD,
>> an everlasting sign that shall not be cut off (55:12–13).

Israel's present spring was preceded by a long winter, which began with the destruction of the First Temple in 586 BC. The return from Babylon and the building of the Second Temple did not basically alter the situation because the fire and the *Shekhinah* did not descend at the consecration of this temple. The times remained cold and dark, so to speak. Perhaps it is very telling that the only season mentioned in the days of Jesus was winter (John 10:22).

14.3.2 The Seven "Seasons": Survey

In this context, this statement by Jeremiah is relevant: "The harvest is past, the summer is ended, / and we are not saved" (8:20). The "summer" was over, and so was the "autumn" (time of the harvest);[21] Jeremiah saw the "winter" approaching, and no salvation for Israel was looming. He could not possibly guess how many centuries this cold and gloomy situation would last.

If we follow this line of thinking, I think the following survey of seven "seasons" is defensible.

---

21. The word "harvest" is etymologically related to what "autumn" is called in other Germanic languages: Dutch *herfst*, German *Herbst*, Swedish *höst*.

(1) *Winter:* Israel's oppression in Egypt was the long winter with which Israel's existence as a nation began. They were "born" in the figurative cold of the Egyptian slavery.

(2) *Spring:* Israel's deliverance from Egypt ushered in the fresh spring season; it was the time of Israel's "bridal days" (Jer. 2:2), which, as in Song 2, correspond with the spring.

(3) *Summer:* The time of the kingship of David and Solomon was like a summer in Israel, a summer that, typologically and prophetically, corresponded to the summer of the Messianic kingdom: "Judah and Israel were as many as the sand by the sea. They ate and drank and were happy. . . . And Judah and Israel lived in safety, from Dan even to Beersheba, every man under his vine and under his fig tree, all the days of Solomon" (1 Kings 4:20, 25; cf. Micah 4:4).

(4) *Autumn:* The wicked (idolatrous, "adulterous") last days of the Davidic monarchy, especially after the godly King Josiah, formed the autumn to which Jeremiah referred, the prophet who saw the harsh winter approaching for Israel.

(5) *Winter.* The long exile from 586 BC until 1948, or 1967—interrupted by the Second Temple period, a period of "thaw," but during which Israel still had to live without the *Shekhinah*—has been Israel's endless winter.

(6) *Spring:* Today, we are experiencing Israel's spring, which must lead to Messiah's bride finally responding to his loving invitation.

(7) *Summer:* The Messianic kingdom will be Israel's ultimate summer, which will not be followed by any autumn; then, for one thousand years, Israel's jubilating response will be heard: "My beloved is mine, and I am his" (Song 2:16). "I am my beloved's and my beloved is mine" (6:3). "I am my beloved's, and his desire is for me" (7:10).

14.4 The Twelve Tribes

14.4.1 The *Tzaddiqim*

We now come to a few important aspects that have not yet been fully examined. One such aspect is the prophecy that all twelve tribes of Israel will be reunited.[22] As mentioned before, this does not mean that the ten tribes are still hidden in some secret area. The "Jews" (i.e. literally, Judeans; therefore we should rather say, the Israelites) living today in *HaAretz* belong to all twelve tribes. Some examples: in the New Testament, we find Jesus from the tribe of Judah, John the Baptist from the tribe of Levi, the apostle Paul from the tribe of Benjamin, and Anna the prophetess from the tribe of Asher. These represent four of the twelve tribes.[23]

The true (converted) Israel from all twelve tribes will be accepted by God as his people; they will be called sons (or, children) of the living God (Hos. 1:10). He will give to each of his faithful a new heart, and will pour out his Spirit upon them.[24] The renewal of these people will include the spiritual cleansing of the Israelites: their iniquities will be atoned, their sins will be washed away, their spiritual wounds will be healed. God will invest them with righteousness, and forever turn away his wrath from them; forever they will be his people, and he will be their God.[25] All the last remains of idolatry will be removed from the country.[26] God will make with them an everlasting covenant of peace, which cannot and will not be broken as long as the present earth lasts.[27]

---

22. See, e.g., Isa. 11:11–16; Ezek. 37:15–28; 48:1–8; Matt. 19:28 and parallels; Acts 26:7; James 1:1; Rev. 7:1–8.
23. A former Israeli colleague of mine, who died in the Yom Kippur War (1973), claimed to have come from the tribe of Simeon.
24. Isa. 32:15; 44:1–5; Ezek. 11:17–20; 36:24–28; 37:1–14; Joel 2:28–29.
25. Isa. 27:9; 33:24; 40:2; 44:22; 54:7; 57:15–16; 60:10, 21; 61:10; Jer. 33:8; 50:20; Dan. 9:24; Hos. 14:2–9; Joel 3:21; Micah 7:18–20; Zech. 3:9; 13:1, 9; Rom. 11:26–32.
26. Isa. 27:9; 42:13–17; Hos. 2:17; 14:4; Micah 5:12–13; Zech. 13:2.
27. Jer. 31:31–34; 32:40; 50:4; Ezek. 16:59–63; 34:25; 37:26; so also many Psalms.

What will be unique about the new Israel is that it will be a people consisting exclusively of "righteous ones" (Heb. *tzaddiqim*), which, of course, has never before been the case: "All the descendants of Israel will be declared righteous (Heb. *yitzd'qu*, from the root *tz-d-q*), and they will praise the LORD" (Isa. 45:25 GW). Although, formerly, God addressed his people as a *redeemed* nation (see Exod. 20:1-2), namely, delivered from Egypt, it was clear from the outset that many of them were not *spiritually* redeemed; that is, they still had their unregenerated hearts: "For forty years [since the exodus] I loathed that generation / and said, 'They are a people who go astray in their heart, / and they have not known my ways'" (Ps. 95:10). "[O]ur fathers were all under the cloud, and all passed through the sea, and all were baptized into Moses in the cloud and in the sea. . . . Nevertheless, with most of them God was not pleased, for they were overthrown in the wilderness" (1 Cor. 10:1-5).

During the Messianic kingdom it will be much different:

> Your people shall *all* be righteous (Heb. *tzaddiqim*);
>   they shall possess the land forever,
> the branch of my planting, the work of my hands,
>   that I might be glorified (Isa. 60:21).

14.4.3 Physical Restoration

The people will be restored not only spiritually, but also physically:

> In that day the deaf shall hear
>   the words of a book,
> and out of their gloom and darkness
>   the eyes of the blind shall see (Isa. 29:18; cf. Matt. 11:5).

> Behold, a king will reign in righteousness,
>   and princes will rule in justice.
> Each[28] will be like a hiding place from the wind,
>   a shelter from the storm,

---

28. GNV and JUB: "And that man shall be . . . ."

> like streams of water in a dry place,
>> like the shade of a great rock in a weary land.
> Then the eyes of those who see will not be closed,
>> and the ears of those who hear will give attention.
> The heart of the hasty will understand and know,
>> and the tongue of the stammerers will hasten to speak distinctly (Isa. 32:1-4).

The Septuagint renders Isaiah 61:1 not as "to bring good news to the poor," but "recovery of sight to the blind," and this is the way Jesus quotes the verse in Luke 4:19.[29] "[N]o inhabitant will say, 'I am sick'; / the people who dwell there will be forgiven their iniquity" (Isa. 33:24).

> Then the eyes of the blind shall be opened,
>> and the ears of the deaf unstopped;
> then shall the lame man leap like a deer,
>> and the tongue of the mute sing for joy (Isa. 35:5-6).

"I will give you as a covenant for the people, / a light for the nations, / to open the eyes that are blind" (Isa. 42:6-7). "I myself will be the shepherd of my sheep, and I myself will make them lie down. . . . I will seek the lost, and I will bring back the strayed, and I will bind up the injured, and I will strengthen the weak, and the fat and the strong I will destroy. I will feed them in justice" (Ezek. 34:15-16).

14.5 Israel During the Messianic Kingdom (2)
14.5.1 God Dwelling In the Midst

Nothing will be greater and more glorious for Israel than the fact that the Lord will dwell in their midst again, as he for centuries had done before:

> Then he led me to the gate, the gate facing east. And behold, the glory of the God of Israel was coming from the east. And the sound of his coming was like the sound of many waters, and the earth shone with his glory. . . And I fell on my face. As the

---

29. Ellicott argues why presumably the Septuagint is to be preferred, also in light of Isa. 35:5 and 42:7; see http://biblehub.com/commentaries/isaiah/61-1.htm.

glory of the Lord entered the temple by the gate facing east, the Spirit lifted me up and brought me into the inner court; and behold, the glory of the Lord filled the temple. . . . I heard one speaking to me out of the temple, and he said to me, 'Son of man, this is the place of my throne and the place of the soles of my feet, where I will dwell in the midst of the people of Israel forever (Ezek. 43:1–7).

We have dealt with this passage before; it is the great and joyful contrast with the sad event described in Ezekiel 9–11: the departure of the Lord's glory in the days of the last king of Judah, just before the destruction of city and temple.

The prophet Zephaniah describes in his own way the glorious dwelling of the Lord in the midst of his people:

Sing aloud, O daughter of Zion;
    shout, O Israel!
Rejoice and exult with all your heart,
    O daughter of Jerusalem!
The Lord has taken away the judgments against you;
    he has cleared away your enemies.
The King of Israel, the Lord, is in your midst;
    you shall never again fear evil.
On that day it shall be said to Jerusalem:
'Fear not, O Zion;
    let not your hands grow weak.
The Lord your God is in your midst,
    a mighty one who will save;
he will rejoice over you with gladness;
    he will quiet you[30] by his love;
he will exult over you with loud singing (Zeph. 3:14–17; italics added).

---

30. AMPC: "He will rest [in silent satisfaction] *and* in His love He will be silent *and* make no mention [of past sins, or even recall them]."

14.5.2 Heavenly and Earthly Saints

During the Messianic kingdom, there will be great difference between two groups of Israelite saints: (A) the risen and glorified saints in heaven and (B) those saints who, with their mortal bodies, will still live on earth.

Group A consists of believers from the time of the Tanakh and Jewish believers within the (New Testament) Ecclesia. Group B—Israelites on earth—consists of those Israelites whose eyes will be opened only at the moment of Christ's second coming, or shortly after (cf. Isa. 66:18-20). Or, to put it differently, group A consists, first, of those who have risen from the dead (1 Thess. 4:14-16), and, second, of those who, without having died, have received their immortal bodies at the coming of Christ (1 Cor. 15:51-54; Phil. 3:20-21). Group B consists of those who have never passed through physical death, and therefore still have their mortal bodies.

To Jesus' (Jewish) apostles, who self-evidently will belong to the glorified saints, he gave the following promise: "[W]hen the Son of Man will sit on his glorious throne, you [the twelve apostles[31]] who have followed me will also sit on twelve thrones, judging the twelve tribes of Israel" (Matt. 19:28; cf. Luke 22:29-30), that is, of course, as viceroys under Christ. Besides this, there will also be an earthly government in Israel; as we saw, Ezekiel speaks of a (mortal) prince or ruler (Heb. *nasi*),[32] whom many consider to be the representative (viceroy) of Christ. He lives on earth (48:21-22), must bring sin offerings also for himself (45:22), and has sons (46:16-18). We must assume that he will be a scion of the house of David.[33]

14.5.3 Navel of the Earth

The position of the land of Israel is already favorable, located at the intersection of three continents, but during the Messianic kingdom, it will once for all be the navel, the organic

---

31. The "twelve" minus Judas, and including the new twelfth apostle, Matthias (Acts 1:23, 26).
32. Ezek. 44:3; 45:7-22; 46:2-18; 48:21-22.
33. Grant (1931, 273); Gaebelein (1972, 314-15).

center, the vein of life between God and the world. One of Israel's eschatological opponents will be Gog, of whom the LORD says,

> "I'm going to invade a country [i.e., Israel] without defenses, attack an unsuspecting, carefree people going about their business—no gates to their cities, no locks on their doors. And I'm going to plunder the place, march right in and clean them out, this rebuilt country risen from the ashes, these returned exiles and their booming economy centered down at *the navel of the earth*[34]" (Ezek. 38:12 MSG; italics added).

The word "navel" (omitted by so many translations) is quite interesting here. The distance from one's navel to the soles of one's feet is one-and-a-half times the distance from the top of the head to the navel. It is the same in Israel: the distance between Jerusalem and Eilat is one-and-a-half times the distance from Kiryat Shmonah to Jerusalem. Jerusalem is like the navel of Israel, as the temple mount is the navel of Jerusalem, the Most Holy place is like the navel of the temple, and the ark of the covenant is like the navel of the inner sanctuary.

Similarly, Israel is like the navel of the (ancient) world. Someone traveling over land from Europe or Asia to Africa, or *vice versa*, had to pass through Israel, that is, between the Mediterranean Sea and the Arabian desert. Such a person followed either the road that passed alongside Jerusalem, or the road along the coast. Notice the importance of this: in the Roman Empire, Judea was no more than a tiny and remote corner of the emperor's territory; but in the Messianic kingdom, not Rome but Jerusalem will be the navel of the earth. Now that we know that the earth has a spherical shape, this has not changed a bit. On the great majority of world maps, Israel is still the center of the map, or very close to it.[35]

---

34. Heb. *tabbur ha'aretz*, appearing further only in Judg. 9:37, where clearly "land" is meant. A similar expression is found in Ezek. 5:5, "Jerusalem . . . in the center of the nations [Heb. *b'tokh haggoyyim*], with countries all around her."

35. On maps where Asia is west, and the Americas are east, there is no such center, or it must be a center in the middle of the Pacific.

A key verse here is Deuteronomy 32:

> When the Most High gave to the nations their inheritance,
> when he divided mankind,
> he fixed the borders [or, territories] of the peoples
> according to the number of the sons of God.[36]
> But the Lord's portion is his people,
> Jacob his allotted heritage (Deut. 32:8-9).

That is, the "sons of God" (angels; cf. Job 1-2) are the national angels, or guardian angels, of the exactly seventy nations (Genesis 10), arranged around Israel. But one territory was *not* placed under a guardian angel: this was the land of Israel, which the Lord kept for himself. The picture of Israel, surrounded by seventy nations, reminds us of the tabernacle, surrounded by the twelve tribes of Israel (Num. 2).

In the Messianic kingdom, this will mean that both the throne of David and the new temple will be located in Jerusalem, and that the city will be the point of attraction for all nations that have been allowed to enter the Messianic kingdom:

> It shall come to pass in the latter days
>   that the mountain of the house of the Lord
> shall be established as the highest of the mountains,
>   and it shall be lifted up above the hills;
> and peoples shall flow to it,
>   and many nations shall come, and say:
> "Come, let us go up to the mountain of the Lord,
>   to the house of the God of Jacob,
> that he may teach us his ways
>   and that we may walk in his paths."
> For out of Zion shall go forth the law [or teaching, Heb. *torah*]
>   and the word of the Lord from Jerusalem.
> He shall judge between many peoples,
>   and shall decide disputes for strong nations far away;
> and they shall beat their swords into plowshares,
>   and their spears into pruning hooks;
> nation shall not lift up sword against nation,

---

36. Thus a Dead Sea Scroll and the LXX; the Masoretic text says, "sons of Israel."

> neither shall they learn war anymore;
> but they shall sit every man under his vine and under his fig tree,
>> and no one shall make them afraid,
>> for the mouth of the Lord of hosts has spoken.
> For all the peoples walk
>> each in the name of its god,
> but we will walk in the name of the Lord our God
>> forever and ever (Micah 4:1–5; cf. Isa. 2:2–4; Jer. 3:17).

Thus, the nations will "go up" to *learn* Torah at Jerusalem, but also to *observe* it:

> Then everyone who survives of all the nations that have come against Jerusalem shall go up year after year to worship the King, the Lord of hosts, and to keep the Feast of Booths. And if any of the families of the earth do not go up to Jerusalem to worship the King, the Lord of hosts, there will be no rain on them. And if the family of Egypt does not go up and present themselves, then on them there shall be no rain; there shall be the plague with which the Lord afflicts the nations that do not go up to keep the Feast of Booths (Zech. 14:16–18).

The Lord will be served, not just by Israel but by all the nations:

> For at that time I will change the speech of the peoples
>> to a pure speech,
> that all of them may call upon the name of the Lord
>> and serve him with one accord (Zeph. 3:9).

"[F]rom the rising of the sun to its setting my name will be great among the nations, and in every place incense will be offered to my name, and a pure offering. For my name will be great among the nations" (Mal. 1:11).

14.6 The Blessings for the Nations

14.6.1 Feast

One of the fine commandments in Israel pertained to the *tzitzit* (or *tzitziyyot*) in Numbers 15:

> Speak to the people of Israel, and tell them to make tassels [*tzitzit*] on the corners of their garments throughout their generations, and to put a cord of blue on the tassel of each corner. And it shall be a tassel for you to look at and remember all the commandments of the LORD, to do them (vv. 38-39).

Some have presumed that the woman with a discharge of blood touched these *tzitzit* when she touched the hem of Jesus' robe (Matt. 9:20; cf. 14:36). Similarly, it is assumed that Zechariah 8:23 refers to the *tzitzit* as well: "In those days ten men from the nations of every tongue shall take hold of the robe of a Jew, saying, 'Let us go with you, for we have heard that God is with you.'" There is a beautiful Talmudic comment on this verse. Rabbi Resh Lakish said that the man observing the *tzitzit* commandment will be served by 2,800 slaves.[37] How did he arrive at this number 2,800? Since the Jewish *tallit* has four *tzitzit*, and traditionally there are seventy "tongues" (§14.5.3), we get 10 x 4 x 70, that is, 2,800 persons per Jewish man. The implication of this is that, in the end times and in the Messianic kingdom, every (godly) Jewish man will be a blessing for 2,800 Gentiles by functioning as a signpost to God. A beautiful thought, as David put it:

> I was glad when they said to me,
>   "Let us go to the house of the LORD!"
> Our feet have been standing
>   within your gates, O Jerusalem! (Ps. 122:1-2).

For restored Israel, the blessings mentioned must be a wonderfulprospect. In those days, the nations that are now oppressing them will come near with trembling, and submit themselves to the Messiah (Micah 7:16-17), and in this way also to his people. Today, the Jews are an "object of ridicule" among the nations,[38] but in that day, Jerusalem will become a song of praise among the peoples.[39] That is, the Gentiles will come to praise the God of Israel (Jer. 3:17). But this will

---

37. Talmud: Shabbat 32b.
38. Deut. 28:37; 1 Kings 9:7; 2 Chron. 7:20; Ps. 44:14; Jer. 24:9; 29:18; 42:18.
39. Jer. 33:9; Zeph. 3:20; Ps. 46:4-11; 48:9-14; cf. Ps. 96-100.

also involve coming to praise the people of the God of Israel. A nation about whom God loves to identify himself as their God must be a people so unique and special that it deserves the honor of all humanity.

During the "times of the Gentiles," when Israel is formally described as *Lo-'Ammi*, God manifests himself in particular as the "God of heaven" rather than the "God of Israel." The prophet Daniel expresses the principle behind this:

> You [Nebuchadnezzar], O king, the king of kings, to whom the God of heaven has given the kingdom, the power, and the might, and the glory, and into whose hand he has given, wherever they dwell, the children of man, the beasts of the field, and the birds of the heavens, making you rule over them all—you are the head of gold (Dan. 2:37-38).

We see three correlative matters here: (a) Israel has moved to the background of the scene, (b) God calls himself the "God of heaven," and (c) the center of the world is no longer a Davidic monarch but the head of the nations. Notice the differences with the Messianic kingdom: (a) again, Israel is overtly God's people, (b) God will again openly be the God of Israel, the God of the land of Israel, the God of the city of Israel, the God of the temple of Israel, and (c) the center of the world will be the great Son of David, who moreover will be the head of the nations. Then again, he will truly be *Adon kol-ha'aretz*, the "Lord of all the earth."[40]

If the nations wish to come near to God, they will not only pray to God in their own religious buildings, but above all, they will go up to Jerusalem. God's temple on Mount Zion will be a "house of prayer for all nations" (Isa. 56:7). Jerusalem will mean to humanity so much more than what Geneva means to the Calvinists, and Wittenberg to the Lutherans, and even more than what Rome means to the Catholics, Constantinople to the Greek Orthodox, Moscow to the Russian Orthodox, Salt Lake City to the Mormons, and Mecca to the Muslims. *God will dwell there* in a way he has never dwelt in any of the cities just mentioned.

---

40. Josh. 3:11, 13; Ps. 97:5; Micah 4:13; Zech. 4:14.

Today, Christ fills the entire Ecclesia, worldwide; he has no preferences. He is not more present in Rome than he is in Rhode Island. But those who, during the Messianic kingdom, wish to come into personal contact with Christ, will have to go up to Jerusalem. It is there that the throne of David will stand, and it is there that the temple will stand, filled with the glory of God. Of course, all the *tzaddiqim* will possess the Holy Spirit dwelling in them, as we have seen, so that they can enjoy fellowship with God in whatever corner of the world they inhabit. It is as in the Psalms, where we heard believers pray to God even when they are far removed from the temple (cf., e.g., Ps. 42:5; 119:19; 120:5). But that did not change the fact that Jerusalem was the place to be if one wished to meet God in a special way.[41]

Jerusalem—the place from where the word and the judgments of the Lord go forth (Isa. 2:2-3). Where the nations will find the Messiah (11:10). Where they find light and glory (60:4). Where they bring their wealth and function as helpers for the Israelites (vv. 10-14; 61:5). Where they will see the horrible memory of God's judgments (66:24), namely, the corpses of the condemned (v. 23; Zeph. 2:11). Where they will bow down before the Lord and offer to him their sacrifices (Isa. 56:6-7). Where they seek communion with the Lord (Zech. 2:11). Where they will beg for his favor (8:20-23). Where they will go annually to celebrate the Feast of Booths (14:16).

There, at that wonderful place, at Zion, the holy mountain,

> the Lord of hosts will make for all peoples
> a feast of rich food, a feast of well-aged wine,
> of rich food full of marrow, of aged wine well refined.
> And he will swallow up on this mountain
> the covering that is cast over all peoples,
> the veil that is spread over all nations.
> He will swallow up death forever;
> and the Lord God will wipe away tears from all faces,

---

41. Ps. 9:11, 14; 48:1-2; 50:2; 65:1; 99:2; 102:21; 116:19; 128:5; 132:13; 135:21; 137:6; 147:12; 149:2.

and the reproach of his people he will take away from all the earth,

for the LORD has spoken (Isa. 25:6-8).

In those days he will "change the speech of the peoples / to a pure speech, / that all of them may call upon the name of the LORD / and serve him with one accord" (Zeph. 3:9). In those days "the earth shall be full of the knowledge of the LORD / as the waters cover the sea."[42]

14.6.2 An Illustrious Trio

In addition to Israel, two other nations will enjoy a particularly blessed position, one to the south and one to the north of Israel (see earlier §10.10):

> In that day there will be a highway from Egypt to Assyria, and Assyria will come into Egypt, and Egypt into Assyria, and the Egyptians will worship with the Assyrians. In that day Israel will be the third with Egypt and Assyria, a blessing in the midst of the earth, whom the LORD of hosts has blessed, saying, "Blessed be Egypt my people, and Assyria the work of my hands, and Israel my inheritance" (Isa. 19:23-25).[43]

Here is an interesting challenge for supersessionism: if "Israel" represents the church here, who would be the church's neighboring "countries," Assyria and Egypt? But also for "Israelists" there is a riddle here: Why are especially these two countries mentioned? Because they have been opponents of Israel? But if that is so, why not Babylon, Media, Persia? Or are Egypt and Assyria viewed here as belonging to the Ishmaelites in the broad sense (see again §10.10)? At least it is important to see that *Ha'Aretz* forms the ancient connection

---

42. Isa. 11:9; Hab. 2:14; cf. Num. 14:21 and Isa. 6:3 (glory); Ps33:5 (steadfast love); Hab. 3:3 (praise).
43. Robertson (2000, 21) drew the strange conclusion that Israel will be the third in ranking after Egypt and Assyria, and that this is a cue that God's attention is focused no longer on Israel, but on the entire world. In the entire book of Isaiah, Israel remains the first in ranking, especially in connection with the Messianic kingdom.

between Egypt and Mesopotamia, and that many battles between these powers were fought in *Ha'Aretz*. In the Messianic kingdom, this will be over; there will even be an open connection between Assyria and Egypt, namely, through Israel.

Isaiah 19:18 spoke of cities in Egypt that will speak the "language of Canaan"—a remarkable expression.[44] It must refer to Hebrew, the language of Israel, linked here with the land where Israel belongs. The language of a neighboring country is naturally foreign to Egypt; but when they begin to know the LORD, the God of Israel, they will also become familiar with the sacred language in which this God has been worshiped in millennia past. (Think of the thousands of Gentile Christian theologians who have learned Hebrew.) Learning to speak that language is embracing the religion of the God of Canaan, the land of Israel, his people.[45]

A third special group, after Egypt and Assyria, is formed by what is called the "Palestinians": the strangers who, already today, live in *Ha'Aretz* (which the Romans called "Palestine," the common name used today). Together with the Israelites, they will receive an inheritance in the Holy Land, as we found in Ezekiel 47:21-23. But also for the foreigners from all other nations there will blessing, available for them in Zion:

> Let not the foreigner who has joined himself to the LORD say,
> "The LORD will surely separate me from his people";
> and let not the eunuch say,
> Behold, I am a dry tree."[46]
> For thus says the LORD:
> "To the eunuchs who keep my Sabbaths,
> who choose the things that please me

---

44. In Dutch, the expression *tale Kanaäns* ("language of Canaan") is used for the mystical language of some hyper-Calvinists; I had two uncles (second and fourth degree) who were renowned specialists in it, evident from their (partially published) letters.
45. Cf. Ezek. 16:3 (about Jerusalem), "Your origin and your birth are of the land of the Canaanites."
46. I.e., let not the castrated man say, "I am only a dead tree," one that cannot sprout (i.e., I cannot have children).

and hold fast my covenant,
I will give in my house and within my walls
    a monument and a name
    better than sons and daughters;
I will give them an everlasting name
    that shall not be cut off.
And the foreigners who join themselves to the LORD,
    to minister to him, to love the name of the LORD,
    and to be his servants,
everyone who keeps the Sabbath and does not profane it,
    and holds fast my covenant—
these I will bring to my holy mountain (i.e., Zion),
    and make them joyful in my house of prayer (i.e., the new temple);
their burnt offerings and their sacrifices
    will be accepted on my altar;
for my house shall be called a house of prayer
    for all peoples" (Isa. 56:3–7).

14.6.3 Questions

Many questions can be raised at this point, which are not answered in the Bible (or I have not been able to find them so far). To mention a few: How will the rule over the various nations occur exactly? In addition to the heavenly rulers—Jesus and the heavenly saints—will there be earthly authorities ruling over these nations? What will the borders between the nations look like? What will be the role of modern technology? We may certainly assume that there will be clean energy, no environmental pollution, and no mountains of garbage. But will there be industry? Will there be electricity, or even nuclear energy, or only water- and windmills? Will Israel be the highly developed technological and digital country that it is today, or will it be a land of livestock owners and farmers, as it was of old? Will the biblical festivals of Israel be agricultural festivals, as they were originally (*Pesach* the feast of the barley harvest, *Shavu'ot* the feast of the wheat harvest, *Sukkot* the feast of the complete harvest, including the grapes and the olives)?

Of course, many authors have expressed their thoughts on these questions. However, because of the lack of biblical data, such speculations may tell us more about the imagination of the authors than about the facts. Nevertheless, I venture to add here a few of my own considerations.

(a) If, during the time when the biblical prophecies originated, there existed very little technology, this does not mean that we must derive a denial of technology from certain Bible passages. For instance, when Isaiah 2:4 and Micah 4:3 tell us that the swords will be beaten into plowshares, and the spears into pruninghooks, we must not necessarily conclude that the only technology during the Messianic kingdom will be agricultural technology. By way of comparison: when the end times prophecies speak only of chariots and horses,[47] we must not conclude that, in the end times, the nations will all have abjured their modern arms (cf. §13.6.1).

(b) If, in principle, all Gentiles are expected to go up to Jerusalem every year (Zech. 14:16)—even though they cannot be there all at the same time—we may presume that humanity will make use of modern means of transport.

(c) If God's words will go forth from Zion (Isa. 2:3; Micah 4:2), we may assume that humanity will avail itself of the modern means of communication (the "media"). Some have even presumed that a statement such as this: "[E]very eye will see him" (Zech. 12:10; Rev. 1:7) might suggest the presence of modern media.

(d) If the Messianic kingdom will be a time of great wealth and prosperity, we can, at least with our present understanding, hardly imagine such a situation without industries, the engine of all economic flourishing. If there is only agriculture and livestock farming, one can feed the world's population, but not build great prosperity for everyone. To this end, the production and consumption of many industrial goods are needed.

---

47. E.g., Isa. 30:16; 66:20; Ezek. 38:4; 39:20; Hos. 1:7; Joel 2:4; Micah 5:9; Hagg. 2:23; Zech. 9:10; 10:5; 12:4; 14:15.

14.7 The New Heavens and the New Earth
14.7.1 One People

Let me finally say a few words about the new earth, and the possible place of Israel in it. Revelation 21:3 said, "Behold, the dwelling place [Gk. *skēnē*, tent, tabernacle] of God is with man [more correctly, with the humans, Gk. *meta tōn anthrōpōn*]. He will dwell with them, and they will be his people [Gk. *laos*; some manuscripts: *laoi*, peoples] and God himself will be with them as their God."

The two designations, "God" and "humans," are remarkable. First, the name here is not YHWH, the LORD, the name that expresses in particular God's special relationship with Israel: "I AM" (Exod. 3:14), that is, "Israel, I am there[48] for you, I will always remain faithful to you." Instead, here God is the God of humanity, the God of all people (or peoples).

Second, notice that "Israel" is no longer mentioned; the Greek term is *laos* or *laoi* (depending on what manuscript reading one prefers). Not even *ethnos* (plural, *ethnē*, "Gentiles") in contrast with Israel. It is simply *anthrōpoi*, human beings. It is humanity in the broadest sense, not distinct nations in the sense of Genesis 10.

The thesis could be defended that the distinction between the nations was the consequence of the confusion of tongues at Babel, and thus a result of sin, namely, that of the false, rebellious unification in Babel (Gen. 10:5, 32; 11:1-9). Therefore, in the eternal state this distinction will be abolished. On the Day of Pentecost, the chasm had already been basically bridged because God was praised in the many languages encountered in the world of those days (Acts 2:4, 7-11). On the new earth, "nations" as such will no longer exist and, as far as I can see, neither will Israel itself be a nation in the sense of a nation distinct from other nations. There will be only the one new *laos*, the people of God, former Jews and former Gentiles without any remaining distinction; or possibly *laoi* (plural) in the sense of "humans" (cf. Matt. 4:23; 27:64; Acts 6:8).

---

48. Cf. Martin Buber's translation of YHWH: *Ich bin da* ("I am there").

Some have thought they could discern a special place for Israel in the eternal state on the basis of this verse: "For as the new heavens and the new earth that I make / shall remain before me, . . . / so shall your offspring and your name remain" (Isa. 66:22).[49] However, no more than Isaiah 65:17 does chapter 66:22 tell us that Israel will continue to enjoy a distinct position *in the new earth*; the latter verse only offers us a comparison. For the rest, Isaiah 65:18-25 and 66:18-24 are evidently descriptions of the Messianic kingdom as looking ahead to the total re-creation at the end of the times known to us (cf., e.g., 65:20 with Rev. 21:4).[50] The mention of the "new heavens and the new earth" is due to a well-known principle in prophecy, namely, to mention in one breath related events, though they may be far apart chronologically. This is the case in Isaiah 9:6-7; 11:1-10; 61:1-2 and Micah 5:2-6, when it comes to the birth and the second coming of Christ. We find it in John 5:28-29 concerning the first and the second resurrection, and in 2 Peter 3:7, 10, 12-13 and 18 concerning the *end* of the "day of the Lord" (i.e., the Messianic kingdom) and the *beginning* of the "day of God" (i.e., the "day of eternity").[51]

As I see it, in the new heavens and the new earth, Israel will not occupy the same privileged position that it has enjoyed since Mount Sinai (Exod. 19 and later). There are two decisive arguments for this claim.

(a) The history of Israel lies embedded in the realities existing *since* the foundation of the world (Matt. 13:35; 25:34), and as a consequence, the position of Israel is earthly and temporary. It does not extend back to what was *before* the foundation of the world,[52] and it does not look forward to what will be *after* the present heavens and earth.

(b) Israel is a model nation: *in* and *through* this nation, God wished to bless all nations of the earth.[53] When the blessing

---

49. Grant (1902, 487).
50. See Ouweneel (2012a, §9.5.3).
51. Ouweneel (1990, 230n56).
52. Cf. John 17:24; Eph. 1:4; 1 Pet. 1:20; Rev. 13:8.
53. Gen. 12:3; 18:18; 22:18; 26:4; 28:14; Gal. 3:8.

of God will one day have extended to all nations, this special role of Israel will have become superfluous, or to put it more beautifully, has come to complete fulfillment. Supersessionism teaches that this is the case already now, "Israelists" believe that this will be the case only on the new earth, in the eternal state. At that time, all earthly, temporary differences will have disappeared. There will only be humans, that is, *tzaddiqim* from all ages and from all nations, in their glorified resurrection bodies, without any national differences.

14.7.2 New Questions

In this respect, new questions can and must be asked, of course. Will there be no distinctions between (a) believers who lived in the time of the Tanakh, (b) believers of the Ecclesia, and (c) the *tzaddiqim* who will live on earth during the Messianic kingdom? The Ecclesia was part of God's *eternal* counsel, she was (in God's mind) from *before* the foundation of the world (cf. note 52). Does this mean she will retain her exceptional position in the eternal state as well?

Here, we can ask more questions than can be answered with any biblical certainty. There is no biblical basis for asserting that the "new heaven" will be for the risen and transformed saints, whereas the "new earth" will form the dwelling place of those who, during the thousand-years reign, were living on earth.[54]

To me, it is doubtful whether the phrase "new heaven" refers here to the dwelling place of God, the angels, and the glorified saints; it seems that the expression "new heavens and new earth" ties in with Genesis 1:1 and many other places.[55] That is, the phrase "heaven and earth" simply means "the cosmos," the totality of God's visible creation. Thus, the "new heavens and new earth" may involve nothing more than the great renewal of God's created world, and may have nothing to do with God's heavenly dwelling place. Especially

---

54. Scott (1920, 417).
55. Gen. 2:4; Isa. 37:16; Jer. 23:24; 33:25; Joel 3:16; Hagg. 2:6,21; Matt. 5:18; 24:35; Acts 17:25; 2 Pet. 3:7; Rev. 14:7.

2 Peter 3 is important here: the former heavens will "pass away with a roar" (v. 10) and give way to new heavens.

We could also imagine that the new earth will be so glorious, and so closely linked with the new heaven, that the distinction between the two will no longer be relevant. Or we might imagine the two spheres to be linked by a "ladder" like the one that Jacob saw (Gen. 28:12), or to which Jesus seemed to allude (John 1:52). It seems that it will become "one world," one everlasting dwelling place for all the *tzaddiqim* of all ages.

14.7.3 The "Tabernacle" On the New Earth

In Revelation 21:3 we read that the tent or tabernacle (Gk. *skēnē*) of God will be with the human inhabitants of the new earth. As we have seen (see chapter 12), the Greek word *skēnē* commonly means "tent."[56] In Latin, one word for "tent" is *tabernaculum*,[57] from which the word "tabernacle" was derived. In Hebrews 8–9, *skēnē* was the word used for the tabernacle of Israel in the wilderness, the tent of God, in which his *Shekhinah* dwelt (see again chapter 12). On the new earth, the *skēnē* is the designation for God's dwelling among people. In Revelation 7:15, we read that God will "spread his tent (or, tabernacle)" over his people who come from the Great Tribulation. Some translations render this as "shelter (or, protect) them with his presence" (ESV), or even: "will put his *Shekhinah* over them" (CJB).

Here, the word *skēnē* seems to suggest two meanings:

(a) It may be a symbolic designation of the Hebrew *sukkah* ("tent, hut, booth") into which God will invite his people for an everlasting Feast of Booths (Heb. *Sukkot*), so to speak. One reason to think in Revelation 7 of *Sukkot* is the reference to the "palm branches" in 7:9, which seem to be a clear allusion

---

56. Matt. 17:4 and parallels; Luke 16:9; Acts 7:43–44; 15:16; 2 Cor. 5:1–2, 4; Heb. 11:9; 2 Pet. 1:13–14; the apostle Paul was a *skēnopoios*, "tentmaker" (Acts 18:3).
57. *Tabernaculum*, "tent" (especially "tent of a seer, diviner"), is a diminutive of *taberna*, "hut, cabin, booth"; cf. the English word "tavern."

to the *lulav*, the bundle of branches that people are waving during *Sukkot*.[58]

(b) *Skēnē* in Revelation 7:15 can also be a symbolic designation of the Hebrew *mishkan*, the "tabernacle," the dwelling place of God between his people, just as in 21:3. Presumably, Israel will no long play a specific role on the new earth, but the designations used here are still derived from the Torah. Thus, Revelation 21:3 seems to say that God's *Shekhinah*, his holy, glorious radiance, will dwell among people on the new earth (CJB: "See! God's *Shekhinah* is with mankind"; OJB: "The Mishkan of Hashem [i.e., God] is with men, and He shall tabernacle with them").

14.7.4 Fourteen Mountains

It may be true that Israel will no longer be mentioned separately, but Israel *was*, from the beginning of its existence, the model (pattern, blueprint) for the glorious state that in the end will arrive in the new heavens and the new earth. On Mount Sinai God showed Moses a pattern of the tabernacle that he had in mind (Exod. 25:40; Heb. 8:5). Compare this with Revelation 21:10: "And he carried me away in the Spirit to a great, high mountain, and showed me the holy city Jerusalem coming down out of heaven from God." Thus, a link is suggested from Mount Sinai all the way to the "great, high mountain," pointing forward to the conditions of the eternal state. These are two of *the* fourteen mountains in the Bible, as a kind of bonus, are briefly summarized here, accompanied by conspicuous references to prayer and praise:

1. Mount *Ararat*, where the ark of Noah landed (Gen. 8:4), after which he thanked God with his sacrifice (v. 20).

2. Mount *Moriah* (*"Zion"*), where Abraham sacrificed his son (Gen. 22:1) and Solomon built his temple (2 Chron. 3:1), the "house of prayer" (cf. Isa. 56:7), and where Jesus prayed as a twelve-year-old boy (Luke 2:41–51).

3. Mount *Horeb* or *Sinai*, where Moses had a first encounter with God (Exod. 3:1); later again, as God gave the Torah to Israel (Exod. 19–Num. 10).

---

58. Cf. Daniélou (2002, 333); see Ouweneel (2001b, §§6.1–6.2).

4. Mount *Nebo*, where Moses had his last living encounter with the LORD, where he saw the entire Promised Land, died, and was buried (Deut. 34).

5. Mount *Tabor*, where Barak, at the instigation of Deborah, fought the Canaanites (Judg. 4, followed by the song of chapter 5); perhaps this was also the "very high mountain," where Jesus was tempted by Satan (Matt. 4:8), and explained to him the essence of worship (v. 10).

6. Mount *Gilboa*, where King Saul and his sons fell in battle against the Philistines (1 Sam. 31), after Saul had sought the face of the LORD in vain (chapter 28).

7. Mount *Carmel*, where, among other things, fire came from heaven on the altar of the prophet Elijah in answer to his prayers (1 Kings 18:36-38).

8. *Har ha'Oshēr*, or the "Mount of Beatitudes" and of Jesus' Sermon on the Mount (Matt. 5-7), in which he spoke so much about prayer (5:44; 6:5-13; 7:7-8, 11).

9. *Qarnē Chittim*, or "Horns of Hattin," where, according to tradition, Jesus chose his twelve disciples after a night of prayer (Luke 6:12-16).

10. *Golan* heights:[59] the mountain where Jesus prayed during the storm on the lake (Mark 6:46-51), and the mountain of the miraculous multiplication of bread after Jesus had given thanks (Matt. 15:29, 36).

11. *Mount Hermon* (e.g., Deut. 3:8), presumably the mountain where Jesus prayed and was transfigured (Luke 9:28-29) (or was this Mount Tabor?).

12. *Mount of Olives* (2 Sam. 15:30; Zech. 4:4), where Jesus began his entrance into Jerusalem (Matt. 21:1-9), where he gave his End Time Sermon (Matt. 24:3; call for prayer: v. 20). It was also the mountain of Gethsemane (threefold prayer: Matt. 26:39, 42, 44), of Jesus' ascension leading to the disciples' worship (Luke 24:50-52), and of Jesus' return (Acts 1:11;

---

59. The Golan numbers several mountains, two of which are mentioned here (if they are not identical); in the Tanakh "Golan" is only the name of one of the cities of refuge, lying among these hills (Deut. 4:43; Josh. 20:8; 21:27; 1 Chron. 6:71).

Zech. 14:4–5).

13. *Calvary* or *Golgotha*, traditionally known as a hill in the form of a skull, where Jesus suffered and died; three of his seven statements on the cross were prayers (Luke 23:34, 46; Mark 15:34).[60]

14. The *"great, high mountain,"* literal or figurative, where John beheld the new "Jerusalem coming down out of heaven from God" (Rev. 21:10).[61]

14.8 The Go'el
14.8.1 The Four Tasks of the Go'el

God addressed the people of Israel many times, but at least once he also directly addressed the land of Israel, *Ha'Aretz*, the Holy Land, the ancient land of his promises: "O land, land, land,[62] / hear the word of the LORD!" (Jer. 22:29). The threefold "land" reminds us of the threefold "temple" in Jeremiah 7:4, "This is the temple of the LORD, the temple of the LORD, the temple of the LORD."

The words in Jeremiah 22:29 were spoken in the context of the judgment pronounced over King Coniah (or, Jeconiah, or Jehoiachin), but they illustrate the significance that God attaches to *Ha'Aretz*. This leads us, as we come to the end of our study, to the important figure of the *go'el*, the "redeemer," the man who buys back what earlier had to be sold because of the owner's distressful circumstances. In ancient Israel, the legislation involving the *go'el* was an important part of the Mosaic Torah.[63] When an Israelite was facing a situation of distress, a close relative[64] was to stand up for him

---

60. The Galilean mountain where the risen Lord appeared to his followers (Matt. 28:16) was presumably either mountain 5, 8, 9, 10, or 11 in the list given.
61. In the Spirit, the elderly prophet Moses saw on Mount Nebo the old Jerusalem, and on that other high mountain the old prophet John saw the new Jerusalem.
62. The word *eretz* here probably refers to the land of Judea, but it is possible to render the Heb. word as "earth" here, so that all the earth was being addressed by God.
63. See especially Lev. 25:23–34; also Num. 35:12; Ps. 69:18; 72:14; 78:35; 103:4; 106:10; 119:154; Prov. 23:11; Ruth 3:9–4:14; other relevant passages are mentioned in the text.
64. Heb. *go'el haqqarob* (Lev. 25:25), the "redeemer who is the nearest relative."

and step into the breach. Prophetically and profoundly, it is God who, as the great *Go'el*, intervened, and will intervene, for his people.

The task of the *go'el* was fourfold:

(1) If an Israelite (usually through his own fault) had fallen into slavery, the *go'el*, namely, his brother or next-of-kin, had the obligation to pay the ransom for his release (purchase his liberation; Lev. 25:35-55).

(2) If the land of an Israelite had fallen into another's hands, the *go'el* had to "redeem" the land, that is, pay the price for it, and return it to the original owner or his nearest relatives: "The land shall not be sold in perpetuity, for the land is mine. For you are strangers and sojourners with me. And in all the country you possess, you shall allow a redemption [Heb. *g'ullah*] of the land" (Lev. 25:23-24).

(3) The *go'el* could also function as a *go'el haddam*, literally, "redeemer of the blood," usually rendered as "avenger" (the one who avenges his kinsman's blood). When a person had been killed by another person, the kinsman of the dead person was to act as *go'el*, here in the sense of killing the manslayer.[65]

(4) If an inheritance that had to be "redeemed" was linked to a woman, namely, the childless widow of the dead owner, the *go'el* was to marry this woman in order to father a son with her who could be the heir of the dead person. Because this *go'el* was usually a brother of this dead man, we speak of a *levirate* marriage (from Latin *levir*, i.e., "husband's brother").[66]

This *go'el* had a profound prophetic significance, as is evident from the fact that the word occurs so frequently in Isaiah 40-66, although not with its inter-human meaning, but in the sense of the relationship between God and Israel (both the people and the land) in connection with the Messianic kingdom. God himself is here the great *Go'el*, and he will faithfully perform the four tasks of the *go'el* in the person of

---

65. Exod. 21:12-14; Num. 35:9-34; cf. Deut. 4:41-43; 19:1-13; Josh. 20:3-9. A striking example is found in 2 Sam. 14:11.
66. Deut. 25:5-10; cf. Ruth 3-4; Matt. 22:24-27 and parallels.

the Messiah. A provisional beginning of this "redemption" was seen with Judah's return from the Babylonian captivity, but the great fulfillment is waiting for the end time. This is shown simply and with certainty by the fact that the four tasks in Isaiah are explicitly linked with the arrival of the Messianic kingdom.

In the imagery described here, God himself is Israel's Brother or Kinsman. Notice again how fluid the metaphors can be in this respect:

(a) We have found that God is often referred to as Israel's Bridegroom or Husband, in which case Israel is the bride or wife.

(b) In one Jewish tradition (see §12.3.3), God is the Father of his daughter, the Torah, who is married to Israel. In this case, God is Father-in-law to Israel, and Israel is son-in-law.

(c) We now find God as Israel's Brother or Kinsman, in which case Israel is God's brother or kinsman.

(d) We may add that God is also described as the Father of Israel, in which case Israel is his (firstborn) son (Exod. 4:22; Hos. 11:1) (in the plural: the Israelites are "sons [and daughters]" of the LORD, Deut. 14:1).

(e) In addition, there are non-familial metaphors: if God is the King of Israel, the Israelites are his subjects or servants.

All these metaphors—Israel as wife, son-in-law, brother (kinsman), or son of God—are meaningful in themselves.

14.8.2 Prophetic Realization

In Isaiah 40-66, God, or the Messiah, who himself is a Jew, was the kinsman who accomplished the four ancient tasks of the *go'el*:

(1) *The redemption of the people of Israel.* This *Go'el* will redeem (buy back) the Israelites fallen into slavery among the nations; that is, he will pay the ransom for their release, and purchase their liberation:

> Thus says the LORD,
>   your *Go'el*, the Holy One of Israel: . . . .
>   the Creator of Israel, your King.

Thus says the Lord,
>   who makes a way in the sea,
> a path in the mighty waters, ...
> for I give water in the wilderness, . . ." (Isa. 43:14-20).

The redemption of Israel is viewed here as entirely parallel with the former liberation of Israel from Egypt,[67] their passage through the Red Sea (". . . who makes a way in the sea"), and the wilderness journey. This was partly fulfilled during the return from Babylon (see Isa. 43:14; 48:20), but the prophecy reaches much further: after having reminded Israel of its sins, the Lord says,

> I will pour water on the thirsty land,
>   and streams on the dry ground;
> I will pour my Spirit upon your offspring,
>   and my blessing on your descendants (Isa. 44:3).

This promise was definitely *not* fulfilled in the time after the Babylonian captivity, but will be fulfilled at the beginning of the Messianic kingdom.[68]

(2) *The redemption of the ancient land of Israel.* This *Go'el* will redeem the lost land—*Ha'Aretz*—that had gotten into foreign hands; that is, he will buy it back in order to give it to the original users, the Israelites:

> Thus says the Lord, your *Go'el*,
>   who formed you from the womb:
> "I am the Lord, . . .
> who confirms the word of his servant
>   and fulfills the counsel of his messengers,
> who says of Jerusalem, "She shall be inhabited,"

---

67. Egypt was called the "house of slavery" (Exod. 13:3, 14; 20:2; Deut. 5:6); liberation from Egypt was liberation from slavery.
68. See Isa. 32:15; 44:3; Ezek. 36:24–27; Joel 2:28–29. In Acts 2:16–21, the apostle Peter compared these verses with what happened on the Day of Pentecost, but, as explained earlier, there was no complete fulfillment on that day: there were no "wonders in the heavens above and signs on the earth below, blood, and fire, and vapor of smoke" (cf. Mark 13:24–25; Luke 21:25 in connection with the coming of the Son of Man).

and of the cities of Judah, "They shall be built,
and I will raise up their ruins" (Isa. 44:24–26).

Here again, the text was speaking primarily about Judah's return under King Kores/Cyrus the Persian (v. 28; 45:1). But the text's meaning was reaching far beyond the past by pointing forward to the time when every knee would bow before God (read, the Messiah), and every tongue would swear allegiance (Isa. 45:23; cf. Phil. 2:9–11). This will be the time when "a *Go'el* will come to Zion, / to those in Jacob who turn from transgression" (Isa. 59:20). This will be the time when "[i]n the Lord all the offspring of Israel / shall be justified [or, declared righteous] and shall glory."[69]

(3) *Revenge on Israel's enemies.* This *Go'el* will also act as the *go'el haddam*, the "redeemer of the blood," the avenger, the one who will render vengeance to Israel's enemies for all the blood of God's people that these nations have shed:

I will make your oppressors eat their own flesh,
and they shall be drunk with their own blood as with wine.
Then all flesh shall know
that I am the Lord your Savior[70],
and your *Go'el*, the Mighty One of Jacob (Isa. 49:26).

Again, the text's meaning extends far beyond the time immediately following the Babylonian captivity:

Thus says the Lord God:
"Behold, I will lift up my hand to the nations,
and raise my signal to the peoples;
and they shall bring your sons in their arms,
and your daughters shall be carried on their shoulders.
Kings shall be your foster fathers,
and their queens your nursing mothers.
With their faces to the ground they shall bow down to you,
and lick the dust of your feet" (Isa. 49:22–23).

---

69. Isa. 45:25; cf. 60:21; Rom. 11:26; Israel will become a nation of *tzaddiqim*.
70. Heb. *moshia'*, from the root *y-sh-'*, "to save," which is also the root of the name *Yēshuah*, "Jesus."

(4) *Marrying the bride involved*. This *Go'el* will again accept the divorced bride, Israel, as his wife:[71]

> ... [Y]ou will forget the shame of your youth,
>   and the reproach of your widowhood you will remember no more.
> For your Maker is your husband,
>   the LORD of hosts is his name;
> and the Holy One of Israel is your *Go'el*,
>   the God of the whole earth he is called.
> For the LORD has called you
>   like a wife deserted and grieved in spirit,
> like a wife of youth when she is cast off, ...
> For a brief moment I deserted you,
>   but with great compassion I will gather you.
> In overflowing anger for a moment
>   I hid my face from you,
> but with everlasting love I will have compassion on you,"
>   says the LORD, your *Go'el* (Isa. 54:4–8).

Notice, here too, the context pointing to the Messianic kingdom:

> I will divide him [i.e., the Messiah] a portion with the many
> and he shall divide the spoil with the strong,
>   because he poured out his soul to death (Isa. 53:12).

> [Y]ou will spread abroad to the right and to the left,
>   and your offspring will possess the nations
>   and will people the desolate cities (Isa. 54:3).

What a wonderful work of God, which one day, in the Messianic kingdom, will become fully visible: a liberated people of Israel, in a restored land of Israel, with no hostile nation threatening them. And a widow, who for a short time was alone, will be accepted as a bride by the *Go'el*: "I will betroth you to me *forever*. I will betroth you to me in righteousness

---

71. Of course, the imagery of a husband re-accepting his repelled wife is not precisely identical with that of the brother-in-law marrying his deceased brother's wife; but the text also speaks of the "widow" whom God will marry.

and in justice, in steadfast love and in mercy. I will betroth you to me in faithfulness. And you shall know the Lord" (Hos. 2:19–20).

14.8.3 Final Remarks

Let me finish with some remarkable biblical statements about God's "eternal people." The last words of this two-volume work on Israel are from the Bible itself.

(1) God says to Israel: "Now therefore, if you will indeed obey my voice and keep my covenant, you shall be my treasured possession among all peoples, for all the earth is mine; and you shall be to me a kingdom of priests and a holy nation" (Exod. 19:5–6).

(2) Moses says to Israel:

> [Y]ou are a people holy to the Lord your God. The Lord your God has chosen you to be a people for his treasured possession, out of all the peoples who are on the face of the earth. It was not because you were more in number than any other people that the Lord set his love on you and chose you, for you were the fewest of all peoples, but it is because the Lord loves you and is keeping the oath that he swore to your fathers, that the Lord has brought you out with a mighty hand and redeemed you from the house of slavery, from the hand of Pharaoh king of Egypt (Deut. 7:6–8).

(3) David says to Jerusalem:

> Pray for the peace of Jerusalem!
> "'May they be secure who love you!
> Peace be within your walls
>   and security within your towers!"
> For my brothers and companions' sake
>   I will say, "Peace be within you!'
> For the sake of the house of the Lord our God,
>   I will seek your good" (Ps. 122:6–9).

(4) God says:

> Behold, I will gather them from all the countries to which I drove them in my anger and my wrath and in great indignation. I will bring them back *to this place* [i.e., *Ha'Aretz*], and I will make them dwell in safety. And they shall be my people, and I will be their God. I will give them one heart and one way, that they may fear me forever, for their own good and the good of their children after them. I will make with them an everlasting covenant, that I will not turn away from doing good to them. And I will put the fear of me in their hearts, that they may not turn from me. I will rejoice in doing them good, and I will plant them in this land in faithfulness, with all my heart and all my soul (Jer. 32:37–41).

(5) God says:

> . . . the land that is restored from war, the land whose people were gathered from many peoples upon the mountains of Israel, which had been a continual waste. Its people were brought out from the peoples and now dwell securely, all of them. . . . [W]hen I have brought them back from the peoples and gathered them from their enemies' lands, and through them have vindicated my holiness in the sight of many nations. Then they shall know that I am the LORD their God, because I sent them into exile among the nations and then assembled them into their own land. I will leave none of them remaining among the nations anymore. And I will not hide my face anymore from them, when I pour out my Spirit upon the house of Israel (Ezek. 38:8; 39:27–29).

(6) The apostle John says:

> I saw another angel ascending from the rising of the sun, with the seal of the living God, and he called with a loud voice to the four angels who had been given power to harm earth and sea, saying, "Do not harm the earth or the sea or the trees, until we have sealed the servants of our God on their foreheads." And I heard the number of the sealed, 144,000, sealed from every tribe of the sons of Israel (Rev. 7:2–4).

(7) The apostle Paul says: "[A]s for all who walk by this rule [of the new creation], peace and mercy be upon them, and upon the *Israel of God*" (Gal. 6:15–16).

Bibliography

Aafjes, B. 1950. *Aren lezen achter de maaiers.* Amsterdam: Meulenhoff.
Aalders, G. Ch. 1949. *De oud-testamentische profetie en de staat Israël.* Kampen: Kok.
Aalders, G. J. D. 1985. *Synagoge, kerk en staat in de eerste vijf eeuwen.* Kampen: Kok.
Aalders, W. 1969. *Schepping of geschiedenis: Over de tegenstelling tussen de christelijke hoop en het moderne vooruitgangsgeloof.* Den Haag: J.N. Voorhoeve.
Acta van het Zending-Congres, gehouden te Amsterdam, volgens opdracht der voorloopige Synode van de Nederduitsche Gereformeerde Kerken, January 28–30, 1890. 1890. Amsterdam: J. A. Wormser.
Adamek, J. 1938. *Vom römischen Endreich der mittelalterlichen Bibelerklärung* Würzburg: Triltsch.
Adams, J. E. 1970. *The Time Is at Hand.* Nutley, NJ: Presbyterian & Reformed Publishing Company.
Alford, H. 1958. *The Greek Testament.* 4 vols. Chicago: Moody Press.
Allis, O. T. 1945. *Prophecy and the Church.* Philadelphia: Presbyterian & Reformed Publishing Company.
Armstrong, K. 1993. *A History of God: The 4000-Year Quest of Judaism, Christianity, and Islam.* New York: A. A. Knopf. *Een geschiedenis van God: Vierduizend jaar jodendom, christendom en islam.* Amsterdam:

Flamingo (Ambo | Anthos).

Bahnsen, G. L. 1999. *Victory in Jesus: The Bright Hope of Postmillennialism.* Texarkana, AR: Covenant Media Press.

Baines, T. B. 1879. *The Revelation of Jesus Christ.* London: G. Morrish.

Bakels, F. B. 2016. *Terug uit Nacht und Nebel: Mijn verhaal uit acht Duitse gevangenissen en concentratiekampen.* 19th ed. Utrecht: Omniboek.

Barnhouse, D. G. 1985. *Revelation: An Expositional Commentary.* Grand Rapids, MI: Zondervan.

Barth, K. 2009. *Church Dogmatics.* Translated by G. W. Bromiley et al. Vol. 1/1. New York: T&T Clark.

Bavinck, H. 2002–2008. *Reformed Dogmatics.* Edited by J. Bolt. Translated by J. Vriend. 4 vols. Grand Rapids, MI: Baker Academic.

Beasley-Murray, G. R. 1974. *The Book of Revelation.* NCB. London: Oliphants.

Bellett, J. G. n.d. *Musings on the Apocalypse.* Oak Park, IL: Bible Truth Publishers.

Berkhof, H. 1986. *Christian Faith: An Introduction to the Study of the Faith.* Translated by S. Woudstra. Rev. ed. Grand Rapids, MI: Wm. B. Eerdmans.

Berkhoff, A. M. 1929. *De Christusregeering, of het in Openbaring in aansluiting bij de gansche Profetie der Heilige Schrift beloofde duizendjarig rijk.* Kampen: Kok.

Berkouwer, G. C. 1972. *The Return of Christ.* Translated by J. Van Oosterom. Studies in Dogmatics. Grand Rapids, MI: Eerdmans.

Bietenhard, J. 1955. *Das tausendjährige Reich.* Zürich: Zwingli-Verlag.

Bland, F. C. 1890. *Twenty-One Prophetic Papers.* London: Pickering & Inglis.

Bloesch, D. G. 2004. *The Last Things: Resurrection, Judgment, Glory.* Downers Grove: InterVarsity.

Blomberg, C. L. and S. W. Chung, eds. 2009. *Premillen-*

nialism: An Alternative to 'Left Behind' Eschatology. Grand Rapids, MI: Baker Academic.

Bober, A., ed. 1972. *The Other Israel: The Radical Case against Zionism.* New York: Doubleday & Co.

Boersma, T. 1978. *Is the Bible a Jigsaw Puzzle: An Evaluation of Hal Lindsey's Writings.* Translated by E. Vanderkooy Roberts. St. Catharines, ON: Paideia Press.

Boettner, L. 1990. *The Millennium.* Phillipsburg, NJ: P & R Publishing.

Boogaard, R., P. Den Butter, and E. F. Vergunst. 1992. *Zijn trouw aan Israël nooit gekrenkt.* Houten: Den Hertog.

Booth, A. E. 1999. *The Course of Time from Eternity to Eternity.* Neptune, NJ: Loizeaux Brothers.

Boteach, S. 2012. *Kosher Jesus.* Jerusalem: Gefen Publishing House.

Bouman, S. M. 1998. *Israël contra Zion.* Amsterdam: Jan Mets/Gent: Scoop.

Braverman, M. 2010. *Fatal Embrace: Christians, Jews, and the Search for Peace in the Holy Land.* New York: Beaufort Books.

Brecht, M. 1985–1993. *Martin Luther.* Translated by J. L. Schaaf. 3 vols. Philadelphia: Fortress Press.

Brener, M. E. 2006. *Richard Wagner and the Jews.* Jefferson, NC: McFarland.

Bruce, F. F. 1969. *The Revelation to John.* New Testament Commentaries. London: Pickering & Inglis.

Brugmans, H. and A. Frank. 1940. *Geschiedenis der joden in Nederland.* Vol. 1. Amsterdam: Holkema & Warendorf.

Brunner, E. 1953. *Das Ewige als Zukunft und Gegenwart.* Zürich: Zwingli-Verlag.

Brustein, W. I. 2003. *Roots of Hate: Anti-Semitism in Europe before the Holocaust.* Cambridge: Cambridge University Press.

Burton, A. H. 1932. *The Apocalypse Expounded.* London:

Advent Witness Office.
Chafer, L. S. 1983. *Systematic Theology.* 15th ed. 8 vols. Dallas, TX: Dallas Seminary Press. Chafer, L. S. 1983. *Systematic Theology,* Vol. I-VIII. Dallas: Dallas Seminary Press (abbrev.: ST).
Chapman, C. 1985. *Whose Promised Land?* Tring, Herts, England: Lion Publishing. 2004. Wiens beloofde land? De voortdurende crisis rond Israël en Palestina. Kampen: Kok (orig.: 2002. Whose Promised Land? Oxford: Lion).
Chater, E. H. 1914. *The Revelation of Jesus Christ.* London: G. Morrish.
Chilton, D. 2007. *Paradise Restored: A Biblical Theology of Dominion.* Fort Worth, TX: Dominion Press.
Clouse, R. G., ed. 1977. *The Meaning of the Millennium: Four Views.* Downers Grove, IL: InterVarsity Press.
Coates, C. A. n.d. *An Outline of the Revelation.* London: Stow Hill Bible & Tract Depot.
Cohen, A. 1983. *The Soncino Chumash.* SBB. London: Soncino Press, 1985.
———. 1985. *The Psalms.* SBB. London: Soncino.
Cohen Stuart, G. H. 2003. *Joodse feesten en vasten: Een reis over de zee van de Talmoed naar de wereld van het Nieuwe Testament.* Kampen: Kok.
Cohn, N. 1967. *Warrant for Genocide: The Myth of the Jewish World-Conspiracy and the Protocols of the Elders of Zion.* New York: Serif Publishing.
Collins, L. and D. Lapierre. 1993. *O Jerusalem!* New York: Simon & Schuster.
Costerus, A. 1608. *Historie der Joden, die tzedert de verstooringhe Jerusalems in alle Landen verstroyt zijn.* Rotterdam: Jan van Waesberghe.
Cullmann, O. 1941. *Königsherrschaft Christi und Kirche im Neuen Testament.* Zollikon-Zürich: Evangelischer Verlag.
———. 1963. *The Christology of the New Testament.* Philadelphia, PA: Westminster Press.

Da Costa, I. 1849. *Israel and the Gentiles: Contributions to the History of the Jews from the Earliest Times to the Present Day*. Translated by M. J. Kennedy. London: James Nisbet and Co.

Daniélou, J. 2002. *The Bible and the Liturgy*. Notre Dame, IN: University of Notre Dame Press.

Darby, J. N. n.d.-a *The Collected Writings of J. N. Darby*. Kingston-on-Thames: Stow Hill Bible and Tract Depot.

———. n.d.-b. *Synopsis of the Books of the Bible*. 5 vols. London: G. Morrish.

De Graaff, F. 1987/1989. *Jezus, de Verborgene*. 2 vols. Kampen: Kok.

DeHaan, M. R. 1944. *The Second Coming of Jesus*. Grand Rapids, MI: Kregel.

De Heer, J. 1934. *Het Duizendjarig Vrederijk*. Doorn: Zoeklicht.

Delitzsch, F. 1975. *Commentary on the Old Testament*. Grand Rapids, MI: Eerdmans.

De Madariaga, S. 1967. *Christopher Columbus*. New York: Macmillan.

Den Boer, W. 2008. *Duplex Amor Dei: Contextuele karakteristiek van de theologie van Jacobus Arminius (1559–1609)*. Apeldoorn: Instituut voor Reformatieonderzoek.

Den Butter, P. 1978. *Volk tussen eeuwigheid en eenzaamheid*. Lisse: De Orchidee.

Dennett, E. n.d. *The Visions of John in Patmos*. Oak Park, IL: Bible Truth Publishers.

Dijk, K. 1933. *Het rijk der duizend jaren*. Kampen: Kok.

———. 1952. *Over de laatste dingen: Het einde der eeuwen*. Kampen: Kok.

———. 1953. *De toekomst van Christus*. Vol. 3: *Over de laatste dingen*. Kampen: Kok.

Donner, F. M. 2012. *Muhammad and the Believers: At the Origins of Islam*. Cambridge, MA: Belknapp Press.

Douma, J. 1996. *The Ten Commandments: Manual for the Christian Life*. Translated by N. D. Kloosterman.

Phillipsburg, NJ: P & R Publishing.

———. 2008. *Christenen voor Israël? Verantwoording van een politieke keus.* Barneveld: De Vuurbaak.

Doyle, R. C. 1999. *Eschatology and the Shape of Christian Belief.* Carlisle: Paternoster Press.

Dumbrell, W. J. 1994. *The Search for Order: Biblical Eschatology in Focus.* Grand Rapids, MI: Baker Books.

Dundes, A., ed. 1991. *The Blood Libel Legend: A Casebook in Anti-Semitic Folklore.* Madison, WI: University of Wisconsin Press.

Du Toit, C. W. M. 1948. *Toekomstige wêreldgebeure in die lig van die Skrif: 'n Verklaring van die boek Openbaring, vir ons tyd bewerk.* Frankfort, OVS: Vrye Christelijke Gereformeerde Kerk.

Eberle, H. R. 2002. *Bringing the Future into Focus: An Introduction to the Progressive Christian Worldview.* Yakima, WA: Winepress Publishing.

——— and M. Trench. 2006. *Victorious Eschatology: A Partial Preterist View.* Yakima, WA: Worldcast Publishing.

Edersheim, A. 1971. *The Life and Times of Jesus the Messiah.* 2 vols. Grand Rapids, MI: Eerdmans.

Ellis, M. H. 2009. *Judaism Does Not Equal Israel: The Rebirth of the Jewish Prophetic.* New York: New Press.

———. 2011. *Encountering the Jewish Future with Wiesel, Buber, Heschel, Arendt, Levinas.* Minneapolis, MN: Augsburg Fortress.

Epstein, I., ed. 1978. *The Babylonian Talmud.* 18 vols. London: The Soncino Press.

Erickson, M. J. 1998. *Christian Theology.* Grand Rapids, MI: Baker Book House.

———. 1999. *A Basic Guide to Eschatology: Making Sense of the Millennium.* 2nd ed. Grand Rapids, MI: Baker Books.

Falk, G. 1992. *The Jew in Christian Theology.* Jefferson, NC: McFarland.

Feinberg, C. L. 1961. *Premillennialism or Amillennialism?*

The Premillennial and Amillennial Systems of Biblical Interpretation Analyzed & Compared. New York: American Board of Missions to the Jews.

Feinberg, J. S., ed. 1988. *Continuity and Discontinuity: Perspectives on the Relationship Between the Old and New Testaments*. Wheaton, IL: Crossway Books.

Finkel, A. Y. 2009. *Nefesh Hachaim: Rav Chaim of Volozhin's Classic Exploration of the Fundamentals of Jewish Belief*. New York: Judaica Press.

Finkelstein, N. 2005. *Beyond Chutzpah: On the Misuse of Anti-Semitism and the Abuse of History*. Oakland, CA: University of California Press.

Flapan, S. 1987. *The Birth of Israel: Myths and Realities*. New York: Pantheon Books.

Flusser, D. 1981. *Die rabbinischen Gleichnisse und der Gleichniserzähler Jesus*. Bern: Lang.

France, R. T. 1989. *Matthew: Evangelist and Teacher*. Exeter: Paternoster.

Fredriksen, P. 2010. *Augustine and the Jews: A Christian Defense of Jews and Judaism*. New Haven, CT: Yale University Press.

Froom, L. E. 1950. *The Prophetic Faith of Our Fathers: The Historical Development of Prophetic Interpretation*. Vol. 1. Washington, DC: Review & Herald.

Fruchtenbaum, A. G. 1994. *Israelology: The Missing Link in Systematic Theology*. 2nd ed. San Antonio, TX: Ariel Ministries Press.

Gaebelein, A. C. 1961. *The Revelation*. Neptune, NJ: Loizeaux Brothers.

_____. 1972. *The Prophet Ezekiel*. Neptune, NJ: Loizeaux Brothers.

Geisler, N. L. 2005. *Systematic Theology*, Vol. IV. Bloomington, MN: Bethany House.

Gentry, K. L. 2009a. *He Shall Have Dominion: A Postmillennial Eschatology*. Draper, VA: Apologetics Group Media.

_____. 2009b. *Postmillennialism Made Easy*. Draper, VA:

ApologeticsGroup Media.

Gesenius, W. 2012. *Der Prophet Jesaia*. 3 vols. Charleston, SC: Nabu Press.

Glashouwer Sr., W. and H. Verweij. 1985. *De komst van Jezus Christus*. Heinenoord: Van der Stoep.

Glashouwer, W. J. J. 2016. *Waarom Israël?* Heerenveen: Royal Jongbloed.

Goldberg, H. M. 1993. *The Jewish Connection*. 3rd ed. Chelsea, MI: Scarborough House.

Goldschmidt, D. and H.-J. Kraus. 1962. *Der ungekündigte Bund*. Stuttgart: Kreuz Verlag.

Golverdingen, M. 1993. *Ds. G.H. Kersten; Facetten van zijn leven en werk*. 3rd ed. Houten, Den Hertog.

Gowan, D. E. 2000. *Eschatology in the Old Testament*. Edinburgh: T. & T. Clark.

Graafland, C. 1978. Het vaste verbond: Israël en het Oude Testament bij Calvijn en het gereformeerd protestantisme. Amsterdam: Bolland.

———. 1979. "De toekomstverwachting der puriteinen en haar invloed op de nadere reformatie." *Documentatieblad Nadere Reformatie* 3:65-79.

Grant, F. W. 1897. *The Numerical Bible: The Gospels*. New York: Loizeaux Brothers.

———. 1902. *The Numerical Bible: Hebrews to Revelation*. New York: Loizeaux Brothers.

———. 1931. *The Numerical Bible: Ezekiel*. New York: Loizeaux Brothers.

———. n.d.-a. *The Revelation of Jesus Christ*. New York: Loizeaux Brothers.

———. n.d.-b. *Present Things as Foreshown in the Book of Revelation*. New York: Loizeaux Brothers.

——— and J. Bloore. 1931. *The Numerical Bible: Ezekiel*. New York: Loizeaux Brothers.

Greijdanus, S. 1965. *De Openbaring des Heren aan Johannes*. KV. Kampen: Kok.

Grenke, A. 2008. From the Holy Land to the New Jerusalem: Specialness, Utopia, Holocaust. Washington,

DC: New Academia Publishing.

Greschat, M. 2004. *Martin Bucer: A Reformer and His Times*. Louisville, KY: Westminster John Knox Press.

Grollenberg, L. H. 1970. *Voor een Israël zonder grenzen: Bijbels geloof en politieke keuze*. Bilthoven: Ambo.

Haak, T. 1918 (repr. 1657). *The Dutch Annotations Upon the Whole Bible*. London: Henry Hills.

Haffner, S. 1979. *The Meaning of Hitler*. New York: Macmillan.

Hamilton, F. E. 1942. *The Basis of Millennial Faith*. Grand Rapids, MI: Eerdmans.

Harkabi, Y. 1972. *Arab Attitudes to Israel*. New York: Halsted Press.

Heering, G. J. 1953. *De zondeval van het christendom: Een studie over christendom, staat en oorlog*. 4th ed. Utrecht: Erven J. Bijleveld.

Heering, H. J., H. De Vries, B. Baanders, R. Munk, F. J. Hoogewoud. 1987. *Vier joodse denkers in de twintigste eeuw: Rosenzweig, Benjamin, Levinas, Fackenheim*. Kampen: Kok.

Herzig, A. and C. Rademacher, eds. *Die Geschichte der Juden in Deutschland*. Hamburg: Ellert & Richter.

Herzl, Th. 1896. *Der Judenstaat: Versuch einer modernen Lösung der Judenfrage*. Leipzig/Wien: M. Breitenstein.

Heyns, J. A. 1988. *Dogmatiek*. Pretoria: NG Kerkboekhandel.

Hilberg, R. 1985. *The Destruction of the European Jews*. Vol. 1. New Haven, CT: Yale University Press.

Hill, C. E. 2001. *Regnum Caelorum: Patterns of Millennial Thought in Early Christianity*. 2nd ed. Grand Rapids, MI: Eerdmans.

Hitler, A. 2018. *Mein Kampf*. Translated by T. Dalton. New York: Clemens & Blair.

Hoek, J. 2004. *Hoop op God: Eschatologische verwachting*. 2nd ed. Zoetermeer: Boekencentrum.

_____. 2010. *Hoe kom ik in de hemel? De betekenis van de*

klassiek-gereformeerde stervensbegeleiding. Enschede: Willem de Zwijgerstichting.

Hoekema, A. A. 1979. *The Bible and the Future*. Grand Rapids, MI: Eerdmans.

Hoekendijk, B. 2001. *De toekomst van Israël: Interviews met Messiaanse leiders*. Putten: Shalom Books.

Holwerda, D. E. 1995. *Jesus and Israel: One Covenant or Two?* Grand Rapids, MI: Eerdmans.

Hoste, W. n.d.-a. *The Vision of John the Divine*. Kilmarnock: John Ritchie.

———. n.d.-b. *Israel, the Church, and Christendom*. Kilmarnock: John Ritchie.

——— and R. M'Elheran, eds. n.d. *The Lord's Return in Grace and Glory*. Kilmarnock: John Ritchie.

Houwaart, D. and S. Gerssen. 1980. *Zionisme en christelijk geloof*. Leusden: Toerustingscentrum.

Huisman, C. 1983 *Neerlands Israel: Het natiebesef der traditioneel-gereformeerden in de achttiende eeuw*. Dordrecht: J.P. van den Tol.

Hulsker, J., ed. 1989. *Vincent van Gogh: Een leven in brieven*. Amsterdam: Meulenhoff.

Ironside, H. A. 1930. *Lectures on the Book of Revelation*. New York: Loizeaux Brothers.

Jama, S. 2001. *L'histoire juive de Montaigne*. Paris: Flammarion.

Jamieson, R., A. R. Fausset, and D. Brown. 1934. *Commentary Critical and Explanatory on the Whole Bible*. Grand Rapids: Zondervan.

Jansen, H. 1981. *Christelijke theologie na Auschwitz. Vol. 1: Theologische en kerkelijke wortels van het antisemitisme*. 's-Gravenhage: Boekencentrum.

———. 2006. *Van jodenhaat tot zelfmoordterrorisme*. Heerenveen: Groen.

Jansen, J. G. B. 1999. *Christelijke theologie na Auschwitz: De geschiedenis van 2000 jaar kerkelijk antisemitisme*. 2nd ed. Amsterdam: Blaak.

Jaspers, K. 1953. *The Origin and Goal of History*. New

Haven, CT: Yale University Press.
Jennings, F. C. 1937. *Studies in Revelation.* New York: Loizeaux Brothers.
Jocz, J. 1949. *The Jewish People and Jesus Christ: A Study in the Relationship.* London: SPCK.
———. 1981. *The Jewish People and Jesus Christ after Auschwitz.* Lanham, MD: University Press of America.
Johnson, H. 2012. *Blood Libel: The Ritual Murder Accusation at the Limit of Jewish History.* Ann Arbor, MI: University of Michigan.
Joseph, M. 2005. *Judaism As Creed and Life.* Whitefish, MT: Kessinger.
Kac, A. W., ed. 1986. *The Messiahship of Jesus: Are Jews Changing their Attitude toward Jesus?* Grand Rapids, MI: Baker Book House.
Kafka, F. 2011. *The Trial.* New York: Tribeca.
Kamenetz, R. 1994. *A Poet's Rediscovery of Jewish Identity in Buddhist India.* San Francisco: HarperCollins.
Kanner, I. Z. 1990. *Joodse sprookjes.* Rijswijk: Elmar (orig.: *Jüdische Märchen*, 1987).
Kant, K. 2015 *Van Eisenach naar Betlehem: Deutsche Christen en Palestijnse christenen over Joden en Israël.* Vledderveen: Toetssteen.
Kasper, W. 1983. *The God of Jesus Christ.* London: SCM Press.
Katanacho, Y. 2012. *The Land of Christ: A Palestinian Cry.* Eugene, OR: Pickwick Publications.
Kelly, W. 1868. *Lectures on the Book of the Revelation.* London: G. Morrish.
———. 1870. *Lectures Introductory to the Study of the Acts, the Catholic Epistles, and the Revelation.* London: W.H. Broom.
———. 1970. *Lectures Introductory to the Study of the Minor Prophets.* London: Hammond.
Kocken, E. 1935. *De theorie van de vier wereldrijken en van de overdracht der wereldheerschappij tot op Inno-*

centius III. Nijmegen: Berkhout 1935.
Koivisto, R. A. 1993. *One Lord, One Faith*. Wheaton, IL: Victor Books.
Kopuit, M., ed. 1977. *Zionisme*. Nijkerk: Callenbach.
Krauss, S. 1902. *Das Leben Jesu nach jüdischen Quellen*. Berlin: Calvary.
Kuhn, T. S. 1996. *The Structure of Scientific Revolutions*. 3rd ed. Chicago: University of Chicago Press.
Kushner, H. S. 1981. *When Bad Things Happen to Good People*. New York: Schocken Books.
Küng, H. 1967. *The Church*. Translated by R. and R. Ockenden. London: Burns & Oates.
Kuyper, A. 1905. *E Voto Dordraceno: Toelichting op den Heidelbergschen Catechismus*. Vol. 2. Amsterdam: Höveker & Wormser.
———. 1931. *Van de voleinding*. Vol. 4. Kampen: Kok.
———. 1934. *Chiliasm or the Doctrine of Premillennialism*. Grand Rapids, MI: Zondervan.
Ladd, G. E. 1974. *The Presence of the Future: The Eschatology of Biblical Realism*. Grand Rapids, MI: Eerdmans.
———. 1977. Historic Premillennialism. In: Clouse, a.w.
———. 1978. *The Last Things*. Grand Rapids, MI: Eerdmans.
Laffin, J. 1989. *De dreiging van de Islam*. Amsterdam: A.W. Bruna (orig.: *Holy War: Islam Fights*, 1988).
LaHaye, T. and J. B. Jenkins. 2010. *Left Behind* 4 vols. Carol Stream, IL: Tyndale House Publishers.
Lang, G. H. 1945. *The Revelation of Jesus Christ*. London: Oliphants.
Lapide, P. 1983. *Opstanding: Een joodse geloofservaring*. Kampen: Kok.
———. 1984. *Is dat niet de zoon van Jozef? Jezus in het hedendaagse jodendom*. Baarn: Ten Have.
———. 2004. *Er predigte in ihren Synagogen: Jüdische Evangelienauslegung*. 8th ed. Gütersloh: Mohn.

———— and K. Rahner. 1984. *Heil uit de joden? Een discussie*. Hilversum: Gooi & Sticht.

Laqueur, W., ed. 1969. *The Israel-Arab Reader: A Documentary History of the Middle East Conflict*. New York: Mazel.

————. 2006. *The Changing Face of Antisemitism: From Ancient Times To The Present Day*. Oxford: Oxford University Press.

Larkin, C. 2009. *Gods Plan met de wereld*. Nunspeet: Gijsbert Versteeg.

Laytner, A. 1990. *Arguing With God: A Jewish Tradition*. Northvale, NJ: Aronson.

Lea, H. C. 2016. *A History of the Inquisition of the Middle Ages*. 3 vols. New York: Wentworth Press.

Lee, F. N. 2006. *Always Victorious! The Earliest Church not Pre- but Postmillennial*. www.dr-fnlee.org/docs5/postmill/postmill.html.

Levinas, E. 1987. *Het menselijk gelaat*. 7th ed. Baarn: Ambo.

Lightfoot, J. 1823. *The Temple-Service, and the Prospect of the Temple*. London: J.F. Dove.

Lindsey, H. 1970. *The Late Great Planet Earth*. Grand Rapids, MI: Zondervan.

Littman, D. G. 1975. *Jews under Muslim Rule in the Late 19th Century* (reprinted from the Weiner Library Bulletin, 1975, vol. 8, New Series Nos. 35/36, London 1975).

McGrath, A. E. 2007. *Christian Theology: An Introduction*. Chichester: John Wiley & Sons. 1997. *Christelijke theologie: Een introductie*. Kampen: Kok.

Maljaars, A. 2015. *Heel Israël zal behouden worden: Een kritisch onderzoek van de gangbare exegese van Romeinen 11, speciaal vs. 26*. Soesterberg: Aspekt.

Mann, G. and A. Heuss, eds. 1951. *Universele Wereldgeschiedenis* 5. Den Haag: Scheltens & Giltay.

Marquardt, F. W. 1990/1991. *Das christliche Bekenntnis zu Jesus, dem Juden: Eine Christologie*. 2 vols. Güter-

sloh: Gütersloher Verlagshaus.
Mathison, K. A. 1999. *Postmillennialism: An Eschatology of Hope*. Phillipsburg, NJ: P & R Publishing.
Maybaum, I. 1965. *The Face of God After Auschwitz*. Amsterdam: Polak & Van Gennep.
Melman, Y. 1992. *The New Israelis: An Intimate View of a Changing People*. New York: Birch Lane Press.
Michael, R. 2015. *A History of Catholic Antisemitism: The Dark Side of the Church*. New York: Palgrave Macmillan.
Miskotte, K. H. 1945. *Hoofdsom der historie: Voordrachten over de visioenen van den apostel Johannes*. Nijkerk: Callenbach.
Moerkerken, A. 2004. *Ons troostboek: Verklaring van de Heidelbergse Catechismus. Houten: Den Hertog*.
Moffic, E. 2016. *What Every Christian Needs to Know About the Jewishness of Jesus: A New Way of Seeing the Most Influential Rabbi in History*. Nashville, TN: Abingdon Press.
Moltmann, J. 1993. *The Crucified God*. London: SCM Press.
_____. 1996. *The Coming of God: Christian Eschatology*. Minneapolis, MN: Augsburg Fortress.
Mordecai, V. 1995. *Is Fanatic Islam a Global Threat?* Jerusalem: Mordecai.
Morris, B. 2000. *Righteous Victims: A history of the Zionist-Arab Conflict, 1881-1999*. London: John Murray.
_____, ed. 2007. *Making Israel*. Ann Arbor, MI: University of Michigan Press.
_____. 2009. *One State, Two States: Resolving the Israel/Palestine Conflict*. New Haven, CT: Yale University Press.
Nadler, S. M. 2001. *Spinoza: A Life*. Cambridge: Cambridge University Press.

Neusner, J. 1997. *The Theology of Rabbinic Judaism: A Prolegomenon*, Atlanta: Scholars Press.

———. 2003. *The Formation of the Babylonian Talmud*. Eugene, OR: Wipf & Stock.

Newton, B. W. 1913. *Expository Teaching on the Millennium and Israel's Future*. London: Lucas Collins.

Noordmans, O. 1956. *Gestalte en geest*. Amsterdam: Holland.

North, G. 1991. *Millennialism and Social Theory*. Tyler, TX: Institute for Christian Economics.

O'Malley, P. 2015. *The Two-State Delusion: Israel and Palestine – A Tale of Two Narratives*. New York: Viking.

Ouweneel, W. J. 1973. *Het Hooglied van Salomo*. Winschoten: Uit het Woord der Waarheid.

———. 1982a. *Het ontstaan van Israël* (with V. I. Kerkhof). Edited by W. J. J. Glashouwer). Hilversum: Evangelische Omroep.

———. 1982b. *'Wij zien Jezus': Bijbelstudies over de brief aan de Hebreeën*. 2 vols. Vaassen: Medema.

———. 1988/1990. *De Openbaring van Jezus Christus: Bijbelstudies over het boek Openbaring*. 2 vols. Vaassen: Medema.

———. 1994. *Godsverlichting: De evocatie van de verduisterde God: Een weg tot spiritualiteit en gemeenteopbouw*. Amsterdam: Buijten & Schipperheijn.

———. 1995. *Alverzoening*. Vaassen: Medema.

———. 1997. *De vrijheid van de Geest: Bijbelstudies bij de Brief van Paulus aan de Galaten*. Vaassen: Medema.

———. 1998a. *De zevende koningin: Het eeuwig vrouwelijke en de raad van God*. Vol. 2 of *Metahistorische trilogie*. Heerenveen: Barnabas.

———. 1998b. *Geestelijke strijd*. Vol. 4 of *Geloofsleven*. Vaassen: Medema.

———. 1999. *Jeruzalem, de stad van de grote Koning*. Vaassen: Medema.

———. 2000a. *Het Jobslijden van Israël: Israëls lijden oplichtend uit het boek Job*. Vaassen: Medema.

———. 2000b. *De zesde kanteling*. Vol. 3 of *Metahistorische trilogie*. Heerenveen: Barnabas.

_____. 2001a. *Hoe lief heb ik uw Wet! De eeuwige Torah tussen Oude en Nieuwe Verbond.* Vaassen: Medema.

_____. 2001b. *Hoogtijden voor Hem: De bijbelse feesten en hun betekenis voor Joden en christenen.* Vaassen: Medema.

_____. 2002. *Israël en de Palestijnen: Waarheid en misleiding.* Heerenveen: Barnabas.

_____. 2003a. *De negende Koning: Het laatste der hemelrijken: De triomf van Christus over de machten.* 3rd ed. Vol. 1 of *Metahistorische triologie.* Soesterberg: Aspekt.

_____. 2004. *Geneest de zieken! Over de bijbelse leer van ziekte, genezing en bevrijding.* 4th ed. Vaassen: Medema.

_____. 2007. *De Christus van God: Ontwerp van een christologie.* Vaassen: Medema.

_____. 2008. *Het plan van God: Ontwerp van een voorbeschikkingsleer.* Vaassen: Medema.

_____. 2009. *Het zoenoffer van God: Ontwerp van een verzoeningsleer.* Vaassen: Medema.

_____. 2010a. *De Kerk van God (I): Ontwerp van een elementaire ecclesiologie.* Heerenveen: Medema.

_____. 2010b. *De kerk van God II: Ontwerp van een historische en praktische ecclesiologie.* Heerenveen: Medema.

_____. 2010c. *Komt er een Grote Opwekking?* Harderwijk: Rock Publ./Highway Media.

_____. 2011. *Het verbond en het koninkrijk van God: Ontwerp van een foederologie en basileologie.* Heerenveen: Medema.

_____. 2012a. *De toekomst van God: Ontwerp van een eschatologie.* Heerenveen: Medema 2012a.

_____. 2012b. *Het Woord van God: Ontwerp van een openbarings- en schriftleer.* Heerenveen: Medema.

_____. 2014a. *Een dubbelsnoer van licht: Honderd grootse joodse en christelijke godsmannen door de geschiedenis heen en hun moeizame relaties.* Soesterberg:

Aspekt.

_____. 2014b. *Wisdom for Thinkers: An Introduction to Christian Philosophy.* St. Catharines, ON : Paideia Press.

_____. 2014c. *What Then Is Theology? An Introduction to Christian Theology.* St. Catharines, ON: Paideia Press.

_____. 2018a. *The Heidelberg Diary: Daily Devotions on the Heidelberg Catechism.* St. Catharines, ON: Paideia Press.

_____. 2018b. *Adam, Where Are You?—and Why This Matters: A Theological Evaluation of the Evolutionist Hermeneutic.* Toronto: Ezra Press.

_____. 2020a. *The Eternal Torah: Living under God.* St. Catharines, ON: Paideia Press.

_____. 2020b. *The Eden Story: A History of Paradise, from Its Demise to Its New Rise.* St. Catharines, ON: Paideia Press.

_____. 2022. *Forever with the Lord: The Bible and the Hereafter.* St. Catharines, ON: Paideia Press.

_____ and de Korte, G. 2010. *Rome en Reformatie: Overeenkomsten en verschillen na vijfhonderd jaar Hervorming.* Heerenveen: Medema.

Paas, S. 2014. *Israëlvisies in beweging: Gevolgen voor Kerk, geloof en theologie.* Kampen: Brevier.

_____. 2015. *Liefde voor Israël nader bekeken: Voor het Evangelie zijn alle volken gelijk.* Kampen: Brevier.

Pache, R. 1968. *De komende Christus.* Laren: Novapres.

Pawson, D. 1995. *When Jesus Returns.* London: Hodder & Stoughton.

Pentecost, J. D. (1958) 1964. *Things to Come: A Study in Biblical Eschatology.* Grand Rapids, MI: Academie Books.

Peters, G. N. H. 1952. *Theocratic Kingdom.* 8 vols. Grand Rapids, MI: Kregel.

Prinz, J. 1966. *Popes from the Ghetto: A View of Medieval Christendom.* New York: Horizon Press.

Reitsma, B. 2006. *Wie is onze God? Arabische christenen, Israel en de aard van God.* Amsterdam VBK Media.
———. 2017. *Kwetsbare liefde: De kerk, de Islam en de drie-enige God.* Zoetermeer: Boekencentrum.
Ritchie, J. 1912. *Man's Future State: An Examination of Scripture Testimony on this Great Subject.* Kilmarnock: John Ritchie.
Robertson, O. P. 2000. *The Israel of God: Yesterday, Today, and Tomorrow.* Phillipsburg, NJ: P&R Publications.
Rosenzweig, F. 1935. *Briefe.* Berlin: Schocken.
Rossier, H. 1961. *Le Langage symbolique de l'Apcalypse.* Vevey: Éditions Bibles et Traités Chrétiens.
———. 1967. *Court exposé et division de l'Apocalypse.* Vevey: Éditions Bibles et Traités Chrétiens.
Rubenstein, R. L. 1968. *De God van de Joden na Auschwitz.* Utrecht: Ambo.
——— and J. K. Roth. 1987. *Approaches to Auschwitz: The Legacy of the Holocaust.* Atlanta: John Knox Press.
Rushdoony, R. J. 1973. *The Institutes of Biblical Law.* Nutley, NJ: Craig Press.
Ryrie, C. C. 1953. *The Basis of the Premillennial Faith.* Neptune, NJ: Loizeaux Brothers.
———. 1965. *Dispensationalism Today.* Chicago: Moody Press.
———. 1995. *Ryrie Study Bible.* Expanded ed. Chicago: Moody Press.
Saada, T. (with D. Merrill). 2008. *Once an Arafat Man: The True Story of How a PLO Sniper Found a New Life.* Carol Stream, IL: Tyndale House Publishers.
——— (with D. Merrill). 2016. *The Mind of Terror: A Former Muslim Sniper Explores What Motivates ISIS.* Carol Stream, IL: Tyndale House Publishers.
Sand, S. 2008. *Comment le peuple juif fut inventé: De la Bible au sionisme.* Paris: Fayard.
Sartre, J.-P. 1946 (1995). *Anti-Semite and Jew: An Explora-*

tion of the Etiology of Hate. Paris: Schocken.

Sauer, E. 1951. *The Triumph of the Crucified: A Survey of Historical Revelation in the New Testament*. Translated by G. H. Lang. Grand Rapids, MI: Eerdmans.

———. 1952. *The Dawn of World Redemption: A Survey of Historical Revelation in the Old Testament*. Translated by G. H. Lang. Grand Rapids, MI: Eerdmans.

———. 1955. *Gott, Menschheit und Ewigkeit*. 2nd ed. Wuppertal: R. Brockhaus.

Schäfer, P. 2007. *Jesus in the Talmud*. Princeton: Princeton University Press.

Schiffman, M. 1996. *Return of the Remnant: The Rebirth of Messianic Judaism*. Baltimore, MD: Lederer Messianic Publications.

Schipflinger, T. 1998. *Sophia-Maria: A Holistic Vision of Creation*. Newbury Port, MA: Weiser Books.

Schmid, A. P., ed. 2011. "The Definition of Terrorism." *The Routledge Handbook of Terrorism Research*. 39–98. Abingdon: Routledge.

Scholem, G. 1960. *Jewish Gnosticism, Merkabah Mysticism, and the Talmudic Tradition*. New York: Jewish Theological Seminary of America.

Schoeps, H. J. 1952. *Philosemitismus im Barock: Religions- und geistesgeschichtliche Untersuchungen*. Tübingen: Mohr (Siebeck).

Scholl-Latour, P. 2000. *Lügen im Heiligen Land: Machtproben zwischen Euphrat und Nil*. Berlin: Wolf Jobst Siedler Verlag.

Schrupp, E. 1992. *Israel und das Reich des Islam*. Wuppertal: R. Brockhaus.

Schwarz-Bart, A. 1985. *The Last of the Just*. Translated by S. Becker. New York: Atheneum Publishers.

———. 2011. *The Morning Star*. Translated by J. Rose. New York: Overlook Duckworth Books.

Scofield, C.I. 1967. *The New Scofield Reference Bible*. New York: Oxford University Press.

Scott, W. 1920. *Exposition of the Revelation of Jesus*

Christ. London: Pickering & Inglis.
Servaas van Rooijen, A. J., ed. 1898. *Oranje-album: Feestbundel ter gelegenheid van het aanvaarden der regeering door H.M. Koningin Wilhelmina op 31 Augustus 1898.* 's-Gravenhage: Lankhout.
Shlaim, A. 1999. *The Iron Wall: Israel and the Arab World.* New York: Norton.
———. 2009. *Israel and Palestine: Reappraisals, Revisions, Refutations.* London: Verso.
Shulam, J. (with H. Le Cornu) 1998. *A Commentary on the Jewish Roots of Romans.* Baltimore: Messianic Jewish Publishers.
———. 2010. *Verborgen schatten: De Joodse manier van uitleg van de Schriften in de eerste eeuw.* Putten: Shalom Books.
Slotki, I. W. 1983. *Isaiah.* SBB. London: Soncino.
Smelik, K. A. D. 2004. *Herleefde tijd: Een Joodse geschiedenis.* Leuven: Acco.
Smith, H. n.d. *The Revelation: An Expository Outline.* Oak Park, IL: Bible Truth Publishers.
Snell, H. H. 1878. *Notes on the Revelation.* London: W.H. Broom.
Spurgeon, C.H. 1969. *Lectures.* Vol. 4: *Commenting and Commentaries.* Carlisle: Banner or Truth Trust.
———. 1982. *Metropolitan Tabernacle Pulpit.* Pasadena, TX: Pilgrim Publications.
Spykman, G. J. 1992. *Reformational Theology: A New Paradigm for Doing Dogmatics.* Grand Rapids, MI: Eerdmans.
Stanley, C. n.d. *The Revelation of Jesus Christ.* London: G. Morrish.
Steinsaltz, A. 2009. *The Essential Talmud.* New York: Basic Books.
Stern, D. H. 1997. *Messianic Jewish Manifesto.* 3rd ed. Clarksville, MD: Jewish New Testament Publications.
———. 1999. *Jewish New Testament Commentary.* 6th

ed. Clarksville, MD: Jewish New Testament Publications.

———. 2009. *Restoring the Jewishness of the Gospel.* Clarksville, MD: Messianic Jewish Publishers.

Strack, H. L. 1945. *Introduction to the Talmud and Midrash.* Philadelphia, PA: Jewish Publication Society.

——— and P. Billerbeck. 1922–1928. *Kommentar zum Neuen Testament Aus Talmud und Midrasch.* 4 vols. München: C.H. Beck.

Susman, M. 1948. *Das Buch Hiob und das Schicksal des jüdischen Volkes.* Zürich: Steinberg-Verlag.

Swete, H. B. 1951. *The Apocalypse of St. John.* Grand Rapids, MI: Eerdmans.

Tatford, F. A. 1947. *Prophecy's Last Word.* London: Pickering & Inglis.

Ten Berge, G. 2011. *Land van mensen: Christenen, joden en moslims tussen confrontaties en dialoog.* Nijmegen: Valkhof Press.

Thurneysen, E. 1931. "Christus und seine Zukunft." *Zwischen den Zeiten* 9:187–211.

Tillich, P. 1968. *Systematic Theology.* 3 vols. Digswell Place, Herts: Nisbett & Co.

Trotter, W. and T. Smith. n.d. *Eight Lectures on Prophecy, or, The Importance of Prophetic Study.* London: Pickering & Inglis.

Van Agt, A. A. M. 2009. *Een schreeuw om recht. De tragedie van het Palestijnse volk.* Amsterdam: De Bezige Bij.

Van Beek, H. M. 2007. *De houding van G.H. Kersten als leider van de SGP tegenover de Joden.* Leiden: Universiteit van Leiden.

Van Campen, M. 2007. *Gans Israël: Voetiaanse en coccejaanse visies op joden gedurende de zeventiende en achttiende eeuw.* 2nd ed. Zoetermeer: Boekencentrum.

Van de Beek, A. 1987. *De adem van God: De Heilige Geest in kerk en kosmos.* Nijkerk: G.F. Callenbach.

Van der Kooi, C. and G. Van den Brink. 2017. *Christian Dogmatics: An Introduction.* Translated by R. Bruinsma with J. D. Bratt. Grand Rapids, MI: Eerdmans.

Van de Poll, E. W. 2008. *Sacred Times for Chosen People: Development, Analysis and Missiological Significance of Messianic Jewish Holiday Practice.* Zoetermeer: Boekencentrum.

Van der Heijden, C. 2008. *Israël, een onherstelbare vergissing.* Amsterdam/Antwerpen: Contact.

Van der Horst, P. W. 2006. *De mythe van het joodse kannibalisme.* Soesterberg: Aspekt.

Van der Kooye, R. 2015. *De Hebreeuwse identiteit: Een onderzoek naar de identiteit van mensen van Afrikaanse afkomst.* CreateSpace Independent Publishing Platform.

Van der Schuit, J. J. et al. 1933. *Rapport over de leer van Ds. A.M. Berkhoff betreffende het duizendjarig rijk en de tweeërlei opstanding.* Zwolle: Generale Synode van de Christelijke Gereformeerde Kerk in Nederland.

Van der Wolf, P. 2010. *Kerk, Evangelie en Israël: De actualiteit van de zendingsopdracht onder de Joden.* Harderwijk: Timotheüs.

Van Genderen, J. 1984. *De verwachting van een duizendjarig vrederijk.* Kampen: Kok.

——— and W. H. Velema. 2008. *Concise Reformed Dogmatics.* Translated by G. Bilkes and E. M. van der Maas. Phillipsburg, NJ: Presbyterian and Reformed Publishing Company.

Van Klinken, G. J. 1996. *Opvattingen in de Gereformeerde Kerken in Nederland over het Jodendom, 1896-1970.* Kampen: Kok.

Van Ryn, A. 1960. *Notes on the Book of Revelation.* Kansas City: Walterick Publishers.

Van Sliedregt, J. 1994. *Naar Schrift en belijdenis.* 10th ed. Houten: Den Hertog.

Van 't Spijker, W., W. Balke, L. van Driel, K. Exalto, and

K. Runia, eds. 1999. *Eschatologie: Handboek over de christelijke toekomstverwachting.* Kampen: De Groot Goudriaan.

———, J. N. Noorlandt, and H. van der Schaaf, eds. 1992. *Een eeuw christelijk-gereformeerd. Aspecten van 100 jaar Christelijke Gereformeerde Kerken.* Kampen: Kok.

Van Vlastuin, W. 1989. *Opwekking.* 4th ed. Utrecht: De Banier.

Verkuyl, J. 1992. *De kern van het christelijk geloof.* Kampen: Kok.

Voorhoeve, H. C. 1922. *De toekomst onzes Heeren Jezus Christus en de daarmee in verband staande gebeurtenissen.* 8th ed. 's-Gravenhage: J.N. Voorhoeve.

———. 1969. *Beschouwing over de Openbaring.* Apeldoorn: Medema.

Wagner, C. P. 2008. *Dominion!: How Kingdom Action Can Change the World.* Grand Rapids, MI: Chosen Books.

Wagner, R. n.d. *Gesammelte Schriften und Dichtungen.* Vol. 5, Leipzig: Siegels Musikalienhandlung.

Walker, P. W. L., ed. 1994. *Jerusalem Past and Present in the Purposes of God.* Grand Rapids, MI: Baker Book House.

Walvoord, J. F. 1949–1951. "The Millennial Issue in Modern Theology; Postmillennialism; Amillennialism; Premillennialism." *Bibliotheca Sacra* 106–108.

———. 1950. *The Return of the Lord.* Grand Rapids, MI: Zondervan.

———. 1957. *The Rapture Question.* Grand Rapids, MI: Zondervan.

———. 1966. *The Revelation of Jesus Christ.* Chicago: Moody Press.

———. 1974. *Matthew: Thy Kingdom Come.* Chicago: Moody Press.

———. 1991. *Major Bible Prophecies: 37 Crucial prophecies that Affect You Today.* Grand Rapids, MI: Zondervan.

Wang, S. and E. R. Nelson. 1998. *God and the Ancient Chinese*. Dunlap, TN: Read Books Publisher.

Warfield, B. B. 1929. *Biblical Doctrines*. New York: Oxford University Press.

———. 1952. "The Prophecies of St. Paul." In *Biblical and Theological Studies*. Edited by S. G. Craig. 463–502. Philadelphia: Presbyterian & Reformed Publishing Company.

Weber, O. 1981. *Foundations of Dogmatics*. Vol. 1. Grand Rapids, MI: Eerdmans. 1955. *Grundlagen der Dogmatik*, Bd. I. Neukirchen: Verlag der Buchhandlung des Erziehungsvereins.

Wexler, P. 2007. "Yiddish Evidence for the Khazar Component in the Ashkenazic Ethnogenesis." In *The World of the Khazars: New Perspectives*. Edited by P. B. Golden, H. Ben-Shammai, and A. Róna-Tas. Handbuch der Orientalistik 17. 387–98. Leyden: Brill.

Whybrow, W. T. 1898. *Addresses on the Revelation*. London: James Carter.

Wiesenthal, S. 1973. *Sails of Hope: The Secret Mission of Christopher Columbus*. New York: MacMillan.

Wijenberg, J. 2011. *De Nederlandse politiek, het Israëlisch-Palestijns conflict, het international recht en de zoektocht naar vrede in het Midden-Oosten*. Eigen uitgave.

Wilckens, U. 1971. "*Sophia, sophos, sophizō*." *Theological Dictionary of the New Testament*. Vol. 7. 465–528. Grand Rapids, MI: Eerdmans.

Wilk, M. 1986. *Jewish Presence in T. S. Eliot and Franz Kafka*. Brown Judaic Studies 82. Atlanta: Scholars Press.

Wilken, R. L. 1982. *John Chrysostom and the Jews*. Berkeley, CA: University of California Press.

Williamson, M. 2013. *Terrorism, War and International Law: The Legality of the Use of Force Against Afghanistan in 2001*. Farnham: Ashgate.

Wilson, M. R. 1989. *Our Father Abraham: Jewish Roots*

of the Christian Faith. Grand Rapids, MI: Eerdmans/ Dayton, OH: Center for Judaic-Christian Studies.

Yamauchi, E. 1988. *Ezra, Nehemia.* EBC. Grand Rapids, MI: Zondervan.

Zijderveld, G. A. n.d. *De wonderen Gods met Israël.* Oostburg: Pieters.

Scripture Index

Old Testament
Genesis
1	95
1:1	663
1:1-3	135
1:26-28	630
1:28	135
2	19, 59
2:2	18
2:2-3	57
4	97
4:9	140
5	490
6:7-8	607
6:8	374
6:9	607
8:4	665
8:9	332
8:20	15, 665
9:4	339
10	98, 652, 661
10:1-31	419
10:5	661
10:6	485
10:7	485
10:32	661 11 98, 490
11:1-9	661
11:10-32	419
11:28-30	193, 12, 10
12:1-3	403
12:3	30, 220
14:18	627
14:18-20	431, 432
14:22	432
15:4-6	32
15:9	15
15:16	467
15:18	440
15:19-21	467
16:1	485
16:3	485, 487
16:9	487
16:10-12	486
16:12	486
17	375
17:1	220
17:17	490
17:20	486
17:20-21	487
17:23	490
18	238, 582
18:18	30
19:36-38	485
20:7	267
21:4	490
21:6	490
21:9	490
21:12-13	487
21:20-21	98
21:21	485
22	598, 600
22:1	665
22:2	458
22:9	396
22:9-13	223
22:14	572
22:17	17
22:18	30
22:24	487
25	32, 488
25:2-3	485
25:3	485
25:8	488
25:8-10	492
25:9-10	98
25:12-1	898
25:13	485
25:13-16	486
25:13-18	488
25:17	488, 490
25:23b	440
25:29-34	121
26:4	30, 27, 440
27:1-40	121
27:29	440
28:1	440
28:12	11, 664
28:14	30
32:6	121
32:24-26	616
33	121
33:13-14	120, 121
33:14	99
35:19	18, 415
35:22	487

35:29	488, 490	19:5	561, 622	33:18-20	133
36:12	485, 487	19:5-6	673	34:1	156
36:16	485	19:6	267	34:4	156
38	193	19:10-14	621	34:6	374
41	193	19:11-13	551	34:28	156
45	99	19:16-17	621	34:6-7	46
45:5	100	20:1-2	647	34:20	13
45:7	100	20:1-17	621	34:26	72
45:1-15	609	20:2	40	35:3	324
49:9	344	20:4	128	40:33-35	559
49:10	10, 190	20:5	46, 254	40:34-35	551, 577, 621
49:33	488	20:8	52		
50:19-20	100	20:8-11	621	40:34-38	602, 552
		20:10	24, 58		
Exodus		20:12	161	**Leviticus**	
1	618	20:13-17	38	1	207
1:8	207	20:20-25	13	1:3	206
1:9-10	208	21:17	161, 486	6:9-13	207
1:21	208	22:25	112	10:1-2	560
1:22	208	22:29	13	10:1-3	601
2:3	208	23:19	72	10:3	566
2:12	472	23:31	617	11	36, 82, 16 64, 212
3:1	665	24:5	13		
3:8	209	24:7-8	256	16:2	552
3:14	553, 661	24:8	15	6:13	552
3-4	471	24:10-11	133	16:16-17	255
4:22	147, 258, 669	24:16	554	16:20-22	232
6:12	542	25:8	546, 554, 558	16:21	111
6:23	565			16:21-22	110
6:30	542	25:23-30	563	16:34	37
12	62, 13, 14 209	25:40	665	17:11	30
		26:7	558	19:8	162
13:2	13	27:21	558	19:18	37, 38, 160, 162
13:11-16	13	28	552		
13:13	486	28-29	13	20:9	161
14:14	481	29:38-46	207	23	36
15:1	615	29:42-46	559	23:3	61
15:13	569, 602	29:45	546, 554	23:4-44	61
15:17	569, 602 16, 59	29:45-46	558	23:15-16	56
		30:20-21	552	25:23	436, 459, 491
16:23-29	57, 17, 481, 482	31:16-17	621		
		31:18	156, 32, 130	25:23-24	668
17:6	176	32:16	156	25:35-55	668
17:20	486	32:32	473	25:36-37	112
19	662, 665	33:16	209	26:19	208

Scripture Index

Numbers
2	652
3:5-13	13
4:1-15	566
4:7	563
4:18-20	552
6	28
6:25	374
12:1	472
12:8	129, 133
15:22-31	264
15:30	264
15:38-39	361, 653, 654
18:22	552
19:1-22	540
20:11-12	233
23	480
24:17a	615-616
24:17b-19	616
30:3-8	253
31	481
33	564
35	139
35:34	554

Deuteronomy
3:8	666
4:12	128
4:15	128
4:20	209
5:6	40
5:7	46
5:8	128
5:14	24, 58
5:12	52
5:16	161
6:4	135, 377
6:5	38, 162
7:6	561
7:6-8	673
7:7-8	423
9:10	156
10:1-5	561
10:12	38
12:5-6	569, 570
12:11	569, 570
14	36, 82
14:1	669
14:21	72
14:24-26	637
16	36
18:15-16	633
23:19-20	112
24:1	623
24:3	623
26:18	561
27:16	161
28:2-6	642
28:23	208
28:32	197
28:68	197
30:1-11	607
30:4	170
30:5	318
30:6	38
31:24-29	561
32:8-9	652
32:10	140, 150, 153, 202, 418
32:35	266
33:5	382
34	666
38-39	361

Joshua
7:2-5	481
10-11	481
15:8	547
15:20-62	629
18:16	547
24:32	415

Judges
4	666
5	666
6:3	485
16:24	437
20:26-27	562

1 Samuel
1-3	277
1:9	562
2:30-34	601
2:35	601
3:3	562
4	596
4:4	557, 564
4:21-22	564, 565, 602
6:19	565
7:1	565
7:2	565
8:1-3	277
10:10	480
13:14	259, 593
13:19	8
14:18	565
17	593
17:40	258
19:23	480
21:6	563
22:1-2	593
22:3-4	603
25:29	247, 258
28	666
31	666

2 Samuel
2:10	6
5	593
5:7	605
5:9	605
6:2	557
6:2-3	565
6:10-11	566
6:12-17	566
7:12-16	606
8	593
8:17	601
11	441
15	601
15:19	232

15:30	666	21:18-19	571	13	193
16:7-8	204	21:26	571	13:23-24	193
17	197	21:29	563		
20:2	6	22	595	**Esther**	
22:45	387	22:1	571	1:1	228
24:24	396	22:8	233	2:5	226
		23:25	554, 574, 583	2:7	227
1 Kings				2:10	227
2:10	599	24:3	601	3	227
2:12	176	25:8	47	3:8	107
2:27	601	28:3	233	3:10	226
2:45	176	29:23	176, 557, 639	3:12	150
3:4	563, 567			4	228
4:20	645			4:8	228
4:25	645	**2 Chronicles**		4:14	228
5	568	1:3	563	4:16	228
6:1	250	2:1	568	8:1	226
8:1	598	3:14	58, 571, 598, 665	9-10	227
8:4	564			9:10	226
8:9	561	5:4-5	564, 568	9:24	226
8:10-11	551, 571, 572	5:13-14	551	10:3	227
		5:14	571, 572		
8:27	546, 547, 548	6:12-42	555	**Job**	
		7:1-2	551	1-2	652
8:29-49	555	7:2	603	1.1	220
8:46	218	13:22	85	1:1-5	157
12:16-17	6	24:27	85	1:5	218, 221
18:21	173	29:18	563	1:8	220
18:36-38	666			1:10	113
21:1	568	**Ezra**		2:3	220
21:10	265	1:3-5	574	2:11	107
21:13	265	1:5	479	6:11	240
		3:1	480	9:33	285
2 Kings		5-6	636	13:15	285
5:7	376	6:13-18	573	19:25-26	139
18:4	129	7:6	81	20	107, 266
		7:10	81, 283	20:5	204
1 Chronicles		7:11-12	81	20:29	204
5:10	485	7:21	81	21:7-33	205
5:19-20	485	10	193	21:19	205
9:32	563			22	107, 266
11:4-7	396	**Nehemiah**		22:6-7	249
13:6	557	2:19	434	22:6-9	114
16:17	37	4:7	434	22:15	204
16:39-40	563	6:1	434	22:18	204

23:12	204, 285	23:1	627	77:19	209
23:13-16	204	23:6	374, 568	78:57-71	604
29:2-25	157	26:8	568	78:59-62	595
29:12-17	114	27:4	567	78:60	546
33:23-24	285	30:3-5	230	78:67-68	605
38:1	285	31:5	260	80:17	226
42	157	37:30-31	159	81:15	594
42:5	157, 217	40:6-8	215	87:1-2	640
42:5-6	238	40:8	159	87:3	640
42:6	124, 238, 285	41:10	248	87:4	74
		42:5	656	90:4	498
42:7	114, 266, 285	42:7	142	92:10-13	3, 95 19
		44	216	95:7-11	18
42:7-8	139	44:17-18	216	95:10	647
42:7-10	221	44:23-24	247	97:7	630
42:8	140	45:2	620	101:7-8	594
42:8-9	221	45:3-4	620	102:13-14	634
42:7-9	119, 213	45:6	620	102:13-17	599, 600,
		45:6-7	378	102:26-27	429
Psalms		45:7	620	103:13	376
1:1-2	279	45:9-14	619	103:21	13
2:2	268	45:10	629	105:7-11	436
2:6	595, 628	45:14	620, 629	105:12-15	266-267
2:6-8	599	46:4	640	110:1	18
2:8	320, 628	48:1	605	110:1-2	597
4:4-5	18	48:2	639	110:3	597
5:7	567-568	51:18-19	638	110:6	597
8	629	53:8	612	115:3	556
9:12	320	55:12-13	248	115:16	556
11:4	557	66:3	387, 594	116:3-5	230
14:7	320, 612	68:29	638	118	500
16:8b	18	69:4	225, 232	118:22-23	125
16:8-11	18	69:5	225	118:26	34, 500
16:10-11	230	69:9a	225	119	47
17:8	150, 153, 202	69:9b	225	119:9	31
		69:21	225	119:12	47
18:44	387	69:35	634	119:19	656
18:44-45	594	69:35-36	226	119:26	47
19:4	16, 20	72:8	126, 617, 629	119:33	47
19:7-8	44			119:44	160
19:9-10	562	72:8-11	490	119:47	44
19:9b-10	203	72:11	629	119:48	44
20:3	320	73	205	119:64	47
22:1	211	73:17	205	119:68	47
22:16b	380	74:18-19	332	119:72	562

119:97	44	27:6	425	9:8	299
119:98	160	27:9	425	10:3	206
119:99	78	28:13	40	10:5	262, 432
119:124	47	30:4	378	10:20	299
119:135	47			10:21-22	607
119:113	44	**Ecclesiastes**		11:1	333, 626
119:127	44, 562	1:18	42	11:1-10	662
119:142	160	4:12	150, 202	11:6-8	520
119:144	160			11:9	127
119:152	160	**Song of Solomon**		11:10	626, 656
119:159	44	1:5	488	11:11	613
119:160	160	2	645	11:11-15	613
119:163	44	2:6	261	11:12	170, 609
119:165	44	2:10-13	643	11:14	169, 482
119:171	47	2:16	203, 645	11:16	170, 613
120:5	485, 656 120,134	4:11	204	12:6	638
		5:16	203,	13:6	4
122:1-2	654	6:3	203, 645	13:9-10	285, 286
122:6-9	673	7:10	203, 645	13:20	485
125:1	608	8:3	261	14:1	299
125:1-3	597	8:6	261	16:1-5	603
126:1-3	608			18:7	611
126:1-4	612	**Isaiah**		19:16-17	492
127:1	638	1:3	487	19:16-25	492
129:5	597, 132 595	1:26	639	19:18	658
		2:2	121	19:18-19	492
132:2-7	570	2:2-3	308, 590, 656	19:20	492
132:11-18	595, 606			19:21-22	493
132:13-18	638, 133 133,134, 638	2:2-4	652-653	19:23	493
		2:3	47, 638, 660	19:23-25	492, 493, 657
139:5-12	550	2:4	127, 336, 337, 660	19:24	493
139:7-10	549			19:25	493
147:2	634	2:5-6	299	21:11	488
		4:2	641	21:13-17	485
Proverbs		6:1	134, 549	21:16	488
1:8	47	6:16	267	25:6-7	275
3:1	47	8:8	169	25:6-8	656, 657
4:2	47	8:14-15	125	26:1-2	641
6:20	47	8:17	299	26:4	627
7:2	47, 202	9:3	169	27:3	627
11:22	575	9:6	335, 379	27:6	299
16:24	204	9:6-7	32, 335, 384, 662	27:13	613
24:13	204			28:16	627
27:6a	418	9:7	530, 620	29:18	647

29:23	299	45:25	614, 647	54:3	672
30:23-24	642	46:9-10	225	54:4-8	624, 625, 672
32:1-4	647, 648	46:13	444, 641		
32:2	627	47:11	206	54:4-10	484
33	582	48:20	670	55:12-13	644
33:17	158, 609, 626	49:2	260	56:2-6	37, 621
		49:3	216, 235, 236	56:2-7	58
33:20	600			56:3-7	219, 658, 659
33:20-21	581	49:6	235, 236		
33:21	582	49:6b	627	56:7	655, 665
33:22	627	49:8	19	56:6-7	637, 656
33:24	648	49:8-26	19	57:13b	441
34	99	49:12	613	57:15	220, 554
34:1-17	617	49:16	260	58:12	634
35:2	158	49:22-23	671	59:20	671
35:5-6	648	49:26	671	60	170, 489
35:10	611	50:1	624	60:1	139, 627
37:22	597	51:3	634, 644	60:4	656
37:27	597	51:16	260	60:5	612, 636
40-66	668, 669	52:1	37, 541, 600	60:6-7	489
40:4	318, 520	52:1-2	600	60:6-9	612
40:11	627	52:5b	235	60:7	488
40:12	260	52:13-53:12	380	60:7-13	637
40:22	550, 555	53	210, 211, 212, 213, 214, 216, 231, 384	60:10	634, 635
40:27	299			60:10-14	656
41:8	299			60:11	636
41:14	111, 299			60:12-13	635
41:19-20	643	53:3	214, 248, 275	60:13	637
42:6-7	648			60:14	308, 600, 639
42:10-12	494	53:4	214		
42:11	488	53:4b	275	60:16	139
42:24	299	53:4-5	110	60:19	627
42-53	211, 226, 229	53:4-6	211, 484	60:21	333, 441, 614, 647
		53:5	210, 231		
43:2	142, 209	53:5a	214	61:1	381, 648
43:2-3	210	53:7	110, 212	61:1-2	662
43:4	259, 622	53:7-8	213, 214	61:4	634
43:14	670	53:8	211	61:5	656 61:6
43:14-20	669, 670	53:8b	214		267, 636
43:16	209	53:9	214	62	640
44:3	670	53:10	231	62:1-5	626
44:24-26	670-671	53:12	384, 672,	62:2	639
44:28	671	54	484	62:3	641
45:1	671	54:1	12, 600	62:4	639
45:23	671	54:2	582	62:9	637

62:12	639	20	238	33:21-22	638
63	99	22:29	667	40:11-12	603
63:1-14	617	23:24	549	49:8	485
63:9	142, 209, 225, 244, 632	23:29	51	50:4-5	611
		25:11-12	412	50:20	614
		25:24	485		
64:4	543	26:4-9	572	**Ezekiel**	
65	501	26:6	596, 604	1:26	134
65:4	37, 541	26:9	596, 604	9:3	572
65:18-25	662	27:5	460	9-11	649
65:17	662	27:10	318	10:18-19	572
65:20	662	28:1-2	437	10:18-22	636
65:20b	594	29:10	412	10:19	580
65:25	520	30:3	610, 611	11:17-20	442
66:1	549	30:7	632	11:22-23	572, 636
66:3	37, 541	30:18	612	11:23	580
66:15-17	541	31:10	627	16	619
66:17	37, 541	31:10-12	611	16:10b	619
66:18-20	650	31:15	333	16:1-14	483
66:18-24	662	30:3-4	7	16:8-14	621, 622
66:22	662	30:7	6	17:22-23	628
66:23	656	30:8	6	18:20	253
66:24	656	30:9	6	18:30-31	278
72:8	495, 591	30:11	6	20:33-43	610, 611
16:19	617	30:16-17	6	20:34-43	439
		30:18-20	7	23	623
Jeremiah		30:21	6	27:21	485
2:2	483, 562, 620, 621, 625, 645	30:24	6	33:25	339
		31	5, 6,	34:15-16	648
		31:4-7	7	34:23	627
2:23-24	487	31:5	20	36:23	235
3:1	623	31:9	7	36:24-28	442
3:2	485	31:15	7, 17	36:25-27	621
3:6-10	623	31:24-25	7	37:14	442
3:16	575, 635	31:27	7	37:15-28	614
3:17	557, 639, 652-653, 654	31:30	6	38:8	674
		31:31	7	38:12	493, 651
3:18	609, 614	31:31-34	5, 6	39:27-29	674
7:4	572, 667	31:38-40	7	40-44	346
7:8-15	572	32:37-41	674	40-48	13
7:12-14	596, 604	33:4	634	40:3	580
8:14b	437	33:6	634	40:34-35	621
8:20	644	33:11	612	40:46	601
10:20	582	33:16	639, 640	40-43	635
12:1-3	205	33:18	638	40-44	540, 547,

Scripture Index

	580		535, 588,	11:1	17, 333, 669
40-48	540, 617		618, 637	11:11	613
43	635	7:9	134		
43:1-4	573	7:11-14	588, 589	**Joel**	
43:1-7	580-581,	7:13	134, 136,	2:27-32	438
	648-649		383-384,	2:28-32	315
43:1-9	603, 637		535, 536	2:30-32	286
43:4-5	551, 621	7:13-14	530, 534,	3	170
43:7	548		629	3:2	445
43:12	635	7:14	318	3:1-3	438
43:13-27	492	7:18	308, 535	3:2-3	263
43:19	601	7:22	134, 308,	3:10	336-337
44:4	551		535	3:17	638
44:6-7	542	7:25	308		
44:7	37	7:27	164, 308,	**Amos**	
44:9	37		534, 535,	6:5	371
44:15	601		589, 590	9:11	582
44-46	635	7:13-14	10, 15, 31		
45-46	37	9	412	**Jonah**	
45:18-46:3	541	9:2-3	412-413	1:12-15	229
45:22	629, 650	9:5-6	146	2	210
46:16-18	629	9:8-9	146	2:2	229
47:13-20	491	9:11	146	2:6	230
47:21-23	98, 393,	9:14-15	146		
	491, 658	9:24	214, 255	**Micah**	
47:22-23	422	9:24-27	531	4:1-2	427, 590
48:21-22	547, 581,	9:26	214	4:1-5	652-653
	650	11	618	4:2	47, 660
48:35	640	12:1	6, 632	4:3	127, 336,
					337, 638,
Daniel		**Hosea**			660
2	522, 588,	1-2	20, 483	4:4	645
	618	1:9	636	5	334
2:34-35	164	1:9-10	164	5:2	334, 379,
2:37-38	637, 655	1:10	19, 520, 646		383, 38
2:40	533	1:11	614	5:2-3	224
2:44	588	2:2-5	622-623	5:2-6	662
2:45	164	2:14-20	625	5:4	627
3	208	2:14-3:5	520	5:4-5	384-385
3:8-12	216	2:19-20	672-673	5:5	386
3:25	141, 210	2:23	19, 20, 164	6:8	41
4	179	3:3	239	7:16-17	594, 654
4:26	179	3:4-5	239		
6:10	458	7:8	173	**Habakkuk**	
7	521, 522,	8:9	487	1:5-11	262

Zephaniah
2:11	656
3:5	594
3:9	653, 657
3:14-17	649

Haggai
2:1-9	573
2:3	573
2:7	573, 635
2:7-9	635

Zechariah
1	615
1:12-17	641
1:18-20	385
2:4-5	640
2:5	627, 641
2:8	140, 150, 153, 202, 418
2:10-11	638
2:11	656
3:9	627
4:4	666
4:6	374, 413, 480
4:7	627
6	615
6:12-13	537, 548, 580
6:13	385, 627
6:15	635
8	598
8:2	641
8:3	554, 583, 600, 640
8:4-8	641
8:20-22	638
8:20-23	656
8:23	616, 654
9:10	126
10:6	610
10:10-11	613
11:7	221
11:10	219, 221
12	615
12:1	592
12:1-9	592
12:2-3	347, 461, 592
12:4	615
12:6	482
12:10	100, 134, 146, 158, 292, 380, 660
12:10-13	592
12:10-14	438, 439
12-14	592
13:1-4	592
13:5-7	592
13:7	592
13:8-9	99, 592
14	170, 334, 615
14:1-7	592
14:4-5	427, 666, 667
14:5	627
14:8-21	592
14:9	627
14:10-11	634
14:16	638, 656, 660
14:16-18	653
14:16-19	37
14:17	627
14:20	615

Malachi
1:4-5	164, 533
1:11	653
2:13-16	472
2:16	623
3:3	638
3:4	638
3:16	579
4:5	4
4:5-6	385, 621

New Testament
Matthew
1	193
1:1-16	380, 381
1:19	242
1:20	380
2:2	376
2:4-6	334
2:11	376
2:15	17, 333
2:17-18	18, 20
2:18	333
2:21	8
2:23	22, 333
3:2	179, 276
4:2	376
4:8	666
4:10	666
4:17	179, 276
4:23	345, 661
5-7	519, 666
5	160, 163
5:5	441
5:17	26, 32, 45, 103, 365, 537
5:17-18	281
5:17-20	162
5:20	178
5:22	160
5:28	160
5:35	639
5:43-45	478
5:44	666
5:48	45
6:1	42
6:1-8	42
6:5-13	666
7:7-8	666
7:11	666
7:21	178
7:28-29	382
8:11	11, 179, 291
8:17	214
9:20	654

Scripture Index

9:35	345	20:28	256	27:26	115
10:5-6	125	21:1-9	666	27:37	629
10:6	123	21:23	381	27:40-43	248, 334
10:28	526, 527	21:42	30	27:46	211
11:5	647	21:42-44	125	27:51	575
11:12	179	22:16	382	27:64	661
11:20-21	276	22:34-40	162	28:1	56
11:29	49	22:35-40	38	28:9	376
12:1-8	376	22:36	382	28:17	376
12:4	230	23	288	28:18	99, 127, 314, 530, 589, 629
12:9-14	376	23:1-33	163		
12:22-32	288	23:2-3	80	28:18-20	519
12:25-28	315	23:3a	84	28:19	46, 47
12:27	95	23:4	43	28:20	47, 482
12:28	156	23:5	42	28:19-20	39
12:32	543, 544	23:13	178		
12:38	382	23:15	24	**Mark**	
12:40	230	23:23	41	1:14-15	471
12:40-41	228	23:23-28	41	2:7	376
12:41	276	23:37-39	499	2:27	58
12:42	593, 628	23:38	499	3:35	387
13:11	315	23:38-39	34	4:37-39	210
13:35	662	24-25	519, 531	4:45-51	666
13:41	535	24:3	345, 666	6:20	242
13:43	502, 589	24:14	345, 519	6:46-51	666
14:33	376	24:15-16	603	7:3-5	82
14:36	654	24:20	666	7:6-13	163
15:1-6	79	24:21	6	7:8-9	73, 79
15:2	82	24:30	31, 535	7:10-13	161
15:4-6	44	24.31	62	7:13	79
15:21-28	125	24:32	643	9:12	214
15:24	123	25:31	529, 531	9:19	482
15:29	666	25:31-46	529	12:29-31	377
15:36	666	25:34	97, 529, 531, 589, 662	13	531
16:17	265			15:34	211, 667
16:18	72	25:45-46	266		
16:23	265	25:46	97	**Luke**	
16:28	535	26:28	5, 256	1:6	31, 49, 242, 278, 283
17:4	291	26:29	502, 589		
18:3	178	26:39	666		1:32 175, 620
18:20	578, 579	26:42	666		
19:16	382	26:44	666	1:32-33	530
19:23	178	26:64	535	1:35	577, 578
19:28	650	26:67-68	146	1:41	49
20:19	99, 115	27:25	33, 141, 252	1:67	49

2:7	144	21:24	531, 596,	4:22	115, 217,
2:14	386, 387		637		221, 224,
2:25	11, 242	21:24-27	286		616
2:38	11	21:28	531	4:42	115
2:41-51	665	22:17	10	5:18	129
2:42	64	22:26	10	5:19	471
3:21-22	381	22:29	15	5:22	13
4:16	64	22:29-30	650	5:25	311, 527
4:18-21	381	22:39	65	5:27	13
4:19	648	22:53	460	5:28	527, 528
4:22	620	23:34	253, 263,	5:28-29	314, 662
5:32	123		667	5:29	528
5:39	69	23:46	260, 667	6:25	382
6:5	3	23:48	223	7:2	62
6:12-16	666	23:50-51	242	7:15	42
8:44	553	24:15-16	296	7:49	41, 262
8:45-48	553	24:20	250, 268	8:24	472
9:28-29	666	24:26	268	8:30-59	288
9:34	577	24:44	38	8:39	296
10:25-37	161	24:50-52	666	8:44	296
11:20	156			8:56	10
11:32	228	**John**		8:58	472
11:42	41	1:1	134, 383	9:41	269
11:52	39	1:1-2	130	10:17-18	576
12	181	1:1-3	576	10:22	644
12:32	15	1:1-18	377	10:33	129
12:40	181	1:14	130, 134,	11	130
12:47	145		376, 383,	11:50	228, 254
12:51	32		553, 575,	12:41	134
12:51-53	387		576	12:43	42
13:28	291	1:18	134	13:34	37
13:28-29	11	1:29	212, 631	13:34-35	365
13:34	33	1:45	296, 363	14:1-3	608
14:14	528	1:47	296	14:3	182
15:4-7	123	1:50	296	14:6	123, 377,
15:7	123	1:51	11		429
15:11-23	269	1:52	664	16:11	525
16:22	181	2:19	577	16:13	66, 76
17:20-21	179	2:19-21	576	17:1-5	377
18:12	55	3:2	382	17:11-15	176
19:42	33, 387	3:3-5	122	18:6	554
20:15-16	125	3:10	287	18:28-40	146
20:38	259	3:26	382	18:36	179
21	531	3:29	621	19:5	111
21:5	575	4:6	376	19:7	129, 251,

	280	6:5	24	17:24	546
19:28	376	6:8	661	17:31	14, 627
		6:9	22	18:4	58
Acts		6:14	22	18:18	27
1:11	666	7	128	20:5-6	56
1:6	534	7:20	208	20:7	56
1:6-7	531	7:47-48	546	20:16	62
1:24	283	7:52	146, 262	21:20	25, 363, 364
2	56, 62, 64,	7:52-53	250	21:21-26	28
	313, 363,	7:55-56	127	21:24	375
	426, 518,	8:32-35	214	21:39	362
	608	9:1-19	278	22:3	42, 86, 104,
2:1	62	9:18	257, 278,		282, 362
2:2	578		291	22:8	22
2:4	661	10:7	24	22:14	127
2:7-11	661	10:25-26	383	22:18	127
2:10	24	10:37-38	381	22:28	590
2:17-21	315	10:38	583	23:1	283
2:22	22	10:42	528, 627	23:6	27, 104, 362
2:23	99, 115, 250,	11:26	22	23:6-9	27, 104
	263, 267	13:27-29	33, 251	24:15	528
2:25-28	18	13:35	230	24:16	283
2:26-27	532	13:43	24	24:17-18	27
2:31	230	13:43-44	58	26:5	199
2:35	18	13:45	33	26:9	22
2:36	115	13:45-51	105	26:20	277
2:38	278	13:50	24	26:28	22
3:1	27	14:1-15	105	28:17	25, 82, 84,
3:6	22	14:2	33		375
3:15	250	14:16	219	28:23-28	519
3:15-18	268	14:19	105		
3:17	263	15	22, 23, 26,	**Romans**	
3:19	277		34, 35, 103,	1:2	30
3:19-21	128, 270,		508	1:16	126
	532	15:5	105, 199	1:16-17	284
3:19-24	633	15:10	48	1:18-32	277
3:21	501	15:14	501	1:20	218
4:10	22, 115, 250,	15:16	583	2:6-11	609
	254	15:21	35	2:7	257
4:13	42	15:28	25, 103, 365	2:10	257
4:26-28	268	16:3	27, 375	2:12-16	42
4:28	263	17:1-2	64	2:13-15	218
5:28	254	17:4	24	2:15	218
5:34-39	282	17:5	33	2:17-24	235
5:34-40	104	17:17	24	2:20	42

715

2:28-29	296, 542	11:12	34	15:51	183
3:1-2	297-298	11:15	34, 229	15:51-54	182, 650
3:2	30	11:25-26	34	16:2	55, 56
3:9	126	11:26	6, 224, 345	16:8	62
3:19	606	11:28	480	16:22	320
3:20	160	11:28-29	291		
3:20-25	606	11:29	221, 483	**2 Corinthians**	
3:21-22	284	12:19	266	1:19-20	32
3:22-25	126	13	349	1:20-21	10
4:11	30	13:8-10	38, 45	3:3	155, 156, 159
4:12	30	14:5-6	53	3:6	5
4:16	606	14:10	13	3:14	609
4:25	214	14:17	292, 386	3:14-15	122, 262
5:1	386	16:26	288	3:14-16	269
5:5	49	28:17	26	3:15-16	158, 257
5:20	606			3:16	609
6:6	525	**1 Corinthians**		4:4	129, 475
6:14	45, 606	2:13	21	5:1-4	579, 580
7:4	280	3	66	5:10	147
7:7	160	3:13-15	65	5:17	32
7:12	46, 375	3:16-17	577	5:18-20	403
8:2	39	4:3	4	6:2	19
8:4	45	5:7-8	24	6:14-15	265
8:9	579	6:19	579	6:16	577
8:11	526, 579	7:18b-19	35	10:3-4	481
8:14	43	7:31	502	11:4	273
8:17	632	8:1-3	42	13:45	32
8:20	162	9:1	127	17:5-8	32
8:33	266	9:21	39, 45, 103		
9:1-29	620	10:1-2	47	**Galatians**	
9:2-3	105, 252	10:1-5	647	1:6-9	273
9:3	288	10:11	6	1:14	42, 82, 282, 283
9:5	619	11:2	84, 282		
9:6	256	12:12-13	72	1:19	25
9:25	19	13:12	241	2:8	25
9:25-26	520	15:3	214	2:19	84
9:26	19	15:20	61, 64	2:19-20	280
10	16, 288	15:23	528	3:16	10, 17
10:1	252	15:24-26	593	3:19	213
10:1-4	285	15:24-28	631	3:28	26, 298
10:4	26, 103, 251	15:25-26	528	4:21-31	12, 490, 600
10:17	158	15:28	523	4:26	75
10:18	16, 20	15:29	72	4:25-26	11
11:5	6, 261, 262	15:45-47	556	4:27	12
11:9	221	15:48-49	556	5:1	375

Scripture Index

5:2	35	1:19-20	386, 631	1:14	579
6:2	24, 26, 40, 45, 103, 365, 509	1:21-22	480	2:12	632
		2:8	73, 79	3:7	79
		2:9	631	3:16	163, 383
6:15-16	675	2:11-12	174	3:16-17	92
6:16	216, 256, 262, 607	2:13	511, 528	4:1	14, 345, 528, 627
		2:16	53		
		3:3	315		

Ephesians

		3:15	386	**Titus**	
1:9-10	4, 630	4:6a	620	1:2	631
1:10	4	4:17	103	2:12-13	9
1:17-18	79, 158			2:13	179
1:22	630	**1 Thessalonians**		2:14	501
1:23	548	1:9-10	9, 276		
2:1	528	2:13	77	**Hebrews**	
2:5	511, 528	2:14-16	33, 105, 252, 288	1:1	5
2:13-16	404			1:2	6, 630
2:14	386	4:13-17	182, 608	1:3	129
2:14-15	36	4:14-16	650	1:5	606
2:17	386	4:16	528	1:6	630
2:20-22	578	5:2	4	1:14	13
3:17	159, 579			2:5	3, 8, 12, 15, 182
4:14	78	**2 Thessalonians**			
4:15	162	2:1	524	2:6-9	10
4:25	162	2:1-12	521, 522	2:8-9	3
4:28	162	2:2	77	2:14	376, 593
5:25	161	2:3	506, 593	2:14-15	525
6:10-12	315	2:15	77, 282	3:1-6	48
6:12	417, 460	3:6	84, 282	3:7-11	18
6:14-20	482			4:9	2, 5, 60
		1 Timothy		4:18	607
Philippians		1:8	375	5:6	345
2:6	129	1:13-14	364	6:5	3, 8, 12, 15, 182
2:9-11	671	1:15	284		
3:3	49	2:5	14, 214	6:18	631
3:5	362	5:18	288	7	627
3:5-6	42	6:14	524	7:27	537
3:5-9	284	6:15-16	557	8	5, 7, 8, 9, 664
3:20	9	6:16	376		
3:20-21	183, 533, 650			8:5	576, 665
		2 Timothy		8:7-9	5
4:7	386	1:3	283	9-10	48
		1:5	277	9:2	576
Colossians		1:9-10	525	9:4	556
1:15	129	1:12	79	9:6	576

717

9:8	576	1:18-19	124	1:13-16	134
9:9	2	1:20	631	2:9	295
9:12	255, 537	2:9	501	2:26-27	532
9:12-14	15	2:10	19	3:2	512
9:14	2	2:22	214	3:9	295
9:15	14, 15, 214	2:24	214	3:10	6
9:21	576	4:2-3	277	3:12	182, 344
9:22	30	4:3	283	3:21	175, 530, 532
9:24	255	4:13	632		
9:28	9	4:16	22	5:5	343, 626
10:1	103	5:8	525	5:10	13, 533
10:4	538, 636			7	591
10:5-10	103	**2 Peter**		7:1-8	596, 597
10:8-10	215	1:11	178	7:2-4	674
10:10	537	1:13-14	580	7:9	664
10:12-13	530	3:7	662	7:14	6
10:19-22	607	3:8	498	7:15	13, 664
10:22	2	3:10	4, 662, 664	11:1	556
10:30	266	3:12	4	11:2-3	531
11:10	7, 10, 182, 183	3:12-13	501, 662	11:15	531
		3:12-14	10	11:15-18	533
11:14-16	8	3:13	179, 594	11:19	13, 255, 556
11:16	7, 11, 182, 177, 183, 545	3:15	380	12	505
		3:16	30, 288	12-13	618
		3:18	4, 662	12:10	266
11:29-30	479			13	168
11:39-40	14	**1 John**		13:6	584
12:22	7, 182, 320, 600, 607	2:7-8	37	14:1	320
		2:17	502	14:1-5	596, 597, 608, 628
12:22-24	12	2:18	6		
12:23	7	3:16	146, 161	14:17	591
12:26-29	15	3:17	162	15:3	627
12:28	3, 8, 182	3:23	37	15:3-4	533
13:8	429	4:14	115	15:5	584
13:14	3, 7, 12, 182	4:19	38	16:13-16	495, 591
		4:21	37	16:19	617
James				17:9-11	618
1:23-25	284	**Jude**		19	311
4:17	145	11	140	19-20	497, 520, 536
5:11	157, 158, 205, 240				
		Revelation		19-21	505, 522
		1:6	13	19-22	497
1 Peter		1:7	100, 292, 660	19:6-9	183
1:7	524			19:10	383
1:13	524	1:10	175	19:11-21	591

19:15	532
19:16	16
20	500, 511, 525, 526, 528, 530, 533, 609
20:1-21:19	498
20:1-3	524, 525
20:1-6	497, 591
20:1-7	308, 310, 311, 316, 498, 499, 500, 522
20:3	311
20:4	10, 530
20:4-6	15, 311, 521, 522, 525, 526, 590
20:5-6	510, 511
20:6	10, 13, 530
20:7-9	594
20:9	638
20:10	616
20:11	501
20:11-15	527, 529
20:12-13	526
20:14	526
21:1	501
21:2	8, 182, 344, 583, 584
21:3	583, 661, 664, 665
21:4	662
21:5-8	632
21:9	344
21:9-10	583, 620
21:9-22	58
21:10	584, 665, 667
21:18	526
21:22-23	584
22:5	523
22:16	626
22:19	584
22:3	16, 40, 281

Subject Index

A

Aaron 97, 110, 131, 132, 371, 469, 552, 559, 560, 565, 593, 601, 604

Abel 12, 18, 96, 97, 140, 353

Abraham v, vi, 7, 10, 11, 17, 21, 30, 32, 65, 98, 123, 179, 192, 198, 211, 220, 221, 223, 237, 238, 267, 290, 291, 296, 334, 343, 348, 353, 366, 367, 369, 370, 375, 396, 411, 415, 431, 432, 436, 440, 457, 458, 464, 469, 485, 487, 488, 490, 492, 497, 519, 521, 558, 571, 582, 599, 600, 665, 701

Abram 403

Adam 122, 166, 168, 173, 319, 328, 469, 556, 629, 630, 693

Adonai 81, 84, 85, 146, 377, 455, 633, 640

amillennialism 74, 309, 310, 311, 312, 313, 314, 315, 316, 317, 318, 319

Amsterdam 131, 148, 154, 325, 326, 327, 351, 352, 353, 354, 677, 678, 679, 684, 686, 687, 688, 690, 691, 694, 697, 698

angels 11, 12, 13, 27, 181, 219, 250, 383, 386, 472, 531, 582, 614, 630, 652, 663, 674

Anglican 52, 71, 140, 171, 194, 298, 312, 315, 328

Anglo-Saxons
    96, 197
animal sacrifices
    15, 27, 48,
    120, 215,
    537, 636
Anointed 22, 137,
    268, 315,
    320, 348,
    380, 470,
    535, 617
anti-Semitism
    33, 35, 60,
    102, 105,
    106, 138,
    142, 185,
    186, 193,
    194, 251,
    252, 286,
    287, 289,
    290, 294,
    321, 327,
    336, 347,
    363, 370,
    423, 428,
    455, 539
apostasy 239, 506,
    521, 522,
    607
apostles 2, 17, 21,
    22, 27, 44,
    48, 57, 67,
    103, 104,
    146, 254,
    255, 288,
    365, 376,
    379, 511,
    537, 538,
    577, 636,
    650

Apostle's Creed
    73
Apostolic Council
    9, 23, 24,
    34, 35, 36
Arabic   301, 321,
    358, 391,
    392, 399,
    404, 405,
    408, 416,
    424, 432,
    433, 457,
    458, 461,
    462, 466,
    471, 485,
    486, 491,
    492, 494,
    612
Ark of the
    Covenant 548, 550,
    555, 556,
    557, 561,
    562, 564,
    566, 567,
    575, 595,
    602, 604,
    606, 635,
    651
Assyria   20, 17,
    168, 170,
    488, 492,
    493, 603,
    612, 613,
    618, 657,
    658
Athanasius 92
atonement
    30, 48, 64,
    110, 213,
    215, 218,
    232, 233,

255, 257,
264, 428,
487, 550,
555, 606,
636
atoning sacrifice
    2, 40, 48,
    636
Augustine
    6, 74, 106,
    142, 166,
    167, 187,
    188, 297,
    298, 299,
    309, 310,
    316, 510,
    515, 528,
    683
authority
    13, 66, 67,
    70, 71, 73,
    74, 87, 90,
    127, 264,
    306, 380,
    381, 382,
    396, 398,
    417, 448,
    454, 471,
    504, 593
    520, 531,
    593, 629

B
Babel   661
Babylonia 89, 90,
    216
Babylonian exile
    81, 109,
    262, 412,
    574, 636

Subject Index

Babylonians
    211, 262,
    492, 588,
    589, 596
Babylonian Talmud
    87, 88, 90,
    682, 691
Balaam
    480, 615
baptism
    i, 8, 24, 35,
    46, 47, 51,
    72, 74,
    173, 174,
    362, 381
Baptists
    72, 350
Barth, Karl
    309, 310
Bathsheba
    441
Bavinck, Herman
    x, 14, 167,
    497, 499,
    678
Belgic Confession
    73, 344
Benjamin
    6, 117,
    118, 283,
    328, 370,
    432, 479,
    547, 581,
    634, 646,
    685
Bethel 562, 563
Bethlehem
    18, 224,
    334, 379,
    383, 384,
    397, 415,
    598
Bible
    v, vii, viii,
    ix, x, 3, 4,
    5, 21, 26,
    29, 36, 43,
    51, 53, 55,
    57, 59, 61,
    63, 65, 66,
    67, 68, 69,
    70, 71, 73,
    75, 76, 77,
    78, 79, 80,
    81, 83, 85,
    87, 89, 91,
    95, 97, 99,
    102, 118,
    138, 145,
    154, 163,
    164, 168,
    175, 179,
    184, 190,
    213, 287,
    295, 297,
    317, 336,
    340, 389,
    391, 397,
    399, 423,
    424, 426,
    427, 429,
    446, 458,
    472, 480,
    486, 499,
    510, 512,
    513, 514,
    516, 525,
    527, 528,
    530, 532,
    544, 545,
    554, 556,
    558, 566,
    568, 575,
    577, 579,
    581, 582,
    584, 592,
    598, 609,
    612, 617,
    641, 642,
    659, 660,
    665, 673,
    678, 679,
    680, 681,
    684, 685,
    686, 693,
    694, 695,
    696, 700
blood 12, 15, 28,
    30, 33, 64,
    76, 96,
    113, 124,
    126, 127,
    139, 141,
    194, 195,
    198, 204,
    206, 229,
    233, 234,
    241, 252,
    254, 255,
    256, 257,
    265, 286,
    304, 305,
    339, 340,
    367, 386,
    392, 404,
    417, 460,
    466, 485,
    486, 542,
    553, 595,
    621, 631,
    636, 654,
    668, 670,
    671

Bunyan, John
13, 180,
182, 183,
184

C

Caiaphas
228, 254,
257, 288
Cain 96, 97,
121, 140
Calvary 105, 525,
537, 667,
688
Calvinism
3, 190,
312, 319
Calvinists
140, 142,
269, 322,
332, 343,
349, 350,
351, 355,
517, 655,
658
Calvin, John
74, 188,
190, 297,
512
Canaan 8, 411,
431, 436,
479, 492,
658
cherubim
546, 547,
548, 549,
555, 557,
564, 565,
572
Christianity
iii, 1, 2, 3,
5, 7, 9, 11
13, 15, 17,
19, 21, 22,
23, 25, 27,
29, 31, 33,
35, 37, 39
41, 43, 45,
46, 49, 51,
63, 65, 81,
83, 95, 96,
99, 104,
105, 106,
110, 111,
116, 123,
128, 132,
137, 138,
164, 170,
171, 172,
184, 186,
213, 248,
271, 272,
273, 276,
280, 296,
297, 298,
300, 306,
307, 313,
320, 327,
328, 340,
344, 363,
375, 376,
377, 379,
430, 459,
462, 478,
499, 506,
507, 511,
515, 539,
678, 685
Christian theology
91, 92,
135, 202
Christmas
63, 192
Christology
158, 318,
681
church ii, 7, 8, 13,
20, 23, 29,
33, 52, 53,
54, 60, 62,
66, 67, 69,
70, 72, 73,
74, 75, 76,
80, 92,
102, 103,
105, 106,
118, 121,
122, 129,
136, 138,
143, 146,
161, 163,
164, 166,
167, 168,
169, 170,
171, 172,
173, 176,
179, 180,
183, 185,
186, 187,
188, 192,
196, 217,
265, 270,
283, 287,
288, 289,
290, 291,
292, 294,
295, 297,
298, 299,
302, 303,
305, 306,
309, 310,
311, 312,

Subject Index

314, 316, 320, 321, 330, 331, 335, 345, 347, 360, 362, 363, 364, 373, 376, 399, 458, 459, 461, 477, 503, 506, 507, 508, 509, 510, 512, 515, 516, 521, 522, 524, 528, 533, 535, 579, 636, 657

church fathers
60, 67, 70, 74, 75, 92, 106, 179, 186, 294, 297, 299, 310, 335, 535

church leaders
288, 312

circumcision
8, 35, 46, 51, 167, 173, 174, 187, 195, 198, 293, 295, 296, 298, 356, 361, 362, 364, 365, 374, 375, 490, 542

Constantine
60, 63, 163, 171, 172, 313, 498, 510, 536

conversion
47, 123, 124, 128, 140, 143, 147, 148, 163, 166, 167, 171, 188, 269, 276, 277, 278, 283, 288, 306, 307, 313, 321, 362, 364, 401, 439, 440, 447, 459, 460, 462, 482, 483, 521, 536

Council of Nicaea
164

Covenant
3, 7, 13, 14, 37, 40, 41, 154, 256, 354, 519, 678, 686

covenant theology
i, 317, 319

Creator
132, 237, 240, 241, 377, 556, 669

D

Damascus
341

Daniel 134, 141, 142, 146, 164, 208, 209, 210, 214, 216, 308, 316, 412, 458, 495, 512, 513, 521, 522, 531, 533, 534, 535, 588, 590, 603, 655

Darby J. N.
ix, 499, 513, 514, 516, 681

Davidic kingdom
583

Day of Pentecost
18, 35, 56, 64, 250, 278, 313, 363, 518, 536, 608, 661, 670

Day of the Lord
4, 11, 56, 175, 285, 286, 662

demons 95, 156, 186, 187, 293, 480, 525

Diaspora 24, 198, 271, 429, 436, 539

disciples 39, 47, 56, 82, 95, 210, 250, 256, 268, 269, 296, 387, 531, 532, 534, 575, 577, 630, 666

Dispensationalism 21, 517, 694

dispensational pre-millennialism 516, 517, 518, 522

E

Easter 62, 63, 172

Eastern Orthodox 29, 65, 298, 312, 359

East Jerusalem 390, 394, 395, 408, 409, 410, 411, 424, 426, 447, 478

Ecclesia 7, 13, 14, 15, 22, 52, 53, 177, 202, 262, 270, 272, 274, 291, 292, 299, 317, 319, 426, 429, 496, 504, 510, 511, 512, 514, 516, 518, 519, 520, 521, 529, 540, 545, 575, 577, 578, 579, 584, 608, 620, 622, 624, 630, 656, 663

Ecclesiology 511, 516, 518

Eden 578, 644, 693

Edom 12, 23, 99, 120, 121, 164, 168, 482, 485, 487, 533, 616, 617, 618

Edwards, Jonathan 506

Egypt 5, 17, 20, 40, 47, 61, 99, 124, 131, 197, 207, 208, 227, 233, 351, 356, 358, 382, 407, 409, 414, 423, 431, 436, 440, 443, 473, 475, 476, 481, 485, 488, 490, 492, 493, 558, 559, 569, 602, 612, 613, 614, 615, 618, 625, 628, 645, 647, 653, 657, 658, 670, 673

election i, 72, 105, 124, 125, 220, 606, 607, 619

Eli 564, 566, 595, 601, 602, 604, 606

Elizabeth 31, 44, 49, 242, 278

Emperor Constantine 60, 63, 313, 510

Enlightenment 20, 68, 147

Esau 23, 98, 99, 120, 121, 440, 534, 615, 616

eschatology 177, 185, 310, 317, 318, 461, 477, 496,

Subject Index

499, 507,
512, 516,
518, 590,
598

eternal life
97, 257,
266, 511

Eternal Torah
3, 12, 153,
155, 159,
693

eternity 4, 7, 9, 72,
134, 135,
171, 281,
337, 377,
379, 529,
554, 557,
587, 662

Ethnic Israel
171, 176,
236

Europe 112, 113,
115, 190,
195, 197,
222, 249,
300, 301,
302, 304,
305, 311,
314, 326,
331, 339,
354, 404,
418, 468,
495, 513,
591, 616,
628, 637,
651, 680

Evangelical
1, 3, 52,
53, 65, 71,
79, 141,
142, 165,

177, 185,
194, 274,
298, 309,
315, 361,
397, 403,
513, 514,
515

Eve 166, 319,
630

exegesis 16, 18, 20,
21, 68, 81,
102, 168,
170, 171,
177, 213,
317, 318,
319, 335,
379, 380,
458

exile 81, 109,
111, 120,
196, 210,
216, 232,
233, 234,
248, 262,
350, 412,
574, 596,
602, 603,
611, 612,
615, 616,
636, 645,
674

Ezekiel 89, 98,
134, 339,
346, 439,
485, 537,
540, 541,
547, 572,
573, 580,
581, 603,
614, 617,
635, 649,

650, 658,
683, 684

Ezra 21, 65, 68,
74, 81, 82,
93, 122,
164, 193,
232, 283,
366, 479,
485, 493,
534, 569,
573, 574,
575, 603,
634, 636,
641, 693,
701

F

faith ii, iii, vi,
14, 19, 22,
23, 26, 30,
31, 32, 36,
52, 65, 72,
73, 81,
104, 118,
126, 133,
137, 142,
158, 159,
169, 174,
177, 178,
188, 236,
242, 259,
264, 277,
278, 282,
284, 290,
298, 321,
324, 329,
332, 350,
352, 361,
363, 373,
376, 377,
386, 402,
403, 419,

THE ETERNAL PEOPLE: GOD IN RELATION TO ISRAEL

445, 464, 466, 476, 477, 479, 480, 481, 482, 483, 494, 497, 512, 553, 579

Feast of Booths
62, 64, 541, 638, 653, 656, 664

firstborn
1, 7, 12, 13, 100, 124, 134, 147, 258, 423, 439, 488, 669

First temple
425

food laws
36, 81, 167, 271, 273, 298, 302, 356, 361, 362, 364, 365, 374, 541

forgiveness
30, 40, 146, 256, 264, 278, 344, 376, 428, 484

France
53, 141, 143, 144, 147, 300, 322, 328, 331, 332, 391, 683

G

Gaza Strip
393, 401, 405, 407, 409, 418, 420, 565

Gentiles
5, 7, 14, 16, 19, 20, 22, 23, 24, 25, 26, 27, 28, 29, 30, 32, 33, 34, 35, 36, 46, 52, 54, 58, 59, 88, 104, 105, 108, 115, 119, 120, 123, 125, 128, 140, 158, 169, 170, 186, 193, 196, 204, 210, 211, 212, 215, 216, 218, 219, 222, 224, 228, 229, 235, 248, 252, 256, 261, 263, 268, 270, 271, 277, 290, 298, 363, 364, 365, 366, 372, 375, 386, 480, 483, 525, 529, 531, 542, 596, 608, 609, 624, 637, 654, 655, 660, 681

God
i, ii, v, vi, vii, viii, 1, 2, 3, 4, 5, 7, 9, 11, 12, 13, 14, 15, 17, 19, 20, 21, 22, 23, 24, 25, 26, 27, 29, 30, 31, 32, 33, 35, 36, 38, 39, 40, 41, 42, 43, 44, 45, 46, 47, 48, 49, 52, 53, 54, 55, 57, 59, 58, 60, 64, 67, 70, 71, 72, 73, 75, 76, 77, 78, 79, 82, 83, 84, 85, 92, 98, 99, 100, 101, 107, 110, 111, 114, 115, 116, 117, 118, 119, 120, 122, 123, 124, 125, 126, 128, 129, 130, 131, 132, 133, 134, 135, 137, 138, 139, 140, 141, 142, 146, 147, 149, 150, 151, 153, 154, 155, 156, 157, 158, 159, 160, 161, 162, 163, 164, 165, 166, 167, 168, 169, 170, 172, 173, 174, 175, 176, 178, 179, 180, 181, 182, 183,

Subject Index

186, 187, 199, 202, 203, 204, 205, 207, 208, 209, 210, 211, 212, 213, 214, 215, 216, 217, 218, 219, 220, 221, 222, 223, 224, 225, 226, 227, 228, 229, 230, 231, 233, 234, 235, 236, 237, 238, 239, 240, 241, 243, 244, 247, 250, 251, 252, 253, 254, 255, 256, 257, 258, 259, 260, 261, 262, 263, 264, 265, 266, 267, 268, 269, 270, 271, 274, 275, 276, 277, 278, 279, 281, 282, 283, 285, 287, 288, 290, 291, 293, 297, 298, 301, 304, 305, 306, 308, 309, 313, 315, 317, 318, 334, 335, 336, 337, 339, 344, 345, 349, 350, 358, 359, 360, 363, 364, 373, 374, 375, 376, 377, 378, 379, 381, 382, 383, 384, 385, 386, 387, 389, 394, 402, 403, 404, 411, 412, 413, 417, 418, 422, 423, 425, 427, 428, 429, 431, 432, 436, 437, 438, 440, 441, 442, 443, 444, 445, 446, 447, 460, 464, 467, 468, 469, 470, 471, 472, 473, 475, 477, 480, 481, 483, 484, 486, 487, 488, 490, 492, 494, 499, 501, 506, 516, 518, 519, 520, 523, 526, 527, 528, 530, 531, 532, 533, 534, 539, 541, 543, 544, 545, 546, 547, 548, 549, 550, 551, 552, 553, 554, 555, 556, 557, 558, 559, 560, 561, 562, 563, 564, 565, 567, 568, 569, 570, 571, 572, 573, 574, 575, 576, 577, 579, 581, 583, 584, 587, 588, 589, 590, 592, 593, 594, 595, 597, 599, 600, 601, 602, 604, 605, 606, 607, 608, 609, 611, 614, 615, 616, 617, 620, 621, 622, 623, 624, 625, 626, 627, 628, 629, 630, 631, 632, 633, 634, 635, 636, 637, 638, 639, 641, 642, 646, 647, 648, 649, 651, 652, 653, 654, 655, 656, 657, 658, 660, 661, 662, 663, 664,

665, 666,
667, 668,
669, 671,
672, 673,
674, 677,
678, 686,
687, 689,
690, 691,
692, 693,
694, 698,
699, 700
go'el 667, 668,
669, 671
Good Friday
297, 373
gospel
i, 9, 16,
19, 26, 97,
106, 113,
126, 127,
170, 177,
183, 184,
185, 251,
255, 256,
263, 273,
311, 344,
345, 349,
386, 401,
428, 429,
430, 475,
479, 480,
509, 519,
527, 533
Great Tribulation
6, 317,
496, 504,
517, 521,
522, 533,
603, 664
Greco-Macedonian
164, 637

Greek ix, 1, 24,
26, 27, 38,
45, 47, 55,
89, 92,
121, 126,
132, 175,
184, 186,
206, 232,
248, 257,
276, 298,
302, 382,
404, 405,
432, 471,
491, 525,
530, 576,
577, 588,
613, 618,
655, 661,
664, 677
Gregory X
303, 307

H
Hades 609
Haggai 573, 603,
635
Halakhic 85
Hananiah
437
heaven 4, 7, 8, 9,
10, 11, 12,
13, 14, 15,
17, 18, 30,
42, 45, 66,
67, 76, 89,
99, 123,
127, 128,
133, 136,
164, 175,
176, 177,
178, 179,

180, 181,
182, 183,
184, 185,
209, 244,
255, 264,
265, 270,
276, 281,
313, 314,
318, 320,
344, 345,
348, 362,
381, 382,
383, 384,
386, 426,
429, 457,
470, 478,
481, 499,
501, 503,
504, 510,
512, 518,
520, 521,
524, 529,
530, 532,
535, 536,
544, 546,
547, 548,
549, 550,
555, 556,
557, 561,
571, 574,
578, 583,
584, 588,
589, 590,
591, 608,
609, 620,
629, 630,
631, 633,
637, 639,
642, 650,
655, 663,
664, 665,

Subject Index

666, 667
Heidelberg Catechism
    73, 180, 284, 344, 693
hell   11, 95, 96, 180, 181, 241, 350, 472, 526, 527
Henry, Matthew
    28, 178, 183, 506
Herodian 22
high priest
    2, 64, 228, 254, 255, 265, 398, 552, 573, 575
historic pre-millennialism
    517, 518
holiness 134, 429, 439, 550, 566, 610, 631, 639, 640, 674
Holocaust
    13, 106, 109, 140, 144, 145, 146, 147, 148, 149, 150, 157, 165, 206, 207, 208, 217, 222, 223, 248, 349, 355, 418, 680, 685, 694

Holy Land
    2, 81, 87, 90, 94, 149, 165, 166, 194, 196, 197, 199, 297, 326, 346, 349, 356, 357, 394, 399, 400, 401, 404, 405, 406, 410, 411, 416, 432, 433, 435, 436, 445, 446, 453, 473, 474, 478, 491, 539, 562, 564, 593, 602, 603, 609, 658, 667, 679, 685

Holy Spirit
    10, 21, 25, 39, 40, 46, 49, 56, 59, 62, 69, 70, 72, 76, 79, 103, 119, 128, 132, 135, 185, 254, 257, 264, 267, 270, 274, 277, 278, 292, 313, 324, 365, 378, 381, 386, 438, 440, 473, 489, 519, 544, 554, 574, 577, 578, 579, 581, 583, 640, 656

holy things
    86, 551, 552, 553

house of Jacob
    187, 299

house of Judah
    5, 609, 610, 614, 615

I

Iberian Jews
    16, 320

idolatry 28, 129, 137, 239, 262, 283, 431, 469, 592, 646

Ignatius of Antioch
    92

image of God
    238, 475

infant baptism
    i, 8, 35, 51, 74, 173, 362

Intercessor 285

Irenaeus	92, 310	467, 469,	139, 140,
Isaac	v, 17, 30,	471, 473,	141, 142,
	89, 98,	475, 476,	143, 145,
	112, 113,	477, 478,	146, 147,
	126, 198,	479, 481,	149, 150,
	201, 223,	483, 485,	151, 153,
	237, 267,	487, 488,	154, 155,
	291, 327,	489, 491,	156, 157,
	353, 369,	678, 682,	158, 164,
	372, 411,	688, 690,	165, 166,
	415, 436,	694, 695	167, 168,
	440, 469,	Ismael 121, 457	169, 171,
	485, 486,	Israel i, v, 2, 5, 6	172, 173,
	487, 488,	7, 8, 9, 10,	174, 176
	489, 490,	11, 13, 14,	178, 180,
	491, 492	15, 17, 18,	181, 184,
Ishmael	20, 51, 98,	19, 20, 24,	185, 186,
	403, 411,	25, 26, 29,	187, 188,
	415, 485,	33, 34, 37,	191, 193,
	486, 487,	44, 46, 47,	194, 195,
	488, 489,	49, 53, 55,	196, 198,
	490, 491,	57, 59, 60,	199, 201,
	492, 493,	64, 74, 75,	202, 203,
	494	76, 80, 81,	204, 205,
Islam	7, 19, 20,	83, 89, 97,	206, 207,
	31, 98,	98, 99,	208, 209,
	190, 196,	101, 103,	210, 211,
	197, 323,	105, 107,	212, 213,
	341, 395,	108, 109,	214, 215,
	402, 416,	110, 111,	216, 217,
	417, 423,	112, 113,	218, 219,
	426, 435,	114, 115,	220, 221,
	443, 445,	118, 119,	222, 223,
	447, 449,	120, 121,	224, 225,
	451, 452,	122, 123,	226, 227,
	453, 455,	124, 125,	229, 230,
	456, 457,	126, 127,	231, 232,
	458, 459,	128, 129,	233, 235,
	461, 462,	130, 131,	236, 237,
	463, 464,	135, 136,	238, 239,
	465, 466,	137, 138,	240, 241,

Subject Index

242, 243, 247, 248, 249, 250, 251, 252, 253, 254, 255, 256, 257, 258, 259, 260, 261, 262, 263, 264, 265, 266, 267, 268, 269, 270, 271, 272, 273, 274, 275, 276, 277, 278, 279, 280, 281, 283, 284, 285, 287, 288, 289, 290, 291, 292, 296, 299, 301, 310, 313, 315, 317, 318, 319, 320, 326, 327, 329, 344, 345, 346, 347, 348, 349, 350, 351, 353, 354, 355, 356, 359, 360, 361, 362, 364, 373, 374,

476, 477, 479, 480, 481, 482, 483, 484, 486, 487, 488, 489, 491, 492, 494, 495, 496, 508, 510, 512, 515, 516, 517, 518, 519, 520, 521, 523, 531, 532, 533, 534, 535, 536, 538, 539, 540, 542, 545, 546, 548, 549, 550, 551, 553, 554, 556, 557, 558, 559, 560, 561, 562, 563, 564, 565, 566, 568, 569, 570, 572, 573, 574, 576, 580, 581, 584, 587, 588, 589, 590, 591, 592, 593, 594, 595, 596, 597,

377, 378, 379, 384, 385, 387, 389, 390, 391, 392, 393, 394, 395, 397, 398, 399, 401, 402, 403, 405, 406, 407, 408, 409, 410, 411, 412, 413, 414, 415, 416, 417, 418, 419, 420, 421, 422, 423, 424, 425, 427, 428, 429, 430, 431, 432, 433, 435, 436, 437, 438, 439, 440, 441, 442, 444, 445, 446, 447, 448, 449, 450, 451, 452, 453, 454, 455, 456, 457, 460, 461, 462, 465, 466, 468, 469, 473, 474,

599, 600,
601, 602,
603, 604,
605, 606,
607, 608,
609, 610,
611, 612,
613, 614,
615, 617,
618, 619,
620, 621,
622, 623,
624, 625,
627, 628,
629, 630,
631, 632,
637, 638,
639, 642,
643, 644,
645, 646,
647, 648,
649, 650,
651, 652,
653, 654,
655, 657,
658, 659,
661, 662,
663, 664,
665, 666,
667, 668,
669, 670,
671, 672,
673, 674,
675, 677,
679, 681,
682, 683,
685, 686,
689, 690,
694, 696

Israelology
v, 20, 75,

J

Jacob

James

99, 683
11, 21, 30,
47, 74, 98,
99, 111,
120, 121,
137, 139,
147, 187,
190, 193,
198, 207,
235, 236,
237, 238,
250, 267,
291, 299,
352, 369,
415, 427,
436, 440,
445, 469,
488, 490,
491, 534,
570, 590,
602, 604,
607, 611,
612, 615,
616, 617,
618, 632,
640, 652,
664, 671
viii, 25, 35,
107, 145,
157, 158,
168, 205,
240, 242,
281, 284,
288, 311,
326, 371,
525, 577,
579, 646,
681, 700

Jehoshaphat
  263, 445
Jeremiah 5, 6, 7, 17,
  20, 51,
  205, 238,
  412, 437,
  548, 572,
  596, 604,
  611, 644,
  645, 667
Jerome 16, 106,
  147, 164,
  194, 293,
  295, 296,
  297, 316,
  533, 534,
  625
Jerusalem
  7, 8, 10,
  11, 12, 23,
  25, 27, 28,
  33, 47, 64,
  75, 81, 83,
  86, 87, 90,
  96, 97, 99,
  101, 104,
  127, 140,
  144, 146,
  157, 158,
  164, 167,
  169, 172,
  182, 183,
  184, 186,
  216, 234,
  236, 237,
  240, 243,
  251, 252,
  254, 265,
  267, 273,
  286, 289,
  308, 313,

Subject Index

318, 320,
323, 344,
347, 348,
352, 353,
354, 357,
358, 385,
387, 390,
393, 394,
395, 396,
398, 403,
406, 408,
409, 410,
411, 412,
415, 424,
426, 427,
428, 432,
434, 435,
438, 447,
453, 455,
457, 458,
459, 461,
465, 466,
478, 479,
482, 492,
499, 500,
531, 534,
535, 537,
539, 540,
544, 547,
550, 554,
556, 564,
566, 567,
568, 570,
571, 573,
574, 576,
578, 581,
583, 584,
585, 590,
591, 592,
595, 597,
598, 599,
600, 602,
603, 613,
615, 617,
619, 620,
621, 622,
626, 628,
634, 635,
638, 639,
640, 641,
642, 649,
651, 652,
653, 654,
655, 656,
658, 660,
665, 666,
667, 670,
673, 679,
680, 685,
690, 699

Jerusalem Talmud 87, 90, 144

Jeshua 479, 573, 593, 636

Jesus Christ i, ii, iii, 2, 7, 9, 17, 19, 22, 29, 31, 36, 45, 64, 72, 103, 116, 131, 136, 146, 158, 178, 184, 212, 215, 217, 250, 256, 270, 278, 293, 295, 314, 386, 401, 402, 403, 428, 429, 470, 477, 502, 505, 518, 524, 530, 533, 575, 580, 584, 591, 606, 620, 630, 631, 636, 678, 680, 684, 687, 688, 696, 697, 700

Jesus-confessing Jews 22, 104, 120

Jewish Council 86, 104, 234, 289, 344

Jewish festivals 37, 195, 294, 298, 360, 364, 374

Jewish state 149, 157, 165, 166, 167, 237, 273, 357, 391, 406, 407, 430, 435, 467, 473, 474, 540

Jewish State 165, 443, 444

Jewish tradition 20, 21, 77,

	83, 150,	127, 128,	275, 276,
	215, 219,	129, 135,	277, 278,
	226, 227,	136, 137,	279, 282,
	232, 233,	138, 140,	283, 286,
	240, 241,	141, 143,	287, 288,
	254, 260,	144, 145,	289, 290,
	384, 385,	146, 147,	291, 292,
	547, 552,	148, 149,	294, 295,
	559, 575,	150, 155,	296, 297,
	616, 617,	157, 158,	298, 299,
	669	159, 164,	300, 301,
Jews	v, 1, 2, 5,	165, 166,	302, 303,
	7, 14, 16,	167, 171,	304, 305,
	19, 20, 22,	172, 173,	306, 307,
	23, 25, 26,	174, 185,	308, 309,
	27, 28, 29,	186, 187,	310, 313,
	30, 31, 32,	188, 189,	320, 321,
	33, 35, 36,	190, 191,	322, 323,
	37, 38, 40,	192, 193,	324, 325,
	41, 44, 46,	194, 196,	326, 327,
	49, 52, 57,	197, 198,	328, 330,
	58, 59, 62,	199, 205,	331, 332,
	63, 64, 65,	206, 207,	333, 334,
	67, 68, 69	208, 209,	335, 336,
	70, 71, 74,	215, 217,	337, 338,
	75, 76, 80,	220, 221,	339, 340,
	81, 82, 83,	222, 224,	341, 343,
	85, 87, 88,	226, 227,	344, 346,
	91, 92, 93,	228, 229,	347, 348,
	94, 95, 96,	231, 236,	349, 350,
	98, 99,	237, 238,	351, 352,
	103, 104,	239, 248,	353, 354,
	105, 106,	250, 251,	355, 356,
	107, 108,	252, 253,	357, 359,
	110, 112,	254, 255,	360, 361,
	113, 115,	256, 257,	362, 363,
	116, 117,	259, 261,	364, 365,
	118, 119,	262, 263,	366, 367,
	120, 121,	267, 270,	368, 369,
	123, 124,	271, 272,	370, 371,
	125, 126,	273, 274,	372, 373,

Subject Index

374, 375,
376, 377,
379, 380,
382, 385,
386, 391,
392, 393,
395, 396,
397, 398,
400, 401,
402, 403,
404, 405,
406, 407,
408, 409,
411, 412,
415, 416,
418, 419,
420, 422,
424, 425,
427, 428,
429, 430,
431, 433,
434, 435,
437, 438,
443, 444,
445, 446,
447, 449,
450, 453,
456, 457,
459, 460,
461, 462,
463, 464,
466, 467,
468, 469,
470, 471,
473, 474,
475, 478,
479, 480,
486, 488,
491, 494,
495, 499,
502, 527,

Job

Joel

532, 534,
536, 538,
539, 540,
541, 542,
543, 545,
576, 599,
607, 608,
609, 611,
614, 616,
618, 629,
646, 654,
661, 679,
681, 683,
685, 687,
689, 701
11, 14,
107, 108,
109, 112,
113, 114,
119, 124,
132, 133,
139, 140,
149, 157,
158, 204,
205, 206,
210, 211,
213, 216,
217, 218,
219, 220,
221, 223,
226, 227,
238, 240,
242, 243,
247, 248,
249, 262,
265, 266,
285, 296,
349, 354,
559, 612,
652, 692
12, 170,

221, 263,
286, 315,
337, 402,
438, 445,
446, 537,
555, 580,
581, 598,
600, 608,
612, 638,
642, 646,
660, 663,
670

John, The Apostle
iii, v, 4, 6,
10, 11, 13,
22, 27, 32,
34, 37, 38,
39, 41, 42,
45, 56, 58,
61, 62, 64,
66, 74, 76,
78, 107,
111, 115,
122, 123,
129, 130,
131, 132,
133, 134,
140, 146,
161, 162,
165, 176,
179, 180,
182, 183,
184, 186,
188, 190,
212, 214,
217, 221,
224, 225,
228, 242,
251, 254,
257, 262,
267, 269,

280, 287,
288, 289,
293, 294,
296, 297,
311, 314,
328, 344,
359, 363,
365, 368,
374, 376,
377, 380,
381, 382,
383, 423,
429, 471,
472, 475,
486, 502,
506, 511,
512, 525,
527, 528,
537, 538,
553, 570,
576, 578,
593, 608,
616, 618,
621, 630,
631, 634,
636, 638,
644, 646,
662, 664,
667, 674,
679, 681,
685, 686,
689, 690,
694, 697,
701

John the Baptist
122, 179,
242, 377,
381, 593,
621, 646

Joseph 14, 74, 89,
98, 99,
100, 108,
112, 129,
193, 207,
211, 223,
227, 242,
329, 352,
354, 361,
363, 371,
380, 384,
385, 415,
433, 469,
488, 490,
595, 605,
609, 610,
617, 687

Joshua 83, 123,
265, 358,
370, 403,
431, 432,
440, 479,
482, 547,
570, 573,
593, 605

Judah 5, 6, 84,
86, 87, 88,
141, 167,
169, 170,
193, 196,
198, 226,
318, 343,
347, 384,
385, 395,
405, 432,
479, 482,
483, 492,
547, 572,
574, 581,
591, 605,
609, 610,
611, 612,
614, 615,
620, 623,
629, 634,
636, 640,
641, 645,
646, 649,
669, 671

Judaism 1, 2, 3, 5,
7, 9, 11,
12, 13, 15,
17, 19, 21,
22, 23, 24,
25, 27, 29,
31, 33, 35,
36, 37, 39,
41, 43, 44,
45, 46, 47,
49, 51, 63,
65, 67, 71,
73, 74, 77,
79, 80, 81,
83, 88, 91,
92, 93, 96,
101, 102,
103, 104,
105, 106,
107, 109,
111, 113,
115, 117,
119, 121,
123, 124,
125, 127,
129, 131,
132, 133,
135, 137,
138, 139,
141, 143,
145, 147,
149, 151,
164, 172,
174, 185,
186, 271,

Subject Index

Judea
272, 273,
275, 276,
281, 282,
287, 288,
297, 300,
307, 312,
313, 321,
322, 323,
324, 325,
327, 336,
347, 348,
361, 362,
363, 365,
377, 397,
416, 423,
430, 450,
455, 457,
459, 464,
469, 473,
678, 682,
683, 687,
691, 695
33, 252,
394, 400,
409, 424,
447, 603,
651, 667

judgment
6, 13, 28,
53, 147,
170, 188,
205, 217,
256, 263,
264, 279,
284, 287,
305, 314,
317, 319,
439, 445,
525, 526,
527, 528,
529, 530,
533, 535,
565, 566,
572, 573,
592, 601,
607, 610,
631, 667

justice
30, 32, 41,
47, 59, 82,
86, 114,
150, 159,
182, 203,
242, 310,
335, 383,
384, 396,
579, 591,
596, 618,
625, 629,
639, 647,
648, 673

justification
ii, 76, 117,
274

K

King Cyrus
215, 588,
634

King David
89, 194,
204, 258,
371, 395,
557, 563,
565, 567,
570, 571,
574, 592,
599, 605

kingdom of God
11, 22,
122, 125,
178, 179,
183, 243,
291, 309,
315, 386,
506, 519

kingdom of heaven
11, 176,
177, 178,
179, 276,
345

kingdom theology
507, 508

King Herod
334, 575

King Nebuchadnezzar
572, 588

King Solomon
89, 176,
193, 250,
546, 548,
563, 567,
571, 575,
601, 628,
634

kosher
273, 321,
541

Kuyper, Abraham
17, 20,
171, 179,
343, 348,
497, 521

Kuyperian
349, 350,
399

L

Latin 295
law i, 24, 28,
36, 38, 39,
40, 41, 43,

44, 46, 47,
48, 49,
103, 189,
201, 215,
228, 234,
235, 250,
251, 280,
282, 283,
284, 328,
332, 387,
394, 395,
396, 399,
400, 411,
412, 414,
417, 419,
420, 421,
424, 441,
447, 448,
467, 473,
476, 513,
560, 561,
564, 590,
606, 635,
638, 652,
669, 672

law of Christ
24, 39, 46,
103

legalism
39, 40, 44,
46, 48, 85,
281, 287,
375

Lo-'Ammi
19, 20,
164, 287,
483, 636,
655

Logos 134, 383

Lord's Day
52, 56,

175
Lord's Supper
256, 538
Lot 98, 485
Lutherans
72, 140,
142, 326,
349, 655

M

Martyr, Justin
92
Marx, Karl
113, 236,
367, 369
Mary 67, 76, 94,
194, 242,
304, 327,
331, 335,
380, 577
Matzot 61, 62, 64,
541
Mecca 426, 457,
458, 655
Mediator 285
Mediterranean
490, 612,
617, 629,
651
Medo-Persian
163, 588,
618, 637
Melchizedek
431, 605,
627
Mesopotamia
658
Messiah 2, 4, 6, 10,
11, 14, 15,
22, 25, 29,
30, 32, 34,

52, 64, 73,
89, 90, 95,
98, 99,
100, 102,
105, 111,
119, 120,
122, 126,
127, 128,
135, 136,
137, 139,
151, 153,
154, 155,
157, 159,
164, 167,
176, 187,
190, 198,
213, 214,
215, 217,
223, 224,
225, 226,
227, 228,
229, 231,
235, 239,
248, 257,
261, 262,
263, 266,
267, 270,
271, 272,
273, 274,
275, 278,
279, 280,
283, 285,
290, 291,
298, 315,
320, 327,
333, 334,
336, 337,
345, 348,
356, 359,
360, 361,
362, 363,

Subject Index

376, 377,
380, 382,
383, 384,
385, 386,
387, 389,
394, 404,
408, 412,
413, 428,
430, 439,
447, 452,
470, 471,
482, 483,
484, 486,
489, 492,
496, 519,
532, 534,
535, 536,
537, 543,
544, 545,
548, 580,
583, 590,
592, 593,
595, 597,
605, 608,
609, 616,
617, 619,
620, 621,
627, 628,
629, 633,
634, 635,
636, 637,
638, 639,
640, 643,
645, 654,
656, 669,
671, 672,
682

Messianic Jews
    2, 23, 36,
    62, 174,
    274, 324,
    360, 361,
    362, 363,
    364, 365,
    375, 403,
    419, 420,
    429, 430

Messianic kingdom
    3, 4, 6, 8,
    10, 11, 12,
    13, 14, 30,
    37, 40, 47,
    58, 59, 60,
    64, 89, 97,
    98, 99,
    125, 127,
    128, 147,
    150, 167,
    169, 174,
    175, 177,
    178, 179,
    180, 182,
    183, 184,
    185, 188,
    227, 233,
    236, 263,
    270, 272,
    275, 287,
    292, 308,
    309, 310,
    311, 312,
    313, 315,
    316, 345,
    374, 384,
    387, 391,
    397, 413,
    422, 440,
    441, 470,
    486, 487,
    489, 491,
    492, 493,
    494, 496,
    499, 501,
    502, 503,
    504, 508,
    510, 511,
    512, 520,
    521, 522,
    523, 528,
    529, 530,
    531, 532,
    533, 534,
    535, 537,
    538, 539,
    541, 542,
    544, 545,
    547, 548,
    551, 573,
    580, 581,
    582, 583,
    589, 590,
    591, 592,
    593, 594,
    596, 601,
    602, 605,
    608, 609,
    616, 626,
    628, 635,
    636, 638,
    641, 642,
    643, 645,
    647, 650,
    651, 652,
    654, 655,
    656, 657,
    658, 660,
    662, 663,
    668, 669,
    670, 672

Middle Ages
    89, 106,
    112, 126,

143, 147, 231, 302, 303, 311, 314, 326, 335, 366, 368, 372, 478, 538, 689

Middle East
  29, 197, 356, 393, 402, 404, 416, 417, 418, 449, 451, 453, 454, 456, 463, 466, 467, 473, 486, 491, 493, 637, 689

Millennial Dispensationalism
  21, 517

Millennium
  16, 313, 314, 316, 500, 518, 679, 680, 683, 691

miracles 95, 131, 157, 275, 280, 381, 455, 471, 472, 473

Mishnah 11, 16, 49, 67, 73, 76, 82, 83, 84, 85, 86, 87, 90, 91, 137, 199, 435

Moab 193, 482, 485, 487, 603, 616

Mosaic Torah
  23, 24, 25, 26, 27, 28, 29, 30, 32, 35, 36, 37, 48, 52, 53, 57, 58, 59, 103, 104, 155, 160, 162, 202, 205, 344, 361, 364, 365, 373, 374, 375, 376, 508, 536, 540, 667

Moses 20, 21, 24, 27, 28, 35, 37, 38, 39, 41, 44, 46, 48, 49, 57, 73, 75, 80, 82, 83, 84, 93, 122, 128, 129, 131, 132, 133, 134, 156, 158, 159, 160, 161, 167, 176, 196, 208, 209, 233, 236, 238, 256, 266, 269, 288, 291, 296, 339, 351, 363, 366, 367, 369, 379, 382, 443, 469, 470, 471, 472, 473, 482, 491, 507, 508, 546, 551, 552, 553, 557, 559, 561, 563, 571, 577, 593, 612, 621, 641, 647, 665, 666, 667, 673

Most High
  vi, 164, 165, 431, 534, 535, 546, 557, 577, 589, 652

Most Holy place
  550, 552, 564, 575, 584, 651

Mount Moriah
  549

Mount of Olives
  65, 258, 403, 426, 427, 428, 592, 666

Mount Sinai
  12, 46, 47, 57, 73, 75, 76, 82, 84,

Subject Index

108, 131,
156, 219,
379, 483,
546, 550,
551, 553,
554, 557,
559, 561,
562, 564,
572, 600,
602, 606,
621, 662,
665
Mount Tabor
389, 666
Mount Zion
7, 12, 99,
286, 425,
438, 555,
595, 596,
597, 598,
599, 600,
605, 606,
608, 609,
611, 655
Muhammad
20, 127,
189, 416,
426, 455,
457, 458,
461, 463,
464, 469,
470, 471,
472, 473,
474, 475,
682
Muslim
eschatology
461

N
Nachmanides
21 74,
126, 127,
128, 154,
333, 336,
337, 338,
368, 487,
488
nations 6, 7, 17,
19, 25, 30,
31, 39,
101, 108,
109, 110,
111, 112,
114, 115,
119, 121,
125, 143,
145, 153,
154, 166,
176, 177,
193, 198,
202, 207,
212, 213,
219, 220,
221, 226,
227, 228,
231, 232,
234, 235,
236, 239,
240, 242,
248, 258,
263, 272,
275, 287,
292, 308,
311, 320,
336, 345,
356, 377,
385, 427,
428, 438,
439, 444,

445, 461,
486, 490,
491, 492,
493, 494,
524, 529,
533, 582,
588, 590,
592, 594,
599, 602,
603, 608,
609, 610,
612, 613,
614, 615,
616, 622,
626, 627,
628, 629,
634, 635,
636, 637,
638, 639,
648, 651,
652, 653,
654, 655,
656, 657,
658, 659,
660, 661,
662, 663,
669, 671,
672, 674
Nazareth 22, 32,
102, 106,
122, 136,
137, 156,
249, 250,
272, 273,
279, 291,
360, 362,
363, 381,
383, 385,
535, 554
Nazirite vow 28
Nazis 13, 113,

743

116, 117,
118, 140,
144, 145,
193, 206,
207, 250,
294, 302,
32
Nehemiah
    193, 434,
    603
neo-orthodox
    309, 513
Netherlands
    v, 74, 140,
    144, 167,
    168, 180,
    190, 191,
    192, 193,
    310, 312,
    320, 324,
    325, 327,
    339, 344,
    346, 349,
    350, 351,
    352, 353,
    355, 369,
    392, 399,
    401, 403,
    477, 478,
    497, 507,
    512, 514,
    515, 589
new birth
    122, 125,
    277
new covenant
    5
new earth
    3, 4, 7,
    10, 166,
    174, 179,

309, 313,
314, 345,
501, 502,
504, 505,
509, 522,
536, 583,
584, 594,
631, 661,
662, 663,
664, 665
new heavens
    3, 4, 7, 10,
    166, 174,
    180, 184,
    309, 313,
    314, 501,
    502, 505,
    509, 522,
    523, 583,
    631, 662,
    663, 664,
    665
New Jerusalem
    236, 344,
    685
New Testament
    v, viii, ix,
    x, 2, 9, 14,
    15, 19, 20,
    21, 23, 25,
    31, 33, 39,
    44, 47, 48,
    52, 53, 54,
    55, 58, 59,
    61, 67, 77,
    78, 79, 80,
    81, 85, 91,
    93, 94,
    102, 128,
    129, 130,
    132, 137,

138, 145,
157, 164,
167, 169,
171, 174,
175, 176,
177, 179,
181, 186,
187, 194,
199, 214,
215, 217,
224, 229,
231, 237,
242, 250,
251, 273,
276, 282,
286, 287,
288, 289,
290, 299,
317, 319,
333, 334,
336, 373,
376, 378,
379, 383,
426, 429,
460, 470,
504, 509,
511, 517,
519, 529,
531, 535,
544, 545,
546, 559,
576, 579,
583, 600,
607, 624,
646, 650,
679, 681,
695, 697,
700
Nicodemus
    122, 287
Noah   98, 137,

Subject Index

208, 219,
339, 374,
469, 485,
558, 607,
665
North America
198, 616
northern kingdom
432, 603,
605
nunc millennialism
313

O

Old Covenant
37, 40
Old Testament
ix, 2, 295,
379, 681,
684, 695
Oral Torah
73, 75, 82,
83, 84, 95,
361, 379
Ottoman Empire
157, 165,
356, 366,
405, 416,
432

P

paganism
115, 117,
164
Palestine v,
104, 144,
149, 165,
166, 196,
197, 357,
359, 391,
395, 400,
403, 404,
405, 406,
408, 409,
415, 416,
421, 430,
432, 433,
434, 436,
445, 449,
450, 454,
456, 466,
467, 468,
474, 479,
491, 658,
690, 691,
696
Palestinians
7, 13, 18,
20, 87, 98,
166, 192,
193, 194,
196, 198,
357, 389,
390, 391,
393, 394,
395, 396,
397, 398,
399, 400,
401, 402,
403, 404
405, 406,
407, 408,
409, 410,
411, 413,
414, 415,
416, 417,
418, 419,
420, 421,
422, 423,
424, 425,
426, 427,
429, 431,
432, 434,
435, 437,
439, 440,
441, 446,
447, 448,
450, 454,
455, 459,
465, 468,
473, 474,
485, 491,
492, 495,
658
Palestinian Torah
88
Papias of Hierapolis
92
Passover
61, 62,
64, 124,
214, 304,
339, 541
Paul, The Apostle
13, 20, 26,
27, 33, 34,
46, 56, 57,
64, 73, 77,
82, 86,
104, 105,
126, 128,
161, 218,
251, 263,
265, 266,
268, 273,
276, 277,
278, 282,
284, 288,
295, 345,
362, 364,
379, 460,

475, 481,
546, 559,
579, 646,
664, 675
patriarchs
  7, 8, 10,
  11, 29, 30,
  57, 267,
  415, 429,
  435, 488,
  490, 558,
  602
Paul, The Apostle
  6, 9, 4, 13,
  14, 16, 17,
  19, 20, 21,
  25, 26, 27,
  28, 33, 34,
  35, 36, 38,
  42, 45, 46,
  56, 57, 64,
  73, 77, 82,
  86, 104,
  105, 126,
  127, 128,
  137, 147,
  156, 158,
  159, 161,
  162, 208,
  218, 251,
  252, 263,
  265, 266,
  268, 273,
  276, 277,
  278, 282,
  283, 284,
  288, 295,
  306, 307,
  309, 322,
  336, 341,
  345, 359,
362, 364,
367, 369,
370, 371,
375, 378,
379, 460,
475, 481,
523, 537,
538, 546,
559, 579,
636, 646,
664, 675,
700
Pentecostal eschatology
  507, 508
people of God
  2, 5, 14,
  19, 164,
  166, 168,
  186, 187,
  236, 290,
  291, 373,
  377, 516,
  661
Persian 89, 107,
  163, 187,
  301, 539,
  569, 588,
  618, 634,
  637, 671
Pesach 55, 61, 62,
  63, 64, 95,
  124, 172,
  273, 321,
  339, 541,
  659
Peter, The Apostle
  18, 19, 25,
  27, 72,
  124, 127,
  178, 250,
263, 265,
270, 277,
278, 284,
288, 291,
315, 323,
379, 383,
454, 460,
463, 498,
508, 532,
537, 538,
553, 577,
581, 636,
662, 664,
670
Pharaoh 207, 208,
  356, 411,
  423, 450,
  490, 615,
  618, 673
Pharisees 62, 73, 80,
  82, 85, 95,
  104, 123,
  160, 162,
  199, 287
Philistines
  20, 74,
  169, 299,
  393, 405,
  437, 446,
  482, 564,
  565, 593,
  595, 596,
  602, 666
Philosemitic
  35, 98,
  146
philosophy
  73, 369,
  370, 372,
  509

Subject Index

physical death 2, 174, 179, 180, 181, 183, 184, 185, 526, 650
Pilate 14, 115, 130, 146, 249, 251, 252, 253, 254, 256, 268, 286, 287, 304, 373, 375
Polish Jews 354
Polycarp 92
Pontius Pilate 115, 130, 268, 373
Pope Gregory I 299
Pope John Paul II 359
post-exilic Jews 75
post-millennialism 316, 318, 500, 503, 507, 509, 512, 522
pre-millennialism 310, 311, 312, 316, 496, 503, 504, 507, 511, 512, 513, 514, 515, 516, 517, 520, 522, 523, 544, 545
Presbyterian ii, iii, 170, 509, 677, 698, 700
pre-tribulationism 496, 516
Priest 256, 385, 537, 605, 607, 627
progressive dispensationalism 506, 517, 518, 519
pro-millennialism 314
Promised Land 7, 8, 24, 48, 150, 153, 166, 186, 233, 270, 278, 280, 358, 402, 436, 439, 441, 472, 481, 483, 562, 568, 570, 600, 601, 602, 609, 666, 680
prophecy 7, 99, 167, 168, 173, 185, 190, 219, 254, 318, 359, 412, 413, 438, 445, 446, 471, 491, 573, 646, 662, 670
prophetic word 103, 390, 438
prophets 11, 32, 33, 128, 136, 150, 187, 220, 229, 251, 252, 267, 268, 270, 291, 296, 334, 363, 377, 402, 471, 473, 516, 532, 537, 543, 577, 579, 591, 593, 603, 622, 626, 628, 633, 637
Protestant 8, 29, 65, 66, 67, 68, 71, 74, 75, 77, 78, 83, 118, 147, 163, 166, 171, 177, 185, 192, 217, 312, 319, 325, 333, 355, 359, 382, 399, 504, 514, 515, 516
Protestant tradition 8, 504

Purim 61, 273
Puritanism 74
Puritans 140, 343, 344

Q
Quran 9, 396, 411, 416, 426, 427, 450, 457, 458, 461, 462, 463, 464, 465, 469, 470, 471, 473, 475, 476, 477

R
Rabbinic Judais 11, 79, 691
rabbinic writings 16, 75, 77
rabbis 16, 24, 34, 44, 48, 68, 78, 80, 86, 87, 88, 90, 91, 93, 94, 96, 120, 129, 210, 227, 261, 287, 333, 334, 335, 336, 355, 380, 382, 398, 435, 439, 488, 577, 579, 613, 615
reconstructionism 507
redeemed 15, 40, 123, 209, 225, 423, 486, 558, 569, 591, 596, 611, 612, 620, 632, 640, 647, 668, 673
Redeemer 120, 137, 139, 190, 285, 608, 624
redemption 11, 14, 15, 22, 40, 44, 123, 124, 126, 139, 255, 318, 481, 518, 531, 612, 668, 669, 670
redemptive history 3, 60, 137, 164, 319, 428, 606
Red Sea 47, 209, 479, 569, 617, 670
Reformational 3, 52, 305, 322, 696
Reformers 60, 310, 511, 512
relativism ii, 78
religion 22, 23, 25, 44, 46, 102, 116, 123, 130, 136, 148, 163, 168, 172, 189, 190, 192, 195, 198, 273, 276, 287, 313, 320, 321, 323, 332, 333, 340, 346, 352, 370, 374, 377, 404, 416, 423, 430, 450, 457, 462, 463, 466, 474, 478, 658
remnant 5, 6, 100, 156, 170, 204, 216, 227, 234, 235, 261, 264, 296, 519, 591, 592, 606, 607, 612, 614, 628, 630, 641

Subject Index

Renaissance 20
repentance ii, 30, 122, 123, 124, 125, 236, 276, 277, 359, 412, 413, 431, 440, 442, 447, 459, 460, 480, 483, 488, 489, 494
replacement theology 102, 167, 174, 177, 317
reprobation i, 72
resurrection 2, 7, 8, 10, 11, 14, 18, 27, 55, 59, 60, 63, 64, 104, 127, 135, 139, 149, 177, 179, 180, 181, 183, 184, 185, 229, 280, 308, 311, 313, 317, 318, 337, 500, 510, 511, 521, 522, 526, 527, 528, 531, 533, 609, 662, 663
Revelation 8, 134, 168, 175, 183, 184, 295, 308, 310, 311, 316, 320, 343, 497, 498, 499, 500, 504, 505, 511, 512, 513, 515, 520, 522, 524, 525, 526, 528, 530, 531, 532, 535, 536, 556, 590, 591, 596, 608, 615, 618, 627, 632, 661, 664, 665, 678, 679, 680, 683, 684, 686, 687, 688, 695, 696, 697, 699, 700
Righteous 96, 140, 250, 385, 639, 690
Righteousness 3, 7, 639
Roman Catholicism 67, 71, 73, 79, 80, 163, 294, 315, 327
Roman Empire 33, 99, 115, 120, 163, 164, 300, 302, 310, 313, 533, 535, 588, 590, 591, 618, 651
Romans 6, 8, 16, 19, 20, 45, 86, 115, 127, 132, 146, 164, 197, 250, 251, 252, 262, 284, 297, 314, 345, 349, 361, 405, 424, 434, 526, 533, 542, 588, 589, 590, 620, 658, 696
root of Jesse 626
Rushdoony, R. J. 507

S

Sabbath 2, 3, 4, 8,

35, 36, 37, 51, 52, 53, 54, 55, 56, 57, 58, 59, 60, 61, 62, 63, 64, 81, 86, 88, 162, 163, 167, 173, 174, 175, 187, 195, 198, 251, 271, 273, 274, 298, 321, 344, 356, 360, 361, 362, 364, 365, 376, 508, 541, 542, 637, 659

sacrifices 15, 27, 28, 30, 48, 58, 86, 103, 120, 187, 215, 218, 221, 228, 489, 537, 538, 540, 567, 570, 602, 610, 635, 636, 637, 656, 659

sacrificial laws 103, 536, 538

saints 8, 11, 13, 14, 15, 65, 72, 164, 165, 179, 230, 326, 330, 510, 522, 523, 530, 533, 535, 589, 591, 608, 627, 650, 659, 663

salvation 9, 22, 26, 44, 45, 111, 115, 120, 125, 126, 150, 155, 166, 180, 188, 217, 221, 224, 229, 231, 232, 236, 250, 263, 280, 281, 293, 319, 334, 362, 374, 375, 377, 428, 429, 444, 494, 501, 502, 504, 511, 612, 626, 627, 641, 644

Samaria 394, 400, 409, 424, 447

Samuel 21, 87, 88, 107, 113, 247, 254, 277, 345, 366, 381, 562, 563, 564, 565, 593

Satan 21, 149, 265, 288, 293, 294, 295, 296, 308, 311, 315, 506, 524, 525, 593, 666

Saul 132, 133, 259, 282, 283, 284, 287, 288, 350, 370, 372, 432, 480, 565, 566, 570, 593, 603, 605, 606, 666

saving grace 277

Saviour 158, 172

Scapegoat 11, 14, 110, 230

Scofield Reference Bible 513, 696

Scripture ii, 30, 64, 66, 67, 70, 71, 73, 74, 75, 77, 79, 92, 163, 168, 213, 214, 269, 270, 319, 359, 380, 402, 446, 462, 468, 471, 499, 526, 694

Subject Index

second coming
8, 9, 64,
99, 168,
177, 178,
179, 180,
181, 182,
183, 184,
188, 255,
275, 280,
309, 311,
312, 313,
315, 316,
318, 335,
384, 387,
497, 499,
504, 505,
506, 507,
509, 510,
511, 512,
514, 516,
521, 523,
524, 529,
530, 531,
532, 533,
539, 592,
608, 650,
662

Second Temple
396, 398,
425, 546,
573, 575,
580, 584,
635, 636,
644, 645

Semites 195, 286,
288, 291,
308, 309,
322, 336,
347, 419,
492

Septuagint
24, 121,
206, 208,
576, 577,
583, 648

Sermon on the
Mount 159, 666

Shavu'ot 62, 64,
541, 659

Shem 106, 122,
286, 419

Shoah 1, 106,
116, 118,
145, 148,
149, 157,
206, 207,
212, 213,
221, 222,
230, 231,
232, 273

sin 9, 30, 46,
48, 76,
111, 126,
134, 140,
145, 171,
172, 212,
213, 214,
215, 218,
231, 233,
242, 255,
264, 387,
441, 470,
501, 525,
538, 614,
629, 631,
636, 650,
661

Sinaitic Covenant
37, 256

slavery 40, 222,
306, 423,
472, 645,
668, 669,
670, 673

Solomon 22, 23, 89,
102, 176,
193, 203,
250, 322,
352, 396,
425, 432,
441, 446,
486, 489,
512, 546,
547, 549,
550, 551,
555, 560,
563, 567,
568, 569,
571, 573,
575, 580,
584, 592,
593, 595,
601, 603,
605, 606,
617, 620,
628, 629,
634, 638,
639, 645,
665

Son of David
6, 583,
592, 606,
607, 620,
626, 627,
655

Son of God
2, 48, 129,
130, 141,
210, 216,
251, 334,
376, 378,
470, 473,

527, 577,
620
Son of Man
    2, 3, 10,
    11, 13, 15,
    134, 181,
    183, 214,
    230, 256,
    316, 521,
    523, 530,
    531, 534,
    535, 536,
    543, 589,
    629, 650,
    670

sovereign grace
    269, 607,
    619
Spain 98, 143,
    147, 148,
    300, 301,
    322, 323,
    324, 326,
    330, 331,
    332, 351,
    352, 466,
    490, 613
Spirit of God
    43, 49,
    156, 281,
    442, 569,
    579
Spiritualism
    318
spiritual Israel
    20, 26,
    138, 168,
    173, 188,
    290, 317,
    320, 345,

364, 516,
520, 521,
624
Stephen 127, 128,
    146, 208,
    250, 323,
    375, 546
Substitution
    11, 110
Sukkot 62, 64,
    541, 560,
    638, 659,
    664, 665
Supersessionism
    9, 101,
    103, 105,
    107, 109,
    111, 113,
    115, 117,
    119, 121,
    123, 125,
    127, 129,
    131, 133,
    135, 137,
    139, 141,
    143, 145,
    147, 149,
    151, 153,
    155, 157,
    159, 161,
    163, 165,
    166, 167,
    168, 169,
    171, 173,
    175, 177,
    178, 179,
    181, 183,
    185, 187,
    189, 191,
    193, 195,
    197, 199,

495, 497,
499, 501,
503, 505,
507, 509,
511, 513,
515, 517,
519, 521,
523, 525,
527, 529,
531, 533,
535, 537,
539, 541,
663
synagogue
    22, 35, 64,
    81, 136,
    186, 187,
    192, 250,
    293, 295,
    299, 306,
    325, 327,
    330, 331,
    352, 355,
    381, 620
Synod of Breslau
    303
Synod of Dordt
    312
Syrian 109, 405,
    448, 465

T
tabernacle
    2, 76,
    546, 547,
    549, 550,
    551, 553,
    554, 557,
    558, 559,
    562, 563,
    564, 565,

Subject Index

	566, 567,	30, 31, 37,		544, 546,
	568, 573,	38, 61, 67,		548, 551,
	576, 577,	70, 73, 74,		559, 564,
	578, 580,	78, 79, 80,		571, 576,
	583, 584,	81, 85, 86,		578, 592,
	585, 596,	91, 92, 93,		598, 599,
	600, 601,	102, 104,		603, 627,
	602, 604,	125, 127,		636, 639,
	652, 661,	133, 134,		650, 663,
	664, 665	135, 141,		666
Talmud	11, 21, 37,	143, 150,	Tannaim	11, 67, 70,
	38, 41, 44,	159, 162,		84, 87, 93
	47, 51, 67,	167, 168,	Tel Aviv	403, 452
	70, 73, 74,	171, 173,	Temple	7, 19, 21,
	80, 85, 87,	174, 176,		22, 24, 27,
	88, 89, 90,	185, 186,		358, 395,
	91, 92, 93,	187, 198,		396, 398,
	94, 95, 96,	202, 224,		410, 425,
	113, 144,	228, 229,		426, 427,
	215, 219,	232, 259,		428, 455,
	226, 227,	268, 283,		457, 458,
	234, 240,	288, 319,		459, 538,
	242, 281,	333, 334,		540, 546,
	295, 306,	339, 344,		551, 555,
	307, 308,	346, 356,		562, 571,
	322, 335,	373, 377,		573, 575,
	336, 337,	378, 379,		580, 581,
	338, 347,	380, 381,		584, 598,
	356, 361,	383, 384,		633, 634,
	367, 379,	411, 416,		635, 636,
	385, 462,	447, 459,		637, 639,
	470, 543,	469, 470,		641, 643,
	561, 573,	471, 472,		644, 645,
	579, 583,	481, 483,		647, 649,
	654, 682,	501, 508,		651, 653,
	691, 695,	509, 516,		655, 657,
	697	517, 520,		659, 661,
Tanakh	v, 2, 4, 9,	521, 522,		663, 665,
	12, 14, 15,	529, 532,		667, 669,
	16, 19, 20,	536, 537,		671, 673,
	21, 25, 27,	538, 540,		675, 689

Temple Mount
19, 425,
426, 427,
428, 457,
458, 459,
598
Temple of Solomon 571
Ten Commandments
24, 40, 48,
52, 57, 59,
156, 162,
253, 682
Tertullian
92, 187,
310
theology i, ii, 2, 21,
66, 68, 71,
91, 92,
102, 135,
163, 167,
174, 177,
185, 194,
202, 232,
290, 295,
317, 319,
320, 355,
365, 412,
499, 507,
508, 509,
512, 513,
544, 598,
607
The Righteous One
96, 250
Thomas à Kempis
180, 181,
182, 183,
184

Throne of David
167, 175,
176, 320,
335, 345,
348, 381,
384, 530,
544, 545,
557, 583,
590, 609,
620, 652,
656
Timothy 26, 92,
277, 375
tithe 41
Torah v, vi, 21,
23, 24, 25,
26, 27, 28,
29, 30, 31,
32, 34, 35,
36, 37, 38,
39, 40, 41,
42, 43, 44,
45, 46, 47,
48, 52, 53,
57, 58, 59,
62, 73, 74,
75, 76, 79,
81, 82, 83,
84, 85, 86,
87, 88, 90,
92, 95,
102, 103,
104, 108,
109, 112,
120, 130,
145, 150,
151, 153,
154, 155,
156, 159,
160, 161,
162, 163,

167, 202,
203, 204,
205, 215,
216, 218,
219, 220,
221, 226,
227, 234,
235, 250,
251, 253,
262, 264,
272, 278,
279, 280,
281, 282,
283, 284,
285, 287,
288, 296,
344, 354,
361, 363,
364, 365,
373, 374,
375, 376,
377, 379,
382, 404,
427, 462,
469, 470,
472, 479,
486, 508,
509, 536,
540, 541,
559, 561,
579, 600,
606, 607,
609, 621,
638, 653,
665, 667,
669, 692,
693
Torah of Christ
10, 26, 37,
45, 46, 59,
167, 365

Subject Index

Traditionalism
  10, 71, 73
Trinity 344, 377, 378
Twentieth century
  1, 87, 94,
  129, 148,
  168, 213,
  294, 309,
  316, 355,
  364, 404,
  405, 431,
  432, 435,
  437, 484,
  497, 512,
  516, 539,
  643
typology 21, 86,
  226, 227,
  592

U
unbelievers
  461, 463,
  475, 511,
  526, 528
United Nations
  166, 357,
  399, 400,
  410, 411,
  420, 425,
  438, 440,
  445, 448,
  456
United States
  6, 113,
  141, 144,
  326, 327,
  328, 401,
  451, 474,
  478, 497

V
Vatican 307, 313, 359
veil 122, 158,
  262, 268,
  269, 271,
  274, 275,
  278, 285,
  296, 551,
  552, 607,
  608, 609,
  656
Visigothic kingdom
  300

W
West Bank
  390, 392,
  394, 400,
  401, 405,
  407, 408,
  409, 413,
  418, 419,
  424, 426,
  434, 438,
  441, 447,
  448, 454,
  455, 478
wilderness
  vi, 62,
  110, 202,
  278, 439,
  473, 489,
  525, 547,
  550, 558,
  563, 564,
  602, 610,
  621, 622,
  625, 643,
  644, 647,
  664, 670
wisdom 67, 77, 78,
  79, 91,
  158, 159,
  277, 331,
  453
Word of God
  11, 31, 70,
  75, 77, 78,
  79, 163,
  282, 288,
  442
World War II
  141, 142,
  144, 206,
  222, 273,
  350, 355,
  390, 456,
  475, 512
worship 13, 58, 59,
  60, 61, 86,
  129, 207,
  376, 383,
  462, 469,
  493, 570,
  601, 613,
  653, 657,
  666
Written Torah
  82, 83
Wycliff, John
  511

Y
Yeshuah
  23, 35, 37,
  84, 94,
  126, 250,
  274, 360

Yiddish
  81, 195, 353, 700
Yom habBikkurim
  61, 62, 63, 64
Yom hakKippurim
  62
Yom Kippur
  62, 64, 110, 306, 325, 358, 409, 465, 541, 552, 558, 646
Yom t'ru'ah
  62, 64

Z
Zechariah
  31, 44, 49, 146, 158, 170, 242, 278, 334, 347, 380, 385, 413, 438, 480, 537, 580, 592, 600, 603, 615, 654

Zephaniah
  295, 649
Zerubbabel
  22, 396, 413, 425, 479, 480, 546, 573, 575, 580, 584, 593, 636
Zionism
  7, 19, 149, 165, 236, 237, 390, 420, 443, 444, 445, 447, 449, 451, 453, 455, 457, 459, 460, 461, 463, 465, 467, 469, 471, 473, 475, 477, 479, 481, 483, 485, 487, 489, 491, 493, 679
Zionist congress
  357
Zipporah 472
Zugot 11, 67, 70, 84, 86, 87

www.ingramcontent.com/pod-product-compliance
Lightning Source LLC
Chambersburg PA
CBHW060646150426
42811CB00086B/2439/J